ExamInsight For The Candidate's Guide to (CFA) Chartered Financial Analyst 2005 Level I Learning Outcome Statements

www.financialexams.com

TOTALRECALL CERTIFICATION SYSTEM FOR CFA Level I 2005

Practice exam provided by
The Financial Certification Center, Inc.
Friendswood, Texas

Authors

Jane Vessey, CFA

M. Afdal Pamilih, CFA

David Stewart

Published by

TotalRecall Publications, Inc.
1103 Middlecreek
Friendswood, TX 77546
281-992-3131

TotalRecall Publications, Inc.

This Book Sponsored by The Center For Financial Certification, Inc.

Printed in United States of America

Printed and bound by Data Duplicators of Houston Texas

Printed and bound by Lightning Source, Inc. in the USA and UK

Printed and bound by Booksurge, LLC around the world

Paper Back

ISBN: 1-59095-914-0

UPC: 6-43977-92501-5

eBook

ISBN: 1-59095-917-5

UPC: 6-43977-92561-9

The sponsoring editor for this book is Bruce Moran and the production supervisor is Corby R. Tate.

This book is dedicated to our fantastic children Adam and Julia who we love very much.

Jane Vessey & M. Afdal Pamilih

This Study Guide is dedicated to the widow(er)s and orphans of the "Silent Spring". Those who have sacrificed loved ones to the obscurity of quiet study and endured weekend sacrifice above and beyond the call of continuing education. On the alter of a profession's highest accreditation these unsung heroes have sacrificed time with their spouse, shopping with Mom, and pitch and catch with Dad. These patient supporters have endured tense attitudes, unfinished chores, extra duties, and received the respect and appreciation of all who have studied throughout the "Silent Spring".

In particular, never ending thanks to:

Carol Lee, Mary Elizabeth, Sophia Victoria, David Todd II

David Stewart

ExamInsight
For
The Candidate's Guide to (CFA)
Chartered Financial Analyst 2005 Level I
Learning Outcome Statements

www.financialexams.com

BY

Authors

Jane Vessey, CFA

M. Afdal Pamilih, CFA

Contributing Author

David Stewart

About the Author:

Jane Vessey

Jane Vessey manages a training company in the United Kingdom specializing in financial analysis and investment. She is a visiting lecturer at Cass Business School teaching classes in asset management and valuation. She also teaches a CFA® revision course at ISMA (the business school at Reading University) and is an associate at a leading London financial training company where she teaches courses covering investment management and related topics. She has developed online training programs for students taking the CFA examinations and teaches CFA courses for UKSIP (the UK Society of Investment Professionals).

Jane graduated in Mathematics from Oxford University, United Kingdom, and is a CFA charter holder. She has some eighteen years experience working in the investment industry, starting out as an equity analyst before becoming an investment manager. She was based in London and Tokyo and took responsibility for managing equity portfolios invested in the Japanese and other Asian markets. In 1990, Jane moved to Indonesia and established and ran an investment management operation on behalf of MeesPierson. She took responsibility for all areas of the business, including investment, operations, marketing and administration. While in Asia, Jane was involved in providing training to capital market participants and state officials and teaching in courses provided by local universities.

M. Afdal Pamilih

Afdal has 18 years' experience working in the finance industry. He started his career with J.P. Morgan, and then with County NatWest Government Securities, in New York specializing in the development of quantitative products for foreign exchange and fixed income markets. After returning to Indonesia in 1989 he was responsible for the development of investment services and subsequently treasury management for leading banks in Jakarta.

Afdal has developed web-based training programs for the CFA examinations and has wide teaching experience, including instructing at the School of Management, University of Surrey, United Kingdom.

He obtained a MSc in Mathematics from the University of Texas at Arlington and holds the Chartered Financial Analyst ("CFA") qualification.

David Stewart:

David Stewart has extensive experience in venture capital and business structural reorganizations. As president of a private client broker dealer firm, he has business valuation and project valuation experience on the venture capital side and portfolio management on the asset management side. His analysis, commentary, books, and study guides have appeared in the financial management, securities, and exam prep industries.

David has collaborated with experts in the field to produce the 2001 through 2004 editions of this study guide. His extensive research into the CFA exam program and past exam histories, field work, and consistent review of CFA Institute information allows him and his co-authors to deliver high quality and up to date information.

About the Book:

The Candidate's Guide to (CFA) teach the full CFA Level I curriculum, eliminating the impossible task of predicating the content of the actual examination.

The purpose of The Candidate's guide is to supply you the information required to pass the CFA Level I certification.

This book is divided into Study Sessions (1 – 18), Appendix A (Exhibits 1 – 3) and a Glossary of Financial Terminology in question format. Appendix A is a collection of Exhibits and flow charts for condensed reference and review. Additional white space was intentionally designed into the book for the candidate's personal notes and remarks.

The 18 2005 CFA Level I Study Sessions breakout is as follows:

Ethical and Professional Standards

Study Session 1: Ethical and Professional Standards

Investment Tools

Study Session 2. Quantitative Methods
Study Session 3. Quantitative Methods
Study Session 4. Economics: Macroeconomic Analysis
Study Session 5. Economics: Microeconomic Analysis
Study Session 6. Economics: Global Economic Analysis
Study Session 7. Financial Statement Analysis: Basic Concepts
Study Session 8. Financial Statement Analysis:
Financial Ratios and Earnings Per Share
Study Session 9. Financial Statement Analysis: Assets
Study Session 10. Financial Statement Analysis: Liabilities
Study Session 11. Corporate Finance: Corporate Investing & Financing Decisions

Portfolio Management

Study Session 12. Capital Market Theory: Basic Concepts

Asset Valuation

Study Session 13. Securities Markets
Study Session 14. Equity Investments
Study Session 15. Debt Investments: Basic Concepts
Study Session 16. Debt Investments: Analysis and Valuation
Study Session 17. Derivative Investments
Study Session 18. Alternative Investments

Download Supplemental Information: To obtain additional printable content visit these download links.
http://snipurl.com/Workbook Preliminary Reading Assignments and Concept Question Workbook
http://snipurl.com/EI-CFA2005 ExamInsight 2005 CFA Level I eBook with two practice exams.

Online Information:

1. CFA Program:

   http://www.cfainstitute.org/cfaprogram/

2. The Code of Ethics (Full Text)

   http://www.cfainstitute.org/standards/ethics/code/

3. International Code Of Ethics And Standards Of Professional Conduct

   http://www.cfainstitute.org/standards/ethics/code/translations.html

4. Interpretations of CFA Institute's Code of Ethics and Standards of Professional Conduct

   http://www.cfainstitute.org/standards/pps/gips_library.html

5. The Standards of Professional Conduct

   Standard I: Fundamental Responsibilities

   Standard II: Relationships with and Responsibilities to the Profession

   Standard III: Relationships with and Responsibilities to the Employer

   Standard IV: Relationships with and Responsibilities to Clients and Prospects

   Standard V: Relationships with and Responsibilities to the Public

   http://www.cfainstitute.org/standards/ethics/conduct/index.html

   http://www.cfapubs.org/ap/issues/v2003n4/toc.html

   http://www.cfainstitute.org/standards/pps/index.html

   http://www.cfainstitute.org/standards/resources.html

6. CFA Institute-PPSTM AIMR Performance Presentation Standards

   http://www.cfainstitute.org/standards/pps/ppsstand.html

7. Global Investment Performance Standards

   http://www.cfainstitute.org/standards/pps/gips_standards.html

8. Soft Dollar Learning Module

   http://www.cfainstitute.org/standards/ethics/soft_dollar/index.html

List of Chapters

Table of Contents

2004 CFA Study and Examination Program Textbooks: Primary Readings

Level I

- 2005 CFA Level I Candidate Readings (CFA Institute, 2004)
- Standards of Practice Handbook, 8th edition (AIMR, 1999)
- Quantitative Methods for Investment Analysis, 2nd edition, Richard A. DeFusco, Dennis W. McLeavey, Jerald E. Pinto, and David E. Runkle (CFA Institute, 2004)
- Economics: Private and Public Choice, 10th edition, James D. Gwartney, Richard L. Stroup, Russell S. Sobel, and David A. Macpherson (South-Western, 2003)
- Fundamentals of Financial Management, 8th edition, Eugene F. Brigham and Joel F. Houston (Dryden, 1998)
- International Investments, 5th edition, Bruno Solnik and Dennis McLeavey (Addison Wesley, 2003)
- The Analysis and Use of Financial Statements, 3rd edition, Gerald I. White, Ashwin Paul C. Sondhi, and Dov Fried (Wiley, 2003)
- Investment Analysis and Portfolio Management, 7th edition, Frank K. Reilly and Keith C. Brown (South-Western, 2003)
- Fixed Income Analysis for the Chartered Financial Analyst® Program, 2nd edition, Frank J. Fabozzi (Frank J. Fabozzi Associates, 2004)
- Analysis of Derivatives for the CFA® Program, Don Chance (AIMR, 2003)

Dates Regarding the June 2005 CFA Examination

15 July 2004 Study Guides available and mailed to applicants

15 July Textbooks available for purchase from book distributor

November Past years' Level III constructed response examination questions and guideline answers available from book distributor

February 2005 Level I and Level II sample examinations and Level III selected response-item set sample examination will be available on the CFA Institute website

21 March Final deadline for special test center requests, disability accommodation requests, and requests for religious alternative dates to be *received by* CFA Institute

4 April Final deadline for all test center change requests to be *received by* CFA Institute

April Examination Admission Tickets distributed

4 June 2005 Examination Day

5 June 2005 Examination Day in Eastern Asia and Oceania

June-July Examinations graded

Late July Examination results distributed to Level I candidates

Mid-August Examination results distributed to Level II and Level III candidates

September CFA charterholders announced for year 2005

Dates Regarding the December 2005 Level I CFA Examination

15 July 2004 Study Guides available

15 July Textbooks available for purchase from book distributor

2 January 2005 Registration and Enrollment Form for December administration available

February Level I and Level II sample examinations and Level III selected response-item set sample examination will be available on the CFA Institute website

19 September Final deadline for special test center requests, disability accommodation requests, and requests for religious alternative dates to be *received by* CFA Institute

3 October Final deadline for all test center change requests to be *received by* CFA Institute

October Examination Admission tickets distributed

3 December 2005 Examination Day

4 December 2005 Examination Day in Eastern Asia and Oceania

December Examinations graded

Late January 2006 Examination results distributed

Note: Fee schedules including registration deadlines can be found on the CFA Institute website at www.cfainstitute.org/cfaprogram/feeschedule.html

Preface

The CFA Level I exam is the preliminary exam in a series of three exams in addition to industry experience needed to obtain the CFA designation. Once you have passed the CFA Level I exam, you are considered to have covered the basics and the general breadth, but not the depth, of the information necessary to function as an analyst in today's global economy. CFA Institute uses a rather large pool from which to select test questions.

In order to pass you must be properly prepared. The **purpose** of The Candidate's guide is to supply you with information, concepts, and practice questions required to pass todays CFA Level I exam.

The Candidate's Guide Tutorials provides two main sections for each Study Session:

1. Book / eBook CFA Curriculum, including Concept Checks
2. Self Help and Interactive Exam Study Aids

You begin your studies with the CFA Curriculum on Page 1. Continue your studies page-by-page; the learning outcome statements (LOS) have been re-ordered, where necessary, to make learning more intuitive than in the CFA Institute's *Study Guide*. Our concise writing style minimizes learning time, and there are numerous Examples to help you master every LOS. Study Guide command words are **boldface** in the LOS title; the examiners expect that your knowledge reflects the command word.

It is suggested that you first read the Learning Outcome Statements to get familiar with the section, and answer the Assessment questions provided within the program to determine your weakest topics.

Each Specific Study Session question database consists of 40+ multiple choice questions with a level of difficulty and design similar to that of the CFA examination itself. Allow 60 minutes to complete each Adaptive Exam (90 seconds per question). Adaptive Exam questions are unique to The Candidate's Guide Tutorials, so if you have also purchased other Level I Mock Exam (Morning or Afternoon Sessions) rest assured that our Adaptive Exam questions will not be repeated there.

Concept Checks complete each Reading Assignment and they consist of questions to reinforce your knowledge. Answers to Concept Check questions are the end of each Study Session.

Your comments are welcome at anytime at support@financialexams.com :
Publishing high-quality learning tools is our business, but errors can slip through. If you think you have found one, please use the Error Reporting Form at www.financialexams.com or www.cfaexams.com. Errors with their corrections will be posted on our website. We will send an e-mail message to you whenever new corrections are posted.

Practice Questions and Answers

After reviewing more intensely the Learning Outcome Statements, use the Financial Analyst Quizzer testing media to solidify what you have learned and to prepare you for testing and passing the exam. Included on the inside back cover of this book is a download option designed to help you study for the CFA Level 1 exam by presenting simulated exams and study sessions using the question and answer format. Drawing questions from a 3000+ question database, the Financial Analyst Quizzer software exam engine gives you the capability of a Study Session, a testing environment, and Flash Card environment with the look and feel of the actual CFA exam. In order to pass you must be properly prepared. CFA Institute uses a rather large pool from which to select test questions. You should also know that if you need to take the exam a second time, you can expect a completely different selection of questions.

CFA Program

The CFA Program is an exhaustive self-study curriculum for developing the fundamentals of financial analysis and portfolio management. It is designed to broaden and deepen your knowledge of the entire field of investment valuation and portfolio management. The program assumes the candidate has mastered undergraduate finance and accounting and seeks to build a platform for individual and sector analysis, equity and fixed income valuation, and asset management emphasizing competence and integrity within the profession of investment management.

Requirements

There are no prerequisites to begin this area of study. This can, however, be considered a fairly comprehensive study if these concepts are totally new to you. CFA Institute assumes you have mastered undergraduate finance and accounting. Although every effort is made to cover all the material you may encounter at exam time, this book does not go into detail in areas that most financial professionals should already know.

http://www.cfainstitute.org/cfaprogram/exam/exam_details.html

Before the Exam

1. Read the CFA Institute Study Guide, since the rules are very strict on what you can or cannot take into the exam room. Don't forget your exam admission ticket and passport, or other form of permitted identification.
2. Remember that the only calculators you can use are the TI BAII plus and HP 12C 11. We strongly recommend you take two calculators or at the very least a spare battery.
3. Ensure you know the location of the exam and how to get there. It is the CFA Institute's policy to close the doors 30 minutes before the exam starts.
4. Read CFA Institute Candidate Bulletins to check for changes to the exam procedures.

Study Program

It is critical that you design a study program. There are no short cuts to passing the CFA exam, and pass rates have been falling. It is a tough exam and you will need to both learn the underlying material as well as do plenty of practice questions to test your knowledge and to get used to the CFA style of questions. Although the The Candidate's Guide Tutorials are designed to cover the entire CFA curriculum and give a concise summary of the material you need to know for the exam, we encourage candidates to also refer to the source text books, particularly for subjects with which they are not so familiar.

The CFA Institute recommends approximately 10 to 15 hours study per study session plus extra time for final revision. That means if you plan to cover one study session per week you will need to start studying in January for the June exam or July for the December exam. The CFA curriculum sets out very clearly what you need to know to pass the exam. Focus on the Learning Outcome Statements (LOS) and the command words. Questions on the exam will relate to the LOS not to other parts of the text.

In addition to doing all the questions in The Candidate's guide Tutorials we recommend you try the sample exam provided by the CFA Institute.

CFA Institute Exam Rules

IMPORTANT:

Use no. 2 or hb pencils for multiple choice answer sheet! Do not use mechanical pencils with synthetic non-graphite (non electrical conducting) compounds which will not be compatible with the electronic scan grading.

CALCULATORS Allowed:

Hewlett Packard 12c

Texas Instruments Baii Plus

TESTING REGULATIONS:

No beepers or cell phones allowed in test area

No removing exam materials from the test room

No writing after the proctor says "stop."

CFA Institute is quite serious about their exam rules, follow them.

Tips for Taking the Exam

Many people do not test well on exams. Often, the student knows the material, but does not know how to take exams. The CFA Level I exam is based upon the multiple-choice format. You receive points for each question answered correctly. No points are subtracted for a wrong or unanswered question. Since the wrong answer is no worse than an unanswered question, never leave an exam with an unanswered question. Any guess is better than a blank. Example: Answering letter "B" throughout the exam will give you approximately a grade of 25. In the last minute finish the exam by selecting a single letter and marking it as the correct answer on all unanswered questions.

The exams have time limits that provide adequate time for you to read and think about the question. You should be able to reach the end of the exam before the time runs out. You should also have time to return to the unanswered questions to provide an answer. You will not have time for to continuously search the answered questions trying to find the ones you later felt you marked wrong. With this thought in mind, be careful to make sure that when you answer a question it is the last time you will read that question. The answer you give is the one you will keep. The following is a blueprint for taking an exam to insure you have answered to the maximum of your knowledge and capability:

Note: Keep in mind that this is a timed test!

A. Starting with the first question, begin to answer the multiple choice questions that you know to be correct.

B. Remember there may not be enough time to go back. If you do not know the exact answer or if it is a choice between two or more answers, skip it. Often later questions will trigger the correct answer to this question for you.

C. Skip all the long scenario questions; they are time consuming, and often you will be better prepared to answer them later in the test session.

D. You should answer at least 50% of the questions with certainty.

E. Return to the beginning and start again on the unanswered questions. Do not take time with the questions you have already answered. If you can narrow a question to two possible answers, pick the best one.

F. You must always finish your test before time runs out! In the last minute quickly answer all remaining questions with your favorite letter!

On the Exam Day

The CFA Level I exam is 100% multiple choice questions, the morning and afternoon paper will each contain 120 questions.

You will be under time pressure in the exam and need to answer on average one question every 1½ minutes so you must keep moving through the questions. We recommend the following strategies:

1. There is a strong argument for working methodically through the questions in the order they are set but you might wish to start with a subject where you feel confident and which you can work through fairly quickly. But avoid hopping from one subject to another, this will waste time and you may end up missing one section of questions out.
2. Don't panic if you hit some difficult questions, you can probably get as many as 30 or 40 questions incorrect on each paper and still pass the exam.
3. Ethics in study session 1 is an important topic, if you are a marginal candidate your ethics score could be the deciding factor whether you pass the exam.
4. There is no penalty for getting an answer incorrect, so if you don't know the answer eliminate any obviously wrong answers and guess which one is correct.
5. Mark questions in the exam booklet when you are not sure of the answer or where the calculation needs checking and come back to them when you have finished all the other questions.
6. Do not get distracted by a question that does not make sense, if the question turns out to be ambiguous then it will be excluded when it comes to grading the paper.
7. Read the questions carefully, particularly when there is a negative statement in the question.
8. Leave time to check your answers on the answer sheet, be careful you don't miss answering a question and mark subsequent answers against the wrong question number on the answer sheet.

***** Make sure that ALL Questions contain an answer *****

2005 CFA Level I Study Guide Outline

Study Session	Topic	Readings
1	Ethical and Professional Standards	*Standards of Practice Handbook*, 8th ed. *2005 CFA Level I Candidate Readings:* Global Investment Performance Standards – Level I Workbook *Global Investment Performance Standards*
2–3	Quantitative Methods	*Quantitative Methods for Investment Analysis,* 2nd ed. (DeFusco, McLeavey, Pinto & Runkle), Ch. 1–8
4–6	Economics	*Economics: Private and Public Choice*, 10th ed. (Gwartney, Stroup, Sobel & Macpherson), Ch. 8, 12–15, 17, 19–24, Special Topic 7 *Fundamentals of Financial Management*, 8th ed. (Brigham & Houston), Ch. 4 *International Investments*, 5th ed. (Solnik & McLeavey), Ch. 1, 2
7–10	Financial Statement Analysis	*The Analysis and Use of Financial Statements*, 3rd ed. (White, Sondhi & Fried), Ch. 2, 3, 6–11 *Investment Analysis and Portfolio Management*, 7th ed. (Reilly & Brown), Ch. 10 *2005 CFA Level I Candidate Readings:* Kieso, Weygandt & Warfield; Schilit (2 chapters)
11	Corporate Finance	*Fundamentals of Financial Management*, 8th ed. (Brigham & Houston), Ch. 1, 9–14
12	Portfolio Management	*Investment Analysis and Portfolio Management*, 7th ed. (Reilly & Brown), Ch. 1, 2, 7, 8
13	Securities Markets	*Investment Analysis and Portfolio Management*, 7th ed. (Reilly & Brown), Ch. 4–6
14	Equity Investments	*Investment Analysis and Portfolio Management*, 7th ed. (Reilly & Brown), Ch. 11, 13, 15, 16 *International Investments,* 5th ed. (Solnik & McLeavey), Ch. 6 *2005 CFA Level I Candidate Readings*: Stowe, Robinson, Pinto & McLeavey
15–16	Debt Investments	*Fixed Income Analysis for the Chartered Financial Analyst® Program*, 2nd ed. (Fabozzi), Ch. 1–7
17	Derivative Investments	*Analysis of Derivatives for the CFA® Program,* (Chance), Ch. 1–5, 7
18	Alternative Investments	*International Investments,* 5th ed. (Solnik & McLeavey), Ch. 8
	Study Review	Online Sample Examination and Guideline Answers

Terminology you must know to take the exam

Analyze	To study or determine the nature and relationship of the parts of by analysis.
Appraise	To judge and analyze the worth, significance, or status of.
Appraisal	For real estate, the process of estimating the current market value of a property.
Arrange	To put into a proper order or into a correct or suitable sequence, relationship, or adjustment.
Calculate	To ascertain or determine by mathematical processes.
Characterize	To describe the essential character or quality of.
Cite	To quote by way of evidence, authority, or proof.
Classify	To arrange in classes; to assign to a category.
Closed-end investment company	An investment company that issues a fixed number of shares, the shares are then traded in the secondary market.
Combine	To bring into such close relationship as to obscure individual characteristics.
Comment	To observe, remark, or express an opinion or attitude concerning what has been seen or heard about the subject at hand.
Comparative sales approach	The value of a real estate is , at the most, the cost of the land and constructing the building at current prices.
Compare	To examine the character or qualities of, for the primary purpose of discovering resemblances.
Compose	To form by putting together; to form the substance of.
Compute	To determine, especially by mathematical means.
Conclude	To make a decision about; to reach a logically necessary end by reasoning.
Construct	To create by organizing ideas or concepts logically and coherently.
Contrast	To compare in respect to differences.
Convert	To change from one form or function to another.
Create	To produce or bring about by a course of action or imaginative skill.
Criticize	To consider the merits and demerits of and judge accordingly; to find fault with.
Critique	To offer a critical review or commentary.
Define	To set forth the meaning of; specifically, to formulate a definition of.

Demonstrate	To prove or make clear by reasoning or evidence; to illustrate and explain, especially with examples.
Describe	To transmit a mental image, an impression, or an understanding of the nature and characteristics of.
Design	To conceive or plan out in the mind.
Determine	To come to a decision as the result of investigation or reasoning; to settle or decide by choice among alternatives or possibilities.
Diagram	To represent by or put into the form of a diagram.
Differentiate	To mark or show a difference in; to develop different characteristics in.
Discriminate	To mark or perceive the distinguishing or peculiar features of; to distinguish by discerning or exposing differences.
Discuss	To discourse about through reasoning or argument; to present in detail.
Distinguish	To perceive a difference in; to separate into kinds, classes, or categories.
Draft	To draw up, compose, prepare, frame.
Draw	To express graphically in words; to delineate.
Estimate	To judge the value, worth, or significance of.
Evaluate	To determine or fix the value of; to determine the significance or worth of, usually by careful appraisal and study.
Explain	To give the meaning or significance of; to provide an understanding of; to give the reason for or cause of.
First-stage financing	Venture capital provided for initial commercial manufacture and sales.
Formulate	To put into a systematized statement or expression; to prepare according to a formula.
Give	To yield or furnish as a product, consequence, or effect; to offer for the consideration, acceptance, or use of another.
Identify	To establish the identity of; to show or prove the sameness of.
Illustrate	To make clear, especially by giving examples or instances.
Income approach	The value of real estate is the present value of it future income.
Indicate	To point out or point to with more or less exactness; to show or make known with a fair degree of certainty.
Infer	To derive as a conclusion from factors or premises.
Interpret	To explain or tell the meaning of; to present in understandable terms.

Judge	To form an opinion about through careful weighing of evidence and testing of premises.
Justify	To prove or show to be valid, sound, or conforming to fact or reason; to furnish grounds or evidence for.
Leveraged buyouts (LBOs)	Capital to fund a management group (a management buyout) or other investors who wish to purchase a business or company.
List	To enumerate.
Investment company	A company that sell its own shares and uses the proceeds to buy stocks, bonds or other financial instruments.
Load fund	A fund that makes an initial sales charge, so the offering price is the net asset value plus a load.
Market capitalization rate	Divide a property's net operating income by the appropriate market capitalization rate to arrive at an estimate for its current market value. It reflects the rate of return required by investors in such a property.
Match	To pair up or put in a set as possessing equal or harmonizing attributes.
Mezzanine (or bridge) financing	Venture capital provided for a company that expects to go public in the near future.
Modify	To make minor changes to give a new orientation to or to serve a new end.
Mutual fund	An open-end investment company.
Name	To mention or identify by name.
No-load fund	Shares are sold at net asset value, with no sales charge added.
Open-end investment company	A company that offers new shares to investors and redeems shares continuously.
Order	To put in order; to arrange.
Outline	To indicate the principal features or different parts of.
Real Estate Investment Trust (REIT)	A closed-end investment company that invests in real estate and mortgages on real estate.
Real Estate Limited Partnership (RELP)	A real estate syndicate that invests in different types of real estate.

Positive leverage	The return from a real estate investment is higher than the cost of debt, an investor will achieve a higher rate of return if he/she uses leverage to purchase the property.
Predict	To declare in advance; to foretell on the basis of observation, experience, or reason.
Prepare	To put into written form; to draw up.
Present	To offer or convey by way of message; to furnish or provide.
Rearrange	To put back into proper order or into a correct or suitable sequence, relationship, or adjustment.
Recommend	To bring forward as being fit or worthy; to indicate as being one's choice for something or as otherwise having one's approval or support.
Record	To set down in writing; to make an answer.
Relate	To show or establish logical or causal connection between.
Respond	To say or write something in return; to make an answer.
Restate	To state again in a new form.
Review	To make a formal or official examination of the state of; to go over or examine critically or deliberately.
Revise	To make a new, amended, improved, or up-to-date version of.
Seed financing	Venture capital provided for product development and market research, the product is still at the 'idea' stage.
Select	To choose from a number or group— usually, by fitness, excellence, or other distinguishing feature.
Separate	To set or keep apart; to make a distinction between; to sort.
Show	To set forth in a statement, account, or description; to make evident or clear.
Solve	To find a solution for a problem.
Start-up financing	Venture capital provided for early stage product development and initial marketing.
State	To express in words.
Subdivide	To divide the parts into more parts.
Summarize	To tell in or reduce to a summary.
Support	To provide with verification, corroboration, or substantiation.
Turnarounds	Capital provided to restructure a company that has problems.
Write	To put on paper; to record, state, or explain.

Important Information:

Visit www.cfaexams.com and register as a new member:For your FREE Gold Member access registeration info send an email to gold@cfaexams.com with your Name, Address, and Phone number.

Please use Gold Member Access in the subject line. We will than email you the Gold Membership registration and login / PW information to www.cfaexams.com

View and Download Supplemental Information:

To obtain additional printable content visit these download links.

http://snipurl.com/Workbook Preliminary Reading Assignments and Concept Question Workbook

http://snipurl.com/EI-CFA2005 ExamInsight 2005 CFA Level I eBook with two practice exams.

STUDY SESSION 1

Ethical and Professional Standards

Overview

Questions on Ethics and Professional Standards have a guideline weighting of 15 percent of the total Level I exam questions, and the score for this section will probably be the deciding factor in marginal pass/fail papers. This is a very important Study Session to master and much of the material will be covered again at level II and III. The material is straightforward, but it needs to be memorized, don't underestimate the amount of time you need to spend on this Session. Care needs to be taken in answering the exam questions, they are not always as easy as you might expect and you will often need to focus on identifying the *best* answer.

Our study notes summarize the Standards of Professional Conduct, and we recommend that you also read the required pages of the *Standards of Practice Handbook*. Given the high number of questions on Ethics and Standards, you will need to know each Standard and how it is applied in a variety of situations. Be aware that the CFA Institute is rewriting the Code of Ethics and Standards of Professional Conduct for 2005/2006. You will not be tested in 2005 on the proposed changes. The last Reading Assignments cover standards for reporting investment performance, or GIPS®, and you will need to know the main requirements and recommendation of the GIPS standards.

Reading Assignments

1-1 "Code of Ethics," p. 1, Standards of Practice Handbook, 8th edition (AIMR, 1999)

1-2 "Standards of Professional Conduct," pp. 2–7, Standards of Practice Handbook, 8th edition (AIMR, 1999)

1-3 "Preface" and pp. 9–159 and 265-283, Standards of Practice Handbook, 8th edition (AIMR, 1999)

1-4 "Global Investment Performance Standards – Level I Workbook" (AIMR, 2002)

1-5 Global Investment Performance Standards (AIMR, 1999)

1-1 Code of Ethics

Introduction

AIMR®, now called the CFA Institute, sees one of its main roles as promoting high standards of ethical conduct which involves educating its members on ethical standards and bringing disciplinary action against members who violate the Code and Standards. It also see its role as providing leadership in the development of global standards and promoting the increasing awareness of ethics and use of the Code and Standards within the investment profession.

The Code of Ethics sets out the ethical standards that members of CFA Institute must follow. Candidates should memorize the Code.

LOS 1-1	the candidate should be able to **state** the four components of the Code of Ethics

The Code of Ethics contains four main components.

Members of the Association of Investment Management and Research (AIMR) shall:

- Act with integrity, competence, dignity, and in an ethical manner when dealing with the public, clients, prospects, employers, employees, and fellow members.
- Practice and encourage others to practice in a professional and ethical manner that will reflect credit on members and their profession.
- Strive to maintain and improve their professional competence and the competence of others in the profession.
- Use reasonable care and exercise independent professional judgment.

Members of AIMR include CFA charterholders, CFA candidates sitting for the current year's exam, and regular members of AIMR.

1-1 View Concept Check Questions Workbook

1-2 Standards of Professional Conduct

Introduction

Candidates are required to be able to identify their responsibilities under each of the five Standards of Professional Conduct. In this Reading Assignment, we set out the Standards. We explain and interpret the Standards in Reading Assignment 1-3.

LOS 1-2 the candidate should be able to **identify** the ethical responsibilities required by the Code and Standards

The Code of Ethics is the underlying philosophy of the Standards of Professional Conduct. The Standards are organized into five broad categories:

I. Fundamental Responsibilities.
II. Relationships with and Responsibilities to the Profession.
III. Relationships with and Responsibilities to the Employer.
IV. Relationships with and Responsibilities to Clients and Prospects.
V. Relationships with and Responsibilities to the Investing Public.

Standard I: Fundamental Responsibilities

Members shall:

1. Maintain knowledge of and comply with all applicable laws, rules, and regulations (including AIMR's Code of Ethics and Standards of Professional Conduct) of any government, governmental agency, regulatory organization, licensing agency, or professional association governing the members' professional activities.
2. Not knowingly participate or assist in any violation of such laws, rules or regulations.

Standard II: Relationships with and Responsibilities to the Profession

A. Use of Professional Designation

1. AIMR members may reference their membership only in a dignified and judicious manner. The use of the reference may be accompanied by an accurate explanation of the requirements that have been met to obtain membership in these organizations.
2. Those who have earned the right to use the Chartered Financial Analyst designation may use the marks "Chartered Financial Analyst" or "CFA" and are encouraged to do so, but only in a proper, dignified, and judicious manner. The use of the designation may be accompanied by an accurate explanation of the requirements that have been met to obtain the right to use the designation.
3. Candidates in the CFA Program, as defined in the AIMR Bylaws, may reference their participation in the CFA Program, but the reference must clearly state that an individual is a candidate in the CFA Program and cannot imply that the candidate has achieved any type of partial designation.

B. Professional Misconduct

1. Members shall not engage in any professional conduct involving dishonesty, fraud, deceit or misrepresentation or commit any act that reflects adversely on their honesty, trustworthiness, or professional competence.
2. Members and candidates shall not engage in any conduct or commit any act that compromises the integrity of the CFA designation or the integrity or validity of the examinations leading to the award of the right to use the CFA designation.

C. Prohibition against Plagiarism

1. Members shall not copy or use, in substantially the same form as the original, material prepared by another without acknowledging and identifying the name of the author, publisher, or source of such material. Members may use, without acknowledgment, factual information published by recognized financial and statistical reporting services or similar sources.

Standard III: Relationships with and Responsibilities to the Employer

A. Obligation to Inform Employer of Code and Standards

Members shall:

1. Inform their employer in writing, through their direct supervisor, that they are obligated to comply with the Code and Standards and are subject to disciplinary sanctions for violations thereof
2. Deliver a copy of the Code and Standards to their employer if the employer does not have a copy

B. Duty to Employer

1. Members shall not undertake any independent practice that could result in compensation or other benefit in competition with their employer unless they obtain written consent from both their employer and the persons or entities for whom they undertake independent practice.

C. Disclosure of Conflicts to Employer

Members shall:

1. Disclose to their employer all matters, including beneficial ownership of securities or other investments, that reasonably could be expected to interfere with their duty to their employer or their ability to make unbiased and objective recommendations.
2. Comply with any prohibitions on activities imposed by their employer if a conflict of interest exists

D. Disclosure of Additional Compensation Arrangements

1. Members shall disclose to their employer in writing all monetary compensation or other benefits that they receive for their services that are in addition to compensation or benefits conferred by a member's employer.

E. Responsibilities of Supervisors

1. Members with supervisory responsibility, authority, or the ability to influence the conduct of others shall exercise reasonable supervision over those subject to their supervision or authority to prevent any violation of applicable statutes, regulations, or provisions of the Code and Standards. In so doing, members are entitled to rely on reasonable procedures designed to detect and prevent such violations.

Standard IV: Relationships with and Responsibilities to Clients and Prospects

A. Investment Process

A.1. Reasonable Basis and Representations

Members shall:

1. Exercise diligence and thoroughness in making investment recommendations or in taking investment actions.
2. Have a reasonable and adequate basis, supported by appropriate research and investigation, for such recommendations or actions.
3. Make reasonable and diligent efforts to avoid any material misrepresentation in any research report or investment recommendation.
4. Maintain appropriate records to support the reasonableness of such recommendations or actions.

A.2. Research Reports

Members shall:

1. Use reasonable judgment regarding the inclusion or exclusion of relevant factors in research reports.
2. Distinguish between facts and opinions in research reports.
3. Indicate the basic characteristics of the investment involved when preparing for public distribution a research report that is not directly related to a specific portfolio or client.

A.3. Independence and Objectivity

1. Members shall use reasonable care and judgment to achieve and maintain independence and objectivity in making investment recommendations or taking investment action.

B. Interactions with Clients and Prospects

B.1. Fiduciary Duties

1. In relationships with clients, members shall use particular care in determining applicable fiduciary duty and shall comply with such duty as to those persons and interests to whom the duty is owed. Members must act for the benefit of their clients and place their clients' interests before their own.

B.2. Portfolio Investment Recommendations and Actions

Members shall:

1. Make a reasonable inquiry into a client's financial situation, investment experience and investment objectives prior to making any investment recommendations and shall update this information as necessary, but no less frequently than annually, to allow the members to adjust their investment recommendations to reflect changed circumstances.
2. Consider the appropriateness and suitability of investment recommendations or actions for each portfolio or client. In determining appropriateness and suitability, members shall consider applicable relevant factors, including the needs and circumstances of the portfolio or client, the basic characteristics of the investment involved, and the basic characteristics of the total portfolio. Members shall not make a recommendation unless they reasonably determine that the recommendation is suitable to the client's financial situation, investment experience, and investment objectives.
3. Distinguish between facts and opinions in the presentation of investment recommendations.
4. Disclose to clients and prospects the basic format and general principles of the investment processes by which securities are selected and portfolios are constructed and shall promptly disclose to clients and prospects any changes that might significantly affect those processes.

B.3. Fair Dealing

1. Members shall deal fairly and objectively with all clients and prospects when disseminating investment recommendations, disseminating material changes in prior investment recommendations, and taking investment action.

B.4. Priority of Transactions

Transactions for clients and employers shall have priority over transactions in securities or other investments of which a member is the beneficial owner so that such personal transactions do not operate adversely to their clients' or employer's interests. If members make a recommendation regarding the purchase or sale of a security or other investment, they shall give their clients and employer adequate opportunity to act on the recommendation before acting on their own behalf. For the purposes of the Code and Standards, a member is a "beneficial owner" if the member has

1. a direct or indirect pecuniary interest in the securities;
2. the power to vote or direct the voting of the shares of the *securities* or investments;
3. the power to dispose or direct the disposition of the security or investment.

B.5. Preservation of Confidentiality

1. Members shall preserve confidentiality *of information* communicated by clients, prospects, or employers concerning matters within the scope of the client-member, prospect-member, or employer-member relationship unless the member receives information concerning illegal activities on the part of the client, prospect, or employer.

B.6. Prohibition against Misrepresentation

- Members shall not make any statements, orally or in writing, that misrepresent
- the services that they or their firms are capable of performing;
- their qualifications or the qualifications of their firm;
- the member's academic or professional credentials.
- Members shall not make or imply, orally or in writing, any assurances or guarantees regarding any investment except to communicate accurate information regarding the terms of the investment instrument and the issuer's obligations under the instrument.

B.7. Disclosure of Conflicts to Clients and Prospects

1. Members shall disclose to their clients and prospects all matters, including beneficial ownership of securities or other investments, that reasonably could be expected to impair the member's ability to make unbiased and objective recommendations.

B.8. Disclosure of Referral Fees

1. Members shall disclose to clients and prospects any consideration or benefit received by the member or delivered to others for the recommendation of any services to the client or prospect.

Standard V: Relationships with and Responsibilities to the Investing Public

A. Prohibition against Use of Material Nonpublic Information

1. Members who possess material nonpublic information related to the value of a security shall not trade or cause others to trade in that security if such trading would breach a duty, or if the information was misappropriated, or relates to a tender offer. If members receive material nonpublic information in confidence, they shall not breach that confidence by trading or causing others to trade in securities to which such information relate. Members shall make reasonable efforts to achieve public dissemination of material nonpublic information disclosed in breach of a duty.

B. Performance Presentation

1. Members shall not make any statements, orally or in writing, that misrepresent the investment performance that they or their firm have accomplished or can reasonably be expected to achieve.
2. If members communicate individual or firm performance information directly or indirectly to clients or prospective clients, or in a manner intended to be received by clients or prospective clients, members shall make every reasonable effort to assure that's such performance information is a fair, accurate, and complete presentation of such performance.

1-2 View Concept Check Questions Workbook

1-3 Standards of Practice Handbook

Introduction

CFA Institute, sees one of their main roles as promoting high standards of ethical conduct which involves educating their members on ethical standards and bringing disciplinary action against members who violate the Code and Standards. They also see their role as providing leadership in the development of global standards and promoting the increasing awareness of ethics and use of the Code and Standards within the investment profession.

Candidates need to understand

(1) the purpose and scope of each Standard
(2) the application of each Standard and
(3) procedures for compliance with each Standard.

Candidates can expect to be given a number of situations in which CFA charterholders are faced with making a decision on the best course of action to take to comply with the Standards. We reemphasize that candidates should purchase their own copy of the Standards of Practice Handbook and work through the numerous examples of applications of each Standard that are provided in the handbook. Candidates should memorize the Code.

LOS 1-3-a	**demonstrate** a thorough knowledge of the Standards of Professional Conduct by recognizing and applying the Standards to specific situations
LOS 1-3-b	**distinguish** between conduct that conforms to the Code and the Standards and conduct that violates the Code and the Standards

Standard I: Fundamental Responsibilities

Members shall:

1. Maintain knowledge of and comply with all applicable laws, rules and regulations (including AIMR's Code of Ethics and Standards of Professional conduct) of any government, governmental agency, regulatory organization, licensing agency, or professional association governing the members' professional activities.

2. Members practicing across many countries must follow the stricter of their own country's laws, the foreign country's laws, or the AIMR Codes and Standards. For example, if a member lives in a country with weak laws but has clients in countries with stricter rules than the Code and Standards, then the member must adhere to the Code and Standards. Members should ensure that they have appropriate knowledge of the laws and regulations of the countries where they do business. Members are responsible for violations that they knowingly or unknowingly participate in or assist.

3. Not knowingly participate or assist in any violation of such laws, rules or regulations.

If the member suspects that a Standard or law has been violated he should seek advice from the firm's counsel. If he knows that a Standard or law has been violated he should report it to his supervisor and get legal advice on who else to notify (he is not automatically required to inform the government or any regulatory organizations). If the situation is not remedied he should disassociate himself from the illegal or unethical activity.

Example 1-1: Fundamental responsibilities

Situation: Marilyn Monteaux, CFA, lives in Mombuta, a country where the securities laws and regulations are less strict than the Code and Standards. Monteaux conducts business with clients who reside in Singaratu, a country where very few securities laws and regulations exist. Mombuta's laws state that the law of the locality where business is conducted applies.

Comment: Monteaux must adhere to AIMR's Code and Standards although the Mombuta laws state that the securities laws and regulations of Singaratu are applicable. The rule of thumb is that a member must adhere to the stricter of the applicable local law and the Code and Standards.

Standard II: Relationship with and Responsibilities to the Profession

A. Use of Professional Designation

AIMR members may reference their membership only in a dignified and judicious manner. The use of the reference may be accompanied by an accurate explanation of the requirements that have been met to obtain membership in these organizations.

To be granted the right to use the CFA designation, a person must meet all of the following requirements:

1. Successfully completed all the Levels of the CFA Program; and
2. Maintain active membership of AIMR and pay annual membership dues; and
3. Make an ongoing commitment to abide by the requirements of CFA Institute's Professional Conduct Program.

Those who have earned the right to use the Chartered Financial Analyst designation may use the marks "Chartered Financial Analyst" or "CFA" and are encouraged to do so, but only in a proper, dignified and judicious manner. The use of the designation may be accompanied by an accurate explanation of the requirements that have been met to obtain the right to use the designation.

The acronym 'CFA' must be used as an adjective not as a stand-alone noun. For example, you should refer to someone as a CFA charterholder rather than as a 'CFA'. On business cards 'CFA' should be in capitals following the charterholder's name and 'CFA' must not be in larger font than the charterholder's name.

Candidates in the CFA Program, as defined in the CFA Institute Bylaws, may reference their participation in the CFA Program, but the reference must clearly state that an individual is a candidate in the CFA Program and cannot imply that the candidate has achieved any type of partial designation.

There is no partial designation for someone who has passed the exams but has not received their charter. Candidates part-way through the Program may only state that they are a candidate for the CFA designation, in which case they must be registered for the next exam. Candidates may also state that they have *completed one or more Levels.*

Example 1-2: Use of CFA designation

Situation: Enesco Fermi has recently passed Level II of the CFA examination. Looking for a new job, he circulates a resumé stating that he has "completed Chartered Financial Analyst II" and he holds the designation "CFA II".

Comment: Fermi has violated *Standard II (A) Use of Professional Designation.* CFA Institute does not award partial designation. However he may say that he passed Level II of the CFA exam or that he is a Level III candidate of the CFA program. Claiming to be a candidate would mean that he is registered to take the next examination; otherwise his statement would not be valid, violating the Standard.

B. Professional Misconduct

1. Members shall not engage in any professional conduct involving dishonesty, fraud, deceit or misrepresentation or commit any act that reflects adversely on their honesty, trustworthiness or professional competence.

This standard addresses compliance with regulations and personal integrity. Dishonest personal behavior reflects badly on the profession, and excessive drinking, multiple minor convictions, and fiddling of expense accounts suggest poor judgment. Members should encourage employers to adopt a code of ethics which all employees must follow, to make clear that dishonest personal behavior reflects badly on the profession, and to check potential employees' backgrounds.

1. Members and candidates shall not engage in any conduct or commit any act that compromises the integrity of the CFA designation or the integrity or validity of the examinations leading to the award of the right to use the CFA designation.

Example 1-3: Professional misconduct

Situation: Melissa White, CFA, runs her own investment advisory firm, and she serves as a proctor for the administration of the CFA examination in her city. She receives copies of the Level II CFA examination many days before the exam day. On the evening prior to the exam, she provides information concerning the examination questions to two stressed candidates whom are also her best-performing advisors.

Comment: White and the two candidates violated *Standard II (B) Professional Misconduct.* Although it does not involve clients' money or an investment recommendation, White and the two members undermined the integrity and validity of the examination.

C. Prohibition against Plagiarism

1. Members shall not copy or use, in substantially the same form as the original, material prepared by another without acknowledging and identifying the name of the author, publisher, or source of such material. Members may use, without acknowledgment, factual information published by recognized financial and statistical reporting services or similar sources.

Examples of plagiarism include basing a report on another analyst's report, using excerpts from an article, using charts or graphs or proprietary computerized spread sheets without giving the original source of the report (or gaining permission, if required). The standard not only covers plagiarism in written materials but also in oral communications, such as client meetings or presentations.

When preparing research reports, keep copies of sources of information used, acknowledge quotations, and cite sources of statistics, if they are not from a recognized data source. A recognized financial and statistical reporting service refers to sources of information that are generally recognized by the investment profession, such as Standard & Poor's Corporation or Moody's Investor Service.

Example 1-4: Plagiarism

Situation: After a few years of employment as a portfolio manager with Truthful Advisors, Bryan Matthews, CFA, starts his own investment business. Prior to his departure from Truthful, Matthews took certain steps to begin his new business, including taking with him a new, proprietary and confidential stock picking methodology. In creating marketing materials for his new firm, Matthews copies and further elaborates on the methodology.

Comment: Matthews violated *Standard II (C) Prohibition against Plagiarism* by copying another company's proprietary materials without permission and without proper credit. Matthews may have also violated *Standard III (B) Duty to Employer* by misappropriating his employer's property.

Standard III: Relationship with and Responsibilities to the Employer

A. Obligation to Inform Employer of Code and Standards

Members shall:

1. Inform their employer in writing, through their direct supervisor, that they are obligated to comply with the Code and Standards and are subject to disciplinary sanctions for violations thereof.
2. Deliver a copy of the Code and Standards to their employer if the employer does not have a copy.
3. 'In writing' means any form of correspondence that can be documented, including e-mail.

Example 1-5: Employer and Code and Standards

Situation: Roberta Johnson is a senior partner of a small brokerage firm. Johnson is neither an CFA Institute member nor a CFA charterholder. Johnson has learned that her firm will be a participant in a large bond offering. She tells her credit analyst, Thomas Black, CFA, to update his last report on the company, which was negative due to the issuer's potential cash flow difficulties. Johnson wants the report to appear more positive with regard to the issuer's prospects. Black tells Johnson that this will violate his profession's Standards of Professional Conduct, but Johnson says she doesn't know what these are. Black submits and rewrites the report with a more favorable opinion of the issuer rather than risk losing his job.

Comment: Black violated *Standard III (A) Obligation to Inform Employer of Code and Standards* because he failed to make Johnson aware of the existence of the Code and Standards. Black should have provided Johnson with a copy of the Code and Standards and informed her of his obligation to comply under the penalty of disciplinary sanctions. (In addition, by rewriting the report, if he did not disclose the firm's participation in the bond offering, Black also violated *Standard IV (A.1), Reasonable Basis and Representations*, and *Standards IV (B.7) Disclosure of Conflicts to Clients and Prospects*.)

B. Duty to Employer

1. Members shall not undertake any independent practice that could result in compensation or other benefit in competition with their employer unless they obtain written consent from both their employer and the persons or entities for whom they undertake independent practice.

When obtaining written permission, the member also needs to include (in writing) details of the types of service to be performed, duration and compensation. To potential clients, the member should disclose the identity of their employer and what the employer would charge for a similar service.

Example 1-6: Duty to employer and clients

Situation: Joanne Reilly, CFA, is an independent registered investment advisor, and she runs her own advisory business advising five high net-worth clients. She specializes in the emerging markets. With a renewed interest in the emerging markets, a local stockbroker asks Reilly to join him as a research analyst. She accepts the offer but keeps her five clients.

Comment: Reilly must seek written consent both from her new employer, the local stockbroker, and her five existing clients to comply with *Standard III (B) Duty to Employer.*

When members plan to leave their current employers there is scope for conflicts to arise, but they still have a duty to act in their employer's best interests until their resignation becomes effective. For example, the member must be careful not to misappropriate trade secrets or misuse confidential information, solicit the employer's clients or misappropriate client lists.

Example 1-7: Duty to employer

Situation: Prior to his departure from Truthful Advisors, Bryan Matthews, CFA, took certain steps to begin his new business, including talking confidentially with the clients of Truthful regarding his intention to start his own advisory firm. He also mentioned his planned fee structure, which would be more competitive than that of Truthful.

Comment: Matthews violated *Standard III (B) Duty to Employer* by soliciting his employer's clients while still employed by them.

C. Disclosure of Conflicts to Employer

Members shall:

1. Disclose to their employer all matters, including beneficial ownership of securities or other investments, that reasonably could be expected to interfere with their duty to their employer or their ability to make unbiased and objective recommendations.
2. Comply with any prohibitions on activities imposed by their employer if a conflict of interest exists.
3. Members should report any beneficial interest they have in securities and any corporate directorships or similar positions that could reasonably be considered to produce a conflict of interest to their employer. If in doubt whether any action could provide a conflict of interest, they should discuss the issue with a compliance officer or supervisor.

Example 1-8: Disclosure of conflicts to employers

Situation: Jason Woodsmith, CFA, covers South East Asian equities for Alpha Beta Investments, which specializes in emerging markets. While on a business trip to Malaysia, Woodsmith learns that index-linked notes that replicate the performance of the Malaysian composite index can be purchased in Singapore. During the Asian financial crisis, Alpha Beta reduces its exposure to Malaysia. Unknown to Alpha Beta, Woodsmith purchases in Singapore the Malaysian index-linked notes for his own account. Later, Alpha Beta increases its exposure to Malaysia, and Woodsmith then purchases the index-linked notes for his pension fund clients. Woodsmith did not sell his own portfolio to his clients, but he has enjoyed an unrealized profit of 30 percent since he bought them.

Comment: Woodsmith violated *Standard III (C) Disclosure of Conflicts to Employers* for not disclosing to his employer his ownership of the index-linked notes. Owning the notes in his personal portfolio may have impaired his professional judgment. (Woodsmith is not in violation of *Standard IV (B.4) Priority of Transaction*s because he did not sell his portfolio.)

D. Disclosure of Additional Compensation Arrangements

1. Members shall disclose to their employer in writing all monetary compensation or other benefits that they receive for their services that are in addition to compensation or benefits conferred by a member's employer.
2. Employers have a right to know that their employees remain faithful to the firm; outside commitments could erode the employee's dedication to the firm. Additional compensation includes payments from clients or from third parties.

Example 1-9: Disclosure of additional compensation

Situation: Theodore Spencer, CFA, is a manager in a small securities company. He also sits on the board of a publicly listed large resort chain. In addition to receiving an annual stipend as a member of the board, he is also given membership privileges for his family at all the resort facilities. Although Spencer discloses his annual stipend, he does not disclose receiving the membership privileges because he believe that he is only obliged to report monetary compensation, not benefits in kind.

Comment: Spencer violated *Standard III (D) Disclosure of Additional Compensation Arrangement* by failing to disclose the total compensation as a member of the board of directors. When dealing with the securities of the resort chain, he may be obligated to disclose this arrangement to clients and prospective clients under *Standard IV (B.7) Disclosure of Conflicts to Clients and Prospects.*

E. Responsibilities of Supervisors

1. Members with supervisory responsibility, authority, or the ability to influence the conduct of others shall exercise reasonable supervision over those subject to their supervision or authority to prevent any violation of applicable statutes, regulations, or provisions of the Code and Standards. In so doing, members are entitled to rely on reasonable procedures designed to detect and prevent such violations.

2. Supervisors are responsible for their subordinates' ethical behavior, even if the employee is not an CFA Institute member. Moreover, if a compliance system is not in place, then the member should not accept the supervisory responsibility until reasonable procedures are in place.

Example 1-10: Responsibilities of supervisors

Situation: Fred Smith is a trainee salesman at Churners Securities, but he is not a member of CFA Institute. Smith recently acquired a sizable private client account and has done an unusually high volume of trades for the account. Anthony Mason, CFA, Smith's supervisor, finds out that the high volume has been derived from trades in a single security, and Smith insists that the trades are performed at the client's request. Mason praises Smith for the large business volume that he generates.

Comment: As a trainee, Smith may lack the necessary judgment as to whether the high volume of trade is appropriate. Mason's failure to adequately review and investigate the unusual high volume of trades violates *Standard III (E) Responsibilities of Supervisors.* Supervisors should be aware of the actual or potential conflicts between their own self-interest and their supervisory responsibilities.

Ideally, compliance procedures should:

- Be easy to understand;
- Outline permissible conduct;
- Be clearly written and accessible;
- Outline the scope of the procedures;
- Implement a system of checks and balances;
- Designate a compliance officer and specify his authority;
- Outline procedures for reporting violations and sanctions;
- Outline procedures to document and test compliance procedures; and
- Describe the hierarchy of supervision and assign duties to supervisors.

Compliance rules should be communicated to all employees and updated periodically. Employees should be partially evaluated on their standards of professional conduct. If a violation occurs then a supervisor must respond promptly, conduct a thorough investigation and put limits on the relevant employee(s)' activities until the investigation is complete.

Standard IV: Relationships with and Responsibilities to Clients and Prospects

A. Investment Process

A.1. Reasonable Basis and Representations

Members shall:

1. Exercise diligence and thoroughness in making investment recommendations or in taking investment actions.
2. Have a reasonable and adequate basis, supported by appropriate research and investigation, for such recommendations or actions.
3. Make reasonable and diligent efforts to avoid any material misrepresentation in any research report or investment recommendation.
4. Maintain appropriate records to support the reasonableness of such recommendations or actions.

Members should analyze the basic characteristics of an investment and the requirements of a client's portfolio. Analysts should maintain files to support their recommendations including sources of information and methodology by which recommendations were made.

Example 1-11: Reasonable basis for recommendations

Situation: Gary Seller, CFA, follows Widget Corporation as a research analyst. All the information he has accumulated and documented suggests that the outlook for the company's existing products is poor. The launch of new products has been delayed. Seller overhears a financial analyst during lunch say that Widget's new products will be superior to those of its competitors. Upon returning to his office, Seller immediately changes his recommendation from "sell" to "buy".

Comment: Seller violated *Standard IV (A.1) Reasonable Basis and Representation* as he should have conducted additional research to make sure that he obtained an adequate and reasonable basis for his recommendation.

A.2. Research Reports

Members shall:

1. Use reasonable judgment regarding the inclusion or exclusion of relevant factors in research reports.
2. Distinguish between facts and opinions in research reports.
3. Indicate the basic characteristics of the investment involved when preparing for public distribution a research report that is not directly related to a specific portfolio or client.

Example 1-12: Research reports

Situation: Judy Wiencek, CFA, is a mining analyst and has written a research report on Noisy Bay Minerals. Included in her report is her own assessment of the extent of mineral reserves likely to be found on the company's land. Based on preliminary core sample results from the company's latest drilling and her own calculations, Wiencek writes, "based on the fact that the company has in excess of 200,000 ounces of gold, we rate Noisy Bay a 'buy'". She omitted to state that potentially serious environmental litigation case that has just been filed by local residents living adjacent to the mining sites.

Comment: Wiencek violated *Standard IV (A.2) Research Reports* as her calculation of the total reserves is an opinion not a fact and her omission of the relevant legal case is not reasonable.

A.3. Independence and Objectivity

1. Members shall use reasonable care and judgment to achieve and maintain independence and objectivity in making investment recommendations or taking investment action.
2. Members may come under pressure from their employers or be given free trips or gifts by corporations that may influence their recommendations or research. Members should avoid these situations which would cause, or be perceived as causing, a loss of independence. When a member visits a company or issuer, he should pay his own transport and accommodation costs. Members should avoid the issuer regularly acting as host.
3. Members should limit receiving gifts, and $100 is the maximum acceptable value.
4. Members should ensure corporate relationships, between colleagues or their employer, are disclosed. If a securities company is unwilling to publish a negative report on a company the company should be put on a restricted list and only factual information should be released.

Example 1-13: Independence and objectivity

Situation: Conrad Hillon, CFA, is an equity analyst with Faith Securities. After in-depth analysis he decides that the stock in Wireworld is overpriced at the current level. He is about to publish an unfavorable report on the company when he receives a copy of the proposal that the investment banking division of his firm has made to Wireworld to underwrite a debt offering. Hillon decided to change his 'sell' recommendation to 'buy' so that the investment banking division can win Wireworld's debt offering.

Comment: To comply with *Standard IV (A.3) Independence and Objectivity*, Hillon's analysis must be objective and based solely on the company fundamentals. Any pressure from other divisions is inappropriate. This conflict could have been avoided if, in anticipation of the debt offering, Faith Securities placed Wireworld on a restricted list.

B. Interactions with Clients and Prospects

B.1. Fiduciary Duties

1. In relationships with clients, members shall use particular care in determining applicable fiduciary duty and shall comply with such duty as to those persons and interests to whom the duty is owed. Members must act for the benefit of their clients and place their clients' interests before their own.
2. A fiduciary is an individual or institution charged with the duty of acting for the benefit of another party in matters coming within the scope of the relationship between them. This means that the fiduciary is in a position of trust. In most cases, the Standard is looking at the case where members or their employers have discretionary authority managing clients' assets.
3. The Standard distinguishes between client types and degrees of fiduciary duty:

Individuals: The manager is responsible for ensuring the client's objectives are realistic and the risks are understood. In most cases recommended investment strategies should relate to the long-term objectives of the client.

Trusts : In the United States, trustees are subject to the 'Prudent Man Rule', which states: "a fiduciary shall exercise the judgment and care, under the circumstances then prevailing, which men of prudence, character and intelligence exercise in the management of their own affairs, not in regard to speculation, but in regard to the permanent disposition of their funds, considering the probable income as well as the probable safety of their capital."

Charitable organizations and public pension plans: In the United States, many pension plans are governed by federal legislation through the Employee Retirement Income Security Act (ERISA) which, for corporate pension plans, requires that fiduciaries:

1. Act within the provisions of the plan documents.
2. Refrain from engaging in prohibited transactions.
3. Diversify the plan's investments to protect it from substantial loss.
4. Act with the care, skill, prudence, and diligence of a prudent person.
5. Act solely in the interests of the plan participants and beneficiaries.

Soft dollar arrangements occur when a manager uses client brokerage to purchase goods or services that benefit the manager. Soft dollar arrangements are not specifically prohibited, but investment firms should disclose to clients the policies being followed and adhere to any laws applicable to soft dollars.

Example 1-14: Soft dollars

Situation 1: Louise Brunn, CFA, is an analyst with Provincial Advisors covering South East Asian equities. She directs most of her trading activities to SEA Securities. SEA Securities has been paying for her travel to the markets that she covers. The commission rates are higher than average but SEA's contacts in the South East Asian region are excellent. SEA has arranged meetings for Brunn with central bank officials, senior officials of the ministries, local economists, and senior executives of local corporations during her recent trip. At the end of the trip Brunn stayed in Bali for five days of vacation that was paid for by soft-dollar commissions.

Comment 1: Brunn violated *Standard IV (B.1) Fiduciary Duties* by not exercising her fiduciary duties to determine whether the trip provides value in relation to making investment decisions and whether the quality of research and execution of SEA Securities justifies the higher commission rates. The five-day vacation is also questionable as it may also be a violation of *Standard IV (B.7) Disclosure of Conflicts to Clients and Prospects.*

Situation 2: Dominique Rhynes, CFA, is a portfolio manager at Dark Cloud Advisors, managing a number of pension fund accounts. She directs most of her trades to JNI Brokerage, despite the higher commission rates, because of the close relationship between the executives of the two firms. The quality of research of JNI is considered average but JNI absorbs overhead expenses of Dark Cloud Advisors such as online information services and magazine subscriptions.

Comment 2: Rhynes and Dark Cloud Advisors breached the fiduciary duty as stated in *Standard IV (B.1) Fiduciary Duties* by not seeking the best value brokerage services to benefit the pension funds and their beneficiaries.

B.2. Portfolio Investment Recommendations and Actions

Members shall:

1. Make a reasonable inquiry into a client's financial situation, investment experience, and investment objectives prior to making any investment recommendations and shall update this information as necessary, but no less frequently than annually, to allow the members to adjust their investment recommendations to reflect changed circumstances.
2. Consider the appropriateness and suitability of investment recommendations or actions for each portfolio or client. In determining appropriateness and suitability, members shall consider applicable relevant factors, including the needs and circumstances of the portfolio or client, the basic characteristics of the investment involved, and the basic characteristics of the total portfolio. Members shall not make a recommendation unless they reasonably determine that the recommendation is suitable to the client's financial situation, investment experience, and investment objectives.
3. Distinguish between facts and opinions in the presentation of investment recommendations.
4. Disclose to clients and prospects the basic format and general principles of the investment processes by which securities are selected and portfolios are constructed and shall promptly disclose to clients and prospects any changes that might significantly affect those processes.

This long list of requirements *really* means that advisors must know their clients prior to giving them advice. In order to comply with the Standard, a member should have an investment policy statement (IPS) for each client. The IPS should include:

- the type and nature of the client and the client's aversion to risk;
- investor objectives in terms of risk and return; and
- investment constraints, such as liquidity, legal requirements, time horizon, tax position, and unique circumstances.

Example 1-15: Portfolio investment recommendations

Situation: Pierre Dauphinais, CFA, an investment advisor, has been advising Delia Moynihan, a risk-averse client, on the use of put options in her equity portfolio. The purpose is to protect the portfolio against stock market declines. Dauphinais educates Moynihan regarding the possible outcomes, including the risks involved and tax implications. He also explained the possible disastrous scenario if stock prices drop precipitously without holding the put options.

Comment: When determining the suitability of investments, the primary issue is the characteristics of the client's entire portfolio, not looking on an issue-by-issue basis. In this case Dauphinais appears to have properly considered the investment in the context of the entire portfolio and thoroughly explained the investment to the client making him comply with *Standard IV (B.2) Portfolio Investment Recommendations and Actions.*

B.3. Fair Dealing

1. Members shall deal fairly and objectively with all clients and prospects when disseminating investment recommendations, disseminating material changes in prior investment recommendations, and taking investment action.

Fair dealing means that the member does not favor one client above any other when disseminating recommendations or taking investment action. This means that material changes to recommendations must be communicated to all clients known to hold the security or to have placed orders contrary to the recommendation. Material changes must be announced to all clients *at the same time.*

Discretionary and non-discretionary clients must be treated equally. New issues should be offered to all clients for whom the issue is an appropriate investment, and if an issue is over subscribed, then it should be distributed on a pro-rata basis.

It is important that members encourage their employers to develop written allocation procedures, particularly for block trades and new issues.

Example 1-16: Fair dealing

Situation: Monica Abidin, CFA, works in the investment management department of a private client firm. She learns that the research department has just issued a "buy" recommendation for ABC Ketchup Inc. She buys a large block of ABC Ketchup stock and allocates it to the mutual finds that are managed internally since these accounts are particularly performance sensitive. She then reviews the firm's other clients and purchases additional shares where appropriate.

Comments: Abidin's activities clearly violate *Standard IV (B.3) Fair Dealing* by giving the mutual funds preferential treatment over other clients.

B.4. Priority of Transactions

1. Transactions for clients and employers shall have priority over transactions in securities or other investments of which a member is the beneficial owner so that such personal transactions do not operate adversely to their clients' or employer's interests. If members make a recommendation regarding the purchase or sale of a security or other investment, they shall give their clients and employer adequate opportunity to act on the recommendation before acting on their own behalf. For purposes of the Code and Standards, a member is a "beneficial owner" if the member has

   a. direct or indirect pecuniary interest in the securities;

the power to vote or direct the voting of the shares of the securities or investments;

the power to dispose or direct the disposition of the security or investment.

Personal transactions are those for the member or someone in his immediate family, although family accounts that are also client accounts should be treated equally with other clients.

Example 1-17: Priority of transactions

Situation: Baillie Trafford, CFA, is a portfolio manager at a local investment firm. His parents opened a retirement account with the firm. Whenever appropriate IPOs become available he firstly allocates the shares to his other clients and then places any remaining portion into his parents' account. He has adopted this procedure to avoid the accusation that he gives favorable treatment to his parents.

Comment: Trafford is in violation of his fiduciary duties to his parents, as stated in *Standard IV (B.4) Priority of Transactions*, by treating them differently to other clients. His parents are entitled to the same treatment as any other fee-paying client of the firm. If Trafford has beneficial ownership to the account, then a pre-clearance for personal transactions is required.

B.5. Preservation of Confidentiality

1. Members shall preserve the confidentiality of information communicated by clients, prospects, or employers concerning matters within the scope of the client-member, prospect-member, or employer-member relationship unless the member receives information concerning illegal activities on the part of the client, prospect, or employer.
2. In general, avoid disclosing any information about a client except to authorized fellow employees. However, a member may want to disclose information of a non-confidential nature in which case they should check if the information is relevant to the work being performed for the client and whether disclosure enables the member to provide a better service to the client. Confidential information can be provided to CFA Institute to cooperate with an investigation.

Example 1-18: Confidentiality

Situation: Roger Warner, CFA, is a portfolio manager. He manages an endowment plan of a university. The university has given Warner a confidential review of the future plans for expansion so he can manage the fund, taking into account projected capital expenditure and cash flow requirements. Geronimo, a friend of Warner, is a local construction businessman who is interested in making a tax-deductible contribution to the endowment plan with the understanding that his company would be favorably considered when bidding for construction work on the future expansion plan. Before speaking to the trustees of the endowment fund, Geronimo insists on meeting with Warner to find out about the future plans of the university.

Comment: Warner owes confidentiality to the endowment fund and its trustees and therefore should refuse to divulge any information to Geronimo. Any confidential information entrusted to a member must be treated as such according to *Standard IV (B.5) Preservation of Confidentiality.*

B.6. Prohibition against Misrepresentation

1. Members shall not make any statements, orally or in writing, that misrepresent
   a. the services that they or their firms are capable of performing;

their qualifications or the qualifications of their firm;
the member's academic or professional credentials.

2. Members shall not make or imply, orally or in writing, any assurances or guarantees regarding any investment except to communicate accurate information regarding the terms of the investment instrument and the issuer's obligations under the instrument.

Example 1-19: Investment guarantees

Situation: Marcus sells mortgage-backed derivatives called interest-only strips (IOs) to his public pension clients and describes them as 'guaranteed by the U.S. government'. The regulations stipulate that public pension clients can only invest in securities guaranteed by the U.S. government. The reality is that IO investors are entitled to the interest stream only, not the principal. The underlying mortgage pool is guaranteed by the U.S. government, but not the interest stream, which can fluctuate depending on many factors.

Comment: Marcus misrepresented the terms and character of the investment and therefore violated *Standard IV (B.6) Prohibition against Misrepresentation.*

B.7. Disclosure of Conflicts to Clients and Prospects

1. Members shall disclose to their clients and prospects all matters, including beneficial ownership of securities or other investments, that reasonably could be expected to impair the member's ability to make unbiased and objective recommendations.
2. Beneficial ownership is the most important issue here, but other issues include a member or the member's firm providing directors or acting as consultant to an issuer, acting as underwriter or broker-dealer relationships.

Example 1-20: Disclosure of conflicts

Martin Bolle, CFA, is an analyst and partner in his firm. He sits on the board of a publicly listed company, and he writes research reports recommending the securities of the publicly listed company.

Comment: *Standard IV (B.7) Disclosure of Conflicts to Clients and Prospects* requires Bolle to disclose his service on the company's board of directors and to his clients and prospects.

B.8. Disclosure of Referral Fees

1. Members shall disclose to clients and prospects any consideration or benefit received by the member or delivered to others for the recommendation of any services to the client or prospect.
2. The disclosure should be in writing and include the nature of the benefit together with an estimate of the dollar value. Members should consult a supervisor and legal counsel concerning any such prospective arrangements.

Example 1-21: Referral fees

Situation: Jerry Weiss, CFA, is a discretionary portfolio manager with Advent Investment Management, responsible for the management of pension fund investments. He is often requested by his contacts to recommend mutual funds for their personal investments. As his firm does not offer retail products, Weiss refers the requests to the portfolio manager of a mutual fund, in a competing firm, whom he has known since his school days. He receives compensation for the occasional sales made. The mutual fund's performance is in the top quartile.

Comment: Although they are not clients of his firm, Weiss is obliged to disclose any such arrangement to personal contacts in order to comply with *Standard IV (B.8) Disclosure of Referral Fees.* Weiss also needs to make a written report to his supervisor in order to comply with *Standard III (D) Disclosure of Additional Compensation Arrangements.*

Standard V: Relationships with and Responsibilities to the Investing Public

A. Prohibition against Use of Material Nonpublic Information

1. Members who possess material nonpublic information related to the value of a security shall not trade or cause others to trade in that security if such trading would breach a duty or if the information was misappropriated or relates to a tender offer.
2. If members receive material nonpublic information in confidence, they shall not breach that confidence by trading or causing others to trade in securities to which such information relates. Members shall make reasonable efforts to achieve public dissemination of material nonpublic information disclosed in breach of a duty.

'Material' means disclosure is likely to have an impact on the price of a security or reasonable investors would want to know the information before making an investment decision. 'Nonpublic' means that if the information has not been disseminated in the market place and investors have not had a chance to react to the information.

However it is acceptable for an analyst to piece together and analyze public information and non-material non-public information to predict events, which would have the same market outcome as receiving material non-public information. This is called mosaic theory.

For tender offers (one company buying the shares of another company, usually at a premium) the possession of non public information triggers trading restrictions.

Example 1-22: Use of nonpublic information

Situation: James Welch, CFA, is a portfolio manager of Churners Securities who was at his son's school party when he overheard another parent saying that she looked at an opened file marked CONFIDENTIAL in her husband's brief case and found out that Woking Corporation is planning to make a purchase offer for a competitor, Guildford Corporation. "The company will pay three times the current market price for Guildford Corporation stock!" Welch returned home and immediately purchased Guildford Corporation shares for his clients.

Comment: First, Welch takes an investment action based on material non-public information regarding a tender offer, which is a violation of *Standard V (A) Material Nonpublic Information*. Second, Welch knows such information has been misappropriated because a confidential file was opened.

Most firms will set up an information barrier, a 'fire wall' to prevent communication of nonpublic information from one department of a firm to another. For example the corporate finance department should be separated from the sales and research departments. Additionally clear procedures need to be in place to ensure that employees can recognize material nonpublic information and report to a supervisor or compliance officer if they receive such information.

B. Performance Presentation

1. Members shall not make any statements, orally or in writing, that misrepresent the investment performance that they or their firm have accomplished or can reasonably be expected to achieve.
2. If members communicate individual or firm performance information directly or indirectly to clients or prospective clients, or in a manner intended to be received by clients or prospective clients, members shall make every reasonable effort to assure that such performance information is a fair, accurate, and complete presentation of such performance.

AIMR has developed the AIMR Performance Presentation Standards (AIMR-PPS℠) and more recently the Global Investment Performance Standards (GIPS℠) as common, accepted sets of standards for the investment management industry. Although compliance is voluntary, members and their firms are encouraged to adopt the standards, and they are becoming increasingly widely used. (GIPS are covered in more detail in the next two sections.)

All performance statements must be fair, accurate, and complete.

Example 1-23: Performance presentation

Situation: Terry Arbuckle, CFA, is a senior partner of Provincial Advisors and circulates a performance sheet of the firm's Technology Funds for the years 1999 through 2004. During a client meeting, Arbuckle states: "All returns are in compliance with CFA Institute Performance Presentation Standards." In fact, returns are calculated in compliance with GIPS Performance Presentation Standards, except that the calculation of the rate of return is money weighted.

Comment: Arbuckle is in violation of *Standard V (B) Performance Presentation* because the performance measurement does not *fully* comply with GIPS. Provincial Advisors must meet all the requirements to be able to claim full compliance.

LOS 1-3-c	**explain** the Rules of Procedure for Proceedings Related to Professional Conduct and **distinguish** among the various sanctions that may be imposed

Disciplinary Procedures and Sanctions

Grounds for discipline

'Covered Persons' (as defined by CFA Institute in its Bylaws) may be disciplined for

- Violation of CFA Institute's Articles of Incorporation and the Code and Standards.
- Imposition of a disciplinary sanction or injunction by governmental or judicial agency or private self-regulatory organization.
- Conviction, or guilty plea, for a felony, or crime punishable by more than one year in prison.
- Being barred for an indefinite period of time from registration under securities laws.
- Each CFA Institute member, CFA charterholder, and candidate in the CFA Program must sign an annual Professional Conduct Statement. Failure to complete, sign and return to CFA Institute the annual professional conduct statement is grounds for discipline.
- Falsification of information on candidate or society membership applications.
- Any good cause including failure to cooperate with CFA Institute in its enquiry into the person's professional conduct.

Sanctions

In increasing order of severity, the disciplinary actions (sanctions) are:

Private censure, although this is announced publicly it does not specifically identify the person.

1. Public censure, announced publicly including giving the person's name.
2. Timed suspension of membership, membership in CFA Institute and affiliated organizations is suspended for a specified period of time.
3. Timed suspension of the right to use the CFA designation, this is suspended for a specified period of time.
4. Revocation of membership, membership in CFA Institute and affiliated organizations is permanently revoked.
5. Revocation of the right to use the CFA designation, the designation is permanently revoked.
6. Summary suspension, automatically removes membership in CFA Institute and affiliated organizations, the right to use the CFA designation and/or the right to participate in the CFA program.
7. Suspension or revocation from further participation in the CFA Professional Designation Study and Examination Program, automatic and/or permanent removal from participating in the Candidate Examination Program.

Investigation

The process of investigation involves:

1. A designated officer is appointed to investigate the matter involving the professional conduct of a person or member.
2. The person is issued with a 'Notice of Enquiry' to which they should respond within 30 days.
3. The designated office will either terminate the enquiry, or serve a 'Notice of Private Censure (for minor violations) or a Stipulation Agreement if a stronger sanction is warranted.
4. When the person receives a Stipulation Agreement they may request a Hearing Panel, which will consist of three to five members. Once the Hearing panel has looked at the evidence supporting the case then it will write a report and determination.
5. In turn a person can then request that a Review Panel reviews the determination of the Hearing Panel. The review Panel's determination is final.

Generally all proceedings are confidential and the records are not made public.

1-3 View Concept Check Questions Workbook

1-4 Global Investment Performance Standards-Level 1 Workbook and

1-5 Global Investment Performance Standards

Introduction

These Reading Assignments look at Global Investment Performance Standards or GIPS® standards which cover the professional and ethical standards that should be followed for the presentation of investment performance. Candidates are expected to know the objectives of GIPS as well as the requirements and recommendations of GIPS and the verification procedures. None of the material is difficult but you will need to allocate time to memorize the long list of requirements and recommendations.

Note:
Reading Assignment 4 does not contain any LOS; however, sections from "Global Investment Performance Standards Level I Workbook" have been incorporated into the LOS for Reading Assignment 5.

LOS 1-5-a **explain** why the GIPS® standards were created

The investment management industry itself is *global*: firms have operations in multiple countries; and the clients and prospective clients reside in different countries.

It is important to have standards that make it easier to compare results between compliant firms. Many countries have not established investment performance standards and, if they do have standards, these may only apply to the specific country and not have broad applicability.

LOS 1-5-b **explain** what parties the GIPS standards apply to and who the standards serve

GIPS apply to two main parties:

1. Investment management firms (firms).
2. Clients and prospective clients (investors), including consultants on behalf of investors.

The clients and prospective clients (the investors with money to be managed) will be the main beneficiaries of the GIPS. The aim is to create a greater confidence amongst investors who deal with firms that choose to comply with GIPS. Those firms who comply with GIPS will give assurances that the performance presentations will be fair and complete. They will also be comparable across compliant firms.

LOS 1-5-c **state** the objectives and key characteristics of the GIPS standards

GIPS objectives

1. To obtain worldwide acceptance of a standard for the calculation and presentation of investment performance in a fair, comparable format that provides full disclosure.
2. To ensure accurate and consistent investment performance data for reporting, record-keeping, marketing and presentation.
3. To promote fair, global competition among investment firms for all markets without creating barriers to entry for new firms.
4. To foster the notion of industry self-regulation on a global basis.

GIPS lay out the *minimum* requirements that a firm must follow in order to ethically calculate and fairly present the investment performance.

Because a single firm can manage hundreds or thousands of investment portfolios, the standards provide the framework of how to fairly and accurately report historical performance to clients and prospective clients.

The characteristics of GIPS

Compliance with GIPS is voluntary and not required by legal or regulatory bodies. They set the minimum requirements that a firm should follow, in some cases providing additional information might give a client or prospective client a clearer understanding.

One of the key concepts is the use of "composites." A composite is a collection of portfolios which are grouped in a set, with reasonable and consistent criteria applied to them, such as the investment strategies, styles or objectives. The criteria should be clearly identifiable and distinguishable. Examples of composites are, European active medium-sized equity portfolios, Japanese passive Nikkei 225 portfolios, emerging market bond index portfolios.

The standards require that all fee-paying portfolios be included in at least one composite under the criteria of ex-ante (prior to the fact based on a pre-established criteria) basis not ex-post (after the fact) basis. This prevents firms "cherry picking" the best performing portfolios for inclusion.

LOS 1-5-d	**state** the scope of the GIPS standards with respect to definition of firm, historical performance record, and compliance

Definition of a firm

There are three ways a firm may define itself:

1. An entity registered with the appropriate national regulatory authority overseeing its investment management activities; or
2. An investment firm, subsidiary, or division held out to clients or potential clients as a distinct business unit; or
3. All the assets that are managed in one or more base currencies fall under the definition of a firm (until January 1, 2005).

The definition of a firm is important to provide the notion of firmwide compliance. For example, if a firm manages bonds and equities then compliance must be claimed for both departments.

Historical performance record

Compliance requires a minimum historical performance record of 5 years. Subsequently firms must build up to a 10-year track record.

Firms can present their entire performance history if they choose to. If a firm has more than 5 years of historical performance, it may present its non-compliant performance results along with its compliant record, provided:

- the compliant track record begins no later than January 1, 2000; and
- the non-compliant periods are disclosed and the reasons for non-compliance are explained.

Compliance

There are only two options for compliance: fully comply with all the requirements or else, if not compliant, no reference to the GIPS is allowed.

Only investment management firms can claim compliance with GIPS. Consultants and software houses can assist investment management firms to meet compliance requirements, but they are unable to claim the compliance themselves.

LOS 1-5-e	**identify** the requirements and recommendations of each of the five main topics of the GIPS standards, i.e., input data, calculation methodology, composite construction, disclosures, and presentation and reporting

Input data

Consistency of input data is critical if investment performance is going to be comparable between firms.

Requirements (compulsory)

1. All data and information used to make calculations and support performance data must be captured and maintained.
2. Portfolio valuations must be based on market values (not cost or book values).
3. Portfolios must be valued at least quarterly, after January 1st 2001 portfolios must be valued at least monthly. After January 1st 2010 it is anticipated that portfolios must be valued each time there is an external cash flow.
4. Trade-date accounting must be used after January 1st 2005.
5. Accrual accounting must be used for fixed-income securities, and other assets that accrue interest income.
6. After January 1st 2005 accrual accounting must also be used for dividends.

Recommendation (voluntary)

1. Sources of exchange rates must be the same for the composite and the benchmark.

Calculation Methodology

The calculation methodology must be uniform firm-wide and across all composites.

Requirements (compulsory)

1. Total return calculations, including realized and unrealized gains plus income must be used.
2. Time-weighted rates of return that adjust for cash flows must be used. Periodic returns must be calculated using geometric averages. After January 1st 2005 adjustment for daily- weighted cash flows must be used. After January 1st 2010, it is anticipated that actual valuations will be required when there is an external cash flow.
3. In both numerator and denominator the market value of fixed-income securities must include income.
4. Composites must be asset weighted.
5. Returns from cash and cash-equivalents held in portfolios must be included in total returns.
6. Performance must be calculated after trading expenses.

7. If a firm sets a minimum asset value for portfolios to be included in a composite, no portfolios below that asset value can be included in the composite.

Recommendations (voluntary)

1. Returns should be calculated net of non-reclaimable withholding taxes on dividends, interest and capital gains. Reclaimable taxes should be accrued.
2. Performance adjustments for external cash flows should be treated in a consistent manner.

Composite Construction

A composite is a group of portfolios that represents a particular investment objective or strategy. The composite return is the asset-weighted average of the returns of the portfolios in the composite.

Requirements (compulsory)

1. All fee-paying discretionary accounts must be included in a composite.
2. Firm composites must be defined according to similar investment objectives and/or styles.
3. New portfolios must be included in a composite.
4. Terminated portfolios must be included in the historical records up to the last full measurement period that the portfolio was under management.
5. Portfolios must not be switched from one composite to another unless for documented reasons. The historical record must remain in the appropriate composite.
6. Convertibles and other hybrids must be treated consistently over time and across composites.
7. When carve-out returns (for example looking at one asset class of a portfolio and excluding cash) are used to create a stand-alone composite cash must be allocated and the allocation method must be disclosed. After January 1st 2005, carve-out returns cannot be included in single-asset class composite returns unless they are managed separately.
8. Composites must include all assets under management and model or simulated portfolios should not be included.

Recommendations (voluntary)

1. Separate composites should be created for different levels of allowed asset exposure.
2. Portfolios that use hedging should be put into separate composites.

Disclosures

These allow firms to elaborate on the performance figures provided.

Requirements (compulsory)

1. The definition of 'firm' used to determine the total assets and firm-wide compliance.
2. Total firm assets in each period.
3. A complete list and description of all the firm's composites must be available.
4. If settlement-date accounting is used.
5. The minimum asset level, if any, for which portfolios are not included in a composite.
6. The currency used for performance calculation.
7. The details of use of leverage and derivatives.
8. Whether performance is calculated gross or net of management fees.

Details on treatment of withholding tax.

1. The percentage of a composite invested in countries or regions not represented in the benchmark (if a benchmark is used).
2. Any inconsistencies between sources of exchange rates in the composite and benchmark.
3. The percentage, if any, of non-fee paying accounts in the composite.
4. If local laws and regulations differ with GIPS, the manner in which they differ.
5. For any performance presented for periods before January 1st 2000 that does not comply with GIPS, the period of noncompliance and why it is not in compliance.
6. If carve-outs have been included, the method used to allocate cash. (Carve-outs refer to, for example, a single asset class being 'carved-out' of a multiple asset class portfolio).

Recommendations (voluntary)

1. Portfolio valuation sources and methods.
2. The calculation method used.
3. The firm's fee schedule, if performance is presented before fees.
4. When performance is net of fees, the average weighted management fee.
5. Any significant changes within the firm (ownership or personnel changes).

Presentation and Reporting

Requirement (compulsory)

1. At least five years of performance, or since inception if shorter, that is GIPS compliant. Thereafter the firm must add each year until they reach ten years' of data that is compliant.
2. Annual returns.
3. The number of portfolios and amount of assets in the composite, and percentage of firm's total assets in the composite.
4. Dispersion of individual portfolio returns around the average composite return.
5. The standard compliance statement indicating firm-wide compliance with GIPS.
6. The composite creation date.
7. Firms linking non-GIPS-compliant performance data must meet disclosure requirements under Disclosures (previous section).
8. Performance for periods of less than a year cannot be annualized.
9. Performance results of a past firm or affiliation can only be disclosed if certain criteria are met.
10. If a compliant firm acquires or is acquired by a non-compliant firm they have a year to bring the non-compliant firms acquired assets into compliance.
11. If a composite is made up of single-asset carve-outs from multiple asset composites additional information must be disclosed.
12. The total returns for the benchmark for the same periods that the composite returns are presented.

Recommendations (voluntary)

The following should be included in the presentation of composite returns or disclosed a supplementary information:

1. Performance gross of investment management fees and custody fees and before taxes.
2. Cumulative returns for composites and benchmarks.
3. Equal-weighted means and median returns for each composite.
4. Volatility over time of the composite return.
5. Inconsistencies with respect to the use of exchange rates.
6. Relevant risk measures for composites and benchmarks (e.g. tracking error, beta, and duration).

LOS 1-5-f **describe** the scope and purpose of verification

Investment firms that claim compliance with GIPS are responsible for their claim. If they wish to claim verification they must hire an independent third party.

Verification covers the *whole firm,* not just specific composites.

The verification tests:

1. Whether the firm is compliant on a firm wide basis and the construction of all the composites follows GIPS requirements.
2. Whether the firm's process and procedures of calculation are incompliance with the GIPS standards.

The initial minimum period for which verification is done is one year, but it is recommended that verification is performed for all periods for which GIPS compliance is claimed.

Verification is not required but is strongly recommended. An independent third-party verification brings credibility to the claim of compliance.

LOS 1-5-g	**describe** the required verification procedures (including pre-verification procedures)

Verification Procedures

The following are the minimum procedures that verifiers must follow when verifying an investment firm's compliance with GIPS.

Pre-verification Procedures

1. Knowledge of the Firm.

Verifiers must look at samples of the firm's performance reports and other information to ensure they have the appropriate knowledge of the firm.

1. Knowledge of GIPS.

Verifiers must have an up-to-date knowledge of GIPS requirements and recommendations.

2. Knowledge of the Performance Standards.

Verifiers must have knowledge of country-specific performance standards, laws and regulations.

Knowledge of Firm Policies.

3. Verifiers must ensure that they are familiar with the firm's policies and procedures, including:
   a. fully discretionary versus non-discretionary accounts

- definition of composites
- timing of inclusion of new accounts
- timing of exclusion of closed accounts
- accrual of interest and dividend income
- market valuation of investment securities
- method for computing time-weighted portfolio returns
- assumptions on timing of capital inflows/outflows
- method for computing composite returns
- presentation of composite returns
- timing of implied taxes due on income and realized capital gains
- use of securities/countries not included in a composite's benchmark
- use of leverage and other derivatives
- other policies and procedures relevant to performance presentation

4. Knowledge of Valuation Basis for Performance Calculations

Verifiers must ensure that they are familiar with the firm's method and policies for recording valuation information, including:

a. classifying fund flows
b. accounting treatment of income, interest and dividend receipts
c. treatment of taxes, tax reclaims and tax accruals
d. recognizing purchases, sales and the opening and closing of other positions
e. accounting for investments and derivatives that is consistent with GIPS

Verification Procedures

1. Definition of the Firm.

Ensure that this has been appropriately defined.

1. Composite Construction.

Verifiers must ensure that:

a. the firm has defined and maintained composites in compliance with GIPS
b. actual discretionary fee-paying portfolios are included
c. definition of discretion has been consistent
d. all accounts are included in their respective composites
e. benchmarks are consistent with composite definitions
f. guidelines for creating and maintaining composites are consistent
g. the list of composites is complete

2. Nondiscretionary Accounts.

Verifiers must take a sample of accounts to check that classification of discretionary and non-discretionary conforms with the account agreements.

3. Sample Account Selection

Verifiers may take a sample of accounts to check GIPS compliance; the following criteria should be used when selecting a sample but are only the minimum criteria to be used:

a. number of composites at the firm
b. number of portfolios in each composite
c. nature of the composite
d. total assets under management
e. system of checks and balances in place

f. number of years under examination

computer applications, external performance measurers and calculation of performance results

4. Account Review.

Verifications should determine:

a. whether the timing of the initial inclusion in the composite is consistent with the firm's policies
b. whether the timing of exclusion from the composite is consistent with the firm's policies
c. whether objectives are consistent with the manager's composite definition
d. the existence of accounts by tracing accounts from client agreement to the composites
e. that portfolios sharing the same guidelines are included in the same composite
f. that shifts between composites meet the guidelines set by the specific account agreement

5. Performance-Measurement Calculation.

Verifiers should check the performance calculation is consistent with the firm's policies by

a. recalculating sample accounts using an acceptable formula as prescribed by GIPS
b. taking a sample of composite calculations to assure accuracy of the asset weighting of returns, calculation of the dispersion and the geometric link of returns

6. Disclosures.

Presentations must include the information and disclosures required by GIPS.

7. Maintenance of Records.

Sufficient records must be maintained by the verifier including a representation letter from the client confirming major policies.

1-4 and 1-5 View Concept Check Questions Workbook

STUDY SESSION 2

Investment Tools:

Quantitative Methods

Overview

Quantitative Methods, covered in Study Sessions 2 and 3, have a guideline weighting of 12% of the questions in the 2005 exams. For candidates without a strong math background parts of these two study sessions can be tough and time consuming but it is vital that you make the necessary effort to master the key principles. They will reoccur in several other study sessions in the level I syllabus and again when you move on to levels II and III. Remember that the focus is not just on learning the equations and quantitative methods but being able to apply them to decision-making in an investment context.

Study Session 2 starts out with the Reading Assignment on time value of money, which establishes the link between present and future values of sums of money, whether they are a single cash flow or multiple cash flows such as annuities and perpetuities. In the second Reading Assignment we move on to the application of time value of money techniques to calculating internal rates of return and net present values of investments to enable us to value securities. The third Reading Assignment provides an introduction to statistical concepts and provides the tools to describe and analyze data. The Study Session concludes with an introduction to probability which will help us to make investment decisions when outcomes are uncertain.

Reading Assignments

Quantitative Methods for Investment Analysis, 2nd edition, Richard A Defusco, Dennis W. McLeavey, Jerald E. Pinto, and David E. Runkle (CFA Institute, 2004)

2-1-A "The Time Value of Money," Ch. 1

2-1-B "Discounted Cash Flow Applications," Ch. 2

2-1-C "Statistical Concepts and Market Returns," Ch. 3

2-1-D "Probability Concepts," Ch. 4

2-1-A "The Time Value of Money"

Introduction

This is one of the most important Reading Assignments at Level I, and you *must* excel at calculating the present value and future value of cash flows. The time value of money is not only important at Level I but also at Levels II and III. Your investment now will pay off in your future studies.

When possible answer questions with your CFA INSTITUTE-approved financial calculator: Hewlett-Packard HP-12C or Texas Instruments BA II Plus. Practicing questions on the HP-12C or BA II Plus from the outset will help bolster your confidence for examination day, and you need not worry about learning new keystrokes at the last minute before the exam.

Note for BA II Plus users: before you attempt any of the examples, change the default number of annual compounding periods from 12 to 1. Do this by following these keystrokes:

2nd [P/Y] 1 ENTER 2nd [QUIT]

LOS 2-1-A-a **explain** an interest rate as the sum of a real risk-free rate and premiums that compensate investors for distinct types of risk

An **interest rate** is simply the rate of return that links cash flow paid or received on different dates, or the required rate of return if a sum of money is received in one year's time rather than today. It is the opportunity cost of money since it is the interest lost if money is spent today rather than saved for a year. The interest rate is often referred to as the discount rate.

The interest rate, denoted by r, is made up of a real risk-free rate plus four risk premiums that compensate for risk.

r = Real risk-free rate + Inflation premium + Default risk premium + Liquidity premium
+ Maturity premium

The **real risk-free rate** is the interest rate for a totally risk-free security assuming expectations of zero inflation. It reflects the underlying preference of individuals to consume today rather than tomorrow.

The **inflation premium** reflects the average inflation rate expected by investors and the inflation premium compensates for the erosion of purchasing power due to inflation. The nominal risk-free rate is approximately the sum of the real risk-free rate and the inflation rate (strictly the product of 1 plus the real risk-free rate and 1 plus the inflation rate). In the US, for example, the nominal risk-free rate is quoted as the Treasury bill rate over the appropriate time horizon.

A **default risk premium** is the compensation for the risk that the borrower will fail to make a payment that is contractually agreed.

The **liquidity premium** reflects the time or the cost involved in converting the asset to cash. A Treasury bill does not pay a liquidity premium but for a bond there might well be a liquidity premium.

A **maturity premium** reflects the increased sensitivity of long-term debt to a change in market interest rates. The difference in interest rates on long-term debt versus short-term debt will partly be explained by a maturity premium.

LOS 2-1-A-b **calculate** the future value (FV) and present value (PV) of a single sum of money

Inflation erodes the purchasing power of money, so one dollar tomorrow will buy fewer goods and services than one dollar today. This LOS answers the question: "what is a dollar to be received sometime in the future worth *today*?"

Future value of a single sum of money

Starting with a known value today (present value), Equation 2-1 finds the future value (FV) for a single sum of money paid over a number of discrete periods:

$$FV_N = PV(1 + r)^N \qquad \textbf{(Equation 2-1)}$$

where

FV_N	=	future value, N periods from today
N	=	number of periods from today
PV	=	present value today
r	=	rate of interest, or required rate of return, per period

If interest rates are assumed to be positive, then FV_N will always be greater than PV.

The raising of the term in brackets by the exponent N is called compounding. As interest is calculated in the first period, it is added to the initial amount to yield the closing balance for the first period. Interest is calculated on this higher closing value, therefore, the second interest payment will be higher than in the first period. This process continues each and every period.

Example 2-1 Future value of a single sum of money

A lump-sum of $1,000 is deposited today into an account that will pay interest at a rate of 10 percent annually for three years. What will be the value of the deposit at the end of three years?

Write down the known variables, and use Equation 2-1 to solve for FV_N

Explicit use of Eq. 2-1:	Calculator keystrokes for:			
$PV = \$1,000$	**HP-12C**		**BA II Plus**	
$r = 10\% = 0.10$	[f] CLEAR [FIN]		[2nd] [QUIT] [2nd] [CLR TVM]	
$N = 3$	1000 [CHS] [PV]	**-1,000.00**	1000 [+/-] [PV]	**PV = -1,000.00**
$FV_N = PV(1+r)^N$	10 [i]	**10.00**	10 [I/Y]	**I/Y = 10.00**
$= \$1,000(1+0.1)^3$	3 [n]	**3.00**	3 [N]	**N = 3.00**
$= \$1,000 \times 1.10^3$	[FV]	**1,331.00**	[CPT] [FV]	**FV = 1,331.00**
$= \$1,000 \times 1.331$				
$= \$1,331.00$				

You can directly enter percentages into the CFA INSTITUTE-approved calculators; only convert percentages to decimals if you are explicitly using Equation 2-1 (and equations to follow).

A time line can also be used to show the relationship between present values and future values. In a time line the index t represents a point in time a stated number of periods from today, so for a time N periods from today t = N. A time line is shown below

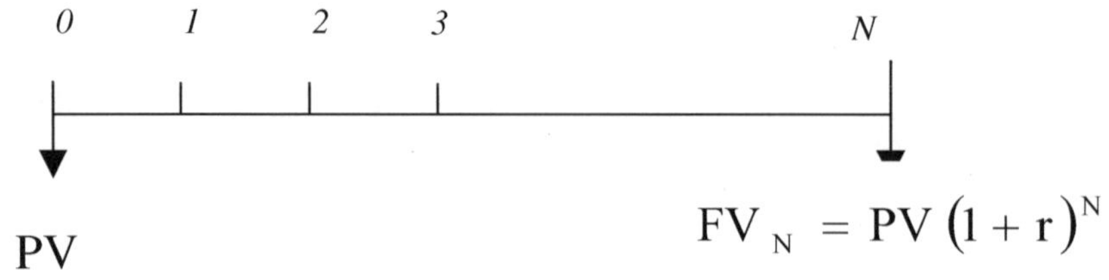

Present value of a single sum of money

Starting with a known future value, Equation 2-1 can be rearranged for present value (PV) for a single sum of money:

$$PV = \frac{FV_N}{(1+r)^N} \qquad \textbf{(Equation 2-2)}$$

where all variables have been defined in Equation 2-1.

The process of bringing distant cash flows to today is called discounting, which is the fundamental quantitative technique of investment analysis.

Assuming that the rate of interest (r) is positive, the denominator in Equation 2-2 will be greater than 1.0, and dividing FV by a number greater than 1.0 will always make PV < FV.

Note that PV does not have the subscript N. Unlike FV_N, PV can only be at one time: today.

Example 2-2 Present value of a single sum of money

An investment will be worth $7,000 in five years' time, and the opportunity cost rate (the best rate of return available on investments of similar risk) over the next five years will be 3 percent. What is the fair value of the investment today?

Write down the known variables, and use Equation 2-2 to solve for PV

Explicit use of Eq. 2-2:	Calculator keystrokes for:			
$FV = \$7,000$	**HP-12C**		**BA II Plus**	
$r = 3\% = 0.03$	[f] CLEAR [FIN]		[2nd] [QUIT] [2nd] [CLR TVM]	
$N = 5$	7000 [FV]	**7,000.00**	7000 [FV]	**FV = 7,000.00**
$PV = \frac{FV}{(1+r)^N}$	3 [i]	**3.00**	3 [I/Y]	**I/Y = 3.00**
$= \frac{\$7,000}{(1+0.03)^5}$	5 [n]	**5.00**	5 [N]	**N = 5.00**
$= \frac{\$7,000}{1.15927}$	[PV]	**-6,038.26**	[CPT] [PV]	**PV = -6,038.26**
$= \$6,038.26$				

The investment will be a cash inflow in five years' time; therefore, [FV] is entered into the calculators as a positive value.

LOS 2-1-A-c	**distinguish** between the stated annual interest rate and the effective annual rate
LOS 2-1-A-d	**calculate** the effective annual rate, given the stated annual interest rate and the frequency of compounding

In all of the previous examples, we have assumed that interest payments are made once a year. In many cases, however, interest is paid more frequently than once a year, even though the interest rate is quoted in annual terms. The stated annual interest rate excludes the reinvestment of interest; whereas, the effective annual rate (EAR) includes the reinvestment of interest. The EAR for m compounding periods per year is given by Equation 2-3

$$\text{EAR} = \left(1 + \frac{r_S}{m}\right)^m - 1 \qquad \textbf{(Equation 2-3)}$$

where

m = number of compounding periods per year
r_s = stated annual interest rate
N = number of years

If interest were paid continuously, then the EAR is given by Equation 2-4:

$$\text{EAR} = e^{r_S} - 1 \qquad \textbf{(Equation 2-4)}$$

If interest is compounded more frequently than once a year ($m > 1$), than the EAR will be higher than the stated rate. If interest is paid annually ($m = 1$), then EAR will equal the stated annual rate.

Example 2-3 Computing effective annual rates

An investment product offers a stated annual interest rate of 6 percent, and interest will be reinvested at the same rate. What is the effective annual rate if interest is paid

1. annually?
2. quarterly?
3. monthly?
4. continuously?

If interest is paid annually, then $m = 1$, and we use Equation 2-3 to solve for EAR:

$$\text{EAR} = \left(1 + \frac{r_S}{m}\right)^m - 1 = \left(1 + \frac{0.06}{1}\right)^1 - 1 = 1 + 0.06 - 1 = 0.06, \text{ or } 6\%$$

If interest is paid quarterly, then m = 4, and we use Equation 2-3 to solve for EAR:

$$EAR = \left(1 + \frac{r_S}{m}\right)^m - 1 = \left(1 + \frac{0.06}{4}\right)^4 - 1 = (1 + 0.015)^4 - 1 = 0.0614, \text{ or } 6.14\%$$

If interest is paid monthly, then m = 12, and we use Equation 2-3 to solve for EAR:

$$EAR = \left(1 + \frac{r_S}{m}\right)^m - 1 = \left(1 + \frac{0.06}{12}\right)^{12} - 1 = (1 + 0.005)^{12} - 1 = 0.0617, \text{ or } 6.17\%$$

If interest is paid continuously, and we use Equation 2-4 to solve for EAR:

$$EAR = e^{r_S} - 1 = e^{0.06} = 1.0618 - 1 = 0.0618, \text{ or } 6.18\%$$

Note that the EAR becomes higher as the compounding frequency increases.

LOS 2-1-A-e	**solve** time value of money problems when compounding periods are other than annual

If payments are made more frequently than once a year we also need to adjust the FV formula. Equation 2-5 is the adjusted FV formula.

$$FV_N = PV\left(1 + \frac{r_S}{m}\right)^{m \times N} \qquad \textbf{(Equation 2-5)}$$

where

m	=	number of compounding periods per year
r_s	=	stated annual interest rate
N	=	number of years

As the compounding frequency increases, FV increases. If taken to the limit, interest can be compounded over an infinite number of periods (m approaches •). This leads to the continuous compounding formula, shown in Equation 2-6:

$$FV_N = PVe^{r_S \times N} \qquad \textbf{(Equation 2-6)}$$

where

e is the natural exponent whose value is approximately 2.7183.

To practice invoking the programmed value of e on your CFA INSTITUTE-approved financial calculator, follow the appropriate keystrokes:

HP-12C	1 [g] [e^x]	**2.7183**
BA II Plus	1 [2nd] [e^x]	**2.7183**

Example 2-4 Comparing FV for different compounding periods

An investment product offers a stated annual interest rate of 6 percent, with a three-year maturity. Interest will be reinvested at the same rate. If an investor buys $1,000 of the product, how much money will he receive in three years' time, assuming that interest is paid

1. annually?
2. quarterly?
3. monthly?
4. continuously?

Write down the known variables:

$$PV = \$1{,}000$$

$$r_S = 6\%, \text{ or } 0.06$$

$$N = 3$$

If interest is paid annually, then m = 1, and we use Equation 2-1 to solve for FV:

$$FV_N = \$1{,}000(1+0.06)^3 = \$1{,}000 \times 1.191016 = \$1{,}191.02$$

If interest is paid quarterly, then m = 4, and we use Equation 2-5 to solve for FV:

$$FV_N = \$1{,}000\left(1+\frac{0.06}{4}\right)^{4\times 3} = \$1{,}000(1+0.015)^{12} = \$1{,}000 \times 1.195618 = \$1{,}195.62$$

If interest is paid monthly, then m = 12, and we use Equation 2-5 to solve for FV:

$$FV_N = \$1{,}000\left(1+\frac{0.06}{12}\right)^{12\times 3} = \$1{,}000(1+0.005)^{36} = \$1{,}000 \times 1.196681 = \$1{,}196.68$$

If interest is paid continuously, then use Equation 2-6 to solve for FV:

$$FV_N = PVe^{r_S \times N} = \$1{,}000e^{0.06\times 3} = \$1{,}000e^{0.18} = \$1{,}000 \times 1.197217 = \$1{,}197.22$$

Note that the FV becomes higher as the compounding frequency (m) increases.

Both CFA INSTITUTE-approved financial calculators can accommodate compounding periods that are more frequent that annually. Here, we demonstrate quarterly compounding over three years for an initial $1,000 deposit:

HP-12C		BA II Plus	
f CLEAR FIN	**0.00**	2nd [QUIT] 2nd [CLR TVM]	
1000 CHS PV	**-1,000.00**	2nd [P/Y] 4 ENTER	P/Y = **4.00**
6 ENTER 4 ÷ i	**1.50**	2nd [QUIT]	
3 ENTER 4 × n	**12.00**	1000 +/- PV	PV = **-1,000.00**
FV	**1,195.62**	6 I/Y	I/Y = **6.00**
		3 2nd [×P/Y] N	N = **12.00**
		CPT FV	FV = **1,195.62**

The HP-12C has special keys to handle monthly compounding, and resetting the BA II Plus restores monthly compounding as the default.

HP-12C		BA II Plus	
f CLEAR FIN	**0.00**	2nd [RESET] ENTER	
1000 CHS PV	**-1,000.00**	1000 +/- PV	**PV = -1,000.00**
6 g 12÷	**0.50**	6 I/Y	**I/Y = 6.00**
3 g 12×	**36.00**	3 2nd [×P/Y] N	**N = 36.00**
FV	**1,196.68**	CPT FV	**FV = 1,196.68**

A series of keystrokes invoking the percentage-change registers will enable both the HP-12C and BA II Plus to handle continuous compounding:

HP-12C		BA II Plus	
f CLEAR FIN	**0.00**	2nd [QUIT] 2nd [CLR TVM]	
1000 CHS PV	**-1,000.00**	2nd [P/Y] 1 ENTER	**P/Y = 1.00**
1 ENTER 6 % g e^x Δ% i	**6.18**	2nd [QUIT] 2nd [Δ%]	
3 ENTER n	**3.00**	1 ENTER	**OLD = 1.00**
FV	**1,197.22**	⇩ 6 % 2nd [e^x] ENTER	**NEW = 1.06**
		⇩ CPT I/Y	**%CH = 6.18**
		2nd [QUIT]	
		1000 +/- PV	**PV = -1,000.00**
		3 N	**N = 3.00**
		CPT FV	**FV = 1,197.22**

LOS 2-1-A-f **calculate** the FV and PV of an ordinary annuity and an annuity due

Series of cash flows (annuities)

In general, an annuity is a series of periodic, equal payments that occur during period *N*, and all payments are assumed to grow at a constant rate of interest (r). For ordinary annuities the first payment is made at the end of the first period.

The **future value** of an ordinary annuity is given by Equation 2-7:

$$FV = A\left[\frac{(1+r)^N - 1}{r}\right] \qquad \textbf{(Equation 2-7)}$$

where FV = future value of the annuity of N equal payments

A = amount of equal annuity payments
N = number of equal annuity payments
r = rate of interest, or required rate of return, per period

The term in brackets in Equation 2-7 is called the future value annuity factor, which gives the future value of an ordinary annuity of $1 per period.

Example 2-5 Future value of an ordinary annuity

An investor will make payments of $2,000 at the *end* of each of the next ten years, and the payments earn interest at an annual rate of 5 percent. Calculate the value of the accumulated funds at the end of the ten years.

Write down the known variables, and use Equation 2-7 to solve for FV

Explicit use of Eq. 2-7:	Calculator keystrokes for:	
$A = \$2,000$	**HP-12C**	**BA II Plus**
$r = 5\% = 0.05$	[f] CLEAR [FIN]	[2nd] [QUIT] [2nd] [CLR TVM]
$N = 10$	2000 [CHS] [PMT]	2000 [+/-] [PMT]
	-2,000.00	**PMT = -2,000.00**
$FV = A\left[\frac{(1+r)^N - 1}{r}\right]$	5 [i] **5.00**	5 [I/Y] **I/Y = 5.00**
	10 [n] **10.00**	10 [N] **N = 10.00**
	[FV] **25,155.79**	[CPT] [FV] **FV = 25,155.79**
$= \$2,000\left[\frac{(1+0.05)^{10} - 1}{0.05}\right]$		
$= \$2,000 \times 12.57789$		
$= \$25,155.79$		

If the first payment is made immediately, rather than paid at the end of the first year, then the annuity is an annuity due. To calculate the future value of an annuity due, multiply by the FV of an ordinary annuity by (1 + r), since all annuity payments will be received one period earlier and will earn an extra period of interest.

Equation 2-8 is the formula for an annuity due:

$$FV = A\left[\frac{(1+r)^N - 1}{r}\right](1+r) \qquad \textbf{(Equation 2-8)}$$

where all variables have been defined previously.

Example 2-6 Future value of an annuity due

An investor will make payments of $2,000 at the *beginning* of each of the next ten years, and the payments earn interest at an annual rate of 5 percent. Calculate the value of the accumulated funds at the end of the ten years.

Write down the known variables, and use Equation 2-8 to solve for FV

Explicit use of Eq. 2-8:	**Calculator keystrokes for:**	
$A = \$2{,}000$	**HP-12C**	**BA II Plus**
$r = 5\% = 0.05$	[f] CLEAR [FIN]	[2nd] [QUIT] [2nd] [CLR TVM]
$N = 10$	[g] BEG	[2nd] [BGN] [2nd] [SET] [2nd]
$FV = A\left[\frac{(1+r)^N - 1}{r}\right](1+r)$	2000 [CHS] [PMT]	[QUIT]
	-2,000.00	2000 [+/-] [PMT]
$= \$2{,}000\left[\frac{(1+0.05)^{10} - 1}{0.05}\right](1+0.05)$	5 [i] **5.00**	**PMT = -2,000.00**
	10 [n] **10.00**	5 [I/Y] **I/Y = 5.00**
$= \$2{,}000 \times 12.57789 \times 1.05$	[FV] **26,413.57**	10 [N] **N = 10.00**
$= \$26{,}413.57$		[CPT] [FV] **FV = 26,413.57***

Note that all variables in this example are the same as those in the Example 2-5 for an ordinary annuity. The future value of an annuity due will always be larger than the future value of an ordinary annuity because all payments will have one extra period to grow, which accounts for the multiplication of the annuity due by (1 + r).

Equation 2-9 gives the present value of an ordinary annuity:

$$PV = A\frac{\left[1 - \frac{1}{(1+r)^N}\right]}{r} \qquad \textbf{(Equation 2-9)}$$

where all variables have been defined previously.

Example 2-7 Present value of an ordinary annuity

An investor will make payments of $2,000 at the *end* of each of the next ten years, and the payments earn interest at an annual rate of 5 percent. Calculate today's value of the accumulated funds.

Write down the known variables, and use Equation 2-9 to solve for PV

Explicit use of Eq. 2-9:	Calculator keystrokes for:	
$A = \$2{,}000$ $r = 5\% = 0.05$ $N = 10$ $PV = A\dfrac{\left[1-\dfrac{1}{(1+r)^N}\right]}{r}$ $= \$2{,}000\dfrac{\left[1-\dfrac{1}{(1+0.05)^{10}}\right]}{0.05}$ $= \$2{,}000 \times 7.72173$ $= \$15{,}443.46$	**HP-12C** [f] CLEAR [FIN] 2000 [CHS] [PMT] **-2,000.00** 5 [i] **5.00** 10 [n] **10.00** [PV] **15,443.47**	**BA II Plus** [2nd] [QUIT] [2nd] [CLR TVM] 2000 [+/-] [PMT] **PMT = -2,000.00** 5 [I/Y] **I/Y = 5.00** 10 [N] **N = 10.00** [CPT] [PV] **PV = 15,443.47**

Equation 2-10 gives the present value of an annuity due:

$$PV = A\frac{\left[1-\frac{1}{(1+r)^N}\right]}{r}(1+r) \qquad \textbf{(Equation 2-10)}$$

where all variables have been defined previously.

You might be surprised that the (1 + r) term is multiplied rather than divided to the formula for the PV of an ordinary annuity. Compared with an ordinary annuity, there is one less discounting period for each payment, which results in the multiplication by (1 + r).

Example 2-8 Present value of an annuity due

An investor will make payments of $2,000 at the *beginning* of each of the next ten years, and the payments earn interest at an annual rate of 5 percent. Calculate today's value of the accumulated funds.

Write down the known variables, and use Equation 2-10 to solve for PV

Explicit use of Eq. 2-10:	Calculator keystrokes for:	
$A = \$2,000$	**HP-12C**	**BA II Plus**
$r = 5\% = 0.05$	[f] CLEAR [FIN]	[2nd] [QUIT] [2nd] [CLR TVM]
$N = 10$	[g] BEG	[2nd] [BGN] [2nd] [SET] [2nd] [QUIT]
$PV = A \dfrac{\left[1 - \dfrac{1}{(1+r)^N}\right]}{r}(1+r)$	2000 [CHS] [PMT] **-2,000.00**	2000 [+/-] [PMT] **PMT = -2,000.00**
	5 [i] **5.00**	5 [I/Y] **I/Y = 5.00**
$= \$2,000 \dfrac{\left[1 - \dfrac{1}{(1+0.05)^{10}}\right]}{0.05}(1+0.05)$	10 [n] **10.00**	10 [N] **N = 10.00**
	[PV] **16,215.64**	[CPT] [PV] **PV = 16,215.64***
$= \$2,000 \times 7.72173 \times 1.05$		
$= \$16,215.63$		

LOS 2-1-A-g **calculate** the PV of a perpetuity

A perpetuity is a special case of an ordinary annuity. A perpetuity's payments begin at the end of the first period, but the periodic payments last *forever.* Because there is not end date for perpetuities, you cannot calculate the FV of them. Thus, you can calculate only the PV of a perpetuity.

Equation 2-11 is the formula for the present value of a perpetuity:

$$PV = \frac{A}{r} \quad \textbf{(Equation 2-11)}$$

where all variables have been defined previously.

Example 2-9 Present value of a perpetuity

A perpetuity makes annual payments of \$1,000, and the current rate of interest is 6 percent. What is the current value of the perpetuity?

Write down the known variables, and use Equation 2-11 to solve for PV:

$$A = \$1{,}000$$

$$r = 6\% = 0.06$$

$$PV = \frac{A}{r}$$

$$PV = \frac{\$1{,}000}{0.06}$$

$$PV = \$16{,}666.67$$

If cash flows or payments are not equal for each period then the cash flows must be discounted individually to calculate the present value, or compounded individually to calculate the future value.

LOS 2-1-A-h **calculate** an unknown variable, given the other relevant variables, in time value of money problems

Up to now we have looked at examples where we have been given the interest rate, number of time periods and either the present value or future values of the cash flows. We can use the same equations to calculate the interest rate, number of payments or periods, or annuity amount when the present or future values are given. The CFA INSTITUTE-approved financial calculators can easily solve for any unknown variable.

Example 2-10 Rate of interest for a perpetuity

A perpetuity with annual payments of $1,000 has a current market price of $7,125. Calculate the implied rate of interest:

Rearrange Equation 2-11 and solve for r

$$A = \$1000$$
$$PV = \$7{,}125$$
$$PV = \frac{A}{r}$$
$$\$7{,}125 = \frac{\$1{,}000}{r}$$
$$r = \frac{\$1{,}000}{\$7{,}125} = 0.140, \text{ or } 14.0\%$$

Example 2-11 Calculate the number of periods

An investor puts $200,000 into a mutual fund and expects to receive a return of 12% per annum. How long will it take to double the size of the investment?

Using Equation 2-1

$$FV_N = PV(1+r)^N$$
$$(1.12)^N = 2$$

Now we need to take the logarithm of both sides

$$N \ln(1.12) = \ln 2$$
$$N = 0.693 / 0.113 = 6.13$$

Or use a financial calculator.

It will take 6.13 years to double the value of the investment.

LOS 2-1-A-i **calculate** the FV and PV of a series of uneven cash flows

When there are unequal cash flows and we need to calculate the PV of this series of cash flows we will need to compute the PV of each cash flow individually and then calculate the sum of these PVs. Similarly to calculate the FV we will need to calculate the FV of each cash flow individually and then take the sum of these FVs.

Example 2-12 FV and PV of a series of uneven cash flows

An investment will pay $5,000 at the end of the first year, $4,000 at the end of the second year, and $3,000 at the end of the third year. If the required rate of return is 12 percent, what will be the value of these payments at the end of three years?

Calculate the FV of each cash flow separately by compounding, and add them together:

Year 1: FV of $5,000	=	$\$5,000 \times (1.12)^2$	=	$6,272.00
Year 2: FV of $4,000	=	$\$4,000 \times (1.12)^1$	=	$4,480.00
Year 3: FV of $3,000	=	$\$3,000 \times (1.12)^0$	=	$3,000.00

Sum = $13,752.00

If the cash flows were paid at the beginning of each year, then all of the cash flows would have been compounded by an extra period.

Calculate the PV of each cash flow separately by discounting, and add them together:

$$
\begin{aligned}
PV &= \frac{\$5,000}{(1.12)^1} + \frac{\$4,000}{(1.12)^2} + \frac{\$3,000}{(1.12)^3} \\
&= \$4,464.29 + \$3,188.78 + \$2,135.34 \\
&= \$9,788.41
\end{aligned}
$$

We could have obtained the same answer by discounting $13,752 for three years:

$$\begin{aligned} PV &= \frac{FV}{(1+r)^N} \\ &= \frac{\$13,752}{(1+0.12)^3} \\ &= \frac{\$13,752}{1.404928} \\ &= \$9,788.40 \end{aligned}$$

You can also use the cash-flow worksheet embedded in your CFA INSTITUTE-approved financial calculator to solve for PV (but not FV) of a series of uneven cash flows:

Calculator keystrokes for:			
HP-12C		**BA II Plus**	
[f] CLEAR [FIN]	**0.00**	[CF] [2nd] [CLR WORK]	**CF_0 = 0.00**
0 [g] [CF_0]	**0.00**	0 [ENTER]	**CF_0 = 0.00**
5000 [g] [CF_j]	**5,000.00**	[⇩] 5000 [ENTER]	**C01 = 5,000.00**
4000 [g] [CF_j]	**4,000.00**	[⇩] [⇩] 4000 [ENTER]	**C02 = 4,000.00**
3000 [g] [CF_j]	**3,000.00**	[⇩] [⇩] 3000 [ENTER]	**C03 = 3,000.00**
12 [i]	**12.00**	[NPV] 12 [ENTER]	**I = 12.00**
[f] [NPV]	**9,788.40**	[⇩] [CPT]	**NPV = 9,788.40**

LOS 2-1-A-j	**draw** a time line, **specify** a time index, and **solve** problems involving the time value of money as applied, for example, to mortgages and savings for college tuition or retirement

Time lines

A time line illustrates cash inflows and outflows for any given financial problem. A **time index** is a scale used on the time line to distinguish between PF, FV, and the intermediate cash flows. By visualizing the problem, a time line can help solve any financial problem.

Consider the time line containing information about a single cash deposit:

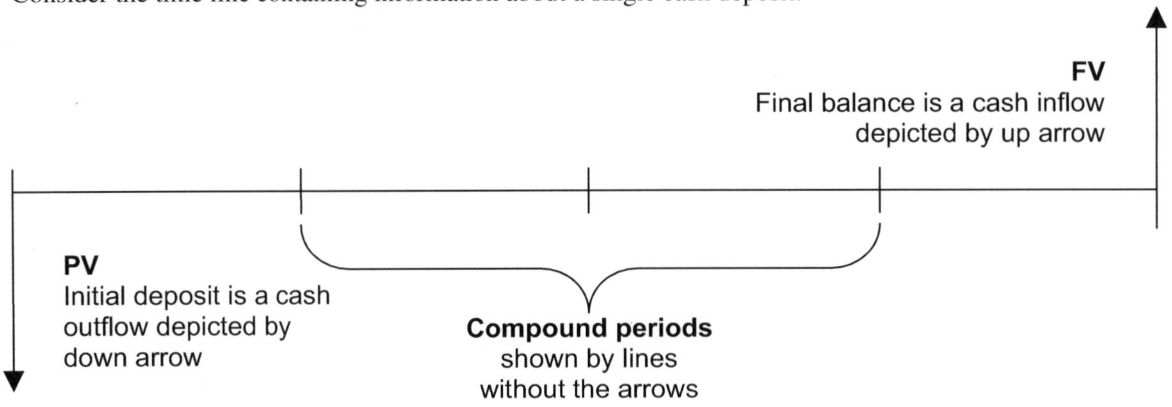

We now look at solving questions on mortgages and savings plans.

Example 2-13 Mortgage payments

A house purchase is financed with a 20-year fixed rate mortgage with monthly payments. $200,000 is borrowed, and the interest rate is 6%. Monthly mortgage payments can be calculated using Equation 2-9 for the PV of an annuity.

PV = $200,000

Periodic interest rate = 6%/12 = 0.5%

Number of periods = 20 x 12 = 240

$$PV = A\frac{\left[1-\frac{1}{(1+r)^N}\right]}{r}$$

$$\$200{,}000 = A \times (200 - 60.4)$$

$$A = \$1{,}433$$

$1,433 is the monthly mortgage payment.

For a mortgage, the borrower receives an initial cash inflow (positive PV) and makes a series of payments (negative outflow) over the life of the mortgage.

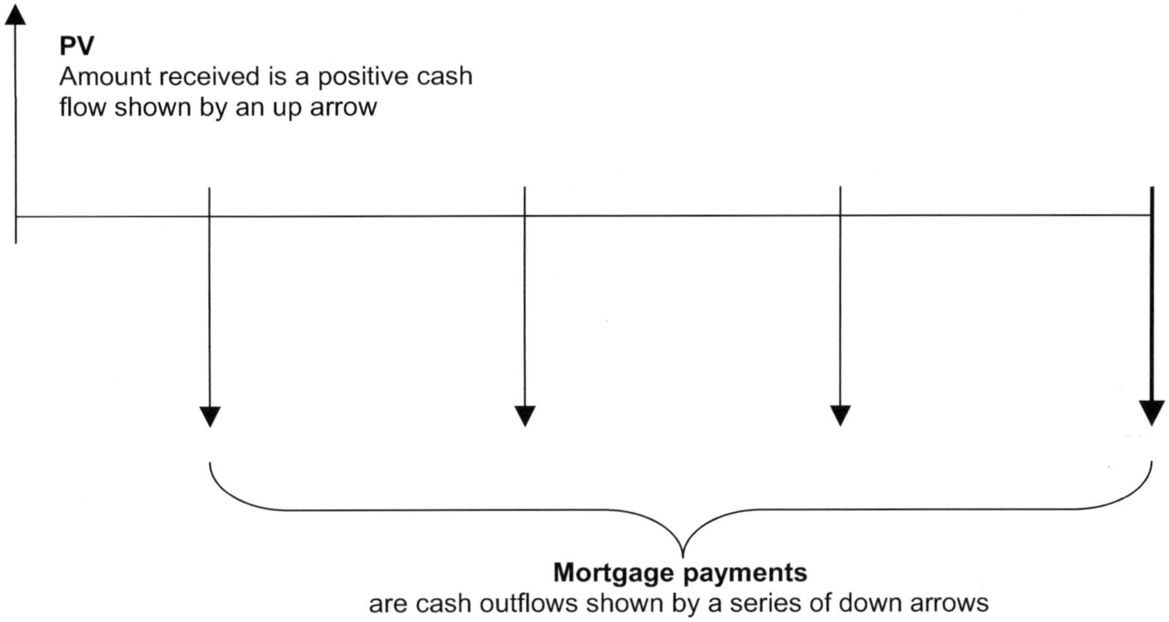

Example 2-14 Saving for retirement

An employee is saving for retirement and can afford to save \$6,000 at the end of each year for the next 25 years. He decides to invest the money in a portfolio of assets that he expects to earn 8% per annum. At the end of 25 years the amount that he estimates will be available is given using Equation 2-7 for the future value of an ordinary annuity.

$$FV = A\left[\frac{(1+r)^N - 1}{r}\right]$$

$$= \$6{,}000\left[(1.08)^{25} - 1\right]/0.08$$

$$= \$6{,}000\,(5.8485)/0.08$$

$$= \$438{,}638$$

LOS 2-1-A-k	**explain** the cash flow additivity principle in time value of money applications

The cash flow additivity principle says that cash flows indexed at the same point of time are additive. We can see this by looking at time lines. Assume two series of cash flows, A and B, as shown below

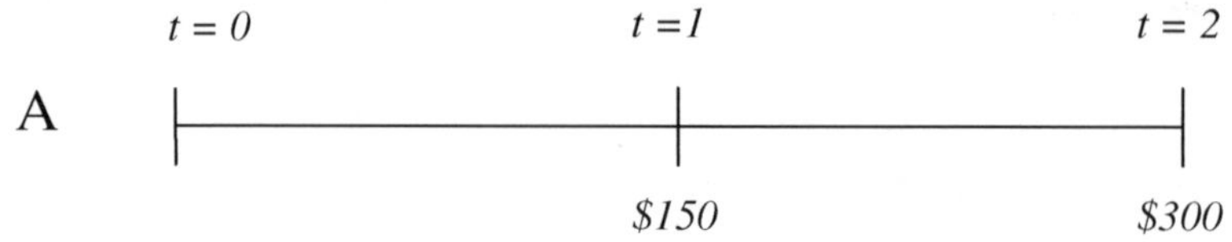

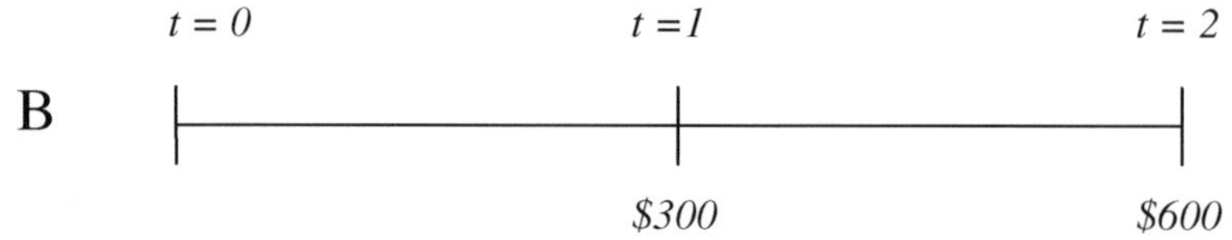

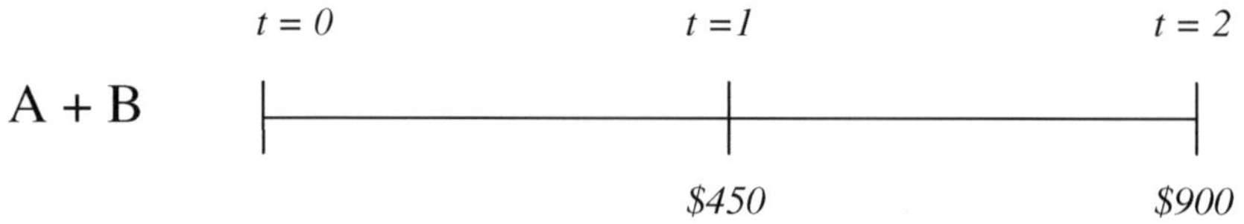

If interest rates are 10% the future value of A's and B's cash flows are

A: $\$150(1.10) + \$300 = \$465$
B: $\$300(1.10) + \$600 = \$930$

The sum of the future values is $1,395. This is the same as the future value of the combined cash flows:

A + B: $\$450(1.10) + \$900 = \$1,395$.

2-1-A View Concept Check Questions Workbook

2-1-B "Discounted Cash Flow Applications"

In the section we apply time value of money analysis to valuing financial instruments. First of all we consider internal rates of return and net present value calculations; these provide a critical input to the decision whether any investment (bond, equity, real estate etc.) is attractive or not. We also consider alternative measures for calculating portfolio returns and the impact of the choice of method on the calculation results. Finally we analyze cash flows from short-term money market instruments and look at the different methods for calculating yields.

LOS 2-1-B-a	**calculate** and **interpret** the net present value (NPV) and the internal rate of return (IRR) of an investment

Net Present Value (NPV)

NPV differs from present value (PV) in that it takes into account cash outflows. In the context of valuing an investment this means the present value is adjusted for the cost (cash outflow) of the investment.

The steps in valuing a project or investment are

Step 1 Identify all the cash inflows and outflows

Step 2 Identify the appropriate discount rate or opportunity cost of capital

Step 3 Calculate the PV of each cash flow, outflows are negative, inflows are positive

Step 4 Sum all the PVs to arrive at the NPV of the project or investment

Step 5 Apply the NPV rule, if the NPV of a project or investment is positive it is expected to add to shareholders' wealth and we should accept the investment, and if it is negative we should reject it.

The formula for NPV is given in Equation 2-12

$$NPV = \sum_{t=0}^{N} \frac{CF_t}{(1+r)^t}$$ **(Equation 2-12)**

where

CF_t	=	expected cash flow at time t
N	=	investment's life
r	=	discount rate or opportunity cost of capital

Example 2-15 Net present value

A company is considering an investment which will cost \$8 million and will generate net cash flows of \$1 million per annum in perpetuity. If the cost of capital is 12% should the investment be accepted or rejected?

$$NPV = CF_0 + \overline{CF}/r$$
$$= -\$8{,}000{,}000 + (\$1{,}000{,}000/0.12)$$
$$= \$333{,}333$$

where

$\overline{CF}$ = the cash flow in perpetuity

Since this is positive the project should be accepted.

Internal Rate of Return

This is the rate of return generated by an investment and it is the rate of return or discount rate which makes the NPV = 0, using Equation 2-12

$$NPV = 0 = \sum_{t=0}^{N} \frac{CF_t}{(1 + IRR)^t}$$

or, if we arrange and the investment equals the initial cash flow

$$\text{Investment} = \sum_{t=1}^{N} \frac{CF_t}{(1 + IRR)^t}$$

The assumption is made that cash flows are reinvested at the IRR.

The decision rule is that if the IRR is greater than the opportunity cost of capital (or **hurdle rate**) then the investment should be accepted, if less then the investment should be rejected.

Example 2-16 Internal rate of return

Using the data in Example 2-15, we need to solve

$$\$8{,}000{,}000 = \$1{,}000{,}000/IRR$$
$$IRR = 0.125 \text{ or } 12.5\%$$

Therefore, if the cost of capital is less than 12.5% then the company should invest, if it is more than 12.5% they should not invest, and if it is equal investment will increase the size of the company but not increase stockholders' wealth.

LOS 2-1-B-b	**contrast** the NPV rule to the IRR rule

The NPV and IRR methods give the same decision for projects which are independent but when a company is making a choice between different projects, of different sizes or with different timings of cash flow, the two methods may produce conflicting recommendations. Since the NPV method uses the market-determined cost of capital, and we are concerned with shareholder wealth, it is the better measure to use.

These concepts are covered again in Study Session 11, LOS 1-C.

LOS 2-1-B-c	**discuss** problems associated with the IRR method

It is important to note that if the cash flows could only be reinvested at a rate less than the IRR, or 12.5% in Example 2-16, the actual return realized will be less than the IRR. Similarly if the reinvestment rates available are higher then the return would be higher.

LOS 2-1-B-d	**distinguish** between money-weighted and time-weighted rates of return
LOS 2-1-B-e	**calculate** the money-weighted and time-weighted rates of return of a portfolio

Measuring Portfolio Returns

Two ways of measuring the return from a portfolio are the money-weighted and time-weighted rates of return.

Money-weighted rate of return

This is the same as the internal rate of return for a portfolio and takes into account the timing and amount of cash flows in and out of a portfolio.

Example 2-17 Money-weighted rate of return

An investor purchases a share at \$100 and a year later purchases another share at \$120. At the end of the second year he sells both shares at \$125 per share. He receives dividends of \$5 per share at the end of each year but does not reinvest the dividends.

PV (outflows) = PV (inflows)

The outflows are the payments for the shares and the inflows are the dividends received and the proceeds of the sale of the shares. So if r is the internal rate of return or the discount factor used:

$$\$100 + \frac{\$120}{(1+r)} = \frac{\$5}{(1+r)} + \frac{\$10}{(1+r)^2} + \frac{\$250}{(1+r)^2}$$

Using a financial calculator to solve for r, r = 13.69%

Note - although the portfolio holding period return in the first year was (\$120 + \$5 -\$100)/\$100 = 25%, and in the second year was (\$250 + \$10 - \$240)/\$240 = 8.33% the money-weighted rate of return is below the average holding period returns. This is because the portfolio performed less well in the second year when there was more money invested in the portfolio.

Time-weighted rate of return

This is the standard measure of performance in the fund management industry. The returns from different periods are averaged over time but it requires doing the following for an exact measure:

1. Value the portfolio before any significant addition or withdrawal of funds, look at subperiods between cash inflows and outflows.
2. Calculate the holding period returns for each subperiod.
3. Compound the holding period returns to obtain the rate of return for the complete year. If required take the geometric mean of the annual returns to obtain the return over a longer measurement period.

Example 2-18 Time-weighted rate of return

Looking at the portfolio returns in Example 2-17 we have calculated the holding period returns to be 25% and 8.33%. Over the two periods we can calculate the time-weighted rate of return, R, by using

$$(1+R)^2 = (1.25)(1.0833)$$

R = 16.37%

This is the return achieved for each \$1 invested in the portfolio at the beginning of the period.

Another example should help clarify the different results obtained from using the money-weighted and time-weighted rates of return.

Example 2-19 Money and time-weighted rate of return

A new fund was started with a value of $100 million, after 3 months the fund was revalued at $125 million and another $25 million was raised from investors. At the end of the year the fund had fallen in value to $140 million.

The money-weighted *quarterly* rate of return is given by r where

PV (outflows) = PV (inflows)

$$\$100 + \frac{\$25}{(1+r)} = \frac{\$140}{(1+r)^4}$$

Solving for r gives r = 3.025%

The annualized money–weighted rate of return is therefore $(1.03025)^4 - 1 = 13.65\%$

To calculate the time-weighted rate of return we need to calculate the rate of return in the first quarter and then the subsequent three quarters:

1Q, R = ($125 - $100)/$100 = 25%
2Q-4Q, R = ($140 - $150)/$150 = -6.67%
The annualized time–weighted rate of return is therefore

(1.25)(0.9333) – 1 = 16.66%

This is higher than the money-weighted performance since the money-weighted performance is dragged down by the negative performance in the second period when there were more funds invested in the portfolio.

LOS 2-1-B-f **calculate** the bank discount yield, holding period yield, effective annual yield, and money market yield for a U.S. Treasury bill

Pure discount instruments are quoted on a bank discount basis, rather than on a price basis, whereas bonds and other longer-term instruments are quoted on a price basis.

1. Yield on a bank discount basis

The yield on a bank discount basis simply annualizes the discount as a percentage of face value, based on a 360-day year.

$$r_{BD} = \frac{D}{F} \times \frac{360}{t}$$ **(Equation 2-13)**

where r_{BD} = annualized yield

D = discount amount
F = face value of the instruments
t = number of days remaining to maturity
360 = convention for the number of days in the year for a bank discount calculation

Example 2-20 Bank discount yield

A T-bill has a face value of $1,000,000 and 270 days until maturity. What is its bank discount yield if it is selling at $950,000?

Applying Equation 2-13:

$$r_{BD} = \frac{D}{F} \times \frac{360}{t} = \frac{\$50{,}000}{\$1{,}000{,}000} \times \frac{360}{270}$$

$= 6.67\%$

The bank discount yield does not meaningfully measure the return earned by an investor since a proper return calculation ought to reflect the return relative to the purchase price and take into account the reinvestment on a compound basis.

There are three other commonly used yield measures:

2. Holding Period Yield (HPY)

The holding period yield looks at the return (not annualized) relative to the purchase price.

$$HPY = \frac{P_1 - P_0 + D_1}{P_0}$$

(Equation **2-14**)

where

P_0 = initial purchase price
P_1 = price at maturity
D_1 = interest or dividend income received during the holding period

Examples 2-21 Holding period yield

The holding period yield of the T-bill in Example 2-20 will be:

HPY= (1,000,000 – 950,000 + 0)/950,000 = 5.26%

3. Effective Annual Yield (EAY)

This is the annualized holding period yield (based on 365 days) and takes into account interest earned on interest.

$$EAY = (1 + HPY)^{\frac{365}{t}} - 1$$

(Equation 2-15)

where

HPY = holding period yield
t = number of days to maturity

Examples 2-22 Effective annual yield

The effective annual yield (EAY) for the T-Bill in Example 2-20 will be:

$$EAY \quad (1 \quad HPY)^{\frac{365}{t}} \quad 1 \quad 1 \quad 0.526^{\frac{365}{270}} \quad 1 \quad 7.17\%$$

This is higher since the HPY calculation was based on only 270 days.

4. Money Market Yield (MMY), or the CD Equivalent Yield

This is the annualized holding period yield, but this time based on a 360-day year, to make it comparable with money market instruments that pay interest on this basis.

$$r_{MM} = (HPY)\left(\frac{360}{t}\right) = (r_{BD})\left(\frac{F}{P_0}\right)$$

In many cases we do not know the Treasury bill price so Equation 2-16 is more useful.

$$r_{MM} = \frac{360 \times r_{BD}}{360 - t \times r_{BD}} \qquad \textbf{(Equation 2-16)}$$

where

r_{BD} = bank discount yield
t = number of days to maturity

Examples 2-23 Money market yield

The MM or CD equivalent for the bond in Example 2-20 will be:

$$r_{MM} = \frac{360 \times r_{BD}}{360 - t \times r_{BD}} = \frac{360 \times 0.0667}{360 - 270 \times 0.0667} = 7.02\%$$

LOS 2-1-B-g	**convert** among holding period yields, money market yields, and effective annual yields

Conversion among HPY, EAY and MMY is illustrated in Example 2-24.

Examples 2-24 Conversion calculations

1. Given the MM (CD) equivalent yield is 7.5%, what would be the HPY for a 120-day T-bill?

Using Equation 2-16:

$$\frac{360r_{BD}}{(360-270r_{BD})}=0.075$$

$$r_{BD}=7.692\%$$

$$HPY=\frac{0.07692/(360/120)}{100-0.07692/(360/120)}=2.63\%$$

2. Given the EAY of 180-day T-bill to be 4.56%, what would be the MM (CD) equivalent yield?

Using Equation 2-15

$$EAY=(1+HPY)^{\frac{365}{t}}-1$$

$$HPY=\sqrt{(1+0.0456)}-1=2.255\%$$

The following relationship holds from Equation 2-14:

$$\frac{P_1-P_0}{P_0}=0.02255$$

Assuming P_1 = 100, P_0 then is 97.79

$$r_{BD}=\frac{100-97.79}{100}\times\frac{360}{2}=4.41\%$$

$$r_{MM}=\frac{360\times r_{BD}}{360-t\times r_{BD}}=\frac{360\times 0.0441}{360-180\times 0.0441}=4.51\%$$

which is the money market yield

LOS 2-1-B-h **calculate** the bond equivalent yield

A convention in bond markets is to double the semiannual yield to arrive at a yield called the bond-equivalent yield.

Example 2-25 Bond-equivalent yield

A bond has a semiannual yield of 3%.

The annualized, or effective annual yield is (1.03)2 – 1 = 6.09%

The bond-equivalent yield is simply 3% x 2 = 6%

2-1-B View Concept Check Questions Workbook

2-1-C "Statistical Concepts and Market Returns"

Introduction

This section provides the tools for describing and analyzing data, and then for drawing conclusions from the analysis. The focus is on return distributions and defining firstly the average or central tendency and secondly the dispersion around this average. We also consider the different types of distributions of returns including normal and skewed distributions. The candidate will be expected to apply these concepts to returns from different investments or portfolios and interpret the implications of different return distributions

LOS 2-1-C-a **differentiate** between descriptive statistics and inferential statistics

Descriptive statistics is the study of how data can be effectively summarized to provide information on a larger group. **Statistical inference** refers to making estimates or judgments about the larger group. This requires knowledge of probability theory which will be covered in later LOSs.

LOS 2-1-C-b **differentiate** between a population and a sample
LOS 2-1-C-c **explain** the concepts of a parameter and a sample statistic

A **population** is *all* members of a specified group; whereas a **sample** is a *subset* of the population, which provides information on the population.

A **parameter** is used to describe a characteristic of a population, and population parameters are often unknown values. Population parameters are denoted by Greek letters. For example, the population mean is denoted by Greek letter μ (mu), while the population standard deviation is denoted by (sigma). A **statistic** is used to describe a sample, in many cases a sample statistic is computed to estimate a parameter of a population.

LOS 2-1-C-d **differentiate** among the types of measurement scales

Data can be measured using four different scales:

1. *Nominal scale*: the weakest level of measurement, where integers (integers are whole numbers: 0, 1, 2, 3, …) are assigned to different groups of data. There is no ranking in a nominal scale.
2. *Ordinal scale*: different groups are ordered with respect to a characteristic.
3. *Interval scale*: the scale is ordered and the difference between each scale value is equal. The Celsius scale for measuring temperature is an example of an interval scale.
4. *Ratio scale*: the strongest level of measurement, the ratio scale is an interval scale level with zero representing zero value, or absence of the item being measured. Rates of return of investments would be examples of a ratio scale.

LOS 2-1-C-e	**define** and **interpret** a frequency distribution
LOS 2-1-C-f	**calculate** and **interpret** a holding period return (total return)
LOS 2-1-C-g	**calculate** relative frequencies and cumulative relative frequencies, given a frequency distribution

A frequency distribution is the grouping of data into a number of non-overlapping classes or intervals, so that the number of observations in each interval can be counted and the data can then be analyzed. The number of observations in each interval is called the **absolute frequency**, and the **relative frequency** is the percentage of the total observations falling into the interval. The **cumulative relative frequency** for an interval is the sum of the relative frequencies for the lowest interval up to an including the interval. It is the total percentage of the observations that are lower than the upper limit of the interval.

Before we can analyze rates of return we need to define the holding period return (HPR). The total return from an investment, or HPR, includes capital appreciation and cash flows paid over the life of the investment, as shown in Equation 2-17:

The total return from an investment, or holding period return (HPR), includes capital appreciation and cash flows paid over the life of the investment, as shown in Equation 2-17:

$$HPR = \frac{EV - BV + D}{BV}$$ **(Equation 2-17)**

where:

BV	=	beginning value of investment
EV	=	ending value of investment
D	=	cash distributions over the period (e.g dividends)

Example 2-26 Calculating the holding period return

If a stock is purchased at $70 and is sold for $85, and during the holding period the investor received a $4 dividend, calculate the holding period return.

rite down the known variables, and use Equation 2-17 to compute HPR:

$$\text{HPR} = \frac{\text{EV} - \text{BV} + \text{D}}{\text{BV}}$$

$$= \frac{\$85 - \$70 + \$4}{\$70}$$

$$= \frac{\$19}{\$70} = 0.271, \text{ or } 27.1\%$$

Note that the HPR does not account for the amount of time over which the investment is held. In our example, the investment could have been held for one day, one month, or one year.

Example 2-27 shows how raw data can be converted into absolute, relative and cumulative relative frequencies.

Example 2-27 Organizing raw data into a frequency distribution

An analyst collects the number of house sales for a 25-month period by a large real estate agent:

254	85	218	162	104
166	193	115	122	97
125	178	66	112	108
130	165	81	145	232
185	210	282	216	297

This is an example of raw, ungrouped data, and the first step towards organizing it as a frequency distribution is to define the intervals. We note that the lowest reading is 66 and the highest reading is 297; for illustrative purposes, we round the lowest number down to 60 and round the highest number up to 300. If we decide to define six intervals, then each interval will be 40 wide. Thus, "60 up to 100" is the first interval; "100 up to 140" is the second interval; and so on. (The choice of upper and lower limits for intervals is flexible, but the intervals must be *mutually exclusive*.)

We count the number of observations in each interval to give the absolute frequency. The relative frequency is the absolute frequency divided by the total number of observations, which in this example is 25:

Number of Houses Sold	Absolute Frequency	Relative Frequency	Cumulative Frequency	Cumulative Relative Frequency
60 up to 100	4	4÷25 = 16%	4	16%
100 up to 140	7	7÷25 = 28%	11	44%
140 up to 180	5	5÷25 = 20%	16	64%
180 up to 220	5	5÷25 = 20%	21	84%
220 up to 260	2	2÷25 = 8%	23	92%
260 up to 300	2	2÷25 = 8%	25	100%

Now that the raw data is arranged into frequencies, we observe that house sales are concentrated (0.68 or 68% of observations) in the range of 100 to 220. The largest absolute and relative frequency occurs in the "100 up to 140" interval. We can see from the cumulative relative frequencies that in 84% of the months 220 or less houses are sold.

LOS 2-1-C-h **describe** the properties of data presented as a histogram or a frequency polygon

A **histogram** is a bar chart showing the absolute frequency on the vertical axis and the intervals on the horizontal axis. The histogram below shows the frequency for the house sales given in Example 2-26:

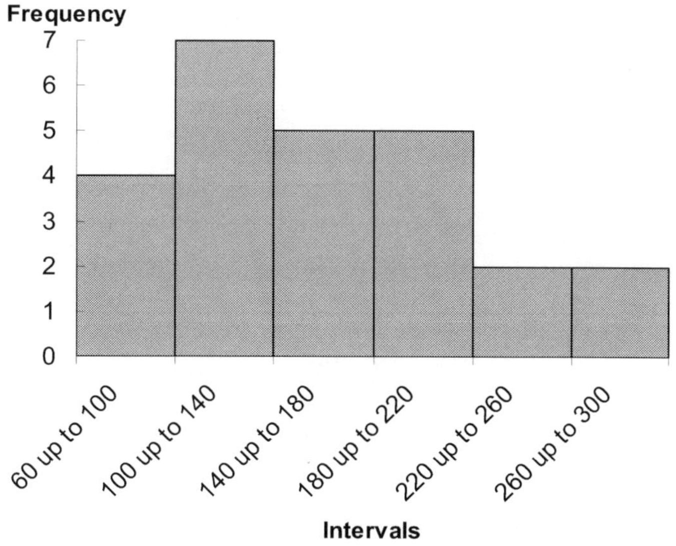

A frequency polygon is a trend line showing the absolute frequency on the vertical axis and the interval midpoints on the horizontal axis. The frequency polygon below shows the frequency for the house sales in Example 2-26.

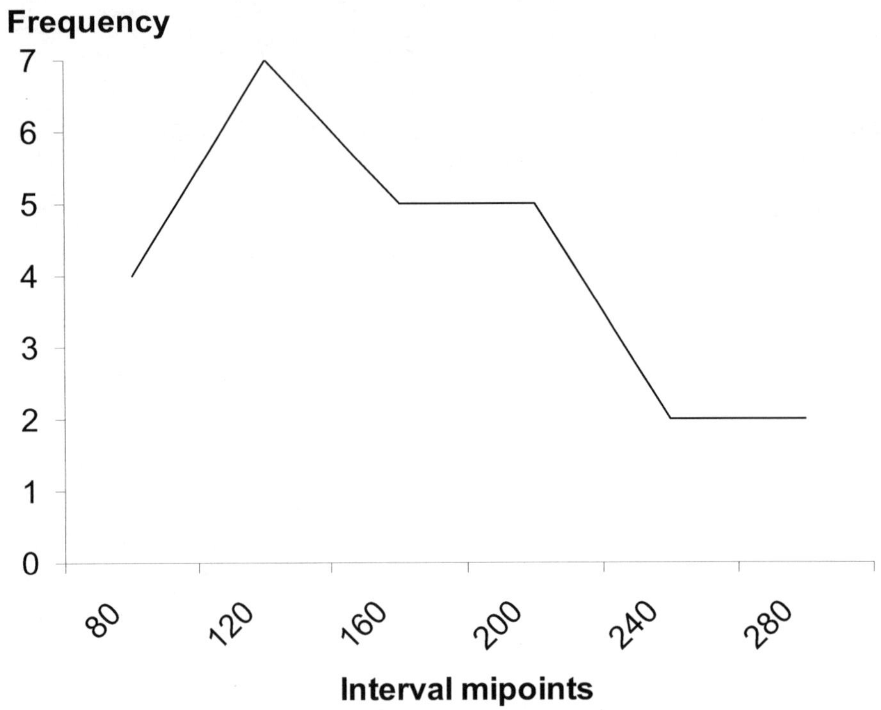

LOS 2-1-C-i	**calculate** and **interpret** measures of central tendency, including the population mean, sample mean, arithmetic mean, median, mode, weighted mean, geometric mean, and harmonic mean

There are two key ways of measuring the characteristics of a population - namely, central tendency and dispersion. First we look at central tendency, or the average, of a set of data.

The population mean is used when we can observe and measure all possible outcomes. Equation 2-18 gives the formula for population mean:

$$\mu = \frac{\sum_{i=1}^{N} X_i}{N}$$ **(Equation 2-18)**

where

μ	=	population mean
X_i	=	ith observation of the data
N	=	number of observations in the population

We use Greek letter μ (mu) to denote the population parameter. There can be only one population parameter, and in practice, knowing all possible outcomes of a population is rare. Rather, we observe a sample, or a subset of data from a population, this might be cross-sectional data when we look at the characteristics of certain items at one point in time (e.g company size at 31st December 2004) or time-series data when we look at data over a time period (monthly historic returns from a stock). We can calculate the sample mean as a statistic, as shown in Equation 2-19:

$$\overline{X} = \frac{\sum_{i=1}^{n} X_i}{n}$$ **(Equation 2-19)**

where

$\overline{X}$	=	sample mean (reads as "X bar")
X_i	=	ith observation of the data
n	=	number of observations in the sample

Observe that the formulas for the population mean and sample mean are the same, only the notation is different.

Example 2-28 Calculating the sample mean

The number of hours of sunshine is recorded on the final day of each month over a two-year period, as shown in the following data set:

2	3	4	5	5	6	8	8	5	4	3
	2									
1	2	3	5	6	7	9	8	6	3	3
	2									

Take the sum of all observations, and use Equation 2-19 to calculate the sample mean:

$$\frac{2+3+4+5+5+\ldots\ldots\ldots\ldots\ldots\ldots\ldots+8+6+3+3+2}{24}=\frac{110}{24}=4.58$$

1. Mean

(i) **Arithmetic mean** is the simple average. It is illustrated by the above population mean and sample mean in Equations 2-18 and 2-19. It has the advantage of being a single value for a set of data and the sum of deviations of each value away from the mean will be zero.

(ii) **Geometric mean** is the nth root of n values. The geometric mean is often used to calculate average returns when a return is given for multiple periods.

The general equation is

$$G=\sqrt[n]{X_1\times X_2\times X_3\times\ldots\ldots X_n}$$ **(Equation 2-20)**

where

G	=	geometric mean
X_i	=	ith observation, which must be greater than or equal to zero.
n	=	number of observations

When used for returns (which could be negative), the equation is modified to:

$$1+R_G=\sqrt[n]{(1+R_1)(1+R_2)\ldots\ldots(1+R_n)}$$ **(Equation 2-21)**

where

R_G	=	geometric mean return
R_i	=	return in ith period
n	=	number of observations

For calculating average historic returns the geometric mean, rather than the arithmetic mean, is the most suitable method. For projecting future returns the arithmetic mean is often used since it better predicts the future portfolio value.

Example 2-29 Arithmetic and geometric means

If the returns from a portfolio are 5%, 12% and –2% over each of the last three years then the average return is given by:

arithmetic mean $= (5\% + 12\% - 2\%)/3 = 5\%$

geometric mean $= \sqrt[3]{(1.05)(1.12)(0.98)} - 1 = 4.8\%$

The geometric mean is always less than or equal to the arithmetic mean.

(iii) **Weighted mean**

If given a set of data where certain values occur more than once then it is quicker to calculate the weighted mean.

$$\overline{X} = \frac{\sum w_i X_i}{\sum w_i}$$ **(Equation 2-22)**

where

$\overline{X}$ = weighted mean

X_i = ith observation

w_i = number of times that X_i occurs.

Example 2-30 Weighted mean

Using the data in Example 2-28:

2	3	4	5	5	6	8	8	5	4	3
	2									
1	2	3	5	6	7	9	8	6	3	3
	2									

The weighted mean is $\dfrac{1(1)+4(2)+5(3)+2(4)+4(5)+3(6)+1(7)+3(8)+1(9)}{24} = 4.58$

2. Median

This is the value of the middle item, or for an even number of readings the arithmetic mean of the middle two items, of an ordered data array. It is particularly useful if a small number of extreme values are distorting the arithmetic mean.

Example 2-31 Median

Using the data in Example 2-28 and putting it in an ordered display gives:

1 2 2 2 2 3 3 3 3 3 4 **4 5** 5 5 5 6 6 6 7 8 8 8 9

The median is the average of the two middle readings, which are 4 and 5. The median is therefore 4.5.

3. Mode

The mode is defined as the most frequently occurring observation. This measure of central tendency has the disadvantage that there may not be an observation appearing more than once or there may be multiple modes. It is useful if you need to select one reading which is the most popular.

Example 2-32 Mode

Using the ordered data display in Example 2-31:

1 2 2 2 2 3 3 3 3 3 4 4 5 5 5 5 6 6 6 7 8 8 8 9

3 is the most frequently occurring observation and therefore 3 is the mode.

For continuous distributions the interval with the highest frequency is the **modal interval**.

4. Harmonic Mean

This is the mean calculated using the reciprocals of the observations using Equation 2-23

$$\overline{X}_H = \frac{n}{\sum_{i=1}^{n}\left(\frac{1}{X_i}\right)}$$ **(Equation 2-23)**

where

$\overline{X}_H$	=	harmonic mean
X_i	=	ith observation
n	=	number of observations.

The harmonic mean is useful if we wish to calculate the average cost of an item when the total amount spent at each date is equal, this is illustrated in Example 2-32.

Example 2-33 Harmonic mean

An investor invests $10,000 in shares of a company at the end of January, February and March. The price she pays per share each month is $40, $42 and $47 respectively. Calculate the average price per share.

The harmonic mean is

$$\overline{X}_H = \frac{n}{\sum_{i=1}^{n}\left(\frac{1}{X_i}\right)} = \frac{3}{\frac{1}{40}+\frac{1}{42}+\frac{1}{47}} = \$42.81$$

An arithmetic mean calculation gives an average of $43, but this does not take into account that more shares will be bought at the lower price, reducing the average cost per share.

LOS 2-1-C-j	**describe** and **interpret** quartiles, quintiles, deciles, and percentiles

Whereas a median divides a distribution in half, **quartiles** divide it into quarters, **quintiles** into fifths, **deciles** into tenths and **percentiles** into hundredths. These are all examples of **quantiles.**

These measures are often used to classify performance, so for example if a fund is in the bottom quartile, it means that the return fell below the first quartile cut off point.

LOS 2-1-C-k	**calculate** and **interpret** 1) a weighted average or mean (including a portfolio return viewed as a weighted mean), 2) a range and mean absolute deviation, and 3) the variance and standard deviation of a sample and of a population

Measures of Dispersion

These measure the dispersion or variability of the data, and therefore indicate whether the mean is a reliable average.

1. Range

The range is the difference between the highest and the lowest value.

2. Mean absolute deviation

This is the mean of the absolute value of the deviations from the mean.

$$MAD = \frac{\sum_{1}^{n} | X_i - \overline{X} |}{n} \qquad \textbf{(Equation 2-24)}$$

where

MAD	=	mean absolute deviation
$\overline{X}$	=	mean
X_i	=	ith observation
$\| X_i - \overline{X} \|$	=	absolute value of the difference between X_i and $\overline{X}$, it is always zero or a positive number
n	=	number of observations

Example 2-34 Mean absolute deviation

The following observations are recorded: 2, 5, 6, 8, 9.

The range is 9 - 2 = 7

The MAD =[|(2 - 6)| + |(5 - 6)| + |(6 - 6)| + |(8 - 6)| + |(9 - 6)|]/5 = 2

3. Variance

Variance is calculated using the squares of the deviations from the mean, so whether a difference from the mean is positive or negative by the time it is squared it is positive. This avoids the problem of positive and negative deviations canceling out. Variance, and standard deviation, are the most common risk measures used in investment.

Variance of a population is calculated as:

$$\sigma^2 = \frac{\sum_{i=1}^{N} (X_i - \mu)^2}{N} \qquad \textbf{(Equation 2-25)}$$

where

σ^2	=	variance of a population
μ	=	population mean
X_i	=	ith observation
N	=	number of observations in the population

4. Standard Deviation

This is the square root of the variance, and it is therefore in the same units as the original data. Standard deviation of a population is:

$$\sigma = \sqrt{\frac{\sum_{1}^{N}(X_i - \mu)^2}{N}} \qquad \textbf{(Equation 2-26)}$$

where

σ	=	standard deviation of a population
μ	=	population mean
X_i	=	ith observation
N	=	number of observations in the population

Example 2-35 Variance and standard deviation

The ages of all the children in a violin lesson are 9, 11, 12, 13, and 15.

First calculate $\mu = 60/5 = 12$

The population variance is calculated as:

$\sigma^2 = [(9 - 12)^2 + (11 - 12)^2 + (12 - 12)^2 + (13 - 12)^2 + (15 - 12)^2]/5 = 4$

The standard deviation = $\sigma = 2$

The larger the standard deviation or variance of a distribution is, the wider the dispersion of the observations away from the mean.

When the data is for a sample, rather than the whole population, then the **sample variance** is given by the equation below:

$$s^2 = \frac{\sum_{i=1}^{n}(X_i - \overline{X})^2}{n-1} \qquad \textbf{(Equation 2-27)}$$

where

s^2	=	variance of a sample
$\overline{X}$	=	sample mean
X_i	=	ith observation
n	=	number of observations in the sample

The denominator in Equation 2-27 is now (n - 1), using n would tend to underestimate the variance if we are using a sample, rather than the whole, of the population.

As before, the standard deviation of the sample is the square root of the sample variance.

LOS 2-1-C-l **contrast** variance to semivariance and target semivariance

It can be argued that most investors are only concerned with downside risk, or the risk of returns falling below the mean. This is measured by semivariance which is the average squared deviation *below t*he mean. The formula for semivariance is given in Equation 2-28, and semideviation can be calculated by taking the square root of the semivariance.

$$s_{semi}^{2} = \frac{\sum_{\text{all } X_i < \bar{X}} (X_i - \bar{X})^2}{n^* - 1} \qquad \textbf{(Equation 2-28)}$$

where

s_{semi}^{2}	=	semivariance of a sample
$\bar{X}$	=	sample mean
X_i	=	ith observation
n^*	=	number of observations that are smaller than the mean

Example 2-36 Semivariance

The returns from a portfolio over six months are -10%,-6%, + 5%, +6%, +8% and +9%.

The sample mean is (- 10% - 6% + 5% + 6% +8% + 9%)/6 = 2%.

Using Equation 2-27 variance of the sample is

$$s^2 = \frac{\sum_{i=1}^{n}(X_i - \bar{X})^2}{n-1} = \frac{12^2 + 8^2 + 3^2 + 4^2 + 6^2 + 7^2}{5} = 63.60$$

To calculate semivariance, note that there are only 2 returns below the mean. Using Equation 2-28 semivariance is

$$s_{semi}^{2} = \frac{\sum_{\text{all } X_i < \bar{X}} (X_i - \bar{X})^2}{n^* - 1} = \frac{12^2 + 8^2}{1} = 208.0$$

This is significantly higher than the variance since the lower readings are well below the means showing relatively high downside risk.

Target semivariance refers to when there is a target return and the target semivariance is calculated by taking the sum of the squared deviations of observations below the target, divided by the number of such observations minus one.

Note:

Other texts use a definition of semivariance where the denominator is (n – 1), the total number of observations in the sample less one. In this case symmetric distributions will have a semivariance that is half the variance.

LOS 2-1-C-m	**calculate** the proportion of observations falling within a specified number of standard deviations of the mean, using Chebyshev's inequality

Chebyshev's Inequality

For both discrete and continuous data distributions Chebyshev's Inequality states that:

For any set of observations at least $1 - 1/k^2$ percent of readings fall within k standard deviations of the mean, when $k > 1$.

Example 2-37 Chebyshev's Inequality

Data is collected on the monthly performance of a mutual fund and the sample mean is 2% and the standard deviation is 0.5%.

k	Interval (% return)	Percent of observations
1.25	1.375 to 2.625	36%
1.50	1.25 to 2.75	56%
2	1 to 3	75%
3	0.5 to 3.5	89%
4	0 to 4	94%

LOS 2-1-C-n	**calculate** and **interpret** the coefficient of variation

Coefficient of Variation

A measure is needed to compare the dispersions of two or more distributions. The coefficient of variation is the standard deviation divided by the mean of a distribution, often expressed as a percentage. The higher the coefficient of variation, the higher the dispersion and vice versa.

$$CV = \frac{s}{\bar{X}} \times 100$$

(Equation 2-29)

where

CV	=	coefficient of variation, as a percentage
s	=	standard deviation
$\overline{X}$	=	sample mean

Example 2-38 Coefficient of variation

Data is collected on (i) the monthly performance of a mutual fund, the sample mean is 2% and the standard deviation is 0.5% (ii) the monthly performance of a pension fund, the sample mean is 1.2% and the standard deviation is 0.4%.

The coefficients of variation are calculated using Equation 2-22

(i) CV(mutual fund)= (0.5%/2%) $\times$ 100 = 25%
(ii) CV(pension Fund) = (0.4%/1.2%) $\times$ 100 = 33.3%

This means that there is more dispersion relative to the mean in the distribution of the returns of the pension fund than the mutual fund.

LOS 2-1-C-o calculate and interpret the Sharpe ratio

An alternative measure is the **Sharpe ratio**, which is used to measure excess returns for each unit of risk taken.

$$\text{Sharpe ratio} = \frac{(\bar{r}_p - \bar{r}_f)}{\sigma_p} \qquad \textbf{(Equation 2-30)}$$

where

$\overline{r_p}$	=	mean return of a portfolio p
$\overline{r_f}$	=	mean return from the risk free asset
σ_p	=	standard deviation of a portfolio p

Example 2-39 Sharpe ratio

A portfolio is providing a mean return of 12% per annum compared with a return of 5% per annum from the risk-free asset, the standard deviation of the portfolio returns is 10%.

Sharpe ratio = (12% - 5%)/10% = 0.7

This indicates the portfolio earned a 0.7% return for each unit of risk; a high Sharpe ratio is more attractive than a low one.

LOS 2-1-C-p	**describe** the relative locations of the mean, median, and mode for a nonsymmetrical distribution
LOS 2-1-C-q	**define** and **interpret** skew, and **explain** the meaning of a positively or negatively skewed return distribution

Symmetric and Skewed Distributions

A symmetric or normal distribution has the following characteristics:

1. The mean and median are equal.
2. The mean and variance completely describe the distribution.
3. 68.3% of observations lie between (mean ± 1 standard deviation)
4. 95.5% of observations lie between (mean ± 2 standard deviations)
5. 99.7% of observations lie between (mean ± 3 standard deviations)

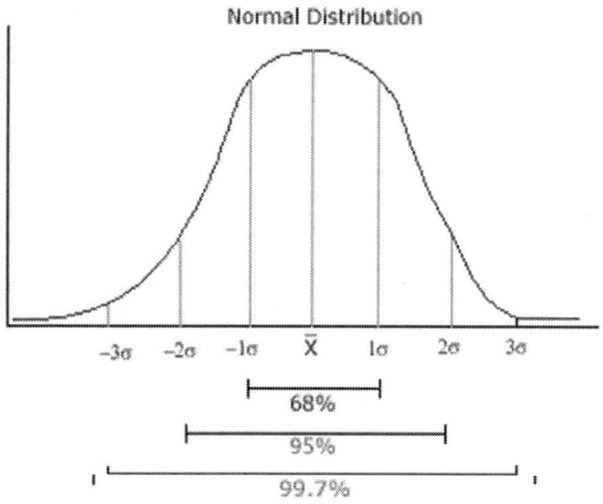

A nonsymmetrical distribution is **skewed**.

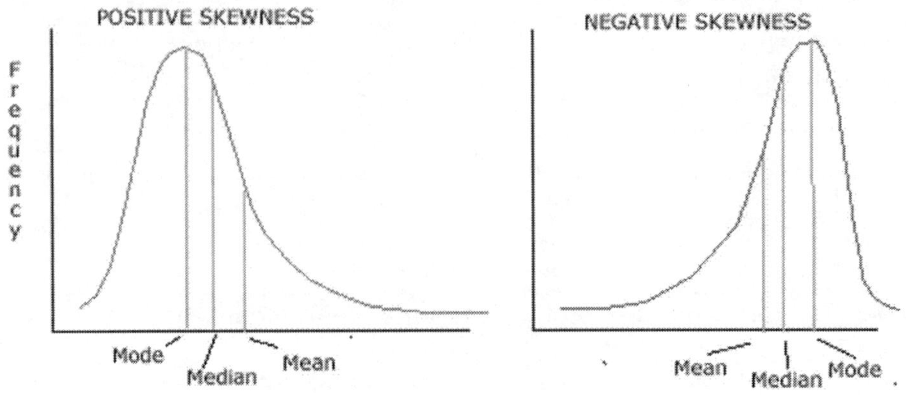

In a positively skewed distribution the mean will be higher than the median, which will be higher than the mode, the opposite will be the case for a negatively skewed distribution.

If a distribution of portfolio returns is positively skewed it indicates that poor returns occur frequently but losses are small, whereas very high returns occur less frequently but are more extreme.

Skewness is calculated using the cubes of the deviations, thereby keeping the 'direction' of the deviations i.e. whether the observations are above or below the mean. When interpreting investment returns positive skewness is considered attractive since it indicates that there is a greater probability of very high returns.

LOS 2-1-C-r	**define** and **interpret** kurtosis, and **explain** excess kurtosis
LOS 2-1-C-s	**describe and interpret** measures of sample skew and kurtosis

Kurtosis

Kurtosis measures whether a distribution is more peaked (leptokurtic) or less peaked (platykurtic) than a normal distribution.

Excess positive kurtosis, or leptokurtosis, would indicate that a distribution has fatter tails than a normal distribution. This is very important since, if a distribution of stock returns exhibits excess kurtosis (a sample excess kurtosis of 1.0 or larger would be considered unusually large) the probability of very good or very bad returns is more likely than if it were a normal distribution. If measures such as Value at Risk (VaR) are used to estimate the probability of a specified loss occurring, and the distribution has been assumed to be normal, then the chance of a major loss will have been underestimated.

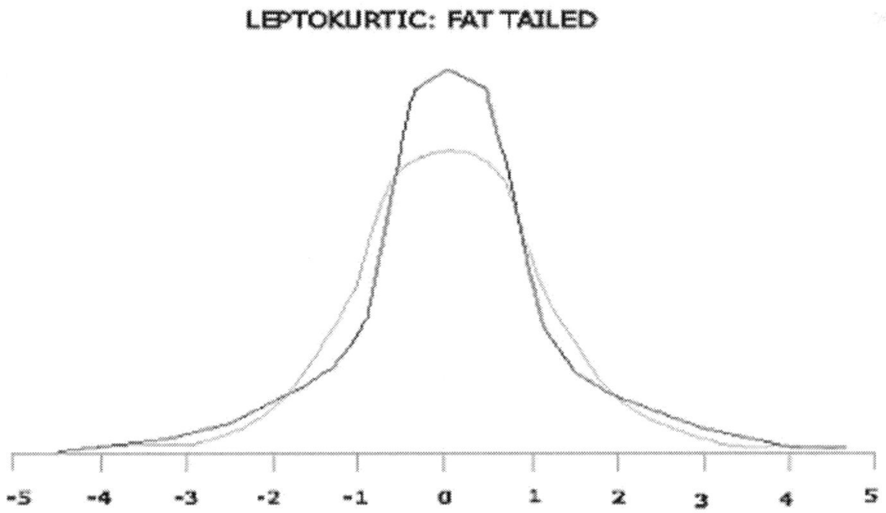

Semi-logarithmic scale

When looking at graphs to assess historic returns, semi-logarithmic scales are often the most appropriate. A semi-logarithmic scale is logarithmic on the vertical axis and arithmetic on the horizontal axis. On a logarithmic scale equal distances represent equal percentage movements.

2-1-C View Concept Check Questions Workbook

2-1-D "Probability Concepts"

This section starts with a definition of the terms and the rules used in probability. It then considers the application to the key concepts used in investment including expected return and variability of returns for both single securities and portfolios. At the end of the Reading there is a summary of shortcuts used for counting possible outcomes. Candidates will be expected to do both the necessary calculations and also to be able to interpret the results of calculations.

LOS 2-1-D-a **define** a random variable, an outcome, an event, mutually exclusive events, and exhaustive events

A **random variable** is a quantity whose future outcomes are uncertain.

The return on a risky investment is an example of a random variable, when the **event** or outcome is not certain.

LOS 2-1-D-b **explain** the two defining properties of probability

The two defining properties of probability are:

1. P(E) stands for the probability of any event E occurring and 0 • P(E) • 1
2. The sum of the probabilities for any list of mutually exclusive and exhaustive events is one.

Mutually exclusive means that only one event can occur at one time.

Exhaustive means that the events cover all possible outcomes.

LOS 2-1-D-c **distinguish** among empirical, subjective, and a priori probabilities

Calculating probabilities

There are different methods for estimating probabilities:

Empirical probabilities – probabilities are estimated from past data.
Subjective probabilities – probabilities are based on personal judgment.
A priori probabilities – probabilities are based on logical analysis.

Empirical and a priori probabilities are classed as objective probabilities, since they are usually independent of the forecaster's own view.

LOS 2-1-D-d **describe** the investment consequences of probabilities that are mutually inconsistent

If one stock price discounts a certain probability of an event occurring and another stock price discounts a different probability, then there is an opportunity to take advantage of the inconsistency.

LOS 2-1-D-e **distinguish** between unconditional and conditional probabilities

The probability that an event A occurs, if it is **unconditional**, is denoted by $P(A)$

This is also known as marginal probability.

Conditional Probability is the probability that A occurs given B has already occurred, it is denoted by $P(A|B)$.

LOS 2-1-D-f **calculate**, using the multiplication rule, the joint probability of two events

Joint Probability is the probability that A and B occur together, it is denoted by $P(AB)$.

General Rule of Multiplication

To calculate the joint probability of two events occurring use the general rule of multiplication:

$$P(AB) = P(A|B)P(B) = P(B|A)P(A) \quad \textbf{(Equation 2-31)}$$

Example 2-40 General rule of multiplication

If 5 out of 100 radios that are manufactured by a company are defective what is the probability, when selecting 2 radios from a shipment of 100 radios, of selecting one defective radio and then another?

Assuming the first radio selected is not replaced in the shipment, and $P(A)$ is the probability of the first radio being defective and $P(B|A)$ is the probability of the second radio being defective given the first defective radio has been taken out, then applying Equation 2-31:

$$P(AB) = P(B|A)\,P(A) = 4/99 \times 5/100 = 0.002$$

LOS 2-1-D-g	**calculate**, using the addition rule, the probability that at least one of two events will occur

General Rule of Addition

To calculate the probability that A or B occurs or that A and B both occur

P(A or B) = P(A) + P(B) - P(AB) **(Equation 2-32)**

Example 2-41 General rule of addition

A company manufactures children's boots in three different sizes - small, medium and large, and makes equal numbers of each size in red, blue, green and yellow colors. What is the probability that a boot chosen at random will be either small or blue?

Using Equations 2-31 and 2-32 with P(A) the probability that the boot is small and P(B) the probability it is blue, then

Probability = 1/3 +1/4 – (1/3 x 1/4) = 0.5

(i.e. 6 out of all possible 12 combinations of color and size will be small or blue)

LOS 2-1-D-h	**distinguish** between dependent and independent events

Two events are **independent** if the occurrence of one event does not affect the probability of the other event occurring. In this case

P(A|B) = P(A), or P(B|A) = P(B)

If they are not independent they are dependent.

LOS 2-1-D-i **calculate** a joint probability of any number of independent events

The Multiplication Rule for Independent Events says that if two events are independent

$P(AB) = P(A)P(B)$ **(*Equati*on 2-33)**

Example 2-42 Multiplication Rule for Independent Events

What is the chance of throwing a double six if two dice are thrown?

Probability $= 1/6 \times 1/6 = 0.027$

Note: events are mutually exclusive if $P(AB) = 0$

Equation 2-33 can be extended to any number of independent events i.e.

$P(ABC\ldots) = P(A)P(B)P(C)\ldots\ldots$ **(Equation 2-34)**

LOS 2-1-D-j **calculate**, using the total probability rule, an unconditional probability

In the investment business we are often interested in using scenarios, which are mutually exclusive, and then looking at the probability of an event, A, happening given certain scenarios. An example of this is saying event A is that the stock market rises over the next year and the different scenarios could be various economic scenarios; high growth, low growth etc.

The total probability rule says:

$P(A) = P(A|S1)P(S1) + P(A|S2)P(S2) + \ldots\ldots\ldots + P(A|Sn)P(Sn)$ **(Equation 2-35)**

This rule expresses an unconditional probability in terms of conditional probabilities, with probabilities used as weights.

LOS 2-1-D-k **calculate** and **interpret** expected value, variance, and standard deviation

The expected value of a random variable X, denoted by E(X), is the probability-weighted average of the possible outcomes of the random variable.

$$E(X) = \sum_{i=1}^{n} P(X_i)X_i \qquad \textbf{(Equation 2-36)}$$

where

E(X)	=	expected value of the random variable X
X_i	=	a possible outcome of the random variable X
n	=	number of possible outcomes

The variance of a random variable is the expected value of the squared deviations of the random variable's expected value. This is given by:

$$\sigma^2(X) = E\{[X - E(X)]^2\}$$

or

$$\sigma^2(X) = \sum_{i=1}^{n} P(X_i)[X_i - E(X)]^2 \qquad \textbf{(Equation 2-37)}$$

where

$\sigma^2(X)$	=	variance of X
E(X)	=	expected value of the random variable X

The standard deviation is the square root of the variance.

Example 2-43 Standard deviation of a distribution

The following probability distribution is provided:

X	**P(X)**
0	0.20
1	0.30
2	0.40
3	0.10

The expected value or mean, using Equation 2-36, is

$$E(X) = \sum_{i=1}^{n} P(X_i)X_i = (0.20 \times 0) + (0.30 \times 1) + (0.40 \times 2) + (0.10 \times 3) = 1.4$$

The variance, using Equation 2-37, is

$$\sigma^2(X) = \sum_{i=1}^{n} P(X_i)[X_i - E(X)]^2$$

$$= 0.2(0 - 1.4)^2 + 0.3(1 - 1.4)^2 + 0.4(2 - 1.4)^2 + 0.1(3 - 1.4)^2 = 0.84$$

The standard deviation is the square root of the variance which is 0.92.

LOS 2-1-D-l	**explain** the use of conditional expectation in investment applications
LOS 2-1-D-m	**calculate** an expected value using the total probability rule for expected value

In investment decision-making we are often using conditional expected values. This refers to the expected value for a random variable X given a scenario or event S, which is denoted by $E(X|S)$.

The total probability rule in Equation 2-35, can also be applied using expected values:

$$E(X) = E(X|S1)P(S1) + E(X|S2)P(S2) + \dots\dots\dots + E(X|Sn)P(Sn) \qquad \textbf{(Equation 2-38)}$$

Example 2-44 Total probability rule

You observe that a portfolio's quarterly returns have a 70% probability of being positive, and a 30% probability of being zero or negative. However you also note that if the previous quarter's returns were zero or negative then the probability of them being positive in the next quarter is only 55%.

Following a positive return you wish to calculate the probability of the next quarter also providing a positive return.

Define S_1 as the scenario that returns were positive in the previous quarter, and S_2 that they were zero or negative and A as the event that returns are positive in the next quarter. We can apply Equation 2-38:

$$P(A) = P(A|S1)P(S1) + P(A|S2)P(S2)$$
$$0.70 = [P(A|S1) \times 0.70] + [0.55 \times 0.30]$$
$$(A|S1) = 0.535/0.70 = 0.764$$

This means that, given a positive return in the previous quarter, there is a 76.4% chance of achieving a positive return in the next quarter. This is higher than the unconditional probability of 70%.

LOS 2-1-D-n **calculate** and **interpret** covariance and correlation
LOS 2-1-D-o **explain** the relations among covariance, standard deviation, and correlation
LOS 2-1-D-p **calculate** the expected return, variance of return, and standard deviation of return on a portfolio

Covariance

When analyzing risk for a portfolio made up of a number of assets we need to know the covariance between the returns from each pair of assets. Covariance measures how closely two assets move together. If on average the return of one asset is above its expected value when the other is below its expected value then covariance will be negative. However when both assets tend to achieve high returns relative to their expected returns at the same time then the covariance will be positive.

Covariance is defined as:

$$Cov(R_i,R_j) = E\{[\,R_i - E(R_i)][\,R_j - E(R_j)]\} \qquad \textbf{(Equation 2-39)}$$

where

R_i = return of asset i

Referring to Equation 2-39, we can see that Cov (R_i,R_i) = $^2(R_i)$, i.e. the covariance of an asset with itself is the same as the variance of the asset.

For a portfolio the variance of the returns is given by:

$$\sigma^2(R_P) = \sum_{i=1}^{n}\sum_{j=1}^{n} w_i w_j Cov(R_i, R_j) \qquad \textbf{(Equation 2-40)}$$

where

R_i = return of asset i
w_i = weighting in asset I

and the expected return is given by:

$$E(R_P) = \sum_{1}^{n} E(R_i) w_i \qquad \textbf{(Equation 2-41)}$$

Example 2-45 Standard deviation of a portfolio

A portfolio is invested in three stock markets A, B and C. 50% of the portfolio is in market A, 30% in B and 20% in C. The expected return from each market is 20%, 15% and 10% respectively. The covariance matrix is as shown below:

Covariance	A	B	C
A	200	90	75
B	90	120	40
C	75	40	100

The expected return from the portfolio is given by Equation 2-41

$E(R_p)$ = (20% x 0.5) + (15% x 0.30) + (10% x 0.20) = 16.5%.

The variance is given by Equation 2-40

$$\sigma^2(R_p) = w_A^2\sigma^2(R_A) + w_B^2\sigma^2(R_B) + w_C^2\sigma^2(R_C) + 2w_Aw_B\text{Cov}(R_AR_B) + 2w_Aw_C\text{Cov}(R_AR_C)$$
$$+ 2w_Bw_C\text{Cov}(R_BR_C)$$

$= [(0.5)^2 \times 200] + [(0.3)^2 \times 120] + [(0.2)^2 \times 100] + [2 \times 0.5 \times 0.3 \times 90] + [2 \times 0.5 \times 0.2 \times 75] + [2 \times 0.3 \times 0.2 \times 40]$

= 50 + 10.8 + 4 + 27 + 15 + 4.8 = 111.6

The standard deviation is given by the square root of the variance, which is 10.56

Correlation

Correlation (denoted by ,) is given by

$$\rho(R_i, R_j) = \frac{\text{Cov}(R_i, R_j)}{\sigma(R_i)\sigma(R_j)} \quad \textbf{(Equation 2-42)}$$

Correlation again describes the way that two variables move together, but it is easier to interpret than covariance since it lies between -1 and +1.

Example 2-46 Correlation

Restating the covariance table in Example 2-45, using Equation 2-42

$$\rho(R_A, R_B) = \frac{90}{\sqrt{200}\sqrt{120}} = 0.58$$

$$\rho(R_A, R_C) = \frac{75}{\sqrt{200}\sqrt{100}} = 0.53$$

$$\rho(R_B, R_C) = \frac{40}{\sqrt{120}\sqrt{100}} = 0.37$$

Correlations	A	B	C
A	1	0.58	0.53
B	0.58	1	0.37
C	0.53	0.37	1

A correlation of 0 indicates an absence of a linear relationship between the two variables

A correlation of 1 indicates a perfect linear relationship

A correlation of -1 indicates a perfect inverse linear relationship

LOS 2-1-D-q **calculate** covariance given a joint probability function

Estimating covariance and correlation

Covariance can be estimated using historical data or by using a **joint probability function**.

A joint probability function, P(X,Y), gives the probability that certain occurrences X and Y occur together. In the case of returns from two assets, R_i and R_j

$$\text{Cov}(R_i, R_j) = \sum_{i=1}^{n}\sum_{j=1}^{n} P(R_i, R_j)(R_i - ER_i)(R_j - ER_j)$$ **(Equation 2-43)**

Example 2-47 Covariance

The returns for two assets, A and B can be calculated under four different economic scenarios. The probability of each scenario is

1. Recession 30%,
2. Slowdown 40%,
3. Slow growth 20%,
4. Strong growth 10%.

The returns under each scenario are given below:

Economic Scenario	Return from A	Return B
1	-10%	2%
2	0%	4%
3	5%	8%
4	20%	10%

First of all calculate the expected return from A and B, using Equation 2-36

ERA = (0.3 x -10%) + (0.4 x 0%) + (0.2 x 5%) + (0.1 x 20%) = 0.0%
ERB = (0.3 x 2%) + (0.4 x 4%) + (0.2 x 8%) + (0.1 x 10%) = 4.8%
Use Equation 2-43 to calculate the covariance

Cov(A,B) = [0.3 x (-10 - 0) x (2 - 4.8)] + [0.4 x (0 - 0) x (4 - 4.8)] +
[0.2 x (5 - 0) x (8 - 4.8)] + [0.1 x (20 - 0) x (10 - 4.8)]
= 8.4 + 0 + 3.2 + 10.4 = 22.0

LOS 2-1-D-r **calculate** an updated probability, using Bayes' formula

Bayes' Formula

Bayes' formula is used when we want to know, given an event (A_1), what was the probability of the scenario that created the event.

Prior probability is the initial probability based on the present level of information.

e.g. $P(A_1)$ is the result that the 'test' is positive, $P(A_2)$ is the opposite.

Posterior probability is the revised probability taking into account additional information, B.

e.g. P(A1|B) is the probability that A1 occurs given B.

Bayes' formula:

$$P(A_1 / B) = \frac{P(A_1)P(B / A_1)}{P(A_1)P(B / A_1) + P(A_2)P(B / A_2)}$$ **(Equation 2-44)**

Example 2-48 Bayes formula

An analyst is looking at data on left-handed people working for a certain company. He notes that 15% of the men are left-handed and 6% of the women are left-handed. 60% of the people working for the company are men. The analyst randomly selects an individual that is left-handed. Using Equation 2-44 we can calculate the posterior probability that this individual is a man.

Define A_1 = man
A_2 = woman
B = left handed

We are looking for the probability that the left handed individual is a man i.e. $P(A_1/B)$

$$P(A_1 \mid B) = \frac{P(A_1)P(B \mid A_1)}{P(A_1)P(B \mid A_1) + P(A_2)P(B \mid A_2)}$$

$$= \frac{0.6 \times 0.15}{(0.6 \times 0.15) + (0.4 \times 0.06)}$$

= 0.09/0.114

= 78.9%

More generally Bayes' formula can be expressed as

Updated probability of an event given new information =

probability of new information given event x prior probability of event

unconditional probability of new information

LOS 2-1-D-s	**calculate** the number of ways a specified number of tasks can be performed using the multiplication rule of counting

Multiplication Rule of Counting

If one thing can be done in n_1 ways, and the next thing, given the first, in n_2 ways, and so on for k things, then the number of ways that the k things can be done is

$$n_1 \times n_2 \times n_3 \times \ldots\ldots\ldots \times n_k \qquad \textbf{(Equation 2-45)}$$

Example 2-49 Multiplication rule of counting

If the first thing can be done in three ways, the second in five ways and the third in six ways then there are 3 x 5 x 6 = 90 ways in which the three steps could be carried out.

LOS 2-1-D-t	**solve** counting problems using the factorial, combination, and permutation notations
LOS 2-1-D-u	**distinguish** among problems for which different counting methods are appropriate
LOS 2-1-D-v	**calculate** the number of ways to choose *r* objects from a total of *n* objects, when the order in which the *r* objects is listed does or does not matter

If you have a certain number of people, n, to be assigned to n jobs and after the first job is assigned there are (n – 1) people left to be assigned to the next job and so on then the number of ways of assigning the jobs is:

$n! = n \times (n-1) \times (n-2) \times .... \times 1$ (this is called **n factorial**) **(Equation 2-46)**

The General Formula for Labeling Problems

This is also called the multinomial formula and it is used when you want to label n objects in k different ways. If n_1 is the first way, n_2 the second and so on then the number of different ways is

$$\frac{n!}{n_1! \times n_2! \times .... \times n_k!}$$ **(Equation 2-47)**

Combination Formula

This is also called the binomial formula and is used in the simpler case when we are looking to choose r objects, when the order does not matter, from a total of n objects. The number of ways is

$${}_nC_r = \binom{n}{r} = \frac{n!}{(n-r)! \times r!}$$ **(Equation 2-48)**

Example 2-50 Combination formula

In we want to know how many ways we can achieve 2 stock moves upwards and 1 downwards over three periods we can use Equation 2-48 and define r as upward moves. The number of ways is

$${}_nC_r = \binom{3}{2} = \frac{3!}{(2)! \times 1!} = 3$$

Permutation Formula

In the case that the order does matter and we are choosing the r objects from n objects we need to use the permutation formula. This states that the number of ways this can be done is

$$ {}_{n}P_{r} = \frac{n!}{(n-r)!} \qquad \textbf{(Equation 2-49)} $$

Example 2-51 Permutation formula

If you have 8 stocks that you follow and you want to select the first and second strongest buys there are

$8!/(8-2)! = 56$ ways that they can be selected.

2-1-D View Concept Check Questions Workbook

STUDY SESSION 3

Investment Tools:

Quantitative Methods

Overview

You will probably find Study Session 3 is more demanding than Study Session 2. We are moving on to focus on the application of the concepts and tools covered in the previous session, and in particular their use in financial analysis and decision making.

In the first Reading Assignment we look at different discrete and continuous probability distributions, and how probability distributions can help us estimate the probability of achieving a specific outcome. In the next two Reading Assignments we study sampling, estimation and hypothesis testing. The objective is to examine the tools which will enable us to test whether a statement or hypothesis is to be 'accepted' or rejected. More specifically we are looking for evidence from a sample that the hypothesis is not correct, a statement that we can make with a certain level of confidence. Hypothesis testing involves understanding the different ways of selecting a sample, confidence intervals and how to select the appropriate test statistic and decision rule, before doing the number crunching to arrive at a decision to reject or not reject the hypothesis being tested.

In the final Reading Assignment we cover correlation and regression. Calculating and interpreting correlation, or the way two variables move together is relatively simple whereas regression analysis is more complex. Here we are looking at the relationship between a dependent variable (e.g. a stock return) and independent variable or variables (e.g. the market index return). We need to know how to calculate a regression equation and also how to apply the equation and test its significance.

Reading Assignments

Quantitative Methods for Investment Analysis, 2nd edition, Richard A Defusco, Dennis W. McLeavey, Jerald E. Pinto and David E. Runkle (CFA Institute, 2004)

3-1-A. "Common Probability Distributions" Ch. 5

3-1-B. "Sampling and Estimation" Ch. 6

3-1-C. "Hypothesis Testing" Ch. 7

3-1-D. "Correlation and Regression" Ch. 8

3-1-A "Common Probability Distributions"

LOS 3-1-A-a	**define** and **explain** a probability distribution
LOS 3-1-A-b	**distinguish** between and **give** examples of discrete and continuous random variables
LOS 3-1-A-c	**describe** the set of possible outcomes of a specified random variable

Introduction

This section focuses on probability distributions which will enable us to make clearer statements about a random variable, for example the return on a stock or earnings per share. Four distributions are considered: uniform, binomial, normal and lognormal distributions. These are used widely in finance, for example to estimate the probability of achieving a certain return and to control risk. Probability distributions will form the basis for understanding hypothesis testing and regression analysis which are covered later in the Study Session. At the end of the section we touch on Monte Carlo simulations, these are analytical procedures which involve identifying risk factors and their probability distributions.

A **probability distribution** lists all possible outcomes of a random variable and the probability that each outcome occurs.

A **discrete** probability distribution is one where the random variable can take on a countable number of possible outcomes. Quoted stock prices are an example, if we are looking at a market where they are quoted in ticks.

A **continuous** probability distribution is one where we cannot count the outcomes. Rates of return are examples of a continuous probability distribution.

The range of possible outcomes can be finite or infinite in both discrete and continuous distributions.

LOS 3-1-A-d	**define** a probability function, **state** its two key properties, and **determine** whether a given function satisfies those properties
LOS 3-1-A-e	**define** a probability density function
LOS 3-1-A-f	**define** a cumulative distribution function and **calculate** probabilities for a random variable, given its cumulative distribution function
LOS 3-1-A-g	**define** a discrete uniform random variable and **calculate** probabilities, given a discrete uniform distribution

A **probability function** specifies the probability that a random variable takes on a specific value eg. $P(X = x)$, written as $p(x)$, or for a continuous function $f(x)$. $f(x)$ is called the **probability density function.**

A probability function has two key properties

$p(x)$ lies between 0 and 1,

the sum of the probabilities $p(x)$ over all values of X is 1.

In the case that we are looking at the probability that X lies within a range we can use the

cumulative distribution function which gives the probability that X is less than or equal to a certain value denoted by P(X • x), this is often denoted by F(x) for both discrete and continuous random variables.

A **discrete uniform distribution** is when the probability of each outcome is the same i.e. it is uniform. In Example 3-1 we look at an example of a discrete uniform random variable, the probability that the random variable takes on any particular discrete value (in this case the integers 1 to 6) is equal.

Example 3-1: Discrete uniform distribution and cumulative distribution function

Taking the example of throwing a dice where the probability of throwing a 1, 2, 3, 4, 5, or 6 is the same.

X = x	Probability function p(x)	Cumulative distribution function F(x)
1	0.167	0.167
2	0.167	0.333
3	0.167	0.500
4	0.167	0.667
5	0.167	0.833
6	0.167	1.000

LOS 3-1-A-h **define** a binomial random variable and calculate probabilities, given a binomial probability distribution

LOS 3-1-A-i **calculate** the expected value and variance of a binomial random variable

Binomial Distributions

Bernoulli trials refer to trials where there are **two** possible outcomes. If p is used for the probability of success, and Y = 1 denotes the outcome being a success and Y= 0 a failure then:

$$p(1) = P(Y = 1) = p$$
$$p(0) = P(Y = 0) = 1 - p$$

Such a random variable is referred to as a **Bernoulli random variable.**

If there are n trials, which are independent with probability p of success, and we define X as the number of successes, X is the **binomial random variable**. When Y_i is the outcome of the ith trial (1 if a success, 0 if a failure)

$$X = Y_1 + Y_2 + ...Y_n \qquad \textbf{(Equation 3-1)}$$

X is described by n and p we write

$X \sim B(n,p)$

This means that X has a binomial random distribution with parameters n and p.

Binomial Probability Distribution

To calculate the probability of x successes from n trials when the trials are independent and the probability of success across trials is constant, use the formula:

$$p(x) = \frac{n!}{(n-x)! \times x!} p^x (1-p)^{n-x} \qquad \textbf{(Equation 3-2)}$$

where

n = number of trials
x = number of observed successes
p = probability of success

Note that the first part of Equation 3-2 is the combination formula from Study Session 2 which is the number of ways of selecting x successes from n trials.

Example 3-2: Binomial probability distribution

A dice is thrown four times, what is the probability of throwing exactly one six?

$$p(1) = \frac{4!}{1! \times 3!} 0.167^1 (1-0.167)^3 = 0.386$$

Mean and Variance of Binomial Random Variables

For a distribution X ~ B(n,p), where X has a binomial distribution with parameters n and p, the mean is np, since the Bernouilli random variable Y ~ B(1,p) takes on the value 1 with probability p and 0 with probability (1 – p) and therefore has a mean of p.

The variance of a Bernoulli trial is p(1 – p), this can be calculated working through Equation 2-39, where variance is $E[(Y - EY)^2]$. Since the trials are assumed to be independent the variance of a Binomial distribution is np(1 – p).

Binomial Trees

Binomial Trees can be used to illustrate a model where a stock price (S) either moves up with constant probability p, or down with constant probability 1- p. If u is 1 plus the return for an upward move, and d is 1 plus the return for a downward move and we look at a three period model, we can use a binomial tree to illustrate the possible outcomes. Each box is called a node and represents a potential value for the stock price.

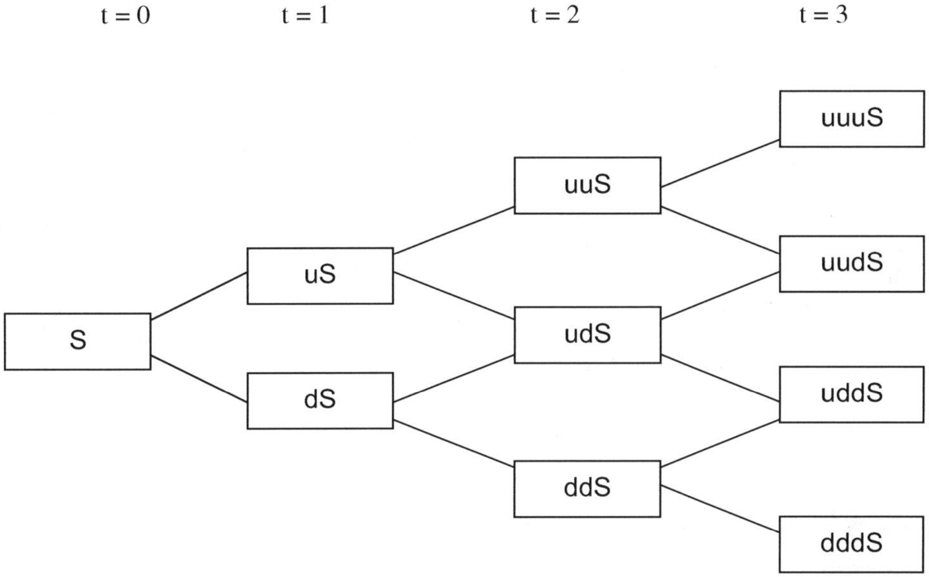

Note that there are four possible terminal prices, but there is only one way to get to either uuuS or dddS but three ways to get both uudS or uddS. Probabilities can be calculated using the probability distribution formula and then the expected stock price can be calculated.

LOS 3-1-A-j	**describe** the continuous uniform distribution and **calculate** probabilities, given a continuous uniform probability distribution

Continuous Uniform Distribution

The probability density function for a uniform random variable is

$$f(x) = \begin{cases} \dfrac{1}{b-a} & \text{for } a \le x \le b \\ 0 & \text{otherwise} \end{cases}$$

In general for continuous distributions when we are concerned with finding the probability that x lies between two values we would find the area under the curve representing the probability density function, this can be done by finding the integral of f(x) between the two points. In the case of a uniform distribution the curve is a horizontal line and the area underneath can be represented by a rectangle so

$$F(x) = \begin{cases} 0 \text{ for } x \le a \\ \dfrac{x-a}{b-a} & \text{for x between a and b} \\ 1 \text{ for } x \ge b \end{cases}$$

Example 3-3: Continuous uniform distribution

A continuous uniform distribution is shown in the graph below

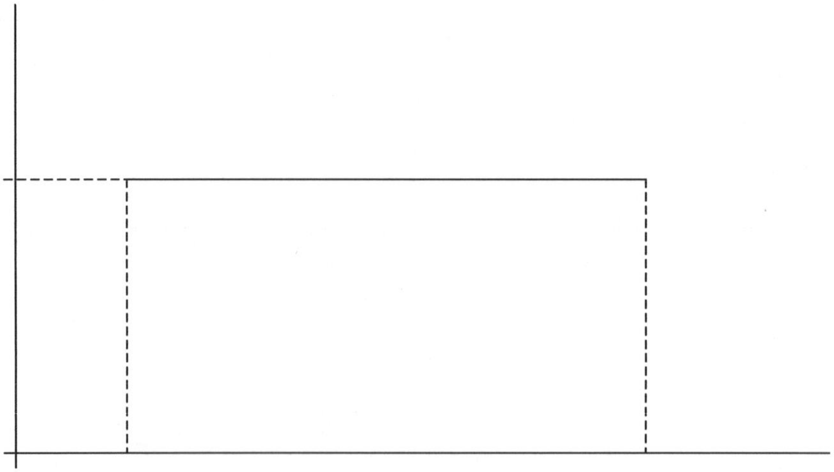

Between x = 1 and 6 f(x) = 1/(6 -1) = 0.2

If we select x = 5

F(5) = (5 – 1)/(6 – 1) = 0.8 which is the area between 0 and 5 on the x axis, which is four fifths of the total probability of 1.

LOS 3-1-A-k **explain** the key properties of the normal distribution

Normal Distribution

A normal distribution is a continuous distribution which is bell shaped and symmetrical with a range of possible outcomes from -• to +•.

The following are also properties of a normal distribution:

The distribution can be described completely by its mean, μ, and variance, ^{2}. A distribution can be denoted by X ~ N(μ, ^{2}). Note that N(0,1) is called the **standard normal distribution.**

Skewness is 0 and the kurtosis (which measures how peaked it is) is 3. The mean, median and mode are the same.

A linear combination of two or more normal random variables is normally distributed.

LOS 3-1-A-l **distinguish** between a univariate and a multivariate distribution
LOS 3-1-A-m **explain** the role of correlation in the multivariate normal distribution

A **univariate distribution** is one which describes a single random variable. A **multivariate distribution** considers probabilities for a number of related random variables. An example of a multivariate distribution is when we examine the distribution of stocks in a portfolio in order to decide whether the distribution of the returns from the portfolio is normally distributed. A multivariate distribution for a portfolio containing a number of stocks is described by

1. the mean returns of the stocks
2. the variance of each stocks' returns
3. the correlations between each pair of stocks' returns.

Note that in the multivariate normal distribution we need to specify correlations whereas in the univariate normal distribution we do not.

LOS 3-1-A-n **construct** and **explain** confidence intervals for a normally distributed random variable

For a normally distributed random variable we can establish confidence intervals, a confidence interval gives the percentage of times that we expect the random variable to fall within the interval.

Some of the most important confidence intervals are

P(X will lie between $\bar{X} \pm 1.645s) = 90\%$

P(X will lie between $\bar{X} \pm 1.96s) = 95\%$

P(X will lie between $\bar{X} \pm 2.58s) = 99\%$

where $\bar{X}$ is the sample mean and s the sample standard deviation.

This was shown graphically in Study Session 2, as below

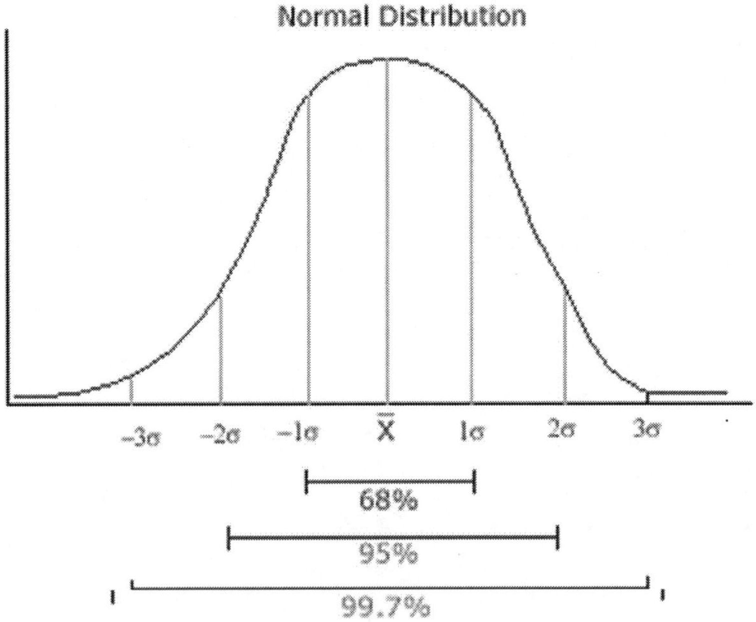

LOS 3-1-A-o	**define** the standard normal distribution and **explain** how to standardize a random variable
LOS 3-1-A-p	**calculate** probabilities using the standard normal distribution

A standard normal distribution is one with a mean of 0 and variance of 1. To standardize a normal distribution, i.e. to get in the format N(0,1), we simply need to subtract the mean from each observation and divide by the standard deviation. This means if $X \sim N(\mu,\ ^{2})$ and we calculate $Z = (X - \mu)/\ $ then $Z \sim N(0,1)$.

Note that Z is the conventional symbol for the standard normal variable; sometimes this is also called a Z-value.

Example 3-4: Z-value

If the mean of a normal distribution is 100 and the standard deviation is 10, what is the Z-value for an observation of 80?

$$\mathbf{Z = \frac{80 - 100}{10} = -2.0}$$

This indicates that an observation of 80 lies 2 standard deviations below the mean.

If the Z-value of an observation X is an integer we can easily work out the probability of the observation lying between the mean and X.

Example 3-5: Interpreting Z-values

If the Z-value of an observation is -2.0, as calculated in Example 3-4, then 47.7% of readings (95.44/2) will lie between the mean and the observation.

If the Z-value is not an integer you will need to use standard normal distribution tables, an excerpt of which is shown below:

P(Z • z) for z • 0

z	**0.00**	**0.01**	0.02
0.0	0.5000	0.5040	0.5080
0.1	0.5398	0.5438	0.5478
0.2	0.5793	0.5832	**0.5871**
0.3	0.6179	0.6217	0.6255
0.4	0.6554	0.6591	0.6628
			Etc.

For example, if Z is 0.22 then 58.71% of observations lie below, or are equal to, 0.22.

If required to find out the probability that an observation will be above or below a certain value then it may be necessary to compute Z-values for two different observations.

Example 3-6: Interpreting Z-values

If the mean of a normal distribution is 0 and the standard deviation is 2, what is the probability of an observation lying between -4 and -2?

First of all calculate Z for -4:

Z = -4/2 = -2.0

Therefore the area between 0 and -4 is 47.7

The Z value for -2 is -1.

Therefore the area between 0 and -2 is 34.1

So the probability that a reading lies between - 4 and -2 is 47.7% - 34.1% = 13.6%.

LOS 3-1-A-q	**define** shortfall risk
LOS 3-1-A-r	**calculate** the safety-first ratio and **select** an optimal portfolio using Roy's safetyfirst criterion

Shortfall risk is relevant when the investor is concerned about the risk of the portfolio value falling below a minimum or threshold level of return (R_L) over a certain time period, in this case safety-first rules should be considered.

Roy's safety–first criterion minimizes the $P(R_p < R_L)$, or selects the portfolio for which $E(R_p) - R_L$ is largest in units of standard deviation. This is the same as maximizing the safety-first ratio which is

$$\text{S F Ratio} = {[E(R_P) - R_L]}/{\sigma_P}$$ **(Equation 3-3)**

where

R_P	=	portfolio return
R_L	=	threshold level
σ_P	=	portfolio standard deviation

Note. This is similar to the Sharpe ratio; the portfolio with the highest Sharpe ratio will be the one that minimizes the probability of achieving a return below the risk-free rate.

Example 3-7: Shortfall risk

An investor needs to ensure that she achieves a return of at least the deposit rate of 5%. Two investment options are suggested, the first has an expected return of 20% with a standard deviation of 10%, the second has an expected return of 12% with a standard deviation of 8%. In order to decide which of the two options is the most attractive use the safety-first criterion and calculate:

S F Ratio(investment 1) = (20 – 5)/10 = 1.5
S F Ratio(investment 2) = (12 – 5)/8 = 0.875

The first investment option is the best according to the safety requirement.

LOS 3-1-A-s	**explain** the relationship between the lognormal and normal distributions

Lognormal distributions

The price of many financial assets is lognormally distributed. A lognormal distribution is defined by Y where $Y = e^x$, where X is the underlying normal distribution. Alternatively we could say that ln Y has a normal distribution. A lognormal distribution is skewed to the right with the lowest value being zero. It is completely described by two parameters, the mean and standard deviation of the underlying normal distribution. Note that the mean and standard deviation of the lognormal distribution are different to those of the underlying normal distribution.

Lognormal distributions have been used to describe price distributions of financial assets, whereas normal distributions are often used to describe return distributions of assets.

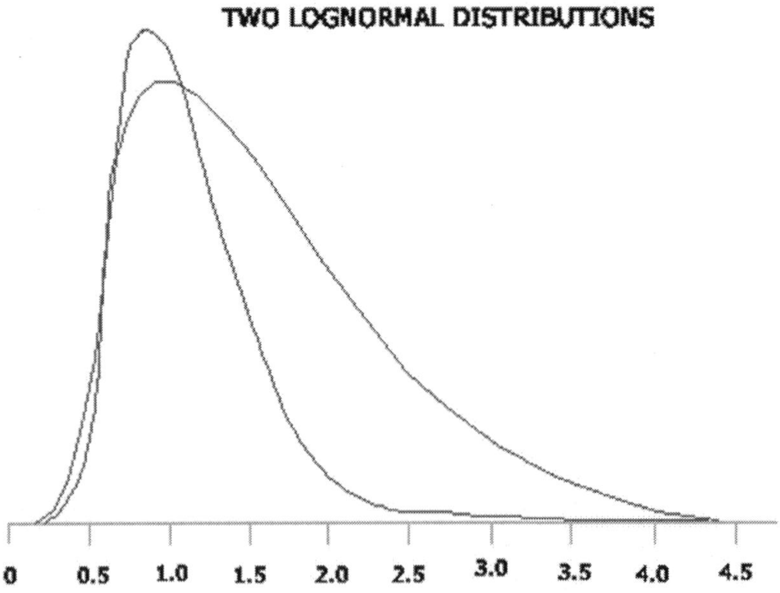

LOS 3-1-A-t	**distinguish** between discretely and continuously compounded rates of return
LOS 3-1-A-u	**calculate** the continuously compounded rate of return, given a specific holding period return

Turning to stock returns and stock prices. We need to define **continuously compounded return**, it is linked to the holding period return by

$$r_{t,t+1} = \ln S_{t+1}/S_t = \ln\left[1 + R_{t,t+1}\right] \qquad \textbf{(Equation 3-4)}$$

where

$r_{t,t+1}$	=	continuously compounded return between t and t+1
S_t	=	stock price at time t
$R_{t,t+1}$	=	holding period rate of return between t and t+1

Example 3-8: Continuously compounded returns

A stock price moves from \$50 to \$60. The return is 20% but the continuously compounded return is ln(\$60/\$50) = ln(1.2) = 0.1823, or 18.23%, less than the holding period return.

Extending the concept we have $r_{0,T} = \ln S_T/S_0$ or $S_T = S_0 \times \exp(r_{0,T})$

If $r_{0,T}$ is normal then S_T can be treated as a lognormal random variable. Even if the continuously compounded returns are not normally distributed a lognormal distribution will effectively describe asset prices.

Calculating portfolio end values using holding period returns will not represent actual returns as well as if the returns were converted to continuously compounded returns and the lognormal distribution was used to forecast end values.

LOS 3-1-A-v **explain** Monte Carlo simulation and historical simulation and **describe** their major applications and limitations

A **Monte Carlo simulation** is when computer models are used to find approximate solutions to complex financial problems. Risk factors are identified and probabilities assigned to the different sources of risk, then random sampling is used to simulate the risk factors. A very large number of simulations would usually be performed.

Examples of when Monte Carlo simulations are used include:

asset/liability planning for pension funds – risks would be stock market returns, interest rates, etc.

estimating Value at Risk – the model provides a distribution for changes in portfolio value which gives an estimate of the probability of portfolio losses exceeding a specified amount.

pricing of complex securities including options.

Historical simulation uses historical records to provide information on distributions. The disadvantage is that it only takes into account risks already reflected in the sample and doesn't include risks not reflected in the historic sample period.

3-1-A View Concept Check Questions Workbook

3-1-B "Sampling and Estimation"

Introduction

This Reading Assignment examines how data in a sample can be collected and then used to provide information on the wider population. Many of the examples are concerned with the mean of the sample being used to estimate the population mean, this is a practice often used in finance. The Central Limit Theorem allows us to make probability statements about a population mean based on sample data. It is imperative that you understand the concept and calculation of confidence intervals for the population mean and when to use the z-statistic or t-statistic before moving on to hypothesis testing in the next section.

LOS 3-1-B-a **define** simple random sampling

There are different ways of selecting a sample from a population. The basic type of sample is a **simple random sample**. In this sample each item or person in the population has an equal probability of being included.

Example 3-9: Simple random sample

Put each member of a population in a sequence and identify each member by a number then use random number tables to select the numbers for a sample (however many numbers needed for the sample size required). Match these numbers to the members of the population to identify the sample.

When it is not practical to assign a number to each item in a population then we might use **systematic random sampling**. In this case the items are arranged and then every *n*th item is included in the sample. This assumes that there is no pattern to the way that the items are arranged.

Example 3-10: Systematic random sample

A chocolate bar manufacturer selects every 100th chocolate bar coming off a conveyor belt for inclusion in a sample to test the weights of chocolate bars being produced.

LOS 3-1-B-b **define** and **interpret** sampling error

Although a random sample will reflect the characteristics of the population in an unbiased way, there is likely to be a difference between the estimate from the sample and the actual population characteristic.

Sampling error is defined as the difference between a sample statistic and the quantity that it is estimating from the population.

Example 3-11: Sampling error

A chocolate bar manufacturer selects every 100th chocolate bar coming off a conveyor belt for inclusion in a sample to test the weights of chocolate bars being produced. The mean weight of chocolate bars in the sample is 105 grams, the mean population weight is 100 grams, and sampling error is therefore 5 grams.

LOS 3-1-B-c **define** a sampling distribution

A **sampling distribution** of a statistic is the distribution of all possible distinct values that the statistic can assume when samples of the same size are randomly taken from the population. For example **the sampling distribution of the sample mean** is the distribution of all possible sample means of a given sample size and the probability of occurrence of each sample mean.

Example 3-12: Sampling distribution

The four employees of a firm have worked for the firm for 3, 7, 8 and 12 years. To calculate the sampling distribution of the sample mean for samples of 2 workers calculate the means for all possible samples

Employees in Sample (years worked)	Sample Mean (in years)
3 and 7	5.0
3 and 8	5.5
3 and 12	7.5
7 and 8	7.5
7 and 12	9.5
8 and 12	10.0

Therefore the sampling distribution of the sample mean is:

Sample Mean (in years)	Probability
5.0	0.167
5.5	0.167
7.5	0.333
9.5	0.167
10.0	0.167

We can see from the example that the mean of the sample mean is the same as the population mean, and the standard deviation of the distribution of sample mean is less than that of the population.

LOS 3-1-B-d **distinguish** between simple random and stratified random sampling

Another method of taking a sample is **stratified random sampling**. In this case we divide the population into subgroups (or strata) and select a sample from each subgroup. If it is a **proportional sample** then the number of items selected from each subgroup will be the same as the size of the subgroup as a proportion to the total population.

Example 3-13: Stratified random sampling

If we wish to study the usage of cars by a population of car owners we might decide to divide car owners into three subgroups by age as shown below.

Age	Percentage of car owners	Number in sample
Under 25 years	15%	300
25 years up to 55 years	60%	1,200
55 years and over	25%	500
Total	*100%*	*2,000*

The number from each group selected for the sample is based on the percentage of car owners in that group.

LOS 3-1-B-e **distinguish** between time-series and cross-sectional data

Two different forms of data are:

1. Time-series data

Time-series data is a sequence of returns collected at discrete and equally spaced time intervals, for example historic monthly stock returns.

2. Cross-sectional data

This is data collected on a characteristic of a group, which might be a group of individuals or companies, at a single point in time. Last year's closing prices for stocks that trade on the NYSE is an example of cross-sectional data.

LOS 3-1-B-f **state** the central limit theorem and **describe** its importance

Central Limit Theorem

For a population with a mean of μ and a variance of ^{2}, the sampling distribution of the sampling mean ($\bar{x}$) of all possible samples of size n will be approximately normally distributed with a mean μ and variance ^{2}/n (assuming n is large, say 30 or over).

To summarize:

Even if the distribution of the population is not normal the sampling distribution of the sampling mean, $\bar{x}$, is approximately a normal distribution.

The mean of the distribution of $\bar{x}$ will be equal to the mean of the population.

The variance of the distribution of $\bar{x}$ will be equal to the variance of the population divided by the sample size.

LOS 3-1-B-g **calculate** and **interpret** the standard error of the sample mean

The **standard error** of the sample mean is

$$\sigma_{\bar{x}} = \frac{\sigma}{\sqrt{n}} \quad \textbf{(Equation 3-5)}$$

This is the standard deviation of the sampling distribution of the sample mean.

If the population standard deviation ( )• is not known, then we can use the sample standard deviation, s, to estimate the standard error, it is then denoted by

$$s_{\bar{x}} = \frac{s}{\sqrt{n}}. \quad \textbf{(Equation 3-6)}$$

where

$$s^2 = \frac{\sum_{i=1}^{n}\left(x_i - \bar{x}\right)^2}{n-1} \qquad \textbf{(Equation 3-7)}$$

Example 3-14: Standard error of the sample mean

If the standard deviation of a population is 10 and a sample of 49 items is taken from the population then the standard error of the sample mean is:

$$\frac{\sigma}{\sqrt{n}} = \frac{10}{7} = 1.4285$$

LOS 3-1-B-h	**distinguish** between a point estimate and a confidence interval estimate of a population parameter

Estimating a population parameter

The formulas that we use to calculate a sample statistic is an **estimator**. The particular value that we calculate using an estimator is an **estimate**.

A **point estimate** is a single estimate calculated from a sample which is used to estimate the population parameter. An example of this would be a sample mean being calculated as a point estimate of the population mean.

Another approach is to make an **interval estimate** of the parameter; this means we find an interval that will include the population parameter with a certain level of probability. This is a **confidence interval.**

LOS 3-1-B-i **identify** and **describe** the desirable properties of an estimator

The three desirable properties of an estimator (or estimation formula) are

1. Unbiased – the expected value (the mean of its sampling distribution) is the same as the parameter it is intended to estimate.
2. Efficient – there is no other unbiased estimate of the same parameter with a sampling distribution of smaller variance.
3. Consistent – the probability of accurate estimates increases as the sample size increases.

Confidence Intervals

This is an interval and the population parameter lies within this interval with a specified probability (1 –). The probability is the **degree of confidence.** The interval is called the (1 –)% confidence interval for the parameter.

The end points of the interval are called the lower and upper **confidence limits**.

A 95% confidence interval can be interpreted by considering the case when we take a large number of samples from the population and construct a confidence interval for each sample. We expect 95% of these confidence intervals to include the population mean. Following on, we can say that we are 95% confident that a single confidence level includes the population mean.

Constructing a confidence interval

A confidence interval is defined by

point estimate ± reliability factor x standard error **(Equation 3-8)**

where

point estimate	=	a point estimate of the parameter
reliability factor	=	a number based on the assumed distribution of the point estimate and degree of confidence for the interval
standard error	=	standard error of the sample statistic providing the point estimate

Applying this to the case where we are estimating the population mean and we are taking a sample from a normally distributed population with known variance. The confidence interval is given by

$$\bar{x} \pm z_{\alpha/2} \frac{\sigma}{\sqrt{n}}$$ **(Equation 3-9)**

where

$\bar{x}$ = sample mean, which is the point estimate of the population mean

σ = population standard deviation

n = sample size

$z_{\alpha/2}$ = reliability factor, the point where $\alpha/2$ of the probability is in the right tail.

Using the characteristics of a normal distribution, we can see that:

$z_{0.05}$ is used for 90% confidence intervals, since it is when 5% of the probability is in the top right tail and 5% in the bottom left tail. $z_{0.05}$ is 1.645.

$z_{0.025}$ which is used for 95% confidence intervals, is 1.960.

$z_{0.005}$ which is used for 99% confidence intervals, is 2.575.

Another way of saying this is that:

90% of the sample means will be within 1.645 standard deviations of the population mean
95% of the sample means will be within 1.960 standard deviations of the population mean
99% of the sample means will be within 2.575 standard deviations of the population mean

For **any** distribution if we do **not** know the variance, and it is a **large** sample, we can use

$$\bar{x} \pm z_{\alpha/2} \frac{s}{\sqrt{n}}$$ **(Equation 3-10)**

where

s	=	sample standard deviation
$\bar{x}$	=	sample mean
n	=	sample size

Therefore

The 90% confidence interval for the mean is $\bar{x} \pm \frac{1.645s}{\sqrt{n}}$

The 95% confidence interval for the mean is $\bar{x} \pm \frac{1.960s}{\sqrt{n}}$

The 99% confidence interval for the mean is $\bar{x} \pm \frac{2.575s}{\sqrt{n}}$

Example 3-15: Confidence intervals

A sample of 81 observations is taken from a normal population, the sample mean is 20 and the standard deviation is 3.

The 90% confidence interval is $20 \pm (1.645 \times 3)/9$ which is 19.45 up to 20.55.

This means we can be 90% confident that the population mean lies between 19.45 and 20.55.

The 95% confidence interval is $20 \pm (1.960 \times 3)/9$ which is 19.35 up to 20.65.

The 99% confidence interval is $20 \pm (2.575 \times 3)/9$ which is 19.14 up to 20.86.

LOS 3-1-B-j **describe** the properties of Student's *t*-distribution

Student's t – distribution

An alternative method for constructing confidence intervals is to use the t-distribution. It is a more conservative method, giving wider intervals, and ideally is used in all cases even when it is a large sample. However when it is a *small sample* (less than 30), when we do not know the population variance, it is essential to use the t-distribution approach.

The **t-distribution** is a symmetrical probability distribution defined by a single parameter, the number of degrees of freedom (df).

LOS 3-1-B-k **calculate** and **explain** degrees of freedom

Degrees of freedom are the number of independent observations used.

Example 3-16: Degrees of freedom

The equation for sample variance $\dfrac{\sum_{i=1}^{n}(X_i - \overline{X})^2}{(n-1)}$

for a sample of size n uses a denominator of (n - 1). This is because there are (n – 1) ways of selecting the sample, if the mean is given (as it is in the numerator of the variance formula). Once you have selected (n – 1) items, the nth item will be determined by the mean. Therefore there are (n – 1) degrees of freedom.

The t-distribution with a mean of 0 and (n – 1) degrees of freedom is given by

$$t = \frac{(\overline{x} - \mu)}{s/\sqrt{n}}$$ **(Equation 3-11)**

It is not normal since there are two random variables, the sample mean and standard deviation. However as the number of degrees of freedom increases the t-distribution approaches the normal distribution, as shown below.

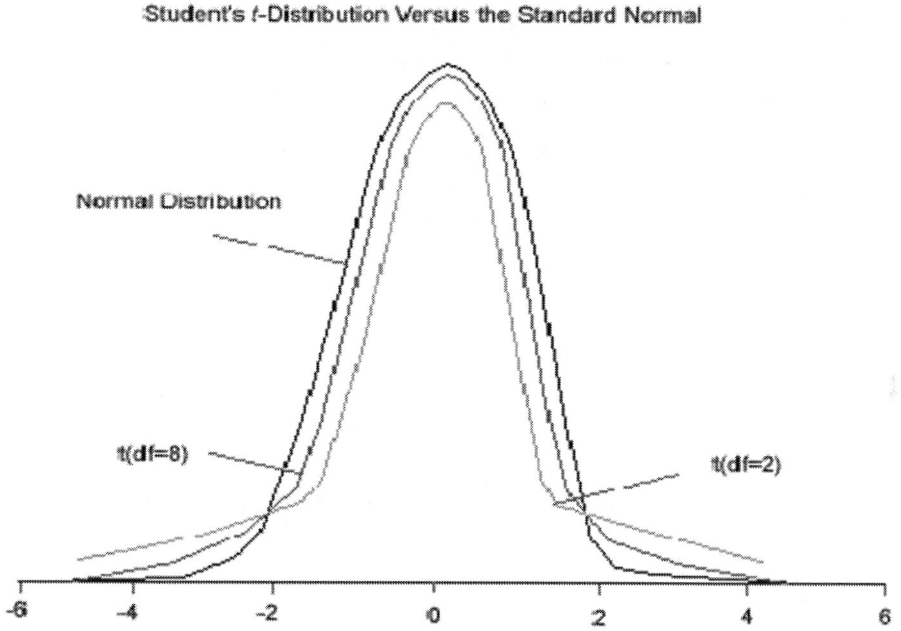

LOS 3-1-B-l **calculate** and **interpret** a confidence interval for a population mean, given a normal distribution with 1) a known population variance or 2) an unknown population variance

LOS 3-1-B-m **calculate** and **interpret** a confidence interval for a population mean when the population variance is unknown, given a large sample from any type of distribution

Confidence Intervals for the population mean

If we are considering a population with unknown variance and either

the sample is large, or

the sample is small but normally distributed, then

The (1 –)% confidence interval is given by

$$\bar{x} \pm t_{\alpha/2} \frac{s}{\sqrt{n}} \qquad \textbf{(Equation 3-12)}$$

where the number of degrees of freedom for $t_{\alpha/2}$ is (n – 1), with a sample size of n.

In order to answer hypothesis questions you may be required to read t-distribution tables to find the critical value of t. We show an excerpt from the tables below. Note that these are for one-tailed tests, so for = 0.05 then p = 0.05, whereas for a two-tailed test you would need to use p = 0.025, which is half the significance level.

For example to find the critical t-value with 5 degrees of freedom and ==0.05 and a one-tailed test the critical t-value would be 2.015. For a two-tailed test (p = 0.025) it would be 2.571.

df	p =0.10	p = 0.05	p = 0.025
1	3.078	6.314	12.706
2	1.886	2.920	4.303
3	1.638	2.353	3.182
4	1.533	2.132	2.776
5	1.476	**2.015**	**2.571**
			Etc.

Example 3-17: Confidence intervals

An investor is looking at the quarterly returns from a mutual fund portfolio which are assumed to be normally distributed and have a mean of 3% and a sample standard deviation of 2%. He looks at 3 years' data and wishes to compute the 95% confidence interval. Since the sample is small he uses Equation 3-12

He will need to use t-distribution tables to look up $t_{0.025}$ for 11 degrees of freedom (since the sample size is 12), this is 2.201.

The confidence interval is $\bar{x} \pm t_{\alpha/2} \frac{s}{\sqrt{n}} = 3\% \pm 2.201 \frac{2\%}{\sqrt{12}} = 3\% \pm 1.27\%$

The 95% confidence interval is between 1.73% and 4.27%

The investor can be confident, at the 95% level, that this range includes the population mean.

In summary, the table below shows which statistic to use for different samples.

Distribution	Variance	Small Sample	Large Sample
Normal	Known	z	z
Normal	Unknown	t	z or t
Nonnormal	Known	Not Available	z
Nonnormal	Unknown	Not Available	z or t

LOS 3-1-B-n **discuss** the issues regarding selection of the appropriate sample size

If a larger sample size is taken then the confidence interval will decrease as the standard error is lower. As you would expect, a larger sample gives more precise results.

LOS 3-1-B-o	**discuss** data-mining bias
LOS 3-1-B-p	**define** and **discuss** sample selection bias, survivorship bias, look-ahead bias, and time-period bias

Biases impacting on data selected:

Data-snooping bias

This is the bias that occurs if you use the empirical results of other analysts' research, or focus on patterns that may have been identified by other research. Ideally you would study new data but unfortunately this may not be practical in financial markets where much of the research is based on historic data.

Data-mining bias

This is when forecasting models are derived from searching through historic data for patterns/trading rules. The problems occur when a large number of models are tested but only the successful ones reported.

Sample selection bias

This occurs when certain data is excluded from the analysis, possibly because the data was not available.

Survivorship bias

This is one type of sample selection bias, which occurs when companies that have gone bankrupt, or funds or portfolios that have been liquidated, are not included in the analysis.

Look-ahead bias

This is when a test uses information that was not available at the test date. An example of this is when the success of valuation ratios is considered but all investors may not have had access to the accounting data incorporated in the valuation ratio at the test date.

Time-period bias

This is when the test period used does not match the conclusion being drawn, perhaps short-term data is being applied to provide long-term forecasts.

3-1-B View Concept Check Questions Workbook

3-1-C "Hypothesis Testing"

Introduction

In order to test statements in finance such as 'have the fund's returns been statistically different to the benchmark's returns?' or 'is the beta of as tock statistically different to 1?' we need to understand the procedure behind hypothesis testing. Essentially we need to state a null hypothesis and then collect data from a sample which will decide whether we have a basis for rejecting the null hypothesis. We will not be certain whether the null hypothesis can be rejected but will be able to state with a certain probability, or confidence level, whether we have evidence to reject it.

The focus of hypothesis testing is on testing a hypothesis concerning the population mean, although you need to be familiar with the tests that are used for population variances, difference between means and differences between variances.

LOS 3-1-C-a **define** a hypothesis and **describe** the steps of hypothesis testing

A **hypothesis** is a statement about one or more populations developed for the purpose of testing.

Hypothesis testing is broken down into a 7-step process:

1. Stating the hypotheses.
2. Identifying the test statistic and its distribution.
3. Specifying the significance level.
4. Stating the decision rule.
5. Collecting the data and performing the calculations.
6. Making the statistical decision.
7. Making the economic or investment decision.

We will now look at each of these steps in turn.

LOS 3-1-C-b	**define** and **interpret** the null hypothesis and alternative hypothesis
LOS 3-1-C-d	**discuss** the choice of the null and alternative hypotheses

1. Stating the hypotheses

We need to state two hypotheses, the null hypothesis and the alternative hypothesis.

The **null hypothesis** is defined as the statement being tested, and is denoted by H_0. The null hypothesis will be considered to be true, and will be accepted, unless the hypothesis test gives evidence that it is false.

Note: the term 'accepted' for the null hypothesis is commonly used although it is misleading, it is better to use 'fail to reject it' since we do not have evidence that it is not true.

The **alternative hypothesis** is the statement that will be accepted if the sample data used in the test suggests that the null hypothesis is false, it is denoted by H_a.

LOS 3-1-C-c	**distinguish** between one-tailed and two-tailed tests of hypotheses

The null and alternative hypothesis can be stated in three ways - as a two-tailed test, or in two different ways as one-tailed tests.

Two-tailed hypothesis test (or two-sided test)

If we are using the sample mean to test for the population mean a two-tailed test would be:

$\mathbf{H_0: \mu = \bar{x}} \quad \mathbf{H_a: \mu \neq \bar{x}}$

In this case the null hypothesis is rejected if the evidence indicates that the population parameter is either smaller or larger than $\bar{x}$.

One-tailed hypothesis test (or one-sided test)

One-tailed tests are used if we want to see if the population parameter is less than or equal to $\bar{x}$, or more than or equal to $\bar{x}$. The two hypotheses to test for the population mean are:

$\mathbf{H_0: \mu \leq \bar{x}} \quad \mathbf{H_a: \mu > \bar{x}}$

$\mathbf{H_0: \mu \geq \bar{x}} \quad \mathbf{H_a: \mu < \bar{x}}$

Note that the null hypothesis must always include the equals sign.

LOS 3-1-C-e **define** and **interpret** a test statistic

2. Identifying the test statistic and its distribution

A **test statistic** is the quantity that is calculated from the sample whose value is used to decide whether to accept or reject the null hypothesis.

In the cases we are looking at, the test statistic is given by

$$\text{test statistic} = \frac{\text{sample statistic - value of parameter in } H_0}{\text{standard error of sample statistic}}$$

For example, when we are using the sample mean to estimate the population mean and we know the population standard deviation, the standard error is $\frac{\sigma}{\sqrt{n}}$, (using Equation 3-5)

The test statistic is $\frac{\bar{x} - \mu}{\sigma / \sqrt{n}}$

If we do not know the population standard deviation we use $\frac{s}{\sqrt{n}}$ instead of $\frac{\sigma}{\sqrt{n}}$.

We are measuring how far the sample mean is from the center of the distribution in standard deviation terms.

Although different distributions can be tested, for the moment we will concentrate on t-tests and on z-tests for standard normal distributions.

LOS 3-1-C-f **define** and **interpret** a Type I and a Type II error
LOS 3-1-C-g **define** and **interpret** a significance level and **explain** how significance levels are used in hypothesis testing
LOS 3-1-C-h **define** the power of a test

3. Specifying the significance level

The significance level reflects how much evidence we require to reject the null hypothesis. This is the level of risk, called α risk, which is the probability of rejecting the null hypothesis when it is true (a **Type I error**). The risk of accepting the null hypothesis when it is false is β risk (a **Type II error**).

Looking at the relationship between a decision and the true situation we can see there are four possibilities.

Decision	True Situation	
	H_0 True	H_0 False
Do not reject H_0	Correct	Type II Error
Reject H_0	Type I Error	Correct

For a given sample, if we want to reduce the probability of a Type I error, we will increase the probability of making a Type II error. We can only reduce the probability of errors occurring by increasing the sample size. The **power** of the test is the probability of correctly rejecting the null hypothesis when it is false.

LOS 3-1-C-i **define** and **interpret** a decision rule
LOS 3-1-C-j **explain** the relation between confidence intervals and hypothesis tests

4. Stating the decision rule

The decision rule is based on deciding a critical value(s) or rejection point(s) for the test statistic, which will decide when the null hypothesis is accepted or rejected. These critical values are determined by the level of significance. For a z-test these are often set at:

Level of Significance	1 Tail	2 Tails
.10	1.28	± 1.65
.05	1.65	± 1.96
.01	2.33	± 2.58

If the z-statistic or z-value is within these values, which means it is within the confidence interval or acceptance range, then the null hypothesis is not rejected, and the result of the test is **not statistically significant**. If it is outside the range then it is in the rejection region and then the null hypothesis is rejected, and the result is **statistically significant**.

The graph below shows the rejection points for the 0.05, or 5%, significance level for a two-tailed test when H_0: $\mu = 0$ H_a: $\mu \neq 0$. We reject the null hypothesis if the z-statistic is greater than 1.96 or less than -1.96.

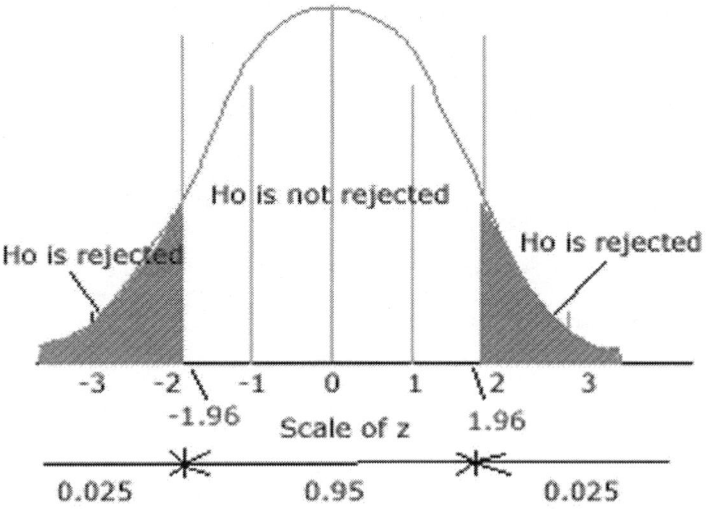

For a one-tailed test the rejection region is at one end of the curve. In this case we have set the null hypothesis as H_0: $\mu \leq 0$ and H_a: $\mu > 0$. At the 0.05, or 5%, significance level, we can reject the null hypothesis if the z-statistic is greater than 1.645. The rejection region is shown below. If H_0: $\mu \geq 0$ and H_a: $\mu < 0$ then the rejection region would be at the lower end of the curve.

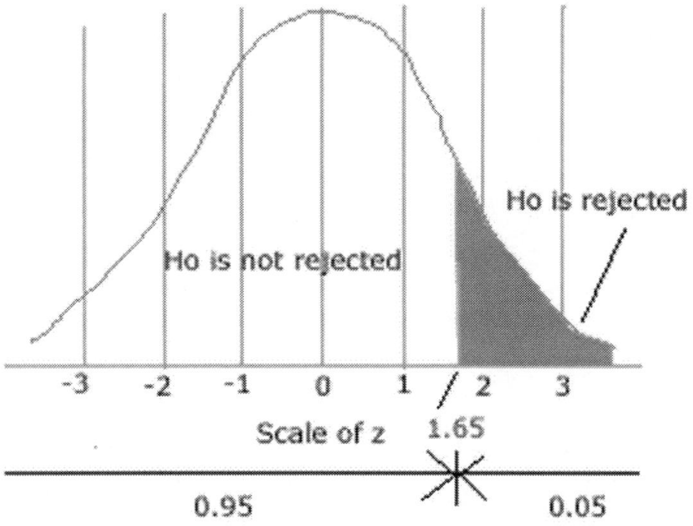

The ***p*-value** is used to measure how confident we can be in rejecting or accepting the null hypothesis, it is the smallest level of significance at which the null hypothesis can rejected. If the *p*-value is smaller than the significance level then H_0 is rejected and vice versa.

The *p*-value is the probability of observing a value as extreme, or more extreme, than the value observed given H_0 is true.

***p*-value less than**	**conclusion**
.10	some evidence that H_0 is not true
.05	strong evidence that H_0 is not true
.01	very strong evidence that H_0 is not true
.001	extremely strong evidence that H_0 is not true

5. Collecting the data and performing the calculations

When collecting data it is important to avoid the biases discussed in the previous section e.g. survivorship bias.

6. Making the statistical decision

This is the decision to accept or reject the null hypothesis based on the decision rule and the calculation of the test statistic.

LOS 3-1-C-k **distinguish** between a statistical decision and an economic decision

7. Making the economic or investment decision

Other economic or investment considerations (for example client's risk tolerance, time horizon, transaction costs) need to be incorporated before the final decision is made.

LOS 3-1-C-I	**identify** the appropriate test statistic and **interpret** the results for a hypothesis test concerning the population mean of a normally distributed population with 1) known or 2) unknown variance

Choice of test

The z-test can be used when the population is normally distributed and the variance is known.

The z-test statistic for a single population mean is

$$z = \frac{\bar{x} - \mu_0}{\sigma / \sqrt{n}} \qquad \textbf{(Equation 3-13)}$$

where

$\bar{x}$ = sample mean
μ_0 = hypothesized value of the population mean.
σ = population standard deviation
n = sample size

If the sample is large, using the central limit theorem, we can use the sample standard deviation as an approximation of the population standard deviation even if the population is not normally distributed.

If the population variance is **not known** we should consider using the t-test. The t-test can be used if the variance is unknown and either (1) the sample is large or (2) the sample is small but the population is normally distributed.

The t-test statistic is

$$t_{n-1} = \frac{\bar{x} - \mu_0}{s / \sqrt{n}} \qquad \textbf{(Equation 3-14)}$$

where

t_{n-1} = t-statistic with (n –1) degrees of freedom for a sample of size n
$\bar{x}$ = sample mean
μ_0 = hypothesized value of the population mean
s = sample standard deviation

Examples 3-18: Hypothesis testing

1. We wish to test, at the 5% significance level, whether the mean of a population has changed from 25. The population standard deviation is 4. A sample of 100 observations is taken from the population and the sample mean is 24.

The null hypothesis is that the mean of the population is 25. So define

$\mathbf{H_0: \mu = 25}$

$\mathbf{H_a: \mu \neq 25}$

In this case we have a large sample with a known population variance so we can use the z-statistic. Using Equation 3-13

$$z = \frac{\bar{x} - \mu_0}{\sigma / \sqrt{n}} = \frac{(24 - 25)}{0.4} = -2.5$$

This is a two-tailed test so the critical values of z are plus or minus 1.96. z is less than -1.96, which is outside the acceptable range, so we reject the null hypothesis. We can conclude that there is statistical evidence that the mean has changed from 25.

2. We wish to test, at the 1% significance level, whether the mean of a population has risen above 100. The population standard deviation is 10. A sample of 70 observations is taken from the population and the sample mean is 102.

Define

$H_0: \mu \leq 100$

$H_a: \mu > 100$

Again we can us the z-statistic since it is a large sample with a known variance.

$$z = \frac{\bar{x} - \mu_0}{\sigma / \sqrt{n}} = \frac{(102 - 100)}{10/8.366} = 1.67$$

This is a one-tailed test so the critical value of z is 2.33. Since 1.67 is less than the critical value we can conclude that we should not reject the null hypothesis and we do not have statistical evidence that the population mean is greater than 100. (At the 5% significance level we would need to reject the null hypothesis).

3. An investor is reviewing his fund's performance using 2 years' monthly data, the mean return is 1% per month with a standard deviation of returns of 3%. Returns are assumed to be normally distributed. He wishes to establish at the 0.05 level of significance whether the performance is consistent with a mean population return of a 1.3%.

In this case apply a two-tailed test with

H_0: $\mu = 1.3\%$
H_a: $\mu \bullet 1.3\%$
We can use the t-statistic since the sample is small but normally distributed.

The rejection points are found in the t-distribution tables with 23 degrees of freedom, they are ± 2.069

Calculate the t-statistic using Equation 3-14.

$$t_{n-1} = \frac{\bar{X} - \mu_0}{s/\sqrt{n}}$$

$$t_{23} = \frac{1.0\% - 1.3\%}{3\%/\sqrt{24}} = -0.489$$

This does not lie outside the rejection points and is within the acceptance range so the null hypothesis cannot be rejected. We can conclude that the results appear to be consistent with a population mean of 1.3%.

LOS 3-1-C-m	**identify** the appropriate test statistic and **interpret** the results for a hypothesis test concerning the equality of the population means of two normally distributed populations, based on independent random samples with 1) equal or 2) unequal assumed variances

Tests for means of two different groups

In this case we want to establish whether the means of two different groups or populations are the same, or whether one is larger than the other. It is assumed that the two groups are approximately normally distributed and the samples are independent of each other. In the first case the populations' variances are assumed to be equal (although they may not be known) and in the second case they are assumed not to be equal.

In the first case the most likely hypotheses to use are

H_0: $\mu_1 - \mu_2 = 0$ $\quad$ H_a: $\mu_1 - \mu_2 \neq 0$
H_0: $\mu_1 - \mu_2 \leq 0$ $\quad$ H_a: $\mu_1 - \mu_2 > 0$
H_0: $\mu_1 - \mu_2 \geq 0$ $\quad$ H_a: $\mu_1 - \mu_2 < 0$
where μ_1 and μ_2 are the population means of the two populations.

When the population variances are equal, we effectively combine or pool the observations and use a t-test based on

$$t = \frac{\left(\overline{X}_1 - \overline{X}_2\right) - \left(\mu_1 - \mu_2\right)}{\left(\dfrac{s_p^2}{n_1} + \dfrac{s_p^2}{n_2}\right)^{1/2}} \qquad \textbf{(Equation 3-15)}$$

where

$$s_p^2 = \frac{(n_1 - 1)s_1^2 + (n_2 - 1)s_2^2}{n_1 + n_2 - 2}$$

$\overline{X}_i$ = the sample mean for group i
μ_i = the mean for population i
which is the pooled estimator of the common variance.

There are $(n_1 + n_2 - 2)$ degrees of freedom.

Example 3-19: Means of different populations

The returns from a fund are shown below

	Mean Weekly Return	Standard Deviation
Year 1	0.45%	2.6%
Year 2	0.20%	2.5%

We assume that the population variances are equal and the data is independent. We wish to establish if the mean returns were statistically different.

Define H_0: $\mu_1 - \mu_2 = 0$ H_a: $\mu_1 - \mu_2 \neq 0$ where μ_1 is the mean return for the fund in Year 1 and μ_2 is the mean return for the fund in Year 2.

Look at the 0.05 and the 0.01 levels of significance. Using tables with 102 degrees of freedom (52+ 52 –2) the rejection points are ±1.984 and ±2.626 respectively.

Using Equation 3-15

$$s_p^2 = \frac{(n_1 - 1)s_1^2 + (n_2 - 1)s_2^2}{n_1 + n_2 - 2}$$

$$= \frac{(51 \times 2.6^2) + (51 \times 2.5^2)}{102}$$

$= 6.51$ **this is effectively the pooled estimate of the common variance**

$$t = \frac{(\overline{x_1} - \overline{x_2}) - (\mu_1 - \mu_2)}{\left(\frac{s_p^2}{n_1} + \frac{s_p^2}{n_2}\right)^{1/2}}$$

$$= \frac{(0.45 - 0.20) - 0}{\left(\frac{6.51}{51} + \frac{6.51}{51}\right)^{1/2}}$$

$= \mathbf{0.49}$

This is not significant at either the 0.05 or 0.01 levels and we can conclude that the means are not statistically different.

If we cannot assume that the population variances are equal the formula becomes

$$t = \frac{\left(\overline{x_1} - \overline{x_2}\right) - \left(\mu_1 - \mu_2\right)}{\left(\frac{s_1^2}{n_1} + \frac{s_2^2}{n_2}\right)^{1/2}} \qquad \textbf{(Equation 3-16)}$$

where the degrees of freedom are given by

$$df = \frac{\left(\frac{s_1^2}{n_1} + \frac{s_2^2}{n_2}\right)^2}{\frac{\left(s_1^2/n_1\right)^2}{n_1} + \frac{\left(s_2^2/n_2\right)^2}{n_2}}$$

LOS 3-1-C-n **identify** the appropriate test statistic and **interpret** the results for a hypothesis test concerning the mean difference of two normally distributed populations (paired comparisons test)

Paired Comparison Tests

When two samples are **not** independent we cannot apply the test statistics shown in Equations 3-15 and 3-16. If, for example, we are comparing the mean returns of two portfolios investing in the U.S. over the same time period, it is likely that the performance will not be independent. This is because they will both be affected by common risk factors, such as the return from the U.S. market.

Denote $d_i = x_{Ai} - x_{Bi}$,where x_{Ai} and x_{Bi} are the ith pair of observations.

Then if μ_{D0} is the hypothesized value of the mean difference (often set at 0) the following hypotheses can be used:

H_0: $\mu_D = \mu_{D0}$. H_a: $\mu_D \neq \mu_{D0}$
H_0: $\mu_D \leq \mu_{D0}$ H_a: $\mu_D > \mu_{D0}$
H_0: $\mu_D \geq \mu_{D0}$ H_a: $\mu_D < \mu_{D0}$
The sample mean difference is given by

$$\bar{d} = \frac{1}{n}\sum_{i=1}^{n} d_i$$

The sample variance by

$$s_d^2 = \frac{\sum_{i=1}^{n}\left(d_i - \bar{d}\right)^2}{n-1}$$

The standard error of the mean difference is

$$s_{\bar{d}} = \frac{s_d}{\sqrt{n}}$$

When the samples are taken from normally distributed populations with unknown variances the t-test is based on

$$t = \frac{\bar{d} - \mu_{d0}}{s_{\bar{d}}} \qquad \textbf{(Equation 3-17)}$$

with (n – 1) degrees of freedom where n is the number of paired observations.

Example 3-20: Paired comparison test

The following information is given regarding the performance of the two portfolios A and B. The performance is monthly over the last five years.

Portfolio	Mean Return	Standard Deviation
A	1.8%	4.5%
B	1.4%	3.6%
Difference	0.4%	1.3%

From the information we can see that

$\bar{d} = 0.4\%$, **and s_d = 1.3% and n = 60**

We wish to establish whether the means of the two performances are equal, at the 0.05 significance level.

Set the hypothesis as

$\mathbf{H_0: \mu_D = 0 \quad H_a: \mu_D \neq 0}$

The test statistic is the t-statistic with 59 degrees of freedom.

Using tables the critical values are t = ± 2.0

Using Equation 3-17

$$t = \frac{\bar{d} - \mu_{d0}}{s_{\bar{d}}}$$

$$t_{59} = \frac{0.4\%}{1.3\% / \sqrt{59}} = 2.36$$

Since this is larger than 2 we reject the null hypothesis and conclude that the difference in mean returns is statistically significant.

LOS 3-1-C-o	**identify** the appropriate test statistic and **interpret** the results for a hypothesis test concerning the variance of a normally distributed population

Testing for Variance

We now look at hypothesis testing in relation to the value of the variance, ^{2}. If we set ${}_0^2$ as the hypothesized value of ^{2} we can set the hypotheses as one of the following.

H_0: $^2 = {}_0^2$	H_a: $^2 \neq {}_0^2$
H_0: $^2 \leq {}_0^2$	H_a: $^2 > {}_0^2$
H_0: $^2 \geq {}_0^2$	H_a: $^2 < {}_0^2$

For a single normally distributed population we use the **chi-square test statistic**, ❹^2. This requires the use of the appropriate distribution tables using (n –1) degrees of freedom for a sample size n. Note that the chi-square distribution is not symmetrical and has a lower bound of zero. It is also sensitive to violations in the assumptions used.

The test statistic is

$$\chi^2 = \frac{(n-1)s^2}{\sigma_0^2}$$ **(Equation 3-18)**

where

s^2 = sample variance
${}_0^2$ = hypothesized value of the variance
and there are (n - 1) degrees of freedom.

Example 3-21: Using a chi-square test statistic

We have the data for monthly returns for a portfolio over the last 5 years.

Mean Return	Standard Deviation
1.8%	4.5%

The managers of the portfolio say that their risk disciplines ensure that the standard deviation of returns is less than 5%.

We wish to test the hypothesis that

H_0: ${}^2 \geq 25$ $\qquad$ H_a: ${}^2 < 25$

The test statistic is the chi-square test statistic with 59 degrees of freedom.

Using chi-square tables and using 0.95 (we have a 95% probability of a test statistic this level or higher), the critical level is 43.188. We will reject the null hypothesis if the test statistic is less than this number.

$$\chi^2 = \frac{(n-1)s^2}{\sigma_0^2} = \frac{59 \times 4.5^2}{25} = 47.79$$

This is more than 43.188 so we cannot reject the null hypothesis, there is insufficient statistical evidence that the standard deviation of the returns of the population is less than 5%.

LOS 3-1-C-p	**identify** the appropriate test statistic and **interpret** the results for a hypothesis test concerning the equality of the variances of two normally distributed populations, based on two independent random samples

Differences between variances

If we are interested in checking whether the variances of two normally distributed populations are the same then we can formulate the hypothesis as follows:

H_0: ${}_1^2 = {}_2^2$ $\quad H_a$: ${}_1^2 \neq {}_2^2$
H_0: ${}_1^2 \leq {}_2^2$ $\quad H_a$: ${}_1^2 > {}_2^2$
H_0: ${}_1^2 \geq {}_2^2$ $\quad H_a$: ${}_1^2 < {}_2^2$

In this case we use the F-test where F is given by the ratio of the two sample variances

$$F = \frac{s_1^2}{s_2^2} \qquad \textbf{(Equation 3-19)}$$

F-distributions are asymmetrical with a lower bound of zero, and again are sensitive to violations in the assumptions. When looking at the differences between variances, we first need to formulate the null and alternative hypothesis, decide the level of significance, and use tables to find the critical values of F. The calculation of F will decide whether there is statistical evidence to reject the null hypothesis or not.

LOS 3-1-C-q	**distinguish** between parametric and nonparametric tests, and **describe** the situations in which the use of nonparametric tests may be appropriate

A **parametric test** is one which is concerned with parameters and/or makes assumptions about the distribution of the sample. A **nonparametric test** is not concerned with the parameter or makes minimal assumptions about the distribution.

A nonparametric test might be used if we want to establish whether a set of data is random or if a distribution is strongly non-normal.

3-1-C View Concept Check Questions Workbook

3-1-D "Correlation and Regression"

Introduction

The last part of this study session looks at correlation and regression, tools that are used to examine the relationship between two or more financial variables. Whereas correlation measures the linear relationship between two variables, regression looks at the relationship between a dependent variable and independent variables. In addition to calculating correlation and regression coefficients you will need to be able to interpret the numbers, test their significance and discuss their limitations.

The last part of this study session looks at ways we can examine the relationship between two or more financial variables.

First of all we look at a **scatter plot**, which is a graph that visually describes the relationship between two series of data in two dimensions.

Example 3-22: Scatter plot

In the table below there is a series of data giving monthly returns for two stock markets, namely the Indopulo and Sheng Sheng Stock Exchanges.

	Indopulo Index Returns	**Sheng Sheng Index Returns**
January 200X	1.1%	-0.8%
February 200X	7.1%	6.8%
March 200X	5.9%	3.1%
April 200X	0.9%	1.2%
May 200X	-3.0%	-5.0%
June 200X	4.1%	3.2%
Average	*2.7%*	*1.4%*

The scatter plot of the two indices is shown below. The x-axis represents the data from the Indopolu index and the y-axis from the Sheng Sheng index, for each month's return there is a single point marked on the graph. Note that a scatter plot does not provide information on which period a point relates to.

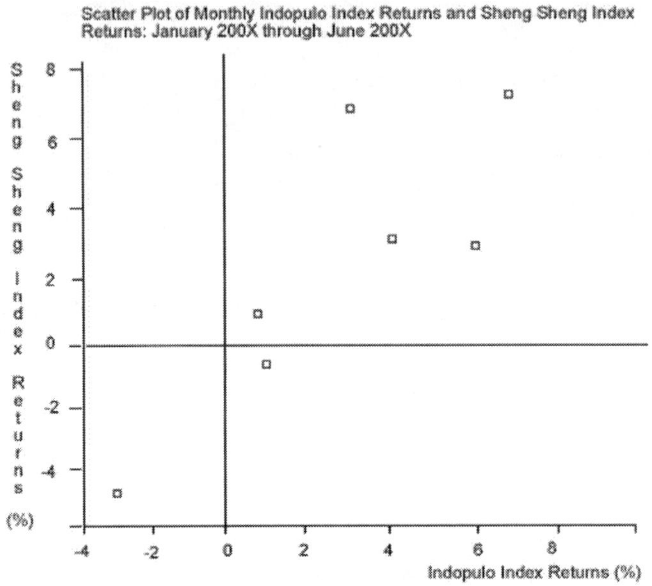

The extent of the association between the two data series can be represented by a single number. This number is called the **correlation coefficient**. A correlation coefficient of 0 indicates that there is no linear relationship between the variables. A correlation coefficient of 1 means that the points on the scatter plot lie on a straight line that is upward sloping, and a coefficient of -1 means that the points lie on a straight line that is downward sloping.

LOS 3-1-D-a **calculate** and **interpret** a sample covariance

Before calculating correlation we will look at another measure of linear association, covariance. In Study Session 2, Equation 2-39, the definition of population covariance is given as the product of the deviations of two random variables from their respective means, i.e.:

$$\mathbf{Cov(R_i,R_j) = E\{[\,R_i - E(R_i)][\,R_j - E(R_j)]\}}$$

For sample covariance with a sample size of n, the formula is

$$\text{Cov}(X,Y) = \frac{\sum_{i=1}^{n}(X_i - \overline{X})(Y_i - \overline{Y})}{(n-1)} \qquad \textbf{(Equation 3-20)}$$

Example 3-23: Covariance

Using the data given in Example 3-22, the covariance of the two index returns can be computed using the cross product data.

	Indopulo Index Returns (Xi)	Sheng Sheng Index Returns (Yi)	Cross Product $(X_i - \overline{X})(Y_i - \overline{Y})$	Squared Deviations $(X_i - \overline{X})^2$	Squared Deviations $(Y_i - \overline{Y})^2$
Jan	0.011	-0.008	0.000351	0.000251	0.000491
Feb	0.071	0.068	0.002378	0.001951	0.002898
Mar	0.059	0.031	0.000542	0.001035	0.000283
Apr	0.009	0.012	0.000039	0.000318	0.000005
May	-0.030	-0.050	0.003647	0.003230	0.004117
Jun	0.041	0.032	0.000253	0.000201	0.000318
Sum	0.161	0.085	0.007208	0.006985	0.008113
Average	0.027	0.014			
Variance				0.001397	0.001623
Stand. Dev.				0.037376	0.040281

$$\text{Cov}(X,Y) = \frac{\sum_{i=1}^{n}(X_i - \overline{X})(Y_i - \overline{Y})}{(n-1)} = \frac{0.007208}{(6-1)} = 0.001442$$

LOS 3-1-D-b **calculate** and **interpret** a sample correlation coefficient

The sample correlation coefficient is

$$r = \frac{Cov(X_i, Y_i)}{s_X s_Y}$$ **(Equation 3-21)**

where

$Cov(X_i, Y_i)$	=	covariance between variables X_i and Y_i
s_X	=	sample standard deviation of X

The correlation, r, always lies in the range of -1 and 1.

r = 1 means the sets of data have a perfect linear correlation
r = 0 means there is no linear relationship between the variables
r = -1 means the sets of data have a perfect negative linear correlation

Example 3-24: Correlation

Following on from Example 3-23

$s_x = 0.037376$ and $s_y = 0.040281$

The correlation coefficient is

$$r = \frac{Cov(X_i, Y_i)}{s_X s_Y} = \frac{0.001442}{0.037376 \times 0.040281} = 0.9577$$

When a correlation coefficient is close to 1, as in this example, it tells us that the variables are highly correlated. So the movements of the Indopulo and Sheng Sheng Stock Exchanges are closely linked.

There may be a strong non-linear association between two variables but zero linear correlation between them. For example, if Y is linked to X by the equation $Y = X^2$, there is a perfect nonlinear association but there is no linear correlation.

LOS 3-1-D-c	**formulate** a test of the hypothesis that the population correlation coefficient equals zero and **determine** whether the hypothesis is rejected at a given level of significance

Hypothesis testing can be applied in assessing whether the existence of a correlation is real or due to chance.

The null hypothesis is that the correlation coefficient is zero. The alternative hypothesis will be that the correlation is not equal to zero so a two-tailed test will be used with

$$H_0 : r = 0$$

$$H_1 : r \neq 0$$

The formula for the t-test is

$$t = \frac{r\sqrt{n-2}}{\sqrt{1-r^2}} \qquad \textbf{(Equation 3-22)}$$

At the .05 significance level the critical values for *t* are ± 3.182, and .01 significance level ± 5.481. If the t-statistic lies outside this range we can reject the null hypothesis and conclude that there is a correlation between the variables.

The critical values of t depend on the degrees of freedom.

Example 3-25: Testing correlation

Use the index returns in Example 3-22. The sample size is 6 and the coefficient of correlation is 0.9577

$$t = \frac{r\sqrt{n-2}}{\sqrt{1-r^2}} = \frac{0.9577\sqrt{(6-2)}}{\sqrt{1-0.9577^2}} = 6.6560$$

We can reject the null hypothesis at a 99% confidence level. The test indicates that the correlation between the index returns is significantly different to zero.

The higher the sample size taken, the larger the t-value, and all else being equal it is more likely that the null hypothesis will be rejected.

The occurrence of outliers can affect the reliability of the computation of a correlation coefficient. **Outliers** are defined to be small number of observations of extreme values occurring in a sample.

Spurious correlation occurs not because the two variables have a theoretical relationship but because there is a relation caused by a third variable.

A good example is the case that in an emerging economy. There is a high correlation between the increase in the number of motorcycles and the number of televisions owned. There is no direct relationship here except that both are correlated to the increase in disposable income.

LOS 3-1-D-d	**differentiate** between the dependent and independent variables in a linear regression

If a linear relationship can be established between two variables, prediction of one variable can be made when the other is known.

Linear regression assumes that there is a linear relationship between the dependent and the independent variables. The **dependent variable** (often denoted by Y) is the variable you are seeking to explain (or to estimate). The **independent variable** (often denoted by X) is the variable that you are using to explain the behavior of the dependent variable (also called the predictor variable).

The general expression of linear regression is:

$$Y_i = b_0 + b_i X_i + \varepsilon_i \qquad \textbf{(Equation 3-23)}$$

where i = 1, …, n

Example 3-26: Independent and dependent variables

Using the example of the Indopulo and Sheng Sheng index returns in Example 3-22, we could designate the Indopulo index returns as the independent variable and the Sheng Sheng index returns as the dependent variable. If we find the regression equation linking the two sets of returns we could work out what the estimated effect of a certain move in Indopulo index has on the Sheng Sheng index.

LOS 3-1-D-e **distinguish** between the slope and the intercept terms in a regression Equation

Using Equation 3-23 the **slope** of the regression line is b_i and the **intercept** is b_0. These are very important in linear regression. The slopes and the intercept are estimated by using a **least square** technique, i.e. finding the slope and the intercept in such a way that minimizes the sum of the squared vertical distances between the observations and the regression line. The least square technique seeks the minimization of these distances which is

$$\sum_{i=1}^{n}(Y_i - \hat{b}_0 - \hat{b}_1 X_i)^2 \qquad \textbf{(Equation 3-24)}$$

where $\hat{b}_o$ and $\hat{b}_1$ are the estimated or fitted parameters (a hat over a symbol indicates an estimated value).

The graphical description of the **best estimate** or **fitted parameters** is given below.

In a regression with a single independent variable, the slope coefficient is

$$\hat{b}_1 = \frac{\text{Cov}(Y_i, X_i)}{\text{Var}(X_i)} \qquad \textbf{(Equation 3-25)}$$

$\hat{b}_o$ can be derived by solving the linear regression equation using the average values of Y_i and X_i.

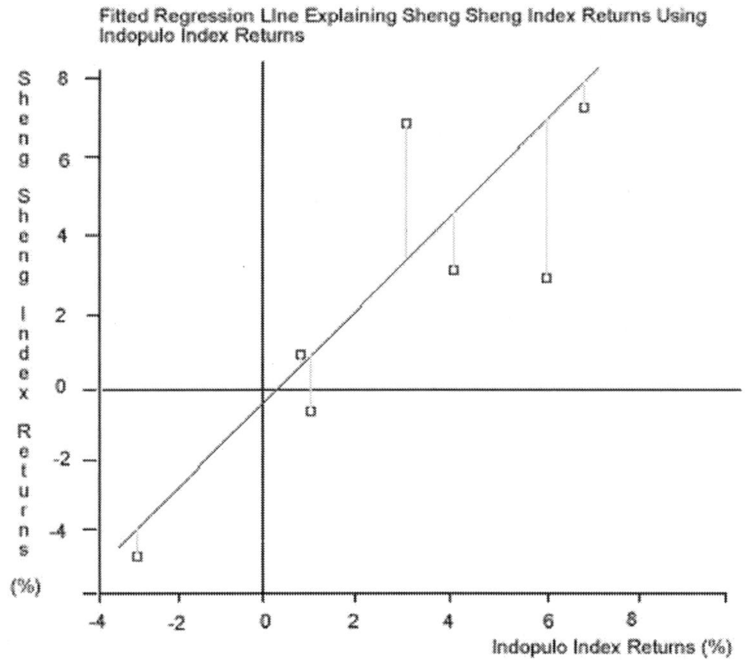

Example 3-27: Regression equation

Using the calculations from the Indopulo and Sheng Sheng indexes:

	Indopulo Index Returns (Xi)	**Sheng Sheng Index Returns** (Yi)	**Cross Product** $(X_i - \overline{X})(Y_i - \overline{Y})$	**Squared Deviations** $(X_i - \overline{X})^2$	**Squared Deviations** $(Y_i - \overline{Y})^2$
Sum	0.161	0.085	0.007208	0.006985	0.008113
Average	0.027	0.014			
Covariance			0.001442		
Variance				0.001397	0.001623
Standard Dev.				0.037376	0.040281

Using Equation 3-25

$$\hat{b}_1 = \frac{\text{Cov}(Y_i, X_i)}{\text{Var}(X_i)} = \frac{0.001442}{0.001397} = 1.0322$$

$\hat{b}_o$ can be found by solving $Y_i = b_0 + b_i X_i + \varepsilon_i$, using the average values of X and Y.

$$b_0 = Y - b_i X_i = 0.014 - (1.0322 \times 0.027) = -0.01357$$

The regression equation is $Y_i = -0.01357 + 1.0322X_i + \varepsilon_i$

LOS 3-1-D-f **explain** the assumptions underlying linear regression

We can only draw valid conclusions from a linear regression if the following assumptions (the classical normal linear regression model assumptions) are **all** met:

1. A linear relationship between the dependent variable Yi, and the independent variable, Xi, exists. The relation is linear in the parameters b0 and b1.
2. The independent variable, Xi, is not random.
3. The expected value of the error term, E(i), is zero. This means that it is an unbiased model.
4. The variance of the error term is the same for all observations: $E(\varepsilon_i^2) = \sigma_i^2$, i = 1, …,n.
5. The error term, i, is uncorrelated across observations. E(i j) = 0 for all i not equal to j.
6. The error term, i, is normally distributed.

LOS 3-1-D-g **calculate** the standard error of estimate

Now we need to assess how well the regression model works, in terms of how well the independent variable explains the dependent variable. Graphically, on a scatter plot, this is illustrated by how close the observations are to the regression line.

For a regression model with one independent variable, the formula for the standard error of the estimate (SEE) is given below

$$\left(\sum_{i=1}^{n}\frac{(Y_i-\hat{b}_o-\hat{b}_1X_i)^2}{n-2}\right)^{1/2}=\left(\sum_{i=1}^{n}\frac{(\hat{\varepsilon}_i)^2}{n-2}\right)^{1/2} \qquad \textbf{(Equation 3-26)}$$

The numerator contains $Y_i-\hat{b}_0-\hat{b}_1X_i$ which is the difference between the actual value of the dependent variable and the predicted value, or the regression residual. The SEE indicates how well the model fits the data and the smaller the SEE, the better the model fits.

Example 3-28: Standard error

From the Indopulo and Sheng Sheng index returns, we have calculated in the table below the squared residuals, using the regression equation calculated in Example 3-27.

The SEE will be $\sqrt{0.000674/(6-2)}=0.01298,\text{ or }1.298\%$

	Indopulo Index Returns	Sheng Sheng Index Returns	Predicted Sheng Sheng Returns	Regression Residual	Squared Residual
Jan	0.011	-0.008	-0.002216	-0.005784	0.000033
Feb	0.071	0.068	0.059716	0.008284	0.000069
Mar	0.059	0.031	0.047330	-0.016330	0.000267
Apr	0.009	0.012	-0.004280	0.016280	0.000265
May	-0.030	-0.050	-0.044536	-0.005464	0.000030
Jun	0.041	0.032	0.028750	0.003250	0.000011
Sum					**0.000674**

LOS 3-1-D-h **calculate** and **interpret** the coefficient of determination

The **coefficient of determination** (R^2) tells us *exactly* how well the independent variable explains the variation of the dependent variable. It is the fraction of the total variance in the dependent variable that is explained by the regression.

The easiest way of computing the coefficient of determination is squaring the coefficient of correlation, r^2. This works well with a **single** independent variable.

A more general way is deriving R^2 is

Total variation = Unexplained variation + Explained variation

$$\mathbf{R^2 = \frac{Explained\ variation}{Total\ variation} = \frac{Total\ variation - Unexplained\ variation}{Total\ variation}}$$

Example 3-29: Coefficient of determination

1. The coefficient of determination for the Indopulo and Sheng Sheng index returns can be calculated using the correlation coefficient calculated in Example 3-24

$$R^2 = r^2 = (0.9576)^2 = 0.9169$$

2. The second way requires using the calculation of squared residuals which were calculated in Example 3-28, the sum of squared residual is the **unexplained variation**. Also recall from Example 3-23 that the squared deviation of the Sheng Sheng index is 0.008113. This is the **total variation**.

$$\mathbf{R^2 = \frac{Total\ variation - Unexplained\ variation}{Total\ variation}}$$

$$\mathbf{= (0.008113 - 0.000674)/(0.008113) = 0.9169}$$

The two methods arrive at the same result.

We can say that 91.69% of the variation in the Sheng Sheng index returns is explained by the variation in the Indopulo index.

LOS 3-1-D-i **calculate** a confidence interval for a regression coefficient

Hypothesis testing can also be applied to the estimation of the regression coefficients, namely the slope and the intercept.

This can be done if we know the following

1. The estimated parameter value, $\hat{b}_o$ and $\hat{b}_1$
2. The hypothesized value of the parameter, b0 and b1
3. A confidence interval around the estimated parameter

Finding the confidence interval that includes the true parameter value, b_1 with a given degree of confidence, is illustrated in Example 3-30.

Example 3-30: Confidence intervals

We have calculated a linear regression model for a stock's returns (Y) which is dependent on the stock market's returns (X) as follows:

Y = 1.25 + 1.5X

In this case the b_1 equals 1.5 and is the beta of the stock.

Also the standard error of the estimate $s_{\hat{b}_1}$ is known to be 0.0175 and the sample size is 32. We decide to use a confidence level of 95%.

The confidence interval for b_1 will be

$$\hat{b}_1 \pm t_c s_{\hat{b}_1}$$

Where t_C is the critical value of t value. With 30 degrees of freedom at the 95% confidence level this is 2.042.

So the confidence interval is 1.5 ± (2.042 x 0.0175), or between 1.464 and 1.535. We can be 95% confident that the beta lies in this range.

Note the t-distribution is often used for this test because we use the sample estimate of the standard error $s_{\hat{b}1}$, rather than the population (true) value of the standard deviation.

The most common statistic to test the population value of a regression coefficient is the **t-statistic** that has a **t-distribution** and (n – 2) degrees of freedom:

$$t = \frac{\hat{b}_1 - b_1}{s_{\hat{b}_1}}$$ **(Equation 3-27)**

It is a two-tailed test.

To formulate null and alternative hypotheses about a population value of a regression coefficient, the following is the procedure

1. For the hypothesized value of B1 and the estimated regression coefficient of $\hat{b}_1$ the null and alternate hypotheses are: $H_0: \quad \hat{b}_1 = B_1$ and $H_a: \quad \hat{b}_1 \neq B_1$
2. Note: that this test must be a two-tailed test.
3. We must know the standard error of the estimated coefficient, $s_{\hat{b}1}$
4. The test statistic is
   $$t = \frac{(\hat{b}_1 - B_1)}{s_{\hat{b}_1}}$$
5.
6. We then select a level of significance, , and the corresponding critical value for the t-statistic, tc.
7. We reject the null hypothesis if the absolute value of t or | t | > tc

Example 3-31: Hypothesis testing

Using the data in Example 3-30, let us test the null hypothesis that the beta of the stock is 1.

$H_0: \quad b_1 = 1.0$ and $H_a: \quad b_1 \neq 1$

We will reject the null hypothesis, at the 95% level if 1.0 does not lie in the confidence interval.

Next we calculate the test statistic, $t = \frac{(\hat{b}_1 - B_1)}{s_{\hat{b}_1}} = \frac{(1.5 - 1.0)}{0.2} = 2.5$

Since 2.5 is greater than 2.042 (the critical value of t) we can reject the null hypothesis and there is evidence that the beta is statistically different to 1.

LOS 3-1-D-j	**identify** the test statistic and **interpret** the results for a hypothesis test about a population value of a regression coefficient
LOS 3-1-D-k	**interpret** a regression coefficient

Example 3-32: Interpreting the results of regression analysis

Using the regression equation in Example 3-30where we have a model for a stock's returns (Y) which is dependent on the stock market's returns (X):

Y = 1.25 + 1.5X

We could follow the same method used in Example 3-31 to calculate whether the intercept of 1.25 is statistically different to zero. Assuming that both coefficients are significant we can use the regression equation to estimate the return of the stock as the market moves.

So for example, if we forecast a return of 10% from the market, the expected return from the stock is

Y = 1.25 + 1.5X = 1.25 + 1.5(10%) = 16.25%

The actual parameter value of a regression coefficient is neither observed nor precisely known. In our prediction or testing we use the estimated values of the coefficients. These estimated parameters are useful to arrive at certain a conclusion given a chosen confidence level.

LOS 3-1-D-l	**calculate** a predicted value for the dependent variable, given an estimated regression model and a value for the independent variable
LOS 3-1-D-m	**calculate** and **interpret** a confidence interval for the predicted value of a dependent variable

There are two sources of errors that are introduced to a predicted value of a dependent variable

1. the error term, i,
2. the uncertainty from the estimated parameters, $\hat{b}_o$ and $\hat{b}_1$.

The standard deviation of the error term can be estimated from the standard error of estimate for the regression equation. There is also uncertainty from the estimated parameters, $\hat{b}_o$ and $\hat{b}_1$.

To calculate the estimated variance of the prediction error (s_f)

$$s_f^2 = s^2\left[1 + \frac{1}{n} + \frac{(X - \overline{X})^2}{(n-1)s_x^2}\right]$$ **(Equation 3-28)**

we must know

The squared standard error of estimate, s^2
The number of observations n

The value of the independent variable to predict the dependent variable
The estimated mean of the independent variable
The variance of the independent variable

To determine the prediction interval, we go through the following steps

1. Make the prediction
2. Compute the estimated variance of the prediction error
3. Choose a significance level,
4. Compute the prediction interval $\hat{Y} \pm t_c s_f$

Example 3-33: Confidence interval for predicted values

Suppose the Indopulo index return is 4.5%. What would be the prediction interval of the Sheng Sheng index return?

Make the prediction: the Sheng Sheng index return will be (using the regression equation in Example 3-27)

$$Y_i = -0.01357 + 1.0322 \times 0.045 = 3.29\%$$

Compute the estimated variance of the prediction error

$$s_f^2 = s^2\left[1 + \frac{1}{n} + \frac{(X - \overline{X})^2}{(n-1)s_x^2}\right] = 0.01298^2\left[1 + \frac{1}{6} + \frac{(0.045 - 0.027)^2}{(6-1)0.001379}\right] = 0.000204$$

$$s_f = 0.014300$$

Choose to be 0.05, we are looking at the 95% confidence interval.

The critical value of t, $t_{c,}$ for the chosen significance level and 4 degrees of freedom is 2.776.

The predicted interval is 0.0329 ± 2.776 x 0.014300, or between – 0.67% and 7.26%.

The predicted interval is wide because the number of observations is small. The larger the number of observations the tighter the interval will be.

LOS 3-1-D-n	**describe** the use of analysis of variance (ANOVA) in regression analysis

Analysis of variance (ANOVA) is a statistical procedure for analyzing the total variability of a set of data into components, which can be attributed to different sources. The application of the ANOVA procedure in regression analysis is to gain information about the usefulness or strength of the independent variable(s) in explaining the variation in the dependent variable.

LOS 3-1-D-o **define** and interpret an F-statistic

The statistical test is the F-test.

The *F*-**statistic** is used to determine whether all of the slope coefficients in a linear regression are equal to zero.

However we need to know four things

1. The total number of observations (n).
2. The total number of parameters to be estimated (slope and intercept).
3. The sum of squared errors or residuals $\sum_{i=1}^{n}(Y_i - \hat{Y}_i)^2$, abbreviated to SSE , or the residual sum of squares.
4. The regression sum of squares $\sum_{i=1}^{n}(\hat{Y}_i - \overline{Y})^2$, abbreviated to RSS, or the amount of total variation in Y that is explained by the regression equation.

The formula for the F-statistic is

$$F_{1,n-2} = \frac{RSS/1}{SSE/(n-2)} = \frac{\text{mean regression sum of squares}}{\text{mean squared error}} \quad \textbf{(Equation 3-29)}$$

Where the subscripts 1 and (n - 2) are the degrees of freedom.

The F-statistic indicates how well the regression equation explains the variation in the dependent variable.

The higher the F-value the better the regression model explains the variation in the dependent variable.

LOS 3-1-D-p **discuss** the limitations of regression analysis

There are three limitations of regression analysis

1. Regression relations change over time. A particular regression may fit for a period of time but may no longer be valid in the other periods of time.
2. The change of regression relations may be caused by a self-fulfilling phenomenon, this is common in the financial industry. This means that once a relationship becomes well known security prices will adjust and the relationship will not hold in the future.
3. If any or several of the classical normal linear regression model assumptions as listed in LOS 3-1-D-f are violated, then the hypothesis test and predictions based on the regression analysis will no longer be valid.

3-1-D View Concept Check Questions Workbook

STUDY SESSION 4

Investment Tools

Economics: Macroeconomic Analysis

Overview

Economics have a guideline weighting of 10% of the exam questions. That is not a lot of questions for three study sessions but the material is relatively straightforward. Study Session 4 focuses on macroeconomics, 5 on microeconomics and 6 on global economic analysis.

In Study Session 4 the Reading Assignments look at the key issues in macroeconomics - the study of economic growth and changes in levels of output, employment and prices. Initially we define and explain how the main indicators of the state of the economy are measured: the main indicators include demand and supply, inflation and unemployment. We then move on to examining how government policy can affect stability and economic growth. This is a key part of the Study Session, candidates need to understand the impact of changes in fiscal and monetary policies on the economy in both the short and long run, and be able to differentiate between the impact when policy changes are anticipated or unanticipated.

For candidates who have studied economics or have knowledge of the basic concepts you will not need to spend much time on the first three Preliminary Reading Assignments. The Preliminary Readings cover measuring GDP and other measures of output and income, inflation, factors that affect aggregate demand and supply, and the basics of Keynesian economics. It is important to note that the CFA Institute states that examination questions are drawn mainly from the subsequent Reading Assignments.

Preliminary Reading Assignments

P1. Economics: Private and Public Choice, 10th edition, James D. Gwartney, Richard L. Stroup, Russell S. Sobel, and David A. Macpherson (South-Western, 2003)

4-P1-A. "Taking the Nation's Economic Pulse," Ch. 7

4-P1-B. "Working with Our Basic Aggregate Demand/Aggregate Supply Model," Ch. 10

4-P1-C. "Keynesian Foundations of Modern Macroeconomics," Ch. 11

Note: http://snipurl.com/Workbook Preliminary Reading Assignments and Concept Question Workbook

4-1-A "Economic Fluctuations, Unemployment, and Inflation"

Introduction

This Reading identifies the different phases of the business cycle and how GDP, inflation and unemployment are key indicators of the stage in the business cycle. We look at how inflation and unemployment are defined and measured. Candidates will need to be able to calculate inflation numbers and describe the harmful effects of unanticipated inflation.

Reading Assignments

Economics: Private and Public Choice, 10th edition, James D. Gwartney, Richard L. Stroup,

Russell S. Sobel, and David A. Macpherson (South-Western, 2003)

4-1-A. "Economic Fluctuations, Unemployment, and Inflation," Ch. 8

4-1-B. "Fiscal Policy," Ch. 12

4-1-C. "Money and the Banking System," Ch. 13

4-1-D. "Modern Macroeconomics: Monetary Policy," Ch. 14

4-1-E. "Stabilization Policy, Output, and Employment," Ch. 15, pp. 349• 365

4-1-F. "The Phillips Curve: Is There a Trade-off between Inflation and Unemployment?"

Special Topic 7, pp. 719• 729

LOS 4-1-A-a **explain** the phases of the business cycle

The Business Cycle

Swings in the output of an economy are referred to as the business cycle, even though the fluctuations in output are often irregular and unpredictable. The four stages are:

1. Peak – this is a boom and it is when businesses are generally operating at full capacity and GDP is growing rapidly.
2. Contraction – the sales of businesses are falling and unemployment is rising. Real GDP is growing at a slower rate or perhaps declining.
3. Trough – this is the bottom of the contraction phase.
4. Expansion – business sales start to rise, unemployment shrinks and GDP starts to increase.

A recession is when GDP declines for at least two consecutive quarters, if it lasts longer than two quarters and there is a sharp decline in GDP it is referred to as a depression.

LOS 4-1-A-b	**describe** the key labor market indicators and **discuss** the problems in measuring unemployment

The Labor Force

The **civilian labor force** is all the people of 16 years and over who are either employed or unemployed. Unemployed means the person is actively seeking employment or waiting for another job. It excludes, for example, students and retired workers.

Rate of labor force participation is the labor force as a percentage of the total civilian population of 16 years and over.

The **unemployment rate** is the number of unemployed as a percentage of the number in the labor force.

Problems with measuring unemployment include:

1. labeling as unemployed workers who have been laid off but waiting to be recalled to their jobs
2. workers who have, for the time being, given up looking for a job who are not counted as unemployed
3. workers in part-time unemployment, but wanting full time work, who are still counted as employed.

LOS 4-1-A-c	**describe** the three types of unemployment

Types of unemployment

Frictional - caused by changes in the economy that lead to qualified job seekers being temporarily unmatched with job openings, due to imperfect information and time taken in the job search by interviews etc.

Structural - due to structural changes in the economy that leave unemployed people not qualified for job openings.

Cyclical - caused by the overall level of economic activity.

LOS 4-1-A-d **explain** full employment and the natural rate of unemployment

Full employment relates to an economy which has frictional and structural unemployment. In other words, an economy at full employment has no cyclical unemployment. The rate of unemployment at full employment is called the natural rate of unemployment.

If output is above full employment (actual unemployment is below the natural rate of unemployment), then inflationary pressures will emerge in the economy.

If output is below full employment (actual unemployment is above the natural rate of unemployment), then disinflationary pressures will emerge in the economy.

If output is at full employment (actual unemployment is at the natural rate of unemployment), then there will be no tendency for the prices to increase or decrease. Output and unemployment will coincide with the position of the LRAS curve.

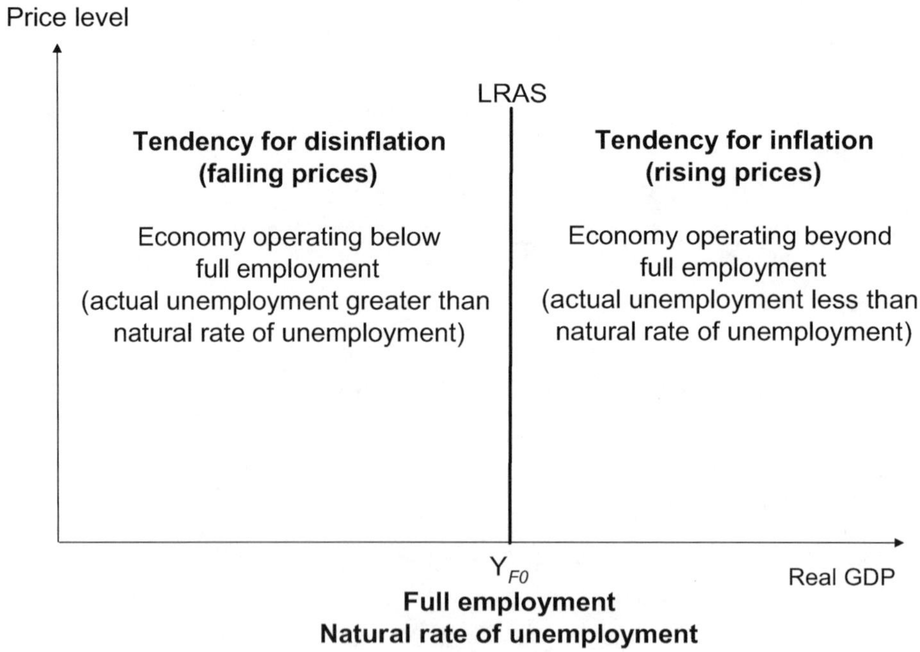

LOS 4-1-A-e **define** inflation and **calculate** the inflation rate

Inflation is the persistent rise in prices that erodes over time the purchasing power of money. Inflation is calculated by comparing the change in a price level over a specified period of time. The most common price level is the Consumer Price Index (CPI).

Equation 4-4 shows the formula for the inflation rate using a generic price level:

$$\text{Inflation rate} = \left[\frac{\text{price index}_{\text{period t}} - \text{price index}_{\text{period t-1}}}{\text{price index}_{\text{period t-1}}}\right] \times 100 \qquad \textbf{(Equation 4-4)}$$

Example 4-4: Calculating the inflation rate

At the beginning of 2002, the Consumer Price Index was 143.7; at the beginning of 2003, the Consumer Price Index was 153.6; and at the beginning of 2004, the Consumer Price Index was 151.3. Calculate the inflation rate for 2003 and 2004.

Use Equation 4-4 to calculate the inflation rate for each year.

$$\text{Inflation rate}_{2003}$$

$$= \left[\frac{\text{price index}_{\text{period t}} - \text{price index}_{\text{period t-1}}}{\text{price index}_{\text{period t-1}}}\right] \times 100 = \left[\frac{153.6 - 143.7}{143.7}\right] \times 100 = 6.9\%$$

$$\text{Inflation rate}_{2004}$$

$$= \left[\frac{\text{price index}_{\text{period t}} - \text{price index}_{\text{period t-1}}}{\text{price index}_{\text{period t-1}}}\right] \times 100 = \left[\frac{151.3 - 153.6}{153.6}\right] \times 100 = -1.5\%$$

LOS 4-1-A-f **discuss** the harmful consequences of inflation

The effects of inflation are felt mainly when changes in inflation are unanticipated. The negative impacts include

1. greater risk in investing in capital goods or other assets
2. distortion in pricing information
3. decision-makers focusing on protecting themselves from inflation rather than productive activities.

The effect of long-term inflation will be to damage the economy and **stagflation** is when there is rapid inflation combined with slow or negative growth in output.

4-1-A View Concept Check Questions Workbook

4-1-B "Fiscal Policy"

Introduction

This Reading investigates the impact of changes in fiscal policy on output, prices and employment, assuming monetary policy is constant. Different economic models – Keynesian, crowding-out, new classical and supply-side models disagree on the impact of an expansionary or restrictive fiscal policy and the candidate needs to be familiar with the effectiveness of fiscal policy according to the four models. This section also looks at automatic stabilizers that take effect without a change in fiscal policy.

LOS 4-1-B-a **explain** the process by which fiscal policy affects aggregate demand and aggregate supply

Fiscal policy is reflected in a government's policy on spending, tax and borrowing. Keynesian economists believe an increase in spending will increase aggregate demand (and vice versa). If personal taxes are decreased this will lead to an increase in consumption reflecting higher disposable incomes (only really effective if the changes are regarded as permanent). A reduction in business taxes would lead to higher investment spending. If the budget deficit is increased, borrowing to finance the deficit will increase.

Under Keynesian economics an increase in government spending or reduction in taxes will lead to a larger increase in demand due to the effect of the expenditure multiplier. So when the economy is operating below capacity the government should adopt an **expansionary** fiscal policy (increase spending on goods and services and/or reduce taxes) and when there is an inflationary economic boom it should adopt a **restrictive** fiscal policy. In other words a counter cyclical government policy can be used to maintain a stable economy. This will take effect much more quickly than waiting for changes in resource prices and real interest rates to impact on demand.

LOS 4-1-B-b **explain** the importance of the timing of changes in fiscal policy and the difficulties in achieving proper timing

There are several timing problems associated with fiscal policy including:

1. the time lag between the forecast of recession/boom and when it actually starts.
2. it takes time to implement a change in fiscal policy.
3. it may take 6 to 12 months for the change in fiscal policy to take full effect.
4. if the timing of a change in policy is incorrect, and the economy's self-correcting mechanism is working, then the impact of the policy change may be to produce economic instability.

LOS 4-1-B-c **discuss** the impact of expansionary and restrictive fiscal policies based on the basic Keynesian model, the crowding-out model, the new classical model, and supply-side model

The benefits of an expansionary fiscal policy will be diluted since higher government borrowing will tend to push up interest rates and reduce private investment. This is called the **crowding-out effect.** Additionally the globalization of financial markets now means that higher interest rates will lead to an inflow of foreign investment thereby strengthening the currency, which will lead to a decline in exports. Under the **new classical model** the benefits of budget deficits will be offset by consumers who will expect taxes to rise in the future, and will therefore reduce current spending. Followers of the new classical model believe that switching between tax and debt is ineffective. **Supply-side economists** believe a reduction in personal tax rates will increase the benefits of earning which will lead to an increase in aggregate supply. High taxes slow growth since they discourage work effort, discourage foreign investment, and switch spending to tax-deductible goods and services.

LOS 4-1-B-d **explain** how and why budget deficits and trade deficits tend to be linked

Budget deficits and trade deficits

A large budget deficit will tend to lead to a substantial increase in net foreign investment into the country leading to an appreciation of the domestic currency. This will in turn make exports more expensive and imports cheaper, leading to an increase in a trade deficit (or decline in a surplus).

LOS 4-1-B-e **identify** automatic stabilizers and **explain** how such stabilizers work

Automatic stabilizers (unemployment benefit, corporate and progressive income taxes) will change fiscal spending automatically. For example, during economic expansion the rising government tax income and lower unemployment benefit payments will reduce the government budget deficit (or increase the surplus).

Overall the timing of the use of fiscal policy is key and changes in fiscal policy should only be used in response to major economic movements.

LOS 4-1-B-f **discuss** the supply-side effects of fiscal policy

The importance of supply-side effects is subject to debate. In the 1980's rates of tax were reduced in the U.S., but this led to only modest increases in output (and a decline in real tax revenues and an increase in the budget deficit). However supply-side economists say that reductions in the highest marginal tax rates are particularly important and also that reductions in taxes have led to long periods of economic expansion. On the other hand it appears that increasing tax rates beyond a certain optimum level leads to a fall in taxes collected and reduces the output of the economy.

Internationally there is evidence that countries such as Ireland that have significantly cut personal and corporate tax rates have seen rapid growth rates. Other European countries, such as France, Germany and the Netherlands, which have high tax rates have experienced slow economic growth rates and a 'brain drain' as highly skilled workers choose to work in lower tax countries.

4-1-B View Concept Check Questions Workbook

4-1-C "Money and the Banking System"

Introduction

We now look at how money supply is defined and how the banking system operates. In particular we examine how the central bank in the U.S., the Federal Reserve System, controls money supply. This section provides the foundation for the next two Readings when we focus on monetary policy and its impact on an economy.

LOS 4-1-C-a	**identify** and **explain** the basic functions of money

The three basic functions of money are:

1. Medium of exchange – using money for transactions reduces the time and cost of transactions.
2. Store of value – money can be used to transfer purchasing power to a future period.
3. Unit of account - it is a unit of measurement for costs and values of assets.

LOS 4-1-C-b	**define** the money supply

Money Supply

Two of the most widely used measures of money supply are:

M1 = currency in circulation + demand and other checkable deposits + travelers' checks

M1 is essentially money and assets that can be converted into money at parity.

M2 = M1 + savings and time deposits (less than $100,000) + money market mutual funds

M2 is a broader definition that includes assets that can be easily converted to checking deposits or cash.

N.B. deposits must be held in depository institutions.

Note that credit card spending is not included in money supply since it is a form of loan, although the usage of credit cards has resulted in people needing to hold less money.

LOS 4-1-C-c	**describe** the fractional reserve banking system

The Banking System

The banking system in the U.S. is under the jurisdiction of the Federal Reserve System.

The three institutions in the banking sector are:

1. Commercial banks.
2. Savings and loans - accept deposits in exchange for shares that pay dividends.
3. Credit unions - cooperative financial institutions for groups of individuals.

The U.S. is a **fractional reserve banking** system which means banks are required by the Fed to hold only a proportion of their deposits in cash or reserves.

LOS 4-1-C-d	**explain** the relationship among the required reserve ratio, potential deposit expansion multiplier, and actual deposit expansion multiplier

The minimum amount of reserves that must be kept available is the **required reserve ratio** and the remainder can be loaned to customers. As money is lent new deposits are made. The **actual deposit expansion multiplier** is the multiple by which an increase in reserves will increase the money supply. The **potential deposit expansion multiplier** is the reciprocal of the required reserve ratio and is the maximum potential increase in the money supply as a multiple of new reserves. The actual will be less than the potential deposit expansion multiplier for a number of reasons, e.g. some borrowers will hold as cash part of the money borrowed, banks may not use all excess reserves to make loans.

Example 4-5: Required reserve ratio

If the required reserve ratio is 5%, then the potential deposit expansion multiplier is 1/0.05 = 20.

LOS 4-1-C-e **describe** the role of a country's central bank and the tools that a central bank can use to control the money supply, and **explain** how a central bank can use monetary tools to implement monetary policy

The main role of a country's central bank is to control money supply and provide a favorable monetary climate for the economy to thrive. In the U.S. the Federal Reserve System, called the Fed, controls the money supply in three ways:

1. Adjusting the Reserve Ratio

Banks will tend to keep the minimum or near-minimum amount in reserves since reserves are not interest bearing. Therefore if the Fed lowers reserve requirements the banks will extend new loans and the money supply will increase. Similarly an increase in reserve requirement will reduce money supply.

2. Open Market Operations

The Fed buys and sells notes and bills to reduce or increase the monetary base. For example if the Fed wishes to increase money supply it would purchase U.S. securities thereby injecting new money into circulation which increases the monetary base (the sum of reserves and money in circulation) which increase money supply.

3. Changing the Discount Rate

This is the interest rate charged to banks borrowing from the Fed. An increase in the discount rate would tend to make banks build up their reserves to avoid the position where they have to borrow funds. Therefore this would be a restrictive policy.

In summary:

Expansionary Monetary Policy	Restrictive Monetary Policy
Reduce reserve requirements	Increase reserve requirements
Purchase U.S. securities	Sell U.S. securities
Lower the discount rate	Raise the discount rate

LOS 4-1-C-f discuss potential problems in measuring an economy's money supply

A number of factors are distorting the money supply numbers and therefore reducing the value of M1 and M2 as indicators of monetary policy:

1. Use of the U.S. dollar overseas is significant which makes measuring the currency component inaccurate.
2. Growth in stock and bond mutual fund investment which is not included in M1 or M2.
3. Use of debit cards and electronic money reduces the need to hold currency thereby reducing money supply growth.

4-1-C View Concept Check Questions Workbook

4-1-D "Modern Macroeconomics: Monetary Policy"

Introduction

A successful monetary policy is critical to providing a stable environment for an economy to grow and to provide high levels of employment. We start the section with looking at the factors that affect the demand and supply of money. We then examine how changes in monetary policy affect the economy in terms of interest rates, output, prices and employment. It is important that candidates understand the short and long-run effects of expansionary and restrictive monetary policies.

Monetarists believe that monetary instability is the major cause of instability in economic growth and rapid growth in the money supply causes inflation.

LOS 4-1-D-a **discuss** the determinants of the demand for and supply of money

There are three chief motivations for people to hold money, rather to invest the proceeds in interest bearing securities:

1. To make regular transactions
2. To deal with uncertainties and emergencies
3. For speculative purposes

However, as interest rates increase, the opportunity cost of holding cash increases. The demand for money is inversely related to interest rates; therefore, the money demand curve is downward-sloping.

The supply of money is independent of interest rates because it is not set by competitive market forces. The supply of money is determined by a nation's central bank (in the United States, the central bank is the Federal Reserve). Therefore, the supply of money is an upward-sloping line.

The intersection of the money demand and money supply curves determines the equilibrium level of interest rates, as shown in the graph below:

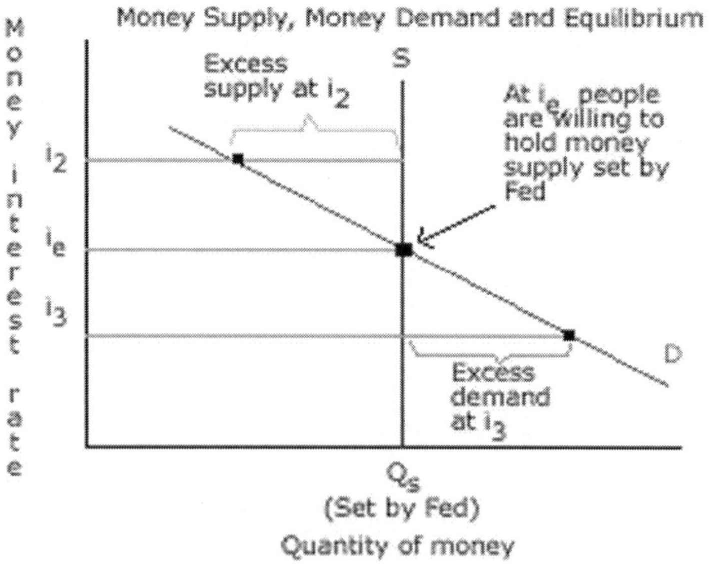

LOS 4-1-D-b	**discuss** how anticipation of the effects of monetary policy can influence the policy's effectiveness
LOS 4-1-D-e	**compare** and **contrast** the impact of monetary policy on the inflation rate, real output, employment, and interest rates in the short run and long run, when the effects are anticipated or unanticipated

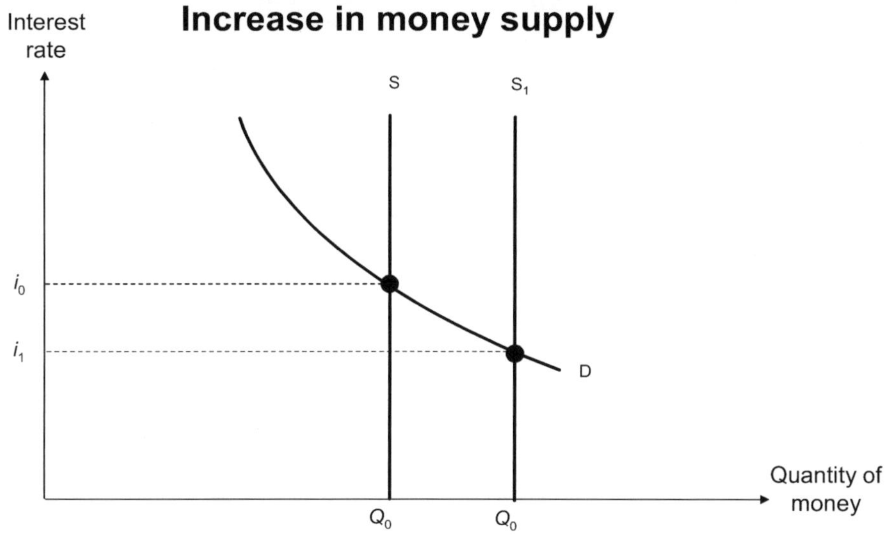

A drop in interest rates would increase gross private business investment, which is a component of aggregate demand. In addition, lower interest rates would cause the domestic currency to depreciate, resulting in an increase in exports and a decrease in imports. The increase in investment and net exports would increase AD curve (shift to the right), causing a short-run increase in output, employment, and the price level. Over time, higher resource price pressures would decrease the SRAS curve, restoring output at full employment, though at a higher price level.

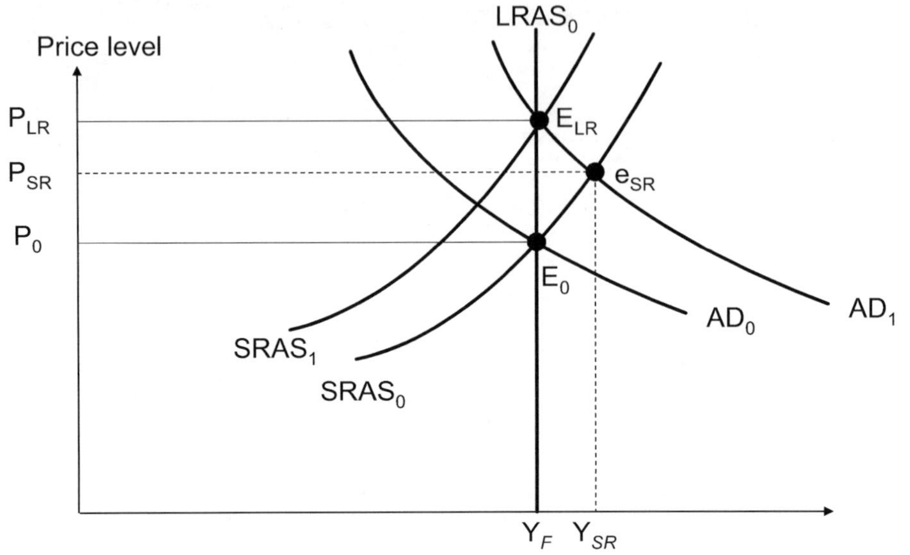

To summarize, if the Fed moves to an **expansionary monetary policy**, it will generally lead to an increase in aggregate demand. If this is unanticipated it will lead to a more rapid rise in prices than costs and a short-term increase in real output and employment. However in the long term the higher price levels will feed through to higher resource costs and unemployment will return to its natural rate. Therefore the long-run result of rapid money growth is inflation.

Similarly a **restrictive monetary policy** will, if the economy is running at full employment, reduce output and it can lead to a recession. However, if the economy is overheated, a restrictive monetary policy can be effective in preventing an inflationary boom.

Monetary policy affects the money supply curve. If the central bank wished to increase output, for example, it would increase the supply of money, which would cause interest rates to fall.

If the effects of a change in monetary policy are anticipated, then costs will rise as quickly as selling prices so output does not rise in the short run. Inflation will result without any short run increase in output.

Interest rates

A move to an expansionary monetary policy will involve injecting new funds into the market and reducing short-term nominal interest rates. However, the long-term interest rates will be affected by inflationary expectations and demand for long-term instruments. Over time higher inflation will also push up nominal short-term rates and increase the velocity of money (as the opportunity cost of holding money increases).

The table below summarizes the impact of changes in monetary policy.

Expansionary monetary policy (opposite impact for restrictive monetary policy).

	Short-run effects when policy is unanticipated	**Short-run effects when policy is anticipated** and **long-run effects**
Inflation	Small increase, depends on excess capacity	Increase
Real output and employment	Increase, particularly if excess capacity	No change
Nominal interest rates	Short-term rates probably decline	Increase
Real interest rates	Decline	No change

LOS 4-1-D-c	**identify** the components of the equation of exchange, and **discuss** the implications of the equation for monetary policy
LOS 4-1-D-d	**describe** the quantity theory of money, and **discuss** its implications for the determination of inflation

The **equation of exchange** states that:

$$MV = GDP = PY \qquad \textbf{(Equation 4-5)}$$

where

M	=	money stock
V	=	velocity of money, the number of times each dollar is used in a year
P	=	economy's price level
Y	=	output, real income or real GDP

The equation says that output (Y) and velocity (V) are determined by factors other than the amount of money in circulation. For example Y is determined by the size of the economy's resource base and technology, these are factors which are insensitive to the money supply. V is affected by factors such as frequency of income payments, the banking system, and the communications system. Therefore Y and V can be assumed to be fairly constant over medium term, say two or three year, time periods.

The **quantity theory of money** says a change in money supply will lead to the same change in price levels, since velocity and output are unaffected by the quantity of money. In the long run this is consistent with the view that the only impact of an expansionary monetary policy is higher prices.

4-1-D View Concept Check Questions Workbook

4-1-E "Stabilization Policy, Output, and Employment"

Introduction

We can now build on the earlier Readings on fiscal and monetary policy to study the impact of expansionary and restrictive policies and discuss the effectiveness of policies in stabilizing the economy. We examine the different theories on how expectations are formed and how expectations decide the effectiveness of policy changes. Candidates also need to be able to differentiate between activist and non-activist approaches to stabilizing the economy.

LOS 4-1-E-a	**describe** the composition and use of the index of leading economic indicators

In order for policy makers to be able to implement effective policies they need to have access to information on the future direction of the economy. The two most widely used sources of information are the leading economic indicators and economic forecasting models.

Index of Leading Indicators

There are ten variables in the composite index. Two or three consecutive declines in the index are a warning that the economy is heading towards a recession. The index has correctly forecast the seven recessions in the U.S. between 1959 and 2001, although it has also indicated recessions that did not happen. The time lag before a recession occurs has been anything between 5 and 30 months.

The ten indicators are:

1. Length of average work week
2. Initial weekly claims for unemployment compensation
3. New orders placed with manufacturers
4. Percentage of companies receiving slower deliveries from suppliers
5. Contracts and orders for new plant and equipment
6. Permits for new housing starts
7. Interest rate spread between 10-year Treasury bonds and the Fed Funds rate
8. Index of consumer expectations
9. Change in stock price index
10. Change in the money supply (M2)

The leading indicators allow policy makers to adopt a counter-cyclical macroeconomic policy to smooth the economic cycle. So, for example, a decline in the leading indicators would usually lead to an expansionary monetary policy. Although the stimulus might be moderate at first if signs of a downturn become more pronounced the policy could be accelerated.

LOS 4-1-E-b **discuss** the time lags that may influence the performance of discretionary monetary and fiscal policy

The timing of changes in monetary and fiscal policy are critical and there are three types of time lag which make timing difficult.

1. Recognition lag

This is the time difference between when a change in policy is needed and when this is recognized by policy makers.

2. Administrative lag

This is the time period between the recognition that a policy change is needed and implementation of the change. The lag for changes in monetary policy is much shorter than fiscal policy.

3. Impact lag

This is the time period between implementation of a change in policy and its impact on the economy. Changes in tax rates will have a faster impact than changes in government spending.

Activists believe that there is time for a government to act to change economic policy to minimize the effects of market downturns. Non-activists believe, for example, that by the time a change to an expansionary policy takes effect a downturn will be over and the policy will contribute to an inflationary boom.

LOS 4-1-E-d	**contrast** the adaptive expectations hypothesis to the rational expectations hypothesis

Expectations

Adaptive expectations hypothesis – this states that future expectations of decision-makers are largely dependent on recent past data. This will lead to systematic error; there will be a time lag before people factor changes in economic policy into new expectations that will be incorporated in their business decisions.

Rational expectations hypothesis – this states that all available information is used to form expectations about the future. Errors will be random, not systematic. In this case the time lag between a change in economic policy and a change in expectations is very much shorter.

Example 4-6: Adaptive versus rational expectations

Money supply growth has been running at 5% per annum and the government adopts an expansionary monetary policy. According to the adaptive-expectations hypothesis people would expect money supply growth to continue at 5% per annum. According to the rational-expectations hypothesis people would expect money supply growth to be higher than 5%, other economic factors being equal.

LOS 4-1-E-c	**explain** the role expectations play in determining the effectiveness of fiscal and monetary policy

The time lag between a change in economic policy and people's expectations changing, and whether errors are systematic or random, is critical to the effectiveness of the change in policy.

Example 4-7: Expectations and policy

If there is a shift to an expansionary monetary policy, under adaptive expectations, there will be a time period before higher inflation changes people's expectations. This means that there will be a period in which higher aggregate demand will lead to higher output. However, under rational expectations, higher prices will be anticipated so costs will rise as rapidly as prices and the result of the shift in policy will be increased prices without a change in output.

The impact of policy changes under adaptive and rational expectations will differ in the short run but be the same in the long run.

The **policy-ineffectiveness theorem** states that any systematic change in policy will be ineffective since decision makers will anticipate the impact of the change in policy and adjust their decisions accordingly.

LOS 4-1-E-e **distinguish** between an activist and a non-activist strategy for stabilization policy

Non-activist strategy

Non-activists believe that:

1. discretionary economic policy increases economic instability.
2. predictable policies based on predetermined guidelines lead to economic stability.

They believe that if the government adheres to a long-term policy regardless of cyclical movements then people will gain confidence in the stability of the policy and private decision-making will be more efficient. This will lead to a stable and higher growth rate for the economy.

Non-activist monetary policy

Non-activists believe that monetary policy should either target a (i) stable growth rate in the money supply or (ii) stable prices.

Non-activist fiscal policy

In theory non-activists would try to run a balanced budget over a business cycle. Many non-activists would try to limit the flexibility of government in running large budget deficits.

4-1-E View Concept Check Questions Workbook

4-1-F "The Phillips Curve: Is There a Trade-off between Inflation and Unemployment?"

Introduction

This is short review of the work of an economist Phillips in the 1960s who proposed that there was a relationship between the rate of inflation and the rate of unemployment which was reflected in the Phillips curve. By the 1970s his views had fallen out of favor partly due to new theories on the role of expectations being incorporated in his original work. The rate of unemployment was then linked to the difference between the actual and expected rate of inflation.

LOS 4-1-F-a **describe** the Phillips curve

The Phillips curve shows the inverse relationship between the inflation rate and unemployment rate. (The Phillips curve is named after an electrical engineer who plotted the inflation rate against the unemployment rate in the United Kingdom between 1861 and 1957). The Phillips curve depicts a macroeconomic trade-off between:

- Low levels of unemployment, but with a high rate of inflation
- Low rates of inflation, but with a high level of unemployment

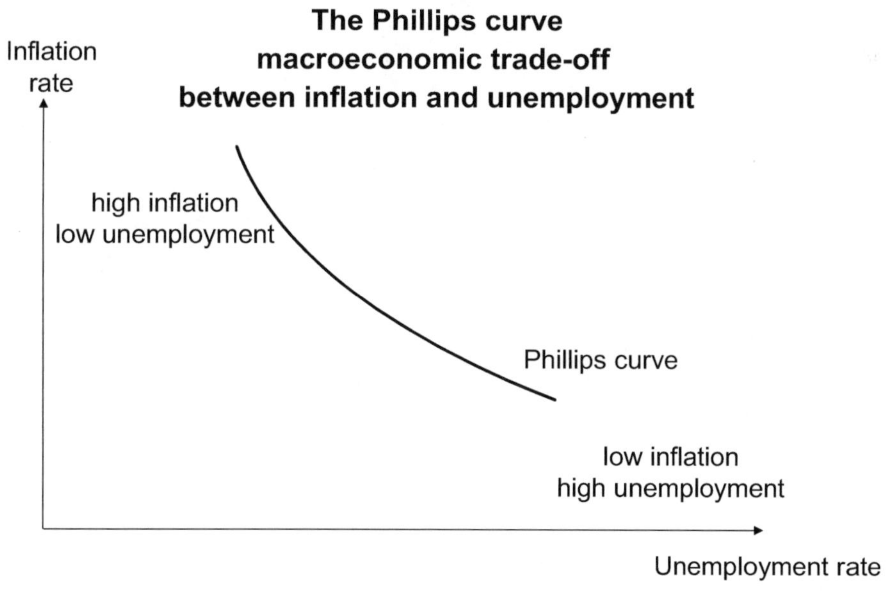

LOS 4-1-F-b **discuss** the trade-off between unemployment and inflation in the context of expectations

In the context of expectations, the original Phillips curve is updated for modern times. Specifically, the relationship is now depicted by the unemployment rate (plotted along the horizontal axis) and the *difference between actual and expected inflation* (plotted on the vertical axis). Recall that the inflation rate by itself was plotted on the vertical axis of the original (naïve) Phillips curve.

Unemployment can fall below its natural rate only when people underestimate the rate of inflation. This is equivalent to an economy operating above full employment output.

Unemployment can rise above its natural rate only when people overestimate the rate of inflation. This is equivalent to an economy operating below full employment output.

Unemployment will be at its natural rate when people correctly anticipate inflation. This is equivalent to an economy operating at full employment output.

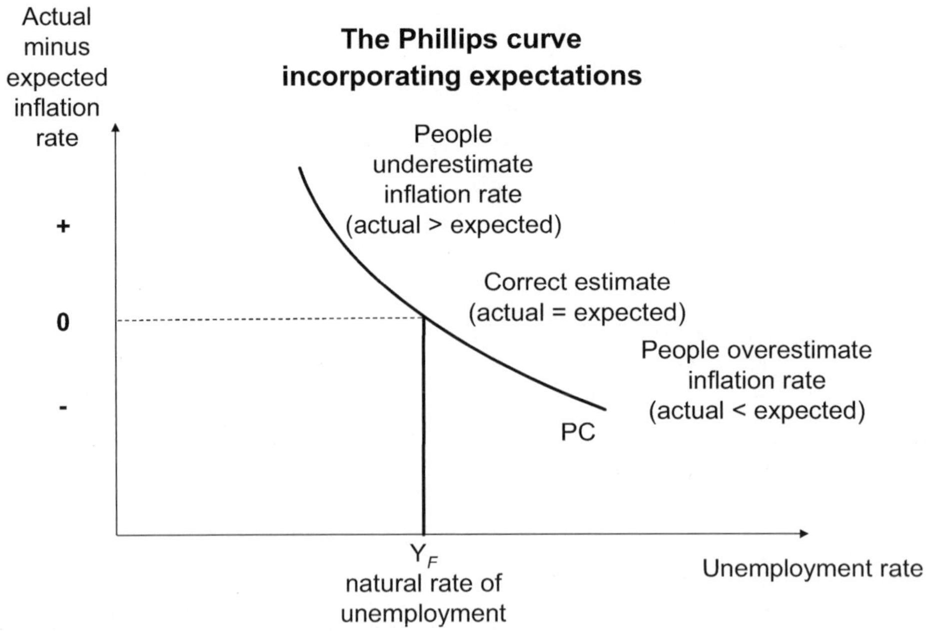

4-1-F View Concept Check Questions Workbook

STUDY SESSION 5

Investment Tools

Economics: Microeconomic Analysis

Overview

In this Study Session the Reading Assignments focus on the key issues in microeconomics - the study of consumers' choices and their influence on demand, how firms operate and their competitive environment, and the choices of resource suppliers.

For candidates who have studied economics or have knowledge of the basic concepts you will not need to spend too much time on the first two Preliminary Readings. The Preliminary Readings cover the laws of supply and demand, market equilibrium, the markets for labor, loanable funds and foreign exchange, and the impact of government controls, black markets and taxes on supply and demand. It is important to note that the CFA Institute states that examination questions are drawn mainly from the subsequent Readings Assignments.

Preliminary Reading Assignments

Economics: Private and Public Choice, 10th edition, James D. Gwartney, Richard L. Stroup, Russell S. Sobel, and David A. Macpherson (South-Western, 2003)

5-P1-A. "Supply, Demand, and the Market Process," Ch. 3

5-P1-B. "Supply and Demand: Applications and Extensions" Ch. 4, pp. 86-105

Note: http://snipurl.com/Workbook Preliminary Reading Assignments and Concept Question Workbook

5-1-A "Demand & Consumer Choice" including "Consumer Choice and Indifference Curves"

Introduction

This section looks at consumer choice and the factors that affect consumer demand. Candidates need to understand the concepts of elasticity and be able to compute price elasticity (change in quantity demanded when the price changes) and income elasticity (change in quantity demanded when income changes) of demand. The section finishes with a discussion of indifference curves (points on an indifference curve are of equal benefit to a consumer) and how they determine optimal combinations of goods for a consumer to purchase.

Reading Assignments

Economics: Private and Public Choice, 10th edition, James D. Gwartney, Richard L. Stroup, Russell S. Sobel, and David A. Macpherson (South-Western, 2003)

5-1-A. "Demand and Consumer Choice," Ch. 19, including addendum "Consumer Choice and Indifference Curves"

5-1-B. "Costs and the Supply of Goods," Ch. 20

5-1-C. "Price Takers and the Competitive Process," Ch. 21

5-1-D. "Price-Searcher Markets with Low Entry Barriers," Ch. 22

5-1-E. "Price-Searcher Markets with High Entry Barriers," Ch. 23

5-1-F. "The Supply of and Demand for Productive Resources" Ch. 24

Fundamentals of Financial Management, 8th edition, Eugene F. Brigham and Joel F. Houston (Dryden, 1998)

5-2. "The Financial Environment: Markets, Institutions, and Interest Rates," Ch. 4, pp. 122• 133

LOS 5-1-A-a **explain** consumer choice in an economic framework

The main assumptions made about consumer behavior are as follows:

1. Since consumers have limited income they must make choices about which goods they can purchase.
2. Choices are made on a rational basis.
3. All goods have substitutes.
4. Decisions are made without perfect information.
5. The law of diminishing marginal utility holds. This says that as consumption rises the marginal benefit of consuming the next unit is less than the last.

The dollar value of a consumer's marginal utility from consuming another unit of a product is called the **marginal benefit**. It is the maximum price that a consumer will pay for an additional unit and will fall as consumption increases. When different products are available a consumer will ensure that the last dollar spent on each product gives an equal marginal utility (MU) per dollar spent. For two products A and B this can be expressed as:

$$\frac{MU_A}{P_A} = \frac{MU_B}{P_B}$$ (Equation **5-1**)

where

MU_A = marginal utility of product A
P_A = price of product A

Example 5-1: Marginal utility

A shopper needs to buy fruit and has \$6 available to spend. He sees that apples and oranges are available and apples cost \$2 per kilogram and oranges cost \$1 per kilogram. The marginal utilities of the first, second and third kilograms of apples are \$3, \$2.50 and \$2 respectively and the marginal utilities of the first, second and third kilograms of oranges are \$2.00, \$1.25 and \$1 respectively. The shopper would benefit most by buying 2 kilograms of apples and 2 kilograms of oranges, the marginal utility of the last kilogram of each per dollar price is 1.25.

Other terms

Substitution effect - the component of an increase/decrease in demand for a good that results from the change in relative price of a good that can be substituted for the original good.

Income effect - the component of an increase/decrease in demand that results from the change in the consumer's real income as the price of a good changes.

Time cost - the time it takes to purchase a good will influence the consumer, and the monetary cost alone will not determine the demand.

Advertising is neither positive nor negative in economic theory. Advertising is a cost which will be passed on to consumers but it is beneficial in that it provides information to consumers, can save them time, and promotes brand names. This gives consumers protection in the sense that once a brand name has value then the producer will strive to maintain the reputation of its product.

LOS. 1. A. b) and LOS. 1. A. c)

(as in preliminary reading)

Shifts in Demand

A shift in the demand curve will be a result of a change in demand due to factors other than price. Other factors include increases in consumer income, changes in taxes on the product, changes in price or availability of competing products, and changes in expectations of future prices. It is important to differentiate between ***changes in demand*** (a shift of the demand curve) and ***changes in quantity demanded*** (a movement along the same demand curve).

LOS 5-1-A-b	**calculate**, and **interpret** price and income elasticity of demand
LOS 5-1-A-c	**discuss** the determinants of price and income elasticity of demand
LOS 5-1-A-d	**describe** the relationships among total revenue, total expenditures, and price elasticity of demand

Price Elasticity of Demand

Demand elasticity is also covered in LOS 5-P1-A-a

$$\text{Price Elasticity of Demand} = \frac{\%\Delta Q}{\%\Delta P} \qquad \textbf{(Equation 5-2)}$$

where

Q = the quantity demanded

P = the price

$\%\Delta Q$ = the percentage change in quantity demanded

Price elasticity of demand is also called the elasticity coefficient.

Example 5-2: Demand elasticity

If the price of televisions produced by manufacturer is increased by 10% then demand is forecast to fall by 15%. The elasticity of demand is, using Equation 5-2:

$$\frac{\%\Delta Q}{\%\Delta P} = \frac{-15\%}{10\%} = -1.5$$

Determinants of Price Elasticity of Demand

1. availability of substitutes - this will increase elasticity.
2. proportion of total spending on the product - if this is small it will tend to decrease elasticity of demand.

Total Expenditures and Demand Elasticity

Looking at total expenditure on a product in an industry:

Total expenditure = price x quantity

This means that if *demand is inelastic*, ie. the price elasticity coefficient is less than 1, the percentage change in price is more that the percentage change in quantity and therefore *a change in price will make total expenditure change in the same direction.*

Conversely, when *demand is elastic, a change in price will cause expenditures to move in the opposite direction.*

Total Revenues and Demand Elasticity

Looking at a firm's demand curve rather than the complete industry

Firm's revenue = price x quantity sold

Using the same analysis, if the product's demand curve is inelastic, total revenues will change in the same direction as price. If the demand curve is elastic, revenues and price will move in the opposite direction.

Income Elasticity

This is also covered in LOS 5-P1-A-a

$$\text{Income Elasticity} = \frac{\%\Delta Q}{\%\Delta I} \qquad \textbf{(Equation 5-3)}$$

where

Q = the quantity demanded

I = income

$\%\Delta Q$ = the percentage change in quantity demanded

Normal goods - income elasticity greater than 0

Luxury goods - income elasticity greater than 1

Inferior goods - income elasticity less than 0

Necessity goods - normal but low elasticity

LOS 5-1-A-e **explain** why the price elasticity of demand tends to increase in the long run

The demand for products is more elastic in the long run than in the short run, as consumers and producers have more time to adjust to the change in price.

LOS 5-1-A-f discuss the characteristics of consumer indifference curves

Consumer Indifference Curves

All of the points along an indifference curve represent bundles of goods that are equally satisfying to an individual consumer.

Example 5-3: Indifference curves

Using an example of a customer who wishes to buy apples and oranges, the curve represents the trade-off he is willing to make between buying different amounts of apples and different amounts of oranges from an initial position of 3 kilograms of apples and 2 kilograms of oranges.

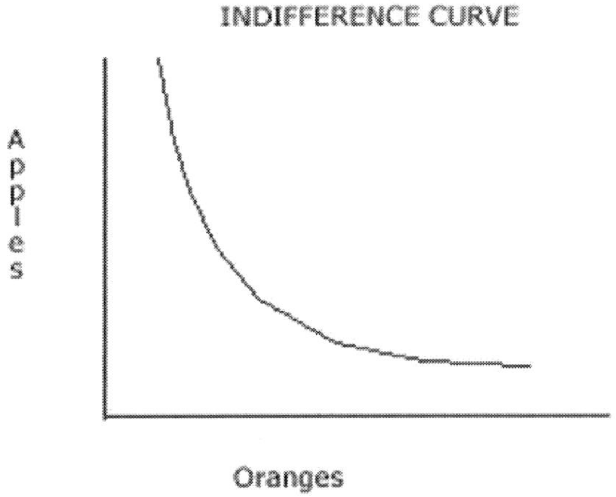

Note that:

1. it is better to have more apples and oranges so curves lying 'above' the indifference curve shown will be preferable.
2. the curve slopes downwards to the right since goods have substitutes.
3. the curves are convex since the value of a good declines as more of it is consumed.
4. indifference curves can be drawn through any point on the diagram.
5. indifference curves do not cross.

LOS 5-1-A-g	**discuss** the role of the consumption-opportunity constraint and the budget constraint in indifference curve analysis

The **consumption-opportunity constraint** differentiates between curves that are attainable and those that are unobtainable. The budget constraint is the constraint due to a limited income and the price of goods.

Example 5-4: Consumption-opportunity constraint

In Example 5-3, if we impose a constraint that the shopper has only \$6 available, and apples cost \$2 per kilogram and oranges cost \$1 per kilogram. We can then add the constraint as shown by the line joining 3 kilograms of apples to 6 kilograms of oranges. The point A, where the line intersects the indifference curve, represents the optimal combination of fruit for the shopper to buy.

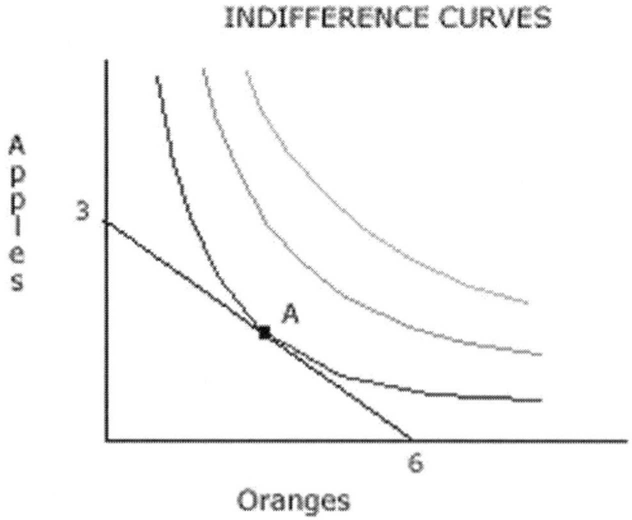

LOS 5-1-A-h	**distinguish** between the income effect and the substitution effect

If the price of a product rises then the **substitution effect** means that the slope of the constraint line will change (holding real income constant), the **income effect** means that the constraint line will move downwards towards the bottom left hand corner.

5-1-A View Concept Check Questions Workbook

5-1-B "Costs and the Supply of Goods"

Introduction

We now move on to looking at firms and their cost bases. First of all candidates have to be able to distinguish between different types of costs, in particular explicit and implicit costs, and the difference between accounting and economic profits. They also have to be able to interpret the components of short-run and long-run costs and relate these to a firm's total cost curves. Finally you need to be able to make the link between the cost structure of firms and the impact on supply.

LOS 5-1-B-a	**describe** the principal–agent problem of the firm

Pprincipal-agent problems - this refers to when the purchaser (principal) does not have full knowledge of the service provided by the agent leading to potentially conflicting objectives. (This is covered in more detail in study session 11).

LOS 5-1-B-b	**distinguish** among the types of business firms

Firms in the U.S. fall into three main categories, namely:

1. Corporations, owned by stockholders whose liability is limited to their investment.
2. Partnerships, owned by two or more individuals who have full liability for the debts of the business.
3. Proprietorships, owned by a single person who has full liability for the debts of the business.

LOS 5-1-B-c	**distinguish** between 1) explicit costs and implicit costs, 2) economic profit and accounting profit, and 3) the short run and the long run in production

Business Costs

Explicit costs – explicit costs have measurable cash flows, the costs relate to payment for resources. Examples are wages, rent, and raw material costs.

Implicit costs – these are opportunity costs of using the firm's resources, they are often not included in the accounting statements. Examples are wages or rental, which are not claimed by the owner of the business.

Total costs - the sum of explicit and implicit costs.

Opportunity cost of equity capital – this is the implicit cost of using the financial resources provided by equity shareholders. It is the normal or market rate of return on financial capital; it must be earned for investors to continue to provide capital to a firm.

LOS 5-1-B-e **differentiate** between economic costs and accounting costs

Economic profit - takes into consideration total economic costs which include both explicit and implicit costs, including the opportunity cost of assets used by the firm. Zero economic profit means that the owners are receiving the normal rate of return on their investment. **Accounting profit** takes into consideration explicit costs, and usually not implicit costs. Accounting profit is therefore usually higher than economic profit.

Example 5-5: Economic and accounting profit

A manufacturing company has sales of $1 million per annum and explicit costs (raw materials, wages, rent, utilities, tax etc.) of $700,000. The accounting profit is $300,000. However the owner of the company, who also owns the factory, is charging a rent of only $25,000 for the factory whereas the rent he could receive in the open market is $75,000. This gives an additional implicit cost of $50,000, reducing the economic profit to $250,000.

With respect to production activities the **short run** is defined as a time period in which a firm cannot alter the size of is production plant. The **long run** is the period in which a firm can alter all of the factors governing production.

LOS 5-1-B-d **define** opportunity costs, sunk costs, fixed costs, variable costs, marginal costs, and average costs

Costs

Definitions are given for different types of a firm's costs:

Variable costs – these are costs that rise as output increases, the average variable cost is the total variable cost divided by the number of units produced.

Fixed costs – these costs do not vary with the level of output. The average fixed costs is the total fixed cost divided by the number of units produced; it will decline as production increase.

Total cost - total fixed costs plus variable costs.

Marginal costs - change in total costs to produce an additional unit of output.

Sunk costs - historical costs incurred due to past decisions, and the decisions cannot be reversed.

LOS 5-1-B-f	**state** the law of diminishing returns and **explain** its impact on a company's costs
LOS 5-1-B-g	**describe** the shapes of the short-run marginal cost, average variable cost, average fixed cost, and average total cost curves

The law of diminishing returns

This law states that as more and more units of a variable resource are allocated to production they will eventually increase output at a decreasing rate. Mathematically, as the marginal costs increase they will become higher than the average total cost, thereby increasing the average total cost.

Example 5-6: Law of diminishing returns

Hiring additional employees (a variable resource) to work at a factory will initially increase output but eventually it will become more and more difficult to generate additional output from the fixed resources (due to plant size and equipment limitations).

The relationship between marginal costs (MC), average total costs (ATC), average variable costs (AVC) and average fixed costs (AFC) is shown below.

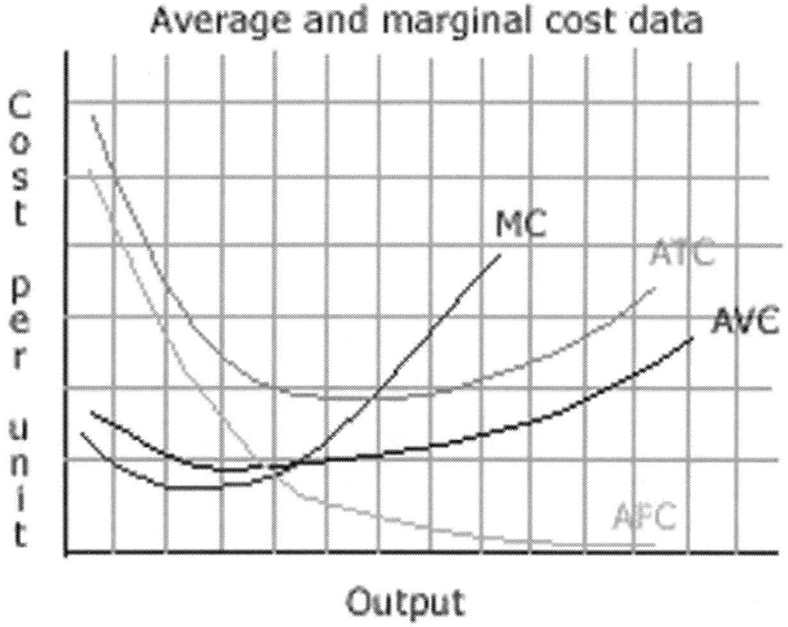

If a firm has the flexibility to alter its plant size then the long run average total cost curve becomes a combination of the short-run average total cost curves.

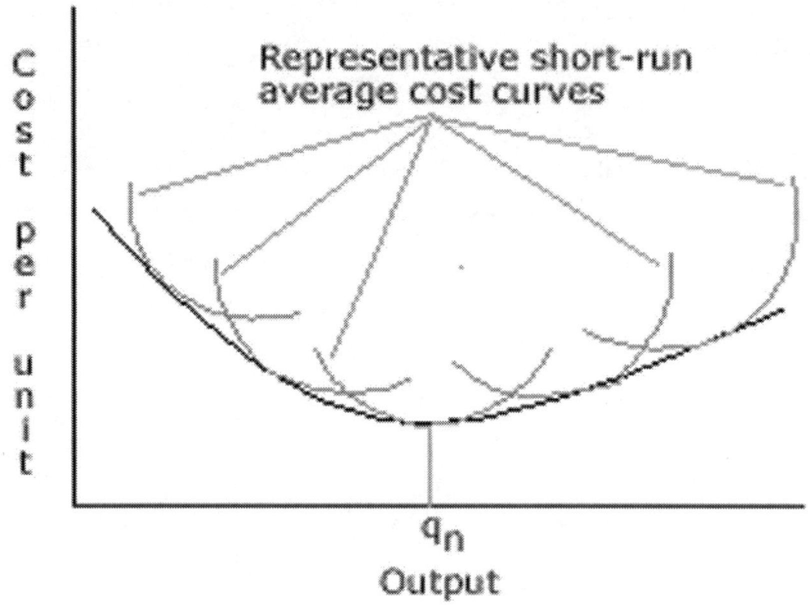

LOS 5-1-B-h	**define** economies and diseconomies of scale, **explain** how each is possible, and **relate** each to the shape of a company's long-run average total cost curve

Economies of scale - refers to when unit costs fall as output increases, the long-run average total cost curve will decline. This is usually a result of mass production, specialized use of resources, and improvements in production techniques due to experience.

However there are cases of **diseconomies of scale** when the long-run average total cost curve rises. This might be due to increasing bureaucracy.

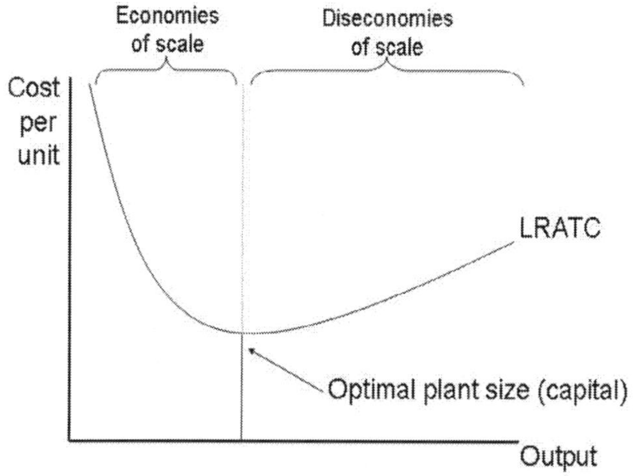

LOS 5-1-B-i	**describe** the factors that cause cost curves to shift

Shifts in the cost curve are caused by a number of factors including:

1. a change in price of resources - marginal cost curves will shift upwards.
2. a change in taxes - depending on the type of tax, it will change the fixed or variable costs.
3. a change in regulations - depending on the type of regulation, it will change the fixed or variable costs.
4. improvements in technology will reduce the resources needed to produce a unit of output.

5-1-B View Concept Check Questions Workbook

5-1-C "Price Takers and the Competitive Process"

Introduction

We continue our analysis of firms by examining price-taker firms, these are firms who have to accept the market price for their products, otherwise their sales will disappear, so they face a perfectly elastic demand curve. Candidates need to understand at what production level price-taker firms maximize profits and be able to describe the short-run and long-run supply curves for different types of price-taker industry.

LOS 5-1-C-a	**distinguish** between price takers and price searchers
LOS 5-1-C-b	**discuss** the conditions that characterize a purely competitive (price taker) market

Price-taker market

A price-taker market is a market characterized by:

1. All firms produce an identical product.
2. There are a large number of firms in the market.
3. Each firm is small relative to the market size.
4. There are no entry (or exit) barriers.

The demand curve is a horizontal line and demand is perfectly elastic, if a firm increases the price of its products above the market price, its sales will be zero.

A price-taker market is also called a **purely competitive market**.

Examples of price-taker markets are to be found in the agricultural sector where producers of agricultural commodities must accept the market price for their goods.

In real economies most companies are not price takers but are price searchers.

Price-searcher market – in a price-searcher market firms face a downward-sloping demand curve but can still set the price for their products.

LOS 5-1-C-c	**explain** how and why price takers maximize profits at the quantity for which marginal cost, price, and marginal revenue are equal
LOS 5-1-C-d	**calculate** and **interpret** the total revenue and the marginal revenue for a price taker

A price taker can always sell more units at the market price so will expand output as long as the marginal revenue, which is the same as the market price, exceeds its marginal cost. Up to this point the production of additional units will add more to revenues than to costs, thereby increasing profits. Profits will be maximized at the point that:

P = MR = MC (Equation **5-4**)

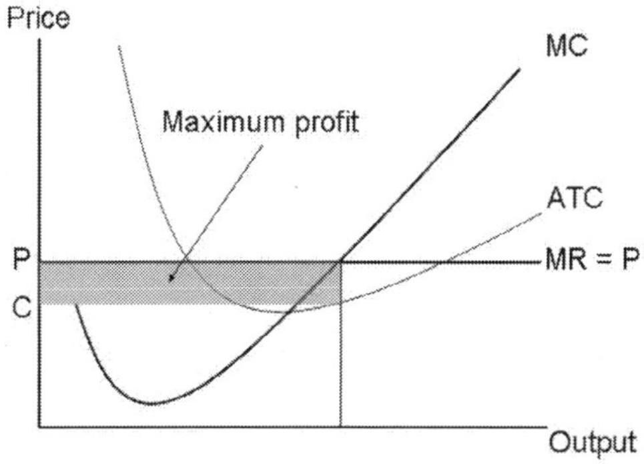

Note - The total revenue is the sales price multiplied by the output, the total cost is the average total cost multiplied by the output.

LOS 5-1-C-e	**explain** the decision by price takers with economic losses to continue to operate, temporarily shut down, or go out of business

If prices are depressed in a price-taker market, a firm has three options:

1. Continue to operate in the short run - if it can cover its variable costs and thinks the downturn is temporary.
2. Shut down temporarily - incur fixed but not variable costs.
3. Go out of business, if market conditions are not expected to change.

LOS 5-1-C-f	**describe** the short-run supply curves for a company and for a competitive market

A firm's short-run supply curve is shown below. The marginal cost curve is the same as the supply curve since it produces to the level where P = MC for a profit maximizing company .

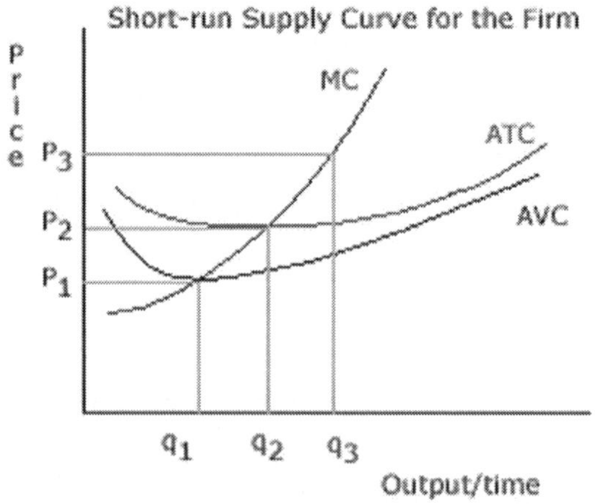

The short-run supply curve for a competitive market, assuming resource prices are held constant, is the sum of the supply curves for the firms in the market.

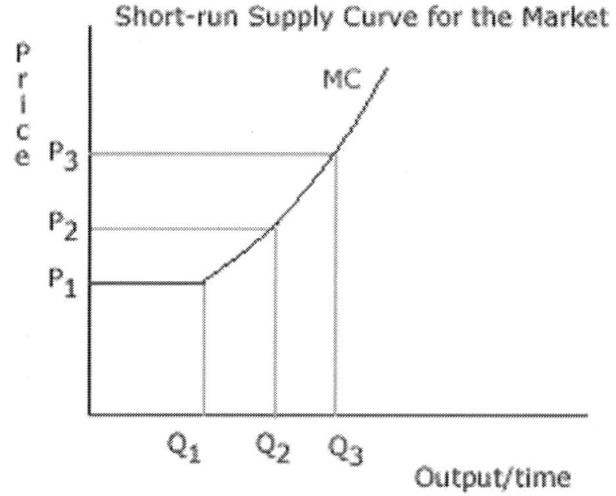

LOS 5-1-C-g	**contrast** the role of constant-cost, increasing-cost, and decreasing-cost industries in determining the shape of a long-run market supply curve

In the short run the supply curve for price takers will slope upwards to the right but in the long run there are three alternatives:

1. Constant-cost industries - costs of production remain constant as output is expanded so the supply curve is horizontal.
2. Increasing-cost industries - costs of production rise as output is expanded so the supply curve will slope upwards to the right. This is usually the case.
3. Decreasing-cost industries - costs of production decline as output is expanded so the supply curve will slope downwards to the right.

LOS 5-1-C-h	**explain** the impact of time on the elasticity of supply

In price-taker markets, in long- run equilibrium, all firms will earn a normal rate of return. If economic profits are available then new firms would enter the business and original companies would expand supply, putting downward pressure on prices. Similarly if firms are making economic losses then they will leave the market thereby reducing supply.

5-1-C View Concept Check Questions Workbook

5-1-D "Price-Searcher Markets with Low Entry Barriers"

Introduction

Price–searcher markets are ones which face downward–sloping demand curves for their products, so if they increase prices they will see demand fall but not completely disappear. Most firms are price searchers, they are looking to maximise profit and they decide what price to charge and how much to produce of their product. In this Reading we look at price-searcher markets with low entry barriers which can lead to a highly competitive environment. Again candidates have to understand how firms make decisions on levels of output and evaluate the efficiency of price-searcher markets.

LOS 5-1-D-a	**describe** the conditions that characterize competitive price-searcher markets

Competitive price-searcher markets

Competitive price-searcher markets are also called **monopolistic competition**, they are characterized by

1. Low entry barriers
2. Firms with downward-sloping demand curves.
3. Firms produce differentiated rather than identical products.

LOS 5-1-D-b **explain** how price searchers choose price and output combinations

The demand curves of price-searcher markets are highly elastic due to the availability of substitutes.

Price searchers will need to decide between different price and output combinations, expanding output will lead to a lower price and vice versa. Firms will expand output until marginal revenue equals marginal cost since this will maximize profits, but due to the large number of competitors the sales of each firm will be below their least-cost capacity level. Prices in a price-searcher market will be slightly above those in a price-taker market.

The diagram below illustrates that over the long-term, if new firms can freely enter the market price will equal unit cost and there will be no economic profits available.

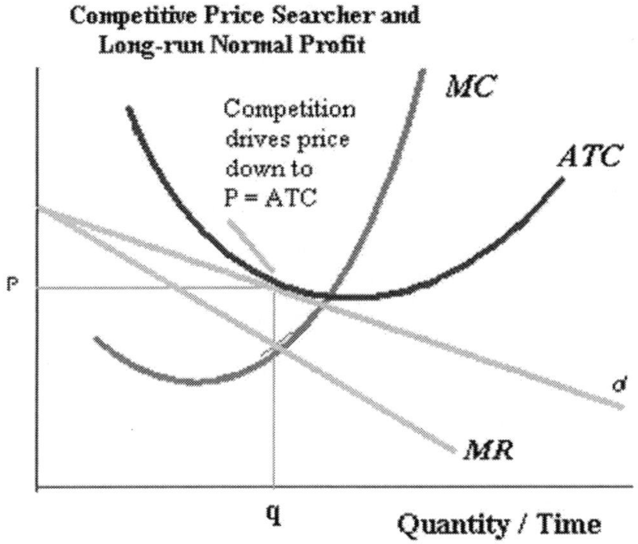

LOS 5-1-D-c	**summarize** the debate about the allocative efficiency of price-searcher markets with low barriers to entry, including the implications of contestable markets and entrepreneurship

A **contestable market** is one where the costs of entry and exit are low. An example of this is an airline route where only a small number of airlines cover the route but they cannot push up prices because other airlines are free to fly the route.

Entrepreneurship - this is important since entrepreneurs make decisions when there is not information available to apply economic models. Therefore entrepreneurs do not have a place in economic models.

Allocative efficiency - the allocation of resources to the production of goods and services most desired by consumers, at the lowest possible cost.

The debate about the efficiency of price-searcher markets with low entry barriers has two sets of arguments:

For

1. incentive to produce efficiently.
4. firms only undertake production if it increases the value of resources used.
5. firms are innovative in developing new products.

Against

1. firms maximize profits when price is higher than marginal cost.
6. long-run average cost is not minimized due to the large number of firms operating in the market.
7. heavy advertising is encouraged.

LOS 5-1-D-d **explain** how price discrimination increases output and reduces allocative inefficiency

Price discrimination is when a producer can charge different prices to different customers for the same product. This is only possible when the customers who are paying less cannot resell at higher prices and when two groups of customers have demand curves with different elasticities.

Example 5-7: Price discrimination

Different pricing of airline fares to different groups of customers. Business travelers have an inelastic demand curve and are generally willing to pay higher prices compared to people on vacation, who have a more elastic demand curve and greater flexibility when they can travel.

Price discrimination increases output and profits and also reduces the allocative inefficiency with prices being set above marginal cost.

There are three main reasons why competition promotes economic progress:

1. Producers need to operate efficiently and meet customers' demands.
2. Producers have an incentive to innovate and find lower-cost methods of production.
3. Producers must adopt an effective business structure and decide the optimum size of business to keep costs low.

5-1-D View Concept Check Questions Workbook

5-1-E "Price-Searcher Markets with High Entry Barriers"

Introduction

Price-searcher markets with high entry barriers (such as legal barriers, patents or economies of scale) have a limited number of participants in the market. In the case of only one participant it is a monopoly, in the case of a few firms it is an oligopoly. Candidates need to recognise the characteristics of monopolies and oligopolies and discuss how they set output levels. Additionally they need to understand the inefficiencies created by entry barriers and look at the rationale behind government policies that protect industries.

LOS 5-1-E-a	**discuss** entry barriers that may protect companies against competition from potential market entrants

Entry barriers

There are four main types of entry barriers which make it difficult or impossible for competitors to enter a business. These are:

1. Economies of scale.
2. Government regulations.
3. Patents.
4. Control over an essential resource.

High entry barriers lead to reduced competition, which means that resources are not used efficiently. Firms may use time in lobbying for government protection rather than focusing on productive activities. The consumer loses through lack of choice and they are usually overpaying for products that are produced inefficiently.

LOS 5-1-E-b **differentiate** between a monopoly and an oligopoly

Monopoly

A monopoly is characterized by:

1. There is only one producer of a well defined product with no clear substitutes.
2. High entry barriers.

Examples of monopolies in the U.S. include local electricity suppliers who have a monopoly in a certain district.

Oligopoly

An oligopoly is characterized by:

1. A small number of producers.
2. Interdependence between producers.
3. High economies of scale.
4. Significant barriers to entry.

Examples of oligopolies in the U.S. include auto producers and steel manufacturers.

LOS 5-1-E-c **describe** how a profit-maximizing monopolist sets prices and determines output

Monopolies face a downward sloping demand curve and will aim to maximize profit. They will also increase production until marginal revenue equals marginal cost.

LOS 5-1-E-d	**discuss** price and output under oligopoly, with and without collusion
LOS 5-1-E-e	**discuss** why oligopolists have a strong incentive to collude and to cheat on collusive agreements
LOS 5-1-E-f	**discuss** the obstacles to collusion among oligopolistic companies

Oligopolies tend to have demand curves that are very elastic and we see a strong link between the prices of different producers. Oligopolists must take into consideration the reaction of their competitors if they change prices. If all the participants in an industry are acting independently then the price will get driven down to the average unit cost of production, since any firm which raises the price above this level would quickly lose sales. Therefore there is a high risk of **collusion,** when firms agree to limit production and/or sell products at, or above, a minimum price. Collusion is attractive since producers want to avoid prices being pushed down to the cost of production. Collusion using a formal organization, which is called a cartel, will try to control supply to maximize the profits of members. An example of this is OPEC.

Collusion is difficult to maintain as there is a strong incentive for individual firms to 'cheat' to increase market share. There are five major obstacles to collusion:

1. An increasing number of firms in the market - each firm will have different objectives depending on its cost base and its estimates of market demand elasticity.
2. Price cutting is difficult to detect - there is a strong incentive for individual firms to cut prices if it cannot be easily detected or prevented.
3. Low entry barriers - a profitable market will attract new entrants.
4. Unstable demand - different demand expectations will make it difficult to reach agreement on pricing and supply.
5. Antitrust legislation.

LOS 5-1-E-g **describe** government policy alternatives that are intended to reduce the problems stemming from high barriers to entry

Problems arising from a market with high entry barriers include:

- Reduced options available to consumers
- Allocative inefficiency - production will not increase until prices fall to the cost level.
- Inefficient firms can make profits even when they are not meeting customers' requirements.
- Resources are used to try to obtain protection from government.

A government can try to improve the efficiency of a monopoly by measures such as:

1. Controlling the structure of the industry to ensure competitors enter the industry, including antitrust laws - this will not tend to be effective when the firms benefit from economies of scale. In this case increasing the number of firms will increase costs and therefore prices. There is a tendency for natural monopolies to form, when production costs continue to fall as output is increased. This will lead to one or a small number of firms dominating an industry.
2. Removing trade barriers and tariffs that limit competition - although this will strengthen competition there are often political reasons to keep trade restrictions in place.
3. Controlling prices charged and output of firms in the market - but fixing prices in relation to profits encourages inefficiency.
4. Supplying the goods by a government owned firm - but a government owned monopoly tends to be less efficient and less subject to scrutiny, leading to higher prices.

5-1-E View Concept Check Questions Workbook

5-1-F "The Supply of and Demand for Productive Resources"

Introduction

Having examined the choices of consumers and firms we turn to the suppliers of resources. These are individuals or firms that are motivated by the income they receive for supplying the resource. Supply and demand for the resource decide the price that they can charge. The candidate is expected to understand the factors that drive demand and how the marginal revenue product from a resource determines demand.

There are two categories of productive resources

1. Human resources - the skill and knowledge of workers.
2. Nonhuman resources
3. physical capital – resources made by humans e.g. tools and machines
4. land
5. natural resources

LOS 5-1-F-a **explain** the relationship between the price of a resource and the quantity demanded of that resource

Demand for a resource is a **derived demand**, which means that the demand is dependent on the demand for the final good that the resource is used to produce.

There is an inverse relationship between the demand for a resource and the quantity demanded. If the price increases producers will (i) turn to substitute resources and (ii) consumers will buy less of the final good as it becomes more expensive. The demand curve is shown below; as prices increase from P_1 to P_2, demand falls from Q_1 to Q_2.

THE DEMAND CURVE FOR A RESOURCE

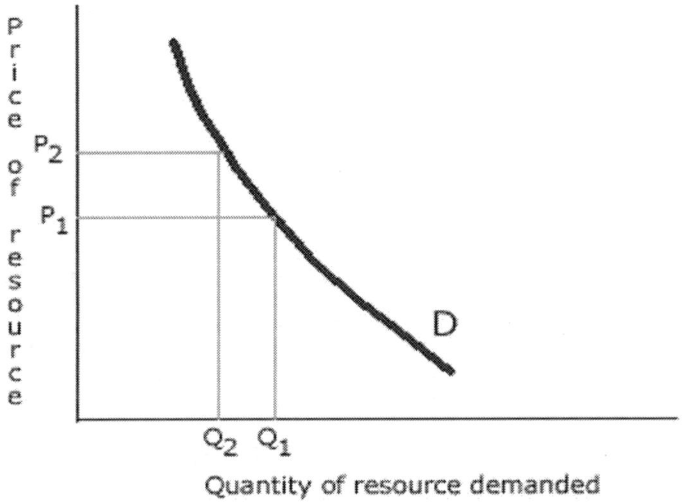

Generally if the demand for the final product is elastic this will lead to demand for the resource being elastic and vice versa. In the long run the demand for a resource is more elastic than in the short run, as producers have more time to substitute another resource. The long-run demand curve will be flatter than the short-run curve. This is shown in the diagram below where the quantity demanded falls by more in the long run (to Q_3) than the short run (to Q_2) when prices increase from P_1 to P_2.

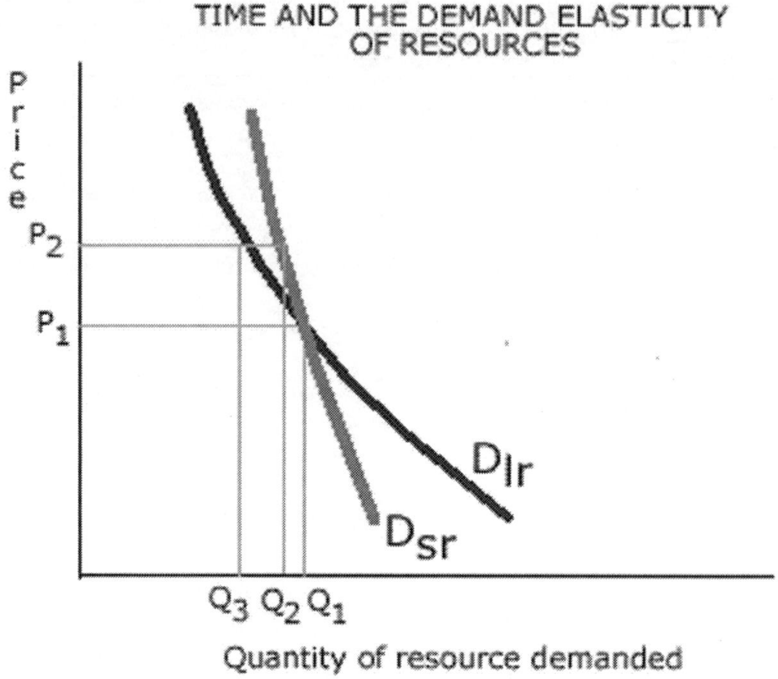

LOS 5-1-F-b	**identify** and **describe** the influence of three factors that cause shifts in the demand curve for a resource

Shifts in the demand curve

Three are three factors that can cause a shift in the demand curve.

1. **A change in demand for the final product** will lead to a similar change in demand for the resources used to make the product, e.g. a fall in demand for technology products leads to workers being laid off in the technology sector.
2. **A change in the productivity of a resource**, a rise in productivity will lead to a rise in demand. Additional capital can be spent to improve productivity (of people or equipment), e.g. skilled labor is more in demand than unskilled labor.
3. **A change in price of a related product**, e.g. higher prices of wood for construction would lead to greater demand for bricks as builders switch from building wood to brick houses.

LOS 5-1-F-c **define** the marginal revenue product of a resource and **explain** how it influences the demand for that resource

The **marginal revenue product** (MRP) of a resource is the change in total revenue of a firm that results from the employment of one additional unit of resource. This is equal to the marginal product (the change in total output) multiplied by the marginal revenue. Following on from the law of diminishing returns, the marginal product (MP) and therefore the MRP of a resource will fall as employment of the resource increases.

For a price–taker firm, because marginal revenue equals market price the MRP equals the resource's value of marginal product (the marginal product multiplied by the selling price of the product it produces). For a price-searcher firm, the MRP is less than the value of MP because marginal revenue is less than the price, since a price-searcher firm must reduce prices to sell more units.

All profit–maximizing firms will expand the use of each resource until the MRP of the resource is equal to the marginal cost of employing the resource.

LOS 5-1-F-d **explain** the necessary conditions to achieve the cost-minimizing employment levels for two or more variable resources

Extending the analysis to the case when a firm is using a number of variable resources, or factors, for a profit-maximizing firm they will expand production until the MP per last dollar spent on each factor is equal. This is because if a marginal dollar spent on one resource increases output by more than if it was spent on another resource, then a firm would increase spending on this resource rather than ones with a higher marginal cost per dollar. However as more and more of a resource are added their MP will fall, until eventually equality is reached.

Example 5-8: Variable resources

A firm is using three variable resources, skilled labor, unskilled labor and machine rental. Unit costs will be minimized when:

$$\frac{\text{MP of skilled labor}}{\text{Price of skilled labor}} = \frac{\text{MP of unskilled labor}}{\text{Price of unskilled labor}} = \frac{\text{MP of machine rental}}{\text{Price of rental}}$$

LOS 5-1-F-e **discuss** the factors that influence the supply and demand of resources in the short run and long run

Supply of Resources

Owners of a resource will sell the resource if the benefit exceeds the costs, and they will sell to the firm that offers them the most for the resource. An increase in the resource price will attract new suppliers and a decrease will lead to a shift of the resource sellers to other activities. The supply curve is upward sloping to the right.

Short-Run and Long-Run Supply

The supply response may well be different in the short and long run. In the short run the response of suppliers to a price change will be less than in the long run. In the long run the suppliers of the resource can adjust their investment to supply more or less of a resource. Therefore supply will be more elastic in the long run than short run, as shown in the diagram below.

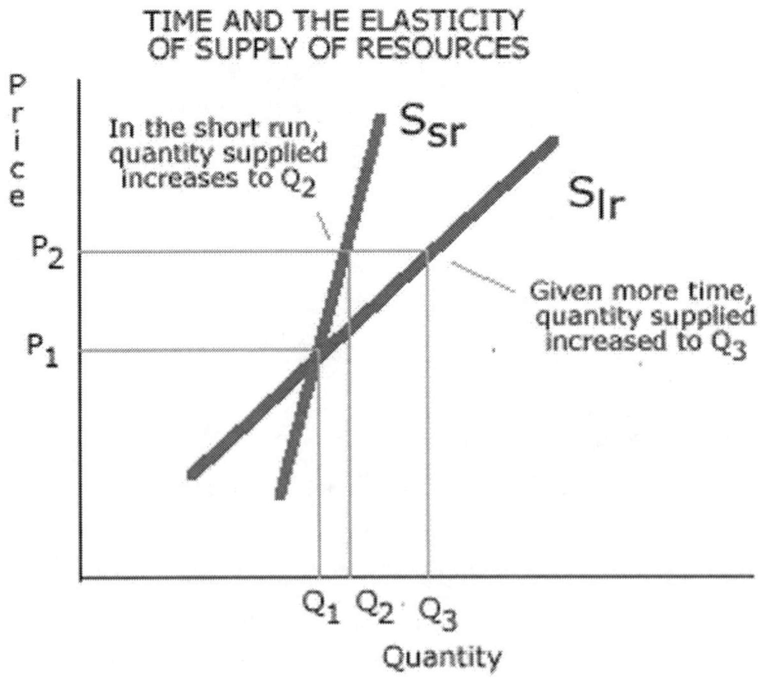

In the short run how quickly supply responds to a change in price of a resource is determined by the **resource mobility**. Resource mobility is how easily the resource can be transferred to another use. High resource mobility leads to an elastic supply curve. Land is often a very mobile resource since it can be used for many different purposes, agriculture, building etc. Machines are usually not very mobile. Labor resources are mobile within a skill level and geographical area but mobility will tend to decline as the skill level increases.

In the long run the supply of resources will naturally decline as machines wear out, people's skills decline etc. However, investment whether in machines or in education and training, can increase the supply of both physical and human resources. The time it takes for the resource supply to adjust to a change in prices will depend on the resource itself e.g. a doctor will take longer to qualify than a truck driver.

LOS 5-1-F-f	**explain** how prices for resources are determined in a market economy

Resource Prices

Resource prices are determined by supply and demand and the equilibrium is when the quantity supplied equals the quantity demanded.

If there is a sudden change in demand the move in price is larger in the short run to long run. For example if there is a sharp increase in demand, the price of the resource will increase. However, in the long run the increased elasticity in the supply curve of the resource will lead to supply adjusting which will put downward pressure on the price, leading to a smaller long-run increase in price.

LOS 5-1-F-g	**explain** the process through which changing resource prices influence resource utilization and the performance of the economic system

Prices in resource markets are critical since they link the actions of firms using a resource and the provider of the resource. They provide information about the scarcity of a resource and provide an incentive to a provider of a resource to invest to increase supply. As consumer preferences change the ability of resource prices to adjust is essential for a properly functioning market system to reallocate the use or resources between industries.

5-1-F View Concept Check Questions Workbook

5-2 "The Financial Environment: Markets, Institutions, and Interest Rates"

Introduction

This section looks at the supply and demand for funds and the link to interest rates. Candidates should be able to differentiate between nominal and real interest rates and the effect of inflation on required returns. We also explore how market interest rates are determined and the premium required for default risk, liquidity risk and maturity risk.

LOS 5-2-a	**identify** and **explain** the factors that influence the supply of and demand for capital

Cost of Capital

There are four main factors which affect the supply and demand for capital and therefore the cost of money (either the cost of borrowing or the cost of equity). These factors are:

Production opportunities - these are the returns available in an economy for investing in productive assets.

Time preferences for consumption – whether consumers prefer to consume today or save for tomorrow.

Risk – this is the risk that investments will not provide the expected returns.

Inflation – the expected rate of future inflation will influence required returns, higher inflation increases the required returns and vice versa.

LOS 5-2-b	**describe** the role of interest rates in allocating capital
LOS 5-2-c	**explain** how the supply of and demand for funds determine interest rates
LOS 5-2-d	**discuss** the factors that cause the supply and demand curves for funds to shift

Interest rates determine the allocation of capital. If a firm has profitable investment opportunities it is wiling to pay more for capital, and a less profitable firm will be able to afford less.

In a low risk market, interest rates will be set by the market at the level where demand for capital equals supply of capital, see the graph in LOS 5-P1-B. In a higher risk market, suppliers of capital will require a higher return and therefore equilibrium will be at a higher interest rate.

There is a different price for each type of capital (eg. equities, home loans, federal loans etc.) and the prices will move as demand fluctuates. In a recession when businesses are not looking to raise capital then short-term interest rates will fall, whereas in an economic boom short-term rates will rise.

LOS 5-2-e **distinguish** between the real and the nominal risk-free rate of interest

Nominal rate of interest

The quoted rate of interest on a debt security is usually the nominal rate of interest. The nominal rate is the real risk-free rate plus premiums that reflect inflation, the risk of the security and the security markets' liquidity. This means that:

$k = k_{RF} + DRP + LP + MRP$ **(Equations 5-5)**

and $k_{RF} = k^* + IP$

where

k	=	nominal rate of interest on a security
k_{RF}	=	the risk-free rate of interest available on a risk-free asset, for example Treasury Bills in the U.S.
k^*	=	real risk-free rate, available on a risk-free asset if zero inflation is expected
IP	=	inflation premium, the expected average annual inflation rate over the life of the security
DRP	=	default risk premium, it reflects the risk the issuer does not pay the interest or principal
LP	=	liquidity or marketability premium
MRP	=	maturity risk premium, long-term securities have a greater risk of price decline

LOS 5-2-f	**explain** the effect of inflation on the real rate of return earned by financial securities and by physical assets
LOS 5-2-g	**define** the inflation premium and **describe** how the inflation premium is determined

Inflation premium

There is a link between inflationary expectations and interest rates, fear of rising inflation will increase interest rates, and investors require a higher rate of return to compensate them for the decline in purchasing power of their capital. However if investors are confident that inflation will remain under control interest rates will ease.

It is important to note that the inflation rate used is the *rate expected over the life of the security.* Although this may be correlated to past trends in inflation it is very likely to be a different rate to the current rate of inflation.

LOS 5-2-h	**describe** the default risk, liquidity risk, and maturity risk premiums

Default risk premium

The default risk premium reflects the risk of the issuer failing to pay the interest or principal back in full. Ratings on corporate bonds give an indication of the default risk. The default risk premium is the difference between the interest rate on a Treasury bond (assumed to have no default risk) and a corporate bond with the same maturity, coupon, liquidity etc.

Liquidity premium

This reflects the risk that the investor cannot sell the security quickly to raise cash, at and if it can be sold he will not receive its fair value.

Maturity risk premium

The maturity risk premium reflects the fact that bonds that have longer to maturity have greater interest rate risk. This premium fluctuates and tends to be higher when markets are more volatile.

Example 5-9: Nominal interest rate

The real risk-free rate is 2% and inflation is expected to be 3% over the next year. A corporate AAA bond with one year to maturity yields 0.5% over a one-year Treasury issue. A highly liquid AAA bond with one year to maturity would have an estimated nominal yield of

Using Equations 5-5

$k = k^* + IP + DRP + LP + MRP = 2\% + 3\% + 0.5\% \qquad = 5.5\%$

we have assumed there is only a very small maturity risk premium.

LOS 5-2-i	**explain** interest rate risk and reinvestment rate risk

Although the maturity risk premium on 30 year Treasury bonds has recently been around one to two percent higher above the risk-free asset the **reinvestment risk** of short-term bills needs to be considered. The reinvestment risk refers to the risk that when short-term paper matures, if interest rates have fallen, the investor will need to accept a lower rate when the proceeds are reinvested.

5-2 View Concept Check Questions Workbook

STUDY SESSION 6

Investment Tools

Economics: Global Economic Analysis

Overview

This is a relatively short Study Session focusing on international trade. There has been rapid growth in the number of cross border transactions and the Session starts with an explanation of the benefits of international trade and the largely negative impact of trade barriers (tariffs, quotas etc.) which are widely used to restrict international trade. It also looks at the mechanics of the foreign exchange markets, how exchange rates are quoted and the main theories explaining forward exchange rates including interest rate and purchasing power parity. Candidates are also expected to understand the impact of government monetary and fiscal policies on currencies and the other factors that make currencies depreciate or appreciate.

Reading Assignments

Economics: Private and Public Choice, 10th edition, James D. Gwartney, Richard L. Stroup, Russell S. Sobel, and David A. Macpherson (South-Western, 2003)

6-1. "Gaining from International Trade," Ch. 17

International Investments, 5th edition, Bruno Solnik and Dennis McLeavey (Addison Wesley, 2004)

6-2-A. "Foreign Exchange," Ch. 1

6-2-B. "Foreign Exchange Parity Relations" Ch. 2, pp. 31• 48

6-1 "Gaining from International Trade"

Introduction

This Reading Assignment concentrates on the benefits for a nation if it exports goods where it has a comparative advantage (can produce goods at a lower opportunity cost than other nations) and import goods where it has a comparative disadvantage. This contributes to economic efficiency for the trading partners. However countries frequently impose trading barriers to protect domestic industries and candidates need to be aware of the beneficiaries and losers (usually the consumer) of barriers such as quotas, tariffs, export constraint and exchange-rate controls.

LOS 6-1-a	**state** the conditions under which a nation can gain from international trade, and **describe** the benefits of international trade

International trade has grown rapidly over recent decades. The principal behind international trade is that individuals and nations benefit from international trade if they buy goods from overseas which cannot be produced cheaply domestically, whereas they can export goods when they have a competitive advantage.

Comparative advantage is defined as the ability to produce goods at a lower opportunity cost than others. This is a relative measure.

Absolute advantage is when a nation can produce more of a product with the same level of resources than another nation.

The **Law of Comparative Advantage** says that trading partners can each benefit by specializing in producing goods where they have a lower opportunity cost, and trade them for goods where they have a higher opportunity cost. As long as the relative costs of producing goods differ between nations there will be mutual advantages in trading.

Example 6-1: Comparative advantage

	Output per worker per month FOOD	Output per worker per month COMPUTERS
France	4	6
Singapore	3	9

In France the opportunity cost of 1 unit of food is 1.5 units of computers, whereas in Singapore the opportunity cost of 1 unit of food is 3 units of computers, therefore France has a relative advantage in the production of food and Singapore in the production of computers. Both countries will benefit if France trades food for Singapore's computers.

It is assumed that the only resource used to produce the goods is labor.

Active trading between nations allows each nation to expand their production and therefore to also expand their consumption. Other benefits of international trade include:

- Domestic producers benefit from economies of scale as their potential markets are not restricted to their home country. This is particularly true for producers in smaller economies.
- Consumers can benefit from purchasing from large scale producers. Take the example of aircraft, It would not be economical for most countries to pay the design and development costs of building aircraft.
- It promotes competition and a wider variety of goods will be available to the consumer.
- In an open economy (one which is open to free trade) the government is under pressure to provide sound institutions and a healthy environment for corporations; if they do not do so capital and labor will move overseas.
- Exporters earn foreign exchange, which allows the country's residents to purchase imports.

LOS 6-1-b	**discuss** the effects of international trade on domestic supply and demand

Impact of free trade on supply and demand

If a country has a competitive advantage in the production of a particular good, and it is able to export the good at the world market price, then producers will benefit since they can sell a larger quantity at a higher price. Consumers will lose since they have to pay a higher world market price for the good; however the gain to producers outweighs the loss to consumers.

On the other hand the lower prices of imports of goods where the country has a competitive disadvantage will benefit consumers. International trade results in lower prices and higher consumption of imported goods and higher prices and lower domestic consumption of exported goods. Overall there will be an increase in output and consumption compared to the situation where there is no international trade or specialization in production.

LOS 6-1-c	**describe** commonly used trade-restricting devices, including tariffs, quotas, voluntary export restraints, and exchange-rate controls
LOS 6-1-d	**explain** the impact of trade barriers on the domestic economy and **identify** who benefits and loses from the imposition of a tariff

Trade restrictions

Despite the benefits of free trade most countries impose trade restrictions. The different types of restriction include:

Tariffs

Tariffs are taxes on imports. Consumers pay the cost of the tariff in the form of higher prices, part of this loss to consumers represents a deadweight loss, due to a reduction in allocative efficiency. The remainder of the cost of the tariff goes to producers who benefit from selling at higher prices and the government which has increased tax revenues. When tariffs are in place a nation's resources are used in producing goods inefficiently rather in the production of goods where the country has a comparative advantage.

Import quotas

Import quotas are, in the same way as tariffs, usually imposed to protect domestic industries. Import quotas are ceilings on the amount of a product that can be imported in a set period. Once again consumers lose as they pay higher prices for goods. However in this case it is domestic producers and the foreign producers who have a license, or quota, to sell into the market who are the beneficiaries. The government does not benefit, so arguably a quota is worse than a tariff for consumers since foreign producers rather than their own government are benefiting from the higher prices they pay for goods.

Governments also use regulations and political pressure to limit foreign competition. An example of this is voluntary export constraints, which is when firms agree to limit the exports of a product to a market, for example Japanese cars to the U.S. These are usually introduced under political pressure, often to avoid a trade barrier being imposed by the importing country. The economic impact is similar to a quota.

Exchange rate controls

This is when a country fixes the exchange rate at a level above the market rate and imposes restrictions on foreign exchange transactions. This will limit exports and therefore there will not be sufficient foreign exchange to pay for imports. The total value of trade will decline.

LOS 6-1-e	**explain** why nations adopt trade restrictions

The three main arguments for a country imposing trade restrictions to protect domestic industries are:

1. They are imposed in order to achieve self-sufficiency in defense industries, this will ensure a supply of arms in the case of international conflict.
2. Trade restrictions can protect infant industries from more established competitors. Although there are arguments for protection as a temporary measure, most protection tends to be difficult to remove.
3. When a nations sees foreign goods being dumped (sold at below cost or at a lower price than they are sold in the producer's domestic market) there is concern that domestic producers will be forced out of business and the foreign producer can establish a monopoly then raise pieces. Dumping is illegal and a government can introduce anti-dumping policies. However the risk is that anti-dumping rules can be applied excessively, at the disadvantage of consumers who will lose access to cheaper foreign goods.

There are strong arguments against these factors being sufficient justification for the imposition of barriers. It is often a case of the producers being represented by strong special interest groups whereas the consumer, who pays the cost of the trade barriers, is either unaware of the impact of barriers or does not have an effective vehicle by which to lobby the government to remove the barriers.

LOS 6-1-f **discuss** the validity of the arguments for trade restrictions

Two of the main arguments given for trade restrictions are;

Trade restrictions that limit imports protect jobs in a nation

Although restrictions may protect jobs in the specific industry being protected they will lead to job losses in other industries. This is because foreigners will have earned less foreign exchange with which they can buy goods from that country, so the export industries will suffer.

In the U.S. in the 1980's and 1990's imports grew faster than GDP but employment also grew rapidly, showing that imports are not a threat to jobs.

Free trade with low wage countries reduces domestic wages

This will not happen since higher wages are paid to workers with higher productivity working with expensive capital equipment. Countries which have low wages often have a work force with low skills and only have a comparative advantage in labor-intensive industries. This produces a comparative advantage which can benefit high and low wage nations.

Studies have been done on the link between economic growth and trade openness. The data for some 91 countries was collected for the period 1980 to 1999. The twelve most open economies had GDP per capita which was almost eight times as large as that in the twelve least open economies. There is a strong relationship between trade openness and per capita GDP and economic growth.

6-1 View Concept Check Questions Workbook

6-2-A "Foreign Exchange"

Introduction

This Reading focuses on the mechanics of the foreign exchange markets or the interbank market where most transactions take place. Candidates have to be familiar with the ways that foreign exchange rates are quoted, and whether they are on a direct or indirect basis. Reasonably simple computations of cross rates, spreads on spot and forward exchange rates, and discounts and premiums on forward rates need to be mastered. Finally, it is important that you understand the relationship between interest rate differentials and forward and spot rates which is called interest rate parity. Again you must be prepared to do calculations based on the interest rate parity equation.

LOS 6-2-A-a	**define** direct and indirect methods of foreign exchange quotations
LOS 6-2-A-d	**convert** direct (indirect) foreign exchange quotations into indirect (direct) foreign exchange quotations

Throughout these notes the notation used for quoting foreign exchange rates will be that /$ means the number of euros per dollar.

/$ = 0.90, means that one dollar can be converted in to 0.90 euros

$/ = 1.11, means that one euro can be converted in to 1.11 dollars

(note that 1.11 is the reciprocal of 0.90)

Direct exchange rates are the most common method of quoting rates, it means that the rate is the amount of domestic currency (DC) needed to purchase one unit of the foreign currency (FC).

In New York and London traders generally quotes the value of the FC in terms of one unit of the DC, this is an **indirect rate.**

Example 6-2: Direct and indirect quotations

In Japan the dollar exchange rate is 120 ¥/$, or 120 Japanese yen per dollar. This is a direct exchange rate quotation.

In New York the yen exchange rate is 120 ¥/$. This is an indirect exchange rate quotation.

Note that when a domestic currency appreciates a direct quote decreases (you need less of the domestic currency to buy a unit of foreign currency) and an indirect quote increases (one unit of domestic currency buys more of the foreign currency).

When quotations involve U.S. dollars, the dollar price of a unit of foreign currency is referred to as **American terms**, a direct quote in the U.S. The amount of the foreign currency for one U.S. dollar is called **European terms**, an indirect quote in the U.S.

LOS 6-2-A-b **calculate** the spread on a foreign currency quotation

Bid-ask spreads

Foreign exchange rates are quoted by dealers as bid-ask prices. The bid price is the price the dealer is willing to buy at and the ask, or offer price, is the price they are willing to sell at. The midpoint is the average of the two.

The bid-ask spread is given by:

$$\text{Percent spread} = \frac{\text{ask} - \text{bid}}{\text{ask}} \times 100 \qquad \textbf{(Equation 6-1)}$$

Example 6-3: Calculating spreads

If the /$ is quoted at 0.90100-0.90150, which means that one dollar will buy 0.90100 euros, or 0.90150 euros are needed to buy one dollar.

The spread is, using Equation 6-1:

$$\frac{\text{ask} - \text{bid}}{\text{ask}} \times 100 = \frac{(0.90150 - 0.90100)}{0.90150} \times 100 = 0.05546\%$$

LOS 6-2-A-c **explain** how spreads on foreign currency quotations can differ as a result of market conditions, bank/dealer positions, and trading volume

The spread will depend on a number of factors:

- volatility of the exchange rate, as volatility increases dealers will increase the spread as they require greater compensation for taking a position in a risky currency.
- spreads are higher for less actively traded currencies

A bank/dealer position such as shortage in a specific currency will lead to them moving the midpoint price, rather than the spread.

LOS 6-2-A-e **calculate** currency cross rates, given two spot exchange quotations involving three currencies

To calculate the exchange rate between two currencies, or the cross rate, it may be necessary to use the exchange rates of each currency against another currency, often the dollar. When calculating a cross rate assume that you are selling at the bid rate and buying at the ask rate.

Note that the DC/FC direct ask exchange rate is the reciprocal of the indirect bid exchange rate, and vice versa.

Mathematically this can be expressed as:

$$(FC_1/FC_2)_{ask} = (FC_1/DC)_{ask} \times (DC/FC_2)_{ask}$$
$$(FC_1/FC_2)_{bid} = (FC_1/DC)_{bid} \times (DC/FC_2)_{bid}$$

(Equations 6-2)

and

$$(FC_2/FC_1)_{ask} = 1/(FC_1/FC_2)_{bid}$$
$$(FC_2/FC_1)_{bid} = 1/(FC_1/FC_2)_{ask}$$

(Equations 6-3)

where FC_1 and FC_2 are the foreign currencies and DC the domestic currency.

Example 6-4: Currency cross rates

Hong Kong dollars are quoted at HK$/US$ = 7.99800-8.00200 (the bid-ask price) and the Thai Baht/US$ = 43.50000–43.53000. The cross rate for the HK$/Baht ask price can be calculated using Equations 6-2 and 6-3

define FC_1 as HK$, FC_2 as Thai Baht and DC as US$

$$(FC_1/FC_2)_{ask} = (FC_1/DC)_{ask} \times (DC/FC_2)_{ask}$$

$$HK\$/Baht_{ask} = HK\$/US\$_{ask} \times US\$/Baht_{ask}$$

$$HK\$/Baht_{ask} = HK\$/US\$_{ask} \times 1/Baht/US\$_{bid}$$

$$= 8.002 \times 0.02299$$

$$= 0.18395$$

LOS 6-2-A-f	**distinguish** between the spot and forward markets for foreign exchange
LOS 6-2-A-g	**calculate** the spread on a forward foreign currency quotation
LOS 6-2-A-h	**explain** how spreads on forward foreign currency quotations can differ as a result of market conditions, bank/dealer positions, trading volume, and maturity/length of contract

Forward exchange rates

In the **spot market** currencies are traded for immediate delivery (within 48 hours after the transaction takes place) whereas in the **forward market** transactions are made to buy and sell currencies for future delivery.

In the same way that spot rates are quoted bid-ask, forward rates are quoted with a spread. If a dealer quoted the six month /$ exchange rate as 0.90600-0.90650, it means that the dealer is willing to commit today to buy dollars at 0.90600 euros, or sell dollars at 0.90650 euros, in six months' time. The spread reflects the volatility and liquidity in the market. The spread tends to increase with a longer maturity contract since these contracts are less liquid.

Dealer positions will move the price, for example if the dealers have large inventory in a currency they are likely to lower the bid and ask prices to attract buyers, although this will not affect the spread.

LOS 6-2-A-i **calculate** a forward discount or premium and **express** either as an annualized rate

Forward premiums and discounts

The profit or loss on a forward transaction reflects the difference between the forward rate agreed in the contract and the spot rate at the time that the contract matures.

In the interbank market forward rates are quoted at a discount or premium to spot rates. The differential is the **swap rate.** There is a **forward discount** if the forward rate is below the spot rate (it is the 'weaker' currency)and a **forward premium** if it is above the spot rate (it is the 'stronger' currency).

To calculate the forward rate from the spot rate simply add the premium, or subtract the discount.

To express the discount or premium as an annualized percentage deviation from the spot rate, use the formula below:

$$\text{Forward premium/discount} = \frac{(F-S)}{S} \times \frac{12}{N} \qquad \textbf{(Equation 6-4)}$$

where

F = the forward rate
S = the spot rate
N = the number of months of the forward contract

Example 6-5: Forward premiums

The spot rate for pounds sterling to the U.S. dollar rate is \$/£ =1.5510 and the 90-day forward rate is \$/£ =1.5625, so pounds sterling are trading at a 115-point premium, points are counted from the last digit quoted.

The forward premium annualized is, using Equation 6-4,

$$= \frac{(F-S)}{S} \times \frac{12}{N}$$

$$= \frac{(1.5625-1.5510)}{1.5510} \times \frac{12}{3}$$

$$= 0.0297$$

or 2.97%

LOS 6-2-A-j explain interest rate parity

Interest Rate Parity

Arbitrage means that, in theory, exchange rates and risk-free interest rates are aligned.

More specifically, **interest rate parity theory** says that in an efficient market, with no transaction costs, the interest differential will equal the forward differential.

So a currency with a forward premium will have a low interest rate and a currency with a forward discount will have a higher interest rate.

Mathematically interest rate parity theory says:

$$\frac{F}{S} = \frac{(1 + r_{FC})}{(1 + r_{DC})} \qquad \text{(Equation 6-5)}$$

where

F	=	forward value of foreign currency per unit of domestic currency
S	=	spot value of foreign currency per unit of domestic currency
r_{FC}	=	foreign interest rate
r_{DC}	=	domestic interest rate

If one country has a higher interest rate than another, there will be forward discount on the currency. Conversely low interest rates will lead to forward premiums. Conceptually it means that if you can earn a higher rate of interest on one currency you will receive a lower exchange rate if you sell it forward than if you sell it today in the spot market. If this was not the case all investors would hold on to the currency offering the highest risk-free rate and sell the currency forward to lock into an 'attractive' exchange rate.

Example 6-6: Interest rate parity

One-year interest rates in the U.S. are 6% and in Japan are 1%. The spot rate is Yen/$ = 112.00 and the forward rate is Yen/$ = 106.72. Interest rate parity holds since:

$$\frac{(1+r_{FC})}{(1+r_{DC})} = \frac{1.06}{1.01} = 1.0495$$

$$\frac{F}{S} = \frac{0.9371}{0.8929} = 1.0495$$

We are defining the FC as the U.S. dollar.

This means that $1,000,000 invested for 1 year earning 6% (giving $1,060,000) will be worth the same as $1,000,000 converted into Japanese yen at 112, invested at 1%, and selling the proceeds of yen 113,120,000 forward into dollars at 106.72.

LOS 6-2-A-k **illustrate** covered interest arbitrage

If an interest rate differential exists it will produce the opportunity to make a profit, this is called **covered interest arbitrage**.

Example 6-7: Covered interest arbitrage

In Example 6-6 let us look at the case where Yen interest rates are 2% and the other data remains the same. We now have an opportunity to arbitrage since interest rate parity no longer holds.

If we borrow $1 million sell them into Yen at the spot rates and place them on deposit for one year, and at the same time sell the proceeds back into dollars in the forward market this will give

$1,000,000 converted to Yen 112,000,000, after one year at 2% gives Yen 114,240,000.
Sold forward at Yen/$ = 106.72, gives $1,070,465
Less borrowing costs for dollars of $60,000.
Profit is $10,465
This assumes zero transaction costs and the borrowing rate is the same as the risk-free rate.

6-2-A View Concept Check Questions Workbook

6-2-B "Foreign Exchange Parity Relations"

Introduction

We now look at different exchange rate systems before focusing on flexible or floating-rate systems where the rate is determined by supply and demand for the currency. Candidates need to be familiar with the main factors (growth in income, inflation and interest rates) that drive exchange rates and the impact of fiscal and monetary policy on exchange rates. The chapter finishes with the review of another parity relationship, the link between relative inflation rates and spot and forward rates.

LOS 6-2-B-a **explain** how exchange rates are determined in a flexible or floating exchange rate system

Flexible exchange rates (the same as floating exchange rates) are determined by supply and demand for different currencies. A flexible exchange rate system has the advantage of providing market-determined exchange rates and allows the government to adopt independent fiscal and monetary policies. The disadvantage is that exchange rates can be quite volatile.

The diagram below illustrates that as demand for foreign currency by U.S. citizens increases, perhaps for purchasing imports, if there is no equivalent increase in foreigners purchasing dollars, there will be a shortage of supply of foreign currency the exchange rate will rise. This will lead to foreign goods becoming more expensive which will reduce future U.S. imports which leads to an increase in supply of the foreign currency.

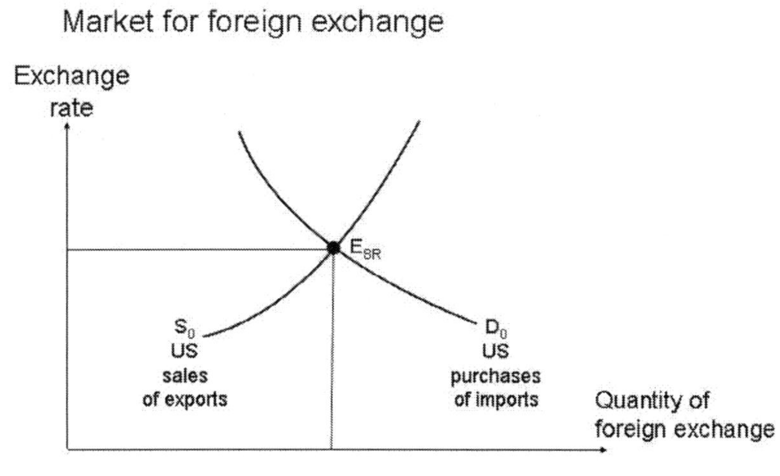

LOS 6-2-B-b	**explain** the role of each component of the balance-of-payments accounts

Balance of Payments

The **balance of payments** is a summary of all financial flows between a country and all other countries over a specific period. It therefore includes exports and imports of goods and services, capital movements, earnings by residents on overseas assets and foreigners' earnings on assets held in the country, and transactions by the central bank and government.

Imports are an example of a debit item since they create demand for a foreign currency whereas exports are a credit item since they create demand for the domestic currency. Foreign exchange markets will ensure that the quantity supplied and quantity demanded of a currency equal, so the total debits must equal the total credits.

Transactions are put into two categories, the current account and the financial account (sometimes called the capital account).

Current Account

The current account includes transactions that are done in the normal business by residents in the country.

The largest item is usually the balance of trade (merchandise exports less imports), but it also includes exports and imports of services (invisible services such as insurance and communication), and net current income on foreign investments and unilateral transfers (such as gifts). The current-account balance will be in surplus if the value of current exports plus earnings from investments abroad is higher than the value of its current imports plus earnings of foreigners on their domestic assets. Alternatively if the debit items are larger than the credit items, the country will have a current-account deficit.

Financial Account

The **financial account** includes (i) cross border direct investment and (ii) portfolio investment in equities, bonds etc. (iii) other investments and liabilities including borrowing from foreign banks.

The sum of the current and financial accounts is called the *overall* balance. If this is not zero, since the balance of payments must balance, then difference is accounted for by an increase or decrease in the central bank's **official reserves**. The official reserves refer to accounts held in foreign currencies and gold, which can be used by central banks to try to adjust or stabilize the exchange rate.

Under a pure flexible exchange rate system the official reserve transactions should be zero, an increase in the current-account deficit would lead to a greater capital-account surplus and so on.

LOS 6-2-B-c	**explain** how current account deficits or surpluses and financial account deficits or surpluses affect an economy

Current-account deficits are neither good nor bad for an economy and can persist over long periods of time. A current-account deficit means that there is a capital-account surplus (under a flexible rate system). The capital-account surplus could be the result of strong inward investment which is needed when domestic savings are insufficient to build an economy. The U.S .has had a persistent current-account deficit reflecting the low savings rate and the attractive investment environment, which brings in foreign investment to offset the current account outflows. On the other hand in the early nineties a number of Asian countries were running large current account deficits. Once foreign investors lost confidence in making investments in the countries leading to a rapid fall in capital inflows there was a major economic crisis and depreciation in the currencies.

LOS 6-2-B-d	**describe** the factors that cause a nation's currency to appreciate or depreciate

Factors affecting exchange rates

Inflation

When a country has a higher inflation rate than its trading partners its goods will look expensive. This will reduce the country's exports and increase its imports, which will increase demand for foreign currency leading to currency depreciation. Similarly relatively low inflation will lead to currency appreciation.

Real interest rates

When a country's real interest rates increase (relative to other countries) it will attract investment from overseas which will lead to currency appreciation. Similarly low real interest rates will lead to currency depreciation.

Economic growth

There are conflicting factors at work and it is unclear which is dominant. A strong economy will tend to attract overseas investors leading to currency appreciation. These flows are based on future expectations.

On the other hand increasing domestic income in a country relative to its trading partners will increase demand for foreign currency to buy imports, leading to depreciation in the currency. This will be a direct effect of strong economic growth. Similarly relatively slow growth in incomes will lead to an appreciation in the currency.

LOS 6-2-B-e	**explain** how monetary and fiscal policies affect the exchange rate and balance-of-payments components

Monetary Policy

An unanticipated move to a more expansionary policy will stimulate growth and net imports, push up inflation and reduce real interest rates. All of these factors will lead to a depreciation of the currency. Similarly an unanticipated move to a more restrictive monetary policy will lead to an appreciation in the currency.

So an expansionary monetary policy will initially tend to move the financial account to a deficit (or smaller surplus) and the current account towards a surplus (or smaller deficit), to offset the financial account deficit. It is assumed that the movement in capital flows, as a result of low real interest rates, takes effect more quickly. The opposite will happen if there is a shift to a more restrictive monetary policy.

However, longer term under an expansionary monetary policy the depreciation of the currency will lead to an increase in net exports.

Fiscal Policy

An expansionary fiscal policy will lead to higher demand and increasing inflation, which will tend to stimulate net imports putting downward pressure on the currency. However it will also lead to higher government borrowing which will increase real interest rates which will in turn pull in foreign capital and put upward pressure on the currency. Of the two conflicting pressures the inflow of foreign capital is likely to have the biggest impact in the short run since investors will be able to move more rapidly than importers and exporters.

A move to a restrictive fiscal policy will lead to lower demand and lower prices. This will help net exports and push up the exchange rate. However, the more immediate effect will be to lower real interest rates, leading to capital outflows and currency depreciation.

The impact of unanticipated changes in monetary and fiscal policies is summarized below:

	Expansionary monetary policy	**Restrictive monetary policy**	**Expansionary fiscal policy**	**Restrictive fiscal policy**
Exchange Rate	Depreciates	Appreciates	Likely to appreciate	Likely to depreciate
Real interest rates	Decrease	Increase	Increase	Decrease
Flow of capital	Outflow	Inflow	Inflow	Outflow
Current account	Towards surplus	Towards deficit	Towards deficit	Towards surplus

LOS 6-2-B-f **describe** a fixed exchange rate and a pegged exchange rate system

We have discussed flexible exchange rate systems, the other two types of exchange rate systems are:

1. Fixed exchange rate systems

In this system a fixed exchange rate is set by government policy rather than market supply and demand. A country that adopts a fixed rate system, in terms of fixing the domestic rate to a foreign currency, loses the flexibility to expand and contract the supply of money. For example, if the country's currency is linked to the U.S. dollar the central bank that decides the supply of money is the Federal Reserve. A currency can be fixed using a **currency board**. The role of the currency board is (i) to issue a currency with a fixed rate of exchange to another currency (ii) to redeem the currency at that fixed rate and (iii) to maintain assets (in the base currency) to back all of the currency issued.

2. Pegged rate systems

This is when the government makes a commitment to use fiscal and monetary policy to maintain the exchange rate at a fixed rate, or near a fixed rate, to another currency. The country must follow a monetary policy consistent with the country to which it has pegged its currency.

LOS 6-2-B-g **discuss** absolute purchasing power parity and relative purchasing power parity

Purchasing Power Parity

In the previous section we covered interest rate parity, as given in Equation 6-5, which links forward and spot rate to interest rate differential.

$$\frac{F}{S} = \frac{(1 + r_{FC})}{(1 + r_{DC})}$$

We now look at another relationship between exchange rates, this time with inflation rates. The inflation rate (I) is defined as the rise in the consumer price index over a specific period. The inflation differential is the difference between the inflation rates in two different countries.

Absolute Purchasing Power Parity (Absolute PPP)

This is based on the concept that the price of a good must be the same in all countries. So if a good costs \$1.00 in the U.S. and the exchange rate is /\$ = 0.90 then it will cost 0.90 in Europe. If in the following year the euro price rises by 10% to 0.99 and the U.S. price rises by 5% to \$1.05, unless the exchange rate adjusts to /\$ = 0.94, the good will have different prices in the two countries and trade flows will increase to take advantage of this differential which will bring the currencies back into line again.

If we look at the average for all goods in an economy we can extend the example to say that the exchange rate should be the ratio of the average price of all goods in the economy.

Relative Purchasing Power Parity (Relative PPP)

This is the most commonly used version of the purchasing power parities. It says that exchange rate movements will offset inflation differentials between two countries. The theory cannot be expected to always be valid, particularly in the short term.

This is expressed as:

$$\frac{S_1}{S_0} = \frac{(1 + I_{FC})}{(1 + I_{DC})} \qquad \textbf{(Equation 6-6)}$$

where

S_0 = spot exchange rate at the beginning of the period, the exchange rate is the foreign price of one unit of domestic currency

S_1 = spot exchange rate at the end of the period

I_{FC} = inflation rate over the period in the foreign country

I_{DC} = inflation rate over the period in the domestic country

Example 6-8: Purchasing power parity

The spot exchange rate for the Australian dollar against the pound (£) is Aus$/£ = 2.25.

Inflation in Australia is running at 5% per annum and in the U.K. at 3%. The end of period spot exchange rate can be calculated as, using Equation 6-6, with the U.K. as the domestic currency, as

$$\frac{S_1}{S_0} = \frac{(1 + I_{FC})}{(1 + I_{DC})}$$

$$\frac{S_1}{2.25} = \frac{1.05}{1.03}$$

$$S_1 = 2.29$$

This means that the pound is expected to strengthen as each pound will buy more Australian dollars in one year's time, reflecting the lower inflation rate in the U.K.

6-2-B View Concept Check Questions Workbook

STUDY SESSION 7

Investment Tools

Financial Statement Analysis: Basic Concepts

Overview

Financial Statement Analysis and Corporate Finance have a guideline weighting of 28% of the exam questions so this is a topic you must do well on. Candidates who are not financial analysts may well find they are not sufficiently familiar with the details of accounting practices such as the treatment of inventory, leases, deferred tax and depreciation. None of the material is difficult but you will need to spend time working through the text and applying your knowledge to practice questions. In many cases you will be required to do calculations but more importantly you must be able to interpret the numbers or ratios computed. The objective of building up knowledge of financial statements and accounting principles is to allow you to use financial statement data to better understand a company's operations and position relative to its competitors and in order to make investment decisions.

In Study Session 7 the main Reading Assignments cover two key topics. The first topic is accounting for income and assets including when items should be recognized on the income statement and balance sheet. The second topic is analyzing cash flows and being able to differentiate between operating, investing and financing cash flows.

Candidates who have studied accounting at an introductory level and are familiar with the relationship between the items on the income statement, balance sheet and cash flow statement and have knowledge of the basic concepts used in financial reporting will not need to spend much time on the Preliminary Readings. It is important to note that the CFA Institute states that examination questions are drawn mainly from the subsequent Reading Assignments.

Preliminary Reading Assignments

Financial Accounting, Belverd E. Needles, Jr., and Marian Powers, 8th edition, (Houghton Mifflin, 2004)

P1-A. "Measuring Business Income," Ch. 3

P1-B. "Financial Reporting and Analysis," Ch. 5, pp. 246–258

P1-C. "Short-Term Liquid Assets," Ch. 7

P1-D. "Inventories," Ch. 8

P1-E. "Current Liabilities and the Time Value of Money," Ch. 9, pp. 412–426

P1-F. "Long-Term Assets," Ch. 10

P1-G. "Long-Term Liabilities," Ch. 11

P1-H. "Contributed Capital," Ch. 12

P1-I. "The Corporate Income Statement and the Statement of Stockholders' Equity," Ch. 13

P1-J. "The Statement of Cash Flows," Ch. 14

The Analysis and Use of Financial Statements, 3rd edition, Gerald I. White, Ashwinpaul C. Sondhi, and Dov Fried (Wiley, 2003)

P2. "Framework for Financial Statement Analysis," Ch. 1, pp. 1–26

Note: http://snipurl.com/Workbook Preliminary Reading Assignments and Concept Question Workbook

7-1-A "Accounting Income and Assets: the Accrual Concept"

Introduction

This Reading looks at the income statement (using accounting income as opposed to economic or other forms of income) and the balance sheet. The Reading focuses on the different methods for revenue recognition and discusses the areas where management has the most discretion with respect to revenue recognition. The balance sheet is also analyzed and in particular the components of stockholders' equity identified. The trickiest part of this Reading concerns accounting for long-term projects using the percentage-of-completion method or completed contract methods. You need to be familiar with the calculations using either method and also understand the impact on the financial statements of the choice of method used.

Main Readings Assignments

The Analysis and Use of Financial Statements, 3rd edition, Gerald I. White, Ashwinpaul C. Sondhi, and Dov Fried (Wiley, 2003)

7-1-A "Accounting Income and Assets: The Accrual Concept," Ch. 2, (including Box 2-5)

7-1-B "Analysis of Cash Flows," Ch. 3, pp. 74• 83, 84 (including Box 3-1) and 87• 99

LOS 7-1-A-a	**describe** the format of the income statement and **describe** the components of net income

The chapter starts with a discussion of different types of income:

Economic earnings – net cash flow plus the change in market value of the firm's assets.

Distributable earnings – amount of earnings that can be paid out as dividends without changing the value of the firm.

Sustainable earnings – level of income that can be maintained in the future given the firm's stock of capital investment (e.g. fixed assets and inventory).

Permanent earnings – the market value of the firm's assets multiplied by the firm's required rate of return.

Accounting income – net cash flow plus change in asset value that generally recognizes changes in value resulting from actual transactions. Using the accrual concept means that cash inflows and outflows are recognized in the relevant accounting period i.e. when services are provided rather than when cash is actually collected.

An example of the format of an income statement is given below.

INCOME STATEMENT

Revenues from sales of goods and services	
-	Operating expenses
=	Operating income from continuing operations
+	Other income and revenues
=	Recurring income before interest and taxes from continuing operations
-	Financing costs
=	Recurring (pretax) income from continuing operations
+/-	Unusual or infrequent items
=	Pretax earnings from continuing operations
-	Income tax expense
=	Net income from continuing operations
+/-	Income from discontinued operations (net of tax)
+/-	Extraordinary items (net of tax)
+/-	Cumulative effect of changes in accounting principles
=	Net income

The income statement starts with revenues generated by the sales of goods and services from the firm's continuing operations. It is important that revenue and income from continuing operations is separated from income from discontinued operations since the income from discontinued operations will not contribute to future profits.

Operating expenses which include both the cost of purchasing or manufacturing the goods sold (COGS = cost of goods sold) and selling, general and administrative expenses (SG&A expenses) are deducted from the revenues to give the operating profit from continuing operations.

Other income may result from investment in other firms, gains or losses on the sale of assets. This income will contribute to the recurring income before income and taxes from continuing operations. This is the profit which is independent of how the firm is financed.

Next, the financing costs or interest expanse is deducted to arrive at recurring income from continuing operations. Items that are classified as unusual or infrequent items (e.g. pretax gains or losses from the sale of assets or investments) are added/deducted and the income tax expense is deducted to arrive at net income from continuing operations.

Finally income from discontinued operations, extraordinary items and the impact of accounting changes made over the period are recorded, all of these items are net of tax. This gives net income for the firm. For analysts the focus is usually on the income for m continuing operations rather income after nonrecurring items.

LOS 7-1-A-b **explain** the importance of the matching principle for revenue and expense recognition

The **matching principle** states that related revenues and expenses should be accounted for in the same time period. This means that operating performance is measured in the period when goods are recorded as sold rather than when collections or expenditures occur.

Example 7-3: Matching principle

The cost of inventory is recorded in the same period as the sale of the inventory is recorded.

LOS 7-1-A-c **identify** the requirements for revenue recognition to occur

Revenue and Expense Recognition

Following on from the accrual concept it is important to address two issues – timing and measurement of revenue and expense. When should they be recognized and how much should be recognized?

There are two conditions for revenue recognition to take place.

1. Completion of the earning process

The firm must have provided all or virtually all of the goods or services and there is no remaining contingent obligation to provide further services. It must be possible to reliably estimate the total associated costs and there must be no significant contingent liabilities outstanding. An example of this is when a firm provides a warranty to replace or upgrade a product and cannot estimate the cost of replacement.

2. Assurance of payment

This means that the sales proceeds have been received, or can reasonably be expected to be collected.

LOS 7-1-A-d	**identify** and **describe** the appropriate revenue recognition, given the status of completion of the earning process and the assurance of payment

The amount of revenue recognized at any point is:

$$= \frac{\text{Goods and services provided to date}}{\text{Total goods and services to be provided}} \times \text{Total expected revenue}$$

Revenues reported in a period will be the total revenue recognized less the revenue recognized in prior periods.

Usually revenue recognition will take place at the time of sale. Additionally revenue recognition can be based on cash expenditures, time or provision of services or goods.

Example 7-4: Revenue recognition

1. Magazine publishers receive subscriptions prior to delivery of the magazine. In this case revenues are recognized in proportion to issues delivered.

2. Credit card fees, revenues are recorded as the right to use the card expires.

3. Revenue from leased equipment is recognized on time or usage basis.

Two factors have increased concern over the application of the principles for recognizing revenues and expenses. The first of these is the growth in technology and the second is the trend towards valuing companies using revenues and gross margins rather than net income.

There is considerable room for management discretion in deciding:

1. Timing - when revenue and expense should be recognized.
2. Measurement - how much revenue or expense should be recognized?

Examples of issue that make it difficult to compare revenues of different firms are shown below.

Revenue Recognition

- Sales incentives – such as discounts to customers are not recorded.
- Barter agreements – goods are supplied in exchange for other goods or services, they may not be recorded at market value.
- Membership fees - recorded as revenue when the agreement is signed rather than over the term of the membership.
- Recording revenues based on estimated usage.
- Agents recording total billings rather than commissions earned.
- Recognizing revenues before a customer has agreed a project is complete.
- Including shipping and handling costs in revenues.

Expense recognition

- Deferral of marketing expenses.
- Deferral of the cost of major maintenance work until work is actually done – an alternative method is to accrue the costs in advance.
- Bad debt expenses – estimating future bad debts and setting up a reserve account is another way of smoothing earnings. When a write-off occurs it is charged to the reserve not earnings.
- Warranty expense – again the estimated future expense can be used to smooth earnings.

Software revenue recognition

Four conditions must be satisfied before a software transaction can be recorded as revenue

- Persuasive evidence of an arrangement between buyer and seller
- Delivery
- A fixed or determinable fee
- Assurance of collectibilty

LOS 7-1-A-e discuss different revenue recognition methods and their implications for financial analysis

In some cases revenue recognition is prior to the sale or delivery. The percentage of completion, completed contract methods which can be used for long–term contracts are discussed in more detail in LOS 7-1-A-k and l.

The two methods below are used when there is uncertainty concerning the collection of the sales revenue or the size of the costs.

Installment method

This method is used when there is no reasonable way to calculate the collectability of receivables. Under the installment method gross profit is recognized in proportion to cash collections, as opposed to recognizing the revenue at the time of sale.

Cost recovery method

Costs to provide a good or service cannot always be reasonably estimated, for example the development of a housing project where future costs may depend on planning decisions. There may be also uncertainty over the collectability of receivables, for example if purchasers are only making small deposits at the time of sale. In these cases the cost recovery method should be used and all cash receipts are used to cover costs before income can be recognized.

These two methods may be used for real estate sales and also for recording franchise sales where the revenue is to be collected over a number of years.

LOS 7-1-A-h	**describe** the types and analysis of unusual or infrequent items, extraordinary items, discontinued operations, accounting changes, and prior period adjustments

Nonrecurring Items

Nonrecurring items can be divided into four categories:

1. **Unusual or infrequent items** (but not both), these should be disclosed separately as a component of income from continuing operations.

Examples include:

- gains or losses from disposal of part of a business sector
- gains or losses from disposal of investments in affiliates or subsidiaries
- provisions for environmental remediation
- impairments, write-offs and restructuring costs
- expenses related to integrating acquired companies

2. **Extraordinary items**. Extraordinary items must be unusual **and** occur infrequently **and** be material in amount. They must be reported separately net of income tax. They are also reported at the earnings per share level.

Examples include:

- foreign government expropriation of a firm's assets
- prior to 2002 gains or losses due to early retirement of debt could be classified as extraordinary items

3. **Discontinued operations**. The business being discontinued must be totally separable from that of the firm to qualify for it to be reported in this category. The date when the management formally decides to sell is defined as the measurement date. Income prior to this is reported separately net of tax. After the measurement date income is offset against the gain or loss on disposal.

4. **Accounting changes** – when a firm changes from one method to another prior year results are not normally restated. The net cumulative effect on net income in prior year periods is reported on the current income statement after extraordinary items and discontinued operations.

Examples include

- changing from LIFO to FIFO for inventory accounting (see study session 8)
- changing to percentage of completion method for accounting for projects
- changing accounting for the value of pension plan assets

It is important that analysts do not rely on a company's classification of which items are nonrecurring and they need to take an independent view. Although the focus of analysis will be on recurring income non recurring items have implications for reported income in prior years (if they are effectively a correction of previously stated income) as well as future earnings (e.g. write downs will reduce future depreciation charges).

It is also important to consider the cash flow implications and distinguish between items that have no cash flow implications (e.g. write downs), affect current cash flows (e.g. company restructuring) and future cash flows.

IAS 8 deals with the treatment of nonrecurring items under IAS GAAP. The treatment is broadly similar to U.S. GAAP with the following exceptions:

- IAS has slightly different definitions of extraordinary items.
- IAS 8 does not require separate reporting of earnings from continuing operations, discontinued operations and before extraordinary items.
- When there are accounting changes under IAS 8 either prior years can be restated or the cumulative effect of the changes can be reported.
- Errors can be corrected by either restating prior periods or including the difference in the current period's earnings (U.S. treatment).

IAS 35 deals with the treatment of discontinued operations. Again there are some differences IAS GAAP and U.S. GAAP.

- Whereas U.S. GAAP accrues estimated losses from a discontinued operation, IAS GAAP requires the loss is reported.
- Under IAS GAAP impairment losses associated with discontinued operations can be reported as part of the loss from continued operations.
- Discontinuation dates may differ under IAS versus U.S. GAAP.

LOS 7-1-A-i	**discuss** managerial discretion in areas such as classification of good news/bad news, income smoothing, big bath behavior, and accounting changes, and **explain** how this discretion can affect the financial statements

There is a fair degree of management discretion as regards to timing of an event and classification of an item (e.g. unusual or extraordinary). The following are ways that management can manipulate earnings:

- Classification of good/bad news - management may report good news as part of continuing operations and bad news as part of discontinued operations or as an extraordinary item.
- Income smoothing - this can be through the choice of the accounting method, timing of expenditures or classificatory smoothing where an item may be classed as either income from ordinary operations or an extraordinary item.
- 'Big bath' accounting - this is when management prefers to record all the bad news in one year so they can move forward to report healthier profits.
- Accounting changes - this includes voluntary and mandatory changes, in many cases they are used to smooth earnings.

LOS 7-1-A-j	**describe** the format and the components of the balance sheet

Balance Sheet

The balance sheet, or statement of financial position, reports the assets (resources), liabilities (claims on the resources) and stockholders' equity at a specific point in time. Assets equal liabilities plus stockholders' equity. The balance sheet is an important source of information for an analyst; it provides information on the resources of a company that can be used to generate future profit. Also creditors will use a balance sheet to provide information on the assets available to repay debt.

Assets are classified as current assets if they are to be converted into cash or used within one year or operating cycle if this is longer than a year. Similarly current liabilities include obligations that are to be settled within one year or operating cycle, if it is longer.

An example of items that are included in a balance sheet is given below:

BALANCE SHEET	Notes
ASSETS	
Current Assets	
Cash and cash equivalents	Risk-free assets, originally purchased with 90-days or less to maturity
Marketable securities	
Accounts receivable	Includes trade receivables (from customers) and notes receivable (from asset sales or loans to management)
Inventories	
Deferred income taxes	These will be reported as an expense in the future
Prepaid expense	These will be reported as an expense in the future
Deferred taxes	
Property, Plant and Equipment	Reported less accumulated depreciation
Capital leases	
Investment in affiliates	
Prepaid pension costs	
Intangible assets	Includes goodwill, brand names etc.

LIABILITIES	
Current Liabilities	
Accounts payable	Includes trade payables (amounts owing to suppliers) and obligations to employees.
Current portion of debt	Debt to be repaid within a year
Income tax liability	
Advance billings	
Long-Term Liabilities	
Bonds payable	
Other long-term debt	
Capital leases	
Deferred income tax	
Minority interests in consolidated subsidiaries	Amount of consolidated net assets that does not belong to the firm

STOCKHOLDERS' EQUITY	
Preferred stock	
Common stock	
Additional paid-in capital	
Retained Earnings	Profits not paid out to stockholders but retained in the company
Cumulative translation adjustment	For foreign currency
Minimum pension liability	
Unrealized gains and losses	
Treasury stock	Shares repurchased by the company

Generally items are recorded on the balance sheet at historic cost, although in some cases these are adjusted to a value closer to net realizable value.

In some cases items that will reduce the value of a long-lived asset will be recorded in a contra account. Similarly an adjunct account can be used to accumulate changes in asset and liability values.

LOS 7-1-A-k **describe** the format, classification, and use of each component of the statement of stockholders' equity

Stockholders' Equity

Generally the components of stockholders' equity are reported in the order of preference in liquidation.

The par value and additional paid up capital of common and preferred stock (but not redeemable preferred) represent the investment in the company by the owners. Retained earnings are the profits that have been reinvested in the company. Additionally the following changes may also be included:

1. Cumulative foreign exchange adjustments
2. Changes in minimum liability for an under funded pension scheme
3. Unrealized gains and losses on cash flow hedges
4. Changes in market values of non current investments
5. Unearned shares issued to stock ownership plans

LOS 7-1-A-f	**identify** the appropriate income statement and balance sheet entries using the percentage-of-completion method and the completed contract method

We discuss below two methods for reporting revenues from long-term and short-term projects, such as building and construction projects.

Percentage-of-completion method

This method should only be used for long-term projects where (i) there is a contract and (ii) reliable estimates for the percentage of the project completed and revenues and costs.

Progress is measured either using engineering estimates or the percentage of costs incurred to total costs. We use the percentage of costs incurred in Example 7-5 below.

When there is a change in estimates the adjustment is made in the same accounting period and prior period adjustments are not made.

Completed contract method

Revenues and expenses are only recognized at the end of the project. It must be used for short-term contracts and when the percentage-of-completion method cannot be used.

The choice of method will have an impact on the income statement and balance sheet of the firm doing the project, this is summarized below.

	Percentage-of-completion method	Completed contract method
Income Statement	Revenues, expenses and income are reported throughout the contract period, based on the percentage of total costs incurred in each period.	Revenues, expenses and income are not recognized until the end of the project.
Balance Sheet	Costs are recorded as an asset (construction in progress). Also gross profit or income is recorded as part of construction in progress Amounts billed to the customer are liabilities (advance billing) and an asset (accounts receivable). Construction in progress and advance billings are netted off in the financial reports.	Expenditures prior to completion are reported as inventory (construction in progress) and cash receipts as advances from customers. these are netted off in the financial reports.

At the end of a project the construction in progress and advance billings are brought to zero and only cash and retained earnings will remain in the accounts.

Example 7-5: Accounting for projects

Towbridge Engineering entered into a contract to build a road. The contract price agreed was $10 million and the estimated cost was $8 million, the project was expected to take 3 years to complete. The following information is provided:

		2002	2003	2004
Costs incurred	**current year**	$2 million	$4 million	$2 million
	cumulative	$2 million	$6 million	$8 million
Amounts billed and cash received	**current year**	$3 million	$3 million	$4 million
	cumulative	$3 million	$6 million	$10 million

Income statement

$million

	Percentage-of-Completion			Completed Contract Method		
	Revenue	**Expense**	**Income**	**Revenue**	**Expense**	**Income**
2002	2.5	2.0	0.5	0	0	0
2003	5.0	4.0	1.0	0	0	0
2004	2.5	2.0	0.5	10.0	8.0	2.0
Total	10.0	8.0	2.0	10.0	8.0	2.0

Note: under the percentage-of-completion method revenue in 2002 is recognized based on the percentage of costs incurred [($2 million/$8 million) x $10 million] using the matching principle. A similar calculation is used in 2003 and 2004.

Balance Sheet

Percentage-of-Completion Method			
$ million	**Assets**	**Liabilities**	**Equity**
2002	1.0	0.5	0.5
2003	1.5	0.0	1.5
2004	2.0	0.0	2.0

assets = cash plus construction in progress (netted against liabilities)

liabilities = advance billings, netted against construction in progress

equity = revenues less costs incurred, refer to income statement above

Notes for 2002

cash = cash received of \$3 million – costs incurred of \$2 million
= \$1 million
construction in progress = costs incurred of \$2 million + recognized profit \$0.5 million
= \$2.5 million
advance billings = \$3 million, this is netted against construction in progress of \$2.5 million, to give liabilities of \$0.5 million

Notes for 2003

cash = \$6 million –\$6 million (use cumulative figures)
= \$0 million
construction in progress = \$6 million + \$1.5 million
= \$7.5 million
advance billings = \$6 million, this is netted against construction in progress of \$7.5 million, to give assets of \$1.5 million

Notes for 2004

cash = \$10 million – \$8 million (use cumulative figures)
= \$2 million
construction in progress = \$8 million + \$2 million
advance billings = \$10 million, this is netted against construction in progress of \$10.0 million, to give liabilities of \$0 million

Completed Contract Method			
\$ million	**Assets**	**Liabilities**	**Equity**
2002	1.0	1.0	0.0
2003	0.0	0.0	0.0
2004	2.0	0.0	2.0

assets = cash plus construction in progress (netted against liabilities)
liabilities = advance billings, netted against construction in progress
equity = revenues less costs incurred, recognized in last year

Notes for 2002

cash = \$1 million
construction in progress = costs incurred of \$2 million
advance billings = \$3 million, this is netted against construction in progress of \$2 million, to give liabilities of \$1 million

Notes for 2003

cash = $0 million
construction in progress = costs incurred of $6 million
advance billings = $6 million, this is netted against construction in progress of $6 million

Notes for 2004

cash = cash received of $10 million – costs incurred of $8 million
construction in progress = costs incurred of $8 million + recognized profit $2 million
advance billings = $10 million, this is netted against construction in progress of $10 million

The percentage-of-completion method is generally preferred by analysts since it gives more information about a company's operating activity.

LOS 7-1-A-g **describe** and **calculate** the effects on cash flows and selected financial ratios that result from using the percentage-of-completion method versus the completed contract method

The impact of a decision to use percentage of completion method on the financial statements is shown below. Note that the differences are throughout the life of the project, when the project is completed the umbers will be the same under both methods. It is assumed that the project is profitable.

Reported cash flows will be the same throughout the life of the project.

	Percentage-of-completion method
Income Statement	Income is higher throughout the project.
Balance Sheet	Total assets are higher, when construction in progress exceeds billings. Liabilities are lower since construction in progress is a larger offsetting item. Equity is higher as income is accrued throughout the project.

The impact on the financial statements will follow through to financial ratios so for example the liabilities to equity will be lower.

It should be noted that the total revenues, expenses and income at the end of the life of the project will be the same under both methods. Also reported cash flows will be the same throughout the life of the project.

7-1-A View Concept Check Questions Workbook

7-1-B "Analysis of Cash Flows"

Introduction

Cash flows are critical, not only do they provide the link between the income statement and balance sheet but they provide data which is less susceptible to being distorted by management choices on accounting methods. A net cash flow number is not particularly helpful; to understand the dynamics of a company the breakdown of the cash flow into cash flow from operating, financing and investing activities is far more useful. Most cash flows fall into the operating category and reflect the ability of the company to generate funds internally. Investing cash flows provide information on the cash being used to buy assets which will maintain current capacity and support future growth. Financing cash flows reflect the capital structure of the company and the cash that is being paid, or collected, from providers of capital (but be careful, interest paid, interest and dividends received are operating cash flows under U.S. GAAP).

For the exam candidates need to be comfortable using the direct and indirect method to compute a statement of cash flows.

LOS 7-1-B-a	**describe** the elements of cash flow from 1) operations, 2) investing, and 3) financing

Statement of Cash Flows

The statement of cash flows reports the cash inflows and outflows for a company over a period. It provides a link between the beginning and end-period balance sheets and provides additional information to that provided by the balance sheet and income statement.

The cash flow is broken into three components:

Cash Flow from Operations (CFO) – this is the amount of cash generated by a firm as a result of its production of goods and services. A company undergoing rapid growth might show negative cash flow from operations. Longer term a company should be able to achieve positive cash flow from operations in order to pay dividends, repay debt and fund expansion.

Cash Flow from Investing (CFI) – this is the amount of cash generated from the purchase and sale of productive assets and investments. This is necessary to maintain and expand a company's operating capacity.

Cash Flow from Financing (CFF) – this is the amount of cash used to pay dividends and repurchase shares, repay borrowings and the cash received from the issue of equity and debt.

LOS 7-1-B-b	**classify** a particular transaction or item as cash flow from 1) operations, 2) investing, or 3) financing

Classification of individual items

The following tables link cash flow items to the income statement and changes in the balance sheet accounts.

Cash Flow from Operations (CFO)	Income Statement	Balance Sheet
Cash received from customers	Sales	Accounts receivable, advances from customers
Cash paid for inputs and operating expenses	COGS, SG&A expense, rent expense	Inventories, accounts payable, prepaid expenses, rent payable, accrued expenses
Interest paid	Interest expense	Interest payable
Income tax paid	Income tax expense	Income tax payable, deferred income taxes
Cash Flow from Investing (CFI)	**Income Statement**	**Balance Sheet**
Capital expenditures	Depreciation and amortization expense	Property, plant and equipment, intangible assets
Cash paid for and received from investments in affiliates	Equity in income of affiliates	Investment in affiliates
Cash paid for and received from investments	Realized gains or losses on investments	Short and long-term investments and gains (losses) on certain investments
Cash paid for acquisitions and received from divestitures		Assets and liabilities resulting from acquisitions and divestitures

Cash flow from financing activities

Cash Flow from Financing (CFF)	Income Statement	Balance Sheet
Increase or decrease in debt		Notes payable, short and long-term debt, bonds payable
Equity financing or repurchase of stock		Increase or decrease in equity
Dividends paid		Retained earnings, dividends payable

It is important to note that an increase/decrease in an asset represents a net cash outflow/inflow respectively. Similarly an increase/decrease in a liability represents a net cash inflow/outflow.

Example 7-6: Cash flows

A company's accounts receivable decline, this means that cash collections have exceeded sales, so this will have a positive influence on cash flow.

LOS 7-1-B-c **compute** and **interpret** a statement of cash flows, using the direct method and the indirect method

To calculate cash flow from operations one can use either the direct or indirect method:

1. Direct method

The direct method identifies the items shown in the tables in the above LOS 7-1-B-c above to compute the cash flow from operations.

2. Indirect method

This method starts with the net income number and adjusts for:

1. Non-cash revenues and expenses
2. Non-operating items in the income statement
3. Changes in operating asset and liability accounts.

Example 7-7: Computing cash flows

Molesely Corp. provides the following information in its financial statements:

2004

Income Statement (in $'000)

Sales	1,000
COGS	(750)
Operating expense	(100)
Depreciation expense	(35)
Rent expense	(15)
Interest expense	(40)
Income before taxes	60
Income tax expense	(20)
Net income after taxes	40

Balance Sheet (in $'000)

	end 2003	**end 2004**
Assets		
Cash	35	50
Accounts receivable	50	60
Inventory	250	300
Property, plant & equip.	170	190 net of acc. depreciation
Total Assets	505	600
Liabilities		
Bank notes	0	50
Accounts payable	30	45
Advances from customers	15	45
Deferred taxes	90	40
Dividends payable	0	0
Stockholders' Equity		
Common stock	120	150
Retained earnings	250	270
Total Liabilities and Equity	505	600

Total dividends of $20,000 were declared.

The cash flow from operations can be calculated two ways:

1. Direct method

Cash collection

Sales	1000
Increase in receivables	(10)
Increase in advances	30

Cash input			
COGS		(750)	
Increase in inventory		(50)	
Increase in accounts payable		15	
Cash expenses			
Operating expense		(100)	
Rent expense		(15)	
Increase in accrued liabilities		0	
Cash taxes paid			
Tax expense		(20)	
Increase in deferred taxes		(50)	
Cash interest paid			
Interest expense		(40)	
Increase in interest payable		0	
Cash flow from operations	**10**		

2. Indirect method

Net income		40	
Adjust for			
Depreciation		35	non cash expense
Increase in deferred taxes		(50)	decrease in liability
Increase in accounts receivable		(10)	increase in asset
Increase in inventory		(50)	increase in asset
Increase in accounts payable		15	increase in liability
Increase in advances from customers		30	increase in liability
Cash flow from operations	**10**		
Cash flow from investments			
Capital expenditure		(55)	
Investment in affiliates		0	
Cash flow from investments	**(55)**		
Cash flow from financing			
Increase in borrowing		50	
Increase in stock outstanding		30	
Dividends paid		(20)	
Cash flow from financing	**60**		
Net cash flow	**15**		

Note: Property, plant and equipment is quoted net of depreciation. To calculate the investing cash flow, add together the increase in net value of property, plant and equipment and the depreciation expense.

The net cash flow is equivalent to the change in cash balances between year-ends.

Molesely Corp. has a small positive cash flow from operations, but insufficient to cover the investment spending. The investment spending has been paid for by an increase in equity and bond financing (cash flow from financing). A weak operating cash flow might indicate the company is in the growth phase, or possibly there are problems such as difficulty collecting receivables, poor inventory management etc.

Analysis of Cash Flows

The cash flow statement is important because it gives a true picture of what events have occurred without the distortion of the choice of accounting assumptions e.g. whether a project uses the completed contract method or percentage-of-completion method of revenue recognition it will produce the same cash flow entries.

Analysis of the cash flow statement gives information on:

1. The company's ability to generate cash flows from its operating activities.
2. The impact of investing and financing decisions.

Problems mainly occur in the classification of different cash flows between operating, investment and financing activities. These include:

- Operating cash flows do not include the cost of using the productive capacity i.e. plant cost. Positive cash flow from operations does not imply that there is sufficient cash flow to replace the productive capacity as needed.
- Cash flows involved in paying operating leases will go through as operating cash flows, whereas an outright purchase of assets is an investing cash flow, this is not consistent.
- If a company has acquired another company and has taken over its inventory the cost of this will be recorded in investing cash flows, but sales of the inventory will go through operating cash flows.
- Interest income and dividends received from investments in other firms are classified as operating cash flows (under U.S. GAAP).
- Interest payments are classified as operating cash flows whereas part of these payments reflects debt financing. However dividends paid are reported in financing cash flows (under U.S. GAAP).

Some transactions do not require cash outlays, such as taking on a mortgage.

LOS 7-1-B-d **describe** and **compute** free cash flow

Free cash flow (FCF) measures the amount of cash available to a company for discretionary spending after making all required cash outlays. The free cash flow can be used for expansion, reducing debt, and paying dividends. The calculation of free cash flow varies from analyst to analyst but a standard definition is:

FCF = cash flow from operations - cash required to maintain the firm's present productive capacity

In many cases capital expenditure is used as a proxy for the cash required to maintain existing capacity due to the difficulty in deciding which capital expenditure is being used for maintenance and which for expansion.

An alternative method is to use cash flow from operations less depreciation, since depreciation is proxy for the cost of using productive capacity. However this is not recommended since depreciation is based on the historic cost of assets.

Another issue is whether we are calculating FCF available to the **firm** which means to all providers of capital whether debt or equity. In this case we should look at the cash flow **before** interest. However if we are looking at FCF available to **equity shareholders** we should calculate the FCF **after** interest, since the debt holders need to be paid first.

Example 7-8: Free cash flow

Using the data in Example 7-7 for Molesely Corp.

Free cash flow to equity shareholders

= cash flow from operations - capital expenditure
= 10 - 55
= (45)

This shows that the company, rather than having cash available to repay debt or pay dividends to stockholders, is depending on raising debt and equity finance for its operations and spending. Further analysis may show that in fact a large proportion of the capital expenditure is for expansion, and the company is in a growth phase which requires outside financing.

LOS 7-1-B-e **distinguish** between the U.S. GAAP and IAS GAAP classifications of dividends paid or received and interest paid or received for statement of cash flow purposes

There are a number of differences between IAS GAAP and U.S. GAAP in the treatment of interest and dividends paid or received. These are summarized in the table below.

	U.S. GAAP	IAS GAAP
Bank overdrafts	A liability- changes shown in cash flow statement	Often part of cash equivalents, changes **not** shown in cash flow statement
Interest and dividends received	CFO	Either CFO or CFI
Interest paid	CFO	Either CFO or financing CFF
Dividends paid	CFF	Either CFO or CFF

7-1-B View Concept Check Questions Workbook

STUDY SESSION 8

Investment Tools

Financial Statement Analysis: Financial Ratios and Earnings per Share

Overview

Analyzing financial statements through the use of ratios is the backbone of this Study Session. Numbers taken from financial statements are, on their own, fairly meaningless. It is only when the relationship between the numbers or ratios are computed that we can start to get an idea of the financial strength and profitability of the company. When we start comparing the ratios of a company with its own past ratios or with ratios of other companies in the industry we get a much clearer idea of the company's relative performance.

The next Reading Assignment looks at the calculation of earnings per share and how to accommodate potentially dilutive securities which, if exercised or converted, would lead to lower earnings per share. Finally there are two Readings on financial shenanigans which are used by companies to manipulate reported earnings. The Readings identify the most commonly used tricks and the effect on revenues, income and liabilities.

Reading Assignments

Investment Analysis and Portfolio Management, 7th edition, Frank K. Reilly and Keith C. Brown (Dryden, 2003)

8-1. "Analysis of Financial Statements," Ch. 10, pp. 319• 358 and Exhibits 10.1, 10.2, and 10.3

Intermediate Accounting, 11th edition, Donald E. Kieso, Jerry J. Weygandt and Terry D. Warfield (Wiley, 2004)

8-2. "Dilutive Securities and Earnings per Share," Ch. 16, pp. 788–801 and Appendix 16B pp. 809-814

Financial Shenanigans, 2nd edition, Howard Schilit (McGraw-Hill, 2002)

8-3-A. "Seek and Ye Shall Find," Ch. 2

8-3-B. "Searching for Shenanigans," Ch. 3

8-1 "Analysis of Financial Statements"

Introduction

This Reading includes the definitions of a large number of ratios and candidates should attempt to memorize the ratios. Although some of the definitions may differ from those you are familiar with the definitions given in the source text, and used in these notes, should be the ones applied in the exam. Candidates will not only be expected to calculate ratios but more importantly to be able to use ratios to draw conclusions about a company's performance both over time and relative to other participants in the market and industry. Ratios not only reflect the profitability of a company and its growth prospects but also its capital structure and the risk inherent in its business and as a result of financing decisions. Finally, the DuPont analysis of return on equity and the calculation of the sustainable growth rate of a company are important topics to revise.

The main categories of analysis where financial ratios are used are as follows:

1. Common size statements
2. Internal liquidity (solvency)
3. Operating performance
    a. operating efficiency
    b. operating profitability
4. Risk Analysis
    c. business risk

a. financial risk
    d. liquidity risk

5. Growth analysis

We will discuss the definition of the ratios used and the application and interpretation of the ratios one by one for Ripley Corporation, whose financial statements are shown below. It is important to always consider ratios in the context of the firm's industry, its major competitors, the market and the overall economy as well as against the company's own history.

Financial information used in Examples 8-1 to 8-7

RIPLEY CORPORATION BALANCE SHEET Year end December 31st 2003 and 2004, US$ million		
	2003	**2004**
Assets		
Current Assets		
Cash and cash equivalents	950	1,350
Accounts receivable	14,200	13,600
Inventories	2,500	4,600
Other current assets	235	765
Total Current Assets	17,885	20,315
Property, plant and equipment (net of accumulated depreciation)	124,000	128,050
Other noncurrent assets	36,600	35,700
Total Assets	178,485	184,065

Liabilities and Shareholders' Equity		
Current Liabilities		
Short-term debt	500	455
Trade accounts payable	8,100	7,345
Accrued expenses and other liabilities	17,885	9,756
Income taxes payable	827	956
Total Current Liabilities	27,312	18,512

Long-term debt	25,000	25,000
Other noncurrent liabilities	0	0
Deferred income taxes	1,050	1,065
Common shareholders' equity		
Common stock	87,000	98,000
Paid-in capital	15,000	18,000
Retained earnings	23,123	23,488
Total Common Shareholders' Equity	125,123	139,488
Total Liabilities and Common Shareholders' Equity	178,485	184,065

RIPLEY CORPORATION INCOME STATEMENT Year end December 31st 2004, US$ million	
	2004
Net sales	184,235
Cost of goods sold	(163,910)
Gross profit	20,325
Selling, general and administrative expenses	(15,424)
Operating profit (EBIT)	4,901
Interest income	60
Interest expense	(1,972)
Operating income before tax	2,989
Provision for income taxes	(1,136)
Reported net income	1,853
Dividends declared	1,488

LOS 8-1-a	**interpret** common-size balance sheets and common-size income statements and **discuss** the circumstances under which the use of common-size financial statements is appropriate

1. Common-size statements

Example 8-1: Common-size statement

The first part of Ripley Corporation's balance sheet is restated as a common-size statement in the right hand column below.

		2004
Assets	**$ million**	%
Current Assets		
Cash and cash equivalents	1,350	0.73
Accounts receivable	13,600	7.39
Inventories	4,600	2.50
Other current assets	765	0.42
Total current assets	20,315	11.04
Property, plant and equipment (net of depreciation)	128,050	69.57
Other noncurrent assets	35,700	19.40
Total assets	184,065	100.00

The common size income statement is shown below

	2004	
	$ million	%
Net sales	184,235	100.00
Cost of goods sold	(163,910)	(88.97)
Gross profit	20,325	11.03
Selling, general and administrative expenses	(15,424)	(8.37)
Operating profit	4,901	2.66
Interest income	60	0.03
Interest expense	(1,972)	(1.07)
Operating income before tax	2,989	1.62
Provision for income taxes	(1,136)	(0.62)
Reported net income	1,853	1.01

LOS 8-1-b	**calculate, interpret**, and **discuss** the uses of measures of a company's internal liquidity, operating performance (i.e., operating efficiency and operating profitability), risk profile, and growth potential
LOS 8-1-d	**calculate** and **interpret** a company's financial ratios relative to its industry, to the aggregate economy, and to the company's own performance over time

2. Internal liquidity (solvency)

Internal liquidity ratios give an indication of a company's ability to pay short-term financial obligations. The most commonly used are:

Current ratio	=	$\frac{\text{current assets}}{\text{current liabilities}}$
Quick ratio	=	$\frac{\text{(cash + marketable securities + receivables)}}{\text{current liabilities}}$
Cash ratio	=	$\frac{\text{(cash + marketable securities)}}{\text{current liabilities}}$
Receivables turnover	=	$\frac{\text{net sales}}{\text{average receivables}}$
Average receivables collection period	=	$\frac{365}{\text{receivables turnover}}$
Inventory turnover	=	$\frac{\text{COGS}}{\text{average inventory}}$
Average inventory processing period	=	$\frac{365}{\text{inventory turnover}}$
Payables turnover ratio	=	$\frac{\text{COGS}}{\text{average trade payables}}$
Payables payment period	=	$\frac{365}{\text{payables turnover ratio}}$
Cash conversion cycle	=	receivables collection period + inventory period – payables payment period

Example 8-2: Liquidity ratios

Using the financial statements for Ripley Corporation, the ratios are calculated below:

Current ratio

2003: $\dfrac{17{,}855}{27{,}312} = 0.65$ 2004: $\dfrac{20{,}315}{18{,}512} = 1.10$

The ratio has improved sharply between the two year ends. At the end of 2003, since the current ratio is less than 1, the company did not have sufficient current assets to meet its current liabilities. By the end of 2004 the current assets had increased and current liabilities had fallen indicating a healthier liquidity position.

Quick ratio

2003: $\dfrac{15{,}150}{27{,}312} = 0.55$ 2004: $\dfrac{14{,}950}{18{,}512} = 0.81$

The quick ratio is stricter than the current ratio in the sense that it considers only relatively liquid current assets, and does not include inventory. Again these look like low ratios for Ripley Corporation, but they are improving, and must be looked at on a comparative basis against the rest of the industry.

Cash ratio

2003: $\dfrac{950}{27{,}312} = 0.03$ 2004: $\dfrac{1{,}350}{18{,}512} = 0.07$

Cash is being kept at very low levels but this may not be a cause for concern if the company has strong credit lines with banks.

Receivables turnover

The average receivables are computed by taking the average of the year-end numbers, 14,000 and 13,800.

2004: $\dfrac{184{,}235}{13{,}900} = 13.25$ times

Average receivables collection period

2004: $\dfrac{365}{13.25} = 27.55$ days

This means that the company collects its receivables in 27.55 days, on average. To see if this is acceptable we would need to look at the company's credit policy and at the collection period for other companies in the industry. Clearly a relatively long collection period indicates that customers are taking a long time to pay and probably too much capital is tied up in receivables.

Inventory turnover

2004: $\frac{163{,}910}{3{,}550} = 46.17$ times

(remember to use COGS and **not** sales)

Average inventory processing period

2004: $\frac{365}{46.17} = 7.91$ days

This measures how long capital is tied up in inventory, if it is too short it might indicate that insufficient inventory is being held, if it is too long it might indicate that the inventory has become obsolete.

Payables turnover ratio

2004: $\frac{163{,}910}{7{,}723} = 21.22$ times

Payables payment period

2004: $\frac{365}{21.22} = 17.20$ days

This means that Ripley Corporation takes just over 17 days, on average, to pay suppliers. The longer the period the better for the company's cash flow.

The cash conversion cycle

2004: 27.55 + 7.91 – 17.20 = 18.26 days

This shows that, after offsetting the period in which capital is tied up in receivables and inventory by the period that the company can wait before they pay suppliers, the period that cash is tied up is just less than 18 days.

3. Operating performance

a. Operating efficiency

Total asset turnover	=	$\frac{\text{net sales}}{\text{average total net assets}}$
Fixed asset turnover	=	$\frac{\text{net sales}}{\text{average net fixed assets}}$
Equity turnover	=	$\frac{\text{net sales}}{\text{average equity}}$

Note: 'net' in total net assets and net fixed assets means the fixed assets are net of depreciation.

b. Operating profitability

Gross profit margin	=	$\frac{\text{gross profit}}{\text{net sales}}$
Operating profit margin	=	$\frac{\text{operating profit}}{\text{net sales}}$
Net profit margin	=	$\frac{\text{net income}}{\text{net sales}}$
Return on total capital*	=	$\frac{(\text{net income + gross interest expense})}{\text{average total capital}}$
Return on total equity	=	$\frac{\text{net income}}{\text{average total equity}}$
Return on owners' equity	=	$\frac{(\text{net income – preferred dividend})}{\text{average common equity}}$

* If a company uses operating leases, for example an airline that leases aircraft, then the return on capital including leases could be calculated. The present value of the leases is added to both the fixed assets and long-term debt. Also the income needs to be adjusted for the implied interest expense and implied depreciation expense. Leases are covered in detail in Study Session 10.

Example 8-3: Operating performance

Using the financial statements for Ripley Corporation the ratios are calculated as below:

Total asset turnover

2004: $\frac{184{,}235}{181{,}275} = 1.02$ times

This is a low number indicating that perhaps Ripley Corporation is in a capital intensive industry, or a new company that is not yet efficiently using its assets.

Fixed asset turnover

2004: $\frac{184{,}235}{126{,}025} = 1.46$ times

Again this is a low number implying a lot of capital is tied up in fixed assets compared to sales.

Equity turnover

2004: $\frac{184{,}235}{132{,}306} = 1.39$ times

Note that equity includes preferred and common stock, paid in capital and retained earnings. If a company decided to change its capital structure this would change the equity turnover. For example, if the company decided to increase the debt financing and reduce the equity financing this would increase the equity turnover.

Gross profit margin

2004: $\frac{20{,}325}{184{,}235} = 11.03\%$

COGS are high as a proportion of sales; the gross profit is only just over 11% of sales.

Operating profit margin

2004: $\frac{4{,}901}{184{,}235} = 2.66\%$

After selling, general and administrative expenses operating profits are reduced to only 2.66% of sales.

Net profit margin

2004: $\dfrac{1{,}853}{184{,}235} = 1.01\%$

In the case of Ripley Corporation the net income is the same as the operating income after tax since there are no non-operating adjustments. These ratios should be calculated using income from continuing operations.

Return on total capital

2004: $\dfrac{1{,}853 + 1{,}972}{181{,}275} = 2.11\%$

Note. Total capital is the total capital being used in the business. Interest expense is not netted off against interest income.

Return on total equity

2004: $\dfrac{1{,}853}{132{,}306} = 1.40\%$

(This is the same as the **return on owners' equity** since there is no preferred stock in issue).

The return on capital and the return on equity look low, the return should reflect the risk of the business. It would suggest that, unless there was a forecast improvement in the return that the company is generating, investors' capital could be used more productively elsewhere.

See LOS 8-1-c for a breakdown and analysis of return on equity (DuPont system).

4. Risk Analysis

Risk analysis looks initially at the internal factors that lead to volatility in the earnings of a company. The two components of this are business risk and financial risk.

Business Risk

Business risk is usually measured by the coefficient of variation of a firm's operating earnings (the standard deviation of operating earnings/mean operating earnings).

Two factors which will contribute to the variability of operating earnings are:

1. **Sales variability** - measured by the coefficient of variation of sales.
2. **Operating leverage** - measures the sensitivity of operating earnings to changes in sales. It reflects the proportion of costs that are fixed as opposed to variable, high fixed costs will increase the operating leverage.

Financial Risk

Financial risk measures the variability of returns to equity shareholders.

Relevant ratios are divided into two categories:

1. Ratios to measure the percentage of capital that is debt financed.

Debt to equity ratio	=	total long-term debt / total equity
If there are leases, this becomes	=	Noncurrent liab. + defd. taxes + PV of lease obligations / Total equity
Long-term debt/total capital ratio	=	total long-term debt / total long-term capital
		Long-term capital is long-term debt plus shareholders' equity
Total debt ratios	=	current liabilities + total long-term debt / total debt + total equity

Note - include deferred taxes in debt if the deferred tax is likely to be actually paid

2. Ratios to measure the cash flow available to meet interest payments

Interest coverage*	=	earnings before interest and taxes / interest expense
	=	net income + interest expense + income taxes / interest expense
Fixed charge coverage ratio	=	EBIT and lease payments / [interest + lease payments + preferred div./(1 – tax rate)]
Cash flow coverage of fixed financial costs*	=	net cash flow from operations + interest expense / interest expense
Cash flow/long-term debt* ratio	=	cash flow from operations / book value of long-term debt
Cash flow/total debt ratio*	=	cash flow from operations / total long-term debt + current interest bearing liabilities

* if the company uses leases then the estimated lease interest expense would be added to the interest expense. The present value of lease obligations is added to the book vale of long-term debt.

Cash flow used is often defined as:

net income + depreciation + change in deferred taxes.

Example 8-4: Risk analysis

Applying these ratios to Ripley Corporation:

Debt to equity ratio

2003: $\dfrac{26{,}050}{125{,}123} = 20.82\%$ 2004: $\dfrac{26{,}065}{139{,}488} = 18.69\%$

Note: Deferred taxes have been included in debt

The debt burden looks relatively low and is falling, partly due to increased equity financing.

Long-term debt/total capital ratio

2003: $\dfrac{26{,}050}{151{,}173} = 17.23\%$ 2004: $\dfrac{26{,}065}{165{,}553} = 15.74\%$

Again this is a low figure and declining.

Total debt ratios

2003: $\dfrac{(27{,}312 + 26{,}050)}{(53{,}362 + 125{,}123)} = 29.90\%$ 2004: $\dfrac{(18{,}512 + 26{,}065)}{(44{,}577 + 139{,}488)} = 24.22\%$

This shows that, in 2004, 24.22 % of the company's assets were financed by debt. This includes both short and long-term debt, some of which is not interest-bearing. The ratio looks relatively low but needs to be seen in the context of other companies.

Interest coverage

2004: $\dfrac{1{,}853 + 1{,}136 + 1{,}972}{1{,}972} = \dfrac{4{,}921}{1{,}972} = 2.52 \text{ times}$

This shows that EBIT could decline by approximately 60% (1.52/2.52) and Ripley Corporation could still pay its interest costs.

To calculate the cash flow coverage ratios we need further information on Ripley Corporation's operating cash flow. This was 1,560 in 2004, this is fairly low partly reflecting the sharp increase in inventories and decrease in accrued expenses.

Cash flow coverage of fixed financial costs

2004: $\dfrac{(1{,}560 + 1{,}972)}{1{,}972} = 1.79 \text{ times}$

This is also looks low but we need to consider the business risk involved in achieving the cash flow.

Cash flow/ long-term debt ratio

$$2004: \quad \frac{1{,}560}{26{,}065} = 5.99\%$$

Cash flow/total debt ratio

$$2004: \quad \frac{1{,}560}{(26{,}065 + 455)} = 5.88\%$$

These figures look low. If the cash flow continues to be poor relative to debt it might be a signal of increased bankruptcy risk.

Liquidity Risk

External market liquidity is measured by the ability to buy and sell an asset without significantly moving the price. This can be measured by the value of shares traded or the bid-ask spread. Other indicators are market value of outstanding securities, number of owners of the security, and the percentage of shares traded in a period.

5. Growth Analysis

The sustainable growth rate depends on the resources the company has to generate earnings and the rate of return it generates on these resources.

Sustainable growth rate	=	earnings retention rate x return on equity
Earnings retention rate	=	$1 - \frac{\text{dividends declared}}{\text{operating income after taxes}}$

In many cases net income is used rather than operating income after tax. In Ripley Corporation's case it does not make a difference since there is no non-operating income.

Example 8-5: Growth analysis

For Ripley Corporation:

Retention rate

$$2004: \quad 1 - \frac{1{,}488}{1{,}853} = 19.70\%$$

Sustainable growth rate

$$2004: \quad 1.40\% \times 19.70\% = 0.28\%$$

This is a low number reflecting the poor return on equity and low earnings retention rate. The company does not appear to be generating an attractive return to shareholders. If the company has few growth prospects it is paying out earnings as dividends rather then reinvesting them in the company for growth.

LOS 8-1-c	**calculate** and **interpret** the various components of the company's return on equity using the original and extended DuPont systems

DuPont System

The DuPont system breaks down return on equity into different components and is useful for analyzing a firm's ROE and looking at ROE on a relative basis to other firms.

Breaking down the ROE into three components under the original DuPont system:

$$\text{Return on equity} = \frac{\text{net income}}{\text{net sales}} \times \frac{\text{net sales}}{\text{total assets}} \times \frac{\text{total assets}}{\text{common equity}}$$

$$= \text{net profit margin} \times \text{total asset turnover} \times \text{financial leverage}$$

Example 8-6: Dupont system

Ripley Corporation's return on equity in 2004

$$\text{Return on equity}$$

$$= \text{net profit margin} \times \text{total asset turnover} \times \text{financial leverage}$$

$$= \frac{1{,}853}{184{,}235} \times \frac{184{,}235}{184{,}065} \times \frac{184{,}065}{139{,}488}$$

$$= 1.01 \times 1.00 \times 1.32$$

$$= 1.33\%$$

Note that we have used end year data for the ratios rather than the average for the year.

The extended DuPont system breaks down the ROE into 5 components, by breaking the net profit margin down further.

$$\text{Return on equity}$$

$$= \frac{\text{net profit}}{\text{pre - tax profit}} \times \frac{\text{pre} - \text{tax profit}}{\text{operating profit}} \times \frac{\text{operating profit}}{\text{net sales}} \times \frac{\text{net sales}}{\text{total assets}} \times \frac{\text{total assets}}{\text{common equity}}$$

$$= \text{tax retention rate} \times (1 - \text{interest expense as \% of pre - tax profits}) \times \text{operating profit margin}$$
$$\times \text{total asset turnover} \times \text{financial leverage}$$

Example 8-7: Return on equity

Ripley Corporation's **return on equity** in 2004

0.62 x 0.61 x 0.03 x 1 x 1.32 = 1.33%

LOS 8-1-e	**discuss** the limitations of financial ratios (e.g., differences in accounting treatment among companies)

Limitations of Financial Ratios

There are a number of limitations as detailed below.

1. Differences between accounting policies used by firms. This is particularly important if making international comparisons. Ideally you should adjust the accounts for major differences before making comparisons.
2. It may be difficult to make industry comparisons if a firm is operating in different industrial sectors.
3. An analyst needs to look at a range of ratios to understand the profile of the firm. Drawing conclusions from one set of ratios may give an overly optimistic or pessimistic indication of the firm's prospects.
4. An analyst needs to look at the acceptable range for the industry for each ratio. A ratio that is either too high or too low may indicate a problem.

8-1 View Concept Check Questions Workbook

8-2 "Dilutive Securities and Earnings per Share"

Introduction

This Reading looks at the computation of basic and diluted earnings per share. Candidates need to be comfortable calculating weighted-average numbers of shares outstanding and adjusting for complex capital structures when there are potentially dilutive securities such as convertible bonds or options outstanding. The calculations are not difficult but remember to adjust for tax on interest payments on convertible bonds and use the Treasury stock method (not a particularly intuitive method) when there are options or warrants outstanding.

LOS 8-2-a	**differentiate** between simple and complex capital structures for purposes of calculating earnings per share (EPS)

Earnings per share (EPS) refer to the income earned by each share of common stock. In terms of calculating earnings per share a **simple capital structure** is when a firm's capital structure consists only of common stock or there is no **potential common stock**. If there is potential common stock which could dilute earnings then it has a **complex capital structure.**

LOS 8-2-b	**describe** the components of EPS and **calculate** a company's EPS in a simple capital structure

In a simple capital structure, **basic EPS** are given by:

$$\text{EPS} = \frac{(\text{net income - preferred dividends})}{\text{weighted average number of shares outstanding}}$$

EPS is also stated before and after extraordinary items.

LOS 8-2-c	**calculate** a company's weighted average number of shares outstanding
LOS 8-2-d	**describe** stock dividends and stock splits, and **determine** the effect of each on a company's weighted average number of shares outstanding

The weighted average number of shares outstanding refers to the shares issued, weighted by the proportion of the period for which they were outstanding. However, in the case of a stock dividend or stock split the additional shares issued are included as if they had been outstanding for the complete period. This is because a stock dividend or stock split does not change the asset base of the firm whereas a new issue will increase the cash position of the firm.

Example 8-8: Weighted-average number of shares

Date	Share Changes	Shares Outstanding
January 1st		100,000
February 1st	Issue 10,000 shares for cash	110,000
October 1st	20% stock dividend	132,000
December 1st	Issue 30,000 shares for cash	162,000

First of all, restate the shares outstanding prior to October for the stock dividend, and then work out the percentage of the year the different numbers of shares were outstanding.

Date	Shares Outstanding	Percentage of the Year
January 1st to February 1st	120,000	1/12
February 1st to October 1st	132,000	8/12
October 1st to December 1st	132,000	2/12
December 1st to December 31st	162,000	1/12

The weighted average number of shares outstanding is

(1/12 x 120,000) + (8/12 x 132,000) + (2/12 x 132,000) + (1/12 x 162,000) = 133,500

LOS 8-2-e	**distinguish** between dilutive and antidilutive securities

Dilutive securities are ones which, if exercised or converted, would lead to lower earnings per share. **Antidilutive securities** are ones which, if exercised or converted, would increase earnings per share.

LOS 8-2-f	**calculate** a company's basic and diluted EPS in a complex capital structure

In a complex capital structure EPS need to be adjusted to take account of the dilutive effect of convertible bonds, options, warrants and any other dilutive securities outstanding.

$$\text{Diluted EPS} = \frac{\text{adjusted income available for common shares}}{\text{weighted average common shares and potential common shares}}$$

LOS 8-2-g	**describe** and **determine** the effects of convertible securities, options, and warrants on a company's EPS

In calculating diluted earnings per share each issue must be considered separately to work out whether it is dilutive or antidilutive. Antidilutive issues should not be included in the calculation since they are unlikely to be converted or exercised. Looking at each of the types of security in turn:

Convertible Securities

There are two steps to adjusting EPS when convertible securities are outstanding:

1. Adjust the net income for the interest saved (if it is a security that pays interest) if the security is converted into common stock. This must be the after-tax adjustment as interest is a tax deductible expense.
2. Increase the weighted average number of shares assuming that the security is converted.

In both cases the adjustment should be done from the beginning of the period, or the time of issue if it was during the period.

Example 8-9: Convertible bonds

Newington Corporation had net income of $5,000,000. There is $1,000,000 of an 8% convertible bond outstanding. Each bond is convertible into one common share. There are 5,000,000 common shares outstanding over the period (weighted average). The tax rate is 30%.

1. Adjusted net income = $5,000,000 + [$80,000 x (1 - 0.30)] = $5,056,000
2. Adjusted number of shares = 6,000,000

EPS (basic) = $5,000,000/5,000,000 = $1.00
EPS (diluted) = $5,056,000/6,000,000 = $0.84

Options and Warrants

When calculating diluted EPS when options or warrants have been issued, it is assumed that proceeds from their exercise are used by the company to repurchase their own stock (treasury stock) at the average market price for the accounting period. However, the option or warrant will only be exercised if the average market price is above the exercise price in the period. This is called the treasury stock method.

Example 8-10: Warrants

Barnsfield Corporation had net income of $3,000,000. There are 600,000 common shares outstanding over the period (weighted average). The average market price of the shares over the year was $70. The company has 100,000 options outstanding, each option gives the holder the right to buy one share at an exercise price of $40.

The proceeds from the exercise of the options would be $4,000,000.

This will be sufficient for the company to buy 57,143 shares (at $70)

Total new shares will be 100,000 - 57,143 = 42,857

Basic EPS = $5.00
Diluted EPS = $3,000,000/642,857 = $4.67

LOS 8-2-h	**compare** and **contrast** the requirements for EPS reporting in simple versus complex capital structures

In summary the different steps for calculating the basic and diluted EPS are shown below:

Simple Capital Structure

a. Compute income applicable to common stock (deduct preferred dividends).
b. Compute weighted average number of common shares outstanding.
c. Basic EPS = (net income- preferred dividends)/weighted average number of shares.

Complex Capital Structure

a. Compute basic EPS.
b. Check each potentially dilutive security to see if it is dilutive or antidilutive, this involves calculating the impact on net income and the adjusted weighted average number of shares, assuming maximum dilution. Only include securities that are dilutive in the final calculation.
c. Diluted EPS = [net income - preferred dividends + interest saving (net of tax)]/(weighted average common shares + potentially dilutive common shares).

8-2 View Concept Check Questions Workbook

3-A "Seek and Ye Shall Find"

3-B "Searching for Shenanigans"

Introduction

These Readings look at tricks or shenanigans that companies use to ensure that their reported earnings are in line with expectations, obviously the intention is often to hide potentially disappointing earnings. The Candidate has to be familiar with specific tricks that are used and the impact on the financial statements, and where they need to look for clues that such shenanigans are being used.

"Shenanigans" refer to a company taking steps to deliberately distort its financial results. These can range from relatively benign actions such as changing accounting estimates to committing fraud.

LOS 8-3-A-a	**explain** the two basic strategies underlying all accounting "shenanigans," and **describe** seven categories of techniques that may be used by management to distort a company's reported financial performance and financial condition

There are two basic strategies underlying accounting tricks, the objective is to either increase current earnings or increase future earnings.

Inflate current period earnings

This is done by inflating current-year revenues and/or deflating current year expenses. See techniques 1, 2, 3, 4 and 5 below.

Deflate current period earnings and inflate future period earnings

Deflate current-year revenues and/or inflate current year expenses. This is done to 'transfer' earnings to a future period when they may be needed.

See techniques 6 and 7 below.

There are seven techniques used to distort financial results:

1. Recording revenue too early, or revenue that is of questionable quality

- Recording revenue when future services still need to be provided.
- Recording revenue before shipment or before the customer has unconditionally accepted the goods/service.
- Recording revenue when the customer is not obligated to pay.
- Selling to an affiliate.
- Giving the customer something of value for doing a transaction.
- Grossing up revenue.

2. Recording bogus revenue

- Recording sales that lack economic substance.
- Recording cash received in lending transactions as revenue.
- Recording investment income as revenue.
- Recording as revenue supplier rebates that are dependent on future purchases.
- Releasing revenue that was held back prior to a merger.

3. Boosting income with one-time gains

- Selling undervalued assets.
- Including investment income or gains as revenue or as a reduction in operating expenses.
- Reclassification of balance sheet accounts to generate income.

4. Shifting current expenses to a later or earlier period

- Capitalizing rather than expensing normal operating costs.
- Changing accounting policies to shift current expenses to an earlier period.
- Amortizing costs too slowly.
- Failing to write-down impaired assets.
- Reducing asset reserves.

5. Failing to record or improperly reducing liabilities

- Failing to record expenses and related liabilities when future obligations remain.
- Reducing liabilities by changing accounting assumptions.
- Releasing questionable reserves into income.
- Creating false rebates.
- Recording revenue when cash is received, even though future liabilities remain.

6. Shifting current revenue to a later period

- Creating reserves and releasing them into income in a later period.
- Improperly holding back revenue just before an acquisition closes.

7. Shifting future expenses to the current period as a special charge

- Improperly inflating the size of a special charge.
- Improperly writing off in-process R&D costs from an acquisition.
- Accelerating discretional expenses in current period.

LOS 8-3-A-c **describe** why "Shenanigans" exist and **explain** where they are most likely to occur

Generally companies that use accounting tricks are attempting to cover up a deterioration in operations. Investors may well lose confidence in management (if they detect the shenanigans) and the share price will perform badly.

Why do people resort to shenanigans?

The text gives three reasons:

It pays to do it

Managers' bonuses and stock options are often linked to the performance of the company. Additionally a poor performing division may be threatened with closure so the managers are motivated to artificially boost revenues.

Analysts' should be concerned if they see a company has a compensation structure that is heavily reliant on a company's income.

It's easy to do

Management has significant discretion selecting accounting policies which are acceptable under GAAP. This is because there is flexibility in interpreting GAAP, GAAP can be applied to boost profits, and there is often a time lag between a financial deficiency being noted and changes in GAAP being made. A good manager will select the policies which give a fair view of the company's position; other managers can use the flexibility to distort results.

An analyst should consider whether accounting polices are overly aggressive, for example the method of accounting for inventory, amortization period and revenue recognition policies. Also they should also look at the strength of internal controls and whether they are a deterrent to management adopting unethical policies.

It's unlikely that you will get caught

In many cases manipulating accounts remains undetected by regulators and auditors. Even if they are detected the penalties are not severe.

Although most companies do not distort their financial reports there are certain warning signs to look out for:

- weak control environment e.g. lack of independent directors or independent auditor
- management under extreme competitive pressure
- management which does not have a good reputation

Pressures may arise when a company's rapid growth rate starts to slow, companies are struggling to survive. Also companies that are newly listed or privately owned that have not been audited and lack strong internal controls have more flexibility to distort accounts.

LOS 8-3-A-b **identify** conservative and aggressive accounting policies

The text looks at two cases, AOL and Medaphis (MEDA). In these cases we find examples of aggressive accounting methods.

Aggressive Accounting Policy	Example
Capitalized normal operating costs	AOL capitalized marketing costs as "deferred subscriber acquisition costs"
Amortized costs too slowly	AOL extended amortization period from 12 to 24 months
Shifted future expenses to the current period as a special charge	AOL wrote off the "deferred subscriber acquisition costs" as a one-off nonrecurring charge
Recorded revenue too soon	MEDA used percentage-of-completion accounting, recording revenue before products were shipped Revenue was recorded before billing
Recorded investment income as revenue	Included net earnings from a joint venture
Capitalized normal operating costs	MEDA capitalized costs which were the equivalent of 52% of pretax earnings in one year
Amortized costs too slowly	MEDA extended amortization period from 5 to 7 years
Operational problems	MEDA's cash flow from operations was deteriorating MEDA's margins were deteriorating MEDA had acquired troubled companies
Shifted future expenses to the current period as a special charge	MEDA recorded a restructuring charge and created reserves.

More generally if company uses conservative accounting principles it suggests that the management is high quality and has integrity.

A summary of aggressive and conservative accounting policies is shown below:

Accounting Policy	Aggressive	Conservative
Revenue recognition	Recognize revenue when sale made, when risk remains with seller	After sale is made and risk passed to buyer
Depreciation method	Straight-line method over long period	Accelerated method over short period
Amortization of goodwill	Over 40 years	Over shorter period
Inventory method, if prices rising	FIFO, which will lead to lower costs	LIFO, which will lead to higher costs
Estimate of warranty costs	Low	High
Estimate of bad debts	Low	High
Treatment of advertising costs	Capitalize	Expense
Loss contingencies	Refer to in footnote	Accrue

LOS 8-3-B-d **list** the documents that an analyst should use to identify "Shenanigans" and **explain** what information to look for in such documents

It is essential that analysts are able to spot indicators that a company has resorted to using shenanigans. The following should be looked at for early signs:

Press releases

Disclosers in press releases, for example warnings that revenues or transactions have not been as positive as previously expected.

Pro forma earnings are an area to watch. Pro forma earnings aim to adjust earnings prepared under GAAP for income items that are not related to the normal operations of the company. They can be useful for new companies or for companies that will be created by a merger. However, there is the temptation to use proforma accounts to present a much more optimistic earnings number than is acceptable under GAAP.

SEC filings

Regular filings with SEC are the main sources of financial information on public companies (in the U.S.). Companies also have to file irregular reports when specific events occur.

Regular filings - annual

Form 10-K – to be filed within 90 days of the fiscal year end. This report contains detailed financial results and must be audited.

Annual report – this is essentially an abbreviated version of form 10-K, and is provided to the shareholders once a year.

Proxy – this contains matters on which shareholders can vote at the annual stockholders' meeting. It also contains information on the directors' and managers' compensation.

Regular filings – quarterly

Form 10-Q – to be filed 45 days after the close of each quarter. it is not audited and less detailed than form 10-K.

Form 8-K- a company must use this form to let the SEC know about special events such as acquisitions, changes in control, or a change in auditor. It must be submitted within 15 days, and in the case of auditor changes within 5 days.

Form 144 – Insiders use this to register when they buy or sell stock.

Registration – A registration statement including a prospectus must be filed when a company plans to issue securities.

International reporting standards are less onerous than those in the U.S.

When an analyst searches for shenanigans they look at the following

Auditor's report

First of all consider the reputation of the auditor. Then read the report to see whether it contains a 'clean' opinion or if it is 'qualified'. A qualified report might mean that the auditor has reservations about the fairness of the financial statements or the company's financial position. Of particular concern would be a 'going concern' qualification where the auditor is doubtful that the company will continue as a going concern.

An analyst should also be concerned if there is no audit committee including members outside the board of directors. This committee will be a buffer between the company and the auditors.

Proxy Statements

These can include important information such as compensation for directors and also lawsuits or continent obligations faced by the company.

Footnotes to the Financial Statements

These are attached to the financial statements and in many cases provide more information than the statements themselves. They provide details of many subjects including changes in accounting policies, related party transactions and contingencies and long-term purchase commitments. These will give an overall indication of the health of the company and whether the company is using aggressive or conservative accounting principles.

President's letter

Don't expect this to be cautious, most presidents' letters are upbeat. It might be useful to compare letters over the last few years to get an indication of whether the company is operating in more 'challenging' or difficult times. Also look if there have been many changes to top management.

Management Discussion and Analysis

This should discuss the current financial position, liquidity and planned capital expenditure. Look for consistency with data given in the footnotes.

Form 8-K

Look for a change in auditors, this might have occurred because the previous auditors disagreed with the management's interpretation of GAAP.

Registration statement

If a company has submitted a registration statement this will give information on the past performance of management and the future plans for the business.

Form 144

Major sales of stock by directors might be a warning signal of bad company news ahead.

The next step for an analyst is to visit the company to collect additional information and meet management. SEC guidelines restrict the information given out.

8-3 View Concept Check Questions Workbook

STUDY SESSION 9

Investment Tools:

Financial Statement Analysis: Assets

Overview

This Study Session looks at some important issues concerning the reporting of assets in financial statements and how different accounting methods can be used. Often the choice of method makes a substantial difference to the reported financial position and profitability of the company. It can also impact on actual cash flows in the form of taxes paid. An analyst needs to consider the necessary adjustments to the reported figures to better understand the underlying position of the company.

In this Study Session we look at two specific issues relating to assets on the balance sheet, these are accounting for inventory and long-lived assets.

Reading Assignments

The Analysis and Use of Financial Statements, 3rd edition, Gerald I. White, Ashwinpaul C. Sondhi, and Dov Fried (Wiley, 2003)

9-1-A. "Analysis of Inventories," Ch. 6, pp. 192• 215

9-1-B. "Analysis of Long-Lived Assets: Part I • The Capitalization Decision," Ch. 7, pp. 227• 240 (including Box 7-1) and pp. 242• 244

9-1-C. "Analysis of Long-Lived Assets: Part II • Analysis of Depreciation and Impairment," Ch. 8, pp. 257• 278 and pp. 280• 282

9-1-A "Analysis of Inventories"

Introduction

When a company sells an item of inventory they must assign a cost to the item. In some cases the company records the cost as that of replacing the item of inventory or more precisely as that of the last unit of inventory purchased (last-in, first-out or LIFO). In other cases they record it as the cost of the first unit of inventory purchased (first-in, first-out, or FIFO). Another method is to use the average cost of items in inventory. The choice of method will not only have a direct impact on the cost assigned to each unit of inventory sold in the income statement but also on the value of the remaining inventory in the balance sheet. It can also have a real (as opposed to only an accounting) effect on the company since cash flows will reflect the tax paid by the company under the different methods. Candidates will need to able to compute financial statement items using the different methods and to work out the effect on financial ratios. The material is relatively straight forward and will hopefully provide some easy marks on the exam.

LOS 9-1-A-a **compute** ending inventory balances and cost of goods sold using the LIFO, FIFO, and average cost methods to account for product inventory

The fundamental relationship between beginning inventory values, ending inventory values, goods purchased and the cost of goods sold is given by:

EI BI P COGS **(Equation 9-1)**

where:

EI = Ending inventory
BI = Beginning inventory
P = Purchases
COGS = Cost of goods sold

Example 9-1: Cost of goods sold

At the beginning of an accounting period the inventory is valued at \$50,000. Purchases are made of \$30,000 and ending inventory is \$45,000. We can use Equation 9-1 to compute the COGS as

$$COGS = BI + P - EI = \$50,000 + \$30,000 - \$45,000 = \$35,000$$

There are three main methods of accounting for the cost of inventory that is sold.

1. FIFO - First In, First Out means that the cost assigned to the unit sold is the one associated with the unit in inventory which that was purchased the first. Therefore the units held in inventory are those purchased last.
2. LIFO - Last In, First Out means that the cost assigned to the unit sold is the one associated with the unit in inventory that was purchased the last. Therefore the units held in inventory are those purchased first.
3. Weighted-Average Cost - Units in inventory are assigned the same average cost as the units sold.

Example 9-2: Accounting for the cost of inventory

A wholesaler had, at the beginning of the year, 1,000 units of inventory, held at a cost of $3.00 per unit. Over the year the company bought 4,200 additional units at steadily increasing prices, as shown in the table below. 4,000 units were sold over the year giving an ending inventory of 1,200 units.

Quarter	Units Purchased	Unit Cost	Units Sold
1	1,000	$3.10	800
2	1,000	$3.20	1,000
3	1,100	$3.30	1,100
4	1,100	$3.50	1,100

Using the different accounting methods we can calculate the COGS and ending inventory values.

FIFO

Under FIFO the first units sold are the ones held in inventory at the beginning of the year, the next are the ones purchased in the first quarter, and so on. The units remaining in the ending inventory are the ones purchased in the third and fourth quarter.

COGS (FIFO)		Ending Inventory (FIFO)	
1,000 units @ $3.00 =	$3,000	100 units @ $3.30 =	$ 330
1,000 units @ $3.10 =	$3,100	1,100 units @ $3.50 =	$3,850
1,000 units @ $3.20 =	$3,200		
1,000 units @ $3.30 =	$3,300		
4,000	$12,600	1,200	$4,180

LIFO

Under LIFO the first units sold are the last purchased. The units remaining in the ending inventory are the ones held in inventory at the beginning of the year and a portion of those purchased in the first quarter.

COGS (LIFO)		Ending Inventory (LIFO)	
1,100 units @ $3.50 =	$3,850	1,000 units @ $3.00 =	$3,000
1,100 units @ $3.30 =	$3,630	200 units @ $3.10 =	$ 620
1,000 units @ $3.20 =	$3,200		
800 units @ $3.10 =	$2,480		
4,000	$13,160	1,200	$3,620

Weighted-average method

The average cost per unit is calculated on based on the units in the beginning inventory plus the units purchased.

Total cost

1,000 $3.00   1,000 $3.10   1,000 $3.20   1,100 $3.30   1,100 $3.50
$16,780

Average cost $\frac{\$16,780}{5,200}$ $3.23

COGS	4,000	$3.23	$12,908
Ending inventory	1,200	$3.23	$3,872

Since unit costs are rising over the period, COGS under FIFO, which takes the cost of items sold as the cost of the first items bought, will be the lowest of the three methods. As a result the remaining inventory will have the highest value.

Applying Equation 9-1 we can check the calculations:

	EI	=	BI	+	P	-	COGS
FIFO	$4,180	=	$3,000	+	$13,780	-	$12,600
LIFO	$3,620	=	$3,000	+	$13,780	-	$13,160
Weighted-average	$3,872	=	$3,000	+	$13,780	-	$12,908

LOS 9-1-A-b **explain** the relationship among and the usefulness of inventory and cost-of-goods-sold data provided by the LIFO, FIFO, and average cost methods when prices are 1) stable or 2) changing

Balance sheet

We can see from the Example 9-2 that if prices rise over a long period then the value of inventory under LIFO or the average cost method will give little indication of the inventory's current value or replacement cost. When analyzing a balance sheet FIFO is generally preferred since the inventory value is closer to its economic value. (GAAP requires the lower-of-cost-or-market valuation for inventories, where market value is defined as replacement cost).

Income statement

If net income is defined as the amount available for distribution to shareholders without impairing a company's operations it would be generally relevant to consider the cost of goods sold to be the replacement cost of the goods. In this case LIFO would be more relevant than FIFO or the average cost method.

LOS 9-1-A-c **discuss** how a company's choice of inventory accounting method affects other financial items such as income, cash flow, and working capital

LIFO versus FIFO - Impact on Income Statement and Balance Sheet

In a period when prices *are rising* and inventory quantities are stable or increasing the impact on the financial statements is shown below. The opposite will hold if prices are decreasing.

	LIFO	FIFO	
COGS	Higher	Lower	Under LIFO costs are assigned to units purchased the most recently
Income before tax	Lower	Higher	Since costs are higher, income before tax under LIFO will be lower
Tax	Lower	Higher	If LIFO is permitted for income tax calculation, the tax paid will be lower
Net income	Lower	Higher	
Cash flows	Higher	Lower	The tax payment is lower under LIFO
Inventory balances	Lower	Higher	Under LIFO the goods in inventory are those purchased the first
Working capital	Lower	Higher	Under LIFO these are lower reflecting lower inventory, although this is partially offset by lower tax payments increasing cash*

*This is illustrated in the Example 9-2 where, using LIFO, with a tax rate of 40%,

COGS is higher by	\$13,160 - \$12,600	= \$560
Tax saving is	\$560 x 40%	= \$224
Ending inventory is lower by	\$4,180 - \$3,620	= \$560
Working capital is lower by		\$336

It should be noted that the main economic impact (as opposed to accounting difference) is the tax payable which will impact on actual cash flows.

The average cost method will result in financial statement items between those calculated by FIFO and LIFO.

LOS 9-1-A-d	**adjust** the financial statements of companies using different inventory accounting methods to **compare** and **describe** the effect of the different methods on cost of goods sold and inventory balances

When prices are rising, inventories using LIFO will have little economic relevance. Therefore companies using LIFO are required to disclose the LIFO reserve, which is needed to make the adjustment to quoting inventories under FIFO.

LIFO reserve is defined by:

$$\text{Inventory}_{\text{FIFO}} \quad \text{Inventory}_{\text{LIFO}} \quad \text{LIFO Reserve}$$ **(Equation 9-2)**

where $\text{Inventory}_{\text{FIFO}}$ refers to inventory calculated using the FIFO method and so on.

Combining Equation 9-2 with Equation 9-1

$$\text{EI} \quad \text{BI} \quad \text{P} \quad \text{COGS}$$

gives the following equation:

$$\text{COGS}_{\text{FIFO}} \quad \text{COGS}_{\text{LIFO}} \text{ - Change in LIFO Reserve}$$ **(Equation 9-3)**

Change in LIFO Reserve is LIFO reserve at the end of the period less LIFO reserve at the beginning of the period, so it is positive if the reserve is increasing.

Example 9-3: LIFO reserve

A company uses **LIFO** in presenting its financial statements which include the following data:

	Year 1	*Year 2*
Inventories	58	67
COGS	355	475
LIFO reserve	42	52

Restating the accounts under **FIFO**, using equations 9-2 and 9-3:

	Year 1	*Year 2*
Inventories	100	119
COGS		465

Adjustment of income to current cost income

Here we consider the adjustments to FIFO and average cost COGS calculations to arrive at an estimate for COGS under LIFO.

$$\text{COGS}_{\text{LIFO}} = \text{COGS}_{\text{FIFO}} + \left(\text{Beginning Inventory}_{\text{FIFO}} \times \text{r}\right) \qquad \textbf{(Equation 9-4)}$$

$$\text{COGS}_{\text{LIFO}} = \text{COGS}_{\text{W}} + \left(\text{Beginning Inventory}_{\text{W}} \times \text{r}/2\right) \qquad \textbf{(Equation 9-5)}$$

where

r is the specific inflation rate for the goods being held as inventory.

$\left(\text{Beginning Inventory}_{\text{FIFO}} \times \text{r}\right)$ and $\left(\text{Beginning Inventory}_{\text{W}} \times \text{r}/2\right)$

are estimates of the gain in value of the inventory under FIFO and the weighted average method, respectively.

The inflation rate, r, may be readily available. For example if the inventory is a commodity the quoted spot price for the commodity can be used. If this is not the case r can be estimated by looking at the LIFO reserve of a competing firm in the same industry and

$$\text{r} = \frac{\text{Change in LIFO Reserve}}{\text{Beginning Inventory}_{\text{FIFO}}} \qquad \textbf{(Equation 9-6)}$$

Example 9-4: LIFO effect

An oil producer uses FIFO accounting and reports the following

$ million	***2002***	***2003***
COGS	1,250	1,300
Ending Inventory	220	180

If the oil price rose by 10% over 2003, then the adjustment to the 2003 COGS to arrive at a current cost COGS (the LIFO effect) is

$$\text{Beginning Inventory}_{\text{FIFO}} \times r = \$220 \text{ million} \times 10\% = \$22\text{million}$$

This reflects the gain in value of the inventory that has been included in the income under FIFO, since COGS under FIFO are understated by this amount.

Using Equation 9-5

$$\text{COGS}_{\text{LIFO}} = \text{COGS}_{\text{FIFO}} + \left(\text{Beginning Inventory}_{\text{FIFO}} \times r\right)$$

= $1,300 million + $22 million = $1,322 million

LOS 9-1-A-e **compute** and **describe** the effects of the choice of inventory method on profitability, liquidity, activity, and solvency ratios

Financial Ratios under LIFO and FIFO

Generally an analyst should use LIFO when calculating ratios from an income statement and FIFO for ratios from a balance sheet.

Gross profit margin: LIFO is more accurate, when prices are rising FIFO will overstate margins since it includes holding gains due to the rising prices.

Working capital ratios: FIFO is more accurate, when prices are rising; inventory under LIFO will be understated leading to understated working capital.

Inventory turnover: use LIFO for COGS and FIFO for inventories, this gives the best approximation of current costs in both the numerator and denominator in the inventory turnover calculation.

Debt to equity ratio: stockholders' equity (if LIFO is used) should be increased by the LIFO reserve. This is a follow through from inventories being understated under LIFO.

LOS 9-1-A-f	**discuss** the reasons why a LIFO reserve might decline during a given period and **discuss** the implications of such a decline for financial analysis

A decline in LIFO reserves may be due to:

1. Liquidation of inventories

If the old inventory was carried at a very low cost the use of this inventory could result in abnormally high profits since LIFO costs are much lower than current costs. This is called LIFO liquidation and it might reflect that the company is in decline and production is being cut. In the case of LIFO liquidations an analyst should exclude the gains from using old inventory from the operating results.

2. Price declines

If prices fall, the difference between LIFO and FIFO cost inventories will also fall leading to a lower LIFO reserve. This means that the LIFO inventory values are not current and should be adjusted. However LIFO-based costs are current and should be used, rather than FIFO-based costs, as in the case of rising prices.

9-1-A View Concept Check Questions Workbook

9-1-B "Analysis of Long-Lived Assets,

Part I - The Capitalization Decision"

Introduction

Now we turn to long-term assets which are not, as in the case of inventory, held for the purpose of selling to customers. Examples would be plant and machinery, computer software and patents. The Reading centers on the rationale behind, and the impact of, a decision to expense versus capitalize the cost of these assets. Candidates need to know the effects of these decisions on the financial statements and ratios.

Long-lived assets are ones that are not bought for re-sale but are used in the company's operations. They include tangible fixed assets as well as intangible assets.

Costs incurred in the acquisition of a long-lived asset prior to it being used should normally be capitalized (including invoice costs, delivery costs, sales tax and installation costs). However there are differences in accounting treatment between firms for a number of items, such as

- Which components of acquisition costs should be capitalized (e.g. interest costs during construction)?
- Should research and development and software development costs be capitalized?
- Which accounting method should be used to decide the amount of costs that will be capitalized?

LOS 9-1-B-a	**compute** and **describe** the effects of capitalizing versus expensing on net income, shareholders' equity, cash flow from operations, and financial ratios

Example 9-5: Capitalizing versus expensing

We look at a very simplified example of two companies, each starts with an asset base of $10 million which generates income of $1,000,000, and neither pay tax. Company A purchases an asset which costs $1 million and their policy is to capitalize the cost, spreading the cost equally over a five year asset life. Company B also purchases an asset which costs $1 million but expenses the cost. The new asset generates income of $300,000 per year for each company, before accounting for the cost of the asset.

In the second year companies A and B each purchase an additional asset at a cost of $2 million which generates an additional income of $600,000 a year and has a five year life. Company A and Company B capitalize and expense the cost, respectively.

Income	**Company A**	**Company B**
Year 1		
Income	$1,300,000	$1,300,000
Less cost of asset	$200,000	$1,000,000
Net income	$1,100,000	$300,000
Year 2		
Income	$1,900,000	$1,900,000
Less cost of assets	$200,000 + $400,00	$2,000,000
Net income	$1,300,000	($100,000)
Year 3		
Income	$1,900,000	$1,900,000
Less cost of assets	$600,000	0
Net income	$1,300,000	$1,900,000
etc.		
Balance Sheet	**Company A**	**Company B**
Year 1		
Assets	$11,000,000 - $200,000 = $10,800,000	$10,000,000
Year 2		
Assets	$12,800,000 - $200,000 -$400,000 = $12,200,000	$10,000,000
Year 3		
Assets	$11,600,000	$10,000,000
etc.		

This illustrates that Company A's decision to capitalize assets increases income in the first two years and leads to a higher asset base. Company B has a lower income in the first two years as the complete cost of the assets is expensed, and the company has a lower asset base.

If we continued the example over time, with each company purchasing further assets, we can see the impact of the capitalizing/expensing decision as shown below.

Impact of capitalizing versus expensing costs

- A company that capitalizes costs will have more stable earnings - capitalized costs will be depreciated over a period of time, whereas costs that are expensed will be charged in one period's accounts. As a company gets larger the variability of earnings will tend to decline.
- Capitalizing costs will tend to increase profitability of a young company since the depreciation cost will be spread over several years, rather than expensing which will have a greater immediate impact. However as the company matures, from a return on equity viewpoint, expensing costs will give a higher return on equity or return on assets since the asset base will be lower.
- The components of cash flow will be different depending on the choice to capitalize or expense costs. If costs are capitalized they will be recorded in the cash flow from investments rather than the cash flow from operations. If costs are expensed they will be recorded in the cash flow from operations. Cash flow from operations will always be higher for a company that capitalizes costs.
- Companies that capitalize costs will have a higher asset base. This will mean that debt to equity ratios will be lower for companies that capitalize rather than expense costs.

LOS 9-1-B-b	**explain** the effects on financial statements of capitalizing interest costs

Capitalization of Interest

In the U.S. it is required to capitalize interest costs on funds used during construction of a long-lived asset, if the company has borrowings. The calculation of interest costs is simplified if specific borrowing has been arranged for a project, the interest cost of this borrowing is the amount capitalized. In the case that there is no separate financing for a project the weighted average interest rate on the company's outstanding debt is used to calculate the interest cost.

The text argues that this treatment is inconsistent because the cost of equity is not capitalized if the firm has no borrowing. Therefore the costs being capitalized result from a financing decision rather than an operating decision. For the purpose of analysis, interest that has been capitalized should be reversed and treated as an expense.

The impact of reversing the capitalization of interest will be:

1. Capitalized interest is added back to interest expense. This will reduce net income.
2. The amortization of interest must be added back if it is a significant amount.
3. Cash flow statements must be adjusted. The interest that was capitalized must be added back to cash flow from investment and deducted from operating cash flow.
4. The interest cover ratio must be adjusted to include the capitalized interest; otherwise the interest expense will be understated leading to the interest cover being overstated.

Internationally there is no single rule whether interest costs during construction or acquisition of assets are capitalized or expensed.

LOS 9-1-B-c	**explain** the circumstances in which intangible assets, including software development costs and research and development costs, are capitalized

Capitalization of Intangible Assets

Intangible assets are identifiable resources controlled by companies that are not tangible and do not have physical substance. Over recent years the growth of internet, telecommunication and service industries has increased the importance of analyzing the accounting treatment of intangible assets.

In general, when an intangible asset is acquired from a third party it is capitalized on the balance sheet at the acquisition costs, which is assumed to represent its market value. In other cases when the asset is internally generated or granted by a government, one alternative would be to value the asset at cost, although in practice this may be difficult to calculate.

Research and Development Costs

The benefits from research and development spending will usually only come through in the medium to long term and due to the uncertainty of any benefit materializing, research and development spending is expensed in the U.S. Outside of the U.S. different treatment is allowed, including capitalization of development costs when the following requirements are met:

1. the product (or process) is clearly defined
2. costs can be clearly identified
3. technical feasibility has been established
4. the firm intends to use the product (or process)
5. the market has been clearly identified
6. the firm has sufficient resources to complete the project

IAS require that companies expense research costs.

Patents and Copyrights

All costs, with the exception of legal fees, incurred in developing patents or copyrights are expensed. However, if they are purchased from another party the complete cost is capitalized.

Under U.S. law patents have a legal life of 17 years and copyrights of 50 years beyond the creator's life. However, in many cases they should be amortized over a shorter period reflecting their economic life.

Franchises

The franchisee should capitalize the cost of purchasing franchise rights.

Brand Names and Trademarks

These can only be capitalized if acquired from a third party. U.S. GAAP and IAS state that they must be expensed if internally generated. IAS applies the same rule to similar items such as customer lists.

Advertising Costs

Generally it is difficult to measure the benefit of advertising and advertising costs are expensed. However direct response advertising costs can be capitalized.

Goodwill

This is the difference between the amount paid for an acquired company and the fair market value of its net assets. It can only be recognized when acquisitions are accounted for using the purchase method.

Software Development Costs

U.S. accounting rules cover the accounting for development costs for software being developed for sale or lease to other parties. Up to economic feasibility being established software development costs must be expensed, thereafter costs can be capitalized as part of product inventory. This means that they will be amortized using the straight-line method or based on product revenues.

9-1-B View Concept Check Questions Workbook

9-1-C "Analysis of Long-Lived Assets,

Part II: Analysis of Depreciation and Impairment"

Introduction

Moving on from the previous Reading we now look in more detail at the accounting treatment of long-lived assets on the balance sheet and income statements. We compare the effects of using different methods of depreciating, or allocating the cost, of tangible assets over their useful life. Candidates will need to be able to compute depreciation expense and net book values using straight-line and accelerated methods. Also candidates need to be familiar with the accounting treatment of impairment of assets which must be recognized when the value of an asset on the balance sheet is more than the cash flows that will be generated by the asset.

Depreciation is the allocation of the cost of property, plant or equipment over its useful life. It is important to appreciate that this is quite different to estimating the fair value of assets, it is a method used to calculate the book value of assets reported in financial statements.

Depletion is allocation of the cost of natural resources on the basis of the rate of extraction or production, usually the units-of-production method is used.

Amortization is applied to intangible assets such as patents, trademarks, and goodwill.

LOS 9-1-C-a	**identify** the different depreciation methods and **discuss** how the choice of depreciation method affects a company's financial statements, ratios, and taxes

Different Methods of Calculating Depreciation

Annuity or Sinking Fund Appreciation

When this method is used the rate of return earned on the asset determines the depreciation expense. This method is not allowed under U.S. GAAP.

Example 9-6 Annuity approach

An asset costs $3 million and generates a return of 10% over a three-year life. It generates a cash flow of $1.2 million per year and will have zero value at the end of three years. The depreciation expense will increase over time in order for the rate of return to be constant.

Year	Opening Balance Asset Value	Cash Flow	Net Income (opening balance x 10%)	Depreciation Expense (cash flow - net income)	Return
1	$3.00	$1.20	$0.30	$0.90	10%
2	$2.10	$1.20	$0.21	$0.99	10%
3	$1.11	$1.20	$0.11	$1.09	10%

The depreciation in the final year should lead to a zero balance at the end of year 3 (errors are due to rounding).

Straight-line Depreciation

This is the method of depreciation that is the most commonly used in the U.S. and internationally.

The straight-line method allocates equal depreciation expenses over each year of the asset's life.

Depreciation expense in each year

$$= \frac{1}{n} \times (\text{Original Cost} - \text{Salvage Value}) \qquad \textbf{(Equation 9-7)}$$

where

n = depreciable life in years

Example 9-7: Straight-line depreciation

Using the example above of an asset that costs $3 million, generates a cash flow of $1.2 million per annum and has zero salvage value we can calculate straight-line depreciation as shown below.

Year	Opening Balance Asset Value	Cash Flow	Depreciation Expense	Net Book Value	Net income	Return
1	$3.00	$1.20	$1.00	$2.00	$0.20	6.7%
2	$2.00	$1.20	$1.00	$1.00	$0.20	10.0%
3	$1.00	$1.20	$1.00	$0.00	$0.20	20.0%

The net book value is the original cost less the accumulated depreciation.

Note that the rate of return is increasing over the asset's life.

Accelerated Depreciation Methods

These depreciation methods attempt to match higher depreciation costs with the greater benefits that can be generated from an asset when it is new. Additionally the maintenance costs are usually higher for an asset when it is old and therefore an accelerated method will tend to lead to more consistent total costs for each year of an asset's life.

Since accelerated depreciation methods give higher depreciation costs in the early years they are often used for tax reporting. There are two main accelerated depreciation methods, the **sum-of-years'-digits method** and the **declining-balance** method.

Sum-of-Years'-Digits Method (SYD)

The depreciation expense in year *i* is given by

$$= \frac{(n - i + 1)}{SYD} \times (\text{Original Cost} - \text{Salvage Value}) \qquad \textbf{(Equation 9-8)}$$

where

n = depreciable life in years

i = the year for which the depreciation is being calculated.

$$SYD = (1 + 2 + \ldots \ \ldots + n) = n(n+1)/2$$

Double-Declining-Balance Method

(An example of a declining-balance method, double since the rate is **2/n**)

In this method the depreciation expense is based on the net book value, or original cost less the accumulated depreciation, of the asset.

Depreciation Expense

$$= \left(\frac{2}{n}\right) \times (\text{Original Cost - Acc. Deprec. Expense}) \qquad \textbf{(Equation 9-9)}$$

where

n = depreciable life in years

Using this method we need to continue to depreciate the asset until the book value is the same as the salvage value. In many cases when the depreciation expense falls below that calculated using the straight-line rate method a company would switch to using the straight-line method for the remainder of the asset's life.

Example 9-8: Accelerated depreciation methods

Assume that an asset has a depreciable life of 3 years, costs $800,000 and has a salvage value of $200,000.

Sum-of-Years'-Digits Method

Using Equation 9-8

Depreciation expense in year i $\dfrac{3 \quad i \quad 1}{6}$ $800,000 - $200,000

Year	Rate	Depreciation Expense	Accumulated Depreciation	Net Book Value
0				$800,000
1	3/6	$300,000	$300,000	$500,000
2	2/6	$200,000	$500,000	$300,000
3	1/6	$100,000	$600,000	$200,000

Double-Declining-Balance Method

Using Equation 9-9

$$\text{Depreciation expense in year i} = \left(\frac{2}{n}\right) \times (\text{Original Cost - Acc. Deprec. Expense})$$

Year	Rate	Depreciation Expense	Accumulated Depreciation	Net Book Value
0				$800,000
1	2/3	$533,333	$533,333	$266,667
2	2/3	$66,667	$600,000	$200,000
3	2/3	$0	$600,000	$200,000

It is important to note that in year 2 the full depreciation expense according to the formula is not charged (it is calculated as $177,778) since the asset's book value has already reached the salvage value.

Units-of-Production and Service Hours Method

These methods calculate the depreciation expense based on usage of the asset. This method will reduce the volatility of earnings since depreciation becomes a variable expense. The disadvantage is that if the company loses competitiveness and/or machinery becomes obsolete leading to lower production the depreciation expense is also declining, but this is the time that the machinery is losing most economic value.

The service hours method bases the depreciation on the number of service hours that the asset is expected to operate for.

Example 9-9: Units-of-production

Use the data on the previous asset which costs $800,000 and has a salvage value of $200,000, and assume that the asset is a piece of machinery that has a total expected output of 120,000 units, 40,000 in the first year, 50,000 in the second year and 30,000 in the third year. The cost per unit is ($800,000 - $200,000)/120,000 = $5.

Year	Units of Output	Depreciation Expense	Accumulated Depreciation	Net Book Value
0				$800,000
1	40,000	$200,000	$200,000	$600,000
2	50,000	$250,000	$450,000	$350,000
3	30,000	$150,000	$600,000	$200,000

Depletion

The accounting treatment for natural resources is similar to those for tangible assets. The cost of acquisition of the resources including exploration and development may be capitalized or expensed. The carrying cost is allocated by the units-of-production method based on the initial estimate of the units in the resource base.

Amortization

Intangible assets can be amortized over their useful lives or the periods set by law or regulations. Straight-line or units-of-production methods are used.

Impact of Choice of Depreciation Method on the Financial Statements

At the beginning of an asset's life

Using accelerated depreciation methods reduces net income and stockholders' equity compared with straight-line methods. The percentage effect on net income is usually greater than that effect on asset values so return ratios (ROE and ROA) tend to be lower.

These methods are considered more conservative.

At the end of an asset's life

Using accelerated depreciation methods increases net income compared with straight-line methods.

For a growing company with rising capital expenditure depreciation expense will usually continue to be higher if they are using accelerated depreciation methods.

Accelerated depreciation methods are considered more conservative but are usually used to decrease the tax burden.

Inflation

In a period of high inflation it is likely that the total depreciation expense over the asset's life will be insufficient to replace the asset, so in effect the depreciation expense has been too low since it is based on historical cost. In this case the firm has effectively over-stated income and the tax paid is too high, and taxes become a tax on capital.

If inflation is an issue using accelerated depreciation methods and short asset lives will increase the depreciation expense.

LOS 9-1-C-b	**explain** the role of depreciable lives and salvage values in the computation of depreciation expenses

Although companies may use the same depreciation methods, comparison between companies' accounts is made difficult if they have different estimates for depreciable lives (useful lives) and salvage values. The assumptions may not be completely transparent, for example companies providing information on useful lives often give the range of periods used rather than precise numbers.

Using long depreciable lives will underestimate annual depreciation expenses. Similarly using high salvage values will reduce the depreciation base (cost minus salvage value) and depreciation expense.

LOS 9-1-C-c	**compute** and **describe** how changing depreciation methods or changing the estimated useful life or salvage value of an asset affects financial statements and ratios

Changes in depreciation method

A company can:

A. Change the method and only apply to newly acquired assets.

Usually this change will have a gradual impact on results since previously acquired assets will be depreciated under the old method. It is not necessary to restate past earnings.

B. Change the method and apply to all assets.

If the change is applied retroactively it will be considered a change in accounting principle and the cumulative effect must be reported separately, net of taxes, in the financial statements. The company must disclose the pro forma impact on prior period results.

C. Change asset lives or salvage values.

These are changes in accounting estimates rather than accounting principles, no retroactive or cumulative changes need to be recognized.

LOS 9-1-C-d	**discuss** the use of fixed asset disclosures to compare companies' average age of depreciable assets, and calculate, using such disclosures, the average age and average depreciable life of fixed assets

Analysis of Fixed Asset Disclosures

Fixed asset data in a company's financial statements can be used to calculate the age of a company's property, plant and equipment. This is useful information since older assets can be less efficient and it will also give an indication if major capital expenditure will be needed in the future. The data can be used to compare firms in similar industries

If straight-line depreciation methods are used the formulae are:

Relative Age as Percentage of Depreciable Life

This gives the average age of assets as a percentage of their useful lives and indicates whether the asset base is old or new.

Relative Age (%)
= Accumulated Depreciation/Ending Gross Investment **(Equation 9-10)**

Average Depreciable Life

This can give useful information of a company's depreciation policy although it will be influenced by the mix of assets the company is using.

Average Depreciable Life
= Ending Gross Investment/Depreciation Expense **(Equation 9-11)**

Average Age

This will give the approximate age of the company's assets, although again it will be distorted by the mix of assets and any acquisitions.

Average Age
= Accumulated Depreciation/Depreciation Expense **(Equation 9-12)**

Example 9-10: Average age and depreciable life

Cobham Industries and Byfleet Industries are both manufacturers of engine parts and the following information is provided on their fixed assets for the previous year.

Machinery and Equipment	Cobham Inds. ($ mn)	Byfleet Inds. ($mn)
Gross Investment	15,600	5,800
Accumulated Depreciation	6,200	1,200
Net Investment	9,400	4,600
Depreciation Expense	750	400
Relative Age %	39.7%	20.7%
Average Depreciable Life	20.8 years	14.5 years
Average Age years	8.3 years	3.0 years

The relative age as a percentage of the depreciable life of assets is much higher for Cobham Inds. This is probably explained by the fact that Byfleet Inds. purchased the machinery more recently.

The average depreciable life is longer for Cobham Industries, this may be the result of a different asset mix or a policy to assume longer depreciable lives. The average depreciable life will also be shortened if one company takes over another company and sets the depreciation balance of the acquired assets to zero.

For Byfleet Inds. the average age is much lower indicting recent heavy capital expenditure or acquisitions.

LOS 9-1-C-e **define** impairment of long-lived assets and explain what effect such impairment has on a company's financial statements and ratios

Impairment of Long-Lived Assets

Impairment is when the carrying value of a long-lived asset cannot be recovered from the expected future level of operations.

Impairments refer to both when a company has decided to dispose of an asset (not discussed here) and to when it will continue to use an asset, albeit at a reduced level.

Accounting standards say that impairment must be recognized when the value of an asset cannot be recovered. Indicators of this include:

- Cost overruns.
- Deterioration in the business environment.
- A significant decrease in the market value of the asset.
- Operating or cash flow losses and a forecast of a decline in the long-term profits that will be derived from an asset.

Impairment must be recognized when the carrying value of an asset is higher than the expected future cash flows from its use plus its disposal value (note, these are undiscounted cash flows).

If impairment is recognized then the value of the loss must be calculated. The loss is either the difference between the carrying cost and the fair value (less the cost to sell the asset), or, if the fair value cannot be determined, it is the difference between the carrying cost and the discounted value of future cash flows. They should be discounted at the company's marginal cost of borrowing.

The loss is reported in pretax income but is not recognized for tax purposes until the asset is disposed of.

The major impacts on the balance sheet will be to reduce:

1. carrying value of plant and equipment
2. deferred tax liabilities (since the reduction in value is not recognized for tax purposes until sale – see Study Session 10 LOS 10-1-A for more on deferred tax)
3. stockholders' equity.

In turn this will increase asset turnover ratios and increase the debt-to-equity ratio.

In the future, impairment write-offs will lead to lower depreciation expense, leading to higher reported earnings and higher return on assets and return on equity. Also the average age of the assets will appear to be extended.

LOS 9-1-C-f **list** the requirements of SFAS 143, Accounting for Asset Retirement Obligations (AROs), and explain the likely financial statement and ratio effects for most firms

The requirements of SFAS 143 come into effect for fiscal years starting after June 15th 2002 and are concerned with Asset Retirement Obligations (AROs). This refers to costs associated with retiring assets such as companies being obliged to remedy environmental damage caused by their operations or restore land to its preexisting condition. This might include removing toxic waste, removing offshore oil platforms at the end off their life etc.

The provisions of SFAS 143 are as follows:

- It applies to all entities and to all legal obligations connected with the retirement of tangible fixed assets
- Affected firms must recognize the fair value of an ARO liability in the period when it is incurred (normally at acquisition)
- Fair value is market value, but if there is no market value use the present value of the expected cash flows required to extinguish the liability, (discount at the credit-adjusted risk-free rate)
- The liability is carried at fair value, and an accretion expense recognized in the income statement for each period. (Accretion expense is calculated using an interest method, this increases the company's interest expense)
- An amount equal to the initial liability is added to the carrying value of the asset, and depreciated over its useful life
- Changes in the estimated value of the ARO liability are accounted for prospectively, and prior years' accounts are not restated

Disclosures include:

1. Description of the ARO and associated asset.
2. Reconciliation of the ARO liability showing new liabilities incurred and liabilities extinguished, accretion expense, revision of the estimated AROs.
3. Fair value of any funds set aside to meet ARO obligations.

Effects on the Financial Statements

Companies that follow SFAS 143 will generally see

- Increase in the carrying value of fixed assets (as the present value of future liabilities is added to asset values)
- Increase in liabilities (as the ARO is added to liabilities)
- Lower net income due to higher depreciation expenses and accretion expense (the accretion expense will tend to increase each year)

The effect on financial ratios is

- Lower asset turnover (assets are higher)
- Lower/higher debt to equity (retained earnings lower, but depends on whether ARO is considered debt or operating liability)
- Lower return on assets
- Lower interest coverage (lower income, higher interest expense)

9-1-C View Concept Check Questions Workbook

STUDY SESSION 10

Investment Tools

Financial Statement Analysis: Liabilities

Overview

This is another Study Session containing important topics in financial statement analysis. The first Reading looks at tax and the differences between accounting for tax in financial statements and in tax reports. The differences give rise to deferred tax assets and liabilities when tax is 'overpaid' or 'underpaid' according to the financial statements. In addition to mastering the different terminology used in the reporting systems candidates need to understand the details of how deferred tax items are created and recorded.

The last two Readings tackle analysis of liabilities. First of all we look at financial liabilities where there is debt as a result of a financing decision. Generally debt is recorded on the balance sheet as the present value of future cash flows (interest and principal repayment) that the company will need to pay on the debt. The Reading focuses on the impact on the financial statements of issuing bonds when they are issued at a premium or discount to par value. Next we look at contractual liabilities such as leases and other forms of off-balance-sheet debt. Candidates need to differentiate between the effect of companies using operating leases (which are an expense and not recorded on the balance sheet) and using capital leases (where the accounting treatment is similar to the company actually owning the asset).

Reading Assignments

The Analysis and Use of Financial Statements, 3rd edition, Gerald I. White, Ashwinpaul C. Sondhi, and Dov Fried (Wiley, 2003)

10-1-A. "Analysis of Income Taxes," Ch. 9, pp. 290• 314 (including Box 9-1)

10-1-B. "Analysis of Financing Liabilities," Ch. 10, pp. 322• 332, 337• 343

10-1-C. "Leases and Off-Balance-Sheet Debt," Ch. 11, pp. 363• 383 (including Box 11-1)

10-1-A "Analysis of Income Taxes"

Introduction

The objectives of financial reporting are to produce statements that are useful to assess the financial position and performance of the company and there is an incentive to reduce the taxes that will have to be paid in the near term. However tax reporting is based on different objectives and often taxable income is calculated using modified cash methods. This, plus differences in reporting methods and estimates, results in differences between income tax expense on the financial statements and taxable income on tax reports. The differences give rise to deferred tax assets (which the company can reclaim in the future) or deferred tax liabilities (which the company must pay in the future). Candidates need to able to differentiate between temporary and permanent differences between the two reporting systems.

The Study Guide says that deferred taxes are applicable globally and therefore are the focus of the Reading Assignment. We look at accounting differences that create deferred tax assets and liabilities in the notes below.

LOS 10-1-A-a define the key terms used in accounting for income taxes

Terms used in Income Tax Accounting

The terms used in the financial statements and tax returns are different; the most important terms are shown below:

Tax Return	
Taxable income	Income subject to tax
Taxes payable (current tax expense)	Tax return liability as a result of current period's taxable income
Income tax paid	Actual cash flow of income taxes paid, including payment made for other years
Tax loss carryforward	Loss that can be used to reduce taxable income in future years
FINANCIAL REPORTING	
Pretax income	Income before income tax expense
Income tax expense	Expense as a result of current period's pretax income. Includes taxes payable and deferred income tax expense
Deferred income tax expense	Accrued income tax expense expected to be paid in future years. It is the difference between income tax expense and taxes payable. Under SFAS 109 it depends on the change in deferred tax assets and tax liabilities.
Deferred tax asset	Balance sheet amount, expected to be recovered from future operations
Deferred tax liability	Balance sheet amount, expected to result in future cash outflows
Valuation allowance	Reserve against deferred tax assets based on the likelihood that assets will be realized
Timing difference	The difference (timing or amount) between tax return and financial statement treatment of a transaction
Temporary difference	Difference between tax and financial statement reporting, which will affect taxable income when the difference reverses.

LOS 10-1-A-b	**explain** why and how deferred tax liabilities and assets are created
LOS 10-1-A-g	**compute** income tax expense, income taxes payable, deferred tax assets, and deferred tax liabilities

First we will consider some of the issues that arise when tax-based and GAAP-based accounting differ by working through an example of how deferred tax liabilities are created in Example 10-1.

Example 10-1: Deferred tax liability

A company pays $60,000 for an asset and for tax accounting purposes the asset is depreciated over three years using the straight-line method. However the company estimates that the asset will generate additional income of $30,000 per annum over its useful life of four years and depreciates the asset over this period using the straight-line method. Other costs are assumed to be zero. The salvage value is estimated to be zero and the tax rate is 40%.

Income Tax Reporting

$'000	Year 1	Year 2	Year 3	Year 4	Total
Revenue	30.0	30.0	30.0	30.0	120.0
Depreciation	(20.0)	(20.0)	(20.0)	(0.0)	(60.0)
Taxable income	10.0	10.0	10.0	30.0	60.0
Taxes payable	(4.0)	(4.0)	(4.0)	(12.0)	(24.0)
Net income	6.0	6.0	6.0	18.0	36.0

Reporting under GAAP and IAS

$'000	Year 1	Year 2	Year 3	Year 4	Total
Revenue	30.0	30.0	30.0	30.0	120.0
Depreciation	(15.0)	(15.0)	(15.0)	(15.0)	(60.0)
Pretax income	15.0	15.0	15.0	15.0	60.0
Tax expense	(6.0)	(6.0)	(6.0)	(6.0)	(24.0)
Net income	9.0	9.0	9.0	9.0	36.0
Taxes payable	4.0	4.0	4.0	12.0	24.0
Deferred tax expense	2.0	2.0	2.0	(6.0)	0.0
Deferred tax liability	2.0	4.0	6.0	0.0	N/A

Note:

Deferred tax expense is the difference between the tax expense under GAAP and the taxes payable under income tax accounting, so deferred tax expense = tax expense – taxes payable.

The deferred tax liability is the amount that will need to be paid in year 4 when the difference in accounting methods reverses. This is entered on the balance sheet.

Deferred Tax Liabilities and Assets

Deferred tax liabilities occur when the future taxable income is expected to be higher than future pretax income. This is due to **timing differences**, when the tax return treatment is different from the financial reporting treatment of an item(s). Similarly a **deferred tax asset** is created when the future taxable income is expected to be lower than future pretax income.

An example of when deferred tax assets are created is when a company issues a warranty on its product. In this case warranty expenses are recognized for financial reporting each year however for tax purposes the cost can only be recognized when the actual repairs are done. Therefore the future taxable income is expected to be lower than future pretax income. Example 10-2 looks at a deferred tax asset created by a warranty expense.

Example 10-2: Deferred tax asset

A company assumes that warranty expenses will cost 10% of each year's revenues so under GAAP the company will record a warranty expense each year. However all repairs will occur in year 4 and for income tax reporting the cost of repairs is only recognized when it actually occurs. Revenues each year are $30,000 and the tax rate is 40%.

Income Tax Reporting

$'000	Year 1	Year 2	Year 3	Year 4	Total
Revenue	30.0	30.0	30.0	30.0	120.0
Warranty expense	(0.0)	(0.0)	(0.0)	(12.0)	(12.0)
Taxable income	30.0	30.0	30.0	18.0	108.0
Taxes payable	(12.0)	(12.0)	(12.0)	(7.2)	(43.2)
Net income	18.0	18.0	18.0	10.8	64.8

Reporting under GAAP and IAS

$'000	Year 1	Year 2	Year 3	Year 4	Total
Revenue	30.0	30.0	30.0	30.0	120.0
Warranty expense	(3.0)	(3.0)	(3.0)	(3.0)	(12.0)
Pretax income	27.0	27.0	27.0	27.0	108.0
Tax expense	(10.8)	(10.8)	(10.8)	(10.8)	(43.2)
Net income	16.2	16.2	16.2	16.2	64.8
Taxes payable	12.0	12.0	12.0	7.2	24
Prepaid tax expense	1.2	1.2	1.2	(3.6)	0
Deferred tax asset	1.2	2.4	3.6	0	N/A

Note: prepaid tax expense = taxes payable - tax expense

The deferred tax asset is the amount that will need to be paid in year 4 when the difference in accounting methods reverses. This is entered on the balance sheet.

Deferred tax assets can also be created for other recurring transactions such as management compensation, bad-debt reserves, and irregular events such as environmental remediation and impairment.

Treatment of operating losses

Tax losses can be carried back to obtain refunds for prior year tax that has been paid. If insufficient prior year tax is available then they can be carried forward as **tax loss carryforwards**. These are treated as deferred tax assets but a **valuation allowance** is made if full recoverability is unlikely.

LOS 10-1-A-c **describe** the liability method of accounting for deferred taxes

The **liability method of tax accounting** focuses on the impact on the balance sheet. This is based on SFAS 109 in the U.S. and IAS 12 internationally. This method measures the balance sheet deferred tax assets and liabilities first on the basis that temporary differences will reverse, and then the reported income is a consequence of the balance sheet amounts. Whereas the deferral method calculates the impact of tax expense on the income statements first, and then calculates the implied impact on the balance sheet, as in Examples 10-1 and 10-2.

LOS 10-1-A-d	**discuss** the implications of a valuation allocation (i.e., when it is required, what impact it has on the financial statements, and how it might affect an analyst's review of a company)

A valuation allowance will reduce the value of a deferred tax asset when management, or the auditor, after analyzing future income streams think it is likely that all or some of the deferred tax asset will be realized. Changes in a valuation allowance are included in income from continuing operations (except when they arise from the change in carrying value of assets and liabilities including investment in securities). If a company has large deferred tax assets it is important that analysts review the company's accounting choices and decide whether the assets are likely to be realized.

LOS 10-1-A-e	**explain** the factors that determine whether a company's deferred tax liabilities should be treated as a liability or as equity for purposes of financial analysis

Deferred Tax Liability or an Increase in Stockholders' Equity?

If deferred liabilities arising from temporary differences in financial and tax reporting are not going to reverse in the future, they arguably should be treated as increases to equity.

When analyzing a company an analyst needs to consider each of the following situations in turn to decide on the treatment of deferred tax liabilities.

Change in tax law and accounting methods

Realization of a future tax liability or asset will depend on the realization of the temporary difference that created the deferred liability or asset in the first place. If tax rates are reduced the size of the deferred assets and liabilities will also be reduced. Changes in GAAP can also impact on deferred taxes e.g. the introduction of accrual accounting for post retirement benefits created sizeable liabilities whereas cash based accounting was being used for tax payments thus creating large tax assets.

Growth rate of company

Growing companies will tend to have a deferred tax liability that increases over time and in this case the liability may never be paid.

Non-recurring items and equity adjustments

Non-recurring items include restructuring charges, early retirement of debt and unrealized gains on market securities. These will have to be analyzed to establish whether they are likely to be reversed.

If the decision is made to continue to treat the deferred tax as a liability an analyst needs to calculate the present value of the liability based on an estimate of when it will actually be reversed. If a deferred tax liability is not going to be treated as a liability then an adjustment to increase stockholders' equity should be made. This is because if the tax expense creating the liability had not been recorded income and equity would have been higher. A decision to increase equity will affect financial ratios such as the debt/equity ratio.

Measures used to assess tax rates

Valuation models often take into account a company's effective tax rate. These can be calculated in different ways.

The reported effective tax rate is

$$\frac{\text{income tax expense}}{\text{pretax income}}$$

However the income tax expense is influenced by management accounting choices so an alternative is to look at:

$$\frac{\text{taxes payable}}{\text{pretax income}} \quad \text{and} \quad \frac{\text{income tax paid}}{\text{pretax income}}$$

LOS 10-1-A-f	**distinguish** between temporary and permanent items in pretax financial income and taxable income

Whereas temporary differences occur between financial statements and tax reporting there are also permanent differences. A permanent difference occurs when there are revenues or expenses reported on financial statements or tax reports but not on both.

Examples in the U.S. of this include interest income on tax-exempt bonds and amortization of goodwill which may be recorded on the financial statements but not on the tax return. Conversely depletion for tax purposes may exceed cost-based depletion that is reported in the financial statements and tax credits.

In the case of permanent differences there are no deferred tax consequences and they are not reported on the financial statements. They will however give rise to a difference between the effective tax rate and the statutory rate.

LOS 10-1-A-h	**calculate** the adjustment to the financial statements related to a change in the tax rate

Changes in tax rates

When a tax rate increase or decrease takes effect there are two adjustments to make:

1. Recalculate the deferred tax liabilities or assets at the new rate.
2. Calculate the deferred tax liability and taxes payable in the current year at the new tax rate.

Tax rate changes are reported in the year that they take effect under the liability method.

Example 10-3: Tax rate changes

Use the data in Example 10-1 and assume that the tax rate is reduced from 40% to 30% at the beginning of year 2. Assume that the change is announced during year 2 and the change is reflected in the year 2 financial statements.

Step 1 – recalculate the deferred tax liabilities in year 1

Year 1 reported deferred tax liability of $2 million, but restating using a tax rate of 30% gives revised deferred tax liability of $1.5 million [($15 - $10 million) x 0.30], a reduction of $0.5 million. This $0.5 million will reduce the year 2 income tax expense.

Step 2 – calculate the deferred tax liability and taxes payable in year 2

Year 2 - increase in the deferred tax liability is $1.5 million, giving a total deferred tax liability of $3 million.

Year 2 - the income tax expense is $4.5 million ($15 million x 30%) less adjustment in deferred tax liability for previous years of $0.5 million. The total income tax expense is $4 million.

10-1-A View Concept Check Questions Workbook

10-1-B "Analysis of Financing Liabilities"

Introduction

This Reading looks at the treatment of bonds on the issuer's financial statements. The liability and interest expense associated with the bond are based on interest rates at the time of issue, not the par value of the bond. The liability is the present value of the cash flows payable to the bond holders, and if a bond is issued at a discount or a premium this discount or premium is amortized over the life of the bond so the liability is equal to the par value at maturity. This method of accounting has an impact on cash flows reporting and candidates must understand the implications for the categorization of cash flow. Interest paid is based on the coupon rate and is a cash outflow from operations, whereas the repayment of capital or amortization of the premium is a cash flow from financing. This leads to inconsistencies in the treatment of cash flow for high versus low or zero coupon bonds.

LOS 10-1-B-a	**compute** the effects of debt issuance and amortization on the income statement, balance sheet, and cash flow statement

Treatment of Debt Issuance in the Financial Statements

Current liabilities, as a result of debt, consist of:

Short-term debt - amounts borrowed from banks or the credit markets to be repaid within one year or less.

Current portion of long-term debt - the portion of long-term debt that is payable within the next year.

Long-term debt

Companies acquire long-term debt by public or private issues, often the debt is purchased by pension funds or other institutional investors. In the examples below we focus on bonds to illustrate the accounting practice, although bonds are only one of the different types of long-term debt.

It is important to remember that

- The liability equals the present value of the future stream of interest and principal payments to be made on the debt.
- Interest expense is the amount paid to the creditor in excess of the amount borrowed.

The **initial liability recorded at issue** is the present value of future coupon payments (coupons are the stated cash interest paid) and principal repayment, discounted at the market interest rate at the time of issue. In the case of bonds, it is usually the amount actually paid by investors for the bonds.

The **effective interest rate** is the market interest rate at the time of issue. This is the constant rate of interest applied over the life of the obligation.

The **balance sheet liability after issue** is the present value of future payments discounted at the effective interest rate.

Whilst the total amount of interest paid is usually known at the time of issue the allocation of the interest expense over different time periods will vary according to the terms of the debt issued.

When the market rate is above/below the coupon rate at the time of issue the bond will be issued at a **discount/premium**. In the case that the bond has been issued at a premium the coupon payment will be broken down into an interest payment and a principal repayment. The principal repayment will reduce the outstanding liability. If the bond was issued at a discount the coupon payment will be less than the interest in which case the difference increases the balance sheet liability. In both cases the balance sheet liability will tend towards the face value of the bond at maturity.

The interest expense, recorded on the income statement, is the effective interest rate multiplied by the balance sheet liability at the beginning of the period. The interest expense will change over time for a bond issued at a discount/premium since the liability is increasing/decreasing.

Example 10-4 examines the different treatment of bonds issued at par, a premium and a discount.

Example 10-4: Accounting for bonds

A. A two-year bond is issued at par on January 1st 2003, with a coupon rate of 8%, making payments semi-annually. The face value is $1,000,000. The market rate (MR) is 8%, or 4% semiannually.

(In $'000)

Period Ending	Opening Liability	Interest Expense (liability x MR)	Coupon Payment	Change in Liability (interest - coupon)
1 Jan. 2003	Proceeds*			
30 June 2003	1,000.00	40.00	40.00	0
31 Dec. 2003	1,000.00	40.00	40.00	0
30 June 2004	1,000.00	40.00	40.00	0
31 Dec. 2004	1,000.00	40.00	40.00	0
Total		160.00	160.00	

*The proceeds are: PV of coupon payments = $145.20

plus: PV of maturity value = $854.80

B. A two-year bond is issued at a premium on January 1st 2003, with a coupon rate of 8%, making payments semi-annually. The face value is $1,000,000. The market rate (MR) is 6%.

(In $'000)

Period Ending	Opening Liability	Interest Expense (liability x MR)	Coupon Payment	Change in Liability (interest - coupon)	Closing Premium
1 Jan. 2003	Proceeds				
30 June 2003	1,037.17	31.11	40.00	(8.88)	28.29
31 Dec. 2003	1,028.29	30.85	40.00	(9.15)	19.14
30 June 2004	1,019.14	30.57	40.00	(9.43)	9.71
31 Dec. 2004	1,009.71	30.29	40.00	(9.71)	0
Total		122.82	160.00	(37.17)	

The proceeds are: PV of coupon payments = $148.68

plus: PV of maturity value = $888.49

C. A two-year bond is issued at a discount on January 1st 2003, with a coupon rate of 8%, making payments semi-annually. The face value is $1,000,000. The market rate (MR) is 10%.

(In $'000)

Period Ending	Opening Liability	Interest Expense (liability x MR)	Coupon Payment	Change in Liability (interest - coupon)	Closing Discount
1 Jan. 2003	Proceeds				
30 June 2003	964.54	48.23	40.00	8.23	27.23
31 Dec. 2003	972.77	48.64	40.00	8.64	18.59
30 June 2004	981.41	49.07	40.00	9.07	9.52
31 Dec. 2004	990.48	49.52	40.00	9.52	0
Total		195.46	160.00	35.46	

The proceeds are: PV of coupon payments = $141.83

plus: PV of maturity value = $822.70

Financial Statement Effects

On the income statement the cost of the bond is recorded as the interest expense. On the balance sheet the liability shown in Example 10-4 above. The cash flow treatment is more complex. The repayment of principal is a cash flow from financing, coupon payments are cash flows from operations.

Example 10-5: Cash flow classification

In all three cases in Example 10-4

(In $'000)

Year	Cash Outflow	
	Operations	**Financing**
2003	80.00	0
2004	80.00	1,000.00
Total	160.00	1,000.00

For bonds that are issued at a premium or discount the cash flow classification incorrectly states the economic transaction. Coupon payments partly represent interest and partly repayment or increase of principal.

Taking the case of a bond issued at a premium and a discount we can reclassify the cash flows as follows

Example 10-6: Reclassifying cash flows

Using the bonds in Example 10-4

(In $'000)

Year	Cash Outflow Bond issued at Premium		Cash Outflow Bond issued at Discount	
	Operations	**Financing**	**Operations**	**Financing**
2003	61.96	18.03	96.87	(16.87)
2004	60.86	1,019.14	98.59	981.41
Total	122.82	1,037.17	195.46	964.54

The proceeds are: PV of coupon payments = $148.68

LOS 10-1-B-b **discuss** the effect on reported cash flows of issuing zero-coupon debt

In the case of a **zero coupon bond**, the bond will be issued at a significant discount. The impact on reported cash flow from operations will be zero and all of the interest costs will be allocated as cash flows from financing. Since the interest is effectively paid as part of the repayment of principal at maturity the reported cash flow will overstate cash flow from operations and understate cash flow from financing.

Convertible Bonds, Warrants, and Convertible Preferred Stock

Note: the LOS on convertible bonds, warrants and convertible preferred stock has been removed from this year's syllabus although it is still covered in the readings. It is presumably unlikely you would get a specific question on this topic.

Convertible Bonds

The accounting treatment ignores the conversion terms at issue, so when the convertible bond is issued the entire proceeds are recorded as a liability and the interest expense is the same as for a conventional bond. An analyst should adjust for the equity feature using one of the following methods:

1. Separate bond and equity components of convertible value using option-pricing models.
2. Look at the financial implications of treating the convertible as a bond or equity, if they are significant then assess the likelihood that the bond will be converted to equity. If the stock price is significantly above the conversion price of the convertible bond it is likely to be converted and vice versa. Then make the necessary adjustments to equity and debt components of the balance sheet.

Bonds with Warrants

When bonds and warrants are issued together it is necessary to allocate the proceeds of the issue between the two instruments. The fair value of the bond is accounted for as a liability and is issued at a discount, as before the interest expense includes the amortization of the discount. The fair value of warrants is accounted for as equity and if they are exercised the additional cash paid by the investor increases equity capital.

In both the case of convertible bonds and bonds with warrants the interest expense is lower than that of a conventional bond. *However this is misleading since the cost of the equity component is ignored.*

Looking at the reporting of a conventional bond versus a convertible bond versus a bond with warrants:

Interest Expense	Balance Sheet Liability	Operating Cash Flow
Conventional bond *higher than*	Conventional bond *equal to*	Conventional bond *lower than*
Bond with warrants *higher than*	Convertible bond *higher than*	Bond with warrants *equal to*
Convertible bond	Bond with warrants	Convertible bond

Preferred Stock

Preferred stock or preference shares have benefits over ordinary shares. Most preferred shares are callable by the issuer and some are also redeemable by the holder. Redeemable preference shares are often classified separately to debt or equity on the balance sheet but an analyst should treat them as debt and the dividend payments as interest. Many of the shares are actually converted into ordinary shares further confusing the issue of whether they should be treated as debt or equity.

LOS 10-1-B-c **discuss** the effect of changing interest rates on the market value of debt and on financial statements and ratios

Changes in Interest Rates

If market interest rates rise after a firm has issued debt, then the market value of the debt falls providing an economic gain to the firm, similarly if interest rates fall then there is an economic loss. These are not reported in the financial statements but for the purpose of analyzing the company's debt position market values should be used. In the U.S. firms are required to disclose the fair value of outstanding debt.

10-1-B View Concept Check Questions Workbook

10-1-C "Leases and Off-Balance-Sheet Debt"

Introduction

This Reading starts with an analysis of leases and a discussion of why lessees generally prefer to structure and report leases as operating leases where they are essentially paying a rental expense for the use of an asset (the asset could be anything from an airplane to a photocopier). However when a company effectively purchases an asset through a lease agreement the lease must be treated as a capital lease. The asset is then reported on the balance sheet and depreciated and a liability is also recorded which is the present value of future lease payments. Candidates need to study the impact on financial ratios of the different methods of lease accounting. Operating leases are often referred to as off-balance-sheet financing. Candidates are expected to be able to describe other forms of off-balance-sheet financing such as the sale of receivables and take-or-pay contracts.

LOS 10-1-C-a **classify** a lease as capital or operating

Classification of Leases

Firms generally acquire the right to use property, plant and equipment by an outright purchase which transfers legal ownership to the firm. However in some case firms decide to use a lease agreement to acquire the use of an asset (and some or all of the benefits and risks of owning the asset) through a lease agreement. There are two types of lease agreement, operating and capital (also called finance) leases.

Lessees must disclose in the notes to accounts future lease obligations for the next five years.

Operating Lease

The concept of an operating lease is that the lessee can use the property for a portion of its useful life. The cost of the lease is reported as an expense by the lessee and the lessor keeps the asset on its balance sheet. This is a form of off-balance-sheet financing for the lessee.

Capital Lease

A longer-term lease transfers the risks and rewards of ownership to the lessee and therefore the accounting treatment is as if the asset had been sold, and the asset is included on the lessee's balance sheet. The lessee depreciates the asset over its life and allocates lease payments to payments of principal and interest.

Generally lessees prefer to structure leases as operating leases whereas lessors prefer to structure leases as capital leases since it allows earlier recognition of revenue and income.

The following rules decide how leases should be classified.

Under U.S. GAAP if **any** of the following conditions hold, a lease is classified as a capital lease. Otherwise it is classified as an operating lease on the lessee's accounts.

1. Title is transferred to the lessee at the end of the lease period.
2. The lease contains an option for the lessee to purchase the asset at a bargain price.
3. The lease term is for 75% or more of the economic life of the asset (not applicable to land or when the lease term begins in the final 25% of the life of the asset).
4. The present value of the minimum lease payments (MLPs), discounted at the minimum of the lessee's incremental borrowing rate or the rate implicit in the lease, is equal to 90% or more of the fair value of the asset, adjusted for the tax credit received by the lessor.

IAS are less stringent and make it easier to classify a lease as an operating lease.

LOS 10-1-C-b **calculate** the effects of capital and operating leases on financial statements and ratios

Entries in financial statements for operating and capital leases.

The different accounting treatment is illustrated in Example 10-7.

Example 10-7: Operating versus financial leases

A firm decides to lease a photocopier and the annual minimum lease payments (MLPs) are $20,000 at the end of each year for three years. The lease agreement starts on January 1st 2001. The discount rate used is 8%.

Operating lease

Balance Sheet: no entries.

Cash Flow: $20,000 cash outflow each year, classified as cash flows from operations.

Income Statement: annual rental expense of $20,000 will be charged on the income statement.

Capital lease

Balance Sheet: at inception the asset and leasehold liability, which is equal to the present value of the MLPs, will be recorded. The asset will be depreciated over the life of the lease and the principal repayments will reduce the size of the liability, see the table below.

Cash Flow: $20,000 total cash outflow each year, the interest payments are cash outflows from operations, and the principal repayments are cash outflows from financing.

Income Statement: annual rental expense of $20,000 will be divided between interest and principal repayments on the liability as shown in the table below.

Calculation of interest and principal repayments for the capital lease:

Year	Opening Liability	Interest (Liability x 8%)	Principal	Closing liability
2001	$51,542*	$4,123	$15,877	$35,665
2002	$35,665	$2,853	$17,147	$18,518
2003	$18,518	$1,482	$18,518	0

* present value of MLPs

Income Statement

	Operating Lease	Capital Lease		
Year	Rental Expense	Depreciation*	Interest	Total Expense
2001	$20,000	$17,181	$4,123	$21,304
2002	$20,000	$17,181	$2,853	$20,034
2003	$20,000	$17,181	$1,482	$18,663
Total	$60,000	$51,542	$8,458	$60,000

*Calculate depreciation using the straight-line method with the cost as the opening liability and the salvage value set at zero.

Balance Sheet (for Capital Lease)

	2001	2002	2003
Assets			
Leased assets	$51,542	$51,542	$51,542
Accumulated depreciation	$17,181	$34,362	$51,542
Leased assets, net	$34,361	$17,181	0
Liabilities			
Current portion of lease obligation	$17,147	$18,518	0
Long-term debt: lease obligation	$18,518	0	0
Total	$35,665	$18,518	0

Cash Flow

	Operating Lease	Capital Lease		
Year	**Operations**	**Operations**	**Financing**	**Total**
2001	$20,000	$4,123	$15,877	$20,000
2002	$20,000	$2,853	$17,147	$20,000
2003	$20,000	$1,482	$18,518	$20,000

Financial Impact of Choice of Lease Classification

1. There is higher total expense (interest plus depreciation) at the beginning of the lease period with a capital lease due to the higher interest payments but as the lease expires the operating lease will have a higher total expense.
2. There are lower operating expenses with a capital lease since part of the expense is interest payment.
3. Ratios - using a capital lease
    - Increases asset values resulting in lower asset turnover and return on assets.
    - Leverage and liquidity ratios will be affected by the addition of current and non-current liabilities.
    - The current ratio and working capital will be lower as a result of an increase in non-current liabilities.
    - The debt-to-equity ratio will usually be higher since a capital lease adds current and long-term debt to the balance sheet.

Total cash flow is unaffected by the lease classification. However with a capital lease both financing and operating cash flows are impacted, with an operating lease only operating cash flows are impacted. Therefore with a capital lease a lessee will report higher operating cash flows.

Analysts should make the appropriate adjustments to the financial statements to restate the impact of using operating leases rather than capital leases.

LOS 10-1-C-c **discuss** the factors that determine whether a company would tend to favor capital or operating leases

Generally the lessee would prefer to treat a lease as an operating lease, since this will give higher operating ratios and lower leverage. The lessor generally prefers to treat a lease as a capital lease since it gives earlier recognition of revenue and income for the lessor. Other factors to consider include:

- The lessee only wants use of the asset for a relatively small part of its life.
- The lessor may be able to resell the asset more easily than the lessee.
- The tax benefits of owning assets will be of most benefit to a high rate taxpayer.
- Bond covenants may limit the flexibility to increase debt, operating leases provide a way to finance off-balance-sheet.
- Management contracts may provide incentives based on the company's return on invested capital.

LOS 10-1-C-d	**describe** types of off-balance-sheet financing
LOS 10-1-C-e	**determine** how take-or-pay contracts, throughput arrangements, and the sale of receivables affect selected financial ratios

Off-Balance-Sheet Financing

Operating leases are one example of financing that gives rise to off-balance-sheet debt. We have considered other types of off-balance-sheet financing below:

Take-or-Pay or Throughput Agreements

This is when one company commits to buy a certain amount of another company's future production, the price is agreed in the contract and may be linked to the market price of the product (often a commodity). The purchaser does not report the assets and liabilities resulting from the commitment on the balance sheet, thereby often understating debt to equity ratios. An analyst should adjust the balance sheet for the present value of future commitments.

Sale of Receivables

When a company sells its receivables to a third party this is usually recorded as a sale, decreasing receivables and increasing cash from operations. However the transaction is effectively borrowing money and using the receivables as collateral, and usually the seller still bears the credit risk. Adjustments should be made to increase the accounts receivable and current liabilities to reflect the receivables sold but not collected and the increase in borrowing. This will decrease the receivables turnover ratio and lead to poorer leverage ratios.

Cash flow should be adjusted so the uncollected amount is classified as a cash flow from financing rather than operations.

Joint Ventures, Investment in Affiliates and Finance Subsidiaries

Joint ventures are used to share opportunities and risks, in many cases these ventures may enter into take-or-pay or throughput arrangements. Joint ventures and affiliates are usually accounted for using equity accounting (if ownership is between 20% and 50%) so only the net investment is shown on the parent's balance sheet.

Finance company subsidiaries or affiliates are set up to provide finance to the parent company. The balance sheets are not consolidated if ownership is kept to less than 50%.

In cases when an analyst sees off-balance-sheet financing the balance sheet should be adjusted to reflect the true liabilities of the company.

LOS 10-1-C-f distinguish between a sales-type lease and a direct-financing lease

Financial Reporting by Lessors

A **sales-type lease** is used by manufacturers and includes a manufacturing or merchandising profit as well as interest income reflecting the financing element of the transaction.

A financial institution uses a **direct-financing lease** when the only profit is from interest income.

For a lessor to treat a lease as a capital lease (which they would generally prefer) it must meet at least *one* of the criteria set out in the above list in LOS 1-C-a and *both* of the following criteria:

1. Collectibilty of the MLPs is reasonably certain.
2. There are no significant uncertainties regarding the amount of reimbursable costs under the lease agreement.

Financial Statement Reporting for a Sales-Type Lease

Gross investment is the sum of lease payments and residual value.

Net investment is the sum of present value of lease payments and residual value.

Gross minus net investment is the **unearned income** or interest component of the lease.

Sales revenue is the present value of lease payments.

COGS are manufacturing costs less the present value of the residual value.

Example 10-8: Accounting for lessors

A firm manufactures and then leases a photocopier, the annual minimum lease payments (MLPs) are $20,000 at the end of each year for three years. The cost of manufacture is $40,000. At the end of the lease the unguaranteed residual value is $10,000. The discount rate used is 8%.

If the lease is treated as a sales-type capital lease the *lessor's* financial reporting at the beginning of the lease agreement will be as follows.

Gross investment in lease

MLPs of $20,000 x 3	$60,000
Residual value	$10,000
	$70,000

Net investment in lease

Present value of MLPs	$51,542
Present value of residual value	$ 7,938
	$59,480
Unearned income	$10,520

At inception, in financial statements

Sales revenue	$51,542
COGS	$32,062
Gross profit on sale	$19,480
Gross investment in lease	$70,000
less unearned income	$10,520
Net investment in lease	$59,480

Thereafter the lease payments received of $20,000 a year are divided between interest income (8% of the net investment) and a reduction in investment.

The interest payment is cash flow from operations and the reduction in investment is an investing cash flow.

If a lease is accounted for as an **operating lease** then:

The assets will continue to be reported on the lessor's balance sheet, they will be depreciated as usual (with a cost of $40,000, salvage value of $10,000).

The lease payments will be rental income and be allocated to operating cash flow.

Financial statement reporting for a direct-financing lease

The treatment here is quite different. These are pure financing transactions and therefore no sale is recognized and only financing income is reported. There are no income or cash flow entries at the inception of the lease. In many cases an allowance for uncollectible payments will be made.

10-1-C View Concept Check Questions Workbook

STUDY SESSION 11

Investment Tools: Corporate Finance

Corporate Investing and Financing Decisions

Overview

This is a long Study Session covering important corporate finance concepts, including cash flow, leverage, cost of capital and how they impact on the value of a company. These concepts also appear in other Level I Study Sessions and throughout the CFA syllabus.

The first Reading looks at agency problems and then we move on to the core of the Study Session. The next four Readings deal with capital budgeting, and the decision-making process for whether potential investments or projects should be undertaken. This involves calculating the cost of capital, estimating the future cash flows from the investments and deciding whether the cash flows will cover the cost of capital. We also consider measures of risk for a company which will give an indication of the level of uncertainty surrounding the cash flow forecasts.

In the last two Readings we look at capital structure and dividend policy. We consider the issues that affect how a company should balance debt and equity financing to maximise its share price. We then look at dividends and how high or low dividend payout ratios will affect the company's share price.

Reading Assignments

Fundamentals of Financial Management, 8th edition, Eugene F. Brigham and Joel F. Houston (Dryden, 1998)

11-1-A. "An Overview of Financial Management," Ch. 1, pp. 18–22

11-1-B. "The Cost of Capital," Ch. 9

11-1-C. "The Basics of Capital Budgeting," Ch. 10

11-1-D. "Cash Flow Estimation and Other Topics in Capital Budgeting," Ch. 11

11-1-E. "Risk Analysis and the Optimal Capital Budget," Ch. 12

11-1-F. "Capital Structure and Leverage," Ch. 13, including Appendix 13A

11-1-G. "Dividend Policy," Ch. 14

11-1-A "An Overview of Financial Management"

Introduction

This is a short Reading which discusses the potential problems that may arise when a principal (shareholder) appoints agents (managers) and gives authority to the latter to make decisions. Conflicts of interest may also occur between stockholders and creditors. Ways to alleviate these agency problems and conflicts of interest are discussed.

LOS 11-1-A-a	**discuss** potential agency problems of stockholders versus: 1) managers and 2) creditors

In general terms an **agency relationship** refers to when **principals** employ **agents** to perform a service, which involves giving the agent some decision-making authority. Two types of agency problems are considered, namely stockholders versus managers and stockholders versus creditors.

Stockholders versus Managers

When an owner-manager sells part of his company to external shareholders this creates a potential agency problem since the owner-manager no longer benefits from all the wealth created by his work, he also no longer pays all the expenses of the company.

Example 11-1: Owner-manager agency problems

An owner-manager stops working hard if he is no longer the sole owner.

An owner-manager takes advantage of perquisites (incidental benefits) if other shareholders are paying part of the cost.

In most large corporations agency problems exist since the managers only hold at most a small stockholding in the company. The managers' objectives should be to create shareholder wealth but in fact their remuneration is largely based on their salaries and benefits.

Example 11-2: Stockholder-manager agency problems

Managers' objectives are often to increase the size of the company thereby

increasing their job security as a hostile takeover becomes less likely

increasing their status and salary packages and

benefiting managers working for them.

Managers use their employers' money to make donations to charities to improve their standing in the community.

Stockholders (through Managers) versus Creditors

Other examples of agency problems arise from the conflicts of interest between the stockholders and the creditors of a corporation. From the creditors' viewpoint the rates at which they lend money will depend on the riskiness of the corporation's cash flows and its ability to repay the interest and capital on the debt. However it is the stockholders that are in a position to take measures that determine the risk of the corporation.

Examples 11-3: Stockholders-creditors agency problems

If a corporation embarks on a major new project that is riskier than the creditors expected then the value of the debt willould decline. Benefits from the project will go to the stockholders rather than the creditors, whose return is decided by the interest rate at which they lent money. Return and risk are borne by different parties.

A corporation issues additional debt and uses the funds raised to buy back ordinary stock. This will increase the default risk of debt issued by the corporation.

Debtors will try to protect their position by placing restrictive covenants in debt agreements. However it is the responsibility of management to act in the best interests of both shareholders and creditors.

LOS 11-1-A-b **describe** four mechanisms used to motivate managers to act in stockholders' best interests

Mechanisms used to motivate managers to act in stockholders' best interests:

1. Managers' compensation

Performance shares - managers are rewarded with shares on the basis of the performance of the company and/or length of service with the company.

Executive stock options - corporations grant stock options to managers, which allow the managers to purchase stock in the future at a specified exercise price. The options will be worthless if the stock price does not rise above this exercise price.

The criteria used to decide the allocation of performance shares will include target earnings per share, return on equity, relative stock price performance or market capitalization of the company.

2. Direct intervention by shareholders

In many cases institutional money managers are the major shareholders and they can try to influence management directly or present shareholder-sponsored proposals at the annual stockholders' meeting.

3. Firing managers

Stockholders can propose their own board of directors at the annual general meeting or indirectly change managers through by putting pressure on managers to resign.

4. Threat of takeover

Managers will generally lose their position if their corporation is subject to a hostile takeover. This is a major incentive for managers to focus on managing the company in a way that supports the stock price.

11-1-A View Concept Check Questions Workbook

11-1-B "The Cost of Capital"

Introduction

All capital has a cost and the true cost of capital is not the same as the cash interest paid on debt or dividends paid to shareholders. This Reading deals with various components of capital in a target capital structures and candidates are expected to be able to calculate the cost of each component. A weighted-average calculation of the cost of capital is also presented, as well as the calculation for marginal cost of capital. Calculations are generally relatively simple but do not forget to adjust for tax in the cost of debt as interest is a tax deductible expense. Candidates are also expected to recognize the factors which affect the cost of capital and identify those which are within and beyond the control of the firm.

LOS 11-1-B-a	**explain** why the cost of capital used in capital budgeting should be a weighted average of the costs of various types of capital the company uses

The cost of capital used in budgeting should be the weighted average cost of capital rather than the cost of financing a specific project. This is because, if a company is a going concern, it will need to raise capital in the future, and the cost of this capital will reflect earlier financing decisions.

Example 11-4: Using weighted average cost of financing

A company funds a project using substantial amounts of debt financing. The next time that the company requires financing it may well find the cost of debt is substantially higher reflecting the company's higher gearing, and it will need to resort to equity financing which is generally more expensive. To avoid these issues the correct way to look at the cost of financing a project is to consider the cost of financing a project as the same as the company's overall cost of funds.

LOS 11-1-B-b	**calculate** the component costs of 1) debt, 2) preferred stock, 3) retained earnings (three different methods), and 4) newly issued stock or external equity

Component Costs of Capital

The component costs of capital that are considered are debt, preferred stock and equity (retained earnings and external or newly issued equity).

These are defined as shown below:

Cost of debt, $k_d(1 - T)$

The cost of debt is calculated *after* tax:

$$\text{cost of debt} = k_d(1 - T) \qquad \textbf{(Equation 11-1)}$$

where

k_d = interest rate on firm's new debt ,(in some case the yield to maturity of existing bonds is used)

T = marginal tax rate

The tax savings on interest paid must be deducted since interest payments are tax deductible for a company. Effectively the government is paying part of the cost of debt.

Note - flotation costs are ignored since they are generally very small.

Example 11-5: Cost of debt

If a company can borrow money at 12% and its marginal tax rate is 30% then the cost of debt is, using equation 11-1:

$$k_d(1 - T) = 12\%(1.0 - 0.3) = 8.4\%$$

Cost of preferred stock (k_{ps})

$$k_{ps} = \frac{D_{ps}}{P_n} \qquad \textbf{(Equation 11-2)}$$

where

D_{ps} = preferred dividend

P_n = net issuing price, the price after deducting flotation costs

Notes - do not adjust for tax since preferred dividend payments are not tax deductible.

Example 11-6: Cost of preferred stock

A company has preferred stock outstanding that trades at \$100 and pays a dividend of \$8 per share. If the company issued new preferred shares its flotation costs would be 3%.

$$k_{ps} = \frac{\$8}{\$97} = 8.2\%$$

Cost of retained earnings (k_s)

This is the rate of return required by common stockholders and it represents the rate of return they could earn elsewhere if the company paid out retained earnings as dividends. It is the opportunity cost involved in the company retaining the capital. It can be calculated by one of the following three methods:

1. Capital Asset Pricing Model (CAPM)

CAPM relates the expected return from a stock to its beta:

$$k_s = k_{RF} + \beta(k_M - k_{RF}) \qquad \textbf{(Equation 11-3)}$$

where

	=	beta of the stock, its sensitivity to movements in the market
k_M	=	expected market return
k_{RF}	=	risk-free rate

CAPM is covered in more detail in Study Session 12.

Example 11-7: Cost of equity using CAPM

If the risk-free rate of return is 6%, the expected market return is 14% and a company's stock has a beta of 1.1 then the required rate of return is given by:

$$k_s = k_{RF} + \beta(k_M - k_{RF}) = 6\% + 1.1(14\% - 6\%) = 14.8\%$$

2. Bond-yield-plus-risk-premium approach

Another more judgmental method to obtain a cost of equity is to add a risk premium to the company's long-term bond yield. Empirically the risk premium has been in the range of 3 to 5%.

$$k_s = \text{bond yield} + \text{risk premium} \qquad \textbf{(Equation 11-4)}$$

Example 11-8: Cost of equity using bond-yield-plus-risk-premium

A company is perceived as being high risk and the yield on their long-term bonds is 15%. An analyst decides to use a risk premium approach to calculate the cost of equity and uses a premium of 4%

$$k_s = \text{bond yield} + \text{risk premium} = 15\% + 4\% = 19\%$$

3. Dividend Valuation Model

The dividend valuation model states that for a company whose dividends are forecast to grow at a steady rate:

$P_0 = \dfrac{D_1}{k_s - g}$ which can be rearranged to

$$k_s = \frac{D_1}{P} + g \qquad \textbf{(Equation 11-5)}$$

where

g = the expected constant dividend growth rate
D_1 = the next year's dividend
P = the current stock price.

Note that D_1/P is the dividend yield of the stock.

and

$$g = (\text{retention rate}) \times \text{ROE} \qquad \textbf{(Equation 11-6)}$$

where

:

retention rate = the percentage of a company's earnings that are retained as opposed to being paid out as dividends, this is (1.0 – payout rate)
.ROE = return on equity.
ROE is return on equity
Here we are assuming that the required rate of return on equity and the expected rate of return are the same.

Example 11-9: Cost of equity using dividend valuation model

A company's current share price is $10025, the last dividend paid was $4 and dividends are forecast to grow at a constant rate of 3%. Then the required rate of return is given by:

$$k_s = \frac{\$4(1.03)}{\$100} + 3\% = 7.1\%$$

Note: Don't forget to use, D_1, the next year's dividend which will be paid in *one year's* time.

Cost of new equity

The cost of new equity or external equity will be higher due to the flotation costs that arise from the issue of new common stock. The equation above needs to be adjusted as follows:

$$k_s = \frac{D_1}{[P_0(1-F)]} + g \qquad \textbf{(Equation 11-7)}$$

where

F = the percentage flotation cost.

$P_0(1-F)$ = net price per share received by the company

Example 11-10: Cost of new equity

A company's current share price is $10025, the last dividend paid was $4 and dividends are forecast to grow at a constant rate of 3%. If the flotation costs are 5% then the cost of new equity is given by:

$$k_s = \frac{\$4(1.03)}{\$100(1.0-0.05)} + 3\% = 7.3\%$$

LOS 11-1-B-c **define** target (optimal) capital structure

A company's target or **optimal capital structure** is the mix of debt, preferred equity and common equity in its balance sheet that will maximize the company's stock price.

LOS 11-1-B-d **calculate** a company's weighted-average cost of capital

Weighted-Average Cost of Capital (WACC)

This is the weighted average of the component costs of debt, equity and preferred stock. The weights are based on the target capital structure of the company. It is the average cost of each dollar of the company's capital.

$$WACC = w_d k_d (1 - T) + w_{ps} k_{ps} + w_s k_s \qquad \textbf{(Equation 11-8)}$$

where w_d, w_{ps} and w_s are the weights in the capital structure of debt, preferred and common equity respectively.

The weights should be based on the market values of debt and equity but if these are not available use the book values.

Example 11-11: Weighted-average cost of capital

A company's target capital structure is 60% debt, 40% equity. Equity financing will come from retained earnings. If the after-tax cost of debt is 10% and cost of equity from retained earnings is 14% then:

WACC = 0.60 (10.0%) + 0.40(14.0%) = 11.6%

LOS 11-1-B-e **calculate** a company's marginal cost of capital

The **marginal cost of capital** (MCC) is the weighted average cost of the last dollar of new capital that a firm raised, or the cost of raising another dollar of capital.

Example 11-12: Marginal cost of capital

Using the above example, a company's target capital structure is 60% debt, 40% equity. The after-tax cost of debt is 10% and cost of equity from retained earnings is 14%, but the cost of new equity is 15%. Once retained earnings have been used the MCC is given by

MCC = 0.6 (10.0%) + 0.4 (15.0%) = 12.0%

LOS 11-1-B-f	**distinguish** between the weighted-average cost of capital and marginal cost of capital

As a firm raises more and more capital the MCC will start to rise. There will be a jump in the MCC when the retained earnings are used up and the firm needs to issue new equity, which will cost more due to flotation costs. This will occur at a **break point,** in this case the retained earnings break point. Additionally the cost of capital will also rise as interest rates rise. Empirical studies show that as more securities are issued in a given period, then the higher the required rate of return of investors in these securities.

LOS 11-1-B-g	**explain** the factors that affect the cost of capital and **distinguish** between those factors that can and cannot be controlled by the company

Factors than affect the cost of capital

Factors that the firm cannot control

1. Interest rates - if interest rates decline the cost of debt will decline and also, indirectly, the cost of equity will decline. If interest rates rise the cost of debt and equity will similarly rise.
2. Tax rates - raising tax rates reduces the cost of debt and makes it relatively more attractive compared to equity and vice versa.

Factors that the firm can control

1. Capital structure policy - since the after tax cost of debt is lower than equity a firm might increase the proportion of debt financing. This would tend to reduce the WACC but using significantly more debt will raise the cost of both debt and equity.
2. Dividend policy - using external equity is more expensive than using retained earnings therefore changes to dividend policy that affect whether a firm has sufficient internal funds to finance investment will impact on the WACC.
3. Investment policy - if a company changes its investment policy to start investing in more or less risky assets this will affect the future WACC.

11-1-B View Concept Check Questions Workbook

11-1-C "The Basics of Capital Budgeting"

Introduction

This is an important section and deals with capital budgeting and evaluation of projects. Four main methods of evaluating whether projects are attractive or not are the payback period, discounted payback period, net present value (NPV), and internal rate of return (IRR). Candidates should know how to evaluate projects using the different methods and identify the advantages and the disadvantages of each method. Using NPV is the preferred method and candidates should understand why the assumption made on the reinvestment of capital is considered more realistic in the NPV than in the IRR method. Calculations are frequently based on the concept of time value of money (NPV and IRR are already covered in Study Session 2) and candidates should practice the calculations using a CFA Institute approved calculator.

LOS 11-1-C-a **define** capital budgeting

Capital budgeting is the process of planning expenditures on fixed assets and projects that extend beyond one year.

Projects are often classified into one of the following categories.

- Replacement, when the maintenance of business requires the replacement of equipment.
- Replacement, when cost savings are possible if out-of-date equipment is replaced.
- Expansion of existing products or markets.
- Expansion into new products and markets.
- Safety and/or environmental projects, in many cases these are mandatory projects.
- Others.

LOS 11-1-C-b **calculate** payback period, discounted payback period, net present value (NPV), and internal rate of return (IRR), and **evaluate** capital projects using each method

Methods for Evaluating Investment Proposals

The four methods of evaluating a project (with respect to the LOS) are summarized below.

1. Payback Period

This is the expected number of years needed to recover the cost of investment in a project based on net after-tax cash flows from the project.

Example 11-13: Payback period

The cost of a project is $150 million and the following cash flows are anticipated.

Year	Net Cash Flow ($ million)
1	25
2	50
3	55
4	40
5	60

After three years the project will have paid back $130 million with $20 million remaining to be paid.

$$\text{Payback} = 3 \text{ years} + 20/40 \text{ years} = 3.5 \text{ years}$$

2. Discounted Payback Period

This is a similar concept to the payback period but it is based on the time taken to recover the investment based on **discounted cash flows,** so the cash flows need to be discounted to their present value. The discount rate used is the project's cost of capital.

Example 11-14: Discounted payback period

The cost of a project is $150 million and the following cash flows are anticipated. The cost of capital is 10%.

Year	Net Cash Flow ($ million)	Discounted Net Cash Flow ($ million)
1	25	22.7
2	50	41.3
3	55	41.3
4	40	27.3
5	60	37.3

$$\text{Discounted Payback} = 4 \text{ years} + 17.4/37.3 \text{ years} = 4.5 \text{ years}$$

The payback period methods are incomplete in the sense that they do not take into account the size of cash flows that will be received after the end of the payback period. Their main value is that they give a feeling for the risk of a project in terms of how long funds will be tied up in the project.

3. Net Present Value (NPV)

To calculate the net present value (NPV) of a project the following steps are needed

1. Estimate future cash flows (inflows and outflows) from the project and discount back to the present value using the cost of capital for the project as the discount rate.
2. Add up the discounted cash flows to give the NPV.
3. If the NPV is positive then accept the project, if negative reject.

$$NPV = CF_0 + \frac{CF_1}{(1+k)} + \frac{CF_2}{(1+k)^2} + \dots\dots + \frac{CF_n}{(1+k)^n}$$ **(Equation 11-9)**

where

CF_t = the expected cash flow in period t
k = the project's cost of capital.

Note: These calculations (NPV and IRR) are quick to do using a financial calculator, make sure you get plenty of practice using your calculator before the exam.

Example 11-15: Net present value

The cost of a project is $150 million and the following cash flows are anticipated. The cost of capital is 10%.

Year	Net Cash Flow ($ million)	Discounted Net Cash Flow ($ million)
0	-150	-150.0
1	25	22.7
2	50	41.3
3	55	41.3
4	40	27.3
5	60	37.3
Total		19.9

The NPV is positive indicating that the cash flows from the project are more than enough to pay back the costs of debtcapital used to pay for the project and give a positive return to stockholders.

Or using a financial calculator the keystrokes are

HP-12C		BA II Plus	
[f] CLEAR [FIN]	**0.00**	[CF] [2nd] [CLR WORK]	**CF_0 = 0.00**
150 [CHS] [g] [CF_0]	**150.00**	150 [+/-] [ENTER]	**CF_0 = 150.00**
25 [g] [CF_j]	**25.00**	[⇩] 25 [ENTER]	**C01 = 25.00**
50 [g] [CF_j]	**50.00**	[⇩] [⇩] 50 [ENTER]	**C02 = 50.00**
55 [g] [CF_j]	**55.00**	[⇩] [⇩] 55 [ENTER]	**C03 = 55.00**
40 [g] [CF_j]	**40.00**	[⇩] [⇩] 40 [ENTER]	**C04 = 40.00**
60 [g] [CF_j]	**60.00**	[⇩] [⇩] 60 [ENTER]	**C05 = 60.00**
10 [i]	**10.00**	[NPV] 10 [ENTER]	**I = 10.00**
[f] [NPV]	**19.95**	[⇩] [CPT]	**NPV = 19.95**

4. Internal Rate of Return (IRR)

Calculate the discount rate that will make the present value of the cash flows from the project equal to the present value of the investment costs. This discount rate is the IRR. If, and only if it exceeds the cost of capital will the project will increase stockholders' wealth. The **hurdle rate** (or cost of capital) is the rate the IRR must exceed if it is to be accepted.

$$0 = CF_0 + \frac{CF_1}{(1+IRR)} + \frac{CF_2}{(1+IRR)^2} + \ldots\ldots + \frac{CF_n}{(1+IRR)^n}$$ **(Equation 11-10)**

where

CF_t = the expected cash flow in period t

IRR = the internal rate of return

Example 11-16: Internal rate of return

The cost of a project is $150 million and the following cash flows are anticipated. The cost of capital is 10%.

Year	Net Cash Flow ($ million)
0	-150
1	25
2	50
3	55
4	40
5	60

$$0 = CF_0 + \frac{CF_1}{(1+\text{IRR})} + \frac{CF_2}{(1+\text{IRR})^2} + \ldots\ldots\ldots \frac{CF_n}{(1+\text{IRR})^n}$$

$$0 = -150 + \frac{25}{(1+\text{IRR})} + \frac{50}{(1+\text{IRR})^2} + \frac{55}{(1+\text{IRR})^3} + \frac{40}{(1+\text{IRR})^4} + \frac{60}{(1+\text{IRR})^5}$$

$$\text{IRR} = 14.6\%$$

Using a financial calculator the keystrokes are

HP-12C		BA II Plus	
[f] CLEAR [FIN]	**0.00**	[CF] [2nd] [CLR WORK]	**CF_0 = 0.00**
150 [CHS] [g] [CF_0]	**150.00**	150 [+/-] [ENTER]	**CF_0 = -150.00**
25 [g] [CF_j]	**25.00**	[⇩] 25 [ENTER]	**C01 = 25.00**
50 [g] [CF_j]	**50.00**	[⇩] [⇩] 50 [ENTER]	**C02 = 50.00**
55 [g] [CF_j]	**55.00**	[⇩] [⇩] 55 [ENTER]	**C03 = 55.00**
40 [g] [CF_j]	**40.00**	[⇩] [⇩] 40 [ENTER]	**C04 = 40.00**
60 [g] [CF_j]	**60.00**	[⇩] [⇩] 60 [ENTER]	**C05 = 60.00**
[f] [IRR]	**14.59**	[IRR] [CPT]	**IRR= 14.59**

LOS 11-1-C-c **explain** the NPV profile

The **net present value profile** is the graph showing the relationship between the NPV of a project and the cost of capital.

If we look at two projects, where project A is a long-term project and project B is a short-term project then the NPV of project A tends to be more sensitive to movements in the cost of capital (the cash flows that will be received far into the future will be most influenced by the discounting process).

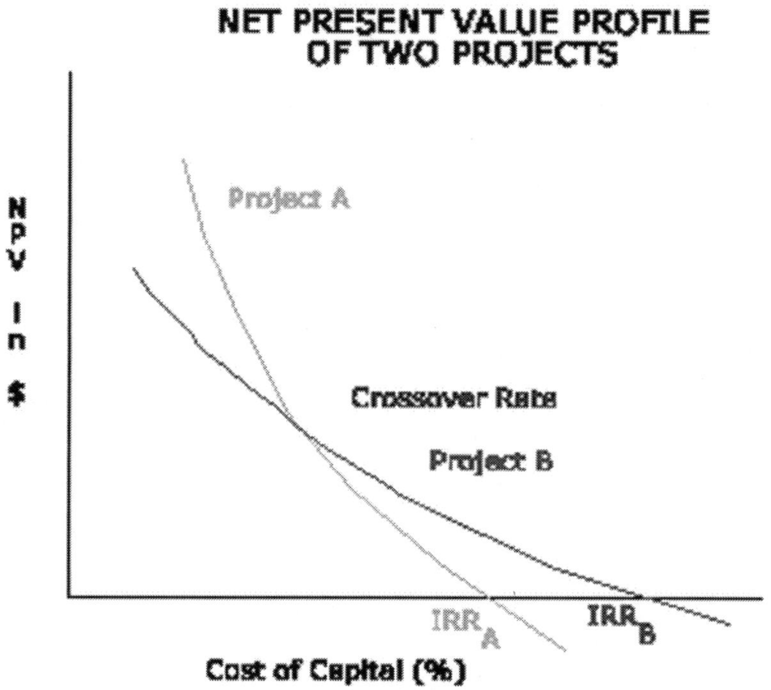

chart page 400

The **crossover rate** is the discount rate at which the NPV of two projects cross. At a cost of capital above the crossover rate project B is more attractive, with the cost of capital below the crossover rate project A is more attractive.

The NPV lines cross the x-axis when the cost of capital is zero. The point that they cross will be the project's internal rate of return.

LOS 11-1-C-d	**explain** the relative advantages and disadvantages of the NPV and IRR methods, particularly with respect to independent versus mutually exclusive projects
LOS 11-1-C-f	**explain** why NPV and IRR methods can produce conflicting rankings for capital projects

If analyzing *independent* projects NPV and IRR analysis will always give the same recommendation to accept or reject each project (the graph shows that if the IRR is greater than the cost of capital, then the NPV will be positive).

If a firm is analyzing two *mutually exclusive* projects then the NPV and IRR analysis may give different answers.

If the cost of capital is less than the crossover rate one project will give a higher NPV, when the cost of capital is more than the crossover rate the other project will give a higher NPV (see graph above). These differences arise when either the cost of the project or the timing of cash flows is different.

The NPV method is considered preferable because it assumes that cash flows are reinvested at the cost of capital, whereas the IRR method assumes that they will be reinvested at the IRR.

LOS 11-1-C-e	**explain** the "multiple IRR problem" and the cash flow pattern that causes the problem

A project has non-normal cash flows if negative cash flows occur after positive cash inflows. In this case the IRR method can give more than one solution, or multiple IRRs. Using the NPV method wouldwill avoid this situation.

Example 11-17: Multiple IRRs

A project has an initial cost of $10 million, will generate a cash inflow of $20 million in year 1 and a cash outflow of $10 million in year 2.

$$0 = CF_0 + \frac{CF_1}{(1+IRR)} + \frac{CF_2}{(1+IRR)^2}$$

$$0 = -10 + \frac{20}{(1+IRR)} - \frac{10}{(1+IRR)^2}$$

$$IRR = 0\% \text{ or } 20\%$$

Using a financial calculator will generate an error message

The LOSs do not require you to be able to describe or compute MIRRs, although it is included in the reading assignment, so we have included a brief description of MIRR for your information.

Modified Internal Rate of Return

In spite of the arguments for using NPV rather than IRR, IRR is often preferred in the corporate world. This has led to the adoption of MIRR as a method for evaluating projects.

The MIRR is the discount rate that will make the present value of the terminal value of the project equal to the cost. The terminal value (TV) is calculated by summing the future cash inflows which are compounded and compounding them at the *cost of capital* until the termination of the project. MIRR is considered more accurate since it assumes that the cash flows are reinvested at the cost of capital, which is generally more realistic than the IRR method, which assumes that they are adjusted reinvested at the IRR.

Example 11-18: Modified internal rate of return

The cost of a project is $150 million and the following cash flows are anticipated. The cost of capital is 10%.

Year	Net Cash Flow ($ million)
1	25
2	50
3	55
4	40
5	60

The Terminal Value (TV) is given by

$$= CF_1(1+k)^4 + CF_2(1+k)^3 + CF_3(1+k)^2 + CF_4(1+k) + CF_5$$

$$= 25(1.10)^4 + 50(1.10)^3 + 55(1.10)^2 + 40(1.10) + 60$$

$$= 36.6 + 66.6 + 66.6 + 44.0 + 60.0$$

$$= 273.8$$

$$\text{Cost} = \frac{TV}{(1+MIRR)^5}$$

$$150 = \frac{273.8}{(1+MIRR)^5}$$

$$MIRR = 12.8\%$$

When assessing two mutually exclusive projects the MIRR will give the same recommendation as the NPV method as long as the two projects are of equal size and life. However Iif they have a different life, the terminal value for both projects must be calculated using the end date of the longest project. However if they are different sizes of projects the NPV and MIRR methods can give different answers. Overall the NPV method is still considered the better method although the MIRR is an improvement on the IRR method in giving a project's correct rate of return.

LOS 11-1-C-g **describe** the role of the post-audit in the capital budgeting process

The **post audit** process refers to the task of (1) comparing the actual results of a project with those predicted and (2) explaining any differences.

It is important since

- If managers know that their actions are being monitored they are more likely to improve their forecasting skills.
- Managers will try to improve their operations to ensure that forecasts are met.

Empirical evidence suggests that companies which put heavy emphasis on the post-audit stage are more successful.

11-1-C View Concept Check Questions Workbook

11-1-D "Cash Flow Estimation and Other Topics in Capital Budgeting"

Introduction

Estimating the cash flows is a first step in applying NPV and IRR methods and the Reading identifies the cash flows which should be used in capital budgeting. Only incremental cash flows, and not sunk costs, are relevant in the process of capital budgeting and opportunity cost, externality and cannibalization need to be considered. Candidates also need to be able to rank a project, either an expansion or a replacement project, using NPV analysis. This will involve identifying three types of cash flows (initial investment outlay, operating cash flows over the project's life and the terminal year cash flows) and candidates have to avoid common pitfalls such as forgetting to adjust for additional working capital requirements at the beginning and end of projects and the impact of depreciation charges on tax.

LOS 11-1-D-a distinguish between cash flows and accounting profits

Defining Cash Flow

It is important to use cash flows and not accounting profits when evaluating a project, this is because it is necessary to consider the two components of cash flow - the return **on** capital (i.e. profit) plus the return **of** capital (i.e. depreciation).

Additionally interest expense or financing costs should **not** be included since we are using a cash flow available to pay the cost of debt, which is incorporated in the weighted-average cost of capital being used to discount the cash flows. The text uses after-tax operating income plus depreciation. Adjustments should be made for all non-cash costs but for most companies depreciation is the largest item.

Example 11-19: Net cash flow

Sales	$120 million
Costs **(including depreciation of $20 million)**	$ 50 million
Operating income	$ 70 million
Tax	$ 28 million
Net income	$ 42 million

Net cash flow = net income + depreciation = $42 + $20 = $62 million

LOS 11-1-D-b **discuss** the relevance to capital budgeting of the following: incremental cash flow, sunk cost, opportunity cost, externality, and cannibalisation

When deciding which cash flows to use, you should use **incremental cash flows**, these are the total cash flows that occur due to a firm as a direct result of taking on a specific project.

Sunk costs

These refer to costs that have already been paid or been committed to, regardless of whether a project is taken on or not. An example might be the cost of a consultancy company preparing a report on the feasibility of a project.

They should **not** to be included as a cost in a capital budgeting decision..

Opportunity costs

These refer to the cash flow that could be generated from an asset if it was not used in the project. For example, if a project is going to use premises that could be used for other purposes by the company.

Opportunity costs should be taken into account in the cash flows used.

Externalities

The impact of a project on other parts of a firm should be taken into account, whether positive or negative. This includes cannibalization, when sales of another side of the firm will be switched to the new area if a new project goes ahead.

Shipping and installation costs

Costs relating to the acquisition of equipment used in a project such as shipping and installation costs should be added to the cost of the project.

LOS 11-1-D-c **explain** the importance of changes in net working capital in the capital budgeting process

In most cases a new project will require additional inventories and financing for higher receivables balances. These will partially be offset by higher payables and accruals. The difference is the change in **net working capital**. If it is positive this indicates the need for additional financing and this must be added to the cost of fixed assets at the beginning of the project. At the end of the project inventories will be sold and receivables collected so the net working capital will be returned.

LOS 11-1-D-d	**determine** by NPV analysis whether a project (expansion or replacement) should be undertaken
LOS 11-1-D-e	**compute** each of the following for an expansion project and a replacement project: initial investment outlay, operating cash flow over a project's life, and terminal year cash flow

Cash flows from an expansion project

An expansion project is a project that is expected to increase sales.

When analyzing an expansion project the following steps need to be taken to calculate the incremental cash flows.

1. Estimate the initial investment outlay. This is the cost of assets required plus increase in working capital requirements (if any).
2. Estimate the operating cash flows over the project's life. This is net operating revenue plus depreciation, interest expense is not included.
3. Estimate the terminal-year cash flows. This will include salvage value of equipment (adjusted for tax) and addition of any previous increase in working capital.

Example 11-20: Expansion project

A company is considering a project to expand its manufacturing facilities with the purchase of a piece of machinery from a competitor. The cost of the machinery is $10 million. The machinery will be completely depreciated for tax purposes over three 3 years although the company estimates that the salvage value will be $1 million at the end of the project's three-year life. Additional working capital will be required of $2 million. The additional operating income after tax generated by the piece of machinery is estimated to be $3 million per annum, the tax rate is 40%. The capital budget analysis should be calculated using a weighted-average cost of capital of 15%.

Initial outlay = $10 million + $2 million = $12 million

$ million	Year 0	Year 1	Year 2	Year 3
Cost of new machine	(10.00)			
Increase in net working capital	(2.00)			
Net operating income		3.00	3.00	3.00
Add back depreciation		3.33	3.33	3.33
Operating cash flow		6.33	6.33	6.33
Return of working capital				2.00
Net salvage value*				0.60
Total cash flows	(12.00)	6.33	6.33	8.93
PV of cash flows	(12.00)	5.50	4.79	5.87

* adjust for tax since the salvage value is $1 million and the book value is zero.

The net cash flow for the project is $4.16 million. If the managers have confidence in their estimates this indicates the expansion project should go ahead.

Cash flows from a replacement project

A replacement project is when new asset(s) are purchased to replacing an existing asset(s).

The above calculation for an expansion project needs to be modified to take account of the sale of the old asset:

Initial investment = cost of assets plus increase in working capital requirements (if any) less after tax cash flow from sale of old asset.

Operating cash flows = adjust for additional net operating revenue and any change in depreciation.

Terminal year cash flow = adjust for salvage value of equipment (net of tax) and addition of any previous increase in working capital.

Example 11-21: Replacement project

A company is considering a project to replace a piece of machinery. The cost of the machinery is $10 million. The machinery will be completely depreciated for tax purposes over three 3 years although the company estimates that the salvage value will be $1 million at the end of the project's three-year life. The old machine can be sold for $2 million although its book value is $3 million; depreciation on the old machine was $1 million each year for the remaining three years of its life after which it was estimated to have zero salvage value. Additional working capital will be required of $2 million. The additional net operating income generated by the replacement of the machinery is estimated to be $3 million per annum; the tax rate is 40%. The capital budget analysis should be calculated using a weighted-average cost of capital of 15%.

Initial outlay = $10 million + $2 million = $12 million

$ million	Year 0	Year 1	Year 2	Year 3
Cost of new machine	(10.00)			
Sale of old machine	2.00			
Tax saving on sale*	0.40			
Increase in net working capital	(2.00)			
Increase in operating income		3.00	3.00	3.00
Increase in depreciation		2.33	2.33	2.33
Increase in operating cash flow		5.33	5.33	5.33
Return of working capital				2.00
Net salvage value				0.60
Total cash flows	(9.60)	5.33	5.33	7.93
PV of cash flows	(9.60)	4.63	4.03	5.21

* adjust for tax since the machine will be sold at $1 million below it book value.

The net cash flow for the project is $4.27 million.

LOS 11-1-D-f **compare** two projects with unequal lives, using both the replacement chain and equivalent annual annuity approaches

Projects with Unequal Lives

Up to now we have compared projects with equal lives, in the replacement project example both machines were assumed to have the same remaining useful life. Now we look at two methods that can be used if we are comparing two mutually exclusive projects with different lives.

Replacement chain approach

This method assumes that each project can be repeated as many times as necessary until they have the same life, and then the NPVs can be compared.

Equivalent Annual Annuity Approach (EAA)

This method calculates the payment each project would make if it were an annuity (calculate NPV and then calculate the EAA, using a financial calculator). Select the project with the highest EAA.

Example 11-22: Projects with different lives

A company is comparing two projects A and B. A has a life of 4 years and B a life of 2 years and the cash flows are shown below. The cost of capital is 8%.

Replacement chain approach

In this case we assume that Project B can be repeated at the end of two years with the same cash flows and costs of capital, the cash flows based on these assumptions are shown in the third column.

	Project A	Project B	Project B extended
Year 0	-30	-12	-12
Year 1	12	8	8
Year 2	10	7	7 – 12 = -5
Year 3	8	-	8
Year 4	8	-	7
NPV	1.92	1.41	2.62
IRR	11.08%	16.67%	16.67%

Initially the NPV of project A ($1.92 million) is higher than B's ($1.41 million) however when we use the replacement chain approach we can see that project B is more attractive.

Equivalent Annual Annuity Approach

Use a financial calculator to work out the EAA for each project

	Project A	Project B
NPV	1.92	1.41
EAA	0.58	0.79

This means that project A is equivalent to an annuity payment of $580,000 per year for four years and project B to an annuity payment of $790,000 per year over two years. The project with the higher EAA will have a higher NPV if they are both extended to the same life.

The calculator keystrokes for project A are as follows

HP-12C		BA II Plus	
[f] CLEAR [FIN]	**0.00**	[2nd] [QUIT] [2nd] [CLR TVM]	
1.92 [CHS] [PV]	**1.92**	1.92 [+/-] [PV]	**PV = -1.92**
8 [ENTER] [i]	**8.00**	8 [I/Y]	**I/Y = 8.00**
4 [ENTER] [n]	**4.00**	4 [N]	**N = 4.00**
0 [ENTER] [FV]	**0.00**	0 [FV]	**FV = 0.00**
[PMT]	**0.58**	[CPT] [PMT]	**PMT= 0.58**

LOS 11-1-D-g **discuss** the effects of inflation on capital budgeting analysis

Inflation

Ideally inflation expectations should be built into the cash flow forecasts since inflation is reflected in the weighted-average cost of capital. If it is not included in the cash flow forecasts there will be a downward bias on the NPV calculation.

11-1-D View Concept Check Questions Workbook

11-1-E "Risk Analysis and the Optimal Capital Budget"

Introduction

Up to now we have assumed that the actual cash flows of a project will match the estimated ones with certainty, but in reality they will not and we need a framework to analyze the risks. In this section we will look into three different types of project risk and we need to be able to distinguish between stand alone, corporate and market risks. Then we investigate three different types of risk analysis techniques which are commonly used, i.e. sensitivity analysis, scenario analysis and Monte Carlo simulation. Finally candidates need to be able to apply the Capital Asset Pricing Model (CAPM) to calculate required returns from projects to compensate for their beta-risk.

LOS 11-1-E-a	**distinguish** among three types of project risk: stand-alone, corporate, and market

Three types of risk can be identified when assessing a project.

1. Stand-alone risk

   In this case the project is seen as independent of a firm's other activities. It is measured by the variability of the expected returns from the project.
2. Corporate risk

   This considers the impact on the overall firm's activities; it is measured by the effect on the uncertainty of earnings of the firm. Corporate risk is more difficult to measure, so stand-alone risk is more commonly used; generally this will be a good proxy since the three types of risk are highly correlated.
3. Market risk

   It is measured by the impact of the project on a firm's beta. For an investor it is the part of risk that cannot be diversified away.

Example 11-23: Types of risk

The example used in the text is General Motors. If General Motors decides to proceed with a major expansion project to produce electric cars the project will have the following risk factors.

Stand-alone risk – high since the project uses new technology.

Corporate risk – the project is expected to do best in a strong economy when car sales are high, this will make the project's performance highly correlated to the performance of General Motor's other business, so the corporate risk is high.

Market risk – the profits are highly correlated with the profits of other corporations so the beta will also be high, so market risk is high.

Investors will tend to be most concerned about corporate risk and market risk (since a firm's beta will be a major determinant of the stock price).

LOS 11-1-E-b	**distinguish** among sensitivity analysis, scenario analysis, and Monte Carlo simulation as risk analysis techniques

Measuring Stand-alone risk

There are two methods for measuring stand-alone risk discussed:

1. sensitivity analysis, measures how much the NPV of a project changes when a specified variable changes. The higher the sensitivities the higher the risk of the project.
2. scenario analysis, different scenarios are assigned probabilities and the dispersion of the NPVs calculated in each scenario is measured, (reference probability distributions which are covered in Study Session 2). The best and worst-case NPV scenarios should be considered.

Scenario analysis has the disadvantage that it considers a number of discrete outcomes. A **Monte Carlo simulation** could be used, using a computer program, which allows for a far larger number of outcomes and their probabilities to be analyzed.

Example 11-24: Sensitivity analysis

A firm is considering a project to build a factory to produce televisions. The most likely scenario is that the factory will produce 1 million televisions a year, which can be sold at $200 each, and costs are estimated to be $180 million a year. The NPV in this case (**base-case NPV**) is $100 million. In sensitivity analysis different variables are considered such as unit sales price, unit volumes of sales, fixed costs, variable costs, cost of capital etc. For example, if the selling price for the televisions is $190 (5% below the estimate), the NPV is estimated to fall to $30 million, a fall of 70%, indicating that the project is highly sensitive to a small error in the unit price estimate.

LOS 11-1-E-c	**describe** how the security market line is used in the capital budgeting process

Beta risk

Beta and the Security Market Line (SML) are covered in much more detail in Study Session 12.

The Security Market Line (SML) links the required return for an investment (k_s) to its risk in terms of beta:

$$k_s = k_{RF} + \beta(k_M - k_{RF})$$

This is the same as Equation 11-3.

A project, from an investor viewpoint, is going to be attractive if the return earned from the project (which should be used as the discount rate to calculate the NPV of the project) compensates for the beta risk of the project.

Example 11-25: Required rate of return

A company is considering a project, which is estimated to have a beta of 1.2. The market return is 15% and the risk-free rate is 4%. The required return for the project, or **the project cost of capital** (k_P), is given by:

$k_P = 4\% + 1.2(15\% - 4\%) = 17.2\%$

This can be analyzed using the SML, if the project lies above the SML the project's expected rate of return is more than enough to compensate for the risk and the project should be accepted, if it lies below the line it should be rejected.

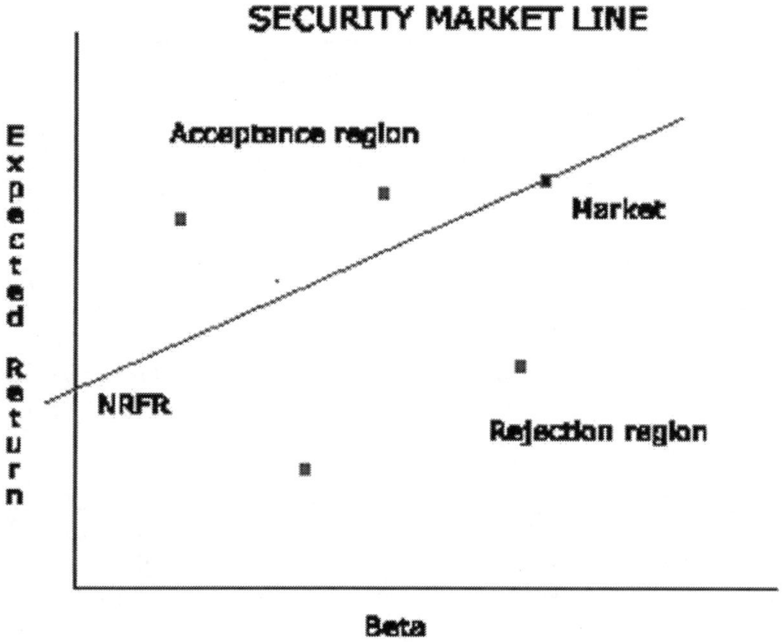

LOS 11-1-E-d	**describe** the pure play and accounting beta methods for estimating individual project betas

Measuring Beta

Two approaches are discussed:

1. The pure play method

First of all identify companies whose only business is the same as the project being analyzed, then take the average betas of these companies as a proxy for the beta of the project.

2. The accounting beta method

If the pure play method cannot be applied then an alternative is to consider a similar project and regress the return of the project against the return on assets for companies in a recognized index (e.g. the S&P Index).

LOS 11-1-E-e	**discuss** the procedure for developing a risk-adjusted discount rate

Risk-adjusted discount rates

One way of adjusting for the risk of a project is to change the discount rate used to reflect the risk, e.g. a high-risk project would be discounted at a higher rate than the firm's cost of capital.

To decide the discount rate, other than using CAPM, a firm might take two steps (1) calculate divisional costs of capital on an operating division basis (2) classify projects within that division by their riskiness.

LOS 11-1-F-f	**define** capital rationing

In theory, a firm should expand operations if marginal revenue exceeds the marginal cost, however in some circumstances there will be a reason to limit their expansion. **Capital rationing** refers to when a firm places a limit on the total size of its capital budget.

11-1-E View Concept Check Questions Workbook

11-1-F "Capital Structure and Leverage"

Introduction

This Reading focuses on optimal capital structures or the balance between debt and equity financing that will maximize a company's share price. Although debt, since interest payments are tax-deductible, appears to be cheaper than equity, the situation is more complex. As a company increases its debt financing the risk will increase pushing up the cost of both debt and equity. There is an optimal balance that can be achieved. Students are also required to know how to measure a company's operating and financial risk by computing degree of operating and financial leverage which, when multiplied together, will give the degree of total leverage.

LOS 11-1-F-a **define** target (optimal) capital structure

When a firm's management is deciding the target capital structure it must balance the following risk and return factors:

- Using more debt generally leads to a higher return
- Using more debt increases the risk for stockholders

The **optimal capital structure** will find a balance between these factors that will maximize the firm's stock price.

LOS 11-1-F-b **describe**, and **state** the impact of changes in, factors that influence a company's capital structure decision

Major factors that influence the capital structure include:

1. Business risk

If business risk (or risk in the company's operations) is higher, the debt ratio should be lower.

2. Tax position

The higher the tax rate the cheaper debt is likely to be (since interest on debt is a tax deductible expense).

3. Financial flexibility

A firm should adopt a lower risk strategy if it anticipates needing additional funds in the future.

4. Managerial style

Aggressive or conservative management will influence the choice of capital structure.

LOS 11-1-F-c	**explain** business risk and financial risk and **discuss** factors that influence each risk

Business and Financial Risk

Business risk is the risk associated with a firm's assets if it is not using debt. It is defined as the uncertainty in forecasting the future return on assets. This will depend on several factors such as:

- demand variability
- sales price variability
- input price variability
- ability to adjust output prices to reflect changes in input prices
- percentage of fixed costs (operating leverage).

Financial risk is the additional risk taken by stockholders if a firm uses debt financing.

LOS 11-1-F-e	**define** operating leverage and **explain** how it affects a project's or company's expected rate of return
LOS 11-1-F-f	**calculate** the breakeven quantity of sales and **determine** the company's gain or loss at various sales levels

Operating Leverage

Operating leverage reflects the percentage of total costs that are fixed costs. High operating leverage means that a firm's operating income (EBIT) is very sensitive to a change in sales.

A company with high operating leverage will tend to have a high **breakeven point** (the level of sales where revenues equal costs and operating income is zero) reflecting the high fixed cost base.

Breakeven will occur when

$$PQ - VQ - F = 0 \qquad \textbf{(Equation 11-11)}$$

where

P	=	average sales price per unit of output
Q	=	units of output
V	=	variable cost per unit
F	=	fixed operating costs

Example 11-26: Breakeven production levels

Consider two companycompanies,'s A and B, who are both manufacturing a product that sells for $10. (The example could be applied in the same way to different projects as well as companies). Their cost structures are different as shown in the table below:

	Company A	Company B
Unit price (P)	$10	$10
Variable cost per unit (V)	$8	$5
Fixed costs (F)	$50,000	$200,000

In both cases the units of output (Q) are expected to be 60,000 per annum

Using Equation 11-11

For A the breakeven point is given by

$$PQ = VQ + F$$

$$Q = \frac{\$50{,}000}{(\$10 - \$8)} = 25{,}000 \text{ units}$$

For B the breakeven point is given by

$$Q = \frac{\$200{,}000}{(\$10 - \$5)} = 40{,}000 \text{ units}$$

The table below gives the sensitivity of each company's EBIT to a change in sales:

$'000		Company A		Company B	
Units sold	**Sales**	**Costs**	**EBIT**	**Costs**	**EBIT**
10,000	100	130	(30)	250	(150)
40,000	400	370	30	400	0
60,000	600	530	70	500	100
80,000	800	690	110	600	200
110,000	1,100	930	170	750	350

We can see from the table that:

1. B has a higher expected return at the anticipated sales level of 60,000 units.
2. The breakeven point is lower for A than B.
3. B's operating profit is more sensitive to a change in sales.

Generally

Higher operating leverage leads to a higher expected return.
The risk of the return (in term of the variability of EBIT and ROE) is higher if the operating leverage is higher.

LOS 11-1-F-g	**define** financial leverage, and describe the relationship between financial leverage and financial risk
LOS 11-1-F-h	**discuss** why the use of greater amounts of debt in the capital structure can raise both the cost of debt and the cost of equity capital
LOS 11-1-F-d	**explain** and **calculate** the effects of changes in sales or earnings before interest and taxes (EBIT) on earnings per share for companies with differing amounts of debt financing

Financial Leverage

Financial leverage is the extent to which fixed-income securities are used in a firm's capital structure. Financial risk is the additional risk placed on the stockholders as a result of financial leverage.

Now we extend Example 11-26 to examine the effect of different levels of financing on EPS.

Example 11-27: Effect of debt financing

Use Example 11-26 above and look at various financing options for Company B. Assume that there are two alternatives:

1. B has $500,000 of debt at an interest rate of 6% and $500,000 of equity (50,000 shares)
2. B has $1,000,000 of equity (100,000 shares)

The tax rate is 40%

$' 000	Company B with 50% debt and 50% equity financing							
Units sold	Sales	Costs	EBIT	Interest	Pre-tax income	Net income	ROE	EPS
10,000	100	250	(150)	(30)	(180)	(108)	(21.6%)	($2.16)
40,000	400	400	0	(30)	(30)	(18)	(3.6%)	($0.36)
60,000	600	500	100	(30)	70	42	8.4%	$0.84
80,000	800	600	200	(30)	170	102	20.4%	$2.04
110,000	1,100	750	350	(30)	320	192	38.4%	$3.84

$' 000	Company B with 100% equity financing							
Units sold	Sales	Costs	EBIT	Interest	Pre-tax income	Net income	ROE	EPS
10,000	100	250	(150)	0	(150)	(90)	(9.0%)	($0.90)
40,000	400	400	0	0	0	0	0%	$0
60,000	600	500	100	0	100	60	6.0%	$0.60
80,000	800	600	200	0	200	120	12.0%	$1.20
110,000	1,100	750	350	0	350	210	21.0%	$2.10

We can see from the table that if there is no debt financing:

1. The expected return to stockholders at the anticipated sales level of 60,000 units is higher.
2. If sales are below the target the potential losses for stockholders are much larger.

If sales are above expectations the return for stockholders is much higher.

The above example illustrates that generally:

- The expected rate of return is higher for stockholders if debt financing is used.
- Increasing the proportion of debt used increases the risk to the common stockholders.

LOS 11-1-F-i	**describe** how changes in the use of debt can cause changes in the company's earnings per share and in the company's stock price

The analysis above shows that whilst debt is generally cheaper than equity, increasing the debt financing will also increase risk and therefore ultimately the cost of both the debt and equity. The key is to find the balance between debt and equity that is the optimal capital structure for the company.

LOS 11-1-F-j	**distinguish** between the value of a company and the value of the company's common stock

Determining the Optimal Capital Structure

The optimal capital structure is the one that maximizes the stock price, and minimizes the weighted-average cost of capital.

Increasing the debt component will reduce costs and increase earnings per share initially but as the level of debt increases the firm will usually have to pay a higher interest rate on the new debt that they issue to reflect the greater risk of default. This will lead to EPS peaking at a certain level of debt. Also, as the debt level rises, the risk for an investor in the firm's stock increases, which will lead to an increase in beta, which in turn increases the required rate or return from equity and the cost of equity capital. The optimal capital structure may be at a lower level of debt than that which maximizes earnings per share.

LOS 11-1-F-k	**explain** the effect of taxes and bankruptcy costs on the cost of capital, the optimal capital structure, and the Modigliani and Miller (MM) capital structure irrelevance proposition
LOS 11-1-F-l	**compare** the MM capital structure irrelevance proposition with the trade-off theory of leverage

Capital Structure Theory

Modigliani and Miller (MM) initially proposed that it was irrelevant how a firm financed its operations (**capital structure irrelevance theory**). However their assumptions, which included the following, were considered unrealistic.

- No brokerage costs
- No taxation
- No bankruptcy costs
- EBIT is independent of the use of debt
- Investors can borrow at the same rate as corporations
- Investors have the same information as management about a firm's future investment opportunities.

The next major paper from MM took into account that interest payments on debt were tax deductible and concluded that, given the other assumptions, companies should be 100% debt financed.

This was later amended to take account of the issue that dividend payments and capital gains, from the investor viewpoint, are taxed at a lower rate than income from bonds. Therefore the investors required rate of return from equities is correspondingly lower.

Bankruptcy costs

MM's theory assumed that there were no bankruptcy costs, this is not the case since bankruptcy leads to legal and accounting costs plus the risk that the firm's assets cannot be sold at the same price as if it were a going concern. Even the threat of bankruptcy will be sufficient to bring problems in terms of keeping employees, finding suppliers and maintaining a customer base. The costs of bankruptcy discourage firms from holding excessively high debt levels.

Trade-off theory

This theory followed on from the earlier work and said that firms must balance cheap debt financing against higher interest rates and bankruptcy costs. There will be an optimal capital structure when the marginal tax benefits from debt financing equal the marginal bankruptcy-related costs.

LOS 11-1-F-m **describe** how a company signals its prospects through its financing choices

Signalling theory

On the basis that managers have better knowledge of their firm's prospects than investors (**asymmetric information**) a decision, for example, to raise money through a new share issue gives a signal about the company's prospects.

If management is positive about a company's prospects they will avoid selling stock to raise capital since this will dilute the benefits to existing stockholders, including management, if the company is successful. On the other hand if a company has poor prospects they will wish to bring in new stockholders to share the future losses.

LOS 11-1-F-n **calculate** degree of operating leverage, degree of financial leverage, and degree of total leverage

Degree of Operating Leverage (DOL)

This measures the change in earnings before interest and tax (EBIT) that results from a change in sales.

DOL = percentage change in EBIT/percentage change in sales

Expressing this another way, the DOL at point Q

$$\text{DOL} = \frac{Q(P - V)}{Q(P - V) - F}$$ **(Equation 11-12)**

Example 11-28: Degree of operating leverage

Use the previous data for Companies A and B and set Q at 60,000 units

	Company A	Company B
Unit price (P)	$10	$10
Variable cost per unit (V)	$8	$5
Fixed costs (F)	$50,000	$200,000

$$\text{DOL}_A = \frac{[60{,}000(\$10 - \$8)]}{[60{,}000(\$10 - \$8) - \$50{,}000]} = \frac{\$120{,}000}{\$70{,}000} = 1.71$$

$$\text{DOL}_B = \frac{[60{,}000(\$10 - \$5)]}{[60{,}000(\$10 - \$5) - \$200{,}000]} = \frac{\$300{,}000}{\$100{,}000} = 3.0$$

For A, a 33.33% increase in sales to 80,000 units will lead to a 57% increase in EBIT, whereas for B, a 33.33% increase in sales will lead to a 100.0% increase in EBIT (as can be seen in the table in Example 11-26)

Degree of Financial Leverage (DFL)

This measures the percentage change in earnings per share (EPS) that results from a percentage change in EBIT.

$$DFL = \frac{\%\text{ change in EPS}}{\%\text{ change in EBIT}} = \frac{EBIT}{EBIT - I}$$ **(Equation 11-13)**

where

I = the interest payment

Example 11-29: Degree of financial leverage

Use the previous data for Company B with 50% debt financing, and Q is 60,000:

$$DFL = \frac{EBIT}{EBIT - I} = \frac{\$100{,}000}{(\$100{,}000 - \$30{,}000)} = 142\%$$

A 100% increase in EBIT would lead to a 142% increase in EPS.

Degree of Total Leverage (DTL)

This measures the percentage change in EPS that results from a percentage change in sales.

$$DTL = DOL \times DFL$$ **(Equation 11-14)**

Example 11-30: Degree of total leverage

The degree of total leverage for company B is given by:

$$DTL = DOL \times DFL = 3.0 \times 1.42 = 4.26$$

11-1-F View Concept Check Questions Workbook

11-1-G "Dividend Policy"

Introduction

Now we move on to the optimal dividend policy and what proportion of earnings should a company pay out to maximize its share price. There are three dividend preference theories you need to be familiar with - the dividend irrelevance theory, the bird-in-the-hand theory and the tax preference theory. Candidates also need to be able to describe dividend payment procedures and the impact of stock dividends and stock splits. Finally the advantages and disadvantages of stock repurchases are discussed.

LOS 11-1-G-a	**describe** the dividend irrelevance theory, the "bird-in-the-hand" theory, and the tax-preference theory
LOS 11-1-G-b	**explain** the dividend irrelevance theory in the context of the determinants of the value of the company
LOS 11-1-G-c	**discuss** the principal conclusion for dividend policy of the dividend irrelevance theory
LOS 11-1-G-d	**describe** how any shareholder can construct his or her own dividend policy

Companies which earn profitsCompanies, which earn profits, can decide to use the profits to:

1. reinvest in the company's business or acquire new assets
2. retire debt
3. pay back funds to stockholders, either as dividends or through stock repurchase programs.

The optimal dividend policy should aim to maximize the company's stock price by balancing investors' requirements for current income against future growth. This will establish the **target payout ratio**, which is the percentage of net income that is paid out as dividends.

There are various theories on the appropriate target payout ratio for dividends:

1. Dividend irrelevance theory (advocated by MM)

This theory says that an investor can combine dividends and buying or selling stock to achieve whatever cash payment they wish to receive from an investment, so the firm's dividend payout policy is irrelevant. This is somewhat simplified since it ignore taxes and transaction costs.

2. Bird-in-the-hand theory

This theory says that a firm's value will be maximized if they set a high dividend payout ratio. Investors prefer to receive cash today rather than an uncertain capital gain in the future.

3. Tax preference theory

Capital gains taxes are generally lower than taxes on dividend payments, also capital gains tax is paid at a later date (and not at all if the investor dies), these factors argue that investors prefer a low payout ratio.

The charts below illustrate the relationship between stock prices and the cost of equity relative to payout ratios under the different theories.

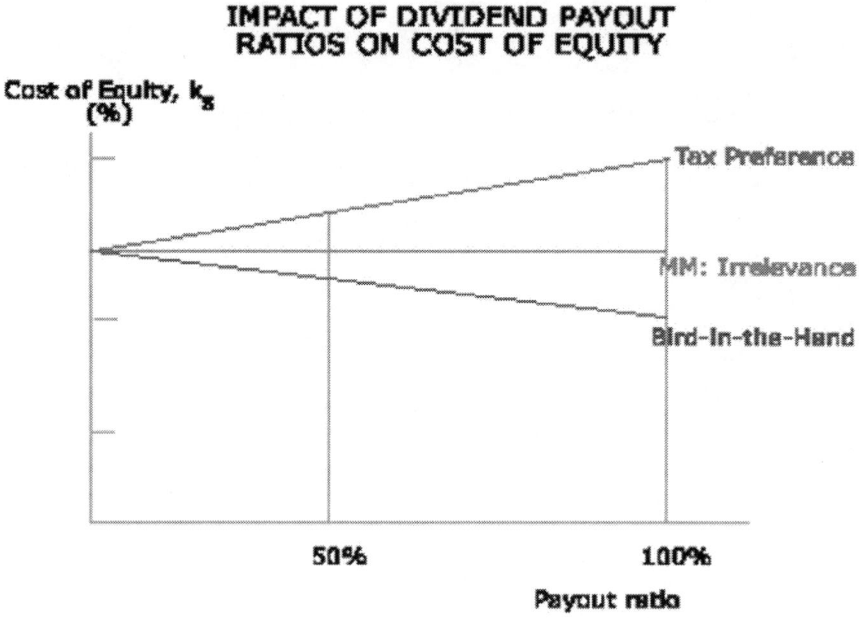

plots y axis stock price

x axis payout ratio

horizontal line- MM irrelevance theory

upward sloping line- bird-in-the-hand theory

downward sloping line- tax preference theory

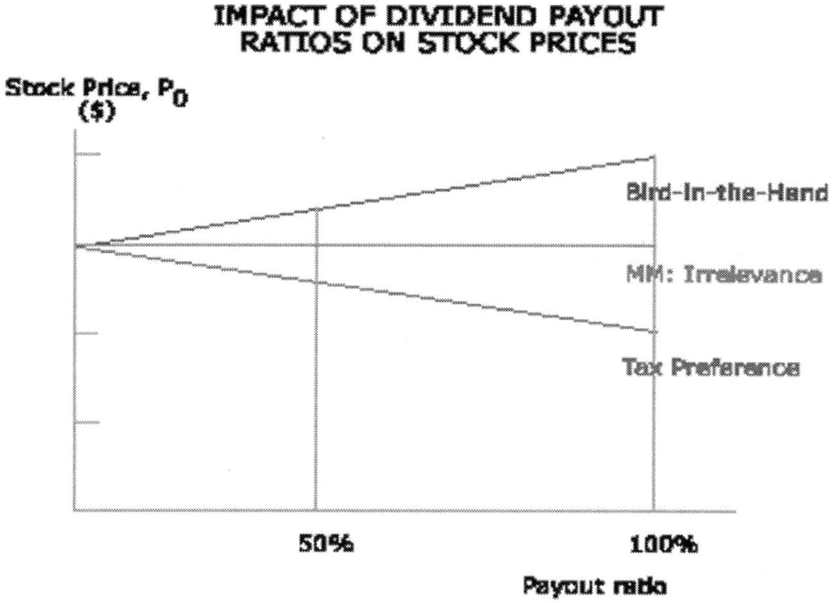

Empirically there is no clear evidence that investors prefer low or high payout ratios, but they do prefer stable policies.

LOS 11-1-G-e **calculate,** assuming a constant return on equity, a company's dividend growth rate, given the company's dividend payout rate

Dividend stability

Investors prefer stable dividends whereas corporations would ideally change the dividends depending on cash available and investment opportunities.

A stable growth rate for dividends is given by g, where

$$g = b \times ROE$$ **(Equation 11-15)**

where

b = the proportion of earnings that are retained, which is 1 minus the payout ratio.

ROE = return on equity

Example 11-31: Dividend growth rates

If a company has a stable return on equity of 15% and a dividend payout ratio of 60%, the dividend growth rate will be:

$$g = (1 - 0.60) \times 15\% = 6\%$$

LOS 11-1-G-f **describe** how managers signal their company's earnings forecast through changes in dividend policy

Signalling hypothesis

Managers are reluctant to cut dividends and will only increase dividends if they are confident that they can maintain the higher dividend level. Therefore a larger than expected increase in dividends is a positive signal from management over future earnings prospects. This explains the better performance of shares following such an announcement, rather than investor preference for a higher payout ratio.

LOS 11-1-G-g **describe** the clientele effect

Clientele effect

The **clientele effect** says that different investors have different preferences regarding dividend policies, and certain firms will tend to attract different types of investors.

Establishing dividend policy

When a firm decides the dividend policy it must take into account four factors:

1. investors' preferences
2. the firm's investment opportunities
3. its target capital structure
4. the availability and cost of external capital

LOS 11-1-G-h **describe** the residual dividend model and **discuss** the model's possible advantages or disadvantages to the company

The **residual dividend model** says that the actual dividends paid should be retained earnings less funds needed to finance the firm's optimal capital budget. If the firm maintains the optimal capital structure through debt and equity financing, where the equity financing comes from retained earnings, it will minimize the marginal cost of new capital (since it avoids issuing costs for new equity). It is important to note the residual discount model should be used to establish dividend payout ratios over the long term, not just for one year.

LOS 11-1-G-i	**describe** dividend payment procedures, including the declaration, holder- of-record, ex-dividend, and payment dates

Dividend Payment Procedures

Dividends are normally paid quarterly and the procedure is described below:

1. Declaration date

This is the date when the directors declare a dividend.

2. Holder-of-record date

The stockholders listed as owners at the close of business on this date will receive the dividend.

3. Ex-dividend date

Usually in the US this is four two days before the holder-of-record date. It is the date that the holder of a stock is no longer entitled to the dividend. If the stock is bought on this date the seller is entitled to the dividend.

4. Payment date

The firm pays the dividend (or mails the checks) to the holders of record.

LOS 11-1-G-j	**describe** stock dividends and stock splits and **explain** their likely pricing effects;

Non- cash Dividends

Stock splits

The number of shares outstanding is increased by giving each stockholder more shares that are worth correspondingly less e.g. a two-for-one stock split doubles the number of shares outstanding. The rationale for a stock split is usually to reduce the share price to make it more affordable to investors who wish to buy a lot of 100 shares.

Stock dividends

This is a dividend that is paid as additional shares rather than cash. e.g. a 10% stock dividend means that each holder of 100 shares receives an extra 10 new shares. This will also reduce the price of the stock, but by less than a stock split, so a stock dividend tends to be given on a regular basis to maintain a lower stock price.

Empirical findings

An announcement of a stock split or a stock dividend tends to lead to a rise in price of the stock, this is explained by the fact that such an announcement is seen as a positive signal from management. However if earnings or dividends are not subsequently seen to improve then the stock price will fall back again.

LOS 11-1-G-k **discuss** the advantages and disadvantages of stock repurchases and **calculate** the price effect of a stock repurchase

Stock repurchases

Stock repurchases have several *advantages* over dividend payments:

- They signal that management thinks that their stock is undervalued
- Stockholders have a choice whether to sell or not
- They can remove stock overhanging the stock market
- Avoids committing management to an increased level of dividends long term
- They can be used to adjust capital structure

Disadvantages are:

- Investors may prefer dividends since they are seen as more dependable
- Stockholders may have insufficient information to make a decision whether to sell stock
- The firm may pay too much for the stock

We can look at the price effect of a stock repurchase by working through Example 11-32.

Example 11-32: Price effect of stock repurchase

ABC Corp. has reported a profit of $5 million. There are 2 million shares outstanding, the shares are trading at $25 a share. ABC has surplus cash of $2.8 million and is considering doing a tender offer to repurchase 100,000 of its shares at $28 per share. The alternative is to use the equivalent amount of money to pay a special dividend of $1.40 per share. The effect of the repurchase on the share price can be calculated as follows

Current EPS = $5 million/2 million = $2.50

Current P/E ratio = $25/$2.50 = 10 times

EPS after repurchasing 100,000 shares = $5 million/1.9 million = $2.63

Expected market price after repurchase = P/E x EPS = 10 x $2.63 = $26.30

The shareholders either receive the benefit of a $1.30 increase in the stock price (if the P/E remains constant) or a special dividend of $1.40 per share. However if the company could pay significantly less than $28 to buy back shares the repurchase could be the more attractive alternative for shareholders.

11-1-G View Concept Check Questions Workbook

STUDY SESSION 12

Portfolio Management

Capital Market Theory: Basic Concepts

Overview

At Level I portfolio management only accounts for one Study Session and a guideline weighting of 5% of the examination questions. However the concepts covered here are an important foundation for both Level II and especially Level III when the syllabus centres on portfolio management.

This Study Session starts with a review of the relationship between risk and return and the components of risk and return. The next section moves on to client policy statements and setting risk and return objectives. These topics are revisited many times in Level III. In the last two Reading Assignments candidates are introduced to modern portfolio theory including how to structure portfolios to obtain the optimal risk and return trade-off. This is followed by an introduction to capital market theory and the Capital Asset Pricing Model (CAPM) which formally links the return of a security or portfolio to its systematic or beta risk.

Reading Assignments

12-1. *Investment Analysis and Portfolio Management,* 7th edition, Frank K. Reilly and Keith C. Brown (South-Western, 2003)

12-1-A. "The Investment Setting," Ch. 1, pp. 16–29

12-1-B. "The Asset Allocation Decision," Ch. 2

12-1-C. "An Introduction to Portfolio Management," Ch. 7

12-1-D. "An Introduction to Asset Pricing Models," Ch. 8, pp. 237• 256

12-1-A "The Investment Setting"

Introduction

This Reading Assignment looks at basic concepts and how risk and return are related in investment. Investors' required returns are derived from the real risk-free rate, plus an inflation premium and a premium for taking on risk. We also consider the difference between risks that can be diversified away in a portfolio and systematic risk which cannot be diversified. The security market line (SML) graphically links the required return to the systematic risk and candidates need to know which factors will lead to a move in the SML.

LOS 12-1-A-a	**explain** the concept of required rate of return and **discuss** the components of an investor's required rate of return
LOS 12-1-A-b	**differentiate** between the real risk-free rate of return and the nominal risk-free rate of return and **compute** both return measures
LOS 12-1-A-c	**explain** the risk premium and the associated fundamental sources of risk

Required Rate of Return

The **required rate of return** is the minimum rate of return an investor needs to receive to compensate for deferring consumption. Different assets provide a wide range of different returns, and returns change significantly over time.

The three components of the required rate of return are (1) the real risk-free rate (2) the expected rate of inflation and (3) the risk premium. These are defined as follows.

1. Real risk-free rate (RRFR) – this is the interest rate assuming there is no inflation and there is certainty regarding receipt of cash flows, it is the pure time value of money. There is a positive relationship between this and the real growth rate in the economy since the opportunities to use money are greater in an expanding economy.

2. Expected rate of inflation – this is linked to the nominal risk-free rate (NRFR) as follows:

$$\text{RRFR} = \frac{(1 + \text{NRFR})}{(1 + \text{Exp. rate of inflation})} - 1 \qquad \textbf{(Equation 12-1)}$$

The NRFR is a stated money market yield such as the return on Treasury bills in the U.S.

3. Risk premium - this is the excess return that must be paid to compensate for the uncertainty of the return being achieved. Different *sources* of risk, which are called fundamental sources of risk, associated with an investment include:

business risk – the uncertainty of a firm's income flows due to the firm's type of business.

financial risk – the uncertainty caused by the way a firm finances its activities.

liquidity risk – the uncertainty over how long it will take to liquidate an investment and the price that will be received.

exchange rate risk – the uncertainty of return created by buying a security in a foreign currency.

country risk – this incorporates both political risk and the risk of a major change in the economic environment in a country.

Total risk is measured as the standard deviation or variance of returns, and is a function of the fundamental sources of risk shown above. Other measures of risk are the coefficient of variation of returns and the covariance of returns with the market return (beta).

Example 12-1: Nominal and real rates of return

If the nominal rate of return on T-bills is 6%, and the rate of inflation is 2%, then the RRFR is given by

$$\text{RRFR} = \frac{(1+\text{NRFR})}{(1+\text{Exp. rate of inflation})} - 1 = \frac{1.06}{1.02} - 1 = 0.0392 \text{ or } 3.92\%$$

The NRFR will also be affected by the supply and demand for capital e.g. a tight monetary policy will in the short run reduce the supply of capital and increase interest rates.

LOS 12-1-A-d **define** the security market line and discuss the factors that cause movements along, changes in the slope of, and shifts of the security market line

The risk premium of an asset can be expressed as a function of its market risk, this is **systematic risk**.

The **security market line** (SML) measures expected return relative to systematic risk (represented by beta).

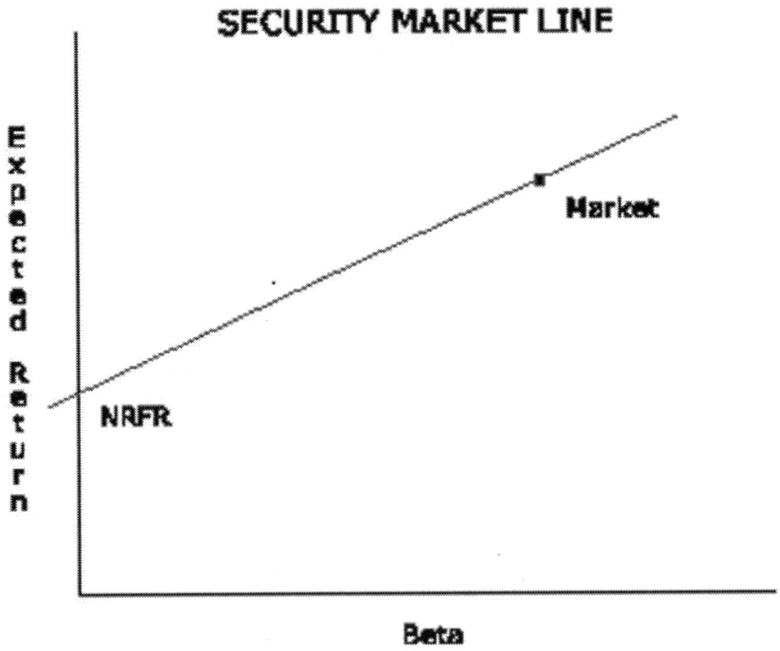

Investors select investments at different points along the line depending on their assessment of the risk of the investment.

A **change in slope of the SML** indicates that investors are requiring a higher, or lower, reward for taking a market risk. This means that the risk premium of the market has changed.

A **shift in the SML** indicates that there has been a change in a factor that affects all investments such as growth or inflation expectations.

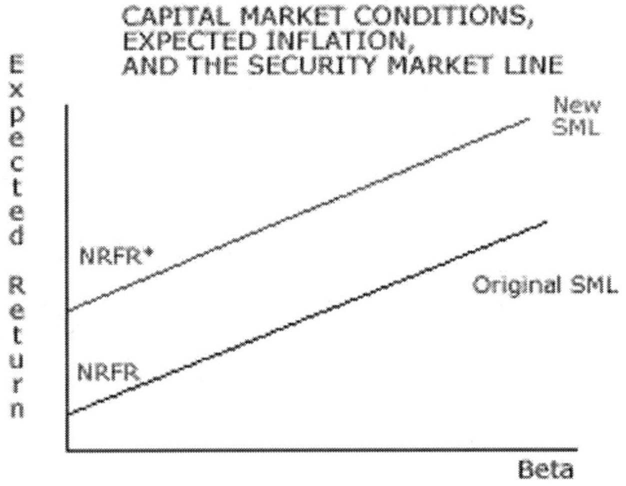

12-1-A View Concept Check Questions Workbook

12-1-B "The Asset Allocation Decision"

Introduction

Asset allocation is the process of deciding how to divide an investor's assets between different countries and asset classes. The asset allocation decision is extremely important since it, rather than stock selection, is the key factor in determining the performance of a portfolio. Studies show that the target asset allocation policy accounts for about 90% of funds' performance. Candidates need to understand how determining a client's objectives and constraints and the subsequent asset allocation decision fit in to the overall investment process.

Asset Allocation for Individual Investors

Risk and return requirements will depend on which *phase of the life cycle* the individual is in, namely:

Accumulation, individuals are using income for their immediate needs, such as house purchases, but are also saving for longer-term commitments such as children's schooling. Net worth will be low but time horizon is long so investors are often looking for high-risk investments.

Consolidation, earnings are higher than expenses so saving is usually for retirement. There is a medium to long-term time horizon so moderate risk investments are appropriate.

Spending, usually when individuals retire, it indicates a move towards safer investments but still a need to maintain the *real* value of capital so equity investments are still a component of their investment portfolio.

Gifting, any excess assets are used to set up charitable trusts, or to assist family and friends.

LOS 12-1-B-a describe the steps in the portfolio management process

Portfolio Management Process

Asset allocation is only one part of the portfolio management process. The portfolio management process can be broken down into **four** steps:

1. Formulate a policy statement that includes the investment objectives and constraints for each client.
2. Analyze current and expected economic, political and social conditions. Investment strategy is dynamic, it reflects changes in the economy, politics, financial markets etc.
3. Construct the portfolio. Meet the investor's requirements with the minimum level of risk.
4. Monitor the portfolio and make adjustments. Changes will made to reflect the changes in market conditions and any changes in the policy statement. Also portfolio performance needs to be evaluated.

LOS 12-1-B-b **explain** the need for a policy statement

The policy statement is needed because it:

1. Allows the investor to formulate his expectations and requirements which will help set realistic financial goals. This process will help the investor understand the characteristics of financial markets and the risks of investing in them.
2. Helps the portfolio manager construct a portfolio which will meet the client's requirements.
3. Provides information needed to judge the portfolio manager's performance. Typically the policy statement will set a **benchmark**, which will reflect the objectives of the client and which performance can be measured against.

LOS 12-1-B-c **explain** why investment objectives should be expressed in terms of risk and return

Objectives

The main objectives are concerned with

1. Return requirements
2. Risk tolerance

If an investor expresses his expectations only in terms of returns, there is a danger that a high target return leads to a portfolio manager investing in higher risk assets, and the risk may not be acceptable to the client.

LOS 12-1-B-d **list** the factors that may affect an investor's risk tolerance

The factors that will influence an individual's risk tolerance include

- Psychological make-up
- Insurance cover
- Cash reserves
- Family situation including number of dependents
- Age and time horizon
- Current net worth and income expectations

LOS 12-1-B-e describe the return objectives of capital preservation, capital appreciation, current income, and total return

Investor return objectives

For private investors, return objectives may be specified in terms such as capital preservation, capital appreciation, current income and total return.

Capital preservation - this is generally for risk-averse investors or short-term funds who want to minimize the risk of loss, usually in real terms. This means they want to achieve a return that is equal to or above the inflation rate.

Capital appreciation – this is usually for longer-term investors where growth in value of the assets is the priority, perhaps to build a retirement fund. Growth usually comes from capital gain.

Current income – this is often for investors who are focusing on income rather than capital gains. Perhaps income from the portfolio is needed to pay for living expenses.

Total return – this is usually for long-term investors and they are looking for growth in value of a portfolio to come from both capital gains and reinvestment of income.

LOS 12-1-B-f describe the investment constraints of liquidity, time horizon, tax concerns, legal and regulatory factors, and unique needs and preferences

In addition to setting out the investor's objectives the policy statement should include constraints that impact on the investments made in the portfolio. These can be put into five categories:

Constraints

1. Liquidity
2. Time horizon
3. Tax
4. Legal and regulatory factors
5. Unique needs and preferences

Example 12-2: Individual investor constraints

An individual investor needs to consider the follow types of issues:

1. *Liquidity*, short-term requirements for major expenses including paying tax bills, the potential loss of employment, the possibility of unexpected bills or medical expenses.
2. *Time horizon,* often reflects the age of the investor and position in the life cycle. Longer time horizons generally imply greater risk tolerance and vice versa.
3. *Tax,* consider the investor's liabilities to capital gains and income taxes.
4. *Legal*, consider whether the funds are in a trust, the role of fiduciary, and securities trading regulations.
5. *Unique needs and preferences*, include socially conscious investing, or restricting investments based on religious beliefs.

Data shows that equities are the only financial asset that performs significantly better than inflation over the long term, this is after adjusting for taxation. Although equity performance is more volatile, it is recommended that if the investor's objectives include capital appreciation or capital protection over a long time period, equities should be a major component of the portfolio.

The following chart illustrates the returns from different asset classes and the effect of taxes and inflation on returns.

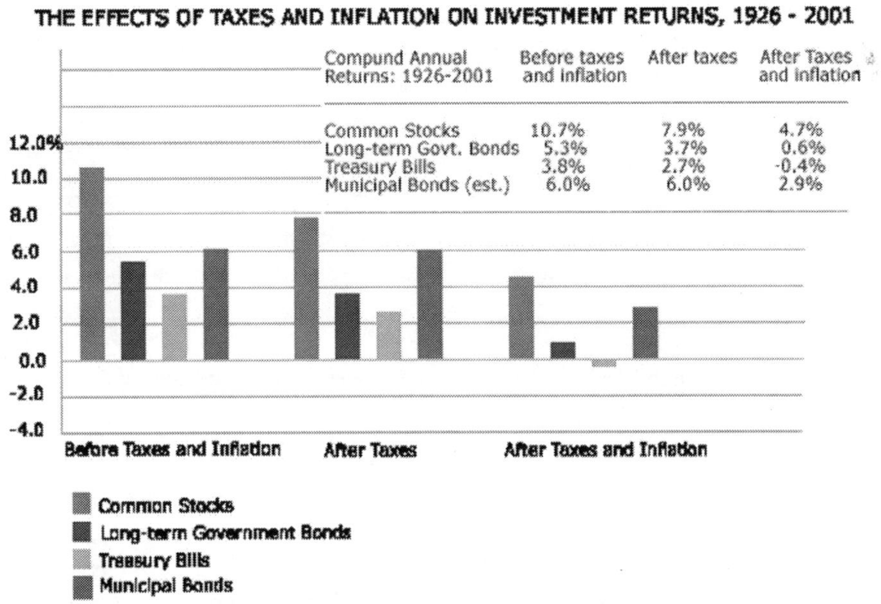

12-1-B View Concept Check Questions Workbook

12-1-C "An Introduction to Portfolio Management"

Introduction

Now we move on to analyzing risk and return in more detail, not just for individual securities_but also for portfolios. Candidates should be comfortable using the equations for computing portfolio return and risk (variance or standard deviation), covariance and correlation. This leads on to studying the Markowitz efficient frontier which determines which portfolios offer an investor the best trade-off between risk and return. This in turn paves the way for the capital market theory covered in the next Reading Assignment.

LOS 12-1-C-a **define** risk aversion and **cite** evidence that suggests that individuals are generally risk averse

Risk aversion

Modern portfolio theory assumes that investors are risk averse and given the choice of investing in two assets with the same expected rates of return they will invest in the one with the lowest risk. This means that there will be a positive relationship between return and risk.

Evidence of risk aversion

Insurance – people are willing to pay a premium to avoid the risk of a future loss.

Bond pricing – investors who hold bonds with higher credit risk require a higher rate of return.

Although there is contrary evidence, such as people buying lottery tickets, that people are willing to pay (have a negative expected return) to take on risk if there is a chance of a big gain. In these cases we are usually looking at small amounts of money being invested.

LOS 12-1-C-b **list** the assumptions about individuals' investment behaviour of the Markowitz Portfolio Theory

Markowitz developed models to measure portfolio risk which led to the importance of portfolio diversification being recognized. There are several underlying assumptions behind the models.

Investors look at each alternative investment as being represented by a probability distribution of expected return over a holding period.

Investors maximize one-period utility; their utility curves demonstrate diminishing marginal utility of wealth.

Investors estimate risk based on variability of expected returns. Investors base decisions solely on risk and return considerations.

For a given level of risk investors prefer high returns to low returns, for a given level of expected return investors prefer low risk to high risk.

An asset or portfolio is considered to be **efficient** if no other asset or portfolio a better risk/return trade-off. We are going to use variance, or standard deviation, as the measure of risk.

LOS 12-1-C-c **compute** expected return for an individual investment and for a portfolio

Expected return of a portfolio

Expected portfolio return = weighted average of expected returns of securities in the portfolio

$$E(R_{port}) = \sum_{i=1}^{n} w_i E(R_i) \qquad \textbf{(Equation 12-2)}$$

where

w_i = percent of portfolio in asset i
$E(R_i)$ = expected rate of return of asset I

Example 12-3: Expected portfolio return

Two securities have expected returns of 8% and 12% respectively. A portfolio is invested with 40% in the first security and 60% in the second. The expected portfolio return is given by:

$$\begin{aligned} &E(R_{port}) \\ &= w_1E(R_1) + w_2E(R_2) \\ &= (0.40 \times 8\%) + (0.60 \times 12\%) \\ &= 10.4\% \end{aligned}$$

LOS 12-1-C-d **compute** the variance and standard deviation for an individual investment

Risk of an individual investment

Although there are various risk measures including the range of returns and semi-variance risk, here we are defining risk as **variance** (^{2}) or **standard deviation** ( ).

$$\sigma^2 = \sum_{i=1}^{n} [R_i - E(R_i)]^2 P_i \qquad \textbf{(Equation 12-3)}$$

where

P_i = the probability of return R_i occurring for asset i
$E(R_i)$ = expected rate of return of asset I

Example 12-4: Risk of an individual investment

The possible rates of return for an asset are shown in the table below:

Possible rate of return	Probability
4%	0.25
10%	0.50
16%	0.25

The expected return is given by:

$$E(R_{port}) = 0.25(4\%) + 0.50(10\%) + 0.25(16\%) = 10\%$$

The variance is given by:

$$\sigma^2 = \sum_{i=1}^{n}[R_i - E(R_i)]^2 P_i = (4\% - 10\%)^2 0.25 + (10\% - 10\%)^2 0.50 + (16\% - 10\%)^2 0.25 = 0.0018$$

The standard deviation is 4.24%

LOS 12-1-C-e **compute** the covariance of rates of return, and **show** how it is related to the correlation coefficient

Risk of a portfolio of assets

Risks are not additive, so when calculating the risk of a portfolio of assets we need further information. In addition to the standard deviation of the individual assets we also need to know the **covariances**, which measures of how closely two assets move together relative to their mean values.

Covariance is 'standardized' to give the **correlation coefficient,** the correlation coefficient lies between -1 and +1. The correlation coefficient, r_{xy}, between two variables x and y is given by

$$r_{xy} = \frac{cov_{xy}}{\sigma_x \sigma_y} \qquad \text{(Equation 12-4)}$$

where

cov_{xy} = the covariance between the returns of x and y
σ_x = the standard deviation of returns of x
σ_y = the standard deviation of returns of y

If r_{xy} is +1, this is perfect positive correlation, it means that there is a perfect liner relationship between the returns from the two assets, the stocks move together in a perfectly linear manner.

If r_{xy} is 0, the returns are not linearly correlated.

If r_{xy} is –1, this is perfect negative correlation, if one return is above its mean then the other will be below the mean by a comparable amount.

Example 12-5: Correlation

If the standard deviations of the returns of two assets are 5% and 10%, and the covariance of the returns is 18 then the correlation coefficient is

$$r_{xy} = \frac{cov_{xy}}{\sigma_x \sigma_y} = \frac{18}{5 \times 10} = 0.36$$

This means that the two assets have a moderately low positive correlation.

> **LOS 12-1-C-f** **list** the components of the portfolio standard deviation formula, and **explain** which component is most important to consider when adding an investment to a portfolio

Standard deviation of a portfolio

Markowitz provided the general formula for portfolio risk as follows:

$$\sigma^2_{port} = \sum_{i=1}^{n} w_i^2 \sigma_i^2 + \sum_{i=1}^{n} \sum_{\substack{j=1 \\ i \neq j}}^{n} w_i w_j \, cov_{ij} \qquad \textbf{(Equation 12-5)}$$

where

σ_i = the standard deviation of returns of asset i

σ_j = the standard deviation of returns of asset j

w_i = the weighting of asset i in the portfolio

cov_{ij} = the covariance between the returns of assets i and j

The formula shows that if a new asset is added to a portfolio the total portfolio risk will *strongly reflect the covariance of this asset with the other assets in the portfolio*. The variance of returns of the individual asset will be a less important factor.

For a two-asset portfolio the equation that gives the risk of the portfolio is shown below:

$$\sigma^2_{port} = w_1^2 \sigma_1^2 + w_2^2 \sigma_2^2 + 2 r_{12} w_1 w_2 \sigma_1 \sigma_2 \qquad \textbf{(Equation 12-6)}$$

(replacing cov_{12} with $r_{12\ 1\ 2}$)

Example 12-6: Portfolio risk

The standard deviations of the returns of two securities are 5% and 10%, with expected returns of 8% and 12% respectively. A portfolio is invested with 40% in the first security and 60% in the second security. Looking at the three cases where the correlation coefficient between the returns of the assets are (1) 1.0 (2) 0 and (3) -1, the return and standard deviation of the combined portfolio are calculated as follows, using Equation 12-6.

$$E(R_{port})$$

$$= w_1 E(R_1) + w_2 E(R_2)$$

$$= (0.40 \times 8\%) + (0.60 \times 12\%)$$

$$= 10.4\%$$

$$\sigma_{port}^2 = w_1^2 \sigma_1^2 + w_2^2 \sigma_2^2 + 2 w_1 w_2 \sigma_1 \sigma_2$$

$$\sigma_{port} = w_1 \sigma_1 + w_2 \sigma_2 = (0.40 \times 5\%) + (0.60 \times 10\%) = 8.0\%$$

$$E(R_{port}) = 10.4\%$$

$$\sigma_{port}^2 = w_1^2 \sigma_1^2 + w_2^2 \sigma_2^2 = 0.0004 + 0.0036 = 0.004$$

$$\sigma_{port} = 6.3\%$$

$$E(R_{port}) = 10.4\%$$

$$\sigma_{port}^2 = w_1^2 \sigma_1^2 + w_2^2 \sigma_2^2 - 2 w_1 w_2 \sigma_1 \sigma_2$$

$$\sigma_{port} = \left| w_1 \sigma_1 - w_2 \sigma_2 \right| = \left| (0.40 \times 5\%) - (0.60 \times 10\%) \right| = 4.0\%$$

Example 12-6 shows that:

The lower the correlation between two assets the lower the risk of the portfolio (other things being equal).

If the correlation between assets is low, or negative, then portfolios can be selected so that the risk of the portfolio is less than the risk of either asset.

If the correlation is –1, risk can be eliminated if the assets are weighted so that $w_1 \sigma_1 - w_2 \sigma_2 = 0$.

LOS 12-1-C-g describe the efficient frontier and **explain** its implications for an investor willing to assume more risk

The Efficient Frontier

Continuing this analysis we can see that for a multiple asset portfolio, if alternative portfolios were plotted on a graph with expected returns measured against risk (standard deviation) then the possible portfolios would fall on and under a curve. This curve is the **efficient frontier**. This is the set of portfolios that offer the maximum rate of return for any given level of risk.

If the expected returns, standard deviations of returns and covariance between returns for a set of assets are known it is possible to construct an efficient frontier.

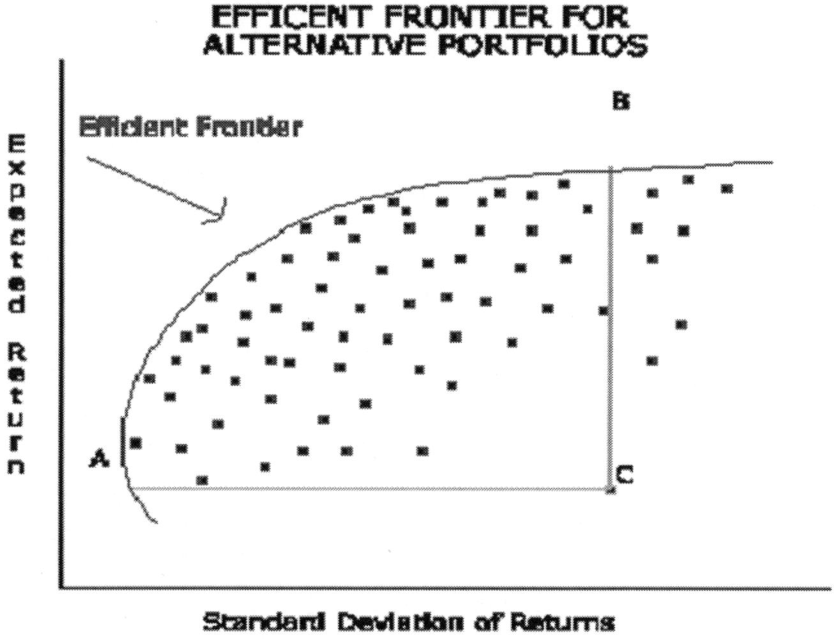

Portfolios A and C have the same level of expected return but A is lower risk, therefore portfolio A is more attractive then portfolio C. Similarly portfolios B and C have the same level of risk, but B offers a higher expected return; therefore portfolio B is more attractive. Portfolios A and B both lie on the efficient frontier, for their levels of risk they offer the highest return.

The curve will flatten for as risk increases; this is because adding more risk leads to diminishing levels of additional return.

LOS 12-1-C-h **define** optimal portfolio and **show** how each investor may have a different optimal portfolio

In order to decide which portfolio on the efficient frontier meets each investor's objectives we can consider the investor's utility curves.

Utility curves

Each investor has a set of utility curves (an infinite number of 'parallel' curves) that represent the trade-off between risk and return. Each point on a single curve is equally attractive to the investor. The steeper the utility curves the more risk averse the investor. The **optimal portfolio** for each investor will be the point where the utility curves are tangential to the efficient frontier.

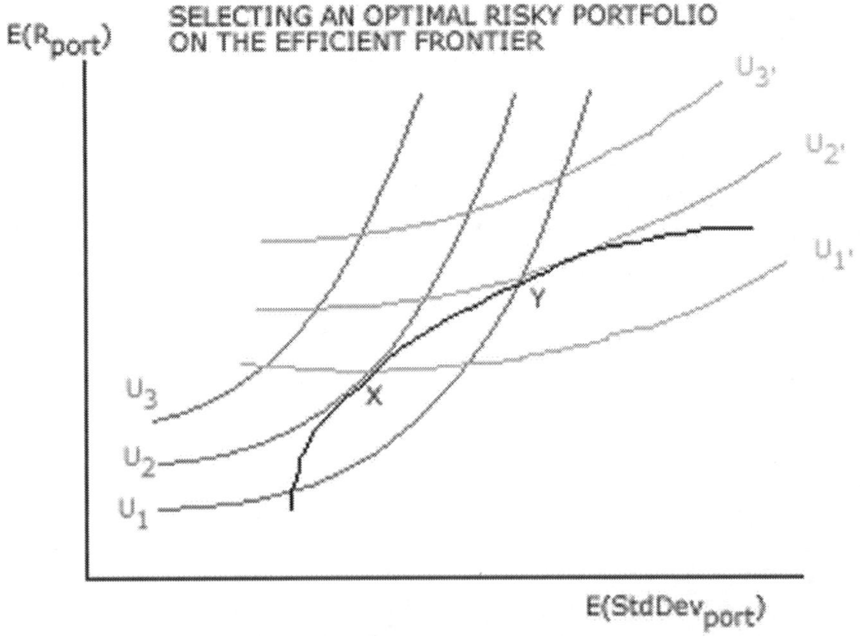

12-1-C View Concept Check Questions Workbook

12-1-D "An Introduction to Asset Pricing Models"

Introduction

This Reading Assignment focuses on the Capital Asset Pricing Model (CAPM). This is a model for pricing risky assets and links the required return to the systematic risk of the asset. Candidates should know the assumptions made by capital market theory, and understand the concepts of a risk-free asset and market portfolio representing a portfolio of risky assets. They should also be prepared to calculate required rates of return using CAPM which can be compared to expected rates of return to decide whether an asset is over or undervalued.

LOS 12-1-D-a list the assumptions of the capital market theory

Capital Market Theory builds on the foundation of Markowitz's work on optimal portfolios. The assumptions made are the previous assumptions in LOS 12-1-C-b plus additional ones:

1. All investors want to invest in points on Markowitz's efficient frontier and the specific portfolio will depend on the individual investor's utility function.
2. Investors can borrow or lend at the risk-free rate. However using a higher borrowing rate does not significantly change the results.
3. All investors have the same return expectations, in terms of the same probability distributions for expected future returns.
4. All investors have the same time horizon, eg. one year.
5. All investments are infinitely divisible, eg. there is no minimum unit size for a holding in an asset.
6. There is no inflation or change in interest rates, or any inflation is fully anticipated.
7. There are no taxes or transaction costs.
8. Capital markets are in equilibrium. Initially all investments are correctly priced in line with their levels of risk.

Although some of the assumptions look unrealistic, relaxing many of the assumptions does not have a major impact on the model. If theories and models based on these assumptions can help explain asset pricing and rates of return then it is useful, despite the assumptions being stringent.

LOS 12-1-D-b **explain** what happens to the expected return, the standard deviation of returns, and possible risk-return combinations when a risk-free asset is combined with a portfolio of risky assets

LOS 12-1-D-c **identify** the market portfolio and **describe** the role of the market portfolio in the formation of the capital market line (CML)

We now look at the impact on the efficient frontier if an investor can purchase a **risk-free asset.** The risk-free asset has zero variance and the rate of return is the NRFR, labeled the RF, which is discussed in LOS 12-1-A. The correlation and covariance between the risk-free asset and any other asset will be 0.

A portfolio that combines the risk-free asset with a portfolio will have an expected return and risk given by:

$$E(R_{port}) = w_{RF}(RFR) + (1 - w_{RF})E(R_i) \qquad \textbf{(Equation 12-7)}$$

where

w_{RF} = the proportion of the portfolio invested in the risk-free asset
$E(R_i)$ = the expected return from portfolio i

Using Equation 12-6

$$\sigma^2_{port} = w_1^2\sigma_1^2 + w_2^2\sigma_2^2 + 2r_{12}w_1w_2\sigma_1\sigma_2$$

We can label the risk-free asset as the first asset and the second asset as portfolio i. We know that $_{RF}$ is zero and the correlation between the risk-free asset and any other asset is zero therefore

$$\sigma_{port} = (1 - w_{RF})\sigma_i \qquad \textbf{(Equation 12-8)}$$

If we now look at the risky asset as a point on the efficient frontier and we pick the point, M, where the line from the risk-free asset to M is tangential to the efficient frontier, we have a set of points representing portfolios described by the equations

$$E(R_{port}) = w_{RF}(RFR) + (1 - w_{RF})E(R_M) \qquad \textbf{(Equation 12-9)}$$

$$\sigma_{port} = (1 - w_{RF})\sigma_M \qquad \textbf{(Equation 12-10)}$$

A new set of optimal portfolios will lie on this line. The line is called the **capital market line** (CML) and the point, M, where the tangent touches the curve is the **market portfolio**. All portfolios on this line will be a combination of the risk-free asset (or borrowing the risk-free asset) and the market portfolio. Theoretically the market portfolio must consist of a completely diversified portfolio which includes all risky assets.

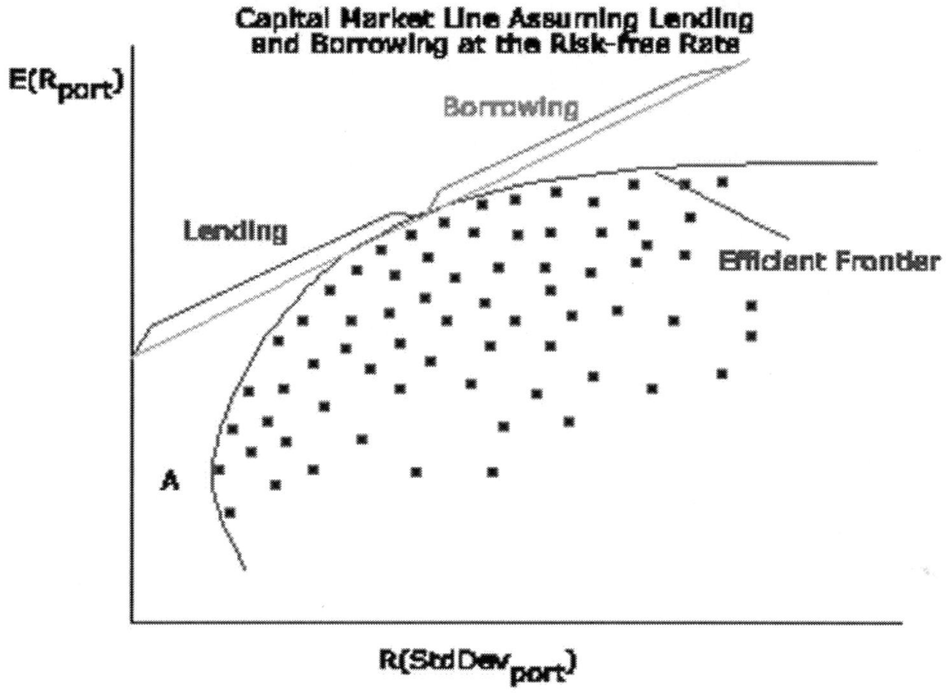

Example 12-7: The Capital Market Line

A portfolio invests 30% in the risk-free asset which earns a return of 5%. The remainder is invested in a market portfolio which has an expected return of 12%, the market portfolio has a standard deviation of returns of 15%.

The expected return of the portfolio is, using Equation 12-9

$$E(R_{port}) = w_{RF}(RFR) + (1 - w_{RF})E(R_M) = (0.30 \times 5\%) + (0.70 \times 12\%) = 9.9\%$$

The standard deviation is, using Equation 12-10

$$\sigma_{port} = (1 - w_{RF})\sigma_M = 0.70 \times 15\% = 10.5\%$$

Another portfolio is more aggressive and has borrowed 30% of the original portfolio value at the risk-free rate.

The expected return for this portfolio is

$$E(R_{port}) = w_{RF}(RFR) + (1 - w_{RF})E(R_M) = (-0.30 \times 5\%) + (1.3 \times 12\%) = 14.1\%$$

The standard deviation is

$$\sigma_{port} = (1 - w_{RF})\sigma_M = 1.30 \times 15\% = 19.5\%$$

We can see that leveraging the portfolio by borrowing has increased the expected return and correspondingly increased the risk.

LOS 12-1-D-d define systematic and unsystematic risk and explain why an investor should not expect to receive additional return for assuming unsystematic risk

Systematic and Unsystematic Risk

Next we consider diversification within a market and how many securities are needed to completely diversify a portfolio. Investing in only a relatively small number of stocks has a dramatic effect on reducing variance. Investment in 12 to 18 randomly selected stocks is sufficient to achieve 90% of the maximum benefits of diversification. Eventually, by adding stocks, variability will be reduced to that of the level of the market. So, for example, if you are investing in U.S. equities, you cannot reduce variance below that of the US equity market itself. The market risk that you cannot diversify away is called **systematic risk.**

NUMBER OF STOCKS IN A PORTFOLIO AND
THE STANDARD DEVIATION OF PORTFOLIO RETURN

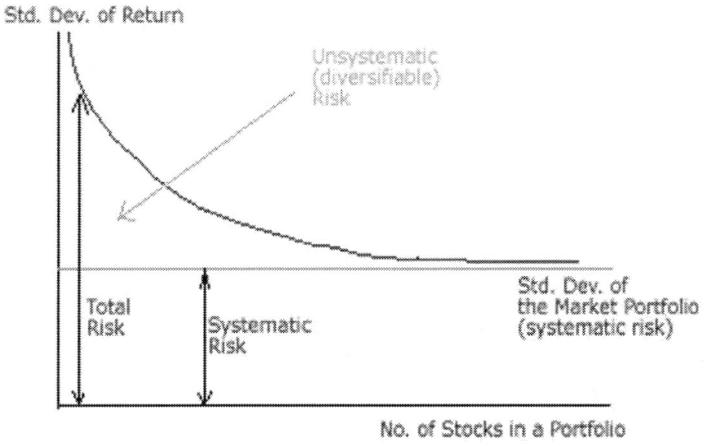

Variance = Systematic Variance + Unsystematic Variance
where

Systematic risk is market risk and cannot be diversified away.

Unsystematic risk is specific risk which can be eliminated by diversification.

Investors should not expect a higher return for taking on unsystematic risk because this can be diversified away by other holdings in the portfolio. Therefore an investor should expect a return which is dependent on the market risk of an asset or portfolio, which is the covariance of the asset with the market portfolio.

LOS 12-1-D-e	**describe** the capital asset pricing model
LOS 12-1-D-g	**define** beta

The Capital Asset Pricing Model (CAPM)

CAPM is concerned with measuring risk as systematic risk since it is assumed that unsystematic risk can be diversified away.

Beta is the measure of a security's volatility in terms of market risk; it is a standardized measure of risk since it compares the covariance of a stock to the variance of the market. For a stock x and market M it is given by:

$$\beta_x = \frac{\text{cov}(x, M)}{\text{var M}}$$ (Equation **12-11**)

where

cov (x,M) = covariance between the stock's return and the market return

var M = the variance of the market portfolio

The beta of the market is 1. If an asset has higher systematic risk than the market the beta will be greater than 1, if lower than the market it will be less than 1. The beta of the risk-free asset, which has covariance of zero with the market, is 0.

The expected return from a security is linked to its beta by the equation

$$E(R_i) = R_f + \beta_i(R_M - R_f)$$ **(Equation 12-12)**

where

R_f = RFR, the risk-free rate

$R_M - R_f$ = the market return less the risk-free rate, which is the **market risk premium**

$_i$ = beta of asset i

This is called the **Capital Asset Pricing Model**.

Example 12-8: Capital Asset Pricing Model

The return on the market portfolio is expected to be 15% and the risk-free rate 6%. If a stock has a beta of 1.5 then the expected return from the stock (or the required rate of return) is

R_x R_f R_M R_f 6% 1.5 15% 6% 19.5%

LOS 12-1-D-f **diagram** the security market line (SML)

The **Security Market Line** (SML) relates the expected return on stock to the risk-free rate (R_f), the market premium and the beta of the stock.

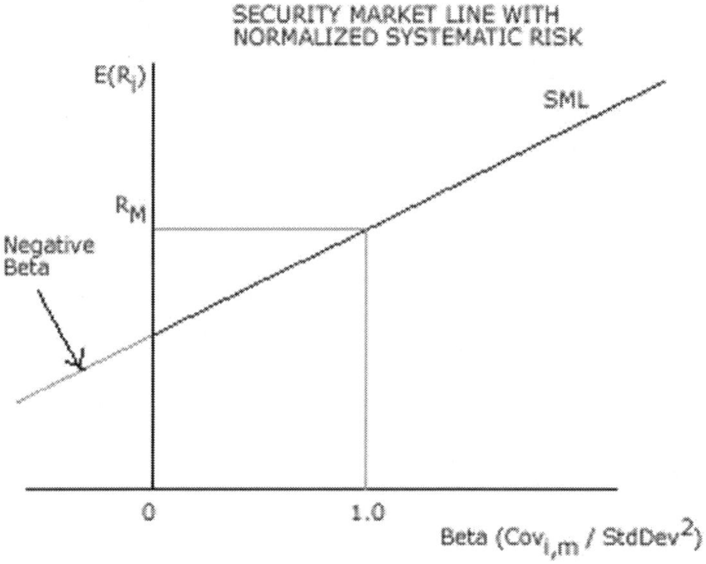

LOS 12-1-D-h **calculate**, using the SML, the expected return on a security and evaluate whether the security is undervalued, overvalued, or properly valued

All stocks should be in equilibrium and lie on the SML, but short term they may be incorrectly priced and lie above or below the line; this provides an opportunity to identify mispriced stocks.

Example 12-9: Security Market Line

An analyst estimates that the return from the same stock (Stock A) in Example 12-8 is 20% (including capital gain and dividend). Plotting the stock against the SML we can see that the estimated return is higher then the required return, so it is above the SML. Assuming that the analyst is correct then the stock is undervalued.

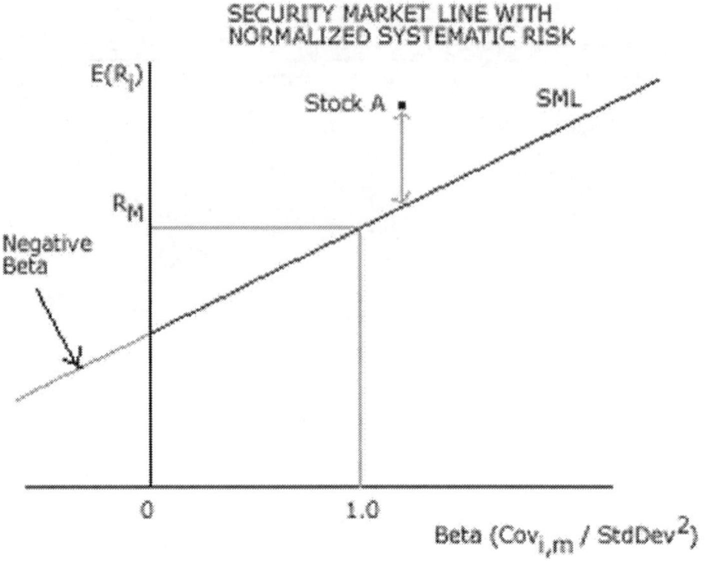

LOS 12-1-D-i **explain** how the systematic risk of an asset is estimated using the characteristic line

Beta

Beta can be estimated using regression analysis to plot the **characteristic line**. This is the line of best fit through a scatter plot of points with the Y-axis being the return from the security and the X-axis the return from the market. For asset i,

$$R_{i,t} = \alpha_i + \beta_i R_{M,t} + \varepsilon \quad \textbf{(Equation 12-13)}$$

where

$R_{i,t}$ = the rate of return for asset i during period t

$R_{M,t}$ = the rate of return for the market portfolio during period t

α_i = the intercept of the regression

β_i = the beta of asset i

ε_i = random error term

There is no single correct time period to use for the regression; there is a trade off between a long time period being used to have a large number of observations, and a short time period which is more relevant to the current beta.

12-1-D View Concept Check Questions Workbook

STUDY SESSION 13

Asset Valuation

Securities Markets

Overview

We now move on to Asset Valuation which makes up a guideline of 30% of the exam questions. In addition to this Study Session on securities markets we look at equities, bonds, derivatives and alternative investments. We have built up knowledge of investment tools from the preceding Study Sessions and we are ready to examine the ways in which asset classes are analyzed and valued. This is a core part of the Level I material as reflected in the guideline weighting.

This is a short Study Session on security markets with a lot of descriptive, rather than analytical, material. We look at how markets function, then how stock and bond indexes are constructed and finally we look at the efficiency of capital markets.

Candidates who are familiar with the basic characteristics of fixed-income, equity, derivative and alternative investments will not need to spend much time on the Preliminary Readings. It is important to note that the CFA Institute states that examination questions are drawn primarily from the subsequent Reading Assignments.

Preliminary Reading Assignment

13-P1. "Selecting Investments in a Global Market," Ch. 3, pp. 78–99, *Investment Analysis and Portfolio Management*, 7th edition, Frank K. Reilly and Keith C. Brown (South-Western, 2003)

13-P1 "Selecting Investments in a Global Market"

Introduction

This Preliminary Readings gives definitions for and describes the main characteristics of different instruments traded both in the U.S. and international markets. We look at each asset in terms of its return, risk and liquidity.

LOS 13-P1-a	**discuss** the characteristics of fixed-income securities available to investors, including U.S. Treasury securities, corporate bonds, municipal bonds, preferred stock, and Eurobonds

Fixed-Income Securities

Investors are lenders to the issuer (except in the case of preferred stock) and will receive periodic interest payments at a predetermined time with the principal being repaid at the maturity of the loan.

Savings accounts – this refers to when money is deposited at a bank or savings and loan association. The deposit earns a fixed rate of interest, which is usually relatively low, reflecting the liquidity and low risk

Certificates of deposit (CDs) – these are for investors with larger sums of money who are willing to give up some liquidity. A CD has a minimum size with fixed durations, there are heavy penalties if CDs are redeemed before expiry, but they can be traded in the secondary market.

Treasury bills (T-bills) - these are short-term obligations of the U.S. government (maturing in 3 to 12 months).

Money market certificates – issued by banks or savings and loan associations, with minimum investments and minimum time to maturity of 6 months, the interest rate paid reflects the T-bill rate.

Capital markets instruments in the U.S.

The following are fixed-income securities that trade in the secondary market.

U.S. Treasury securities

These are bills, notes or bonds depending on the time to maturity at issue. Bills mature in 1 year or less, notes in 1 to 10 years and bonds in over 10 years' time. U.S. government securities are viewed as being free of credit risk and are highly liquid.

U.S. government agency securities

These are issued by various government agencies but are not direct obligations of the government, although the default risk is very low. Examples of agencies are the Federal National Mortgage Association (issues Fannie Maes) or the Government National Mortgage Association (issues Ginnie Maes). They are relatively liquid.

Municipal bonds

These are issued by local governments as general obligation (backed by taxes of the municipality) or revenue bonds (interest is paid from revenue from specific projects). The interest received by residents of the issuing state is tax-exempt.

Corporate bonds

These are issued by corporations to raise funds for investment. They can be segregated in terms of issuer, credit quality, maturity etc. The *indenture* is the legal agreement specifying the obligations of the issuer; *call provisions* give the issuer the right to buy back the bonds prior to maturity. A *sinking fund* provision specifies payments the issuer must make to redeem a percentage of the outstanding issue prior to maturity.

Corporate bonds can be categorized based on seniority, this means some bonds have prior claim on assets in the case of default. In order of seniority:

Secured bonds are pledged against assets and have the lowest risk of default.

Mortgage bonds are backed by a claim on land and/or buildings, in the case of bankruptcy these assets will be sold to repay the mortgage bondholders.

Collateral trust bonds are backed by financial assets such as stocks or other high-quality bonds.

Equipment trust certificates are backed by specific pieces of equipment e.g. airplanes.

Debentures are not backed by any specific collateral.

Subordinated bonds are similar to debentures but in the case of bankruptcy holders will be paid back only after senior bond and debenture holders have been repaid.

Income bonds only pay interest to the holder when the issuer makes sufficient income to make the payment to the holder. If the issuer does not make sufficient income to pay the interest then this is not grounds for the investor to force the issuer to go bankrupt. Missed interest payments are considered to be in arrears and if the company has sufficient income it must pay them in the future.

Convertible bonds give the holder the option to exchange the bonds for common stock. They are almost always subordinated to the nonconvertible debt.

Preferred stock makes payments to holders in the form of dividends; dividends are pre-specified as a dollar amount or as a percentage of face value. The obligation to pay a dividend is not as legally binding as a coupon payment.

International bonds

Eurobonds are international bonds where the currency in which they are denominated is different to that of the country of issue.

Yankee bonds are issued by foreign corporations or governments in the U.S. market, and are denominated in dollars.

International domestic bonds are sold by an issuer in its own country, in that country's currency.

LOS 13-P1-b **discuss** the characteristics of equity securities available to investors, including classes of stock and American Depository Receipts

Equity Securities

Equity securities returns are quite different because the payments made are not contractual.

Common stock

This represents ownership of a firm. For analysis purposes, stocks are often categorized by the industry of the issuer. Alternatively stocks may be viewed on the basis of the country where the issuer is based in, but it is becoming increasingly relevant to view stocks by their industrial sector rather than on a geographic basis.

The following are four ways to buy foreign common stock:

1. American Depository Receipts – certificates of ownership that represent indirect ownership of shares in a foreign company. They are priced in U.S. dollars and dividends are received in dollars (although the return will reflect the movement of the foreign currency against the dollar as well as the movement in the foreign share price).
2. American shares – securities listed in the U.S. by an agent acting on behalf of a foreign firm.
3. Direct purchase - this applies to either buying a foreign company which has its shares listed in the U.S., or buying shares in an overseas market.
4. International or global mutual funds – either a global fund investing in both U.S. and foreign stocks, or an international fund investing outside the U.S. This may be a convenient way for a small investor to diversify into overseas markets.

LOS 13-P1-c **discuss** the characteristics of derivative investments (e.g., options, futures)

Derivatives are covered in detail in Study Session 17.

Equity Derivatives

Options - the right to buy (a call option) or sell (a put option) a security at a pre-specified price over a period of time, or at a specific date. Warrants are a form of option.

Futures - the agreement to buy or sell a security at a future date at a pre-specified price.

LOS 13-P1-d	**discuss** the characteristics of various alternative investments (e.g. investment companies, real estate, low-liquidity investments).

Alternative Investments

Alternative Investments are covered in detail in Study Session 18.

Investment company, this is often called a mutual fund. An investment company sells shares in itself and uses the money raised to purchase money market instruments, bonds, stocks etc. An investor in an investment company owns part of the underlying portfolio of securities.

Real estate investment is either by direct real estate investment or via a real estate investment trust.

Low liquidity investments include antiques, art, coins and stamps etc. Although some of these investments have reported high rates of return they are often very illiquid.

Historic Risk/Return Data for Assets

Reilly and Wright studied the historical rates of return for major international asset classes between 1980 and 1999. The results were broadly consistent with the concept that high returns are matched by higher risk.

Looking at the correlations between assets over this period we see that U.S. equities have a high correlation with Canadian and U.K. equities (0.77 and 0.64 respectively) but low correlation with Japanese and emerging market equities (0.31 and 0.35 respectively). U.S. equities have almost zero correlation with non-U.S. world government bonds and very low correlation with U.S. bonds (0.005). This supports the argument for diversification between equities and bonds and internationally.

Art and antiques – there is a wide range of return and risk data from different segments of the market. A well-diversified portfolio can reduce risk to relatively low levels.

Real estate – reliable data is difficult to obtain due to illiquidity of the market and lack of a centralized source of data. Overall the returns from U.S. real estate were lower than from common stocks but the risk was also lower. However real estate has low and sometimes negative correlation with other assets, which makes them a very useful asset from the point of view of including real estate in a portfolio to reduce risk.

13-1-A "Organization and Functioning of Securities Markets"

Introduction

This Reading looks at the operation of primary and secondary bond and stock markets. Primary markets are for the issue of new securities to investors and secondary markets for trading between investors. We review the different dealing systems, role of participants in the markets, types of orders and the mechanics of margin transactions.

Main Reading Assignments

13-1. *Investment Analysis and Portfolio Management*, 7th edition, Frank K. Reilly and Keith C. Brown (South-Western, 2003)

13-1-A. "Organization and Functioning of Securities Markets," Ch. 4

13-1-B. "Security-Market Indicator Series," Ch. 5

13-1-C. "Efficient Capital Markets," Ch. 6

LOS 13-1-A-a describe the characteristics of a well-functioning securities market

Characteristics of a well-functioning market

Availability of information

Timely and accurate information needs to be available for investors to decide what price to pay for a security. This includes information on prices and volumes of dealing.

Liquidity

There are two factors that indicate liquidity.

Price continuity which means that prices do not change significantly between transactions, unless there is major news released.

Depth meaning that there are many buyers and sellers who wish to deal above and below the current price.

Low transaction costs

This is called *internal efficiency*. Investors clearly prefer markets where the transaction costs are a small percentage of the value of a trade.

Prices rapidly adjust to new information

This is called *external efficiency* or *informational efficiency*. Investors prefer markets where the prices reflect supply and demand for the security.

LOS 13-1-A-b	**distinguish** between competitive bids, negotiated sales, and private placements for issuing bonds

Primary markets

Primary markets are where governments, municipalities or companies sell new issues of bonds or shares to raise fresh funds.

Treasury bills, notes and bonds are sold by Federal Reserve System auction.

Municipal bonds are sold by one of the following three methods.

1. Competitive bid – the issue is sold to the underwriting syndicate that submits the bid with the lowest interest rate.
2. Negotiation – an underwriter is appointed to help prepare the issue and has the exclusive right to sell the issue.
3. Private placement – the issuer sells the issue directly to a small group of investors.

The underwriter provides three services.

1. Origination - design and planning of the issue.
2. Risk-bearing - the underwriter takes on the issue at an agreed price and takes the risk that it will not be able to sell the issue on at the same or higher price. Alternatively an investment bank can act on a best-efforts basis.
3. Distribution - selling to investors, usually with the assistance of a selling syndicate.

In a negotiated bid the underwriter carries out all three roles. In a competitive bid the issuer may have paid a fee for advice from an investment bank on the design and pricing of the issue, and the risk-bearing and distribution function will probably be taken on by a different underwriter.

Corporate bonds are usually sold as a negotiated transaction through an investment bank acting as an underwriter.

Stock issues fall into two categories:

1. Seasoned new issues – issues from companies that already have publicly listed stock outstanding.
2. Initial public offerings (IPOs) – when stock is being sold to the public for the first time.

Both types of issue are usually arranged and underwritten by an investment bank, although they can be done on a private placement basis.

LOS 13-1-A-d **distinguish** between primary and secondary capital markets and **explain** how secondary markets support primary markets

Secondary markets

Secondary markets are where trading takes place of bonds or stocks that are already in the public's ownership.

Secondary markets are important because they provide liquidity to the investors who bought issues in the primary market. They also provide pricing information which is used to price securities in the primary market.

LOS 13-1-A-c **compare** and **contrast** the secondary markets for U.S. government/municipal bonds to the secondary markets for corporate bonds

Secondary bond markets

U.S. government and municipal bonds are traded by bond dealers which include some of

the largest banks and investment banking firms. There are 35 primary dealers for buying and selling Treasury bonds but there is no formal set of dealers for government agency securities. The major market makers for municipal bonds are banks and investment firms.

Secondary corporate bond markets are now all in the over-the-counter (OTC) market whereas previously they were traded on the NYSE. The major market makers are the large investment banking firms who are also underwriters.

LOS 13-1-A-e **distinguish** between call and continuous markets

Secondary equity markets

Trading in equities is done on listed securities exchanges and the over-the-counter (OTC) market which includes trading in securities not listed on an exchange.

Looking first of all at securities exchanges there are different types of trading systems. The first is a **pure auction market** where potential buyers and sellers submit bid and ask prices to an independent party who matches orders. This system is price-driven in the sense that the investor who offers to pay the most will be the buyer, and the investor willing to accept the lowest price will be the seller. The other system is a **dealer market** where dealers make a market in stocks (quoting bid-ask prices) and are willing to take positions on their own books. This provides liquidity.

Auction and dealer markets can be either call or continuous markets. In a **call market** trading for each stock takes place at a specified time. After all information on buy and sell orders have been collected, the exchange will decide the single price at which all transactions will be processed. Call markets are more common in a new exchange when there are only a few stocks listed and a few traders. Also exchanges can use a call market system to clear a build up of orders that has occurred overnight or after a stock has been suspended.

In a **continuous market** trades occur at any time when the market is open. These are either dealer or auction markets.

LOS 13-1-A-f	**compare** and **contrast** the structural differences among national stock exchanges, regional stock exchanges, and the over-the-counter (OTC) markets

Secondary equity markets are classed as (i) national exchanges (ii) regional stock exchanges and (iii) OTC markets.

National stock exchanges

In the U.S. the New York Stock Exchange (NYSE) and the American Stock Exchange (AMEX) are considered to be national exchanges due to the number, prestige and geographical diversity of the companies listed, as well as the broad range of investors using the exchanges. Internationally, examples of national exchanges are the Tokyo Stock Exchange and the London Stock Exchange.

There are two trends internationally. The first is that new stock exchanges are being set up in emerging economies. The second trend is the consolidation of the exchanges in mature economies. The Global 24-hour market refers to the fact that it is possible to trade almost continuously in one of the New York, London or Tokyo markets.

Regional stock exchanges

Regional exchanges are important because they have less strict listing requirements. They list smaller local companies that are not big enough to list on the national exchanges. Many countries have one national exchange accounting for the majority of trading and several regional exchanges. The operating procedures are usually the same as in the national exchanges.

OTC markets

This includes trading in stocks not listed on the national and regional exchanges and it also includes trading in listed stocks. There are more stocks traded on the NASDAQ system (the OTC trading system) in the U.S. than the NYSE and AMEX combined, although NASDAQ is not the largest in terms of value of transactions. The OTC market is not a formal organization with membership; any security can be traded if a registered dealer is prepared to make a market in the security.

The OTC market is a negotiated market in the sense that investors negotiate directly with dealers. If an investor wishes to buy shares in a company his broker would look at the prices being offered by dealers.

Dealer	Bid	Ask
1	20.25	20.55
2	20.50	20.75
3	20.30	20.60

The broker will check the prices and will buy shares from Dealer 1 since this is the lowest offering or ask price. If the investor had been a seller they would sell the shares to Dealer 2 who has the highest bid price.

The dealer or market maker will adjust their prices based on their inventory in the stock and their expectations of future price movements.

The **third market** refers to trading in listed stocks outside the exchanges that they are listed on.

Trading in stocks directly between investors without using a broker is referred to as the **fourth market.**

LOS 13-1-A-g **compare** and **contrast** major characteristics of exchange markets, including exchange membership, types of orders, and market makers

Exchange membership

There are four major categories of members.

Market makers (specialists)

In the U.S. a market maker is called a specialist. Specialists act as brokers and dealers. As a broker they match orders and handle special limit orders. As a dealer they are expected to maintain a fair and orderly market and provide liquidity by buying and selling for their own accounts when necessary.

Commission brokers

These are employees of a member firm who buy and sell securities on behalf of the firm's clients.

Floor brokers

These are independent members who act as brokers for other members, for example when a commission broker is too busy to execute all his own trades.

Registered traders

These are members who buy and sell for their own account. Arguably they have better access to information and can avoid paying commission costs. Their transactions increase market liquidity.

Types of orders

Market order

This is the most common type of order, it is an order to buy or sell a security at the best current price.

Limit order

This order specifies the buying or selling price. It might be for a specific period of time, or might be open-ended.

Stop loss order

This is when the investor gives an order to sell a stock if it falls to a certain price. If the stock does fall to the specified price the order becomes a market order. It will be executed at the best price available, which won't necessarily be exactly the same as the price specified.

LOS 13-1-A-h	**describe** the process of selling a stock short and **discuss** an investor's likely motivation for selling short

Short sales

This refers to the sale of stock that is not owned. This is usually done with the intention of buying the stock back later at a lower price. The investor is clearly motivated by the anticipation of a fall in the price. The stock is borrowed from another investor who is given collateral. There are certain restrictions on short sales:

- The price of a short sale must be done at a higher price than the last traded price (an *uptick* trade), or at the same price but the last traded price must be higher than the price of the previous trade (*zero uptick*).
- The short seller must pay any dividends due to the lender of the stock.
- The short seller must deposit margin, the margin can take the form of another unrestricted security that is owned by the short seller.

Sometimes a short seller uses a *stop buy order* to limit a loss on a short sale if the stock price begins to rise.

LOS 13-1-A-i	**describe** the process of buying a stock on margin, and **compute** the rate of return on a margin transaction
LOS 13-1-A-j	**define** maintenance margin and **determine** the stock price at which the investor would receive a margin call

Margin transactions

When an investor pays for part of the cost of purchasing shares by borrowing, usually from the broker, this is called buying on margin. The **initial margin requirement** is the percentage of the total transaction that must be paid for in cash (**percent margin**).

Buying on margin is effectively a leveraged transaction; the leverage factor is 1/percent margin.

After the initial purchase the proportion of the investor's equity (the market value of the stock less the amount borrowed) to the total market value of stock must not fall below the **maintenance margin level**, if it does a **margin call** will be made, and the investor will be required to deposit additional funds with the broker. The margin call occurs when:

value of equity < maintenance margin level x value of stock **(Equation 13-1)**

Example 13-1 Margin transactions

An investor buys 1,000 shares on margin at a price of \$100. The initial margin requirement is 40%, so the investor pays \$40,000 of the \$100,000 cost in cash and borrows the remaining \$60,000. If the stock price rises to \$110, the investor's equity is now \$50,000 (\$110,000 – \$60,000) or 45.45% of the market value of the stock.

The return on the \$40,000 investment is \$10,000 or 25%. The leverage factor is 1/0.40 = 2.5.

(This assumes there is no interest cost in borrowing or trading commission).

If the maintenance margin is 25%, the investor will receive a margin call if the stock price declines to a price below P. P can be found by using Equation 13-1:

value of equity = maintenance margin level X value of stock

$$1{,}000P - \$60{,}000 = 0.25 \times 1{,}000P$$

$$P = \$80$$

So if the price falls to \$75 the margin call (M) would be for the amount which will bring the equity back to 25% of the total value of the account value. The equity would be : $(\$75 \times 1{,}000) - \$60{,}000 + M$ and the value of the account would be $[(\$75 \times 1{,}000) + M]$

$$[(\$75 \times 1{,}000) + M] \times 0.25 = (\$75 \times 1{,}000) - \$60{,}000 + M$$

$$\$3{,}750 = 0.75M$$

$$M = \$5{,}000$$

LOS 13-1-A-k discuss major effects of the institutionalization of securities markets

Institutionalization of Securities Markets

The growing institutionalization of the U.S. markets is shown by the rapid growth in the use of block trades which make up more than half of the volume on the NYSE. Block trades are trades of 10,000 or more shares and therefore almost always originate from financial institutions. The growth in block trades has led to the establishment of block houses who have sufficient capital to handle block trades. The institutionalization has had a number of effects on the market, discussed below.

Negotiated commission rates

The move to allow all commissions to be negotiated in the U.S has had a dramatic effect. Institutions typically only pay commission of 5 cents per share and individuals can access low commission rates by dealing through discount brokers. As a result many small research firms have disappeared as institutions find it cheaper to buy research from the big brokerage firms, and many medium and small-size investment firms have merged or gone out of business.

Influence of block trades

Specialists did not have sufficient capital to commit to block trades and block houses have been set up. Block houses are investment firms that deal in block trades; they are usually well capitalized with good contacts in the institutions.

Impact on stock price volatility

Although there is a belief that block trades are linked to increased price volatility there is little empirical evidence to support this.

Development of National Market System (NMS)

Many institutions are looking for a NMS that would provide a centralized system for reporting of transactions, quotations, and a centralized limit order book. They also want to see greater competition between market makers.

13-1-A View Concept Check Questions Workbook

13-1-B "Security-Market Indicator Series"

Introduction

Security-market indicator series, also called stock and bond market indexes, are widely used by market participants and investors in order to judge the strength or weakness of the market and measure portfolio performance. In order to use indexes it is important to understand how they are constructed and the implications of the different methods of weighting securities in an index.

Security market indexes

Security market indexes or series are used:

- To measure portfolio performance.
- For the construction of index funds.
- To examine factors that influence aggregate security price movements.
- By technical analysts.
- For beta calculation.

When constructing an index it is important to consider:

- The sample in the index must be representative of the population.
- The weighting given to the individual members in the sample (there are price-weighted, market-value-weighted and unweighted series).
- The mathematical method of calculating the index (arithmetic or geometric averaging or base period weighting).

LOS 13-1-B-a	**distinguish** among the composition and characteristics of the three predominant weighting schemes used in constructing stock market series
LOS 13-1-B-b	**discuss** the source and direction of bias exhibited by each of the three predominant weighting schemes

The three main weighting systems used in constructing a series or index are:

Price-Weighted Series

This is the arithmetic average of current prices divided by a divisor which reflects the number of stocks in the index. The Dow Jones Industrial Average (DJIA) is a price–weighted average and on day t the index is calculated using

$$DJIA_t = \sum_{i=1}^{30} p_{it} / D_{adj} \qquad \textbf{(Equation 13-2)}$$

where

$DJIA_t$ = the value of the DJIA at day t

p_{it} = the closing price of stock i on day t

D_{adj} = the adjusted divisor on day t

When there is a sock split the divisor will adjust to ensure the index is the same before and after the split.

Example 13-2 Stock splits and divisor calculation

Look at the example when there are three stocks, A, B and C, used to compute an index and stock A has a four-for-one stock split. The stock prices are shown below, with the index and divisor calculations.

	Share Price before split	**Share Price after split**
A	\$100	\$25
B	\$50	\$50
C	\$10	\$10
Total	\$160	\$85
Divisor	3	\$85/53.33 = 1.59
Index	53.33	53.33

This means that high-price stocks carry more weight than low-price stocks in a price–weighted series. Adjusting for stock splits tends to have a long-term downward bias as rapidly growing or successful companies have rising stock prices leading to more stock splits. Another example of a price-weighted series is the Nikkei Stock Average.

Market-Value-Weighted Series

This is the total value of shares in the series (current market price X number of shares outstanding) divided by the value of the series at a selected base date, this is multiplied by the index's beginning value. The index on day t is given by

$$\text{Index}_t = \frac{\sum P_t Q_t}{\sum P_b Q_b} \times \text{Beginning Index Value} \qquad \textbf{(Equation 13-3)}$$

where

P_t = closing price for stock on day t

Q_t = number of outstanding shares on day t

P_b = closing price for stock on base day

Q_b = number of outstanding shares on base day

A stock split will not have an impact on the index since the market value of the company will not be changed. Examples of m**arket-value-weighted series** are the S&P, NYSE, and MSCI indices.

Unweighted Index Series

An equal dollar investment in each stock in the index is assumed, share price and market capitalization are irrelevant. Examples are the Value Line Indexes. Most academic work uses arithmetically averaged unweighted indices but both the Value Line Indexes and Financial Times Ordinary Share Index use the geometric means of security price moves. The geometric mean will be lower than the arithmetic mean for the same stock movements, the arithmetic mean will give the actual return earned on a portfolio holding the same stocks as the index. They are sometimes referred to as equal-weighted indexes.

LOS 13-1-B-c	**compute** a price-weighted, a market-weighted, and an unweighted index series for three stocks

Example 13-3 Computing indexes

Consider a market in which there are three stocks A, B and C.

	Number of Shares	Share Price end 2003	Market Cap. end 2003
A	2,000,000	\$100	\$200 million
B	10,000,000	\$50	\$500 million
C	100,000,000	\$10	\$1,000 million
Total		\$160	\$1,700 million

Price-weighted index

If the divisor is 3, using Equation 13-2

$$\text{Index} = 160/3 = 53.33$$

Market-value-weighted index

Set the beginning index equal to 100.

Look at the following two scenarios:

Scenario 1. At the end of 2004 the share price of A has doubled and the share prices of B and C have not changed.

Scenario 2. At the end of 2004 the share prices of A and B have not changed, but the share price of C has doubled.

	Scenario 1		Scenario 2	
	Share Price end 2004	Market Cap. end 2004	Share Price end 2004	Market Cap. end 2004
A	\$200	\$400 million	\$100	\$200 million
B	\$50	\$500 million	\$50	\$500 million
C	\$10	\$1,000 million	\$20	\$2,000 million
Total	\$260	\$1,900 million	\$170	\$2,700 million

Price-weighted index

Scenario 1

$$\text{Index} = 260/3 = 86.67$$

$$\text{Rise in index} = \left[(86.67 - 53.33)/53.33\right] - 1 = 62.5\%$$

Scenario 2

$$\text{Index} = 170/3 = 56.67$$

$$\text{Rise in index} = \left[(56.67 - 53.33)/53.33\right] - 1 = 6.3\%$$

Market-value-weighted index

Scenario 1

Using Equation 13-3

$$\text{Index}_t = \frac{\sum P_t Q_t}{\sum P_b Q_b} \times \text{Beginning Index Value}$$

$$\text{Index} = \frac{\$1{,}900}{\$1{,}700} \times 100 = 111.8$$

$$\text{Rise in index} = 11.8\%$$

Scenario 2

$$\text{Index} = \frac{\$2{,}700}{\$1{,}700} \times 100 = 158.8$$

$$\text{Rise in index} = 58.8\%$$

Unweighted index

	Scenario 1		Scenario 2	
	Share Price end 2004	**Rise %**	**Share Price end 2004**	**Rise %**
A	$200	100%	$100	0%
B	$50	0%	$50	0%
C	$10	0%	$20	100%

Scenarios 1 and 2

Arithmetic mean = (0% + 0% + 100%)/3 = 33.33%
Rise in index = 33.33%

Geometric mean = $[1.00 \times 1.00 \times 2.00]^{1/3} - 1 = 0.26$

Rise in index = 26.00%

Example 13-3 illustrates that:

- The price-weighted index is sensitive to moves in high-price stocks.
- The value-weighted index is sensitive to moves in the share prices of companies with large market capitalizations.

LOS 13-1-B-d	**compare** and **contrast** major structural features of domestic and global stock indexes, bond indexes, and composite stock-bond indexes

Bond market series are more complex than equity market series since:

- the universe of bonds is wider
- the universe is constantly changing as bonds mature and new bonds are issued
- volatility changes as duration changes
- collecting bond prices is more difficult

Most of the bond indexes are market-value weighted and include total rates of return (price change plus accrued income plus coupon income reinvested). Domestic bond indexes are produced for both investment grade bonds and high–yield bonds.

Indexes are also produced for global bonds, these tend to be dominated by government rather than corporate issues.

Composite stock-bond indexes measure the performance of all securities in a market with a weighting system that is close to using market values.

13-1-B View Concept Check Questions Workbook

13-1-C "Efficient Capital Markets"

Introduction

We now consider the efficiency of capital markets and whether all the information available about a security is already reflected in its price. Candidates need to examine the different forms of the Efficient Market Hypothesis (EMH) and the tests which support or disprove the hypothesis. Candidates also have to understand the implications of efficient markets for the portfolio manager and the rationale for the growth in index fund investing.

LOS 13-1-C-a	**define** an efficient capital market and **discuss** arguments supporting the concept of efficient capital markets

Definition

An **efficient market**, or to be more precise an **informationally efficient market,** is a market where security prices adjust rapidly to the arrival of new information and therefore current security prices reflect all the information available about the securities.

Assumptions

1. There are a large number of competing, independent, profit-maximizing participants who are analyzing and valuing securities.
2. New information comes to the market in a random fashion, the timing of one announcement is generally independent of others.
3. Investors attempt to adjust the security prices rapidly to reflect new information. Although price adjustments will not always be perfect they are unbiased.

If these assumptions hold then the expected security returns should only reflect the risk of the security. This means all stocks should lie on the market's Security Market Line, their returns are consistent with their risk.

LOS 13-1-C-b **describe** and **contrast** the forms of the efficient market hypothesis (EMH): weak, semistrong, and strong

The Efficient Market Hypothesis (EMH) is broken down into three forms as follows:

Weak-form EMH

This says that stock prices reflect all security-market information e.g. price and volume data. The implication is that past rates of return should have no relation to future rates of return.

Semistrong-form EMH

This says that stock prices adjust rapidly to all *public* information released. This includes non-market information such as earnings and dividend announcements, valuation measures etc. This means that basing decisions on information that is already in the public domain will not consistently lead to outperformance on a risk-adjusted basis.

Strong-form EMH

This asserts that stock prices reflect all information from public and private sources. This means that no group of investors has sole access to a certain type of information and can consistently outperform on a risk-adjusted basis. Information has no cost and is available to all investors. The strong-form includes the weak-form and semistrong-form EMH.

LOS 13-1-C-c **describe** the tests used to examine the weak form, the semistrong form, and the strong form of the EMH
LOS 13-1-C-d **identify** six market anomalies and **explain** their implications for the semistrong form of the EMH
LOS 13-1-C-e **explain** the overall conclusions about each form of the EMH

The evidence on the EMH is mixed and extensive work has been done to test the validity of the different forms of the hypothesis.

Tests for the weak-form EMH

Tests can be broken down into two categories.

1. Testing the independence between rates of return. This involves testing for correlation of stock returns and testing for runs. Tests have indicated little correlation between stock returns over time, although more recent tests have found evidence of correlation for small companies. Tests for runs found no evidence of patterns of movement (increases followed by decreases) that could not be explained by random movements.
2. Testing trading rules. Tests have focused on relatively simple trading rules based on using past market data. There are problems applying rules (some trading rules use subjective interpretation of data and there are unlimited potential trading rules) plus high theoretical trading costs. Generally, but not in all cases, tests support the weak-from hypothesis i.e. buying and selling securities based on trading rules does not outperform a buy and hold policy.

Tests for the semistrong-form EMH

Tests can again be broken down into two categories:

Studies to predict future returns using public non-market information. This includes time-series analysis using valuation measures. There is evidence from these studies that markets are not semistrong-form efficient due to anomalies (see below) which conflict with the markets being efficient.

Event studies. These examine how fast security prices react to public announcements. For example, announcements regarding stock splits, accounting changes, as well as economic news. Generally the findings support the hypothesis, although studies on stock price movement after an exchange listing indicate that there are some short-term opportunities to make an excess return.

Anomalies to the semistrong-form EMH

The following are anomalies that provide evidence that the markets are not semistrong-form efficient. Note that performance is being measured on a risk-adjusted basis relative to the market.

- Stock prices do not respond as rapidly as expected to earnings surprises, there is evidence of abnormal returns 13-26 weeks after an announcement.
- January effect. Investors sell loss-making stocks in December and then reinvest in January, leading to a superior relative performance of security prices in January. This is possibly explained by tax year-end dates in the U.S.
- The weekend effect. Average relative returns between Friday's close and Monday's open are negative for large firms and during Monday's trading are negative for small firms.
- Low P/E (price-earnings ratio) stocks perform better.
- Stocks with high BV/MV (book value to market value) tend to outperform, these are generally classified as value stocks. Outperformance is particularly noted in periods of monetary expansion.
- Small company stocks perform better although the performance is not stable. The differential may be accounted for by higher transactions costs and the risk of smaller companies may not be adequately explained by beta.
- Neglected company stocks perform better. Neglected means stocks that are only followed by a small number of analysts.

These anomalies illustrate that the market is not completely semistrong-form efficient.

Tests for the strong-form EMH

Tests have focused on looking at investors who have access to non-public information or an ability to react to new information before other investors.

Corporate insiders

Corporate insiders, such as company directors, are required to report to the SEC transactions in the stock of the firms where they are insiders. Analysis indicates that insiders achieve above average returns as a result of these transactions.

Stock exchange specialists

Specialists have access to information about unfilled limit orders that is not available to other investors. Specialists appear to be able to make money from selling shares at higher than the purchase price and also from trading in blocks of shares and after unexpected announcements.

Security analysts

Studies have looked at the performance of stocks that have high versus low rankings by Value Line (a well known research and advisory firm in the U.S.). Changes in a stock's ranking are usually reflected very rapidly in the stock's price and it is not possible to obtain excess returns from investing on the basis of these rankings, after taking into account transaction costs.

There is some evidence of superior analysts who are accessing private information. They appear to have market timing and stock-picking skills.

Professional money managers

These are generally highly trained professionals and although they do not necessarily have access to monopolistic information they have the opportunity to interview the management of listed companies. Studies show that professional managers on average underperform the market, after taking into account fees.

The results from the four groups are mixed but much of the evidence supports the strong-form of the hypothesis, the main exceptions are the results from corporate insiders and specialists. Money mangers did not outperform, so from the point of view of the majority of investors the hypothesis holds.

LOS 13-1-C-f **explain** the implications of stock market efficiency for technical analysis and fundamental analysis

In conclusion the markets appear to be efficient with regard to much of the information available but there are a number of instances where the markets are not efficient.

The evidence that the capital markets are weak-form efficient indicates that technical analysis using historic market information will not lead to outperformance on a risk-adjusted basis, after transaction fees.

Fundamental analysts believe that market valuations and intrinsic valuations can be different, but eventually these differences will be corrected. The EMH suggests that using historic data will not help because prices adjust very quickly to news. However analysts can add value by forecasting economic variables that lead to long-term market movements. Understanding how these variables impact on security returns can lead to superior performance if estimates are both correct and different to the consensus. Also it should be possible to achieve superior returns by exploiting the anomalies to the weak-form of the EMH, e.g. by focusing on neglected companies.

LOS 13-1-C-g	**discuss** the implications of efficient markets for the portfolio management process and the role of the portfolio manager

Implications for Portfolio Managers

If portfolio managers have access to superior analysts then they should use these analysts for recommendations for part of a portfolio, taking into account the risk preferences of the client. Analysts should be asked to focus on mid or small sized stock that are not so widely followed so there is a greater chance of identifying undervalued stocks. Also they should focus on stocks with low BV/MV.

Portfolio managers who do not have superior analysts should do the following:

1. Quantify their clients' risk tolerance.
2. Construct a portfolio which has the appropriate risk profile and maintain this risk level on an ongoing basis.
3. Diversify to eliminate any unsystematic risk by investing globally.
4. Minimize costs including taxes, transaction costs and holding illiquid stocks.

LOS 13-1-C-h	**explain** the rationale for investing in index funds

The EMH justifies the move to the use of index funds. Index funds have the objective of duplicating the performance of selected market indices at the lowest possible research and trading cost.

13-1-C View Concept Check Questions Workbook

STUDY SESSION 14

Asset Valuation

Equity Investments

Overview

This Study Session covers a diverse number of topics related to equity analysis and valuation. It works through stock market analysis, industry analysis and individual security analysis. The emphasis is on fundamental analysis and using discounted cash flows and relative approaches (for example price earnings ratios and price to book value multiples) to value equities. However a later Readings looks at technical analysis and the philosophy and the indictors used by analysts are examined. The Study Session consists of Readings taken from different source texts so the candidate is exposed to a number of different approaches to equity valuation.

Reading Assignments

Investment Analysis and Portfolio Management, 7th edition, Frank K. Reilly and Keith C. Brown (South-Western, 2003)

14-1-A. "An Introduction to Security Valuation," Ch. 11

14-1-B. "Stock-Market Analysis," Ch. 13, including p. 435

14-2. "Equity: Concepts and Techniques," Ch. 6, pp. 256-273, *International Investments,* 5th edition, Bruno Solnik and Dennis McLeavey (Addison Wesley, 2003)

Investment Analysis and Portfolio Management, 7th edition, Frank K. Reilly and Keith C. Brown (South-Western, 2003)

14-3-A. "Company Analysis and Stock Valuation," Ch. 15, pp. 540-544 and 559–577

14-3-B. "Technical Analysis," Ch. 16

14-4. "Introduction to Price Multiples," John D. Stowe, Thomas R. Robinson, Jerald E. Pinto, and Dennis W. McLeavey (AIMR, 2003)

14-1-A "An Introduction to Security Valuation"

Introduction

In this Reading we focus on the application of discounted cash flow techniques in equity valuation. When valuing equities it is important to remember that the cash flows are not contractually agreed (as they usually are with a bond or money market instrument) so we need to adjust for the uncertainty of cash flows with a discount factor that includes an appropriate risk premium. Discounted cash flow concepts are core to this Reading but we also look at other issues including different valuation approaches and the drivers of a P/E multiple.

LOS 14-1-A-a	**explain** the top-down approach, and its underlying logic, to the security valuation process

Approaches to the valuation of securities

There are two general approaches to the valuation process which can be used by both fundamental and technical analysts.

Top-down approach

This is also called the three-step approach. This approach is based on the belief that the return from investing in a stock is heavily dependent on which economy, market and industry the issuer is in. Analysis using a top-down approach follows the steps shown below.

1. Analyze alternative economies and securities markets

The objective is to decide the country allocation and the allocation between bonds, equities and cash in each market. Analysts of economies will study a government's fiscal and monetary policies, inflation, interest rates, corporate and consumer expenditure, and exchange rates. Other macro factors include international events such as wars and political changes.

Generally if a country is expected to move into recession equity investors would tend to underweight a market (relative to its weight based on market value) and focus on defensive investments. On the other hand if the economic outlook is positive they will tend to overweight a market.

2. Analyze alternative industries

The next step is to use economic and market analysis to decide which industries will benefit and which will suffer in the expected environment. Other factors to consider are issues such as demographics and the industry's international exposure. These factors will determine which industries should be overweighted and which should be underweighted relative to the market weightings.

Industry analysis is an important step, it is very difficult for a company to perform well if it is operating in an industry that faces difficulties and all companies' profitability will be affected by their industry environment.

3. Analyze individual companies and securities

Individual companies are analyzed within the industries selected. This will include analyzing each company's past performance and forecasting its future prospects and then determining its value. Once the value has been compared to the market price you can decide whether it is an attractive investment.

The last objective is to purchase securities that fit in with the other securities in a portfolio; this will involve looking at data such as correlation between the securities. (This is covered in Study Session 12)

The top-down method is preferred by the authors due to its logical process and empirical support. It has been shown that stock prices and a company' earnings are linked to the economic environment and that the rate of return for industries and stocks within the industry are linked.

Bottom-up approach

This is stock picking. Followers of this approach believe that they can select stocks that are under priced and will outperform regardless of the industry and market outlook.

LOS 14-1-A-b **explain** the various forms of investment returns

The next step is to look at the valuation of securities and we first need to explain the different types of return.

Investment returns

The return, or cash flow, can be received by an investor in different forms e.g. earnings, dividends, cash flow, interest payment, capital gains. Valuation models are based on different types of return and more than one model should be used to get an accurate valuation of an investment.

In addition to forecasting the returns themselves it is necessary to estimate the timing of returns and the growth rate of returns.

We now look at how securities are valued. If the estimated value is greater than the market price it is a buy signal and if it is lower it is a sell signal.

LOS 14-1-A-c **calculate** the value of a preferred stock, assuming a perpetual dividend

Value of preferred stock

The holder of a preferred stock receives a dividend in perpetuity. The value of a preferred stock is given by:

$$\text{value} = \frac{\text{dividend}}{k} \qquad \text{(Equation 14-1)}$$

where

dividend	=	annual dividend paid
k	=	the investor's required rate of return.

Example 14-1: Valuing preferred stock

A preferred stock pays a dividend of \$10 a year and trades in the market at \$80. If an investor's required rate of return is 12% then the value of the preferred stock to the investor is, using Equation 14-1,

$$\frac{\$10}{0.12} = \$83.33$$

Since the market price of \$80 is below the estimated value the investor should consider buying the stock.

There are two main approaches to equity valuation, the first is using discounted cash flow techniques and the second is using relative measures (e.g. price/earnings and price/book value ratios). The first method we look at is the dividend discount model which is when we consider the value of the cash flows (dividends) that are paid to the equity investor.

LOS 14-1-A-d	**calculate** the value of a common stock, using the dividend discount model (DDM) for both a one-year holding period and a multiple-year holding period
LOS 14-1-A-e	**calculate** the value of a common stock, using the infinite period DDM
LOS 14-1-A-f	**calculate** the value of a common stock for a company experiencing temporary supernormal growth

Dividend Discount Model

This model values equities as the present value of future dividends to be paid to the investor.

$$\text{Value} = \frac{D_1}{(1+k)} + \frac{D_2}{(1+k)^2} + \ldots\ldots.. + \frac{D_\infty}{(1+k)^\infty}$$ **(Equation 14-2)**

where

k = the required rate of return

D_i = the dividend in period i

If the stock is to be sold at the end of period n, for price P, the equation becomes

$$\text{Value} = \frac{D_1}{(1+k)} + \frac{D_2}{(1+k)^2} + \ldots\ldots.. + \frac{P + D_n}{(1+k)^n}$$ **(Equation 14-3)**

If it can be assumed that (i) the share is going to be held indefinitely, (ii) the growth rate(g) of dividends is constant and (iii) k is greater than g, then Equation 14-2 can be simplified to:

$$\text{Value} = \frac{D_1}{(k-g)}$$ **(Equation 14-4)**

Example 14-2: Dividend Discount Model

1. A stock's last dividend was \$5 per share and dividends are expected to grow by 6% per annum indefinitely. If the investors' required rate of return is 12% the value of the stock is given by

$$\text{Value} = \frac{D_1}{(k-g)} = \frac{\$5(1.06))}{(0.12-0.06)} = \$88.33$$

Note: it is important to use *next* year's dividend in the numerator.

2. An analyst forecasts a company will pay dividends of \$2 in the first year, \$3 in the second year and \$3.50 in the third year. After the third year dividends are forecast to grow at 4% per annum. If an investor's required rate of return is 12% the value of the stock is calculated as follows:

First, calculate the value of the stock at the end of year three, using Equation 14-4.

$$\text{Value} = \frac{D_4}{(k-g)} = \frac{\$3.50(1.04)}{(0.12-0.04)} = \$45.50$$

Using Equation 14-3, the value of the stock today is the sum of the present values of the first three years' dividends plus the present value of the end-year-three value.

$$\text{Value} = \frac{D_1}{(1+k)} + \frac{D_2}{(1+k)^2} + \frac{P+D_3}{(1+k)^3} = \frac{\$2}{(1.12)} + \frac{\$3}{(1.12)^2} + \frac{\$45.50+\$3.50}{(1.12)^3} = \$39.05$$

LOS 14-1-A-g	**show** how to use the DDM to develop an earnings multiplier model, and **explain** the factors in the DDM that affect a stock's price-to-earnings (P/E) ratio

Earnings Multiplier Model (or P/E)

P/E = current market price of stock/expected 12 month earnings per share
Using Equation 14-4,

$$P/E = \frac{(D_1/E_1)}{(k-g)} \qquad \text{(Equation 14-5)}$$

So P/E is dependent on:

5. The expected dividend payout ratio, D_1/E_1
6. The estimated required rate of return, k
7. The expected growth rate of dividends, g

Example 14-3: Price-to-earnings ratio

If a firm has a dividend payout ratio of 70%, a required rate of return of 15% and a growth rate of 8% then the P/E is, using Equation 14-5

$$P/E = \frac{(D_1/E_1)}{(k-g)} = \frac{0.70}{(0.15-0.08)} = 10.0$$

Note: As the payout ratio decreases g will increase and the P/E will increase (assuming the ROE is higher than k).

LOS 14-1-A-h	**explain** the components of an investor's required rate of return (i.e., the real risk free rate, the expected rate of inflation, and the risk premium)

There are two inputs that are used in several valuation methods, the required rate of return and the expected growth rate in earnings; we look at these in turn.

Calculation of k, the required rate of return

The required rate of return will depend on:

The economy's real risk-free rate (RRFR).
This is the minimum rate of return that an investor requires.

The expected rate of inflation E(I).
The nominal risk-free rate (NRFR) takes into account the expected rate of inflation,
NRFR = [1 +RRFR] [1 + E(I)] - 1

A risk premium.
This reflects the additional return required from investment in different securities, it reflects the risk of each investment.

LOS 14-1-A-i	**discuss** the risk factors to be assessed in determining a country risk premium for use in estimating the required return for foreign securities

Country risk premium

When analyzing international investments it is important to look at the risk components that vary between different countries. The major factors are as follows:

1. Business risk, reflects operating activity and operating leverage.
2. Financial risk, this measures the financial leverage used.
3. Liquidity risk, the U.S. has the most liquid capital markets, many emerging markets are illiquid.
4. Exchange rate risk, uncertainty of returns reflecting exchange rate movements.
5. Country risk, this reflects uncertainty due to factors such as political or economic turbulence in a country.

LOS 14-1-A-j	**estimate** the dividend growth rate, given the components of return on equity and incorporating the retention rate
LOS 14-1-A-k	**describe** a process for developing estimated inputs to be used in the DDM, including the required rate of return and expected growth rate of dividends

Estimating the growth rate, g

The growth rate of dividends will depend on the growth in earnings and the percentage of earnings paid out as dividends, as opposed to being retained by the company. Many analysts assume that the payout ratios are relatively stable in which case the growth rate of dividends equals the growth rate of earnings.

The growth rate is determined by the amount of earnings retained and the return on equity that it can generate on these earnings.

g = earnings retention rate x return on equity **(Equation 14-6)**

Example 14-4: Estimating the growth rate

If a firm retains 50% of earnings and has a return on equity of 8% then its long-term growth rate g is given by

$g = 0.50 \times 0.08 = 0.04$ or 4%

Using DuPont analysis we can break down the return on equity (ROE) into three components,

ROE = profit margin x total asset turnover x financial leverage **(Equation 14-7)**

An increase in any of these ratios will increase ROE, and when an analyst estimates ROE he must look at the estimates for each of the three components.

Additionally analysts should look at historic trends for cash flow, earnings and dividends. This might take into account the averages of historic returns, or use linear regression models and log-linear regression models.

14-1-A View Concept Check Questions Workbook

14-1-B "Stock-Market Analysis"

Introduction

In this Reading we focus on estimating the future price level of a stock market index or series. The method used is to initially estimate the future P/E ratio based on the payout rate, investors' required return and the sustainable growth rate. The second step is to forecast earnings for the index based on sales, profit margins, tax and interest costs. Once these are combined we have an estimate for P, the index level. Again candidates will be expected to know which variables lead to a change in the P/E of an index.

LOS 14-1-B-a **calculate** the earnings per share (EPS) of a stock market series

If we can estimate the EPS for a stock market series and then estimate the P/E, we will be able to multiply them together to arrive at a price or value for the series. First we look at estimating the EPS, then at estimating the P/E.

The calculation of EPS for a stock market series

The calculation involves the following steps:

1. Estimate the average sales per share. This will reflect the estimate for GDP which can be linked to the change in sales using regression analysis.
2. Estimate the operating profit margin, defined here as EBITDA (earnings before interest, tax, depreciation and amortization).
   This will involve estimating the:
   a. capacity utilization rate
   b. unit labor costs
   c. rate of inflation
   d. impact of foreign competition
3. Estimate depreciation per share. This can be estimated by time-series analysis where depreciation depends on capital expenditure.
4. Estimate interest expense per share. This will involve looking at the amount of debt outstanding and the average interest rate paid on the debt.
5. Estimate the corporate tax rate. Look at the current tax rate and any government legislation that will lead to changes in the tax rate.

LOS 14-1-B-b **calculate** the expected P/E ratio (earnings multiplier) of a stock market series, using the series' expected dividend payout ratio, required rate of return, and expected growth rate of dividends

If we wish to estimate the P/E we can use Equation 14-5,

$$P/E = \frac{(D_1/E_1)}{(k-g)}$$

Again the most difficult parameters to estimate are k and g.

Required rate of return, k

In this case k is the NRFR for the time to maturity that is similar to an investor's holding period, plus an equity market risk premium.

Equity risk premium

The premium can be calculated in different ways.

Research by Ibbotson and Sinquefield for the period 1926 to 2001 for the U.S. market suggests that if we use geometric averages of returns from stocks versus Treasury bills the premium is 7.5%. However if we are considering the risk premium against an intermediate government bond (since most investors have a time horizon that is longer than a Treasury bill's) the appropriate long-term historical risk premium is about 6.5%.

However there are problems using a historic risk premium calculated over a very long time period. One criticism is that the bond market volatility has increased relative to equity market volatility so the premium will be lower in the future. Studies indicate the current risk premium should be in the range 2.5% to 6%.

Growth rate of dividends, g

Remember Equation 14-6

g = earnings retention rate x return on equity

These numbers need to be calculated for the market. The annual earnings retention rate is between 45% and 60% for the U.S. market but is quite volatile and heavily influenced by changes in earnings. It is more appropriate for the long-term investor to base estimates on long-term trends rather than short-tem differences.

The return on equity needs to be calculated by considering the individual components (net profit margin, asset turnover and financial leverage) for the market.

LOS 14-1-B-c **estimate** the value of, and explain the level of and changes in, the earnings multiplier of a stock market series

Calculation of the earnings multiplier for a stock market series

Using the formula for the earnings multiplier

$$P/E = \frac{(D_1/E_1)}{(k - g)}$$

The earnings multiplier is much more volatile than EPS since it is very sensitive to changes in k and g.

There are two ways to calculate the earnings multiplier:

1. The direction of change approach - use the current earnings multiplier and estimate the change based on the estimates for the three components (D/E, k and g). Specifically this will involve forecasting the direction and extent of change in:
   a. the dividend-payout ratio
   b. the real RFR
   c. the rate of inflation
   d. the risk premium for common stock
   e. the earnings retention rate
   f. the return on equity
2. The specific estimate approach - make specific estimates for the three components (D/E, k and g). Generally an analyst should consider different scenarios to derive optimistic and pessimistic estimates.

LOS 14-1-B-d **calculate** the expected rate of return for a stock market series

The calculation of the expected rate of return on a stock market series.

The expected rate of return is given by:

$$E(R_t) = \frac{IV - BV + Div}{BV} \quad \textbf{(Equation 14-8)}$$

where

$E(R_t)$= estimated rate of return during period t
IV = intrinsic value of the stock market series
BV = beginning value of the stock market series
Div = expected dividend on the stock market series during the investment horizon.

It is expected that the market price will move towards its intrinsic value.

Example 14-5: Expected rate of return

A stock market series is expected to rise from 500 to 550 over one year and the estimated dividend per share over the period is 18. The expected rate of return is:

(550 – 500 + 18)/500 = 13.6%

If an investor's required rate of return is higher than 13.6% they should underweight the index, if it is lower they should overweight the index.

LOS 14-1-B-e **explain** how the top-down approach can be used to analyze the valuation of world stock markets

Valuation of world stock markets

The valuation of international markets follows the same methodology. It uses a top-down approach where the relevant components of a country's economy are forecast first (e.g. GDP, capital investment, inflation, interest rates). The next step is to look at the corporate data, including forecasts for earnings and dividend growth, which leads to market valuation measures being estimated.

14-1-B View Concept Check Questions Workbook

14-2 "Equity: Concepts and Techniques"

Introduction

We now look at stocks in the context of their global industry. Whilst the country where a company is domiciled is clearly important an investor will also need to analyse its competitors on a global basis. This Reading looks at the factors that need to be considered when evaluating a company in a global setting. It starts with an introduction to country analysis and the economic variables that analysts follow. When looking at economic growth it is important to differentiate between business cycles and long-term sustainable growth. Economic growth will feed thought to corporate profits and stock returns.

LOS 14-2-a	**classify** business cycle stages and **identify**, for each stage, attractive investment opportunities

The business cycle

In the short term business cycle conditions can be favorable or unfavorable for investments in different asset classes or sectors. However the turning points of business cycles are very difficult to predict as they are determined by many factors in the private and government sector. In an ideal world an investor would be fully invested in stocks at the trough and bonds at the peak of the cycle.

The text quotes Calverley (2003, pp. 15-19) for the classification of the different business cycle stages:

Recovery – the economy is picking up from a slowdown or recession. Buy the country's cyclical stocks and commodities. Buy riskier assets as the recovery is confirmed.

Early Upswing – confidence has picked up and the economy is gaining momentum. Buy the country's stocks and commercial and residential property.

Late Upswing – boom mentality is in place. It is not a good time to buy stocks; commodity and property prices are also peaking. It is time to buy the country's bonds, as yields are high, and buy interest rate sensitive stocks.

Economy Slows or goes into Recession – economy is declining. Hold on the country's bonds which will perform well as the country's interest rates fall, similarly interest rate sensitive stocks will also perform well.

Recession – monetary policy will be eased but will take time to stimulate the economy. Towards the end of the recession move in to the country's stocks and commodities.

Business cycle synchronization

Global economies are becoming more integrated so strong economic growth in one country will have a beneficial effect on companies exporting goods to that country helping to stimulate growth in foreign countries.

However full synchronization between countries' economies has not happened, and is unlikely to happen, given the importance of national economic factors. There are still benefits to investors who diversify internationally.

Growth theory

This is the study of the factors (including labor, capital and productivity) which lead to different rates of sustainable long-term growth. When analyzing an economy it is important to establish the source of growth, whether it is input-driven (e.g. from capital inflows from overseas) or efficiency-driven. Increased productivity or efficiency will have a more sustainable impact on growth than input-driven growth.

It is important to look at the relationship between country and industry analysis. For multinational companies the country of domicile may not be particularly relevant as the majority of their sales are in other countries.

LOS 14-2-b	**discuss,** with respect to global industry analysis, the key elements related to return expectations

Industry analysis and return

Global analysis is performed with the objective of finding companies that can earn on a sustainable basis a return on equity above the required rate of return. This means analysts must focus on sources of growth and sustainable competitive advantage rather than current levels of profits or cash flows. We outline below the key areas to analyse in order to identify investment opportunities.

Demand analysis

Demand is studied by (1) the use of regression equations to help forecast demand and (2) market surveys. Demand forecasts are critical for all capacity and production decisions.

Value creation

The value chain is the process by which raw material is transformed into a product or service. Upstream refers to activities which are close to raw material supply and downstream as being activities close to the consumer. Each transformation in the chain adds value; the amount of value added depends on:

- *Learning/experience curve* – cost per unit declines as a company gains experience.
- *Economies of scale* - average cost declines as output expands.
- *Economies of scope* - as a company moves into related products experience and reputation with the original product may help demand.
- *Network externalities* – some products and services gain value as more and more customers use them.

An analyst will be studying the value chain and the position of each company in the chain. Their position will help determine their ability to make profits and over time there will be profit migration between different parts of the value chain.

LOS 14-2-c **describe** the industry life cycle and **identify** an industry's stage in its life cycle

Industry life cycle

One popular method of analysis divides the life of an industry into five stages based on the rate of growth in sales.

LIFE CYCLE FOR AN INDUSTRY

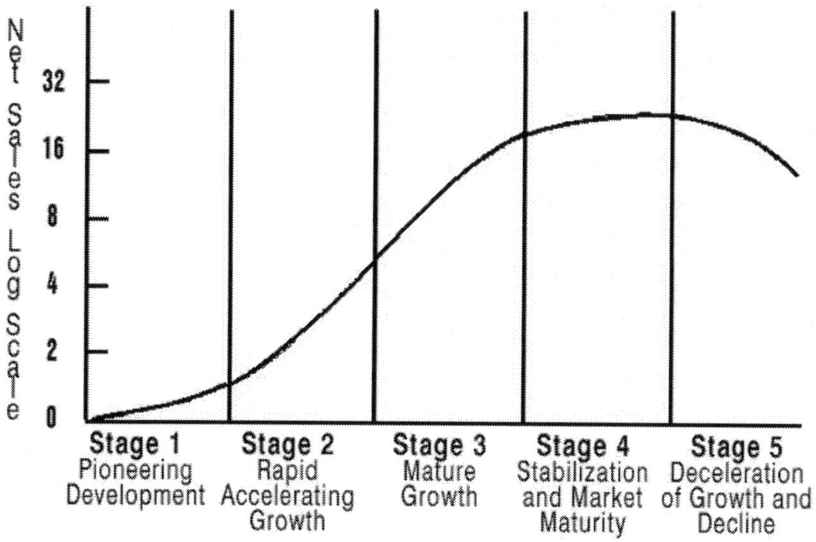

Pioneering development

This is the start-up stage when an industry has slow sales growth and small profits, or losses. There are probably major development costs.

Rapid accelerating growth

The firms in the industry experience strong sales growth as demand for the products rises rapidly. There is little competition, leading to high profit margins and very rapid profits growth.

Mature growth

During this stage there is higher growth in sales than in the overall economy, but competitors have entered the market and profit margins stabilize.

Stabilization and market maturity

In this stage the industry grows in line with the economy. It becomes highly competitive on a price basis which reduces profit margins, and returns on capital decline to a long-term competitive level.

Deceleration of growth and decline

Sales growth declines because of demand shifts and/or the availability of substitutes. Profit margins fall and the focus is on improving efficiency.

LOS 14-2-d **calculate** a concentration ratio and a Herfindahl index

Competitive environment

One of the most important steps in analyzing an industry is to look at the competitive structure of the industry which will determine the ability of firms to earn above-average rates of return.

One method is to look at the N firm concentration ratio which is the combined market share of the largest N firms in the industry. An alternative measure is the Herfindahl index. This is defined by:

$$H = M_1^2 + M_1^2 + \dots\dots\dots + M_1^2$$ **(Equation 14-9)**

where

H = Herfindahl index

M_i = market share of ith firm

The Herfindahl index will have a value less than or equal to one, and a large number (above 0.18) indicates that the industry is dominated by a few players (ologopolistic) and a small number (less than 0.1) that the industry is competitive with no dominant participants. Between 0.1 and 0.18 indicates moderate concentration. If there are N firms which all have equal market share then the index is simply 1/N.

The N firm concentration ratio is useful because it is an easily recognized measure of the dominance of the largest firms whereas the Herfindahl index is useful because it includes data on all firms, although it gives a greater weighting to firms with a large market share.

Example: 14-6

An analyst is comparing two industries A and B. The following data is given on the market shares of the largest participants in the industries:

Industry A	Industry B
One firm has 50%	Six firms have 16.67%
Four firms have 10%	
Five firms have 2%	

Industry A

Five firm concentration ratio is 60%

The Herfindahl index = $H = M_1^2 + M_1^2 + ... + M_1^2 = 0.50^2 + 4(0.10)^2 + 5(0.02)^2 = 0.292$

Industry B

Five firm concentration ratio is 83.33%

The Herfindahl index = 1/6 = 0.1667

Although the five firm concentration ratio is higher for industry B the Herfindahl index is lower reflecting lower concentration than industry A. Industry A is dominated by one participant with 50% of the market.

Competitive advantage

Porter, a leading academic in the area of competition, looked at the factors that give one location a competitive advantage over another. Four factors that can lead to a competitive advantage are:

Factor conditions such as human capital which could be measured by years of schooling.

Demand conditions such as size of the domestic market.

Related supplier and support industries.

Strategy, structure and rivalry such as management practices and corporate governance.

Competitive strategies

There are three competitive strategies identified by Porter which a firm can use:

Cost leadership – be the lowest cost producer.

Differentiation – provide products not provided by the competitors.

Focus – target a market niche.

Sector rotation

Many investors use the business cycle as an indicator for when certain industries are going to outperform. For example they purchase consumer durables and consumer non durables in a recovery or early upswing since these industries do well in a strong economy. However consumer staples are more defensive and will do better in a recession. This type of strategy can be dangerous - although demand for an industry's products may depend on the stage of the business cycle this may not feed through to higher profits.

LOS 14-2-e	**discuss**, with respect to global industry analysis, the elements related to risk

Industry analysis and risk

An investor needs to look at potential returns in relation to the risks involved. We now look at the risks in relation to the industry sector. Risks will differ from sector to sector, in some cases the main risk will be the business cycle, in others technological change may pose the greatest risk.

Market competition

Here we need to evaluate the likely success of competitive strategies. In many cases we are looking at firms who are trying to maintain a competitive advantage which will involve deterring new entrants or promoting exit strategies. Using pricing strategies such as predatory pricing (pricing below cost) can help drive competitors out of the market. When evaluating a company it is important to assess the risk that it will be unable to maintain its competitive advantage.

Value chain competition

Companies must also compete within the value chain. Workers' wages are an example of this; workers are suppliers of a resource and may well demand a higher proportion of potential profits. There are also co-opetition risks; co-opetition refers to cooperation along the value chain. Co-opetition risks include risks that the suppliers of materials may delay delivery or that their distributors may decide to use other producers. Generally suppliers of commodities, rather than differentiated products, will have less ability to extract profits from other participants in the value chain.

LOS 14-2-f **describe** the basic forces that determine industry competition

Five Forces

Porter believed that five factors determined the competitive environment and the importance of each will vary according to the industry. The factors are shown below in some cases slightly modified or extended (ref. Oster):

1. *Rivalry amongst existing competitors*, this includes issues such as foreign competitors, the cost base of the industry and exit barriers. Coordination between participants can reduce rivalry and create excess profits.
2. *Substitutes*, considerations include how similar are the potential substitutes and how are they priced.
3. *Bargaining power of buyers*, if buyers have much larger businesses they have more power than individuals. Standardization of products increases the buyers' power because they can purchase elsewhere. High buyer power tends to reduce profitability for the producer.
4. *Bargaining power of suppliers*, the more suppliers in the industry the less the supplier power. Standardized products reduce supplier power since the supplier does not have a differentiated product. Also watch out for the potential of buyers to integrate backwards and cut out the suppliers.
5. *Threat of new entrants*, this will include considering barriers to entry. The higher the potential profits the more likely it is that new firms will try and enter the industry. High exit costs will discourage new entrants.

Other factors to consider are:

Government participation – governments may decide to subsidize certain companies, not only does this create a risk of poor profitability for competitors but creates uncertainty over future policy. Other issues are government policies on wages and benefits, and exports and imports.

Risks and covariance – here we are looking at standard deviations of returns for a stock or industry. Part of standard deviation can be diversified away so then we need to look at beta which is related to the covariance between return and the market returns. Betas will vary due to factors such as the business cycle and the competitive environment.

14-2 View Concept Check Questions Workbook

14-3-A "Company Analysis and Stock Selection"

Introduction

In this Reading we use the same methodology used in the valuation of a stock market index covered in Reading 14-1-B. To value individual stocks we estimate the earnings multiplier (P/E) and earnings in order to arrive at an estimate for the future price of the stock. Candidates are also expected to be able to differentiate between the definitions for a growth, defensive, cyclical and speculative stock and company.

LOS 14-3-A-a	**differentiate** between 1) a growth company and a growth stock, 2) a defensive company and a defensive stock, 3) a cyclical company and a cyclical stock, and 4) a speculative company and a speculative stock

It is important to differentiate between company analysis and stock selection. Company analysis may identify a company that is highly attractive in terms of growth and management. However, when it comes to looking at the valuation of the stock it may be that the market has already discounted the favorable prospects in the share price and the shares are trading above their intrinsic value. In this case the stock should probably be avoided. On the other hand, there may be a company with less attractive prospects where the stock price is trading below its intrinsic value, which makes it a more attractive investment.

Growth companies and growth stocks

Growth companies – these are traditionally companies that have shown above average growth in sales and earnings, although they can also be defined as companies that have the potential to earn a rate of return that is above the required rate of return or cost of capital.

Growth stock – A growth stock is one that has achieved a higher risk-adjusted return than other stocks in the market. Growth stocks are not limited to being stocks of growth companies. They are stocks that at some stage were undervalued by the market but during the adjustment to a fair value exhibited superior performance.

It should be noted that growth companies' share prices have not generally provided superior performance in the past, meaning they are not always growth stocks.

A **defensive** company is one whose earnings are resilient to economic downturn. A defensive stock is one that has a low or negative beta so the stock price is expected to fall by less than the market in a downturn.

Similarly a **cyclical** company is heavily influenced by the business cycle whereas a cyclical stock has a high beta and is expected to rise or fall by more than the market.

A **speculative** company is one where the business is risky but there is the potential for a large gain. A speculative stock is one with a high probability of poor returns and a small probability of spectacular returns.

Value versus growth investing

Value stocks are ones which are undervalued on some measure other than their growth potential, such as a low price/book or price/earnings value. In this comparison we are looking at growth stocks to mean something different to the definition above, in this case we are looking at growth stocks as ones which have above average sales or earnings growth. They will often trade at high price/earnings and price/book values.

LOS 14-3-A-b	**describe** and **estimate** the expected earnings per share (EPS) and earnings multiplier for a company

Estimating a company's earnings per share

Once again the earnings per share forecast will depend on the sales and profit margin forecasts.

1. *Estimate sales*, look at the company's sales performance with respect to its industry and the economy, as well as factors that will influence the individual company's ability to increase sales e.g. potential to expand capacity.
2. *Estimate the company's profit margin*, look at the firm's performance relative to the industry environment, its competitive position, and general company trends.

Estimating a company's earnings multiplier

Two methods can be used to calculate the earnings multiplier:

1. Use macroanalysis to estimate the P/E by looking at the economy and its industry.
2. Calculate the three components of the earnings multiplier; the dividend payout ratio, the required rate of return and growth rate.

14-3-A View Concept Check Questions Workbook

14-3-B "Technical Analysis"

Introduction

This is a broad introduction to technical analysis, the philosophy or assumptions made by technical analysts, and the challenges to their work. Technical analysts differ from fundamental analysts in that they believe prices are driven by both rational and irrational factors. The Reading also looks at the signals technical analysts use to indicate that the market or an individual security price is moving into a new trend.

LOS 14-3-B-a **explain** the underlying assumptions of technical analysis

Technical analysis involves examining past trading prices and volume data to identify trends that can be used to predict future market and security price movements.

Assumptions of technical analysis

The assumptions made by technical analysts include:

1. Prices are decided by supply and demand.
2. Supply and demand are driven by rational and irrational behavior.
3. Prices move in trends that persist for long periods of time.
4. The shifts in supply and demand can be seen in market price behavior.

LOS 14-3-B-b **explain** how technical analysis differs from fundamental analysis

The main difference between fundamental analysts, technical analysts and followers of EMH is in the time that they believe security prices take to react to news. EMH says that prices react almost immediately to news, fundamentalists believe there is a little longer to make decisions and technical analysts believe that it takes time for a new equilibrium price to be established. Technical analysts also believe that new information that affects supply and demand comes into the market over a period of time rather than at one specific point in time.

LOS 14-3-B-c discuss the advantages of technical analysis

Advantages of technical analysis

- There is no need to analyze financial statements and adjust accounting data for different accounting methods.
- Technical analysis incorporates psychological and fundamental reasons for price moves.
- Technical analysis signals buys and sells without needing to justify why other investors are buying and selling.
- Technical analysts have more time to decide whether a new trend for a stock price is being established.

LOS 14-3-B-d discuss the challenges to technical analysis

Challenges to technical analysis

- Results of testing correlations between prices and runs and the use of trading rules, with respect to the weak-form Efficient Market Hypothesis, has shown that technical analysis based on past market data does not provide superior performance.
- If sufficient technical analysts are operating in a market then they will drive price moves. This will lead to technical analysis working, but only in the short term, since if a price move is not based on fundamentals the price will return to its equilibrium.
- If a trading rule is found to be successful several technical analysts would follow the rule so it is unlikely to continue to generate profits.
- Trading rules are subjective, different analysts will reach different conclusions when presented with the same market data.

LOS 14-3-B-e identify examples of each of the major categories of technical indicators

When referring to technical analysts it is important to differentiate between:

1. **Contrarians** who believe that as the market approaches peaks and troughs investors will generally become over-bullish or bearish, and
2. Analysts who **'follow the smart money'**; they wish to follow the positive sentiment of sophisticated investors.

Contrary-opinion technical analysts

This group of analysts uses the following indicators to assess what the majority of investors are doing, and then take the opposite view.

1. Mutual fund cash positions, the percentage held in cash varies between about 5 and 13%. Contrary-opinion analysts believe that mutual funds generally have a high percentage of cash near the trough of markets so a high cash position is read as a bullish indicator. On the other hand a low cash position would be seen as a bearish indicator.
2. Investor credit balances in brokerage accounts, investors sell stocks and leave the cash balances in brokerage accounts if they expect to reinvest the money in the short term. Therefore if the credit balances increase it is seen as a build up of purchasing power and is a buy signal. Alternatively a decline in credit balances is a sell signal.
3. Investor advisory opinions, based on the view that most investment advisors are trend followers therefore if the 'bearish sentiment index' (bearish opinions/total opinions) is more than 60% this would be seen by technicians as a bullish indicator and if it were lower than 20% technicians would see it as a bearish indicator.
4. OTC volume versus NYSE volume, OTC trading is considered to be speculative compared to NYSE trading and the percentage of speculative trading is highest at market peaks.
5. Put/Call Ratio, a high ratio is read by technicians to be a bullish indicator, and a low ratio a bearish indicator.
6. Futures traders bullish or bearish, technical analysts will look at the percentage of speculators in stock index futures who are bullish or bearish and then take the opposite view.

Follow the smart money

Technical analysts who wish to **follow the smart money** use the indicators below:

1. Confidence Index, this is published by Barron's and is the average yield on the 10 top grade corporate bonds divided by the yield on the Dow Jones average of 40 bonds. The ratio will be high, approaching 100, when investors are confident and relatively happy to invest in lower grade bonds.
2. T. Bill - Eurodollar Yield Spread, when the spread is large, typically at times of international crisis, it shows that investors are keen to invest in Treasury bills as a safe-haven investment.
3. Debit balances in brokerage accounts, these represent margin borrowing. An increase could be read as a bullish sign, a decrease as a bearish sign.

Other Indicators

These are often used to obtain a view of overall market sentiment by technical analysts.

1. Breadth of Market, this measures the number of securities that have risen versus the number that have declined. This can be measured by following the advance-decline series which is the net advances, or declines, relative to the market to see if they move in the same direction. If they move together is shows that the market move is broadly based, if not, it indicates that the market is near a peak or trough.
2. Short interest ratio, this is equal to the outstanding short interest/average daily trading volume. A high ratio is considered bullish since potentially the short sellers will need to buy back stock in the market.
3. Share prices relative to moving average:
4. If more than 80% of stocks are above the 200-day moving average then the market is overbought. If less than 20% of stocks are above the 200-day moving average then the market is oversold.
5. Block uptick - downtick ratio, is an indicator of institutional sentiment. A low ratio indicates an oversold market and a high ratio indicates an overbought market.

Price and Volume Analysis

Dow Theory, prices move in major, intermediate and short-term trends. Followers are hoping to identify the major trends. A major upward trend may be broken by intermediate downward trends but if each peak was higher than the last and upward moves are accompanied by high volumes this would be seen as a bullish signal.

Support and resistance levels are useful in determining price trends. A *support level* is the price range at which a substantial increase in demand for the stock is expected which will reverse a declining trend. A *resistance level* is the price range at which a substantial increase in supply of the stock is expected which will reverse a rising trend.

Moving-average lines, when moving-average lines cross, it can signal a reversal in trend.

Relative strength, technicians believe that if a stock or industry is outperforming the market it will tend to continue to do so.

Charts

Analysts who are looking for repetition of past trends often use charts, the charts used include bar charts and point-and-figure charts.

Technical analysis of bond markets

Similar trading rules used for bonds are used in equity markets. One problem with bonds is that, since trading is mainly OTC, volume data is not available.

14-3-B View Concept Check Questions Workbook

14-4 "Introduction to Price Multiples"

Introduction

This Reading discusses four of the most commonly used price multiples or ratios, price to earnings (P/E), price to book value (P/BV), price to sales (P/S), and price to cash flow (P/CF). The multiples are fairly simple to calculate, and readily accessed in newspapers etc. They can be used for comparing a stock to another stock, to an industry or a market. Ratios give a measure of the price of a stock relative to its earnings or assets, or other measure of value. If the characteristics of two companies are very similar the one trading on the lower multiple offers the better value.

We look at each of the four multiples in turn and consider the rationale for using the multiple and how it is defined and calculated.

LOS 14-4-a	**discuss** the rationales for the use of price to earnings (P/E), price to book value (P/BV), price to sales (P/S), and price to cash flow (P/CF) in equity valuation
LOS 14-4-b	**discuss** the possible drawbacks to the use of each price multiple
LOS 14-4-c	**calculate** and **interpret** P/E, P/BV, P/S, and P/CF

Price to Earnings (P/E)

Rationales for using P/E are

- Analysts see earnings as the main driver of value (followed by cash flow, book value and dividends).
- It is widely recognized and used by investors.
- Empirical research shows low P/E stocks tend to outperform the markets over long periods.

Disadvantages in using P/E include

- Earnings per share (EPS) can be negative, in which case the P/E is meaningless.
- EPS may not reflect ongoing or recurring earnings of the company.
- EPS will reflect management's choice of accounting practices and not be comparable with EPS reported by other companies.

Determining Earnings

Whilst the current price of a stock is usually readily available, different EPS can be used to compute the P/E.

Trailing P/E – this is the same as the current P/E, and the EPS used are those for the most recent four quarters.

Leading P/E – this is the forward or prospective P/E, and the EPS used are the next year's expected EPS.

Usually an analyst is looking forward so a leading P/E is more useful, however if earnings are unpredictable a trailing P/E might be used. Issues to consider in the calculation of EPS are:

1. The company's non-recurring earnings, these are generally removed by the analysts and underlying earnings are used. Examples of non-recurring earnings are extraordinary items, restructuring costs, effects of changes in accounting methods, asset write-downs and merger costs.
2. Transitory components due to the industry or business cycle. Business-cycle-adjusted EPS is referred to as normal EPS and it is the EPS that is expected mid-cycle. Normal EPS can be calculated as the average over the last business cycle, or as the average ROE over the last business cycle multiplied by the current book value per share.
3. Differences in accounting methods. In order to compare P/Es between two companies it is important to ensure that the same accounting methods are used (e.g. LIFO versus FIFO), and if not, adjust the accounts so that they are comparable.
4. Potential dilution of EPS - use earnings that are diluted to reflect convertibles, options and warrants outstanding.

Earnings yield is E/P, in this case if we rank stocks highest to lowest the most expensive stocks have the lowest E/P and the cheapest the highest. One advantage of looking at E/P is that stocks with negative P/Es can be ranked on the same basis using E/P and the lower the negative E/P the less attractive.

Example 14-7: P/E calculation

ABC Commodities is sensitive to the economic cycle; they have also been through a period of restructuring. You decide that the six years ending 2004 reflect a business cycle for the company and collect the following data, EPS and BVPS in US$.

	1999	2000	2001	2002	2003	2004
Reported EPS	1.25	2.70	6.50	2.25	3.25	1.00
Adjusted* EPS	1.30	2.65	5.50	4.30	3.25	1.00
ROE* %	0.04	0.13	0.22	0.18	0.12	0.03
BVPS						32.00

* Adjusted for non-recurring items

The current share price of ABC Commodities is $30.00

In order to calculate the normalized EPS there are two methods that can be used

1. Use the average of the recurring EPS over the six-year period and

Normal EPS = (1.30 + 2.65 + 5.50 + 4.30 + 3.25 + 1.00)/6 = 3.00

P/E = 30.00/3.00 = 10.00

2. Use the average ROE over the period, and multiply by the current book value.

Average ROE = (0.04 + 0.13 + 0.22 + 0.18 + 0.12 + 0.03)/6 = 0.12

Normal EPS = 0.12 x 32.0 = 3.84

P/E = 30.00/3.84 = 7.81

The P/E using the second method is lower, this is because it is calculated using the current size of the company, rather than on the average size over the last six years.

Price to Book Value (P/B)

Here we are comparing the price of the shares to the investment the shareholders have made in the company. Book value is shareholders' equity, or total assets minus total liabilities.

Rationales for using P/B are

- Book value is generally a positive number.
- It is more stable than EPS.
- Book value is viewed as appropriate for valuing companies with mainly liquid assets, where the market value is approximately the same as the book value e.g. banks, insurance and finance companies.
- Book value may be appropriate for companies that are not expected to continue to operate as a going concern.
- Empirical research shows low P/B stocks tend to outperform the markets over long periods.

Disadvantages in using P/B include

- Other assets, not included on the balance sheet are often significant, for example human capital.
- It is not a good measure for comparing companies with very different levels of assets being employed.
- Accounting differences between companies will invalidate comparisons between different companies, and especially those in different countries.
- Book value may not reflect the market value of a company's assets, particularly in an inflationary environment.

Calculation of BV

BV per share is common shareholders' equity divided by the number of common stock shares outstanding.

Some adjustments may be made to book value in order to make it better reflect the value of shareholders' investment.

- **Tangible book value** is book value less reported intangible assets. Whilst goodwill should probably be deducted other items such as patents may be considered individually.
- Adjust for off-balance-sheet assets and liabilities and for difference in fair value and historic cost of assets.
- Adjust to comparable accounting methods.

Price to Sales (P/S)

Rationales for using P/S are

- Sales numbers are less subject to accounting manipulation.
- Sales are positive.
- Sales are more stable than EPS.
- P/S is viewed as appropriate for valuing mature, cyclical and zero-income companies.
- Empirical research shows that P/S can be linked to stock performance.

Disadvantages in using P/S include

1. A business can generate positive sales without being profitable or generating positive operating cash flow.
2. It can not be used for comparing companies with different cost structures.
3. There is still potential to manipulate sales figures.

Price to Cash Flow (P/CF)

Rationales for using P/CF are

- Cash flow is less subject to manipulation by management.
- Cash flow is generally more stable than EPS.
- Using cash flow can avoid the issues of quality of earnings between different companies.
- Empirical research shows that P/CF can be linked to stock performance.

Disadvantages in using P/CF include

1. When approximations for cash flow, such as earnings plus non-cash charges, are used then important items such as changes in working capital are often ignored.
2. Free cash flow to equity is the preferred cash flow that should be used, but tends to be a more volatile measurement of cash flow.

14-4 View Concept Check Questions Workbook

STUDY SESSION 15

Asset Valuation

Debt Investment: Basic Concepts

Overview

There are two Study Sessions covering debt investments. Study Session 15 provides definitions and descriptions of the main characteristics of different types of fixed income instruments, plus an introduction to the basic concepts behind bond valuation. Study Session 16 looks in greater detail at the methods of analyzing and measuring interest rate risk of fixed income instruments.

Study Session 15 starts with a description of the typical features that define fixed-income securities i.e. the principal and coupon cash flows and the factors that may affect the regularity of such cash flows. In the second Reading the different types of risks related to investing in bonds are discussed. Interest rate risk is covered in greater detail as interest rates are the main determinant of the price movement of most high grade bonds. The third Reading familiarises the candidates with the features of a variety of bond sectors, such as government and corporate bonds. The last Reading delves into the concept of yield spread, i.e. the additional yield on a bond relative to a given benchmark, as well as the external factors that may influence the level of yields expected by an investor.

Reading Assignments

Fixed Income Analysis for the Chartered Financial Analyst® Program, 2nd edition, Frank J. Fabozzi (Frank J. Fabozzi Associates, 2004)

15-1-A. "Features of Debt Securities," Ch. 1

15-1-B. "Risks Associated with Investing in Bonds," Ch. 2

15-1-C. "Overview of Bond Sectors and Instruments," Ch. 3

15-1-D. "Understanding Yield Spreads," Ch. 4

15-1-A "Features of Debt Securities"

Introduction

This Reading looks at the main features and characteristics of different categories of bonds including the types of cash flows paid out by a bond issuer to an investor. We also examine the options given to investors or issuers resulting in the modification of the pattern of the principal and coupon cash flows and various provisions for the early retirement of debt. As with other Readings in this Study Session many candidates who are not working in the U.S. debt markets will meet a lot of new terminology that they need to become familiar with.

LOS 15-1-A-a **explain** the purposes of a bond's indenture, and **describe** affirmative and negative covenants

Indentures

A bond's indenture is a legal contract that sets forth in great detail the promises of the issuer (also called debtor or borrower) and the rights of the bond holders. Bondholders (also called investors or creditors) will know what to expect from the issuer as long as they hold the bonds. Since the bonds might change hands among investors, to help monitor that the issuer abides by the terms of the indenture, a third independent party needs to be appointed. This third party who acts on behalf of the bondholders is called an indenture trustee and is usually a bank.

Covenants

Affirmative covenants require the issuer to perform certain actions. The common ones are:

- to pay the interest and the principal on a timely basis
- to pay all taxes and claims when due
- to maintain that the borrower's properties are in good working order
- to submit periodic reports that the borrower is in compliance with the loan agreement

Negative covenants call upon the issuer not to perform certain actions. The main ones are limitations on taking on additional borrowings that would potentially compromise the ability of the issuer to keep its promises to the current bondholders, unless certain tests are met. These tests may include leverage level, liquidity level, etc.

It is in the bondholders' interest to impose the strictest restrictions on the borrowers, whereas the borrowers would prefer the least restrictive loan agreement. A balance is struck and diligently set out in an indenture. The balance will be a trade-off between interest costs and the restrictions. Failure to adhere to the covenants may be considered a violation or a default situation.

LOS 15-1-A-b	**describe** the basic features of a bond (e.g., maturity, par value, coupon rate, provisions for redeeming bonds, currency denomination, options granted to the issuer or investor)

A **fixed income security** is defined as a financial obligation of an entity (an issuer) to pay a specified sum of money at specified future dates. Generally the financial obligation consists of a promise to pay interest and to repay principal (amount borrowed). The terms *bonds* and *fixed income securities* are often interchangeable.

Maturity or **term to maturity** is the number of years over which the issuer has promised to pay interest and to repay the principal. The **maturity date** of a fixed income security is the date after which the debt will no longer exist and at which time the issuer repays the amount borrowed.

The **par value** of a bond is the amount that the issuer agrees to repay the bondholder by the maturity date. Synonyms are the **principal, face value, redemption value** and **maturity value**. Bonds can have any par value. Bond prices are quoted as a percentage of par, in increments of 1/32.

The **coupon rate**, also called the **nominal rate**, is the annual rate of interest that an issuer agrees to pay. The annual amount of the interest payments is called the **coupon**, where:

coupon = coupon rate x par value **(Equation 15-1)**

In the U.S. it is common practice for the coupons to be paid twice a year (semiannually). Mortgage-backed and asset-backed securities normally pay the coupon monthly, reflecting the payment structure of the underlying assets, i.e. mortgage loans whose borrowers pay monthly installments. In other countries, the frequency of the coupon payments can be quarterly, semiannually, or annually depending upon market practice.

Provisions for redeeming bonds is the agreement by the issuer on how the principal is repaid. Provisions include:

- call and funding provisions
- prepayments
- sinking fund provisions
- index amortizing notes

Further explanation is given in subsequent Readings.

Fixed income securities can be issued in any currency as long as it is legal and practical to do so. For instance, a Japanese company can legally issue a British pound-denominated bond in the United Kingdom as long as the regulatory requirements of the issuance are met.

It is common to grant issuers and/or bondholders an option to take an action against the other party; these are called options granted to the issuer or investor. These are explained in the subsequent Readings. The exercise of such options such as an early repayment of principal could modify the cash flows of the bonds, which in turn affects the value of the bonds as an investment.

Example 15-1: Par values

The longest maturity of bonds is typically 30 years, this is the case with U.S. Government bonds, or it can be anything from 1 to 100 years. Dollar prices are linked to quoted prices as follows:

Par values

Quoted Price	Price per $ par value	Par value	Dollar price
89 ½	0.8950	$5,000	4,475
103 3/32	1.0309375	$100,000	103,093.75

A bond with a 7.5% coupon rate and a par value of $10,000 will pay annual interest of $750, i.e. 0.075 x $10,000, (using Equation 15-1).

LOS 15-1-A-c **describe** the various coupon rate structures (e.g., zero-coupon bonds, step-up notes, deferred coupon bonds, floating-rate securities)

Coupon rate structures

Bonds have different coupon rate structures, depending upon the desired cash-flow pattern from the issuers' perspective or other considerations.

Zero-coupon bonds are those where the coupons are not paid-out periodically but accrued and realized at the date of maturity. The bonds are sold at a discount that reflects the accrued coupon. Another type is **accrual bonds,** which are similar to zero-coupon bonds in the way that the coupons are accrued and realized at the maturity date, but the difference is that the bonds are issued at par, not at a discount.

Step-up notes are those where the coupon rate is increased over time. There are **single step-up notes** as well as **multiple step-up notes**.

Deferred coupon bonds are those which offer no coupon payments for a specific period, but a lump-sum payment of the accrued interest at a specified later date. Regular periodic payments of the coupons resume after the specified date.

Floating-rate securities, often called **variable-rate securities**, have coupon rates that are reset periodically according to particular rules or reference interest rate.

Example 15-2: Coupons

1. When a zero-coupon bond with a 2-year maturity and par value of \$10,000 is quoted at 87½, it means that the (100 – 87½) x \$10,000 = \$1,250 is the compound interest portion.

2. An accrual bond with a 3-year maturity and a 7% coupon paid in arrears and compounded annually, and a par value of \$10,000, will at maturity pay \$12,250.43 including accrued interest.

3. A bank issues a step-up note with the following schedule:

   6.0% from March 3, 1999 to March 2, 2002
   6.25% from March 3, 2000 to March 2, 2003
   6.5% from March 3, 2001 to March 2, 2004

4. A floating-rate bond is quoted with a coupon formula of: 6-month LIBOR + 125 basis points (semiannual reset), meaning that the coupon rate is 1.25% above the prevailing 6-month LIBOR rate. If the current 6-month LIBOR rate is 6.25% then the coupon rate of the bond for the period until the next reset date will be (6.25% + 1.25%) = 7.5%.

LOS 15-1-A-d **describe** the structure of floating-rate securities (i.e., the coupon formula, caps and floors)

Floating-rate securities

The structure of floating-rate securities, such as the coupon formula and the caps and floors features, and the mechanics of the payments and the coupon rate resetting are now examined.

The typical **coupon formula** is

coupon rate = reference rate + quoted margin **(Equation 15-2)**

The **reference rate** generally reflects the market conditions, often represented by the risk-free rates in the market such as yields of government bonds or interbank offer rates,

The **quoted margin** is the additional interest rate that the issuer agrees to pay above the reference rate. It indicates the additional compensation that an investor requires. The quoted margin can occasionally be a negative value creating a coupon rate lower than the reference rate.

To protect an issuer from rampant hikes in interest rates, often a maximum limit is set. A **cap** is a maximum rate for a coupon that can be reached regardless of how high the reference rate goes. Caps are naturally unattractive to investors.

Conversely, a **floor** is its minimum, which is in place to protect the investor. If a bond has a cap and a floor, the feature is called a **collar**.

There are various different types of floating-rate securities, which are often structured with the use of derivative instruments. Following is a list of examples:

1. Inverse floaters or reverse floaters.

The coupon formula is

coupon rate = K – L x (reference rate),
where K and L are values specified in the prospectus or the indenture for the issue in such a way that the movement of the resulting coupon rate is opposite to the market move.

2. Dual-indexed floaters

The coupon formula

coupon rate = ($R_1 - R_2$) + quoted margin
where R_1 and R_2 are two pre-specified reference rates.

3. Ratchet bonds

The issuer can only adjust their coupon rates downwards based on the coupon formula. Once the coupon rate falls due to the reference rate drop, the coupon rate cannot be adjusted up if the reference rate subsequently rises.

coupon rate = R + quoted margin
where R will always be equal to the lowest recorded reference rate during the life of the issue.

4. Stepped spread floaters

The quoted margin of this type of a security can be adjusted up or down at certain intervals during the life of the security as specified in the indenture. The quoted margin will be stepped down if it is expected that the issuer's risk will improve during the course of time, or stepped up if the issuer's risk deteriorates.

coupon rate = reference rate + QM
where QM, the quoted margin, will follow a resetting schedule over the life of the issue.

5. Reset Margin Determined at Issuer Discretion

A floating-rate security where the coupon rate can be changed depending on market conditions, so the issue will trade at a pre-determined price, is called an extendible reset bond. The new rate will reflect the market interest rate and the required margin. Unlike a typical floater with a fixed quoted margin, this coupon formula will take into account the dynamics of the market perception of the issuer risk.

coupon rate = reference rate + QM
In this case the sum of the reference rate and QM, the quoted margin, will usually make the issue trade at a minimum of par value.

6. Non-interest rate index floaters

The reference rate in the coupon formula can take a wide variety of indices other than an interest rate or an interest index. With the latest financial engineering techniques, any reference rate can now be used, such as the price of a commodity (e.g. gold or crude oil), the return of an equity index (e.g. S&P 500), or others.

Another popular reference rate is an inflation index. The U.S. Department of Treasury issued Treasury Inflation Protection Securities (TIPS), and other commercial entities have already begun issuing inflation-indexed bonds.

7. Deleveraged floater is a floating rate security with the following coupon formula:

coupon rate = b x (reference rate) + quoted margin
where b is between 0 and 1

8. Drop-lock bonds change their floating-rate coupons to fixed-rate when certain conditions are met.

Example 15-3: Floating-rate securities

1. A deleveraged floater is quoted with a coupon formula of: 0.60 x (1-year LIBOR) + 300 basis points and a minimum coupon rate of 6%.

2. An inverse floater has a coupon formula: coupon rate = 10% – 0.8 x (reference rate), so if the reference rate moves up from 5% to 7%, the coupon rate decreases from 6% to 4.4%.

3. A dual-indexed floater may have a coupon rate = (1-year LIBOR – 3-month LIBOR) + 7%. If the 1-year LIBOR is 6.5% and the 3-month LIBOR is 5.5%, the coupon will be 8%.

4. A ratchet bond has a coupon rate = R + 1.5%. When R increases from 6% to 7%, the coupon rate remains at 7.5%, since it stays at the lowest rate.

5. Non-interest rate index floaters, J.P. Morgan issued a 15-year bond that pays the CPI plus 400 basis points. If the CPI is 2.1%, the coupon rate will be 6.1%.

LOS 15-1-A-e **define** accrued interest, full price, and clean price

Accrued interest

Accrued interest is the amount of interest that has been earned by the seller of a bond but is paid to the buyer (as the holder of record date for the next coupon payment). It is the interest earned between the previous coupon payment date and the date of the transaction. There are a number of different conventions depending on market practice as to how the accrued interest is calculated. What is important is that at the transaction date both parties know exactly what portion of the coupon belongs to each party.

Full price is when the price of the bond traded includes the accrued interest. It is a convention in the United States that bonds trade at full price, or **dirty price**. **Clean price** is when the price excludes the accrued interest.

LOS 15-1-A-f **explain** the provisions for early retirement of debt, including call and refunding provisions, prepayment options, and sinking fund provisions

Early retirement provisions

The issuer may be given the flexibility (a right not an obligation) to retire bonds prior to the stated maturity date. Remember that this is an option that modifies the cash flows of a bond hence may affect the expected return.

This early retirement would be achieved with,

1. A **call provision** is the right of an issuer to redeem all or part of an outstanding issue prior to the stated maturity date. An example of a call provision is that an issuer may redeem say a 10%-coupon bond when the market interest rate decline to a certain level, say 5%.

The price that the issuer must pay to retire the bond using this call option is called the **call price**. The call price is in most cases higher than par and there is typically a call schedule, i.e. different call prices on different call dates. The higher call price is intended to compensate the investors for the loss of maturity.

Issuers are restricted on the earliest date they can exercise the call option. It is typically a number of years after the issue date, because the investor must be given the assurance that the bond is initially intended as a medium- or long-term instrument, otherwise investors might as well invest in short-term money market instruments. This feature of an issue is called a **deferred call**. The **first call date** is the date when the bond may first be called. The implication of call provisions is that there will be different computed yields for different call dates.

An issuer can call the bond in its entirety or simply in part. When it is called in part, there are two ways that an issuer can select which certificates are to be redeemed, i.e. on a random or on a **pro rata basis**. The pro-rate basis is rare for a public issue due to administrative difficulties. The random selection requires transparency of the process such as publication of the actual serial numbers and how they were selected.

2. A **refunding provision** is the right of the issuer to replace an outstanding issue with another with a lower coupon. This is different from a call provision because the intention of refunding is to replace the outstanding bond with a similarly structured but lower coupon thus saving the issuer some interest expense. The investors are given the same number of bonds, unlike in a call provision when investors receive cash.

Watch for non-refundable and non-callable provisions. Non-callable means there is absolute protection that an issuer is not permitted to redeem the bond prior to maturity. Non-refundable means that the issuer can only call the bond as long as it is not for refunding purposes, for example to reduce their debt level.

3. A **prepayment option** is similar to a call option in that the issuer may retire a portion of the principal borrowed. However, unlike a call option, there is no pre-specified price associated with the retirement of the debt principal. The term is commonly used and associated with mortgage-backed securities but not generally practiced with corporate bonds. With mortgage-backed securities the behavior of the individual mortgage borrowers are independent of the legal contract between the issuer and the investor of the securities.

4. A **sinking fund provision** can also be seen as an early retirement option rather than a provision for paying off the bonds. A stipulation in the indenture may require that the issuer retire a specified portion of the bond each year. For example, a 10-year $100 million bond can be retired at $5 million per year so at maturity the outstanding bond is only half of the original principal. Often there is an additional option for the issuer to retire more than the amount specified in the sinking fund provision. This is called **accelerated sinking fund** provision.

5. **Index amortizing notes** are bonds with an *accelerated principal repayment* provision based on a pre-determined reference rate. Like a floating-rate coupon structure, the provision is triggered when the reference rate is met or exceeded but unlike the floating-rate structure the provision applies to the principal not the coupon.

LOS 15-1-A-g	**differentiate** between a regular redemption price and a special redemption price

Regular redemption prices or **general redemption prices** refer to call prices that are standard, meaning they are commonly above par until the first par call date. As we recall, the call provision is to an issuer's advantage so an investor will be compensated by a higher price than par when the issuer exercises the option.

There are **special redemption prices**, usually at par value, at which the bonds are redeemed when certain regulatory or legal requirements are met. The requirements could be the presence of a sinking fund provision or the event of a legal restructuring of the firm. Generally, the regulatory or legal requirements are very specific and rarely come about in the course of the issuer's normal business. Investors however are often concerned that the provision of special redemption prices may encourage issuers to use all possible means to call their bonds at par. This is called the **par call problem**.

LOS 15-1-A-h **explain** the importance of options embedded in a bond issue, and **indicate** whether such options benefit the issuer or the bondholder

It is frequent to grant issuers and/or bondholders an option to take an action against the other party regarding the money owed, either with the principal or the coupons. Such an option has a significant effect on the behavior of the bond price because the potential modification of the cash flows that the action may cause. Although not explicitly priced in the market, the option carries implicit economic value and will be reflected in the prices of the bonds.

These options are called **embedded options**, to distinguish them from the bare options, i.e. stand-alone options that are traded in the markets.

The presence of options embedded in a bond issue makes it more difficult to project the cash flows of the bond. Sophisticated modeling will be required to value a bond with embedded options, which has to take into account the projected changes in interest rates and the paths they take during the life of the security, and the economic conditions that will encourage the issuer to benefit from exercising the options.

The options will have value to either the issuer or investor depending upon to whom the option is favorable, described below.

1. Embedded options granted to issuers

- call provisions
- the right to prepay a portion of the principal in excess of the scheduled principal repayment
- an accelerated sinking fund provision
- caps on a floating-rate bonds

From the issuer perspective, the call provisions, prepayment options and accelerated sinking funds are valuable when interest rates fall. When exercised, the issuers no longer have to pay the higher coupon rates and can replace the outstanding bonds with those with a lower coupon rate.

2. Embedded options granted to investors

- conversion privileges, e.g. the option to convert bonds to equities
- put provisions, i.e. the right of investors, at their discretion, to demand repayment from the issuer
- floors on floating-rate bonds

From the investor perspective a put option is beneficial when interest rates rise. The investor benefits from being able to sell back the bond at a specified price that is higher than the prevailing market price at the higher level of interest. A conversion option is likewise valuable when the stock price is strong so the investor can take advantage of the upside price movement.

LOS 15-1-A-i	**describe** methods used by institutional investors in the bond market to finance the purchase of a security (i.e., margin buying and repurchase agreements)

A **repurchase agreement** is the sale of a security with a commitment by the seller to buy it back at a pre-determined price on a pre-determined future date. The price is called the **repurchase price** and the date the **repurchase date**. The difference between purchase and repurchase price reflects an implied interest rate, which is called the **repo rate**. This is a form of collateralized borrowing, i.e. a borrowing using securities as collateral. The main motivation is to obtain funding with a lower cost than bank financing.

Another type of collateralized borrowing is **margin buying**, although it is more prevalent in common stock investment (both retail and institutional) and retail bond investment. The difference is that the funds borrowed to purchase the security are provided by the broker who obtains the money from a bank. The interest rate charged by the bank is called the call money rate. To the investor, the broker adds a service charge on top of the call money rate. The main motivation is to gain exposure to an investment but only pay a fraction of the purchase cost.

There is not one single repo rate used in repurchase agreements because of the variety of transactions. Certain securities used for collateral are in demand and difficult to obtain. Such collateral is called **hot collateral**, otherwise it is called **general collateral**. Hot collateral can obtain a lower repo rate.

15-1-A View Concept Check Questions Workbook

15-1-B "Risks Associated with Investing in Bonds"

Introduction

Investors in bonds face a number of risks when buying bonds. Numerous different risks are listed in this Reading but the main risks to focus on are interest rate risk, credit risk, reinvestment and prepayment risk. Candidates are introduced to the concept of duration, duration measures the interest rate risk of a bond or portfolio of bonds, duration will be covered in more detail in the next Study Session.

LOS 15-1-B-a	**explain** the risks associated with investing in bonds (e.g., interest rate risk, call and prepayment risk, yield curve risk, reinvestment risk, credit risk, liquidity risk, exchange-rate risk, volatility risk, inflation risk, and event risk)

Risks in bond investment

The major risks to bond investors are listed below:

1. Interest rate risk.
3. Call and prepayment risk.
4. Yield curve risk.
5. Reinvestment risk.
6. Credit risk.
    a. default risk
    b. credit spread risk
    c. downgrade risk
7. Liquidity risk.
8. Exchange rate risk (currency risk)
9. Volatility risk.
10. Inflation risk.
11. Event risk.
    a. natural catastrophe risk,
    b. corporate restructuring risk
    c. regulatory change risk
    d. political change risk

LOS 15-1-B-b	**identify** the relationship among a bond's coupon rate, the yield required by the market, and the bond's price relative to par value (i.e., discount, premium, or equal to par)

The inverse relationship that exists between changes in interest rates and bond prices is best explained mathematically in the subsequent Readings. However the following example will explain it descriptively:

Example 15-4: Effect of yield changes

Suppose a bond with a 10-year maturity and coupon rate of 7% is sold at par value (100% price). When an investor buys the bond he will obtain a 7% yield.

Assuming that, due to changes in market conditions, the yield for a 10-year bond of similar creditworthiness (quality) has now increased to 7.5%. If there is another issuer who wants to issue a 10-year bond, it must be priced to yield 7.5% to match the market conditions. So the coupon rate of the new bond will have to be 7.5% in order to be sold at par.

Now if the investor who bought the 7% coupon bond wants to sell it, he must sell it to yield 7.5% otherwise why should anybody buy a 10-year bond yielding 7% if there are bonds of the same maturity and quality yielding 7.5% available in the market? Since this is a fixed-rate bond, investors cannot force the issuer to raise the coupon rate from 7% to 7.5%, so the bond must be sold at a certain price other than the original par value so that the yield will be 7.5%. By calculation it turns out that the bond will have to be sold at 96.5259%, i.e. less than par value, in the bond market this is referred to as the bond being at a discount.

The opposite is true, suppose that the yield changes to 6%, the price of the 7% coupon bond will be 107.4387%, which is at a premium.

Example 15-4 illustrates that between interest rates (yields), coupon rates and bond prices the following relationships hold:

1. If the coupon rate = yield, then price = par value.
2. If the coupon rate < yield, then price < par value (discount) or
3. If the coupon rate > yield, then price > par value (premium).
4. If interest rates increase, then the price of a bond decreases
5. If interest rates decrease, then the price of a bond increases

LOS 15-1-B-c **explain** how features of a bond (e.g., maturity, coupon, and embedded options) affect the bond's interest rate risk

Interest rate risk

The degree of sensitivity of a bond price to interest rate changes is called the **interest rate risk**. A bond is said to be more sensitive to interest rate changes when a small change in the interest rates creates a relatively large swing in the bond price, and vice versa. Interest rate sensitivity is a function of the maturity, the coupon of and the presence of an embedded option in the bond.

In the next Study Session, the mathematical calculations of bond values will better explain these effects. The link between interest rate risk and the characteristics of a bond can be described as follows:

1. The interest rate risk increases with a longer maturity.

Intuitively, we would say that we do not know what the future holds. So the longer the maturity, the higher the uncertainty between now and the maturity date therefore the higher the risk becomes.

2. The interest rate risk increases with a lower coupon rate.

We could intuitively also say that the lower the coupon an investor receives the less the cash cushion he has to offset future uncertainty.

3. The interest rate risk depends on the embedded options:
   a. When interest rates decline, the interest rate risk decreases with an embedded call option

The probability becomes higher of the issuer calling the bond when interest rates decline, so the price of the bond will converge to the call price and become less sensitive to small changes in interest rates.

   b. When interest rates increase, the interest rate risk decreases with an embedded put option

Likewise the probability becomes higher of the investor demanding repayment of the bond when interest rates increase, so the price of the bond will converge to the put price and then become less sensitive to small changes in interest rates.

LOS 15-1-B-d **identify** the relationship among the price of a callable bond, the price of an option-free bond, and the price of the embedded call option

The relationship between the price of a callable bond, an option-free bond and the price of the embedded call option is as follows:

Price of callable bond
= price of option-free bond – price of embedded call option **(Equation 15-3)**

The implication of this relationship is that the price of the callable bond would have to be lower than the equivalent noncallable bond since the issuer holds the right to exercise the option. The call option is valuable to the issuer at the expense of the investor.

LOS 13-1-B-e **explain** how the market yield environment affects the interest rate risk of a bond

All other factors held constant, the higher the market yield level of a bond, the lower the price sensitivity. The mathematical model will be explained in more detail in the next Study Session, but an illustration is provided below. This feature is called 'tapering off' and refers to a bond having lower price sensitivity at a higher level of interest rates.

Example 15-5: Interest rate risk

Bond A has a 6% coupon and 15-year maturity and is traded at par, giving a 6% yield. If the required yield is increased by 100 basis points, the price of the bond will fall to 90.8040, a decrease of 9.1690%.

If the same bond was traded at a 10% yield the price would be 69.2551. If the required yield were to be increased by 100 basis points, the price would be 63.6656, a decline of 8.0708%.

The higher market yield leads to lower sensitivity.

LOS 15-1-B-f **explain** the interest rate risk of a floating-rate security and why such a security's price may differ from par value

Common sense would tell us that all floating-rate securities should always be traded at par value as the coupon rates continually adjust to changing market yields.

There are however three reasons why a floating-rate security price may differ from par.

1. Coupons are reset at pre-specified intervals; say every 6 months or annually. Prices will adjust to the prevailing yield level until the next resetting date. This is the time lag effect. It is more obvious with the longer time between resetting dates.
2. The quoted margin is generally fixed during the life of the security. However investor's perception of the issuer's risk may change during the life of the bond. Changing risk perception will lead to a changing level of risk premium. Risk premium is reflected in the margin, so the bond price may change due to the change in the level of the quoted margin, while the reference rate remains constant.
3. Many floating-rate securities have a cap. When the cap is reached while the market interest rates are still moving upwards, the bond price will behave like a fixed-rate bond, as the coupon will be fixed at the cap rate. The security price will have to adjust down; this type of risk is called the cap risk.

LOS 15-1-B-g **interpret** the meaning of the duration of a bond

The most important interpretation of the duration of a bond is how sensitive is the price of the bond to changes in market interest rates. The estimate of the percentage change in the bond price for a 100 basis points (1%) change in the interest rate is called **duration**.

Different bonds have different durations. Depending upon the investment strategy, an investor may look for bonds with higher (long) or lower (short) durations. A more accurate calculation is made using calculus or a bond-pricing model. A reliable valuation model is a pre-requisite to accurate calculation of duration.

LOS 15-1-B-h **compute** the duration of a bond, given the bond's change in price when interest rates change

The formula for duration is:

$$\frac{\text{price if yields decline} - \text{price if yields rise}}{2 \times (\text{initial price}) \times (\text{change in yield in decimals})}$$

(Equation 15-4)

Example 15-6: Duration

Let us look at the bond in Example 15-5, which trades at the initial price of 90.9040 yielding 7.0%.

If yields decline by 50 basis points, price = 95.2545
If yields rise by 50 basis points, price = 86.6281
Change in yield in decimals = 0.005
The duration = (95.2545 – 86.6281)/(2 x 90.9040 x 0.005) = 9.49
The interpretation is that for every 100 basis points interest rate change, the price of the bond will change by 9.49%.

Remember from LOS 15-1-B-b that the bond price will go up when the interest rate goes down. This inverse relationship means that if the interest rate increases by 100 basis points, then the price of the bond would decline by 9.49%, and vice versa.

LOS 15-1-B-i	**compute** the approximate percentage price change of a bond, given the bond's duration
LOS 15-1-B-j	**compute** the approximate new price of a bond, given the bond's duration and new yield level

Example 15-7: Price and duration

Looking at the bond in Example 15-6 with duration of 9.49.

What happens to the price of this bond if the yield rises by 150 basis points?

The answer is that the percentage change will be 150/100 x 9.49% = 14.24%.

So the dollar price will change by the same percentage to be 90.9040 x (100% - 14.24%) = 77.9593 (Remember that bond prices decline when yield increases).

Using a bond-pricing model, the price of the bond is 79.0262 at that yield, showing that the duration is a reasonable (linear) approximation of the percentage change of the price although not completely accurate.

Often traders use the term **dollar duration**, i.e. the translation of the percentage change to monetary value. For instance, if the nominal value of the bond in the above example is $1,000,000 then the dollar duration will be the dollar equivalent of the 9.49%, i.e. $94,900. It says that for every 100 basis point change in the yield, the value of the bond will change by $94,900.

LOS 15-1-B-k	**explain** why duration does not account for yield curve risk for a portfolio of bonds

Yield curve risk

There are various interest rates in the market. Interest rates differ from each other depending upon the maturities and the credit risks of the fixed-income securities.

When these different interest rates/yields are plotted against their respective maturities, the graphical description is called the **yield curve**. The yield curve is subject to change in the form of parallel shifts, i.e. when every interest rate in the yield curve changes by the same amount and the same direction, or nonparallel shifts, where the interest rates in the yield curve do not change by the same amount and/or direction.

A bond portfolio consists of a variety of bonds with different maturities and coupon rates. The different patterns of interest rate changes will affect the value of the individual bonds in the portfolio differently.

The risk that affects a bond portfolio due to different patterns of the changes of the various interest rates in the economy is called the **yield curve risk.**

Because of this, a single duration number is not sufficient to explain the interest rate risk of a portfolio of bonds. A **rate duration**, which defined to be the sensitivity of the change of bond price with respect to a particular (spot) rate, is a more useful measure.

The following is a table, which illustrates yield curve risk.

1. Effect of a *parallel* shift of +50 basis points of the yield curve

Bond	Coupon	Maturity	Original Yield	Par Value	New Yield	New Bond Price
X	6.00%	2	6.00%	100.00	6.50%	99.08
Y	6.25%	5	6.25%	100.00	6.75%	97.91
Z	6.75%	10	6.75%	100.00	7.25%	96.49
Total				300.00		293.48

2. Effect of a *non-parallel* shift of the yield curve

Bond	Coupon	Maturity	Original Yield	Par Value	New Yield	New Bond Price
X	6.00%	2	6.00%	100.00	5.50%	100.93
Y	6.25%	5	6.25%	100.00	6.75%	97.91
Z	6.75%	10	6.75%	100.00	6.50%	101.82
Total				300.00		300.66

The 'New Yield' columns of both tables show the different types of the yield curve shifts. In table (1) the yields increased uniformly by 50bp while in table (2) they all moved differently. The resulting new bond prices are also correspondingly different thus showing the different total sensitivity of the portfolio to the change of the yield curve.

In practice, only select key maturities are of interest, such as 2-year, 5-year, 15-year, etc. The rate duration for each of the key maturities is called a **key rate duration**. A portfolio with a "5-year rate duration" of 2.5 means that the portfolio value will change by 2.5% for a 100 basis points change in the 5-year yield.

LOS 15-1-B-l **identify** the factors that affect the reinvestment risk of a security

Reinvestment risk

Reinvestment risk occurs when:

1. The yields of reinvestment opportunities are lower than the original yield.
2. The computation of the yield depends on the reinvestment rate of the coupon payments.

LOS 15-1-B-m **explain** the disadvantages of a callable or prepayable security to an investor

A **call provision** may be included in a bond, i.e. the right of the issuer to retire all or part of

the issue before the stipulated maturity date. The main disadvantages of a callable or prepayable security for investors are

1. The cash flow pattern will be uncertain.
2. Since bonds are generally called when the interest rate is lower than the bond's coupon rate, investors will face reinvestment risk.
3. Price compression will often occur, i.e. the price appreciation potential will be less than the comparable option-free bonds.

LOS 15-1-B-n **explain** why prepayable amortizing securities expose investors to greater reinvestment risk than nonamortizing securities

Prepayable amortizing securities expose investors to greater reinvestment risks because the proceeds of principal repayment, coupon, and prepayments might only be able to be reinvested at a lower yield, particularly during a declining interest rate environment.

The targeted yield may not be achieved since the yield-to-maturity calculation *assumes* that the reinvestment yield is the same as when the bonds were purchased.

LOS 15-1-B-o	**describe** the various forms of credit risk (i.e., default risk, credit spread risk, downgrade risk)

Credit risk

There are three types of credit risk:

Default risk

This is when an issuer fails to meet the obligation of interest and principal payments. A single delay in an interest payment on the coupon payment date is considered a default. An investor does not necessarily lose the whole amount of the principal and accrued interest when a default occurs. The percentage amount recoverable in a case of a default is called the **recovery rate**. Based on the historical data on default rates and recovery rates of outstanding bonds in the market, credit rating agencies evaluate and classify the creditworthiness of the issuers or issues.

Credit spread risk

This is when the yield spread of a particular issue or sector widens against the risk-free benchmark causing the price of the bond to decline (usually due to macroeconomic factors). Similar to floating-rate securities, fixed-rate bonds are priced by two components: (1) the yield of a risk-free bond with a similar maturity and (2) a premium above the yield of the similar risk-free bond. This premium is similar to a quoted margin i.e. the price of the credit risk. It is the compensation required by the investor for taking on an additional credit risk vis-à-vis the risk-free bond. This premium can increase or decrease depending upon the market's perception of the credit risk.

Downgrade risk

This is when a rating agency (e.g. Standard & Poor's, Moody's or Fitch) decides the individual creditworthiness of a bond has deteriorated. The credit spread will widen due to the downgrade which will lead the bond price to decline. The rating agencies' opinions on individual issues are very influential in the bond market.

LOS 15-1-B-p	**explain** why liquidity risk is important to investors even if they expect to hold a security to the maturity date

Liquidity risk

This is the risk which is faced by investors when they are forced to sell a bond at a price below its true value perhaps due to a temporary imbalance of supply and demand for the individual bond. The market liquidity of an issue is reflected by the level of the bid-ask spread quoted by dealers. The wider the bid-ask spread, the less liquid is the issue in the market. Market liquidity should not be confused with the financial liquidity of the issuer as a going concern.

Liquidity risk is important to investors who mark their portfolios to the market, regardless of whether they intend to hold a security to maturity or sell it the next day. Mark-to-market is an exercise to revalue the portfolio based on the current market prices of the individual securities that make up the portfolio.

Liquidity risk changes over time according to the market environment, as illustrated below:

Sector	**Bid-ask spread (% of price)**	
	Typical	**Distressed**
Treasuries		
Bills	0.002	0.005
On-the-run notes and bonds	0.003	0.006
Off-the-run notes and bonds	0.006	0.009
Corporate bonds		
A-rated Finance	0.120	0.500
B-rated Industrials	0.500	5.000
Mortgage-backed Securities		
Fixed-rate	0.060	0.250

(Fabozzi, 2000)

Newly introduced fixed-income structures or instruments generally have wide bid-ask spreads because of the limited number of investors and market makers. As the new structures or instruments become more popular, the bid-ask spreads narrow as liquidity improves.

Often a market sector becomes unpopular and is avoided by investors and market makers. In such a case, the bid-ask spread may widen considerably. An example of this is the derivative mortgage market when an important player, say a hedge fund, collapses creating a dramatic widening in the bid-ask spreads as the dealers withdraw from the market.

LOS 15-1-B-q	**describe** the exchange rate risk an investor faces when a bond makes payments in a foreign currency

Exchange rate risk

This is also called **currency risk**; it is the risk that the currency of the investment moves adversely against the home currency causing the local currency value of coupon payments and the principal repayment to decrease.

Example 15-8: Exchange rate risk

A British Pound denominated bond has a 7% annual coupon and matures in three years. It was purchased at the par value of £100,000 when the exchange rate was $/£ = 1.50. The coupon and principal cash flows are as follows.

	Coupon 1	**Coupon 2**	**Coupon 3**	**Principal**
Amount in £	£7,000	£7,000	£7,000	£100,000
Exchange rate	$/£ = 1.60	$/£ = 1.55	$/£ = 1.45	
Amount in $	$11,200	$10,850	$10,150	$145,000

The investor received a declining coupon income due of the deprecation of the US$.

In practice, diversification across currencies is often recommended to reduce exchange rate risk.

LOS 15-1-B-r	**describe** inflation risk and **explain** why it exists

Inflation risk

This is the risk that the purchasing power of income from bonds is reduced due to the erosion in its value by inflation. The identical amount of coupon paid out on different coupon payment dates will decrease in value according to the prevailing inflation rate. It exists because inflationary pressure is almost always present in different economies. Investing in inflation protection bonds can mitigate this type of risk.

Example 15-9: Inflation risk

If a bond investor receives a coupon rate of 10% and the inflation rate (CPI) is 6%, investors' purchasing power due to the coupon will only increase by 4%.

LOS 15-1-B-s	**explain** how yield volatility affects the price of a bond with an embedded option and how changes in volatility affect the value of a callable bond and a putable bond

Volatility risk

Changes in the expected volatility of yield change the value of embedded options in a bond. Option theory says that the value of an option is directly related to the level of volatility therefore when the volatility of the expected yield rises, the value of the embedded option will rise. Equation 15-3 stated:

Price of callable bond = price of option-free bond – price of embedded option

So, in the case of a callable bond, its price will fall when yield volatility increases, as the value of the embedded option is subtracted from the price of the option-free bond.

Price of putable bond

= price of option-free bond + price of embedded option **(Equation 15-5)**

Conversely with a putable bond, its price will rise with an increase in the level of expected yield volatility.

LOS 15-1-B-t	**describe** the various forms of event risk (e.g., natural catastrophe, corporate takeover/restructuring, and regulatory risk) and the components of sovereign risk

Event risk

This risk occurs very infrequently but with a serious impact on the issuer's ability to honor its debt obligation. There are four main factors:

1. **Natural catastrophe risk**, including the risk of an earthquake, hurricane, floods or industrial accidents. This type of event will lead to a downgrade but is normally confined to individual issuers.
2. **Corporate restructuring risk**, such as occurred with RJR Nabisco's bonds during the leverage buyout (LBO) wave in the 1980's. Investors demanded an additional yield of 250 basis points after the LBO of RJR Nabisco was announced. The announcement subsequently affected the whole sector as investors temporarily withdrew from the market.
3. **Regulatory change risk**, an example was the passing of the Financial Institutions Reform, Recovery and Enforcement Act (FIRREA) in 1994. The legislation drastically limited the exposure of the Savings and Loans industry to non-investment grade bonds. As a result the ensuing divestments from such bonds created a collapse in the market. Prices declined by 20% to 25% without any fundamental change in their creditworthiness.
4. **Political change risk**, most often occurs in emerging countries where there is a change in government policies in terms of debt repayment. This is often a case of a change in willingness rather than the actual capacity to repay debt.

15-1-B View Concept Check Questions Workbook

15-1-C "Overview of Bond Sectors and Instruments"

Introduction

This Reading starts with a description of the different types of international bonds and then moves on to look at the U.S. bonds that are available in the market. It describes the characteristics of different categories of Treasury securities and corporate bonds including bankruptcy issues and credit ratings. We also look at the differences between corporate bonds, MTNs and commercial paper. Again the Study Session contains a lot of detail and new terms; candidates will have to make the required effort to remember the key expressions.

In some cases the terms used in the LOS refer to the first edition of Fabozzi. To reflect the most recent edition of the textbook, new terms, e.g. internal and external bond markets, are also given in this section.

LOS 15-1-C-a	**describe** the different types of international bonds (e.g., foreign bonds, Eurobonds, global bonds, sovereign debt)

International bonds

These are generally classified as:

1. Foreign bonds

These are issued by entities not domiciled in the country of issuance. The bonds are denominated in the currency of the country of issue. Examples are Yankee bonds which are issued in the U.S. by companies not domiciled in the U.S. and are regulated by the U.S. authorities, Samurai bonds are issued in Japan by firms not domiciled in Japan, etc.

A US Dollar bond issued in the U.S. by Japanese-based Sony Corporation is a Yankee bond. A Japanese Yen bond issued in Japan by U.S.-based Ford Motor Company is a Samurai Bond.

2. Eurobonds

These are foreign bonds that have the following features

a. Underwritten by international syndicates
b. Offered simultaneously to investors in a number of countries
c. Outside the jurisdiction of any single country
d. Issued in unregistered form

They are classified based on the currency of issue so US Dollar denominated bonds are called Eurodollar bonds and the Japanese Yen denominated are called Euroyen bonds.

3. Global bonds

These are securities that are traded both in the foreign bond market of one of more countries and the Eurobond markets. The main requirements of a global bond offering are that the issue size is large (in excess of US$1 billion) and the issuer has a high credit rating.

4. Sovereign debt

These are bonds that are issued by central governments of countries around the world. These bonds rely on the creditworthiness of the individual governments.

Note: The new text classifies the bond market sectors into the following,

Overview of the Sectors of the Bond Market

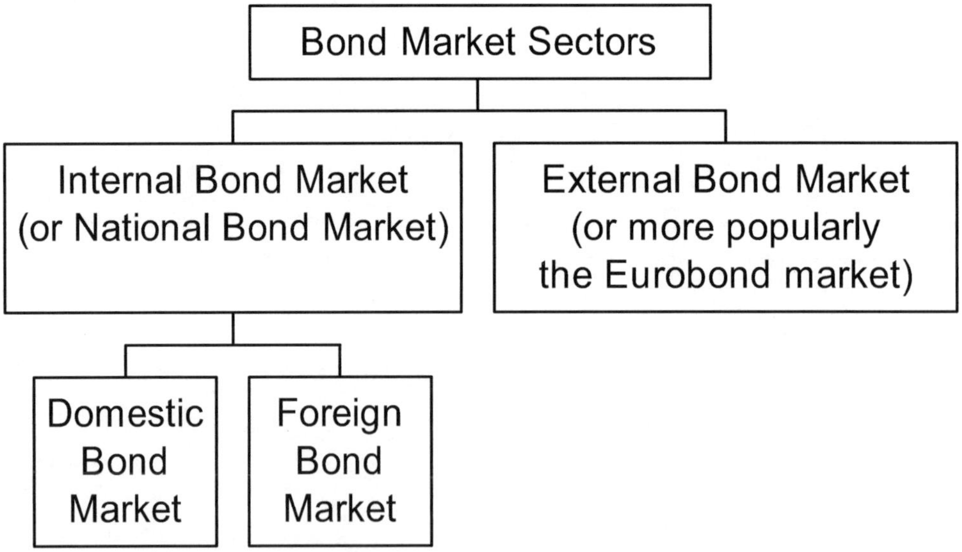

(Fabozzi, 2004)

The **foreign bond market** is part of the **internal bond market**, also called the **national bond market**. The internal bond market is divided into the domestic bond market and foreign bond market. The Eurobond market, which is popularly known as the **external bond market,** is also called the **international bond market** or the **off-shore bond market**.

LOS 15-1-C-b **describe** the types of securities issued by the U.S. Department of the Treasury (e.g. bills, notes, bonds, and inflation protection securities)

United States Treasury Securities

The U.S. Department of Treasury securities are considered to have no credit risk, implying that the U.S. Government will not go bankrupt or cease to honor its financial obligations. They often serve as a benchmark for risk-free securities.

Treasury issues are categorized into three types, i.e. **fixed-principal securities, inflation-indexed securities** and **Treasury STRIPS.**

Overview of US Treasury Debt Instruments

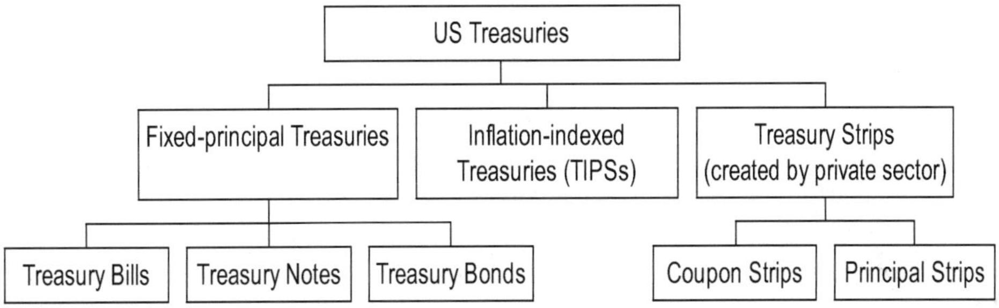

(Fabozzi, 2004)

1. Fixed-principal Securities

- Treasury Bills are discounted securities that mature at par and are priced to reflect the prevailing yield. The terms to maturity are under 1 year, i.e. 3-month (91 days), 6-month (182 days) and 1-year (364 days). They are popularly known as T-bills.
- Treasury Notes are fixed-principal securities with maturity of more than 1 year and no longer than 10 years.
- Treasury Bonds are fixed-principal securities with initial maturities longer than 10 years. They are generally noncallable save for a few exceptions.

2. Inflation-indexed securities

Treasury Inflation Protection Securities (TIPS) are Treasury notes and bonds that carry fixed coupons but have the feature of an **inflation-adjusted principal**. The inflation index used is the City Average All Items Consumer Price Index for All Urban Consumers (CPI-U).

The adjustment for inflation is applied to the principal of TIPS and is computed semi-annually at coupon settlement dates. The inflation index is published daily.

Example 15-10: Inflation protection securities

A TIPS bond has a principal of $1,000,000, coupon 3.5% and maturity 30 years. The inflation index is CPI-U, and it was bought on June 30, 2000.

On January 1, 2001 the CPI-U is 3% annualized and on June 30, 2001 is 2.8%.

What would be the coupons on these dates?

The principal on January 1, 2001 will be adjusted by the 3% annual inflation rate, or 1.5% semiannually, to

1.015 x $1,000,000 = $1,015,000.
The coupon for the semiannual coupon period will be: 0.0175 x $1,015,000 = $17,762.50.

The principal on June 30, 2001 will be inflation rate adjusted to

1.014 x $1,015,000 = $1,029,210.
The coupon will be 0.0175 x $1,029,210 = $18,011.18.

As can be seen in Example 15-10 the income continuously reflects the inflation-adjusted principal. In the case of deflation, there is a clause for the redemption to be the larger of the inflation-adjusted principal and par value.

Treasury STRIPS

The Treasury Department does not issue zero coupons, but it recognizes their market demand and set up the Treasury's Separate Trading of Registered Interest and Principal Securities (STRIPS). Individual coupons and the principal of a bond are stripped and they are treated and registered as individual securities. These securities only have a single cash flow at maturity and therefore behave like zero coupons.

Coupon strips are created from stripping the coupons and **principal strips** are from the principal payment. They are distinguished from each other due to tax reasons.

Often banks independently offer stripped Treasury products. Please look at LOS 15-1-C-d for further details.

LOS 15-1-C-c	**differentiate** between on-the-run and off-the-run Treasury securities

Since U.S. Treasury securities are continuously issued, the most recently auctioned is called an **on-the-run issue**. These on-the-run issues are important because they best reflect the prevalent interest rate environment and are most liquid right after the moment of issue.

Those that are replaced by new on-the-run issues are called **off-the-run issues**. As time moves on and bonds approach their respective maturities, there is often more than one off-the-run issue with approximately the same remaining term to maturity as the on-the-run one.

LOS 15-1-C-d **discuss** how stripped Treasury securities are created, and **distinguish** between coupon strips and principal strips

The U.S. Treasury does not issue zero-coupon bonds but there is plenty of demand for risk-free zero-coupon bonds. Zero-coupon bonds can be created from a coupon security. Each and every cash flow from the coupons and principal are treated as securities. They are effectively zero-coupon instruments as each cash flow has a maturity value (the amount of the coupon or principal) and a maturity date (coupon date or redemption date).

Since 1985, a program called Separate Trading of Registered Interest and Principal Securities (STRIPS) was launched to facilitate the creation and trading of zero-coupon instruments.

Example 15-11: Stripped Treasury securities

A $10 million Treasury note with maturity of 5 years and semiannual coupon of 10% will generate 10 coupon cash flows and 1 principal repayment. The first security created from the first coupon will have a term to maturity of 6 months; the second will have 12 months and so on. Each one of them has a maturity value of $500,000. The principal will be a 5-year zero coupon with a maturity value of $10 million.

The market distinguishes between zero-coupon instruments created from the cash flow of a coupon and from the cash flow of the principal. The former are called **coupon strips** and the latter **principal strips**. The coupon strips are identified with "ci" and the principal strips with "np" or "bp".

The distinction has to do with different taxation treatments of coupons and principals by foreign tax authorities as applied to non-U.S. entities.

LOS 15-1-C-e **describe** a mortgage-backed security, and **explain** the cash flows for a mortgage-backed security

Mortgage-backed securities

Mortgage loans are loans that are secured by collateral of a certain property. A classic example is a home loan is when a family borrows money from a bank to purchase a home and the collateral is the property itself, be it a house or an apartment. The bank, who is the lender, is given the right to foreclose (lien) the property if the borrower is not satisfying the obligation, i.e. missing the monthly installment payments.

When these mortgage loans are pooled together, a new type of security can be formed by combining the cash flows generated by the underlying loans. The new security is called a **mortgage-backed security** (MBS) which includes pass-through securities, **collateralized mortgage obligations** (CMOs) and stripped mortgage-backed securities.

In a pass-through, the pooled cash flow pattern mimics the underlying pool of mortgage loans, this consists of,

a. Net interest
b. Scheduled principal repayment
c. Prepayments

The cash flow is distributed on a pro rata basis to the holders of the pass-through MBSs.

CMOs and stripped MBSs are derivatives of MBSs since they are constructed from a pool of MBSs.

LOS 15-1-C-f **define** prepayments and **explain** prepayment risk

Prepayment is the repayment of a portion or all of the outstanding balance of the principal that is made ahead of the scheduled date.

Curtailment is a prepayment that is not for the full amount of the outstanding balance of the principal.

Prepayment risk is the risk that the outstanding balance of the principal is paid off prior to the scheduled date. If the principal payment is made after the scheduled date it is called a default.

LOS 15-1-C-g **describe** the types and characteristics of securities issued by federal agencies (including mortgage passthroughs and collateralized mortgage obligations)

Federal agency securities

Depending upon the issuers, federal agency securities can be categorized as

1. **Federally related institutions**, which are arms of the federal government, such as Government National Mortgage Association (Ginnie Mae), Tennessee Valley Authority (TVA). They do not normally issue securities directly to the marketplace although, with a few exceptions, they carry the full faith and credit of the U.S. government.

2. **Government sponsored enterprises (GSEs)**, which are privately owned but publicly chartered so their investors are exposed to credit risk. These institutions issue securities directly to the market place.

The GSEs issue two types of securities:

1. Agency debentures. Uncollateralized debt issued by a GSE, the repayment depends on the ability of the entity to generate sufficient cash flow to meet the obligation.
2. Agency mortgage-backed securities. Securities that are backed by mortgage loans. The cash flow generated by the mortgage loans will be the primary source of repayment of the coupon and principal.

LOS 15-1-C-h **state** the motivation for creating a collateralized mortgage obligation

Both a **mortgage pass-through security** and a **collateralized mortgage obligation** are securities that are backed by a pool of mortgage loans. The pool of mortgage loans will generate the cash flows that will be passed on to the holders of the securities.

The main difference is that with a mortgage pass-through security there is *no* modification of the cash flows. In other words, whatever is received from the pool of mortgage loans will be distributed pro rata to the security holders, less legitimate servicing and other fees. The cash flow of a unit of participation will reflect scheduled principal repayment, net interest and prepayments of the loan pool.

A collateralized mortgage obligation on the other hand **modifies** the cash flows by following more than one distribution rule that are applied to the different **tranches**. A tranche is a class of bond that is part of the obligation having a unique distribution rule. The sum of all the cash flows passed on to the tranches (inclusive of servicing fees, and other legitimate outflows) should be equal to the total cash flows generated by the pool of mortgage loans. A holder of two different tranches from the same CMO will however see two different patterns of cash flows. This approach is taken with the motivation to redistribute the prepayment risk to different tranches to meet the different risk tolerances of investors.

LOS 15-1-C-i **describe** the types of securities issued by municipalities in the United States

Municipal bonds

Municipal bonds are issued by local governments or related bodies to investors in the state who are usually exempt from paying tax on the bond. The bonds are categorized based on the sources of repayment as follows:

1. Tax-backed debt
   a. general obligation debt
   b. appropriation-backed obligations
   c. debt obligations supported by public credit enhancement programs
2. Revenue bonds
3. Special bond structures
   a. insured bonds
   b. prerefunded bonds
4. Municipal derivative securities

General obligation debt is the broadest type of tax-backed debt. It is backed by the general taxing powers of the issuers.

Appropriation-backed obligations are the obligations of agencies or authorities of several states and carry a potential state liability to make up shortfalls if they occur. The appropriation must obtain the state legislatures approval but the moral obligation is there.

LOS 15-1-C-j **distinguish** between general obligation bonds and revenue bonds

General obligation bonds are the broadest definition of tax-backed debt. They are municipal securities that are backed by some form of tax revenues. The issuer can be a state, a county, a special district, a city, a town or a school district that is given the right to levy taxes or some other form of taxing power.

Revenue bonds are issued by entities that pledge the revenues from specific enterprises to the bondholders. These enterprises have the capacity to generate revenues from the completed projects themselves. Revenue bonds include utility revenue bonds, transportation revenue bonds, housing revenue bonds, higher education bonds, and health care revenue bonds.

LOS 15-1-C-k **describe** insured bonds and prerefunded bonds

Insured bonds are additionally backed by insurance policies from commercial insurance companies. The insurance company will take over the payments to the bondholders in case of default.

Prefunded bonds are escrowed or collateralized by a portfolio of U.S. government securities. The cash flows of the collateral match the obligations of the issuers. This is the safest type of municipal bond.

LOS 15-1-C-l **summarize** the bankruptcy process and bondholder rights

Bankruptcy

In the U.S. the Bankruptcy Reform Act of 1978 governs the bankruptcy process. It contains the rules for corporations that are about to be either liquidated or reorganized.

Liquidation means that all the assets are distributed according to claims of the creditors and finally to the shareholders if any assets are left. After liquidation, the legal corporate entity is dissolved and no longer exists. **Reorganization** means that a new corporate entity will emerge at the end of a bankruptcy proceeding. The process will often involve some creditors being paid back in cash, not necessary in full, and some receiving securities in the new company.

Once a petition of bankruptcy is filed, a company will be given protection from its creditors.

The petition can be filed by the company itself as a **voluntary bankruptcy** or by its creditors as an **involuntary bankruptcy**. The status of the company will be a "debtor-in-possession" and allowed to continue its business operations under the supervision of the court. This provides some time for the company to decide whether to reorganize or go into liquidation as well as time to execute the ensuing reorganization or liquidation plan.

The equity holder's claims are subordinated to those of the creditors. In liquidation, the distribution of the proceeds will follow the **absolute priority rule** to the extent assets are available. There is typically a seniority ranking of the debts in a company. The senior debts are paid off in full first before the more junior debts are paid. The equity holder receives whatever is left, if anything at all. This rule generally holds in liquidation. In reorganization, there will typically be a variety of schemes offered to the creditors making it unusual to uphold the absolute priority rule.

LOS 15-1-C-m **explain** the factors considered by rating agencies in assigning a credit rating to a corporate debt instrument

Credit ratings

In assessing credit risk, rating agencies look into the following factors to determine credit quality:

Character

Rating agencies assess the quality of the management in terms of integrity and reputation. Are they professionally competent and do they keep their word? Many cases of default are not caused the company's *inability* to pay but more by *unwillingness* to pay for one reason or another.

Capacity

Rating agencies assess the ability of the issuer to generate sufficient cash flow to meet the interest payments and principal repayment. If the company's cash flow generation is declining, it is a cause for concern.

Collateral

The quality and value of the assets pledged to back up the debt are assessed. Often the quality and value of the pledged assets deteriorate during the life of a debt so they are no longer sufficient to back up the debt. Rating agencies have to feel reassured that the collateral value provides the expected level of protection in case of a default.

Covenants

Rating agencies review the limitations and restrictions currently imposed on the borrower to assess the level of protection for the investors. These covenants are spelled out in the indenture documents of the outstanding debt. Rating agencies will assess the position of the debt being reviewed vis-à-vis the other outstanding ones.

LOS 15-1-C-n describe secured debt, unsecured debt, and credit enhancements for corporate bonds

Secured debt

A debt is secured when an identifiable asset is pledged as a main source of repayment of the debt. The creditors are given a lien, i.e. a right to repossess a property in case of a default. The investors of secured debt will have a priority claim over the pledged property, meaning they will be in the queue ahead of other creditors.

Unsecured debt

These are often called **debenture bonds**. The general creditors have a claim on all the remaining assets that are not pledged to the secured creditors. It does not mean that for unsecured debt the creditors have no claim at all on the assets but in this case it is subordinated, meaning the claim comes later in the queue.

The credit rating of corporate bonds can be enhanced by a **third party guarantee**. This says that if the issuer is unable to honor its obligation, the third party guarantor will step in and assume the obligation. The obligation of the third party and the events that trigger it are clearly spelled out in the indenture. The third party that provides such **credit enhancement** can be the parent company or an unrelated entity such as a bank.

LOS 15-1-C-o distinguish between a corporate bond and a medium-term note

Medium-term notes (MTNs) are debt instruments that are shelf-registered with the Securities and Exchange Commission, and are issued continuously with a variety of maturities, usually between 9 months and 30 years. Shelf-registered means that the issuer has the flexibility to design the coupon formula and maturities to satisfy its funding requirements as long as certain guidelines and covenants are met.

The difference between MTNs and corporate bonds are:

- MTNs are issued continuously while corporate bonds typically have a single offering period.
- Issuers file shelf registration with the Securities and Exchange Commission for MTN issuance while corporate bonds have regular registration.
- Method of distribution: MTNs are typically distributed on a 'best-efforts basis' while corporate bonds are often underwritten. 'Best effort basis' here mean that the dealer is only responsible to sell how much he or she can in the market.

MTN programs generally suit larger corporations with good credit standing where there is strong demand for their paper.

LOS 15-1-C-p **describe** commercial paper, and **distinguish** between directly-placed paper and dealer-placed paper

Commercial paper (CP) is a short-term unsecured promissory note that is usually in the form of a zero-coupon instrument. The maturity is typically less than 270 days with 50 days maturity being the most common. It is a convenient short-term funding tool for a corporation as it does not require SEC registration if the maturity is less than 270 days. Investors are generally comfortable with short-term unsecured papers issued by highly rated companies.

The issuers of CPs can be financial or non-financial companies. Financial companies, such as banks and leasing companies, usually issue their CPs as **directly-placed paper**, i.e. the debt instruments are sold directly to the investors without the need of a broker, dealer of other intermediary.

Non-financial companies, such as industrial firms, more often appoint intermediary agents to sell their papers, hence the term **dealer paper**. The reason that the agents are needed is that as non-financial entities these issuers may not be directly involved in the financial markets.

LOS 15-1-C-q **define** an asset-backed security

Asset-backed securities can be defined to be securities that are collateralized by an identifiable pool of receivables.

Take an example of a construction company, ABG Ltd., which does a variety of construction projects for large companies. Assuming that the construction company is rated BBB and its customers are all rated AAA, let us look at the balance sheet of ABG Ltd. Its receivables from its customers are all payables of AAA companies. If those receivables are taken out from ABG Ltd.'s balance sheet, they can be pooled and structured as a security that can probably be rated higher then ABG itself. The investors will have direct claim to the receivables, bypassing the balance sheet of ABG Ltd. The higher the rating of a security, the lower the interest rate will be. This is the principle and motivation behind asset securitization.

LOS 15-1-C-r **describe** the role of a special purpose vehicle in an asset-backed securities transaction

The asset securitization scheme described above will require a legal separation of the receivables from the balance sheet of ABG Ltd. This legal separation ensures that once the receivables are identified and isolated, they can no longer be claimed back by the issuer.

The usual method is for ABG Ltd., in the example above, to legally and irrevocably sell the receivables to a separate legal entity, which in turn will issue the securities. The legal entity is called a **special purpose vehicle** or **special purpose company**. The entity is legally structured in such a way that the creditors to ABG Ltd. will have no claim to the receivables sold to the SPV. This concept is called **bankruptcy remote**.

LOS 15-1-C-s **state** the motivation for a corporation to issue an asset-backed security

The main motivation for asset securitization is to obtain funding which is lower in cost than the corporation's rating allows. As we recall, the cost of funding depends on the credit rating. The higher the credit rating, the lower the funding cost.

LOS 15-1-C-t **describe** the types of external credit enhancements for asset-backed securities

There are three common types of **external credit enhancement**:

1. A corporate guarantee

This is when a separate entity agrees to provide cover for the financial obligations of the issuer in case of a default.

2. A letter of credit

This is a similar form of guarantee but extended by a financial institution such as a bank.

3. Bond insurance

The investor is protected by insurance policies underwritten by commercial insurance companies.

15-1-C View Concept Check Questions Workbook

15-1-D "Understanding Yield Spreads"

Introduction

The Reading starts with looking at how interest rates are determined and the tools that are available to central banks to set the level of interest rates. Theories concerning the shape of the yield curve are also explained.

A yield spread is the additional yield over and above that offered by the risk-free benchmark security, to compensate investors for taking additional risk. The Reading investigates the different kind of risks associated with the different kinds of yield spreads and the factors that may affect the behavior of the yield spread such as the presence of embedded options, the liquidity of an issue or even the size of an issue.

LOS 15-1-D-a	**identify** the interest rate policy tools available to a central bank (such as the U.S. Federal Reserve)

A central bank, such as the Federal Reserve has the following tools available to manage the level of interest rates in an economy:

a. open market operations
b. the discount rate
c. bank reserve requirements
d. verbal persuasion to bankers to increase or decrease lending

An open market operation is when the Fed injects funds into the market or withdraws funds from it. Injecting funds is done by buying U.S. Treasury securities from the market while withdrawing funds is performed by selling Treasury securities into the market. These actions influence the level of the **fed fund rate**; the interest rate that banks lends to and borrow from each other. The discount rate is the interest rate at which banks can borrow on a collateralized basis at the Fed's discount window.

Changing bank reserve requirements and verbal persuasion are less commonly used.

LOS 15-1-D-b describe a yield curve and the different yield curve shapes observed

The relationship between the interest rates (yields) and time to maturity for any class of similar-risk securities is called the **term structure of interest rates**. The graphical description is called the **yield curve**.

The yield curve can take different 'shapes' including upward sloping, downward sloping and flat, as shown below:

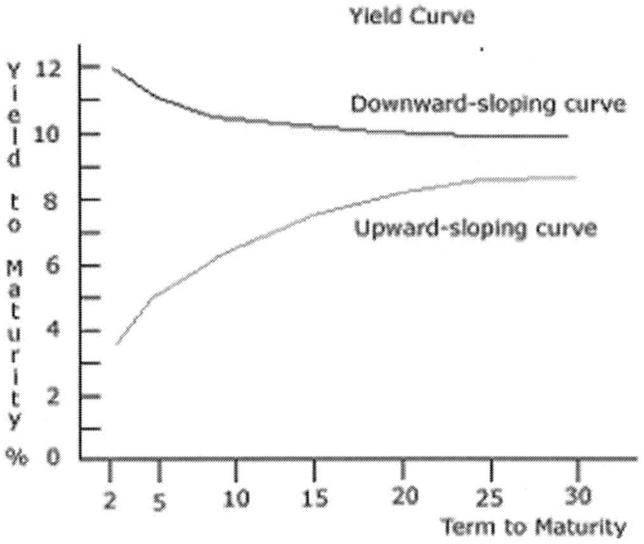

Each 'shape' indicates a different interest rate environment as a result of macroeconomic cycles or policies. There are two factors that complicate the relationship between yield and maturity:

1. the yields of on-the-run issues can be distorted by high demand and high liquidity due to their being sought as hot collateral,
2. although they have similar maturities, the on-the-run and off-the-run securities may be different with respect to their profiles of interest rate risk.

Therefore when the market mentions the interest rates used to value a security they refer to another relationship, i.e. the relationship between the yield on zero-coupon securities and their maturity. **Spot rates** are yields on zero-coupon securities. **Treasury spot rates** are the yields of zero-coupon securities synthetically created from Treasury securities.

The seven on-the-run Treasury securities are the 3-month, 6-month and 1-year T-bills, the 2- and 5-year T-notes and the 10- and 30-year T-bonds. Since there are only 7 on-the-run securities, an interpolation is required to arrive at yields for other maturities.

LOS 15-1-D-c	**explain** the basic theories of the term structure of interest rates (i.e., pure expectations theory, liquidity preference theory, and market segmentation theory)

There are three main theories which explain the shape of the yield curve.

1. Pure Expectations Theory

The theory explains the shape of the yield curve by investor expectations of future short-term interest rates. There is a link between interest rates and investor expectations about future inflation, the higher the expected inflation, the higher the interest rate demanded by investors.

2. Liquidity Preference Theory

Investors want to be compensated for the risk of holding a long-term bond because they are subject to higher price volatility when interest rates change during the holding period, since the longer the duration, the higher the price volatility. The required compensation is in the form of higher yields.

3. Market Segmentation Theory

This theory suggests that the debt market is segmented into maturity sectors, and that the supply and demand for funds within each maturity segment determines interest rates. For example certain groups of institutional investors (e.g. pension funds, insurance companies) may have demand for long-term bonds, due to their liabilities, which outstrips the supply of available bonds pushing the prices of the bonds up hence driving down the interest rates in this segment of the yield curve. The yield curve changes according to the relationship between the supply and demand within all maturity segments and the segments are independent from each other.

LOS 15-1-D-d	**describe** the implications of each theory for the shape of the yield curve

The implications for the shape of the yield curve are described below.

1. Pure Expectations Theory

A rising term structure or upward-sloping yield curve indicates that the market expects short-term yields to rise in the future.

Shape of yield curve	Implication according to pure expectations theory
Upward sloping	Rates expected to rise
Downward sloping	Rates expected to decline
Flat	Rates not expected to change

2. Liquidity Preference Theory

A normal curve is upward sloping indicating that there is a maturity premium, although the upward slope could be a result of investors' expectations that interest rates are going to rise.

A downward-sloping curve is explained by the theory that the expectation is that there will be lower short-term rates in the future.

3. Market Segmentation Theory.

The implication of this theory is that any shape of the yield curve is possible since the shape is independently determined within each sector.

All of the three theories work in conjunction to explain the shape of a yield curve.

LOS 15-1-D-e	**explain** the different types of yield spread measures (e.g., absolute yield spread, relative yield spread, yield ratio), and **compute** yield spread measures given the yields for two securities

Yield spread is the additional yield over and above the benchmark Treasury issue with the same remaining term to maturity.

Spread sectors are the sectors in the bond market that offer a yield spread to Treasury securities. Most sectors are spread sectors.

The securities in the spread sectors are called **spread products**.

Absolute yield spread = yield on bond A – yield on bond B **(Equation 15-6)**

$$\text{Relative yield spread} = \frac{\text{yield on bond A} - \text{yield on bond B}}{\text{yield on bond B}}$$

(Equation 15-7)

$$\text{Yield ratio} = \frac{\text{yield on bond A}}{\text{yield on bond B}}$$

(Equation 15-8)

In many cases bond B is the benchmark on-the-run Treasury issue.

Example 15-12: Yield spread measures

Assume bond A yields 8.5% and the on-the-run Treasury security yields 6.95%. Using Equations 15-6, 15-7 and 15-8

Absolute yield spread = 8.5% - 6.95% = 1.55% or 155 basis points
Relative yield spread = (8.5% – 6.95%)/6.95% = 0.223 = 22.3%
Yield ratio = 8.5%/6.95% = 1.22

LOS 15-1-D-f **explain** why investors may find a relative yield spread to be a better measure of yield spread than the absolute yield spread

The **relative yield spread** is a better measure than the **absolute yield spread** since the magnitude of the yield spread is affected by the actual level of interest rates (yields of the on-the-run Treasury securities).

Example 15-13: Relative yield spread

Assume that the on-the-run Treasury security yield drops to 5.75% and the absolute yield spread remains the same at 155 basis points.

The relative yield spread will be 27.0%. The yield ratio becomes 1.27.

The important question is not the yield spread measure per se but rather the factors that cause the yield spread between two fixed income securities.

Bonds are classified based on the type of issuer. The different types of issuer indicate the different risk and reward profiles that are offered to investors.

The major sectors of the bond market in the United States are the:

a. U.S. government sector
b. U.S. government agencies sector (GSEs)
c. corporate sector
d. mortgage sector
e. asset-backed sector
f. foreign sector (also called Yankees).

Each sector can be further broken down into sub-sectors with common economic characteristics. The grouping based on these common characteristics provides a picture of the nature of the issuer, as it is a key feature of a debt obligation.

Sub-sectors within the corporate sector are, for example, industrial companies, utility companies, finance companies and banks. Within the sub-sectors are further subdivisions.

LOS 15-1-D-g **distinguish** between an intermarket and intramarket sector spread

Intermarket sector spread is the yield spread that occurs between two distinguishable sectors, for instance between the bank sector and the industrial sector.

Intramarket sector spread is the yield spread that occurs between two issuers within a sector, for instance between Ford and General Motors, both from the automotive sector.

The factors that are responsible for the intermarket and intramarket yield spreads can be identified as follows:

a. the comparative credit risks between the two issues
b. the presence of any embedded options
c. the market liquidity of an issue
d. the taxability of the interest

LOS 15-1-D-h **describe** a credit spread and **discuss** the suggested relationship between credit spreads and the economic well being of the economy

Credit spread, sometimes referred to as **quality spread,** is the yield spread which reflects the credit risk of an issue against the corresponding Treasury issue that is identical in maturity and has no embedded option.

Credit spreads change with the change in economic prospects. During an economic contraction or a recession, the credit spreads are expected to widen. This is because it is anticipated that the corporate issuers will have a tighter cash flow as sales revenues decline. The widening of the spread can also be caused by a 'flight to quality'; investors switch to risk-free Treasury securities and sell the corporate bonds at lower prices as they are concerned about corporate default.

Another way is to look at yield spreads of cyclical versus non-cyclical industries. It is argued that during an economic expansion, the cyclical industry will benefit more so the improvement of the cash flow is more significant than that of a non-cyclical industry.

LOS 15-1-D-i **identify** how embedded options affect yield spreads

Embedded options affect yield spreads in the following ways:

1. If the embedded options are favoring the issuer, the investors require a higher yield spread to compensate for it.
2. If the options are favoring the investors, they are happy to accept a lower yield spread.

Nominal yield spreads are the reported yield spreads that are raw, meaning that they have not taken into consideration the value of the embedded option.

Option-adjusted spreads are the preferred calculation as they take into account the valuation of the embedded option.

Recall Equations 15-3 and 15-5:

Price of callable bond = price of option-free bond – price of embedded option
Price of option-free bond = price of callable bond + price of embedded option

It can be explained as follows: when a yield spread of a callable bond is quoted we must look at the yield spread **without** the value of the embedded option. We subtract the option value from the reported yield spread resulting in a lower figure for an option-adjusted spread. Since yields move inversely to prices, the higher the price the lower the yield. The converse is true, that with a putable bond, the option-free bond yield is higher.

Example 15-14: Option-adjusted spread

A callable bond is quoted with a nominal spread of 161 basis points (bp) over its equivalent Treasury bond. However, its option-adjusted spread is considerably less, e.g. 63 bp. The difference reflects the valuation of the embedded option.

LOS 15-1-D-j **explain** how the liquidity of an issue affects its yield spread relative to Treasury securities and relative to other issues that are comparable in all other ways except for liquidity

The yield spreads of non-Treasury securities (the spread sector) versus the benchmark Treasury securities of similar characteristics (maturity, coupon, etc) often vary due to market liquidity.

A clear case is between the on-the-run and off-the-run corporate bonds. On-the-run bonds are normally more liquid than equivalent off-the-run issues and enjoy lower repo rates as they are sought after in the market. This higher level of market liquidity is reflected in the reported yields.

LOS 15-1-D-k **describe** the relationships that are argued to exist among the size of an issue, liquidity, and yield spread

The relationship between the size of an issue, yield spreads and liquidity is as follows:

The higher the issue size the higher the liquidity hence the yield spread is tighter.

A global bond offering is generally larger in size than a comparable local offering and attracts a wider base of investors. The probability that the bonds will trade among the investors, thus creating liquidity, will be higher as well. This liquidity will cause a tighter yield spread.

LOS 15-1-D-l **compute** the after-tax yield of a taxable security and the tax-equivalent yield of a tax-exempt security

The **after-tax** yield on a taxable bond is computed as follows

After-tax yield = pre-tax yield x (1 – marginal tax rate) **(Equation 15-9)**

Or, we can also find the **taxable-equivalent yield** or **tax-equivalent yield** offered on a bond issue which gives the same after-tax yield as a tax-exempt issue.

$$\text{Taxable-equivalent yield} = \frac{\text{tax-exempt yield}}{(1 - \text{marginal tax rate})}$$

(Equation 15-10)

Example 15-15: Tax and yields

Suppose a New York Municipal bond if offered at a tax-exempt yield of 5.25% per annum. The taxable-equivalent yield for an investor in a marginal tax bracket of 36% will be:

5.25% /(1 - 0.36) = 5.25/0.64 = 8.23%

15-1-D View Concept Check Questions Workbook

STUDY SESSION 16

Asset Valuation

Debt Investments: Analysis and Valuation

Overview

This Reading moves on to more interesting material and some key topics are covered, not only are they important for the Level I exam but they provide a foundation for Level II and Level III debt investments.

We start to analyse and value bonds. In the first Reading we look at different valuation methods, including the arbitrage-free valuation free approach. In the second Reading we examine different ways of measuring yield and candidates need to be comfortable switching between spot and forward rates. The next concept that is looked at in more depth than in the previous Study Session is duration which measures a bond's interest rate sensitivity. Candidates need to understand the differences between alternative definitions of duration, be able to calculate effective duration for option-free bonds, and work out the movement in price of a bond due to a specified change in interest rates. Convexity is also covered; it is used to obtain a closer approximation of the interest rate sensitivity of a bond.

Reading Assignments

Fixed Income Analysis for the Chartered Financial Analyst® Program, 2nd edition, Frank J. Fabozzi (Frank J. Fabozzi Associates, 2004)

16-1-A. "Introduction to the Valuation of Debt Securities," Ch. 5

16-1-B. "Yield Measures, Spot Rates, and Forward Rates," Ch. 6

16-1-C. "Introduction to the Measurement of Interest Rate Risk," Ch. 7

16-1-A "Introduction to the Valuation of Fixed Income Securities"

Introduction

The Reading covers the fundamentals of valuing a bond. It starts with the general principle of valuation, that the value of a financial asset is the present value of its expected future cash flows. The steps in the valuation process are examined, starting with estimating the cash flows, determining the appropriate discount rates and discounting the expected cash flows. The difficulties often come with correctly estimating the cash flows and with selecting the appropriate discount rates. Candidates are expected to be able to compute the value of a bond using a discounted cash flow approach.

The Reading also investigates the price volatility of bonds (interest rate sensitivity) and the factors that affect volatility. Bonds, like any other assets can be mispriced, here we learn how to calculate the intrinsic value of bonds and how dealers can take advantage of the mispricing.

LOS 16-1-A-a **describe** the fundamental principles of bond valuation

Bond Valuation

The fundamental principle of valuation is that the value of any financial asset is the present value of the expected cash flows which is the same as the sum of the present values of each expected cash flow.

The three steps in valuing a financial asset are:

1. **Estimate** the expected cash flows.
   To correctly estimate the cash flows for a bond with options see LOS 16-1-A-b.
2. **Determine** the discount rate or rates.
   The interest rate(s) that are chosen as discount rate(s) must be appropriately selected. Using multiple interest rates that incorporate the relevant risk premium is now the norm.
3. **Calculate** the present value of each of the cash flows using the discount rate(s) and take the sum of these to arrive at a value for the bond.

A bond's cash flow is simply the cash that is expected to be received in the future from investment in a bond. This cash flow consists of coupon and principal.

LOS 16-1-A-b	**identify** the types of bonds for which estimating the expected cash flows is difficult and **explain** the problems encountered when estimating the cash flows for these bonds

Sometimes it is difficult to estimate the expected cash flows, in terms of the amount and the timing, if the bond has the following features:

1. There are **embedded options** that allow the issuers or the investors to alter the contractual date of principal repayment, such as callable bonds, putable bonds, mortgage-backed securities, etc.
2. The coupon formula includes a **resettable coupon rate** or depends on some **variable value(s)** such as reference rates, exchange rates and market indices, e.g. floating rate notes, index floaters, etc.
3. There is an **option for the investor**, at his discretion, to convert or exchange the bond into another type of security, such as common stock, e.g. convertible bonds, exchangeable bonds.

The difficulty in estimating the cash flows lies in the ability to forecast the economic and market factors that the reference rates depend upon, such as interest rates, market indices, etc., and also to predict with reasonable certainty the reaction of borrowers and issuers to such changes. With mortgage-backed securities, for instance, one cannot determine with certainty how many percent of the underlying mortgages will prepay when the mortgage interest rate falls by a certain amount.

LOS 16-1-A-c	**determine** the appropriate interest rates for valuing a bond's cash flows

The **discount rate** is the interest rate that is used to discount the cash flows in Step 2 of the valuation process. The discount rate should be at least the **risk-free rate**, i.e. the yield available in the market that reflects a default-free cash flow. In the United States the yields of the Treasury Securities represent the default-free discount rates.

Higher discount rates indicate that there exists an element of additional risk. The **risk premium**, or the difference between the discount rate and the risk-free rate, signifies the additional risk. This premium is the additional compensation given to an investor for the risk taken. A single discount rate can be used but using multiple rates to discount a bond is preferred.

LOS 16-1-A-d **compute** the value of a bond, given the expected cash flows and the appropriate discount rates

Now, let us look at an example of valuing a bond based on the steps given in

LOS 16-A-1-a.

Example 16-1: Bond valuation

Consider a bond with a 12% coupon, payable annually in arrears, a 3-year maturity and $1,000 principal value. The discount rate used is 10%.

Step 1: The cash flow schedule will be as follows:

End of year 1: First coupon of the bond will be 12% x $1,000 = $120

End of year 2: Second coupon of the bond will be 12% x $1,000 = $120

End of year 3: Third and last coupon of the bond will be 12% x $1,000 = $120 plus the repayment of the principal of $1,000, totalling $1,120.

Step 2: The discount rate is given to be 10%.

Step 3: Compute the present values of the cash flows:

Year 1: $\$120/(1.1)^1 = \$109.09$

Year 2: $\$120/(1.1)^2 = \$99.17$

Year 3: $\$1,120/(1.1)^3 = \$841.47$

The value of the bond is $109.09 + $99.17 + $841.47 = $1,049.74.

LOS 16-1-A-e **explain** how the value of a bond changes if the discount rate increases or decreases and **compute** the change in value that is attributable to the rate change

What happens when we alter the discount rate in calculating the bond value in Example 16-1?

1. Assume the discount rate is now 11%. The bond value will be:

$\$120/(1.11)^1 + \$120/(1.11)^2 + \$1,120/(1.11)^3 = \$1,024.44$

2. Assume the discount rate is now 9%. The bond value will be:

$\$120/(1.09)^1 + \$120/(1.09)^2 + \$1,120/(1.09)^3 = \$1,075.94$

We can see that:

If the discount rate *increases* the present value is *lower* and, conversely, if the discount rate *decreases* the present value is *higher*.

We can also compute the effect on the price of the bond when the discount rate changes.

If the discount rate increases by 1.0% (100 basis points) the security value declines by:

\$1,049.74 - \$ 1,024.44 = \$25.30

Alternatively, if the rate drops by 100 basis points, the value of the bond goes up by:

\$1,075.94 - \$1,049.44 = \$26.50

The effect is not a linear one, i.e. the effect of an increase of the discount rate is not the same as that of a decrease of the same amount.

LOS 16-1-A-f	**explain** how the price of a bond changes as the bond approaches its maturity date and **compute** the change in value that is attributable to the passage of time

Pull to par value

What happens to the price of the bond when it approaches maturity?

Using the bond in Example 16-1, the bond price at the end of year 1 with 2 cash flows remaining can be computed as:

Year 2: $\$120/(1.1)^1 = \$109.09$
Year 3: $\$1{,}120/(1.1)^2 = \$925.62$
So, the value is: \$1,034.71.

The bond price at the end of year 2 with 1 cash flow remaining can be computed as:

Year 3: $\$1{,}120/(1.1)^1 = \$1{,}018.18$.

The price of the bond, with the discount rate unchanged, will move towards its par value. This characteristic is called "**pull to par value**".

Similarly we can calculate the effect of passage of time on the bond price:

Year 2 the price declines by \$1,049.74 - \$1,034.71 = \$15.03
Year 3 the price declines by \$1,034.71 - \$1,018.18 = \$16.53

Again, the effect of the change is not linear. Both the changes of the bond price due to the change in discount rate and the passage of time are not linear, i.e. they are convex.

LOS 16-1-A-g **compute** the value of a zero-coupon bond

Zero-Coupon Bonds

In valuing a zero-coupon bond, the calculation is more straightforward since there are no coupon payments prior to maturity.

The present value is simply the maturity value discounted by the discount rate over the number of years to maturity. However in practice, the formula is aligned to the pricing of semiannual coupon bonds, so the formula is for the value is:

$$\frac{\text{Maturity value}}{(1+ i/2)^{\text{no.of years} \times 2}}$$

(Equation 16-1)

where

i = the annual interest rate

Example 16-2: Value of a zero-coupon bond

A 4-year zero-coupon bond with a maturity value of $1,000 discounted at a 9% interest rate is priced at

$\$1{,}000/(1 + 0.09/2)^{4 \times 2} = \$703.19$.

LOS 16-1-A-h **explain** the arbitrage-free valuation approach and the market process that forces the price of a bond toward its arbitrage-free value

Arbitrage-Free Valuation Approach

The preferred valuation method for bonds is called the **arbitrage-free valuation approach**, meaning there is no arbitrage opportunity in the pricing of a bond since the market price is the same as the 'theoretical' or intrinsic price.

For each of the cash flows of a Treasury bond, the discount rate will be the **theoretical rate** that the U.S. Treasury would have to pay if it issued a zero-coupon bond with a maturity date equal to the maturity of the cash flow. This zero-coupon Treasury rate is called **Treasury spot rate**. The value of a bond using the Treasury spot rates as the multiple discount rates is called the **arbitrage-free value**.

Market forces will assure that the prices of Treasury bonds do not depart materially from their arbitrage-free values. When a bond is undervalued, the price will be bid up until the fair valuation is reached. Likewise when a bond is overvalued, there will be dealers in the market who would short sell the bond so the price will come down to its fair value.

LOS 16-1-A-i **determine** whether a bond is undervalued or overvalued, given the bond's cash flows, appropriate spot rates or yield to maturity, and current market price

To determine whether a bond is mispriced, i.e. either undervalued or overvalued, we compare its current market price and its arbitrage-free value (or theoretical value).

Consider a 4-year Treasury bond with an 8% coupon discounted at 6%. A Treasury spot curve is given in the data below:

Period	Cash flow	Discount rate	Present value (1)	Spot rate	Present value (2)	Arbitrage profit
1	$4	6%	$3.8835	3.0000%	$3.9409	$0.0574
2	$4	6%	$3.7704	3.3000%	$3.8712	$0.1008
3	$4	6%	$3.6606	3.5053%	$3.7968	$0.1362
4	$4	6%	$3.5539	3.9164%	$3.7014	$0.1475
5	$4	6%	$3.4504	4.4376%	$3.5843	$0.1339
6	$4	6%	$3.3499	4.7520%	$3.4743	$0.1244
7	$4	6%	$3.2524	4.9622%	$3.3694	$0.1170
8	$104	6%	$82.0986	5.0650%	$85.1414	$3.0428
			$107.0197		$110.8797	$3.8600

The discount rates and spot rates are annual rates. To obtain the semiannual discount rate take one-half of the annual rate. For example in the first period, using a discount rate of 6%, the present value (1) is given by $4/(1 + 0.03) = $3.8835. If the spot rate is 3.0% the present value (2) is given by $4/(1 + 0.015) = $3.9409.

Here the market value as presented in the Present value (1) column, $107.0197, is lower than the arbitrage-free value as shown in Present value (2) column, $110.9797. The difference is $3.86. Since the market value is lower that the arbitrage-free value, the bond is *undervalued.*

LOS 16-1-A-j explain how a dealer can generate an arbitrage profit

If a Treasury bond is priced lower than its **arbitrage-free value**, a dealer can buy it and strip it into zero-coupon bonds and sell them to make a profit. Breaking apart a coupon bond into individual zero coupon bonds is called **stripping**.

Conversely, if the bond is priced higher than the arbitrage-free value, a dealer can buy a set of strips to create a synthetic bond and sell them as a bond at a profit. This process is called a **reconstitution**, the opposite of stripping.

LOS 16-1-A-i describes an arbitrage opportunity that appears when a bond is valued using the Treasury spot rates.

The value of the bond using spot rates is also called the arbitrage-free value of the bond, which is $110.8797, in this case it is higher than the market value of $107.0197 (at a 6% discount rate) providing an arbitrage opportunity to make a profit of $3.86. So a dealer could buy the bond and strip it into a package of zero coupon bonds and pocket the difference in value when he sold off all of the zero coupon bonds.

16-1-A View Concept Check Questions Workbook

16-1-B "Yield Measures, Spot Rates, and Forward Rates"

Introduction

Yields are the main measure of investment performance of bonds. Here we look into a variety of yield measures and in what circumstances they are used. We also investigate the reinvestment risk, i.e. the risk that might prevent an investment from generating its expected yield or yield to maturity. We then explore what spot and forward rates are, how they are derived and why they are important. Candidates are expected to be able to value bonds using these different discount rates.

LOS 16-1-B-a	**explain** the sources of return from investing in a bond (i.e., coupon interest payments, capital gain/loss, reinvestment income)

There are three sources of return from a bond investment:

1. The **coupon** payments.
2. Any **capital gain** or **loss** when the bond is sold or matures; as demonstrated in LOS 16-1-A-d bonds can increase and decrease in price depending on the movement of interest rates.
3. **Income from reinvestment** of the interim cash flows; this is mainly from the reinvestment of the coupons although, in the case of amortizing securities, can be from the scheduled principal repayments.

LOS 16-1-B-b	**compute** the traditional yield measures for fixed-rate bonds (e.g., current yield, yield to maturity, yield to first call, yield to first par call date, yield to refunding, yield to put, yield to worst, cash flow yield)

Yield Measures

Yield measures vary, the most important ones are:

1. Current yield

This is calculated based on the current market price.

current yield = annual dollar coupon interest/current price **(Equation 16-2)**

2. Yield to maturity

This is the discount rate that will make the present value of the cash flows equal to the market price plus accrued interest. Since the cash flows of a typical bond occur semiannually, the discount rate is the semiannual yield.

The convention is to double the semiannual yield to arrive at the bond equivalent yield (BEY).

The following relationships hold:

Bond selling at	Relationship
Par	Coupon rate = current yield = yield to maturity
Discount	Coupon rate < current yield < yield to maturity
Premium	Coupon rate > current yield > yield to maturity

3. Yield to first call

This is similar to yield to maturity, but it is calculated until the first call date using all the coupon payments and the call price as the cash flows, plus accrued interest.

4. Yield to first par call date

This is calculated to the first par call date using all the coupon payments and the par price as the cash flows, plus accrued interest.

5. Yield to put

This is similar to yield to maturity, but it is calculated to the put date using all the coupon payments and the put price as the cash flows, plus accrued interest.

6. Yield to worst

When a bond has several call and put dates, the yields can be calculated to each of these dates as well as the yield to maturity. The lowest yield is called the yield to worst.

7. Cash flow yield

With mortgage-backed or asset-backed securities, the cash flow contains uncertainty of early prepayments on the underlying pool of loans. The basis on which **prepayments** are made needs to be taken into account. The rate at which the borrowers prepay is called the **prepayment rate**.

Example 16-3: Traditional yield measures

1. Current Yield

A bond has 6 years to maturity, an 8% coupon and a current price of $98.75, what is the current yield?

If the par value is $100, the annual coupon payment will be 8% x $100 = $8.

The current quoted price is $98.75, so the current yield is $8/$98.75 = 8.10%

2. Yield to maturity

A bond has a 10% semiannual coupon, 5 years to maturity and the following price-yield relationship:

Semiannual interest rate	5.0%	5.1%	5.2%	5.3%	5.4%
Present value	100.00	99.23	98.47	97.72	96.97

The bond pays a $5 coupon every 6 months, so when the semiannual interest rate in the market is 5%, the bond is priced at par. When the semiannual interest rate in the market is 5.1% the price of the bond is $98.23, at 5.2% the price is $98.47, and so on, (calculated using a financial calculator).

The following calculations are based on the bond below:

a. Coupon = 10%
b. Maturity = 5 years
c. Not callable for the first 2 years
d. First call date in 2 years, call price $103
e. First par call date in 3 years (call price $100)
f. First put date in 4 years at $101
g. The price of the bond is $110.75

3. Yield to first call

The calculation produces a 2.84% semiannual yield or a BEY of 5.68% if the bond is called at the end of 2 years at a call price of $103.

4. Yield to first par call

The calculation produces a 3.01% semiannual yield, or a BEY of 6.02% if the bond is called at the end of 3 years with a par call price, i.e. $100.

5. Yield to put

The calculation produces a 3.54% semiannual yield, or a BEY of 7.08% for the yield to first put at the end of 4 years at $101.

6. Yield to worst

The semiannual yield to maturity, assuming no put or call options are exercised is 3.69%, or a BEY of 7.38%.

The yield to worst in this example is the yield to first call of 5.68%.

LOS 16-1-B-c	**explain** the assumptions underlying traditional yield measures and the limitations of the traditional yield measures

The traditional yield to maturity calculation makes the following two major assumptions:

1. The coupon payments are reinvested at the rate equal to the yield to maturity
2. The bond is held to maturity

Remember in Study Session 11 the calculation of internal rate of return (IRR) assumed reinvestment of cash flows at the IRR. The yield to maturity is the IRR of the bond.

Similarly the **cash flow yield** calculation makes the following two major assumptions

1. The projected cash flows are reinvested at the cash flow yield.
2. The securities are held until the final payoff of the loans based on some prepayment assumption. (Note: Since the securities are an amortizing type, the timing of the full amount of principal repayment can not be known with certainty as it is dependent on the probability of prepayment).

LOS 16-1-B-d	**explain** the importance of reinvestment income in generating the yield computed at the time of purchase, and **calculate** the amount of income required to generate that yield

As stated above, the yield to maturity is achieved only if the income is reinvested at the rate equal to the yield to maturity.

If the cash flows cannot be reinvested at the rate equal to the yield to maturity then there is **reinvestment risk**. If the bond is not held to maturity, it may have to be sold for less than its purchase price. This is **interest rate risk.**

In both cases the actual yield obtained will be different to the expected yield to maturity. Following is an illustration of how reinvestment income plays a role in generating the yield computed at the time of purchase (expected yield to maturity).

Example 16-4: Reinvestment income

Let us take the case of a bond with a 10% coupon (payable semiannually) yielding 10% with a remaining term to maturity of 4 years, priced at par of $1,000.

The future value of the bond at the date of maturity	$\$1,000 \times (1.05)^8 = \$1,477.46$
The return of principal	= $1,000.00
The total dollar return	= $ 477.46
Without reinvestment income	4 x $100 = $ 400.00
Capital gain	
= $ 0.00	
Dollar return without reinvestment income	= $ 400.00

The dollar shortfall = \$477.46 - \$400.00 = \$77.46, was obtained from the reinvestment of the coupons at 10% for 4 years, as follows:

First coupon	$\$50 \times 1.05^7 - \$50 = \$20.36$
Second coupon	$\$50 \times 1.05^6 - \$50 = \$17.01$
Third coupon	$\$50 \times 1.05^5 - \$50 = \$13.81$
Fourth coupon	$\$50 \times 1.05^4 - \$50 = \$10.76$
Fifth coupon	$\$50 \times 1.05^3 - \$50 = \$\ 7.88$
Sixth coupon	$\$50 \times 1.05^2 - \$50 = \$\ 5.13$
Seventh coupon	$\$50 \times 1.05^1 - \$50 = \$\ 2.50$
Eighth coupon	$\$50 \times 1.05^0 - \$50 = \underline{\$\ 0.00}$
Total	\$77.46

We show here that the reinvestment income of \$77.46 is crucial in making the realized yield to be 10%, i.e. equal to the yield to maturity.

If the coupons cannot be invested at a 10% yield, than the reinvestment income will be lower and therefore the realized yield will be lower than 10%.

LOS 16-1-B-e **discuss** the factors that affect reinvestment risk

Factors that affect reinvestment risk are maturity and coupon rates:

1. The longer the time to maturity the more the bond is dependent on the reinvestment income.
2. The higher the coupon rate the more the bond is dependent on the reinvestment income.

Zero-coupon bonds do not have reinvestment risk. For bonds bought at a premium, the reinvestment income is more important that ones bought at par, this is because the reinvestment income is needed to compensate for the capital loss made due to the amortization of the premium. In contrast, for bonds bought at a discount dependence on the reinvestment income is less.

LOS 16-1-B-f **compute** the bond equivalent yield of an annual-pay bond and **compute** the annual-pay yield of a semiannual-pay bond

It is common practice to pay the coupons semiannually in the U.S., while the annual payment of coupons is often the norm internationally.

The **bond-equivalent yield** (**BEY**) of an annual-pay bond is

$$= 2\left[(1 + \text{yield on annual-pay bond})^{0.5} - 1\right] \qquad \textit{(Equation } \textbf{16-3)}$$

Another way, which is more commonly used with Eurobonds or in Europe, is to quote yield on an annual basis, i.e.:

Yield on an annual basis or **annual-pay yield** is linked to BEY as follows

= [(1 + yield on a bond-equivalent basis/2)^2 – 1] (Equation **16-4**)

Example 16-5: Bond-equivalent yield and annual-pay yield

1. Given the annual-pay yield is 9%, the BEY yield is 2[(1 + 0.09)$^{0.5}$ – 1] = 8.81%

The BEY is always lower that the annual-pay yield due to the compounding effect in the annual-pay yield calculation.

2. Given the BEY of 9%, the annual-pay yield is [(1 + 0.09/2)^2 - 1] = 9.20%

The annual-pay yield is always higher.

LOS 16-1-B-g **compute** the value of a bond using spot rates

Valuing a bond using **spot rates** is straightforward, since each cash flow is discounted using a corresponding spot rate.

Recall from LOS 16-1-A-h that a zero-coupon Treasury rate is called a Treasury spot rate.

Example 16-6: Valuation using spot rates

Given the 1-year spot rate is 3.56%, 2-year spot rate is 4.01% and 3-year spot rate is 4.87%, the value of a 6% annual coupon bond with remaining term to maturity of 3 years and par value of $1,000 will be:

$\$60/1.0356 + \$60/(1.0401)^2 + \$1{,}060/(1.0487)^3$
$= \$57.9374 + \$55.4627 + \$919.0773$
$= \$1{,}032.48$

If not all the spot rates are available across the maturity spectrum, it is possible to construct a **theoretical spot curve**, i.e. what the spot rates would be if there are zero-coupon bonds available to represent the maturity spectrum.

LOS 16-1-B-h **compute** the theoretical Treasury spot rate curve, using the method of bootstrapping and given the Treasury par yield curve

One way of building a theoretical spot rate curve is by a method called **bootstrapping.** See Example 16-7 for a bootstrapping calculation.

Example 16-7: Bootstrapping

Period	Years	Annual Yield to Maturity (BEY) %	Price	Spot Rate (BEY) %
1	0.5	4.00		4.0000
2	1.0	4.30		4.3000
3	1.5	4.65	100	4.6606
4	2.0	4.75	100	4.7618
etc.	etc.	etc.	100	etc.
30	15.0	7.00	100	etc.

In the first two periods the rates are given for Treasury bills so these are already spot rates.

We will use the notation z_m as one-half the theoretical m/2 year spot rate.

Period 3

First we calculate z_3 which is one half the theoretical 1.5 year spot rate.

We can see in the table that z_1 is 2.00% and z_2 is 2.15% (half the six-month and one-year spot rates respectively).

The yield to maturity of a bond which is priced at 100 is the same as its coupon rate.

Therefore we can say that the price of the bond (100) is equal to the coupons of 4.65/2 = 2.325 discounted back at the appropriate spot rates over the one and a half year period.

$$100 = \frac{2.325}{1+z_1} + \frac{2.325}{(1+z_2)^2} + \frac{102.325}{(1+z_3)^3}$$

$$100 = \frac{2.325}{1.02} + \frac{2.325}{(1.0215)^2} + \frac{102.325}{(1+z_3)^3}$$

$$95.4924 = \frac{102.325}{(1+z_3)^3}$$

$$z_3 = 1.023303 - 1 = 2.3303\%$$

The spot rate on a BEY basis is 4.6606%

Period 4

Using the same method to calculate z_4.

$$100 = \frac{2.375}{1+z_1} + \frac{2.375}{(1+z_2)^2} + \frac{2.375}{(1+z_3)^3} + \frac{102.375}{(1+z_4)^4}$$

$$100 = \frac{2.375}{1.02} + \frac{2.375}{(1.0215)^2} + \frac{2.375}{(1.0233)^3} + \frac{102.375}{(1+z_4)^4}$$

$$93.1791 = \frac{102.375}{(1+z_4)^4}$$

$$z_4 = 1.023809 - 1 = 2.3809\%$$

The spot rate on a BEY basis is 4.7618%

Continue using the same method for the following periods.

$$100 = \frac{2.375}{1+z_1} + \frac{2.375}{(1+z_2)^2} + \frac{2.375}{(1+z_3)^3} + \frac{102.375}{(1+z_4)^4}$$

$$100 = \frac{2.375}{1.02} + \frac{2.375}{(1.0215)^2} + \frac{2.375}{(1.0233)^3} + \frac{102.375}{(1+z_4)^4}$$

$$93.1791 = \frac{102.375}{(1+z_4)^4}$$

$$z_4 = 1.023809 - 1 = 2.3809\%$$

The spot rate on a BEY basis is 4.7618%

Continue using the same method for the remaining periods.

LOS 16-1-B-i **explain** the limitations of the nominal spread

The **nominal spread** is traditionally calculated as the difference between a bond's quoted yield and the benchmark Treasury bond's yield, or in other words the premium over its benchmark yield.

Example 16-8: Nominal spread

The nominal spread between a T-bond with a remaining life to maturity of 5 years, a coupon rate of 6% and yielding 6.12%, and a bond with the same remaining life, a coupon rate of 8% and yielding 8.25%, would be: 8.25% - 6.12% = 2.13%

Recent findings show that there are limitations of nominal spread:

1. The yield fails to take into account the term structure of the spot rates, i.e. it is only relative to one point on the yield curve. It is important to understand the behavior of the spread across the yield curve.
2. In the case of embedded options, such as call and put options, expected interest rate volatility may alter the cash flows of the bond rendering the information carried by the spread of little worth.

LOS 16-1-B-j	**differentiate** among the nominal spread, the zero-volatility spread, and the option-adjusted spread for a bond with an embedded option, and **explain** the option cost

Nominal spread is traditionally the difference between a bond's quoted yield and its benchmark Treasury bond's yield, or in other words the premium over its benchmark yield.

The **zero-volatility spread**, also called the **Z-spread** or **static spread** is the spread over the entire Treasury spot rate curve for a non-Treasury bond, if the bond is held until maturity, unlike the nominal spread that is only relative to one point on the yield curve. The Z-spread represents the non-Treasury risk premia relative to the Treasury spot rate curve, due to credit risk, liquidity risk, embedded options risk, etc.

Option-adjusted spread (OAS) is a spread measure that takes into account the embedded option in the security. The calculation is model dependent and assumes that the interest rate has a volatility that is non-zero. Z-spread assumes otherwise and therefore is also called zero-volatility OAS.

The difference between the two spreads is the **option cost**,

Option cost = Z-spread – OAS (Equation **16-5**)

LOS 16-1-B-k	**explain** a forward rate, and **compute** the value of a bond using forward rates

Forward Rates

Forward rates are the implied market's expectations of future short-term rates and are derived from an extrapolation of the spot rate curve. In short they are the market consensus of future interest rates.

For example from the spot rate curve we can calculate the

6-month forward rate 3 years from now

3-year forward rate 6 months from now, etc.

A spot rate can be calculated from forward rates, e.g. a two-year spot rate is a product of the one-year spot rate and the one-year forward rate one year from now.

We next look at calculating the value of a bond using forward rates.

Example 16-9: Bond valuation using forward rates

Using the bond in Example 16-6, the value of an annual 6% coupon bond with remaining term to maturity of 3 years and par value of $1,000 is using spot rates:

Year	Spot rate	Cash flow	PV of Cash flow
1	3.56%	$60	$57.9374
2	4.01%	$60	$55.4627
3	4.87%	$1,060	$919.0773
			$1,032.48

For Year 1, the PV is derived from $60/(1.0356) = 57.9374, for year 2 the PV = $\$60/(1+0.041)^2$ = $55.4627, etc.

Using forward rates:

Year	Spot rate	Forward rate	Cash flow	PV of Cash flow
1	3.56%	3.56%	$60	$57.9374
2	4.01%	4.64%	$60	$55.3683
3	4.87%	6.43%	$1,060	$919.0773
				$1,032.38

In year 1, the forward rate is the same as the spot rate. In year 2, the one-year forward rate is one year from now is calculated to be 4.64%, the PV of the cash flow is $60/[(1.0356)(1.0464)] = $55.3683. In year 3 the one-year forward rate two years from now is given to be 6.61%, so the PV of the cash flow will be

$1,060/[(1.0356)(1.0464)(1.0643)] = $919.0773

There should be no difference, other than rounding errors, in the result of the computation of the value of the bond.

LOS 16-1-B-I **explain** and **illustrate** the relationship between short-term forward rates and spot rates

Short-term forward rates and spot rates are related through the formula

$${}_1f_m = \frac{(1+z_{m+1})^{m+1}}{(1+z_m)^m} - 1 \qquad \textbf{(Equation 16-6)}$$

${}_1f_m$ is the notation used for determining the 6-month forward rate m (6-month) periods from now. To get the 6-month forward rate on a BEY basis we need to double the answer.

So, the 6-month forward rate 3 years from now will be 2 x ${}_1f_6$

The market observes at any point of time how the Treasury yield curve, Treasury theoretical spot curve and short-term forward rate curve plot against each other. An example is shown below:

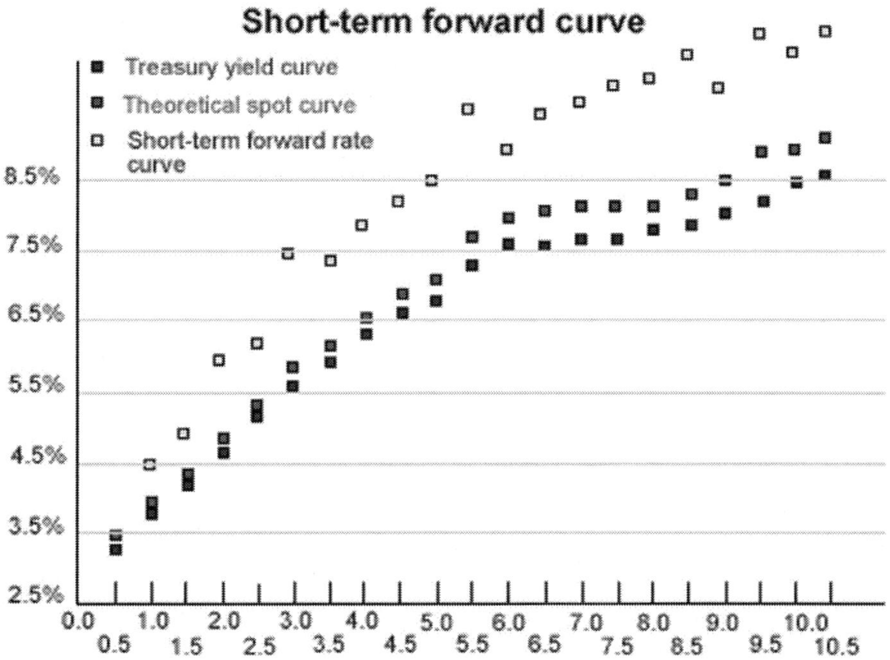

Notice that the short-term forward rates lie above the spot rates and the yields. This is generally true when the yield curve is upward sloping.

LOS 16-1-B-m	**compute** spot rates given forward rates, and forward rates given spot rates

To compute spots rates from forward rates use the following formula

$$z_T = [(1+z_1)(1+{}_1f_1)(1+{}_1f_2)(1+{}_1f_3)...(1+{}_1f_{T-1})]^{1/T} - 1$$ **(Equation 16-7)**

Example 16-10 Spot and forward rates

Using the bond in Example 16-7

Period	Years	Annual Yield to Maturity (BEY) %	Price	Spot Rate (BEY) %
1	0.5	4.00		4.0000
2	1.0	4.30		4.3000
3	1.5	4.65	100	4.6606
4	2.0	4.75	100	4.7618
etc.	etc.	etc.	100	etc.
30	15.0	7.00	100	etc.

We can use Equation 16-6 to calculate the six-month forward rate six months and one year from now

$$_1f_1 = \frac{(1+z_2)^2}{(1+z_1)^1} - 1$$

$$= \frac{(1.0215)^2}{(1.02)} - 1$$

$$= 2.3002\%$$

Therefore the six-month forward rate six months from now is double this, 4.6004%

$$_1f_2 = \frac{(1+z_3)^3}{(1+z_2)^2} - 1$$

$$= \frac{(1.023303)^3}{(1.0215)^2} - 1$$

$$= 2.6919\%$$

The six-month forward rate one year from now is double this, 5.3838%

Using Equation 16-7 we can check the 1.5 year spot rate

$$z_3 = [(1+z_1)(1+{}_1f_1)(1+{}_1f_2)]^{1/3} - 1$$

$$= (1.02)(1.02300)(1.02692)^{1/3} - 1$$

$$= 2.3303\%$$

The annual rate is double this, 4.6606%.

16-1-B View Concept Check Questions Workbook

16-1-C "Introduction to the Measurement of Interest Rate Risk"

Introduction

This is perhaps the most important topic in bond risk analysis: interest rate sensitivity which is also known as price volatility. As the name suggests, it revolves around the relationship between price and yield of a bond. Firstly we look at the different approaches of measuring the interest rate sensitivity, either using a full valuation approach or using duration/convexity measures. Then we explore the behaviour of the price volatility of a bond either with or without the presence of embedded options. Candidates are expected to be able to calculate the price change of a bond when the duration is known. We also look at different types of duration and their limitations and the convexity of a bond and its importance.

LOS 16-1-C-a	**distinguish** between the full valuation approach (the scenario analysis approach) and the duration/convexity approach for measuring interest rate risk, and **explain** the advantage of using the full valuation approach

To measure interest rate risk, the obvious approach is the **full valuation** method. Each bond in the portfolio is revalued under different interest rate scenarios and the resulting total losses/gains of the portfolio are calculated.

Another approach is the **duration/convexity** approach where the sensitivity figures are determined and the total loss/gain is calculated using the sensitivity figures.

The main advantage of the full valuation approach is that it can account for non-parallel shifts in the yield curve, namely changes in interest rates that are not uniform across the maturity spectrum.

LOS 16-1-C-b **compute** the interest rate risk exposure of a bond position or of a bond portfolio, given a change in interest rates

Example 16-11: Interest rate risk exposure

Look at the interest rate exposure for a parallel shift in the yield curve for the following bond:

Bond: 8% coupon, 4 years to maturity.

Price: 105.2097

Yield: 6.5%

Par value: $1,000,000

Market value of position: $1,052,097.

Yield increase	Price	Market value	Percent change
50bp	103.4370	$1,034,370	-1.69%
100bp	101.7007	$1,017,007	-3.34%
200bp	98.3341	$983,341	-6.54%
300bp	95.1032	$951,032	-9.61%

LOS 16-1-C-c **demonstrate** the price volatility characteristics for option-free bonds when interest rates change (including the concept of "positive convexity")

Convexity

Looking at the bond in Example 16-11

Yield	Price	Price change (from previous price)	Percent change
9.00	96.7021	3.2979	-3.4104
8.00	100.0000	1.7007	-1.7007
7.50	101.7007	1.7363	-1.7073
7.00	103.4370	0.8817	-0.8542
6.75	104.3187	0.8852	-0.8198

6.51	105.1739	0.0358	-0.0340
6.50	105.2097	---	---
6.49	105.2455	0.0358	0.0340
6.25	106.1100	0.8645	0.8214
6.00	107.0197	0.9097	0.8573
5.50	108.8679	1.8482	1.7270
5.00	110.7552	1.8873	1.7336
4.00	114.6510	3.8958	3.5157

This relationship can be presented in the following graph, if the yield increases from Y_1 to Y_2 then the price falls from P_1 to P_2 and so on.

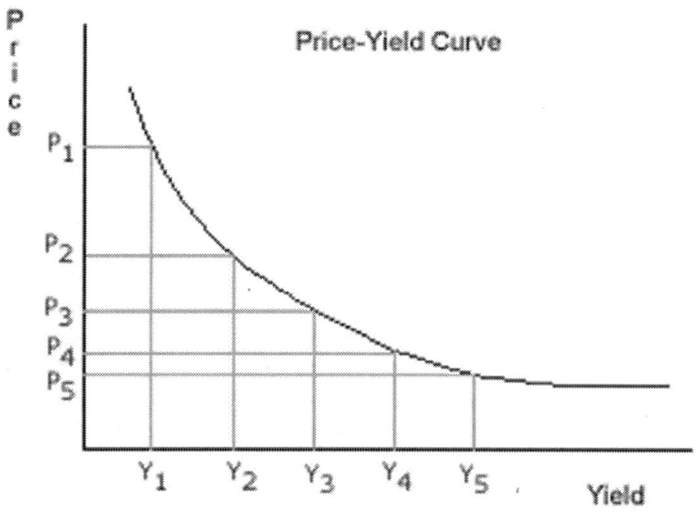

A particular characteristic shown by the relationship is called the **positive convexity**, which means:

1. The percentage price change for a given yield change is not the same for all bonds.
2. For small changes in yield, the percentage changes are roughly the same, whether the yield increases or decreases.
3. For a large change in yield, the percentage price change is not the same for an increase in yields as it is for a decrease in yields.
4. For a large change in yield, the percentage price increase is greater than the percentage price decrease.

LOS 16-1-C-d	**demonstrate** the price volatility characteristics of callable bonds and prepayable securities when interest rates change (including the concept of "negative convexity")

For bonds with embedded call options, we can observe **negative convexity**. Negative convexity is the 'tapering off' feature of the price curve that for the same amount of yield decrease, the increase in price is progressively less. This is caused by the higher probability of prepayments or the bond being called when interest rates decline. So the price of the security gravitates toward par or its call price instead of going to a premium. This is also known as **price compression**.

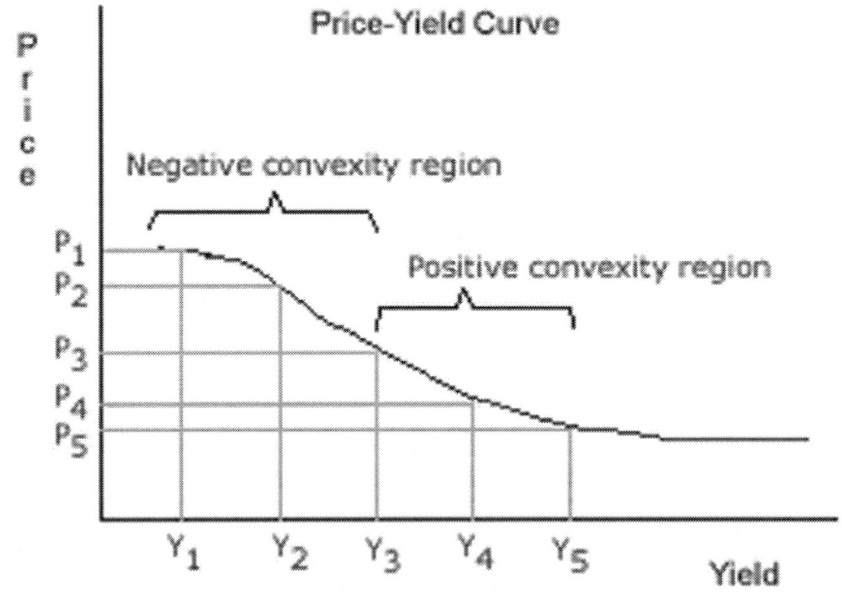

In this illustration, the call price or par is P_1. When the yield reaches Y_1 the issuer is likely to call the bonds so the price will not go higher than P_1. Negative convexity only appears at lower yields, as at higher yields the bond behaves like an option free-bond.

LOS 16-1-C-e **describe** the price volatility characteristics of putable bonds

When a bond contains an embedded put option, the opposite behaviour from one with a call option is shown. As yields increase, the decrease in price is progressively less. This behaviour appears at higher yields, as at lower yields the bond behaves like an option free-bond.

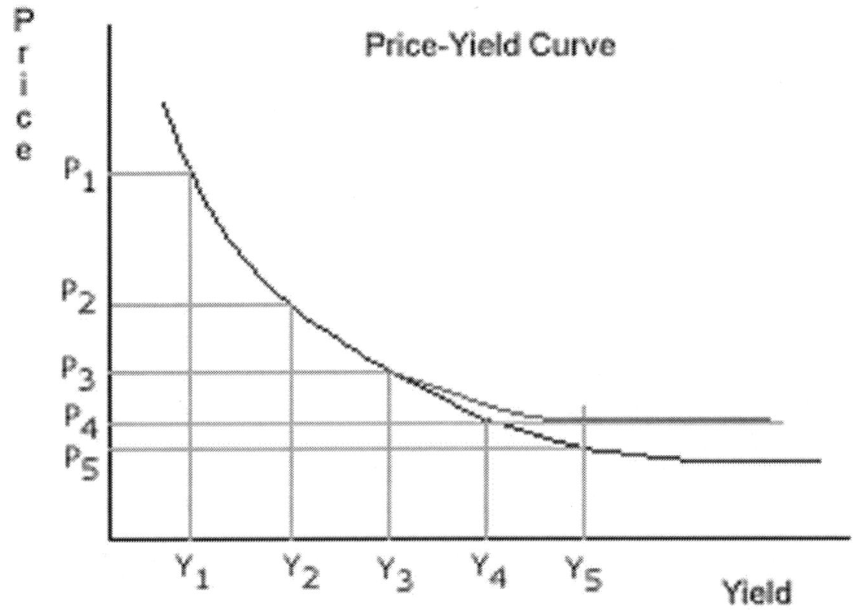

That behaviour can be illustrated in the graph above. The put price has been set at P_4. As the yield increases toward Y_4, the price will be sliding toward P_4. When the yield reaches Y_4, it is very likely that the bondholders would request the issuer to repay the principal at P_4. If the yield drops to Y_5, the price will not reach P_5 because the bonds would have been put back to the issuer at the price P_4.

LOS 16-1-C-f	**compute** the effective duration of a bond, given information about how the bond's price will increase and decrease for given changes in interest rates

Calculating Effective Duration

The effective (sometime called option-adjusted) duration formula can be expressed as

$$\text{duration} = \frac{V_{-} - V_{+}}{2(V_0)(\Delta y)} \qquad \text{(Equation } \mathbf{16\text{-}8}\text{)}$$

where

•y = change in yield in decimals, e.g.100 basis points is 0.01
V_0 = initial price
V_- = price if yield declines by •y
V_+ = price if yield increases by •y

Example 16-12: Duration

Consider the bond in Example 16-11. The table of price changes due to changes in yields is given. Take •y = 50 basis points for the bond at a 6.50% yield, when the price is 105.2097.

$$\text{duration} = \frac{V_{-} - V_{+}}{2(V_0)(\Delta y)} = \frac{(107.0197 - 103.4370)}{2(105.2097)(0.005)} = 3.4053$$

This measure says that the price of the bond will change by 3.4053% for a 100 basis points change. At the yield of 7.50% the price is $101.7007 (a 3.3352% change) and at 5.50% the price is $108.8679 (a 3.4771% change). Note that the price increase is larger which agrees with the characteristics of positive convexity.

LOS 16-1-C-g	**compute** the approximate percentage price change for a bond, given the bond's effective duration and a specified change in yield

We can also compute the approximate percentage price change, given the duration measure and the change in the yield. The formula:

Approx. percentage price change = - duration x •y x 100 (Equation **16-9**)

where

•y = change in yield in decimals

Example 16-13: Approximate percentage price change

Using the bond in Example 16-12, let us take a 25 basis point change in yield, then

Approx. percentage price change = - 3.4053 x 0.0025 x 100
= 0.8513%

The prices in the table show a 0.8469% change for a 25 bp increase and a 0.8557% change for 25bp decrease, therefore Equation 16-9 gives a good approximation of the price change.

LOS 16-1-C-h	**distinguish** among modified duration, effective (or option-adjusted) duration, and Macaulay duration

Types of Duration

We need to distinguish between the different types of duration.

Modified duration assumes no changes in the expected cash flows.

Effective duration can be used for bonds which have embedded options. At Level I we do not cover the model for valuing V_- and V_+ when there are uncertain cash flows due to options; we simply apply the formula **(Equation 16-8)** to an option-free bond.

The relationship between the Macaulay (generic) duration and the modified duration is as follows:

$$\text{Modified duration} = \frac{\text{Macaulay duration}}{(1 + \text{yield}/k)}$$

(Equation 16-10)

where

k =number of periods, or payments, per year

Macaulay duration is defined to be the weighted-average time to receive the cash flows, the weighting being the present values of the cash flows as a percentage of the bond's full price.

$$\text{Macaulay duration} = \sum_{i=1}^{n} \frac{t \times PVCF_t}{k \times \text{Price}}$$

(Equation **16-11)**

where

k	=	number of periods, or payments, per year
n	=	number of periods until maturity
t	=	period in which the cash flow is expected to be received
$PVCF_t$	=	present value of the cash flow in period t discounted at the yield to maturity
Price	=	bond's price (total present values of all cash flows)

(**Note** - the LOS suggests that you are probably not required to memorize Equation 16-11).

The difference in the duration calculation between the **modified duration** and **effective duration** of bonds with embedded options can be dramatic.

The book mentions two examples: a callable bond could have a modified duration of 5 but an effective duration of 3, while a CMO could have a modified duration of 7 and an effective duration of 20!

LOS 16-1-C-i	**explain** why effective duration, rather than modified duration or Macaulay duration, should be used to measure the interest rate risk for bonds with embedded options

Effective duration is considered a better measure since it takes into account the expected alteration of cash flows due to a change in yields.

Duration has been described in more than one way:

1. Interest rate sensitivity
2. First derivative of the price-yield function of the bond
3. The weighted-average number of years to receiving the present value of the cash flows

The most important interpretation is point (1) above which tells investors the effect of changing interest rates on the value of their investments. The other interpretations are mathematical concepts and often not valid for more complex instruments.

For example, certain derivative instruments such as an interest-only security might have a duration measure of -4. This implies that for a 100 basis points rate increase the price of the bond will increase by 4%. A weighted-average number of years calculation cannot explain negative duration.

LOS 16-1-C-j	**describe** why duration is best interpreted as a measure of a bond's or portfolio's sensitivity to changes in interest rates

Let us look at how each of the three descriptions of duration can be applied:

1. A portfolio duration of 4.5 indicates that the value of your portfolio will change by approximately 4.5% when interest rates change by 1% or 100 basis points.
2. A portfolio duration of 4.5 is the first derivative of the price-yield function, or slope of the price-yield curve, for the bonds in the portfolio.
3. A portfolio duration of 4.5 means that the weighted-average number of years to receive the present value of the portfolio's cash flows is 4.5 years.

The first interpretation obviously makes better practical sense in investment analysis although there is nothing wrong conceptually with the other two.

LOS 16-1-C-k **compute** the duration of a portfolio, given the duration of the bonds comprising the portfolio

The duration of a portfolio is the *weighted average* of the durations of each of the bonds comprising the portfolio where the weighting is the market values. The calculation can be mathematically expressed as follows:

$$D_P = w_1D_1 + w_2D_2 + w_3D_3 + ... + w_kD_k \qquad \text{(Equation 16-12)}$$

where

w_i =market value of bond i/market value of the portfolio

D_i =duration of bond i

k =number of bonds in the portfolio

Example 16-14: Portfolio duration

Given bonds with the following market values:

	Market price	Par Amount	Market Value	Duration
Bond A	98.825	$1 million	$ 988,250.00	5.5
Bond B	100.250 $	2 million	$2,005,000.00	7.8
Bond C	104.500 $	1 million	$1,045,000.00	9.3
			$4,038,250.00	

The portfolio duration = ($988,250/$4,038,250) x 5.5 + ($2,005,000/$4,038,250) x 7.8 + ($1,045,000/$4,038,250) x 9.3 = 1.35 + 3.87 + 2.41 = 7.63

LOS 16-1-C-l **explain** the limitations of the portfolio duration measure

A critical assumption made when using Equation 16-12 for the portfolio duration is that the yields of all the bonds must change by the same amount. In other words, the yield curve makes a parallel shift. In reality the yields of bonds in a portfolio do not move in parallel.

Different yield changes will affect individual bonds differently so a single duration measure is not sufficient to explain interest rate sensitivity.

LOS 16-1-C-m **discuss** the convexity measure of a bond

Convexity

An important concept is presented here: **convexity**, which explains the non-linear behavior of the interest rate sensitivity (duration) for large moves in interest rates.

If we look at the example in LOS 16-1-C-c, the price of the bond for 150 and 250 basis points moves are:

Yield	Price	Price change	Percent change
9.00	96.7021	-8.5076	-8.0863
8.00	100.0	-5.2097	-4.9517
6.51	105.1739	-0.0358	-0.0340
6.50	105.2097	-	-
6.49	105.2455	0.0358	0.0340
5.00	110.7552	6.5455	5.2709
4.00	114.6510	9.4413	8.9738

Had the price movement been linear, the bond prices at 9.00% yield would have been 96.2597 and at 4% would have been 114.1597.

The difference can be explained by the

$$\text{convexity} = \frac{V_+ + V_- - 2V_0}{2V_0(\Delta y)^2} \qquad \text{(Equation 16-13)}$$

where

•y = change in yield in decimals
V_0 = initial price
V_- = price if yield declines by •y
V_+ = price if yield increases by •y

From our example above

$$\text{Convexity measure} = \frac{107.0197 + 103.4370 - 2(105.2097)}{2(105.2097)(0.005)^2}$$

= 7.0906

LOS 16-1-C-n	**estimate** a bond's percentage price change, given the bond's duration and convexity measure and a specified change in interest rates

How do we use the convexity measure to adjust the percentage price change?

Convexity adjustment to percentage price change
$= \text{Convexity measure} \times (\bullet y)^2 \times 100$ (Equation **16-14**)

Examples 16-15: Convexity adjustment

1. From the data above when yields move from 6.5% to 4%,

Estimated change using duration	$-3.4053 \times -0.025 \times 100$	= 8.5133
Convexity adjustment:	$7.0906 \times (.025)^2 \times 100$	= 0.4432
Total estimated percentage price change		= 8.9565

This is close to the observed 8.9738% change in the above price table.

2. Another example of the total estimated price change in percentage terms is:

Duration = 4.5670%
Convexity = 81.0935
Yield increases by 300 basis points

Estimated change using duration	$-4.5670 \times 0.03 \times 100$	= -13.7010
Convexity adjustment:	$81.0935 \times (.03)^2 \times 100$	= 7.2984
Total estimated percentage price change		= -6.4026

In this case convexity is large and we are considering a big move in interest rates, therefore the convexity adjustment is significant.

Convexity measures are not quoted in a standard scaling, namely they may be derived from slightly different formulas although they convey the same concept. Convexity measures are meaningful only in the context of an adjustment to the price change. Bonds that exhibit '**price compression**' have negative convexity measures.

LOS 16-1-C-o **differentiate** between modified convexity and effective convexity

Analogous to that of the duration, convexity can take either form of **modified** or **effective** convexity. Effective convexity is applicable when the cash flows are expected to change when the yield changes.

LOS 16-1-C-p **compute** the price value of a basis point (PVBP), and explain its relationship to duration

The **price value of a basis point** (PVBP), also called the **dollar value of a 01** (DV01), is the absolute value of the change in the price of a bond for a 1 basis point change in yield.

Example 16-16: Price value of a basis point

Given an initial price of 125.3900 of a bond having duration of 20.9994, the PVBP is

$20.9994 \times 0.0001 \times 125.3900 = \$0.2633$

The relationship is straight forward. Dollar duration is based on 1% or 100 basis point change while PVBP is on 0.01% or one basis point. PVBP is simply a special case of dollar duration as described in Session 15.

16-1-C View Concept Check Questions Workbook

STUDY SESSION 17

Asset Valuation

Derivative Investments

Overview

This is a long Study Session and provides an introduction to the characteristics and pricing of the main types of derivatives – forwards, futures, options and swaps. Some of the calculations are reasonably demanding but candidates should make every attempt to comprehend the material and make the necessary calculations. Derivatives are a key topic and will be important at Level II and III when you will explore further how they are used by managers to hedge risk or alter risk–return characteristics of portfolios to meet client objectives.

The first Reading is a general overview of derivatives; all the concepts are revisited in later Readings. The next four Readings examine the characteristics of forwards, futures, options and swaps in more detail and candidates will become familiar with the main contracts based on different underlying assets. The final Reading looks at how options can be used to manage risk.

Reading Assignments

Analysis of Derivatives for the CFA® Program, Don Chance (AIMR, 2003)

17-1-A. "Derivative Markets and Instruments," Ch. 1

17-1-B. "Forward Markets and Contracts," Ch. 2, pp. 25-37

17-1-C. "Futures Markets and Contracts," Ch. 3, pp. 81-103

17-1-D. "Option Markets and Contracts," Ch. 4, pp. 159-194

17-1-E. "Swap Markets and Contracts," Ch. 5, pp. 269-285

17-1-F. "Risk Management Applications of Option Strategies," Ch. 7, pp. 411-429

17-1-A "Derivative Markets and Instruments"

Introduction

This is very much an introductory chapter which looks briefly at the two categories of derivatives, forward contracts and contingent claims, and how they are traded, OTC or on an exchange. It gives an introduction to the terminology used in forwards, futures, swaps and options markets and outlines the main concepts. All of the terms are covered in more detail later in the Study Session.

LOS 17-1-A-a	**define** a derivative

Definition of a derivative

A derivative is a financial instrument that provides a return that depends on the price of another underlying asset.

A derivative has a finite life and usually the payoff or return on the derivative is decided at the expiry date.

LOS 17-1-A-b	**differentiate** between exchange-traded and over-the-counter derivatives

Exchange-traded derivatives have standard terms and are dealt in an organized derivatives market or exchange. Over-the-counter derivatives are ones which are traded between two parties outside the exchange.

LOS 17-1-A-c	**define** a forward commitment and identify the types of forward commitments

Derivatives are either forward contracts or contingent claims. Forward contracts or commitments are ones where two parties agree to do a transaction at a later date at a price decided at the start. We will look at exchange-traded contracts which are called futures contracts and over-the-counter contracts which consist of forward contracts and swaps.

LOS 17-1-A-d	**describe** the basic characteristics of forward contracts, futures contracts, and swaps

Forward Commitments

Forward contract - a contract is agreed at one point in time, the performance is in line with the terms of the contract and settlement occurs at a subsequent time. The forward contracts discussed are ones which involve an exchange of one asset for another with the price agreed in the initial contract.

Forwards are often non-standardized contracts and are traded in unregulated markets, so the parties bear the counterparty risk i.e. that the party who bears a loss as a result of the transaction defaults on the payment.

Futures contract – futures are a form of forward contract since one party agrees to accept or deliver an underlying asset, or cash equivalent, to another party, at a future expiration date, at a price determined at the beginning of the contract. A futures contract differs from a forward contract since it has standardized contract terms and is traded through an exchange. The contract is effectively guaranteed by the **clearinghouse** (a financial institution associated with the futures exchange), a deposit (margin) must be deposited at the clearinghouse by futures traders.

Swap – this is an agreement between two parties (the counterparties) to exchange a series of cash flows over a period of time (the **tenor**) in the future. It is effectively a series of forward contracts. These cash flows are often dependent on exchange rates (**currency swaps**) or interest rates (**interest rate swaps**). The swap market is largely unregulated and parties must take into account counterparty risk.

LOS 17-1-A-e **define** a contingent claim and **identify** the types of contingent claims

Contingent Claims

Whereas a forward contract is bonding on both parties the other category of derivatives is contingent claims. They are often referred to as options and here a payoff occurs only if a specific event takes place.

LOS 17-1-A-f **describe** the basic characteristics of options and **distinguish** between an option to buy (call) and an option to sell (put)

Options - these are either call options or put options. The holder has the right to buy (a call option) or sell (a put option) an underlying asset at a pre-specified price (the **exercise price** or **strike price**) up to/at a certain date. It is important to differentiate between a future where the holder has the obligation to buy or sell and an option where the holder has the choice whether to buy or sell. The seller of the option is the **option writer**, he/she receives a payment from the buyer but is obliged to buy or sell the underlying asset if the holder of the option wishes to do so. The payment is the option price, sometimes called the **option premium.**

An option can be either exchange-listed or over-the-counter. If they are exchange-listed they are standardized contracts and guaranteed by the exchange, whereas with over-the-counter options there is the possibility that one party will default.

Several types of financial instruments containing options and are forms of contingent liabilities. These include convertible bonds where the holder can decide whether to participate in a rise in the underlying stock price, callable bonds where the issuer can buy back the bond prior to maturity and asset-backed securities where the borrower holds a prepayment option.

LOS 17-1-A-g **discuss** the purposes and criticisms of derivative markets

Purposes of derivative markets

1. Price discovery
   Futures prices provide useful information on the price of the underlying asset (the current price of the underlying asset is called the **spot** price). A short-term futures price is sometimes used as a proxy for the spot price.
   Options prices provide information about the volatility of the underlying security.
2. Risk management
   An important use of derivatives is to control risk including removing certain types of risk from investment.
3. Market completeness
   This means that all potential payoffs can be obtained by trading securities available in the market. The inclusion of derivatives in a market adds to the different risk/return combinations available.
4. Speculation
   Taking on risk in pursuit of additional profit.
5. Trading efficiency
   Investing in a derivative can be a more attractive alternative then investing in the underlying instrument, this might be a result of greater liquidity or lower transaction costs in the derivatives market.

Criticisms of derivative markets

- Many of the criticisms of derivatives stem from their complexity, which leads to commentators misunderstanding their role, or investors purchasing derivatives without understanding the risks involved.
- Derivatives are often seen as legalized gambling. This is an unfair criticism since derivatives have the benefit of making financial markets work better and provide a means for people to manage risk, whereas it is difficult to argue that gambling improves society as a whole.

LOS 17-1-A-h **explain** the concept of arbitrage and the role it plays in determining prices and in promoting market efficiency

An **arbitrage** is when it is possible to trade and generate a risk less profit, without needing to make an investment. This opportunity might occur if the same security was priced differently in different stock markets or derivatives were mispriced. The text assumes that there are no arbitrage opportunities (the **no-arbitrage principle**) since arbitrage opportunities will not exist in a relatively efficient market.

17-1-A View Concept Check Questions Workbook

17-1-B "Forward Markets and Contracts"

Introduction

We now look one-by-one at the different types of derivatives. We start with forwards, a forward contract is a commitment between two parties to do a transaction at a later date with the price and terms set in advance. It is assumed that no money changes hands at the beginning of the contract. In addition to describing the characteristics of forward contracts and how they are settled candidates need to be familiar with the payments made at expiration on contracts where the underlying is a bond, equity or equity index, interest rate or currency rate.

LOS 17-1-B-a	**discuss** the differences between the positions held by the long and short parties to a forward contract in terms of delivery/settlement and default risk

Long and short parties

A forward agreement is between two parties, one is the buyer (called the long) and the other the seller (the short), who agree to do a transaction at a future date at a specified price. No money changes hands when the agreement is made. A forward transaction locks in the price, so the parties are unaffected by price changes between the date when the contract is agreed and the expiry of the contract.

An example of an investment manager using forwards would be if a manager has to meet redemptions from a fund and will need to sell U.S. securities in two months' time. He could enter into a forward transaction today where he takes a short position thereby locking in the sale price of the securities.

LOS 17-1-B-b	**describe** the procedures for settling a forward contract at expiration

Expiration

On expiry of the contract there are two ways that the parties can settle.

Delivery, the long accepts delivery of the underlying asset and pays the agreed price to the short.
Cash settlement, the long and short exchange the net payment, the difference between the agreed price and the current price of the underlying asset. These contracts are called nondeliverable forwards.

In either case both parties are subject to default risk, the party who has made a profit bears the risk that the other party does not settle.

LOS 17-1-B-c	**discuss** how a party to a forward contract can terminate a position prior to expiration and how credit risk is affected by the way in which a position is terminated

Termination of a contract

Usually both parties enter into a forward contract on the basis that they will hold it through to expiry. However there are situations where one party will wish to terminate the contract prior to expiry. The party can go into the market and enter into an offsetting contract. For example if the party who wishes to terminate the contract had a long position they could enter into a new contract with the same underlying asset and expiry date, this time taking the short position. This will remove the net exposure to the asset.

Alternatively the party could look at entering into a second contract with the same party to avoid having two sets of counterparty risk outstanding. In this case the contracts will be cancelled and the parties will exchange the present value of the value of the contract at expiry.

Example 17-1: Terminating contracts

An investor has a long position to purchase an asset at $100. He decides he wishes to terminate the contract but the prices in the forward market have moved and when he takes a short position to deliver the same asset at the same expiry date the price is $105. If he takes on the short position then at expiry the investor will pay $100 for the asset (if it is for delivery) and sell the asset for $105, netting a profit of $5.

If the short position was taken with the same counterparty they would cancel the contracts and the investor receive the present value of $5.

LOS 17-1-B-d	**differentiate** between a dealer and an end user of a forward contract

The two types of participants in the forward markets are dealers and end users. The dealers are usually major investment banks. The end user may simply be taking a position in a market or asset in anticipation of a price move but more often they are using forwards to hedge out the risk of an existing position. The end user will go into the market and look for the best bid-ask prices being quoted by dealers. The dealer is taking on the risk from the end user, they will in turn try to pass on this risk by entering into another derivative or spot transaction, with another end user or with another dealer. The dealer is aiming to make a profit on the spread between the different prices that he is quoting in the market.

LOS 17-1-B-e	**describe** the characteristics of equity forward contracts

We now look at the different types of forward contracts, they are categorized on the basis of the underlying asset to the contract.

Equity forwards

These are contracts for the purchase of individual stocks, a portfolio of stocks or a stock index.

Example 17-2: Equity forward

An investment manager wishes to gain $1,000,000 exposure to the S&P Index but will not have cash available in the fund for another 3 months. She decides to lock in the purchase price today and takes a long position in a forward contract. The price given by the dealer for the contract is 1150. If, at expiry, of the contract the index has fallen by 5% to 1092.50, the manager will need to pay the dealer (assuming cash settlement) $1,000,000 x 0.05 = $50,000.

Equity forwards make payments based on the return of the index or price movement of the stock, which does not include dividends, unless a total return index is specifically referred to.

LOS 17-1-B-f	**describe** the characteristics of forward contracts on zero-coupon and coupon bonds

Bond forwards

A forward contract on a bond or bond index is similar to an equity forward. However there are some differences, a forward contract on a bond must expire before the bond matures and a forward contract must specify what happens if a bond defaults (and how a default is defined). Also if a bond has an embedded option or convertibility this must be considered in the terms of the contract.

If we look at the forward contract for a risk-free zero-coupon bond, in this case a Treasury bill, the prices are quoted in terms of the discount rate. The interest is deducted from the face value of the bill and is calculated based on a 360-day year (e.g. if a 180-day T-bill is selling at a discount of 3%, its price will be $1.00 – 0.03(180/360) = $0.985.

Forward contracts on coupon bond prices are usually quoted with accrued interest, and prices are often quoted by stating the yield.

LOS 17-1-B-g **explain** the characteristics of the Eurodollar time deposit market
LOS 17-1-B-h **define** LIBOR and Euribor

Before we look at interest rate forwards (called forward rate agreements or FRAs) we need to examine the underlying interest rates.

Eurodollar time deposits

The main instrument used for time deposits is the Eurodollar, which is a dollar deposited outside the U.S., the main market for Eurodollar time deposits is in London. Banks borrow from each other and the lending rate is called the London Interbank Offer Rate (LIBOR). Interest rates are based on a 360-day year but interest is added-on to the face value (unlike the discount method used for T-bills). If a bank borrows $1,000,000 at 3% for 180 days they will need to repay $1,000,000 + 0.03(180/360) = $1,015,000.

Rates are also quoted for other currencies including Euroyen and Eurosterling. Euribor and the less commonly used EuroLIBOR are interest rates on euro deposits.

LOS 17-1-B-i **describe** the characteristics of forward rate agreements (FRAs)
LOS 17-1-B-j **calculate** the payment at expiration of an FRA and **explain** each of the component terms

This is a contract where the underlying is an interest rate payment made in US dollars or another currency at a relevant rate for that currency. In this case the party with the long position will benefit if rates rise and the short position will lose.

The payoff is calculated based on the difference between the underlying rates adjusted for the number of days the instrument has to maturity, which is then discounted back to reflect the fact that the payment is be made at expiry. The formula for the payoff for the party with the long position is

$$\text{Notional Principal} \times \frac{[(\text{underl. rate at expiry} - \text{forward contract rate})(\text{days in underl. rate}/360)]}{[1 + \text{underl. rate at expiry (days in underlying rate}/360)]} \qquad \textbf{(Equation 17-1)}$$

Example 17-3: FRA

A dealer quotes on a 90-day FRA, where the underlying is 180-day dollar LIBOR, at a rate of 4%. The end user is looking for rates to fall and takes a short position, with a notional principal of $1 million.

At expiration the rate on 180-day LIBOR is 5%. To calculate the payoff use Equation 17-1.

$$\$1,000,000\left[\frac{(0.05-0.04)(180/360)}{1+0.05(180/360)}\right]=\$1,000,000\left(\frac{0.005}{1.025}\right)=\$4,878$$

The end user pays $4,878 to the dealer, his anticipation that rates would fall was incorrect.

FRAs are available for a number of different maturities; non-standard contracts are called *off the run.* The FRA market uses terminology that refers to the periods in months, a n x m contract expires in n months and the interest is paid on the underlying time deposit m months after the initial contract. So in the Example 17-3 the contract is 3 x 9, it is a 90-day contract and the interest calculated on an underlying deposit maturing 90 + 180 days from the initial contract.

LOS 17-1-B-k **describe** the characteristics of currency forward contracts

Currency forwards

Currency forwards are widely used in the investment business and also by banks and corporations to manage currency risk.

Example 17-4: Currency forward

A French manufacturer will receive US$500,000 from a customer in six months' time, but wishes to lock in the exchange rate that it uses to convert the dollars into euro. They go to a dealer who quotes a six-month forward rate of $1.10, this would allow the manufacturer to convert US$500,000 to 454,545.45. Of course if the US dollar weakens over the six months the manufacturer will have benefited from locking into the rate, but if the US dollar strengthens they would still have to settle at the relatively unfavorable rate agreed in the contract.

17-1-B View Concept Check Questions Workbook

17-1-C "Futures Markets and Contracts"

Introduction

We next turn to futures contracts which are in many ways similar to forward contracts except that they are exchange traded and have standardized contracts. This has some important implications including the requirement for an investor using futures to deposit margin. Candidates will be expected to know the characteristics of futures contracts and be able to compute margin payments and the pricing of different types of contract.

LOS 17-1-C-a	**identify** the institutional features that distinguish futures contracts from forward contracts
LOS 17-1-C-b	**describe** the characteristics of futures contracts

Futures versus forwards

A futures contract is dealt on a recognized exchange and there are a number of ways in which futures and forwards differ:

1. A forward transaction is a private transaction whereas a futures transaction is reported to the futures exchange, the clearing house and often a regulatory authority.
2. A forward transaction is customized whereas in a futures transaction all the terms (expiry, underlying asset etc.), with the exception of the price, are set by the exchange.
3. Since futures contracts are standardized they can be traded more easily in the secondary market making them more liquid than forward cataracts.
4. The clearinghouse of a futures exchange guarantees that trades settle, by acting as the counterparty to both sides of a futures transaction. In a forward transaction each party takes on the risk that the other party will default.
5. A futures contract is **marked to market**, also called daily settlement, which means that gains and losses to each party's position is calculated daily and credited or debited to their account.
6. In most markets futures contracts are regulated by the government.

An exchange will set the expiration dates; these are often set at three month intervals, eg. March, June, September and December. Many contracts are only available for a maximum period of one year, although some are for longer. The exchange also sets which specific day of the month is the expiry day.

In the U.S., trading of futures in an exchange takes place in the trading **pit** by a system of open outcry or by electronic trading. The hours of trading, the contract size and the minimum price movement are also set by the exchange.

As in the case of forward transactions, a party to a futures transaction takes either a long or short position. If a party wishes to close or terminate a position prior to expiry they can enter the market and do an offsetting order (this feature means that futures contract are **fungible**), for example the holder of a long position can go into the market and take a short position in exactly the same contract. Because the clearinghouse acts as the counterparty for the settlement of each transaction the two transactions can be offset.

LOS 17-1-C-c	**differentiate** between margin in the securities markets and margin in the futures markets
LOS 17-1-C-f	**define** initial margin, maintenance margin, variation margin, and settlement price
LOS 17-1-C-g	**describe** the process of marking to market
LOS 17-1-C-h	**compute** the margin balance, given the previous day's balance and the new futures price

Margin Requirements

Margin requirements make the futures market safer since they provide an assurance that traders will be able to meet their financial obligations. This is different to a margin in the securities market which refers to a loan being made.

Before a trader enters into a futures transaction he must deposit funds with a broker. These funds are called the **initial margin**, the dollar amount per contract is usually set by the clearinghouse. This is a deposit against future liabilities and once a transaction is settled it is returned, with interest that has accrued, to the trader.

Each day the contract is marked-to-market. If a trader starts to lose money on a transaction and the value of his equity with the broker falls to the **maintenance margin** level (often around 75% of the initial margin) he will receive a **margin call**, and will need to deposit sufficient funds (the **variation margin**) to bring the account back *to the initial margin level.* This is the process of daily settlement or marking to market. Alternatively if a trader is making profits they can withdraw funds as long as the account's equity value stays above the initial margin.

The clearinghouse collects margin payments from clearing members only, so if a broker is not a member it will clear all trades with a clearing member.

Example 17-5: Margin requirements

The initial margin requirement for a futures contract is $10 which is deposited with the broker. The maintenance margin requirement is $8. A trader takes a long position in 100 contracts. Assuming no excess margin is withdrawn, the table below shows the margin position as the futures price moves.

Day	Beginning balance in margin account	Additional funds deposited in the margin account	Futures price	Gain/loss (futures price change x 100 contracts)	Ending balance
0	0	$1,000	$10		$1,000
1	$1,000	0	$12	$200	$1,200
2	$1,200	0	$9	$300	$900
3	$900	0	$7	$200	$700
4	$700	$300	$8	$100	$1,100
5	$1,100	0	$10	$200	$1,300

Initially the trade deposits $1,000 representing the $10 initial margin for each of the 100 contracts. On day 4 the balance in the margin account has fallen below the maintenance margin level so the trader is required to deposit an additional $300 variation margin to bring it back to the initial margin requirement.

LOS 17-1-C-i **explain** price limits, limit move, limit up, limit down, and locked limit

Limit moves

In some futures markets there are price limits, which is the maximum permitted price move in the day, usually expressed in dollar rather than percentage terms. If the price is stuck at one of the limits it is called a **limit move**. If, for example the price is moving upwards and the maximum permitted price is reached this is called a **limit up**. If a transaction cannot take place because it is stuck at one of the limits this is a **locked limit.**

LOS 17-1-C-d	**describe** how a futures trade takes place
LOS 17-1-C-e	**describe** how a futures position may be closed out (i.e., offset) prior to expiration
LOS 17-1-C-j	**describe** how a futures contract can be terminated by a close-out (i.e., offset) at expiration, delivery, an equivalent cash settlement, or an exchange-for-physicals

Terminating a futures position

A futures contract can be terminated in three ways:

1. Delivery or cash settlement.
2. Offset, a reversing trade where a party sells exactly the same contract that was originally bought (or vice versa).
3. Exchange-for-physicals, two traders privately agree to exchange the physical good underlying the futures transaction prior to the delivery date.

LOS 17-1-C-k	**explain** delivery options in futures contracts

Delivery options

A futures contract can specify cash settlement or delivery. In the case of cash settlement at he expiration day the margin accounts are marked to market. If the contract is for delivery, that actual delivery may take place a number of days after the contract expiration. In some case the holder of the short position will have a choice on the exact asset being delivered and the location of delivery (frequently this is the case with commodity contracts).

LOS 17-1-C-l distinguish among scalpers, day traders, and position traders

Members of a futures exchange

A futures exchange is owned by its members, who hold seats. Each member is acting as a floor trader (called locals) or broker (called futures commission merchants or FCMs).

Floor traders are market makers quoting bid and ask prices for contracts and they provide the liquidity in the market. There are different types of floor traders.

Scalpers – they hold positions in futures for extremely short time periods and attempt to profit from the spread between bid and ask prices.

Day traders – they hold positions longer than a scalper but close out all their positions at the end of each day.

Position traders - they hold positions overnight. Position traders and day traders try to anticipate the direction of the market.

FCMs are executing transactions on behalf of other parties from outside the exchange.

LOS 17-1-C-m describe the characteristics of the following types of futures contracts: Treasury bill, Eurodollar, Treasury bond, stock index, and currency

Financial and currency futures

Treasury bill futures

This is priced based on a 90-day $1,000,000 T-bill. It is priced as a discount instrument (see LOS 17-1-B-f).

The pricing of the futures is

$$1-\left(\frac{\text{rate}}{100}\right)\left(\frac{90}{360}\right) \qquad \textbf{(Equation 17-2)}$$

This is different to the IMM index which is the reported and publicly available price based on 100 minus the rate.

Example 17-6: T-bill future

If the rate priced into the futures contract is 5% then the quoted price is 100 - 5.00 = 95.00. Using Equation 17-2 the actual futures price is

$$\$1{,}000{,}000\left[1-\left(\frac{\text{rate}}{100}\right)\left(\frac{90}{360}\right)\right]=\$1{,}000{,}000\left[1-\left(\frac{5}{100}\right)\left(\frac{90}{360}\right)\right]=\$987{,}500$$

For convenience the IMM price is often used to calculate the gain or loss on a futures position by traders, since every basis point move in the IMM index is equivalent to a $25 move in the futures price (in Example 17-6 it is 500 basis points which is equivalent to $12,500).

Eurodollar futures

See LOS 17-1-B-g for information on LIBOR. The futures contract is based on a $1 million notional principal of 90-day Eurodollars, so in Example 17-6 the price of a Eurodollar future with a rate of 5%, would be the same, $987,500. The quoted price and actual futures price differ as in the case of T-bill futures, note that here we are quoting on a discount interest basis rather than on an add-on basis.

The minimum tick size, or price movement is $25 and there are monthly expirations for the closest two months and then March, June September and December expiry dates.

Treasury bond futures

This is based on delivering a Treasury bond with a maturity of at least fifteen years, and any coupon. If it is callable then the first call date must be more than fifteen years after the delivery date. The holder of the short position has an advantage in that they can select between a number of bonds to deliver, however the exchange adjusts by a conversion factor the amount of money the holder of the long position must pay, it is based on the coupon of the bond being delivered versus a hypothetical 6% coupon bond. Despite the adjustment there will always be a **cheapest-to-deliver** bond, the one where the amount received on delivery exceeds the market price by the largest margin.

Treasury bond futures have quarterly expiry dates. Prices are quoted in points and 32nds, so a price of $96\frac{15}{32}$ is equal to 96.4688.

There are also contracts available on Treasury notes.

Stock index futures

Some of the most popular futures contracts are those quoted on stock market indexes, such as the S&P 500 Stock Index. The price is based on the index level adjusted by a multiplier. For the S&P futures the multiplier is $250, so a futures price of 1,100 gives an actual price of $250 x 1,100 = $275,000.

Stock index futures expire at quarterly intervals although trading is concentrated in the contracts that are closest to expiry.

Currency futures

Different contracts have different sizes and quotations, most expire quarterly. For example the euro contract covers 125,000 and a futures price of $1.1050 is equivalent to a contract price of 125,000 x $1.1050 =$138,125.00.

17-1-C View Concept Check Questions Workbook

17-1-D "Option Markets and Contracts"

Introduction

This Chapter examines options. Options are quite different to forwards and futures since the holder of an option has the right, but not the obligation, to buy or sell an underlying asset. Also the option buyer must pay the option seller for this right or option at the beginning of the contract. In addition to covering definitions and characteristics of options candidates have to be able to calculate option payoffs, understand lower bounds for option prices and put-call parity. Some of the formulas and calculations look somewhat intimidating but the concepts behind the formulas are not difficult and the candidate should attempt to master the concepts to help them memorize the formulae.

LOS 17-1-D-a	**identify** the basic elements and **describe** the characteristics of option contracts

A **call option** gives the holder the right to buy at a pre-specified price (called the **exercise price, strike price** or **striking price**) and a **put option** the right to sell at the exercise price. For example, the owner of a call option has a choice whether to exercise the option or not, whatever they do they pay the price of the option (the **option premium**) and if they decide to exercise the option they must pay the exercise price to the option seller in order to buy the underlying asset. On the other hand the seller, or writer, of the call option keeps the premium but is obliged to sell the underlying asset to the option holder if he decides to exercise the option.

An option has an expiry or **expiration date,** and an option that has not been exercised by this date expires worthless. If the holder of a call option decides to exercise he must pay the exercise price and will be delivered the underlying asset or an equivalent cash sum. If the holder of a put exercises the option he will deliver the underlying asset, or cash equivalent, and receive the exercise price.

Options can be traded on exchanges or over-the-counter. Note that if they are dealt over-the-counter the credit risk is unilateral, only the option writer can default.

The most common exchange traded options in the U.S. are stock options, index options, foreign currency options and options on futures.

LOS 17-1-D-b	**define** European option, American option, moneyness, payoff, intrinsic value, and time value

An **American option** can be exercised at any time prior to or at expiration, a **European option** at expiration only. So for equivalent options, an American option is worth more, since in certain situations it may be advantageous to exercise the option prior to expiry.

A call option is **in-the-money** if the stock price is higher than the exercise price, **out-of-the-money** if the stock price is lower than the exercise price and **at-the-money** if the stock price is equal to the exercise price (and the opposite holds for put options). Options that are far in-the-money are called **deep-in-the-money** and far out-of-the-money are called **deep-out-of-the-money.**

Example 17-7: Moneyness

1. A call option on a stock has an exercise price of $50 and the stock is trading in the market at $55. The option is $5 in-the-money, since the immediate exercise of the option would give a cash inflow of $5 (ignoring transaction costs).

2. A put option on a stock has an exercise price of $30 and the stock is trading in the market at $35. The option is $5 out-of-the-money.

Intrinsic value

The value of a call option at expiry is either zero or the stock price (S) minus the exercise price (X). This is the **intrinsic value** of the option, the value of the option if it was exercised immediately. If the intrinsic value is positive the option is in-the-money, if it is zero then the option is out-of-the-money or at-the-money.

A put option will have a value at expiration of Max [0, (X– S)], this is the intrinsic value. Prior to expiration an option will usually trade at a market price above its intrinsic value, the difference between the price and the intrinsic value is the **time value**.

LOS 17-1-D-c	**differentiate** between exchange-traded options and over-the-counter options

Over-the-counter options

These are customized contracts (price, exercise price, time to expiry etc are decided by the two parties), and the parties are usually institutional rather than retail investors. The option buyer runs the risk the writer will default, and sometimes will require collateral. The markets are essentially unregulated.

Exchange-traded options

The exchange standardizes all the terms of the option contract, only the price is decided by the participants. Usually there are options available with an exercise price close to the trading price of the underlying asset.

The exchange decides which companies (in the case of stock options) will be listed for options trading. The participants in the exchange are usually either market makers or brokers.

As in the case of futures the transactions are guaranteed by the clearing house. The clearing house also has to protect itself against the writers defaulting so the premium paid is deposited in the option writer's margin account and the writer must deposit additional money in the account. The amount will depend on whether the option is in or out-of-the money and whether the writer has hedged the risk.

Since the contracts have standardized terms an option holder can go to the market and sell

the same contract and the positions will be cancelled.

Generally at expiry an in-the-money option will be exercised and out-of-the-money options will expire unexercised. Most exchange-traded options require actual delivery of the stock rather than cash settlement, in this case the decision to exercise will take into account the transaction costs involved with trading the stock or settling in cash.

LOS 17-1-D-d	**identify** the different types of options in terms of the underlying instruments

Financial options

We now look at the different types of financial options available. They are categorized in terms of the underlying instrument.

Stock options

These are options (sometimes called equity options) on individual stocks and are popular in the market.

Index options

These are options on stock indices, such as the S&P 500 Index, which are for cash settlement (based on a multiplier times the index level).

Bond options

Bond options are not popular with the retail investor and most of the trading is between institutions in the over-the-counter market. They can be for actual delivery or for cash settlement and would be based on a notional principal which is quoted terms of the face value of the bond.

Example 17-8: Bond options

An investor buys a call option with $10 million face value on a bond with an exercise price of $1.02 per $1.00 par value. The expiration day must be well before the maturity date of the bond. If the buyer of the call option exercises it when the bond price is $1.04 then the seller pays the buyer (1.04 – 1.02)$10,000,000 which equals $200,000, if it is cash settlement.

LOS 17-1-D-e	**compare** and **contrast** interest rate options to forward rate agreements (FRAs)
LOS 17-1-D-f	**explain** how option payoffs are determined, and **show** how interest rate option payoffs differ from the payoffs of other types of options

Interest rate options

We will consider options on LIBOR as an example of interest rate options. Note that there is not an underlying financial instrument but an interest rate that is used to calculate the payoff.

First of all let us look back at LOS 17-1 when we discussed FRAs. In the case of FRAs the payoff is based on the discounted spot rate of a LIBOR payment. Interest rate options are options where the underlying asset is an interest rate so rather then exercise price we have an **exercise rate** or **strike rate**. An FRA is a commitment to make and receive an interest rate payment at a later date and the payment is made immediately when the contract expires. An interest rate option is the right to make one interest payment and receive another.

An interest rate call is an option where the holder has the right to make a known interest rate payment and receive an unknown payment, an interest rate put is an option where the holder has the right to make an unknown interest rate payment and receive another known payment. Interest rate options and FRAs have a notional principal. The options are usually European style and settle for cash. They are often dealt in by the same dealers that make prices in FRAs.

The payoff on an interest rate call is given by

Not. principal x [Max (0, underlying rate at expir. – exercise rate)
x (days in underlying rate) 360 **(Equation 17-3)**

Example 17-9: Interest rate options

Using the same data as in Example 17-3, we will now consider an option expiring in 90 days where the underlying is 180-day dollar LIBOR, at an exercise rate of 4% with a notional principal of $1 million.

At expiration the rate on 180-day LIBOR is 5% and the call option is in-the-money. The payoff will be

$$\$1,000,000(0.05-0.04)\left(\frac{180}{360}\right)=\$5,000$$

The payoff is **not** made immediately but in 180 days' time.

LOS 17-1-D-g **define** interest rate caps and floors

When interest rate options are being used for hedging, for example to hedge the risk on a floating rate loan, then the buyer is purchasing a series of interest rate options. This series of call options is called an **interest rate cap**, or a cap. A series of interest rate put options is called an **interest rate floor**, or floor. An interest rate cap is defined as a series of call options on an interest rate, with each option expiring at the date on which the rate on the floating rate loan will be reset, each option has the same exercise rate. Each call option is a **caplet**. Similarly each component of an interest rate floor is a **floorlet**. The price of the interest rate cap or floor is just the sum of the constituent options.

An interest rate collar is a combination of a long cap and short floor or vice versa.

Currency options

A currency option gives the holder the right to buy or sell an underlying currency at a fixed exercise rate, which is an exchange rate.

Example 17-10 Currency options

A U.S. company is going to require 100 million to fund their European operations in six months' time. It is concerned that the euro will strengthen against the US dollar and it decides to buy a call option on the euro, the exercise price is $1.30 per euro.

If the euro expires above $1.30, at say $1.40, then the company exercises its option to buy 100 million at $1.30.

If the euro expires below $1.30, at say $1.20, then the company buys 100 million at the market rate of $1.20 and lets the option lapse.

A call on the euro is equivalent to a put on the dollar. If the dollar declines they can use the option to sell dollars at a rate of 1/1.30 = 0.77. If the dollar rises the company can sell at the market rate.

Options on futures

This is an option where the underlying is a futures contract, a call option gives the holder to go long of the futures at a fixed price and a put option the right to go short. The fixed futures price is the exercise price. There are arbitrage opportunities and in some cases the options are essentially an option on the spot price of the underlying asset (when the options and futures expire on the same date).

Example 17-11 Options on futures

An option is based on a Eurodollar futures contract. An investor buys a call option which has an exercise price of 95.00 and is priced at $6.00. The underlying futures price is 96.00. The contract size is $1 million. So a buyer of the call option pays 0.06 x $1,000,000 = $60,000 for the right to buy the futures contract at a price of 95.00. If, when the option expires, the futures price is 97 the investor would exercise the option and receive a long futures position at a price of 95, since the futures price is 97 his margin account is credited with the difference of 2.00,or 0.02 x (90/360) x $1 million equals $5,000, since the future is based on a 90-day Eurodollar rate. The party on the short side will be charged the $5,000 gain that the long position has made.

LOS 17-1-D-h	**identify** the minimum and maximum values of European options and American options

Option pricing

We now look at the pricing and valuation of options. Options always have a positive value for the holder up until expiration.

The notation used throughout is

S_0, S_T	=	price of underlying asset today, price of underlying asset at time T
X	=	exercise price
r	=	risk-free rate
T	=	time to expiration, expressed as number of days divided by 365
c_0, c_T	=	price of European call option today and at expiry
C_0, C_T	=	price of American call option today and at expiry
p_0, p_T	=	price of European put option today and at expiry
P_0, P_T	=	price of American put option today and at expiry

Looking first at the value at expiration, or the **payoff,** of a long call position we can see that if the underlying price is less than the exercise price, the option will lapse with zero value. If the underlying price is higher than the exercise price then the long call position has a value equal to $(S_T - X)$. The short position will have a value which is the negative of the value of the long position.

At expiration both European and American options have the same payoff, they are the same instruments at this point, so

$$c_T = \text{Max}\ [0, S_T - X] \text{ and } C_T = \text{Max}\ [0, S_T - X] \qquad \textbf{(Equations 17-4)}$$

Example 17-12: Value of a call option at expiration

The value of a call option at expiration, if the exercise price is \$100, is illustrated in the graph below.

If, for example, the stock price is \$110 at expiry the payoff on a long call position is

Max [0, $S_T - X$] = Max [0, \$110 - \$100] = \$10, and for a short call is -\$10.

If the stock price is \$80 the payoff for a long or short call is

Max [0, $S_T - X$] = Max [0, \$80 - \$100] = \$0

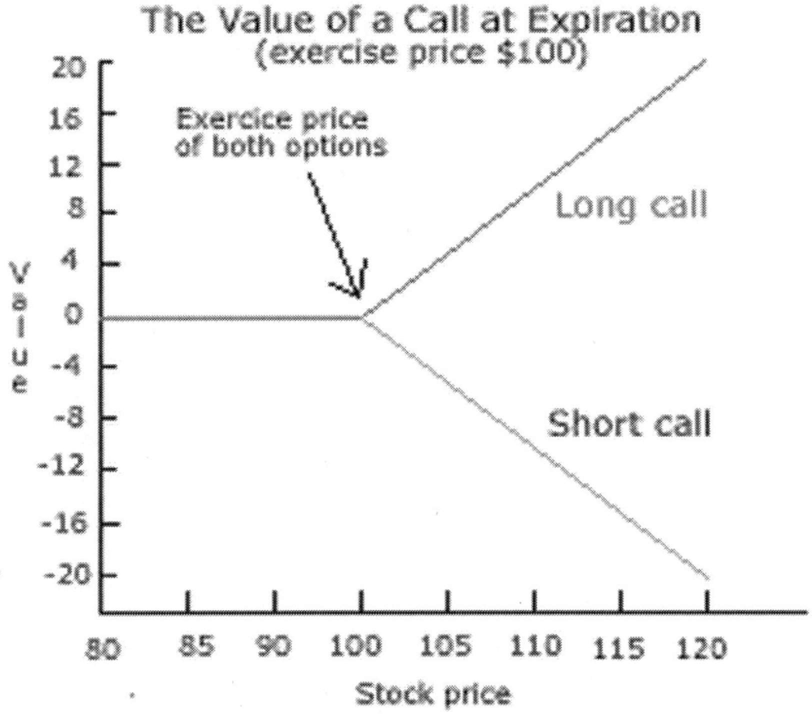

With a put option if the underlying price is higher than the exercise price, the option will lapse with zero value. If the underlying price is lower than the exercise price then the long put position has a value equal to ($X - S_T$). At expiration

$p_T = $ Max [0, $X - S_T$] and $P_T = $ Max [0, $X - S_T$] **(Equations 17-5)**

Example 17-13: Value of a put option at expiration

The value of a put option at expiration when the exercise price is \$100 is illustrated in the graph below.

If the stock price is \$110 at expiry the payoff on a long or short put position is

Max [0, X - S_T] = Max [0, \$100 - \$110] = \$0

If the stock price is \$80 the payoff for a long put is

Max [0, X - S_T] = Max [0, \$100 - \$80] = \$20 and for a short put is -\$20.

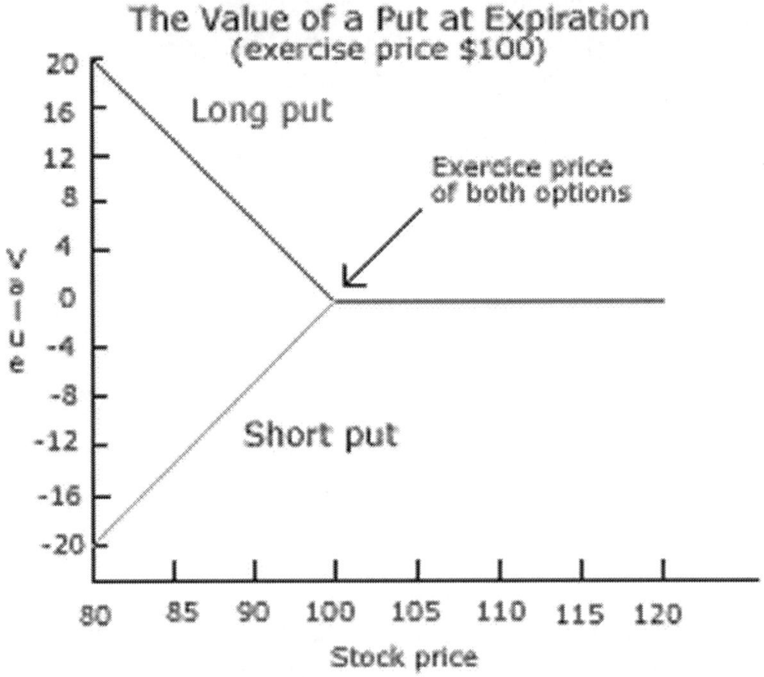

LOS 17-1-D-i	**explain** how the lower bounds of European calls and puts are determined by constructing portfolio combinations that prevent arbitrage, and calculate an option's lower bound
LOS 17-1-D-j	**determine** the lowest prices of European and American calls and puts based on the rules for minimum values and lower bounds

Lower bounds

Since an American option can be exercised at any time the lower bound of its value is its intrinsic value, otherwise it could be exercised for an immediate gain. However for a European option the lower bound is a function of the present value of the exercise price, since we cannot exercise until the expiry date.

so

$c_0 \bullet$ Max $[0, S_0 - X/(1 + r)^T]$ $p_0 \bullet$ Max $[0, X/(1 + r)^T - S_0]$ **(Equations 17-6)**

$C_0 \bullet$ Max $[0, S_0 - X]$ $P_0 \bullet$ Max $[0, X - S_0]$

An American call must always be worth at least as much as a European call so we can say that

$C_0 \bullet$ Max $[0, S_0 - X/(1 + r)^T]$ **(Equation 17-7)**

but the lower bound for an American put is higher than a European put so we cannot adjust the formula for the put which remains, $P_0 \bullet$ Max $[0, X - S_0]$.

Note that the concept of intrinsic value and time value is not strictly applicable for a European call since European calls cannot be exercised until expiry so prior to that the concept of intrinsic value does not exist.

Example 17-14: Lower bounds

Options are available for an underlying asset which has a price of 30, the risk-free rate is 4% and T = 0.25. The lower bounds for calls and puts, with exercise prices of 25 and 35 can be calculated for European and American options as follows:

	European	**American**
X = 25	$c_0 \bullet$ Max $[0, 30 - 25/(1.04)^{0.25}] = 5.24$ $p_0 \bullet$ Max $[0, 25/(1.04)^{0.25} - 30] = 0$	$C_0 \bullet$ Max $[0, 30 - 25/(1.04)^{0.25}] = 5.24$ $P_0 \bullet$ Max $[0, 25 - 30] = 0$
X = 35	$c_0 \bullet$ Max $[0, 30 - 35/(1.04)^{0.25}] = 0$ $p_0 \bullet$ Max $[0, 35/(1.04)^{0.25} - 30] = 4.66$	$C_0 \bullet$ Max $[0, 30 - 35/(1.04)^{0.25}] = 0$ $P_0 \bullet$ Max $[0, 35 - 30] = 5$

LOS 17-1-D-k	**describe** how a portfolio (combination) of options establishes the relationship between options that differ only by exercise price

Exercise Price

Let us consider the case where we have two call options with the same terms except for the exercise prices. The first is a European call with an exercise price X_1 and the second a European call with an exercise price X_2, which is larger than X_1. We will refer to these as $c_0(X_1)$ and $c_0(X_2)$ respectively. If we look at a portfolio where we buy $c_0(X_1)$ and sell $c_0(X_2)$ we can calculate the value at expiration, for the three possible prices of the underlying S_T as follows:

	Value at expiration		
	$S_T \bullet X_1$	$X_1 < S_T < X_2$	$S_T \bullet X_2$
$\mathbf{c_0(X_1) - c_0(X_2) =}$	0	$S_T - X_1$	$S_T - X_1 - (S_T - X_2) = X_2 - X_1$

In all three cases the value is zero or positive, so we can conclude that the value of $c_0(X_1)$ is higher than $c_0(X_2)$.

A call option with a lower exercise price has a higher or equal value to one with a higher exercise price. This holds for both European and American calls.

Using the same methodology we can show that **the value of a put with a higher exercise price has a higher or equal value to one with a lower exercise price.**

LOS 17-1-D-l	**explain** how option prices are affected by the time to expiration of the option

Time to Expiry

Now we look at two call options with the same terms except for the time to expiry. The first is a European call with a time to expiry T_1 and the second a European call with a longer time to expiry T_2. We will refer to these as $c_0(T_1)$ and $c_0(T_2)$ respectively.

When the first option expires it has a value of Max $[0, S_{T1} - X]$ and at this point the call with a longer time to expiry will have a value of at least Max $[0, S_T - X/(1 + r)^{T2-T1}]$, this is worth at least as much as the shorter-term call. The same will be true for American call options.

We have shown that **longer-term calls are worth at least as much as shorter-term calls**. This is intuitively correct, the longer you can hold the option the more chance there is of making money.

For European put options the case is not so clear because if you exercise a put you receive money which can earn interest. However usually a longer-term put will be worth more and all longer–term American put options are worth more than shorter-term ones (which can be exercised at any time so there is no penalty in waiting to expiration).

LOS 17-1-D-m **explain** put-call parity for European options, given the payoffs on a fiduciary call and a protective put

Put-call parity

Next we look at the relationship between call and put options. A **fiduciary call** is defined as a European call option plus a risk-free bond that matures on the expiration day and has a face value equal to the exercise price. We also look at the value of a **protective put** which is a European put plus the underlying asset. We show in the table below that the payoff from a fiduciary call and a protective put is the same whether the underlying price is above or below the exercise price at expiry.

	Value at expiration	
	$S_T \bullet X$	$S_T > X$
$\mathbf{c_0 + X/(1 + r)^T}$	$0 + X = X$	$S_T - X + X = S_T$
$\mathbf{p_0 + S_0}$	$X - S_T + S_T = X$	$0 + S_T = S_T$

Therefore we can see that the fiduciary call and the protective put have the same value, this is called **put-call parity** and it is expressed by the equation:

$$c_0 + X/(1 + r)^T = p_0 + S_0 \qquad \textbf{(Equation 17-8)}$$

Note that this equation only holds for European options, not for American options.

Re-ordering the equation we can see that

$$c_0 = p_0 + S_0 - X/(1 + r)^T$$

The right-hand side of the equation is the equivalent to a call and is referred to as a **synthetic call**. Alternatively we can rewrite the equation as

$$p_0 = c_0 - S_0 + X/(1 + r)^T$$

and the right-hand side is now a **synthetic put.**

Arbitrage opportunities

If Equation 17-8 does not hold there is an opportunity for arbitrage, the side that is overpriced should be sold and the side that is underpriced should be purchased. At expiry a risk-free gain will be realized.

Example 17-15: Put-call parity

A one-year call option exists which is priced at \$5, has an exercise price of \$50 and the underlying is priced at \$45. The one-year risk-free rate is 5%. The put with the same expiry and underlying is priced at \$4.

Using Equation 17-8

$c_0 + X/(1 + r)^T = \$5 + \$50/(1.05) = \$52.62$

$p_0 + S_0 = \$4 + \$45 = \$49.00$

The fiduciary call is overpriced so there is an arbitrage opportunity. We should write the call and borrow sufficient to buy the put and the stock. This will generate a gain of \$3.62 and at expiry there will be no net payout.

LOS 17-1-D-n	**explain** the relationship between American options and European options in terms of the lower bounds on option prices and the possibility of early exercise

Early exercise of American options

Generally it would not be logical to exercise an American option early; it is more attractive to sell the option to another investor than exercise it. By exercising the option you lose the time value of the option and only realize the intrinsic value.

For a call option the exception is if the underlying is making a cash payment such as a dividend or an interest payment. In this case if the dividend is high enough it may be worth more than the time value. In this case the American option is worth more than the European option.

For a put option an example of when it is attractive to exercise early is if the underlying stock's issuer is going bankrupt. In this case it is better to exercise today and be able to earn interest on the proceeds.

LOS 17-1-D-o	**explain** how cash flows on the underlying asset affect put-call parity and the lower bounds of option prices

Cash flows on the underlying asset

In the case that there are cash flows on the underlying assets we need to adjust the lower bounds for option values that were given in Equations 17-6. We need to restate the underlying price by the present value of the cash flows. If we call the present value of the cash flows over the life of the option PV(CF, 0, T)

$$c_0 \bullet \text{Max}\ \{0, [S_0 - PV(CF, 0, T)] - X/(1 + r)^T\}$$ **(Equations 17-9)**

$$p_0 \bullet \text{Max}\ \{0, X/(1 + r)^T - [S_0 - PV(CF, 0, T)]\}$$

LOS 17-1-D-p	**identify** the directional effect of an interest rate change on an option's price

Interest rates

The other factors that influence option prices are interest rates and volatility.

When interest rates increase this will increase call option prices, and decrease put option prices.

This is because when interest rates are high it is relatively more attractive to buy a call option today but delay paying for the underlying to a later date. However if interest rates are high it is relatively more attractive to sell the underlying today (and earn interest on the proceeds) than hold a put option to sell it in the future.

Higher volatility increase option prices since there is a greater possibility of the underlying price rising and the call option holder having an increased profit on the upside, or for a put option the holder having an increased profit due to the downside movement. Volatility is a more critical variable than interest rates in the pricing of options.

17-1-D View Concept Check Questions Workbook

17-1-E "Swap Markets and Contracts"

Introduction

This is the last chapter which examines the characteristics of a specific type of derivative. We look at swaps which are essentially a series of forward rate agreements. The two parties agree to exchange payments, usually at least one party will make a payment which is dependent on a variable such as an interest rate or equity index level. Candidates should be able to calculate the payments for currency, interest rate and equity swaps.

LOS 17-1-E-a **describe** the characteristics of swap contracts

Swap contracts

In a swap agreement tThe counterparties to a swap agree to exchange a sequence of cash flows over a period in the future. One party (or sometimes both parties) is usually agreeing to make payments that depend on the price of a random outcome such as the level of interest rates, currency rates or commodity prices. These payments are referred to as variable or floating. The party paying the floating rate is called the floating- or variable-rate payer, the other party the fixed-rate payer.

Each date when payments are made is called a settlement date and the time between the settlement dates is the **settlemen**t period. If payments are being made in the same currency they will be **netted** off against each other.

The swaps market is virtually unregulated and offers privacy for the counterparties entering into a transaction however the parties take on the risk that the other party defaults on the transaction.

LOS 17-1-E-b **explain** how swaps are terminated

If a party wishes to terminate a swap prior to the termination or expiration date they are a number of alternatives:

- A swap has a market value, this can be calculated and **if** both parties agree, the payment is made by the party holding the negative market value to the other and this will terminate the swap.
- A party can enter in to a separate and offsetting swap agreement with another party. If, for example the party is making floating-rate rate payments, they could enter into another swap where they receive floating-rate payments. This can be designed to eliminate the interest rate risk but default risk will remain with both counterparties.
- The swap could be sold to another party, although they will need the permission of the first counterparty.
- Use a swaption, this is an option to enter a swap agreement, and could be used to enter an offsetting swap agreement.

LOS 17-1-E-c **define** and **give** examples of currency swaps

Currency swaps

In a plain vanilla currency swap each party holds one currency that they wish to convert to the other party's currency. In this case the principal is swapped and then paid back at the end of the tenor of the swap. Each party will pay interest on the currency it received from the other party. The payments can be fixed or floating rate according to the swap agreement, but in a plain vanilla currency swap one party would pay a floating rate on dollars and the other a fixed rate on the foreign currency. Payments might be annual or for a shorter period in which case the number of days between settlement dates is usually divided by 360, eg semi-annual interest is calculated using 180/360. The payments are usually made in arrears.

Example 17-16: Motivation for currency swap

A U.S. company can borrow dollars at 5% in the U.S. but must pay 7% to borrow pounds sterling in the U.K. A U.K. company can borrow pounds sterling at 6½% in the U.K. but must pay 6% to borrow dollars in the U.S. The U.S. company has a comparative advantage in borrowing funds in the U.S. and the U.K. company has a similar comparative advantage in borrowing in the U.K. If the U.S. company needs to borrow pounds sterling and the U.K. company needs to borrow dollars then both companies can benefit from entering into a fixed-for-fixed currency swap. If, for example, the interest rates were agreed at 5½% on the dollars and 6¾% on the pounds sterling this would reduce the cost of borrowing for both parties.

US company	UK company
pays 5% to lender in U.S. for US dollars	pays 6½ % to lender in the U.K. for pounds sterling
swaps US dollars for pounds sterling receives 5½% for dollars from the U.K. company pays 6¾ % for pounds sterling to the U.K. company	swaps pounds sterling for US dollars pays 5½% for dollars to the U.S. company receives 6¾% for pounds sterling from the U.S. company

The Comparative Advantage Fixed-for-Fixed Currency Swap
(Exchange of Currencies at Initiation)

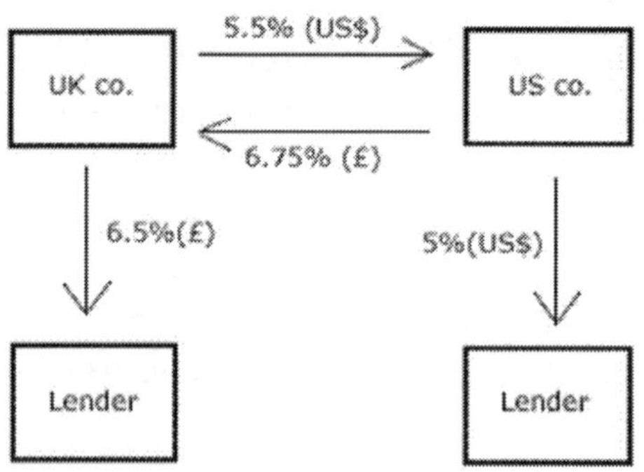

LOS 17-1-E-d calculate the payments on a currency swap

Here we look at an example where two parties are effectively exchanging a fixed-rate loan in US dollars to a fixed-rate loan in Swiss Francs. There are many variations on this type of swap, for example floating-rate interest rates could have been used.

Example 17-17: Currency swap payments

Two parties, X and Y, enter into a three-year plain vanilla currency swap agreement with a principal of $10,000,000. X wants to borrow dollars and Y wants to borrow Swiss Francs. The exchange rate when the agreement is signed is $1 = SF 1.70 and U.S. interest rates are fixed at LIBOR, which is 5%. The interest rate to be paid on the Swiss Francs is fixed at the one-year Swiss Franc rate which is 3%. After one-year LIBOR moves up to 6½% and at the end of the second year to 7%. Payments would be as follows:

Year	X pays Y	Y pays X
0	SFr 17,000,000	$10,000,000
1	5% x $10,000,000 = $500,000	3% x SFr 17,000,000 = SFr 510,000
2	6½% x $10,000,000 = $650,000	3% x SFr 17,000,000 = SFr 510,000
3	$10,000,000 + (7% x $10,000,000) = $10,700,000	SFr 17,000,000 + (3% x SFr 17,000,000) = SFr 17,510,000

This could be illustrated by a box and arrow diagram as shown below:

LOS 17-1-E-e define and give an example of a plain vanilla interest rate swap

Interest rate swaps

In a plain vanilla interest rate swap one party agrees to pay a series of fixed-rate interest rate payments and the other party to pay a series of floating rate payments, over a period of time called the **tenor** of the swap. The payments are based on the interest rate calculated on a **notional principal**. The notional principal does *not* change hands.

Payments are usually determined in advance and paid **in-arrears**, this means that the floating-rate payments are decided by the floating rate benchmark (e.g. LIBOR) at the previous settlement date. Usually only the difference between the two payments, the **net payment**, is made.

LOS 17-1-E-f	**calculate** the payments on an interest rate swap

In this example we look at a plain vanilla swap where the payments are the same as if party A had issued a fixed-rate bond and party B a floating-rate bond.

Example 17-18: Interest rate swap payments

Two parties, A and B, enter into a three-year plain vanilla interest rate swap agreement. A agrees to pay a fixed rate of 10% the LIBOR rate and B agrees to pay the LIBOR rate a fixed rate of 10%, on a notional principal of $10 million. LIBOR was 11% when the agreement was signed, stands at 10% at the end of the first year, and stands at 9% at the end of the second year. If payments are made in arrears the payments will be as follows:

Year	LIBOR	A pays 10% fixed rate	B pays LIBOR	Net payment
0	11%			
1	10%	$1,000,000	$1,100,000	B pays A $100,000
2	9%	$1,000,000	$1,000,000	no payment
3	n/a	$1,000,000	$900,000	A pays B $100,000

This could also be illustrated by the cash flow diagram shown below:

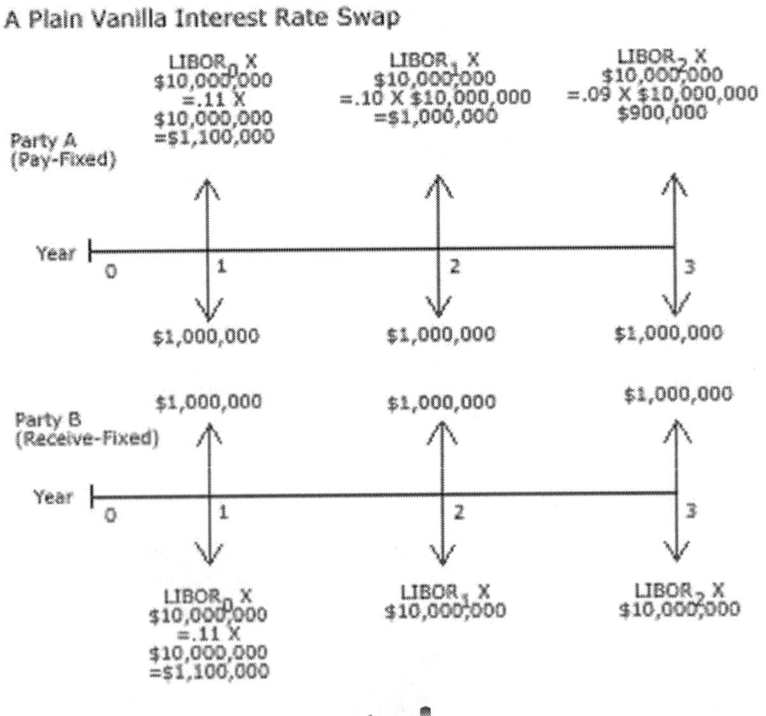

LOS 17-1-E-g **define** and **give** examples of equity swaps

Equity swaps

In this case the variable is the return on a stock or stock index. Since the return from a stock can be negative we could have one party paying a fixed rate plus an equity-related payment. Another difference between equity swaps and interest rate and currency swaps is that the stock prices are only known at the end of the settlement period. Equity swaps are often structured to include both dividends and capital gains.

LOS 17-1-E-h **calculate** the payments on an equity swap

Equity swaps are often used by investment managers to adjust their exposure to an equity market without having to buy or sell the underlying securities.

Insert chart on page 618

Example 17-19: Equity swap payments

ABC Asset Management are running a fund whose returns are linked to the performance of the S&P Index. They have a US$100 million cash inflow and they decide to use a swap agreement to gain exposure to the market. They enter into a one-year agreement with XYZ investment bank where XYZ agree to pay the return on the S&P Total Return Index and ABC will pay a fixed rate of 5% on a notional principal of US$100 million. The payments are to be made quarterly with the first payment on the last day in March and the payments will be based on the actual day count/365 basis.

The S& P Index return is calculated over each quarter (based on the change between the beginning and end of the quarter) and the payments are calculated as follows

Year	ABC pays 5% fixed rate	S&P Index return	XYZ pays	Net payment
March 31st	\$100m x 5% x 90/365 = \$1,232,877	+10%	\$10,000,000	XYZ pays \$8,767,123
June 30th	\$100m x 5% x 91/365 = \$1,246,575	+3%	\$3,000,000	XYZ pays \$1,753,425
Sep. 30th	\$100m x 5% x 92/365 = \$1,232,878	-12%	(\$12,00,000)	ABC pays \$13,232,878
Dec. 31st	\$100m x 5% x 92/365 = \$1,260,274	+1%	\$1,000,000	ABC pays \$260,274

17-1-E View Concept Check Questions Workbook

17-1-F "Risk Management Applications of Option Strategies"

Introduction

This is a brief introduction to how derivatives, in particular options, can be used to manage risk. Options allow the holder to capture much of the upside if prices move in one direction and limit their losses if prices move in the other direction making them attractive for portfolios managers meeting specific client risk-return objectives. In this Reading we look at strategies that are frequently used by equity managers and candidates need to be able to interpret the relevant payoff diagrams as well as calculate profits, losses and breakeven prices.

LOS 17-1-F-a	**determine** the value at expiration, profit, maximum profit, maximum loss, breakeven underlying price at expiration, and general shape of the graph of the strategies of buying and selling calls and buying and selling puts, and **explain** each strategy's characteristics

We are now going to look at some of the investment strategies that can be implemented using options. We will use the same notation as we used in LOS 17-1-D

S_0, S_T	=	price of underlying asset today, price of underlying asset at time T
X	=	exercise price
r	=	risk-free rate
T	=	time to expiration, expressed as number of days divided by 365
c_0, c_T	=	price of European call option today and at expiry
p_0, p_T	=	price of European put option today and at expiry

We will only look at European options, since we are looking at the return for a strategy up to the expiration date, the calculations are the same for American options.

Profit on call options

Taking into account the cost of the option, the premium P, the profit made from the **long call position** is

Profit = Max $[0, S_T - X] - c_o$ **(Equation 17-10)**

Options are a **zero-sum gain** in the sense that the profit made by the purchaser of the option will be equal to the loss made by the option writer (or vice versa), so the profit made from the **short call position** is

Profit = c_o - Max $[0, S_T - X]$

Example 17-20: Profit and loss on a call option

The profit and loss on a call option at expiration when the exercise price is $100 and the premium is $5 is illustrated in the diagram below. Note that for the long position there is unlimited upside but the maximum loss is limited to the premium.

Insert diagram page 311

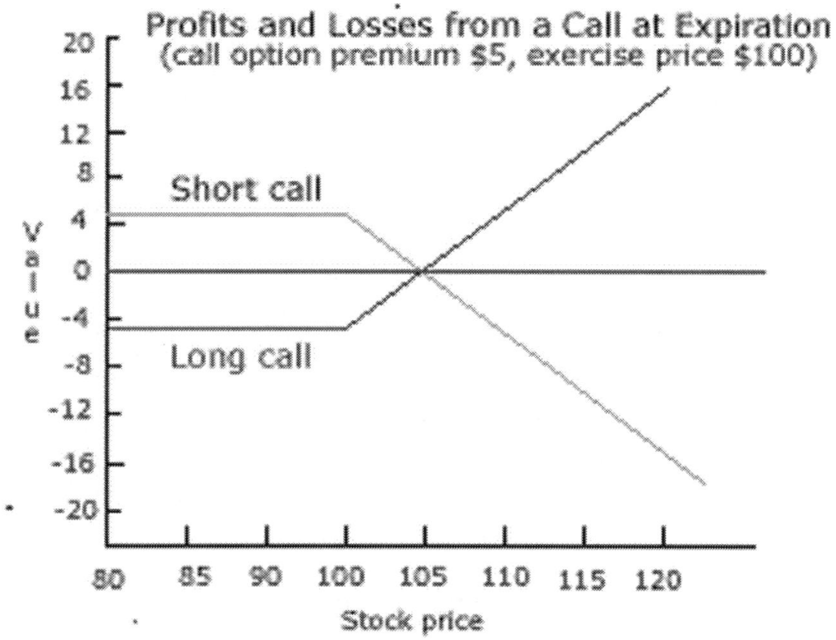

Breakeven will occur when

$0 = S_T - X - c_o$

when $S_T = X + c_o$ (Equation **17-11**)

In Example 17-20 the breakeven is \$105.

Profit on put options

When we take into consideration the option premium the profit on a **long put position** is

$\text{Profit} = \text{Max}\,[0, X - S_T] - p_o$ **(Equation 17-12)**

And on a **short put position** the profit is given by:

$\text{Profit} = p_o - \text{Max}\,[0, X - S_T\,]$

The corresponding diagram for a put option is shown in Example 17-21.

Example 17-21: Profit and loss on a put option

The profit and loss on a put option at expiration when the exercise price is \$100 and the premium is \$5 is illustrated in the diagram below. For the long position there is large potential upside (\$95 in the case that the price of the underlying goes to zero) but the maximum loss is limited to the premium.

Insert diagram page 315

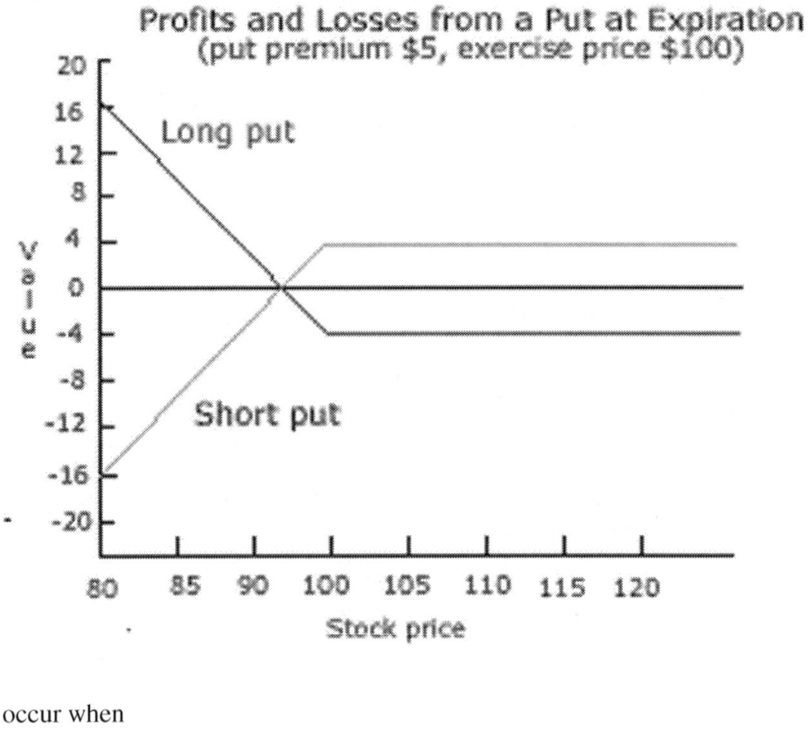

Breakeven will occur when

$0 = X - S_T - p_o$

when $S_T = X - p_o$ (Equation **17-13)**

In Example 17-21 the breakeven is \$95.

Example 17-22: Calculating the profit and loss from option positions

1. The value of an asset is $50 and an investor purchases a call option with a value of $6 and an exercise price of $52. The price at which the investor will breakeven is given by

$S_T = X + c_o = \$52 + \$6 = \$58$

The breakeven point is $58 and if the price rises above this there will be a profit.

2. A trader writes a put option on a stock with an exercise price of $40 and a premium of $5, if the stock falls to $38 at the expiration date the profit made by the trader is given by

Profit = $5 - Max [0, ($40 – $38)] = $3

LOS 17-1-F-b **determine** the value at expiration, profit, maximum profit, maximum loss, breakeven underlying price at expiration, and general shape of the graph of the covered call strategy and the protective put strategy, and **explain** each strategy's characteristics

Covered call

A **covered call**, is when an investor owns the underlying asset and writes a call option on the asset. The investor will receive income in the form of the premium paid to them by the buyer of the option. However, in the case that the stock price rises to above the exercise price plus the premium, the investor is worse off than if they had not written the call, they will lose the potential capital gain on the underlying asset.

The profit on a covered call is

$S_T – S_0$ (the profit on the underlying) plus c_o - Max [0, $S_T – X$] (the profit on a short call)

Profit = $S_T – S_0 + c_o$ - Max [0, $S_T – X$] **(Equation 17-14)**

Breakeven will occur when X is greater than S_T, and the option is not exercised so it will occur when

$S_T = S_0 - c_o$ (Equation **17-15**)

Example 17-23: Covered call

The profit and loss diagram is shown below for a covered call with an exercise price of $110 and premium of $4. The initail price of the stock is $100.

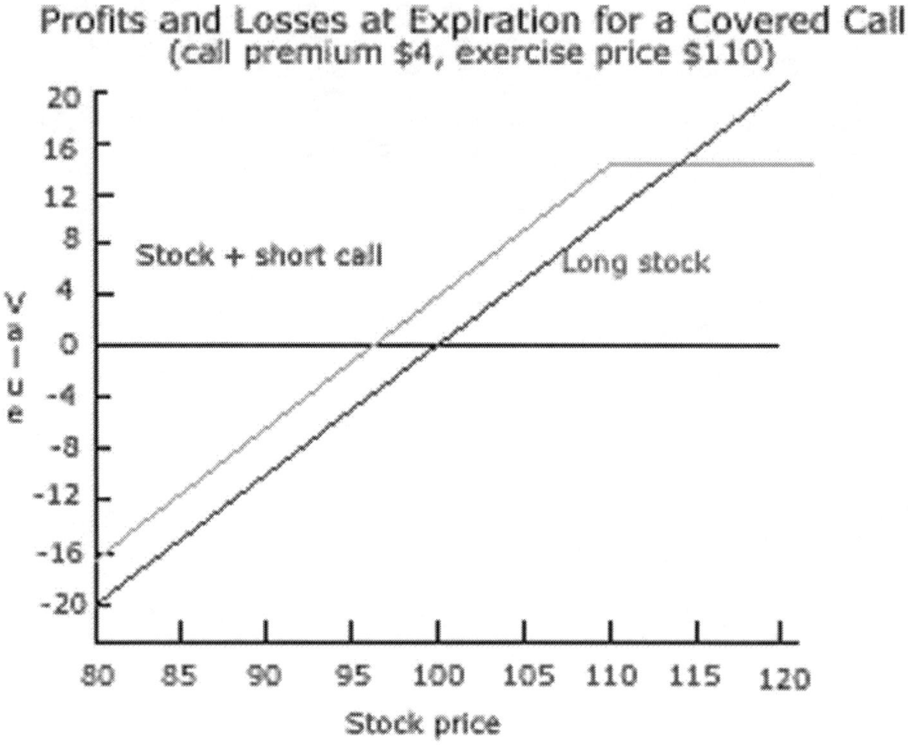

Breakeven is when $S_T = S_0 - c_0 = \$100 - \$4 = \$96$

Example 17-24: Value of a covered call

An investor holds 1,000 shares in ABC Corp. which has a current market price of \$58. The investor sells 1,000 call options on the shares at a premium of \$5 and exercise price of \$60. In the case that ABC shares (i) rise to \$80 (ii) fall to \$50, calculate the value of the combined portfolio at the expiration date.

The value of the combined value of the portfolio is

(i) (1,000 x \$80) + 1,000{premium - maximum [0, (S – X)] }
= \$80,000 + 1,000(\$5 - \$20)
= \$65,000
(ii) (1,000 x \$50) + 1,000{premium - maximum [0, (S – X)] }
= \$50,000 + 1,000(\$5 - \$0)
= \$55,000
If the investor had not sold the option then the value of the shares would be higher in the first case (the call option has capped his capital gain) and lower in the second case since he has the benefit of the premium income.

Protective put

This is sometimes called **portfolio insurance**. It is an investment strategy which uses hedging to protect the value of a portfolio from falling below a certain level. It is executed by combining holding an asset and buying a put option on the asset.

In the case that (i) the asset price falls below the exercise price, then the value of the combined position will fall by the cost of the put option, since losses on the asset will be offset by the payoff on the put option. (ii) the asset rises above the exercise price, then the value of the position will rise in line with the asset, less the cost of the put option, since the option lapses worthless. The cost of the put option is essentially the cost of insuring the portfolio.

The profit can be calculated using Equation 17-12

$\text{Profit} = S_T - S_0 - \{\text{Max}\,[0, X - S_T] - p_o\}$ **(Equation 17-16)**
and breakeven is when

$S_T = S_0 + p_o$ (Equation **17-17)**

Example 17-25: Portfolio Insurance

The diagram below shows the payoff for an insured portfolio, which combines a long position in the index and a put option on the index. The initial level of the index is $96, the exercise price $96 and the premium $4. In this case the breakeven is when the index is $96 + $4 = $100.***Insert diagram page 339***

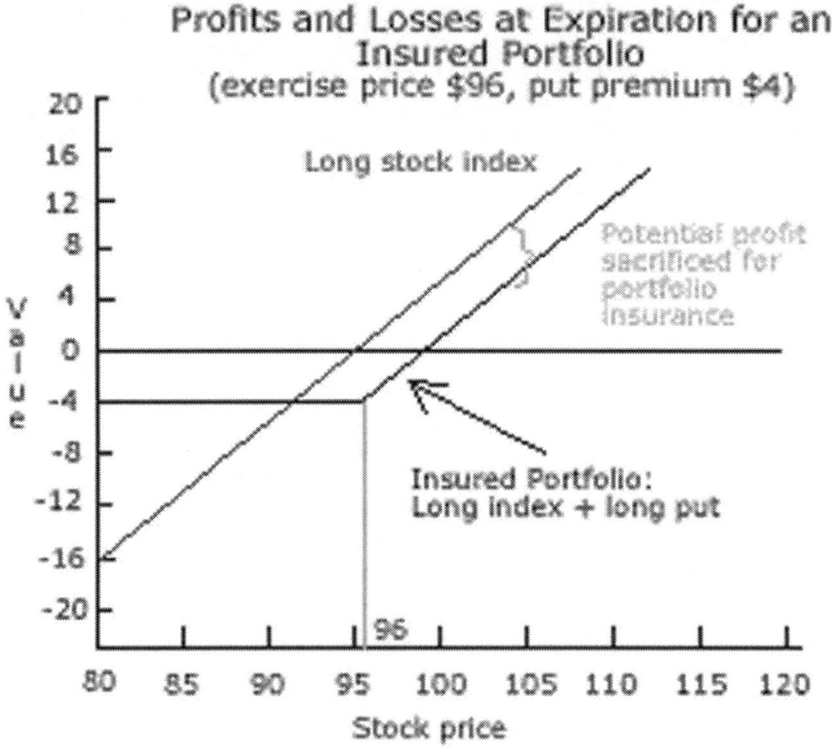

17-1-F View Concept Check Questions Workbook

STUDY SESSION 18

Asset Valuation

Alternative Investments

Overview

This is a short Study Session that gives a brief introduction to alternative investments. 'Alternative investments' are arefer to a variety of investments, including real estate and venture capital, that broad category. They complement the 'traditional' asset classes such as stocks, bonds and other instruments traded in the financial markets. It is also often used to refer to alternative strategies which mostlymay use the traditional assets classesbut have a different objectives such as search oftargeting absolute returns. Hedge funds, for example, belong touse alternative strategies.

The Study Session looks at the characteristics of alternative investments including risk and return and how investments are valued. The Study Session is based on just one chapter and it works through a range of different investments: open and closed-end funds, exchange traded funds, real estate, venture capital, hedge funds, closely-held companies and finally commodities.

Reading Assignments

International Investments, 5th edition, Bruno Solnik and Dennis McLeavey (Addison Wesley, 2004) 18-1. "Alternative Investments," Ch. 8

18-1 "Alternative investments"

Introduction

Alternative investments differ from traditional investments; they tend to be less liquid, to be in inefficient markets and require longer holding periods. Often investing in them involves particular legal or tax considerations.

The main features of alternative investments are:

- Illiquidity.
- Difficulty in determining current market values.
- Limited historical risk and return data.
- Extensive investment analysis required.

The main attraction of alternative investments is the potential for earning a higher alpha than is available t can be found compared to thein more efficient markets. Recall that alpha is the excess risk-adjusted return. in excess of required rate of return.

Candidates will be expected to be familiar with the unique characteristics and advantages and disadvantages of investing in each asset. They will also need to be able to apply appropriate methods to value real estate and venture capital investments.

Investment Companies

An investment company is a financial intermediary that pools investors' funds and invests them on their behalf giving a proportional share of the pooled fund performance to each investor. An investment company (usually a corporation) invests a pool of funds collected from a number of individual investors in a portfolio of investments. The investments can be in any specified asset class or combination of asset classes. An investment management company is appointed by the directors of the investment company to do the actual management of the investments.

Investment (Fund) Companies

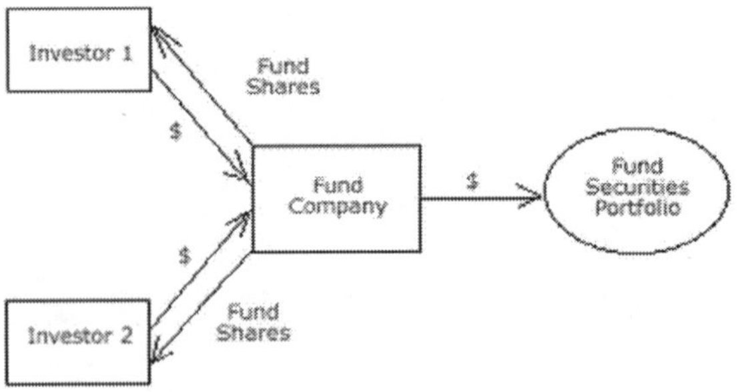

Open-end investment companies offer a redemption feature. Howeverand closed-end funds issue shares that are types of investment companies that are distinguished by their readiness to offerare traded in the secondary market.

LOS 18-1-a **distinguish** between an open-end and a closed-end fund

Closed-end investment company

A closed-end investment company does not offer new shares or redeem shares except through a new share offering or a stock repurchase. Shares are dealt in the secondary market and the investor pays the market price plus regular trading commission. Closed-end funds usually trade at a different price, at a premium or more commonly a discount, to their NAVs.

Open-end investment company (mutual fund)

An open-end investment company continues to buy and sell shares after the initial offering. A loadmanaged or load fund fund is when the offering price is the NAV plus an initial charge called a **front-end load.**

An open-end investment company continues to buy and sell shares after the initial offering. A managed or load fund is when the offering price is the NAV plus an initial charge called a **front-end load.** The redemption price is usually the NAV, but can be the NAV less a redemption fee or a **back-end load.** This fee is often charged if the shares are sold in less than a specified period of time, to discourage the investors from selling their shares too quickly. A no-load fund has no initial sales charge so the offering price is the NAV redemption feature.

LOS 18-1-b **explain** how the net asset value of a fund is calculated

An investment company is a financial intermediary that pools investors funds and invest them on their behalf giving a proportional share of the pooled fund performance to each investor.

- An open-end fund
- A closed-end fund
- Net asset value (NAV)

Net asset value (NAV)

Shares in investment companies are valued based on their NAV. The NAV per share is a company's assets minus liabilities divided by the number of shares outstanding. The asset value is calculated using the market value of the securities held, liabilities will include items such as fees payable to the investment manager. Fees are charges on an annual basis and for an unmanaged fund all or some of the set up costs will be passed on by selling the shares initially at a price higher than NAV. Open-end funds also charge purchase and redemption fees.

LOS 18-1-c **explain** the nature of various fees charged by investment companies

Fees

To summarize the dDifferent types of fees charged are:

1. Front-end loadfees or sales charge - commission charged at the time of purchase.

2. Redemption fees or deferred sales charge - a charge to exit the fund.

3. Annual expenses - ongoing expenses throughout the life of the fund, which generally consist of:

- Distribution fees, fees paid to the party who arranged the initial sales on a continuing basis.
- Management fees, the fees paid to the investment manager(s).
- Other expenses, such as custodian fees. and other expenses

Example 18-1 shows how fees are calculated.

Example 18-1: Investment company fees

We will look at a mutual fund that has issued three classes of shares. Each class holds the same underlying portfolio of securities but the expense structures differ.

	FundClass A	**FundClass B**	**FundClass C**
Front-end fees	4%	None	None
Redemption fees	None	5% in the first year but declining by 1% point each year thereafter	1% for the first 23 years only
Annual expenses			
	0.30%	0.30%	0.30%
Distribution fees	0.75%	1.00%	1.00%
Management fees	0.20%	0.20%	0.20%
Other expenses	1.25%	1.50%	1.50%

1. What would be the ending value for each of the classes of shares if an investor invests $1 for thea period of 5 years, assuming the fund grows by 8% annually?

2. What would the investor receive if he or she decides to redeem the shares after two years?

Answer

1. Fund A. Due to the front-end fee of 4%, only \$0.96 from the \$1 will be available to invest. At the end of 5 years, \$1 invested in the the fund will be worthreturn $\$0.96\ \text{x}\ (1.08)^5\ \text{x x}\ (1 - 0.0125)^5 = \$1.3246$, or a return of 32.46% compounding growth.

Fund B and Fund C will have the same return since the annual expenses are the same and there is no front-end fee for botheither of them. At the end of 5 years, \$1 invested in the funds will be worthwill return $\$1\ \text{xx}\ (1.08)^5\ \text{xx}\ (1 - 0.015)^5 = \$1.3624$, or a return of 36.24% compounding growth.

2. Fund A. There is no redemption fee, so the investment in the fundfund after 2 years will be worth produce $\$0.96\ \text{xx}\ (1.08)^2\ \text{xx}\ (1 - 0.0125)^2 = \$1.0919$, or a return of 9.19% compounding growth.

Fund B, after 2 years the redemption fee will be 4%, i.e. a decline of 1% point from 5%. The investment in the fund The fund after 2 years will be worthproduce $\$1\ \text{xx}\ (1.08)^2\ \text{xx}\ (1 - 0.015)^2\ \text{x x}\ (1 - 0.04) = \$1.0864$ or a return of 8.64% compounding growth.

Fund C, after 2 years the redemption fee will be 1%. The investment in the fund after 2 years will be worth $\$1\ \text{x}\ (1.08)^2\ \text{x}\ (1 - 0.015)^2\ \text{x}\ (1 - 0.01) = \$\ 1.1204$ or a return of 12.04%.

LOS 18-1-d	**distinguish** among style, sector, index, global, and stable value strategies in equity investment

Investment companies mainly invest in equities although they can invest in a wide range of asset classes. Different equity investment strategies include:

Style – for example growth versus value, or large versus small capitalization stocks.

Sector – investment is focused in a certain industrial sector.

Index fund – the objective is to perform in line with a specified index, perhaps by owning all the shares in the index with the same weighting as their representation in the index.

Global – invest in securities from around the world (an international fund only invests in securities from outside the home market).

Stable value – invests in short-term fixed income securities and guaranteed return investment contracts.

LOS 18-1-e	**distinguish** among exchange traded funds (ETFs), traditional mutual funds, and closed-end funds

Exchange traded funds (ETFs)

Exchange traded funds are funds that trade on a stock market and investors can buy shares in the fund. The investor is buying shares in an open-end fund or unit investment trust that holds a portfolio of shares which are selected to track the performance of an underlying index (for example an equity, fixed-income or sector index). Usually an ETF is an open-end fund with a choice of three legal structures (1) managed investment company, the most flexible structure in that shares or derivatives can be used to match the underlying index performance, (2) unit investment trust, a slightly more restrictive structure which only allows investment in the underlying securities in the index and dividends received must be held until they are paid out to investors, (3) grantor trust, this is not a recognized investment company so investors indirectly own an unmanaged basket of securities.

In-kind creation and redemption

A special feature of ETFs is the creation and redemption process. Creation and redemption units are for large multiples of ETF shares, say 50,000 shares, and they can be traded by ETF market makers or authorized participants. When there is demand for ETF shares the market makers will deposit with the trustees of a fund a portfolio of the underlying shares used to track the index and in return will receive a creation unit or block of ETF shares which they can sell to the end investors. To redeem shares the market maker will return a large block of ETF shares and will receive a portfolio of the underlying shares in the index.

CREATION/REDEMPTION PROCESS OF
EXCHANGE TRADED FUNDS

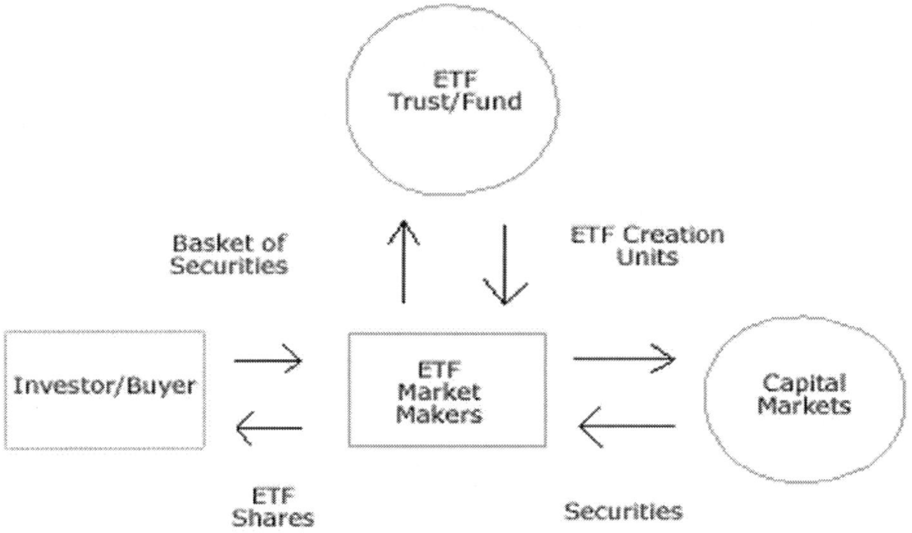

Source: Solnik, et al, 2004

This process is quite different to the redemption of an open-end fund and means that no capital gain (or loss) is realized in the fund since the underlying shares are not sold to meet redemptions. This can have tax advantages for the remaining holders of the ETF shares. Redemption for cash is discouraged for small ETF shareholders by time delays and additional fees. Individual shareholders will prefer to sell their shares in the market, and the share price will stay close to the NAV, if it moves away arbitragers can use the in-kind creation and redemption process to make a risk-free gain which will bring the prices back in line with the NAV.

LOS 18-1-f explain the advantages and risks of ETFs

Advantages of ETFs

ETFs are attractive to investors for a number of reasons.

Diversification

Investors gain exposure to a diversified portfolio of stocks or bonds represented by the underlying index. ETFs can also be sold short or bought on margin.

Continuous trading

ETFs trade throughout the trading day, whereas mutual funds usually only trade based on the once-a-day closing prices.

Improved risk management

Futures and options often trade with the same underlying indexes so the ETFs can be used for risk management.

Transparency

The constituents of the fund are published daily.

Cost effectiveness

There are no load fees and the expense ratio (which includes management and custody fees) is lower than for actively managed funds.

Avoidance of significant premium/discount

The price stays close to the NAV, this is not the case with closed-end funds which often trade at a significant discount to their NAVs.

Tax-saving

The capital gains tax liability is lower within the fund due to in-kind redemptions.

Immediate dividend reinvestment

Dividends received by the fund are usually reinvested immediately so there is no cash drag.

Disadvantages of ETFs

Narrow-based index

In some markets there are only ETFs available for the large capitalization stock indexes.

Intra-day trading

Investors with long time horizons do not need intra-day trading.

Bid-ask spread

If the volume of trading in ETFs is low then the bid-ask spread can be wide.

Cost efficiency

For large investors it may be more cost or tax efficient to invest directly or have an actively managed portfolio.

Risks

The risk will depend on the type of ETF and the index it is tracking, but potential risks are:

- Market risk – the NAV will reflect moves in the underlying market.
- Asset class/sector risk – if the index is for a specific sector it may underperform the wider market.
- Trading risk – the bid–ask spread might widen or the price move away from NAV, particularly if there is low liquidity in the shares.
- Tracking error risk – this arises if the share price performance deviates from the index performance.
- Derivative risk – if the ETF uses derivatives this introduces additional risks such as counterparty risk.
- Currency and country risk – for ETFs investing in international markets.

ETFs are used in many ways by investment managers, for implementing asset allocation, and gaining exposure to new markets, managing cash inflows, and managing portfolio risk.

LOS 18-1-g **describe** the forms of real estate investment

Real estate is a tangible asset and covers land and buildings, including offices, industrial, retail as well as residential properties. First we look at the different types of real estate investment.

Forms of real estate investment

Free and clear equity

This is sometimes called "fee simple" and means full ownership of a property for an

indefinite period of time. The owner has the right to lease out the property or resell the property.

Leveraged equity

This refers to the same ownership rights but subject to debt or a mortgage and a requirement to transfer ownership of the equity in case of a default on the debt.

Mortgages

These are mortgage loans, and are a real estate investment vehicle in the form of a debt investment. The holder will receive interest, scheduled repayments of the debt and possibly prepayments which give uncertainty over the cash flows.

Aggregation vehicles

These are collective vehicles giving investors access to a diversified portfolio of real estate investments.

Real estate limited partnerships (RELPs) are syndicates that invest in different types of property. The manager is a general partner and takes unlimited liability whereas the other investors are limited partners. Real estate investment trusts (REITs) are closed-end investment companies that invest in various types of real estate and real estate mortgages. Equity REITs invest in property using leverage whereas mortgage REITs makes construction loans and mortgage loans to real estate investors. REITs pay out the majority of their income as dividends and are similar to a bond investment.

.

LOS 18-1-h	**explain** the characteristics of real estate as an investable asset class

Characteristics of real estate

Investing in real estate is quite different to buying securities in a financial market. Its characteristics are:

- Properties are immovable and indivisible, (indivisible means that you usually cannot sell just part of the investment).
- Each property is unique and not directly comparable to other properties.
- Property is relatively illiquid.
- There is no central market place so it is difficult to assess the market value of a property.
- Real estate investment involves high transaction costs and management fees.
- The real estate market is inefficient and information is not freely available.

LOS 18-1-i	**describe** the various approaches to the valuation of real estate
LOS 18-1-j	**calculate** the net operating income (NOI) from a real estate investment
LOS 18-1-k	**calculate** the value of a property using the sales comparison and income approaches

Valuation of real estate

There are four main methods used to appraise the value of real estate.

1. Cost approach

This approach is used for new buildings; it says that the value of a property is at most the cost of the land and the construction of the buildings at current prices.

2. Sales comparison approach

This involves looking at selling prices of similar properties as a benchmark. A related method is hedonic price estimation, which means that the major characteristics of the property are identified and then the value is calculated based on the properties' exposure to these characteristics. See Example 18-2 for a calculation of a property value using this method.

Example 18-2: Sales comparison approach

A real estate appraiser has identified three factors that affect house prices in an area, the number of rooms, size of the plot and distance from the railway station. Using data collected on recent house sales he has used regression analysis, with the selected characteristics as the independent variables, to produce the following data

Characteristic	Units	Slope coefficient in euro per unit
Intercept		80,000
Number of rooms	Number	25,000
Size of plot	Square meter	40
Distance from railway station	Kilometer	- 5,000

A house has 10 rooms, a plot of 1,000 square meters and is 5 kilometers from the station. The appraisal price is

80,000 + (10 x 25,000) + (1,000 x 40) + (5 x -5,000) = 80,000 + 250,000 + 40,000 – 25,000
= Euro 345,000

3. Income approach

This approach calculates a property's value as the present value of income that will be received from the property using a perpetuity discount model. Income is defined as nWhere net operating income (NOI) which is gross potential rental income less vacancy losses, operating expenses and property taxes.

More specifically, if we assume a constant annual net operating income

Appraisal value = NOI **(Equation 18-1)**

Market cap rate

The market cap (or capitalization) rate reflects the rate of return required by investors and is based on benchmark transactions (for a single or several comparable transactions).

$$\text{Market cap rate} = \frac{\text{Benchmark NOI}}{\text{Benchmark transaction price}} \quad \textbf{(Equation 18-2)}$$

Example 18-3: Income approach

An investor is considering purchasing an office building as an investment, and the following information has been collected. The figures are on an annual basis.

Gross potential rental income	$1,000,000
Estimated vacancy and collection losses	5%
Insurance and taxes	$80,000
Utilities	$30,000
Repairs and maintenance	$60,000
Depreciation	$70,000
Interest on proposed financing	$90,000

NOI = gross potential rental income minus expenses

= $1,000,000 – (0.05 x $1,000,000) - $80,000 - $30,000 - $60,000

= $780,000.

Note the expenses for this calculation do not include depreciation (it is assumed that repairs will maintain the building in good condition indefinitely) and interest expense.

A similar office building had NOI of $400,000 and sold for $3,200,000.

Using Equation 18-2,

Market cap rate = $400,000/$3,200,000 = 12.5%

Using Equation 18-1, we can apply this market cap rate to give an appraisal value for the office building of

Appraisal value = $780,000/0.125 = $6,240,000

LOS 18-1-l	**calculate** the after-tax cash flows, net present value, and yield of a real estate investment

Discounted after-tax cash flow approach

This method looks at the underlying factors that determine real estate values and looks at the value from the individual investor's viewpoint. This means that issues such as borrowing costs and the investor's tax position can be incorporated into the valuation, as well as future expectations of factors that determine real estate prices.

This method discounts after-tax cash flows by the required rate of return. After-tax cash flows are the annual cash flows earned on an investment, net of expenses, debt payments and taxes. Depreciation of a building is important since for tax purposes it is a non-cash cost that can reduce tax payments. The net present value (NPV) is the present value of the cash flows generated by the property less the initial investment in the property, if it is a positive number it indicates it is a good investment, a negative number suggests it is a bad investment.

Example 18-4: Discounted cash flow approach

An investor is considering buying a house that he will rent out. The cost of the house is $350,000. He will finance 80% of the purchase price with a mortgage on which he will make annual payments $18,000, of which $14,000 represents interest and is tax deductible. He forecasts that he can sell the house at the end of three years for $400,000 net of selling expenses and tax. His net operating income per annum is $24,000, he will make tax savings on the deprecation of $5,000 per annum on the building. His marginal tax rate is 30%.

The after-tax cash flow is the same for the first two years.

After-tax net income

= (NOI – depreciation – interest)(1 – tax rate)
= ($24,000 - $5,000 - $14,000)(0.70) = $3,500

After-tax cash flow

= after-tax net income + depreciation – principal payment on mortgage
= $3,500 + $5,000 - $4,000 = $4,500

In the third year we must add the $400,000 cash inflow from the sale of the house, and deduct the mortgage that must be repaid, which will be the amount borrowed less the principal repayments, ($280,000 – $12,000) so the after-tax cash flow is

$4,500 + $400,000 -$268,000 = $136,500.

The initial investment (I) is 20% of the purchase price. If the investor's required rate of return (r) is 12% the NPV is calculated as

$$NPV = \frac{CF_1}{(1+r)} + \frac{CF_2}{(1+r)^2} + \frac{CF_3}{(1+r)^3} - I$$

$$= \frac{\$4{,}500}{1.12} + \frac{\$4{,}500}{1.12^2} + \frac{\$136{,}500}{1.12^3} - \$70{,}000$$

$$= \$4{,}018 + \$3{,}587 + \$97{,}158 - \$70{,}000$$

$$= \$34{,}763$$

This is positive so it is an attractive investment from the point of view of this investor.

To calculate the IRR we can use a financial calculator. It is the rate of return that will make the NPV = 0

IRR = 28.85%

LOS 18-1-m explain the various stages in venture capital investing

Venture capital

Venture capital is a form of private equity, which is equity that is not traded on exchanges. Venture capital covers investment from investing in start-ups through to the exit via an IPO or buyout. Typically investors have long time horizons and are attracted to venture capital by the possibility of making very high returns on a successful investment (although many investments will end in failure). Investment is usually through a limited partnership so the liability is limited to the size of the investment.

Stages in venture capital investing

Seed financing, for product development and market research, the product is still at the 'idea' stage.

Early-stage financing for companies moving towards commercial manufacturing.

- **Start-up financing**, for product development and initial marketing, this is usually before the company's products are being sold commercially.
- **First-stage financing**, for initial commercial manufacture and sales.

Up to this point financing is referred to as **formative-stage financing**.

Later-stage financing

- **Second-stage financing**, for initial expansion of the company.
- **Third-stage financing**, for major expansion, product improvement and/or marketing.
- **Mezzanine (or bridge) financing**, for a company that expects to go public in the near future.

LOS 18-1-n	**discuss** venture capital investment characteristics and the challenges to venture capital valuation and performance measurement

Characteristics of venture capital investments

- Illiquidity – the main exit routes are IPOs or the arrangement of a buyout, there is usually no short-term exit route.
- Long-term commitment – investors who can afford to make long-term investments can expect to be rewarded with a liquidity risk premium.
- Difficulty in determining current market value – since there is little trading of venture capital investments it is difficult to establish market values.
- Limited historical risk and return data – a result of there being little trading data.
- Limited information – it is difficult to assess the prospects of the companies in terms of cash flow forecasts etc.
- Entrepreneurial/management mismatches – entrepreneurs often don't make good managers and as a company grows different management skills are needed.
- Fund manager incentive mismatches – it is important that the fund managers are rewarded based on the performance of their investments.
- Lack of knowledge of how many competitors to a start-up company exist – since information on competitors with similar ideas may be difficult to find.
- Vintage cycles – when funds available for investment in venture capital are high the expected returns will fall, also poor financial conditions may make finding financing difficult for venture capital firms.
- Extensive operations analysis and advice may be required – it is important that venture capital managers can help entrepreneurs by applying their financial and operating knowledge and skills.

The main exit routes for the venture capital investor are trade sales (sales or mergers for cash or stock of the acquiring company) or IPOs where shares are issued for public trading. Other exit routes are write-offs and voluntary liquidations which may result in a payout to investors, also some companies will go bankrupt. In other cases the entrepreneur buys out the venture capital investors

Challenges in valuing venture capital investments

Valuation is made difficult because of the uncertainty of future cash flows. Even if entrepreneurs have an innovative and potentially successful product they may lack the management experience to make it a success, and even then it is difficult to tell how long it will take to achieve that success. Some of these risks can be diversified by holding a portfolio of different venture capital investments. Valuing a venture capital investment will involve:

- Estimating the payoff at time of exit, if the venture is successful.
- Estimating the time it will take to exit.
- Assessment of the probability of failure.

Challenges to performance management

Performance of venture capital investments is usually done by estimating the internal rate of return (IRR) using forecast cash flows and an end-of-period valuation. Some of the challenges to performance measurement include:

- The difficulty in determining precise valuations with no market values, valuations might be based on applying an average historical IRR to the managers average investment costs for current investments.
- Lack of meaningful benchmarks by which to measure the performance.
- The long-time period needed to reliably assess the performance.

LOS 18-1-o	**calculate** the net present value (NPV) of a venture capital project, given the project's possible payoff and conditional failure probabilities

Example 18-5: \NPV of a venture capital project

An investor is looking at investing $1 million in a project, where the expected payout is $10 million at the end of five years. However there is a significant risk of failure and the probability of failure in any year is given in the table below. The probability is based on the condition that the project has survived the previous year.

Year	1	2	3	4	5
Probability of failure	0.40	0.35	0.25	0.20	0.20

The probability that the project survives throughout the five years is given by the product of the individual probabilities it survives each year, which is

$(1 - 0.40)\ (1 - 0.35)\ (1 - 0.25)\ (1 - 0.20)\ (1 - 0.20) = 18.7\%$

If the project survives the present value is $10 million/$(1.10)^5$ - $1 million = $5.2 million

If the project fails the present value is - $1 million.

The expected NPV is the weighted average of the two NPVs, which is

0.187($5.2 million) + 0.813(- $1 million) = $159,400

This is a positive NPV so the project is attractive.

LOS 18-1-p **discuss** the descriptive accuracy of the term "hedge fund" and **define** hedge fund in terms of objectives, legal structure, and fee structure

The original concept of a hedge fund was a bet against the market using derivative instruments, such as futures, short selling, etc.

Today its definition in terms of investment objectives is to **search for absolute returns**. Whilst the recent trend in the wider investment management industry has been to focus on investment performance relative to pre-assigned benchmarks, e.g. an investment manager tries to outperform the S&P 500 Index; hedge funds have reacted against this trend. They are essentially isolating a specific bet to generate alpha. It is more appropriate to name them isolation funds.

The most common legal structure is limited partnership (in the U.S.) or an offshore corporation. The legal structure gives the fund managers the freedom to implement a variety of strategies such as taking long and short positions in an asset, using derivative instruments, and leveraging the fund without restrictions. In the U.S. the limited partnership structure is under section 3 (c) (1) of the Investment Company Act, therefore exempt from most SEC regulations.

The fee structure generally consists of a base management fee plus an incentive fee. The base management fee is a percentage of the value of assets under management, typically 1% to 3%. The incentive fee is usually in the range of 15% to 30% of total profits. Often the incentive fee is only triggered when the performance is above the risk-free rate and sometimes includes a "high water mark" clause stating that following a year of decline, the fund must recover the losses before the incentive fee kicks in.

Example 18-6: Net return calculation

A new hedge fund has a base management fee of 2% and an incentive fee of 25% of profits above the risk-free rate.

If the risk-free rate is 5% and the total return of the fund is 45%, what would be the net return after fees?

Answer

Fee = 2% + 25% x (45% – 5%) = 2% + 10% = 12%

The net return = 45% - 12% = 33%.

LOS 18-1-q describe the various classifications of hedge funds

Types of hedge fund

The classification of hedge funds is somewhat arbitrary due to the variety and the diversity of fund strategies, but we look at some of the commonly used classifications below.

Long/short funds

These are the traditional type of hedge fund and represent a large proportion of hedge funds assets. They often take long and short positions in common stocks based on their forecast returns, and often have long and short market exposure. The funds often use leverage and currently operate in many markets around the world. A subgroup within this classification is funds with a systematic short bias, also known as dedicated short funds or short-seller funds.

Market-neutral funds

These funds attempt to hedge against a general market move by a combination of long/short positions. The bets are on mispricing of individual securities within some market segment. The market-neutral long-short strategy means that the total value of long positions is offset by an equivalent value of short positions to give a net zero market exposure (**dollar neutrality**). This strategy also creates **beta neutrality**. Various techniques that are used include:

- Equity long/short
- Fixed-income hedging
- Pairs trading
- Warrant arbitrage
- Mortgage arbitrage
- Convertible bond arbitrage
- Closed-fund arbitrage
- Statistical arbitrage

Note that the term 'arbitrage' or 'neutral' in their labels does not mean that the strategy is riskless because there is no such thing as a perfect hedge. Losses can occur if the model is imperfect and can be severe due to the high leverage used.

Global macro funds

These funds bet on the direction of markets, interest rates, currencies, commodities or macroeconomic variables. The funds tend to use derivatives extensively and be highly leveraged. Subgroups in this category are:

- Futures funds (or managed futures funds), which take long or short positions using futures contracts.
- Emerging-market funds, which take bets on all type of securities in emerging markets. These markets are generally less efficient and less liquid compared to major developed markets. Volatility is fairly high, as prices are highly influenced by economic and political factors.

Event-driven funds

These funds bet on some event specific to a company or security that has significant effect on the pricing of the security. The resulting price fluctuations create opportunities that can be exploited. There are a number of subgroups, namely,

- **Distressed securities funds**, these funds invest in debt and/or equity securities of companies facing financial distress which are in the bankruptcy reorganization stage, or emerging from reorganization, or likely to announce bankruptcy. The funds take long positions if the managers believe that the financial situation will improve, or short positions if they believe that the financial conditions will deteriorate.
- **Risk arbitrage in mergers and acquisitions**. These funds take advantage of the discounted pricing of the target company prior to or when a merger or acquisition is announced. The funds simultaneously buy the stock (take a long position) in the target company and sell short (take a short position) the stock of the acquiring company. If the merger or acquisition goes through, this strategy will create a profit since generally the acquired stock price will rise and the acquiring one will fall after the completion of the merger or acquisition. There is however also a chance that the merger or acquisition fails, perhaps for regulatory reasons, creating large losses when the bets are funded by high leverage.

LOS 18-1-r **discuss** the benefits and drawbacks to fund of funds investing

Fund of funds

A fund of funds (FOF) is created for both small and institutional investors who wish to invest in hedge funds. A FOF invests in a number of hedge funds allowing investors to have access to funds which normally require a large minimum size of investment.

Benefits of FOF

- **Retailing**. With the same money, an investor can access a large number of hedge funds instead of a single hedge fund.
- **Access**. An investor can be given access to funds that are already closed to new investments.
- **Diversification**. A FOF can invest in a number of hedge funds that are diversified across different markets.
- **Expertise**. Investors often choose a FOF because they believe that the managers of a FOF have expertise in selecting the hedge funds. The information about hedge funds is often difficult to obtain and managers are expected to have intimate knowledge of the hedge funds selected.
- **Due diligence process**. The due diligence process may be too time consuming for an institutional investor when selecting hedge funds, considering the secretive nature and complex investment strategies of the funds. The FOF will have performed the specialized due diligence on behalf of the investors.

Drawbacks of FOF

- **Fees**. Fees are charged by the manager and administrator of the FOF in addition to those charged by each of the hedge funds.
- **Performance**. The future performance of the FOF cannot be relied on due to the selection process of the individual hedge funds. They are mainly selected on the basis of past performance.
- **Diversification is a two-edged sword**. The expected return on a portfolio of hedge funds may be lower, but the fees remain high.

LOS 18-1-s **discuss** the leverage and unique risks of hedge funds

Use of leverage

Arbitrage profits are generally very small so hedge funds use leverage to magnify the profits, but it also magnifies the losses. Hedge funds managers create leverage by

- Borrowing external funds to invest, or selling short by more than the equity capital of the fund.
- Borrowing through brokerage margin accounts.
- Using derivatives that require posting margins rather than buying the cash securities out right.

The leverage ratio often runs from 2:1 to 10:1 or even to 100:1 depending upon the assets held and strategies used. There have been cases of much higher ratios, the Long Term Capital Management hedge fund, at one time registered a ratio of 500:1.

Prudent hedge funds now determine the upper limit of permitted leverage but allow the managers considerable flexibility within the limit.

Unique risks

- **Liquidity risk.** Lack of liquidity in thin or illiquid markets is a known factor. But it may also appear under extreme market conditions, even in major markets where the presence of liquidity is normally expected.
- **Pricing risk**. Particular pricing risk occurs with over-the-counter complex securities. The broker-dealers might price them conservatively during periods of high volatility leading to a higher level of margin calls. This higher level of margin calls may cause a severe cash drain on the hedge funds.
- **Counterparty credit risk**. Hedge funds will face counterparty credit risk as they deal with brokers, dealers and other financial institutions when trading or buying on margin.
- **Settlement risk**. This risk is associated with the failure of any counterparty involved in the transaction to deliver the money or security at the settlement date. This risk is often higher in emerging or less developed markets.
- **Short squeeze risk**. The risk when short sellers must close their positions when prices are rising.
- **Financing squeeze**. Sometimes due to margin calls or marking positions, the funds are forced to raise additional cash when their borrowing capacity is reached. They might have to reduce their leveraged positions at a loss.

LOS 18-1-t **discuss** the performance of hedge funds and the biases present in hedge fund performance measurement

Performance of hedge funds

The performance of hedge funds creates a strong case for investing.

- The net returns after fees are usually higher than equity or bond market returns.
- The risk level, as measured by the volatility of returns, is lower than equity investments
- The Sharpe ratio of hedge funds during 1996-2002 was higher than that of equity and bond investments.
- The correlation with conventional investments is generally low although still positive.

Net Return and Risk of Hedge Funds and Conventional Investments January 1996 – September 2002, Annualized

	HFR Fund Weighted Composite	HFR Fund of Funds	EACM 100	CSFB/ Tremont	S&P 500	Lehman Gov/Corp Bond Index
Annualized Return	10.92%	8.29%	9.96%	11.55%	5.86%	7.24%
Standard Deviation	8.59%	7.00%	4.93%	9.34%	17.49%	3.99%
Sharpe Ratio	0.74	0.54	1.10	0.75	0.08	0.68
Correlation with HFR Fund Weighted Composite	1.00	0.91	0.88	0.77	0.73	-0.11
Correlation with HFR Fund of Funds	0.91	1.00	0.94	0.91	0.56	-0.04
Correlation with EACM 100	0.88	0.94	1.00	0.88	0.52	0.01
Correlation with CSFB/Tremont	0.77	0.91	0.88	1.00	0.51	0.13
Correlation with S&P 500	0.73	0.56	0.52	0.51	1.00	-0.04
Correlation with Lehman Gov/Corp Bond Index	-0.11	-0.04	0.01	0.13	-0.04	1.00

CSFB/Tremont, EACM and HFR are hedge fund indexes

Source: Solnik, et al, 2004

The reported performance data of hedge funds is subject to a number of biases. Additionally since the hedge fund industry does not adhere to rigorous performance standards, unlike publicly listed funds, extreme caution must be taken when analyzing the performance data.

LOS 18-1-u	**explain** the effect of survivorship bias on the reported return and risk measures for a hedge fund data base

Survivorship bias

In the investment industry, only the successful funds present their performance track record in order to seek new investors. The unsuccessful ones tend to fade away and either not be reported or taken away from the data base. It is also often the case that managers only report the better performing ones from all the hedge funds under management. Additionally hedge funds with high volatility of returns tend to disappear leaving the ones with strategies that have low volatility in the data base. There is no guarantee

Other biases

- Hedge fund managers decide themselves whether to submit their funds for inclusion in a data base, they will not do so of they have a poor track record.
- Smoothed pricing, since some assets trade infrequently so estimates of fair value are made, this tends to smooth out the price movements.
- Many managers use options or follow option-like strategies, so returns are not symmetric. Using standard deviation or Sharpe ratios may underestimate the risk of large losses.
- Past risk measures may not be a good indicator of future risk, incentive fees and high water marks encourage managers to take higher risks if their recent performance has been poor.

LOS 18-1-v	**explain** how the legal environment affects the valuation of closely held companies

Closely held companies

Closely held companies are organized under different legal structures, such as tax-advantaged corporations, general partnerships, limited partnerships, and sole proprietorships. These different legal forms have different tax implications. Depending upon the jurisdiction, a variety of definitions of valuations is in use, such as intrinsic value, fundamental value and fair value, with different legal interpretations. There has been a lengthy argument for and against using projected cash flows as a basis of valuation versus using recently received cash flows. Valuation of closely held companies requires extensive knowledge of the law and the purpose of the valuation.

LOS 18-1-w	**describe** alternative valuation methods for closely held companies and **distinguish** among the bases for the discounts and premiums for these companies

Alternative valuation methods include:

The **cost approach,** this approach simply determines what it would cost to replace all the assets of the company.

The **comparables approach**, this approach looks at the valuation relative to a benchmark value. The benchmark value may be of similar companies that are actively traded, or the average or median value of such companies.

The **income approach**, discounting the future economic stream of income is considered to be one of the most appropriate approaches to valuation.

Analysts often apply discounts or premiums to the valuation of closely held companies. The bases for the discounts and premium are as follows:

- **Marketability discount.** Closely held companies are as a rule not actively traded, therefore investors must be compensated for the illiquidity. The base of a comparable market value is firstly established, and then an appropriate marketability discount is applied.
- **Minority interest discount.** The base value is the value arising from ownership of all rights of control. The minority discount is then applied.
- **Control premium.** The base is the minority ownership, i.e. without rights of control, and then the control premium is applied.

LOS 18-1-x	**discuss** distressed securities investing and the similarities between venture capital investing and distressed securities investing

The definition of distressed securities is securities of companies who have filed for or are on the verge of filing for bankruptcy court protection, or who are seeking out-of-court debt restructuring. The valuation of this type of security is very complex requiring legal, financial and operational analysis.

Analysts must appreciate the differences in the positions between bondholders and stockholders in term of hierarchy of claims. Bondholders have a priority of claims over the stockholders. Distressed security investing may mean investing in the bonds of the company with a view to being an equity holder when the reorganization is completed.

There are similarities between distressed securities and venture capital investing:

- The investments are illiquid.
- They require a long time horizon to realize a profit.
- They require participation of investors in directing the companies.
- They offer possibilities of mispricing.
- They are laden with business volatilities and/or high leverage.

LOS 18-1-y	**discuss** the role of commodities as a vehicle for investing in production and consumption

Investing in commodities, such as crude oil, gold, grain, cattle or metals, is investing directly in the production and consumption of an economy instead of in the stocks of the companies who process them.

Indirect ways to invest in commodities include:

- Futures contracts.
- Bonds indexed on some commodity price.
- Stocks of the companies producing the commodity.

LOS 18-1-z	**discuss** the motivation for investing in commodities, commodities derivatives, and commodity-linked securities

The motivation for investing in commodities and commodities' derivatives are:

For passive investors:

- Risk diversification benefits, commodities' returns have negative correlation with stock and bond returns.
- Positive correlation with inflation, so they provide a good inflation hedge.

For active investors

In addition to the benefits described above for passive investors, active investors are also looking for the following:

- Superior performance in periods of economic growth.
- Superior returns due to an active timing strategy.

LOS 18-1-aa **discuss** the sources of return on a collateralized commodity futures position

A collateralized position in commodity futures is a long position in futures for a given amount of underlying exposure and simultaneously investing the same amount in government securities such as Treasury bills. The return therefore comes from the interest income from the Treasury bills plus the change in futures price.

The risk of managed futures can be achieved through:

- Diversification.
- Liquidity monitoring, because illiquid contracts might be included when the universe is large.
- Volatility dependent allocation, where weights in different contracts depends on the historical or implied volatility.
- Qualitative techniques such as VaR and stress tests.
- Risk budgeting on various aggregation levels to detect undesired concentration.
- Limits on leverage.
- Use of derivatives to eliminate unwanted currency risk
- Care in model selection and avoiding biases.

The sole return from investing directly in commodities is from the price increase. Investors can now invest in securities, bonds and equity whose return is indexed to the price of commodities. By investing in these commodity-linked securities, an investor can achieve both a return from the increase in value of the securities due to the commodity link, plus income.

18-1. View Concept Check Questions Workbook

Thank you for reading our book

Appendix A: Exhibits

Exhibit 1: Accounting Statements

Exhibit 2: Puts and Calls

Exhibit 3: PE Breakdown

Exhibit 4: Ratios

Exhibit 1: Accounting Statements

Income Stmt: Particular moment in the life of an asset

Convert assets into profit to return to Inv or Stkhldrs Equity

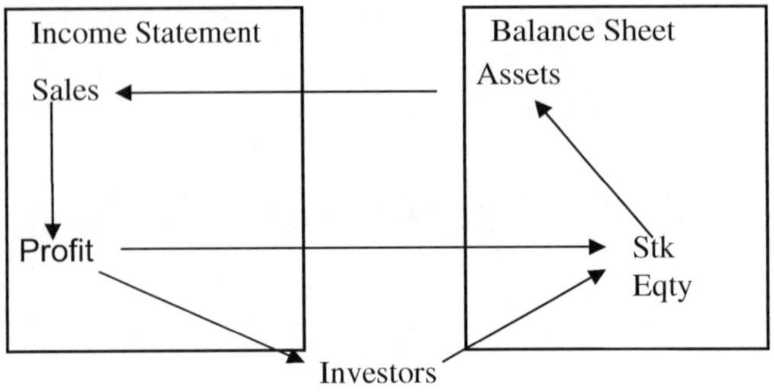

Assets come into Balance Sheet in SE to get to Assets

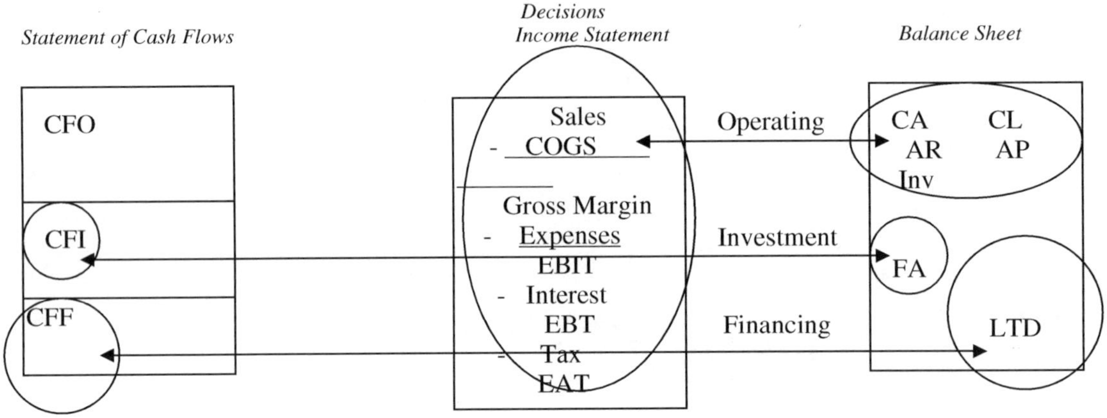

CEOs look at things from viewpoint of Cash Flow ... to pay bills, liquidity

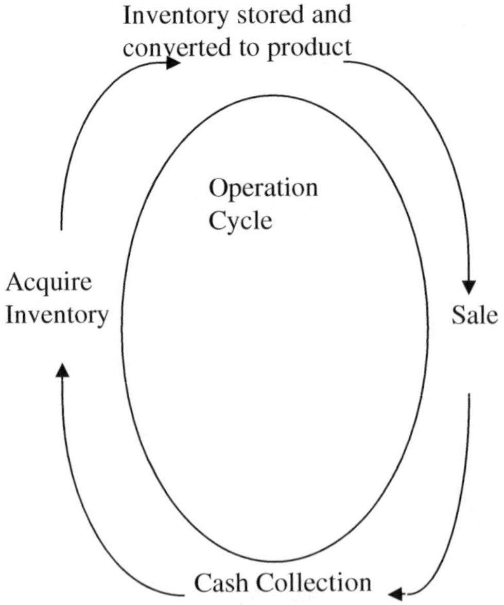

A growing company never has enough cash collection to grow the inventory.

CEO is always looking for something which will grow cash.

Newspaper cycles daily,
Boeing could take years

Notes:

Exhibit 2: Puts and Calls

Interpret the diagrams that depict the expiration-day **values** of the long call, short call, long put and short put strategies; (X = strike price, S = Stock price, C = cost of Call, P = cost of Put)

Long Call

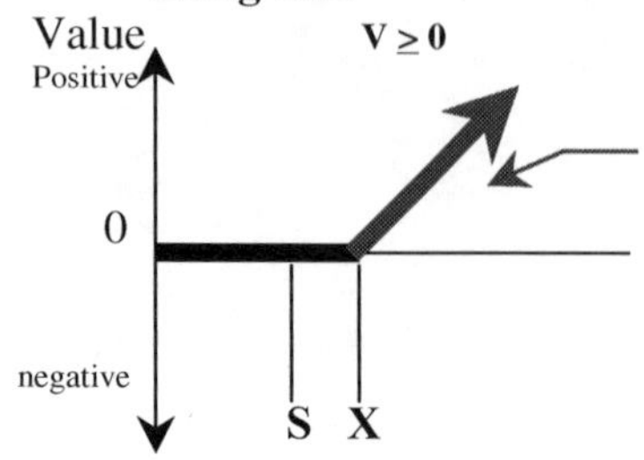

Value of the long call will be the **amount over strike** the stock is trading. **Long call will never have a value less than zero.**

Long Put

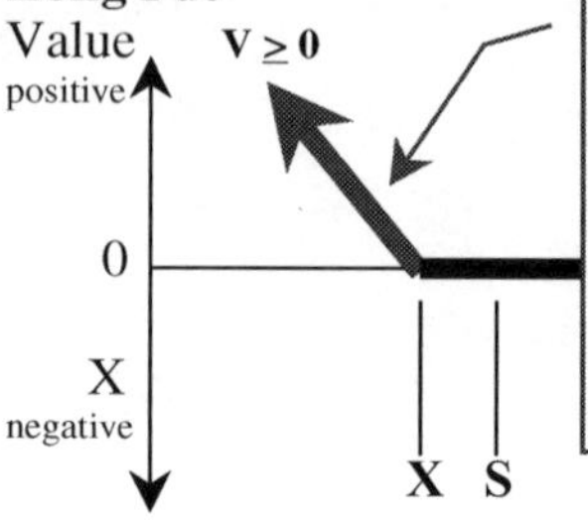

Value of the long put will be the **amount less than the strike** that the stock is trading. **Long put will never have a value less than zero.**

Short Call

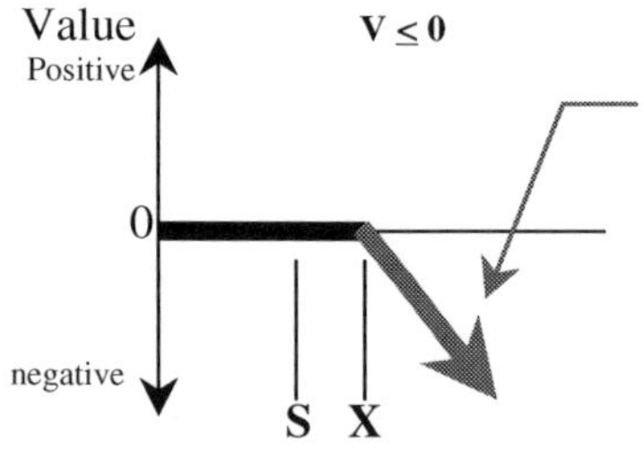

Value of the short call will be the **amount over the strike** the stock is trading. **Short call will never have a value greater than zero.**

Short Put

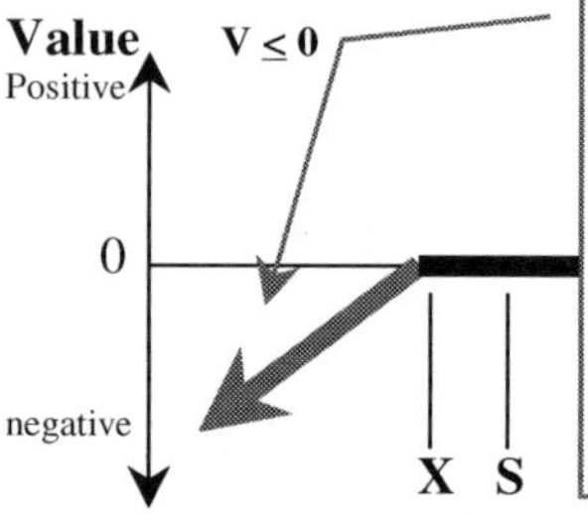

Value of the short put will be the **amount less than the strike** the stock is trading. **Short put will never have a value greater than zero.**

Interpret the **profit/loss** diagrams for the long call, short call, long put, and short put strategies;

Long Call

Loss ≤ C, Profit > X+C

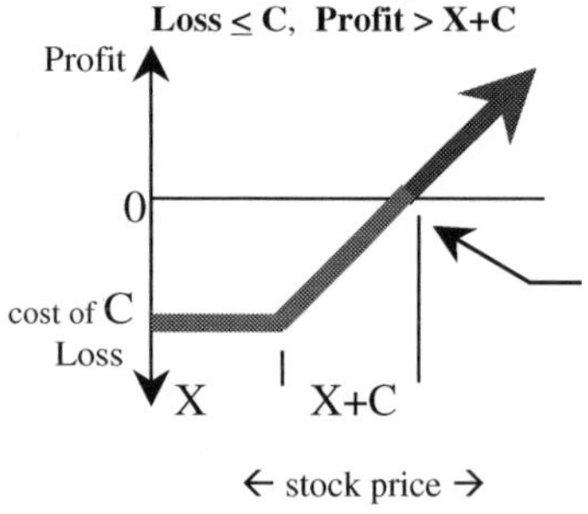

Profit of the long call is the amount over the strike + cost of the call (X+C). Loss on the call is the amount the stock is under the call + strike, not to exceed the cost of the call.

Long Put

Loss ≤ X+P, Profit < X

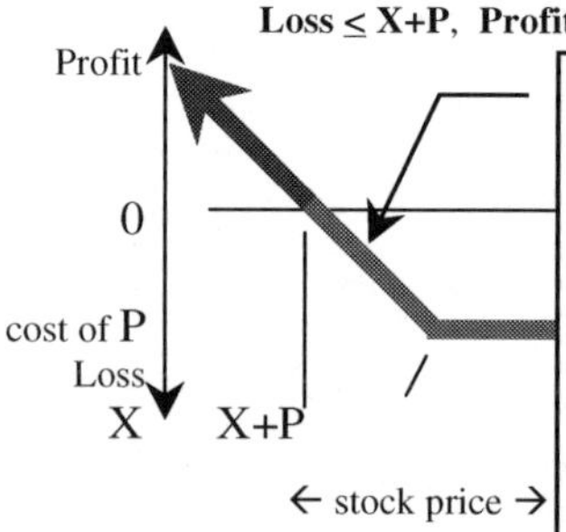

Profit the long put is the amount under the strike and cost of the put. Loss on the put is the amount the stock is over the strike, not to exceed the cost of the put.

Short Call

Loss ≥ X+C, Profit < X+C

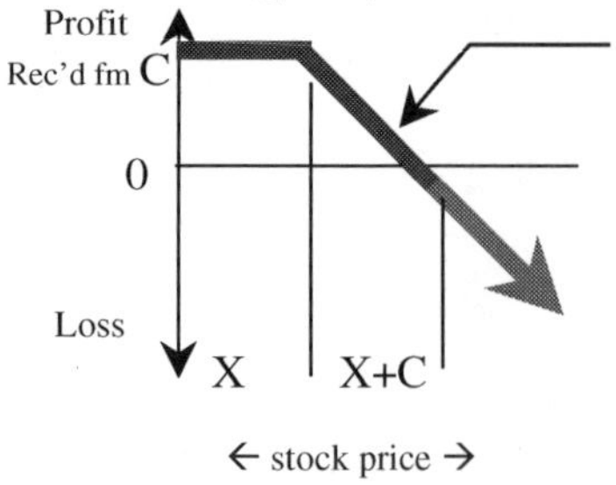

Profit of the short call is the amount under the strike + cost of the call (X+C), not to exceed the proceeds received from the call. Loss on the call is the amount the stock is over the call + strike.

Short Put

Loss ≥ X, Profit > X

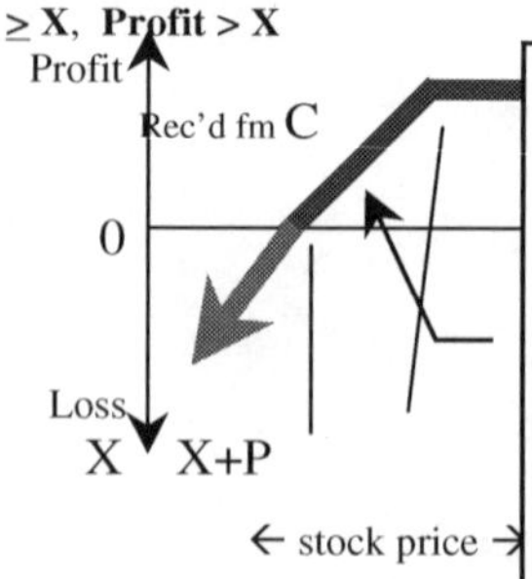

Profit the short put is the amount more than the strike of the put, not to exceed the proceeds received from the put. Loss on the put is the amount the stock is less than the strike.

Notes:

Exhibit 3: PE Breakdown

Note: 3 Stage ROE	Profit Margin	*	Total Asset Turnover	*	Financial Leverage
	NI	*	Sales	*	Total Assets
	Sales		Total Assets		Equity

Editor's Review:

Income Statement

Sales	
- COGS	
Gross Margin	
- Expenses	(mgmt hides it's perks if EAT is OK)
EBIT	
- Interest	Bank happy
EBT	What mgmt earns for shareholders
- Taxes	Gov't happy
EAT	Stockholders happy

EAT = EBT - EBT(t)

EAT = EBT(1-t)

Expected EPS = Expected Sales/share * Expected Net profit Margin

Income Stmt: Next year's projected

[(S) (EBDIT) - D - I] (1-t)

pending sales | ratio | Depr per shr | Inter Exp | tax adj

We know last year's P & P/E

Can calc next year's earnings

then Proportion via P/E to get $P_{proj\ EOY}$

$P_{proj\ EOY} = (E_{Proj\ EOY})\ (P/E)$

Earnings, DDM & ROE Calc

$\frac{P}{E} = \frac{Div / Earn}{k - g}$ $\frac{\text{Dividend pay-out}}{k - g}$

(Retention) (ROE)

k = Real Rate + Interest Prem + Risk Prem

Nominal rate should really multiply

Tax Reten Rate * Interest Burden * Oper'g Profit Margin * Asset Turnover * Financial Leverage

$k = R_f + \beta(R_m - R_f)$ β is # units of risk in the stock

Stockholders want and pay for k, k determines the P

$\frac{NI}{EBT} * \frac{EBT}{EBIT} * \frac{EBIT}{Sls} * \frac{Sls}{Assets} * \frac{Assets}{Equity}$

$P_0 = \frac{D_1}{k - g}$

WACC = $(w_e k_e) + (w_d k_d)$

[Oper Profit Margin * Total Asset Turnover - Interest Expense Rate] * Financial Leverage ***Multiplier*** * Tax Retention ***Rate***

[$\frac{EBIT}{Sls} * \frac{Sls}{Assets} - \frac{Int}{Assets}$] * $\frac{Assets}{Equity}$ * (1 - T)

Note: tax ret (1-t)

$P_0 = \frac{D_1}{k - g}$

$Return_{Estimated} = \frac{\text{Cash Div} + Price_{End} - Price_{Now}}{Price_{Now}}$

Bad side of

Good side of leverage

$P_0 = \frac{D_1}{k - g}$ restate: $k = \frac{D}{P} + g = k = R_f + \beta(R_m - R_f)$ also $k = (1+RR)(1+IP)(1+RP)$

real infl risk

should be in equilibrium

Exhibit 4: Ratios

calculate the financial ratios in each major category of analysis and discuss the uses of those ratios;
Common Size Statements: B/S in percent of Total Assets, I/S in percent of Sales
Quickly compare two different size firms, same firm trends over time, structure of firm's financial statements
Internal Liquidity (Solvency): ability of firm to meet future short term obligations, compare near term obligations with current assets or cash flows

Current Ratio:	$\frac{\text{Current Assets}}{\text{Current Liabilities}}$	Working Capital = CA - CL	
Quick ratio	$\frac{\text{Cash + mkt sec + AR}}{\text{CL}}$	not include. inventory	
Acid Test	$\frac{\text{CA - Inv}}{\text{CL}}$	a.k.a. Quick Ratio	
Cash ratio	$\frac{\text{Cash + mkt sec}}{\text{CL}}$	even more conservative	
Receivables Turnover	$\frac{\text{Net Annual Sales}}{\text{Avg Receivables}}$	Avg collection:	$\frac{365}{\text{Annual Turnover}}$
Days Receivable	$\frac{365}{\text{Avg Receivables}}$	Avg # of days to get paid	
Working Cap / Sales	$\frac{\text{CA - CL}}{\text{Net Sales}}$	higher % indicates more liquidity	
Payables Turnover	$\frac{\text{COGS}}{\text{@ AP}}$	@ payable period: (do they pay their bills)	$\frac{365}{\text{Annual Turnover}}$

Operating Performance: How well management is operating the business

Operating Efficiency Ratios: How management uses its assets and capital

Activity ratios: sales per something

Inventory Turnover	$\frac{\text{COGS}}{\text{@ Inventory}}$	@ Inventory period	$\frac{365}{\text{Inventory Turnover}}$
Total Asset Turnover	$\frac{\text{Net Sales}}{\text{@ Tot Net Assets}}$	high or low relative to industry? low: tie up too much assets	
Fixed Asset Turnover	$\frac{\text{Net Sales}}{\text{@ Net Fixed Assets}}$	utilization of fixed assets hi: old depr equipment	

Equity Turnover $\frac{\text{Net Sales}}{\text{Average Equity}}$ excludes CL & LT Debt

Receivables Turnover $\frac{\text{Net Annual Sales}}{\text{Avg Receivables}}$ Avg collection period: $\frac{365}{\text{Annual Turnover}}$

Operating Profitability: rate of profit on sales, % return on capital
(How good is mgmt turning profits into sales)
Note: Run down Income Statement and ratio to Sales (GP, EBIT, EBT, EAT)

EBIT: Mgmt earns

Tax: Government earns

Interest: Banker's earn

EBT: Stockholder's earn

Gross Profit Margin $\frac{\text{Gross Profit}}{\text{Net Sales}}$ (GP = Sls - COGS)
relative cost price position in industry?

Operating Profit Margin $\frac{\text{Operating Profit}}{\text{Net Sales}}$ (EBIT)
variability is business risk indicator

Net Profit Margin $\frac{\text{Net Income}}{\text{Net Sales}}$ NI = EAT

EBT Margin $\frac{\text{EBT}}{\text{Net Sales}}$ before tax profit margin

Common Size Income Statement
lists all expense and income items as a % of sales
(Inc Stmt: / Sls) (Bal: / Sls or Tot Assets)

Return on Total Capital $\frac{\text{Net Income + Interest Expense}}{\text{Average Total Capital}}$ Debt, Pref. Stock, C Stock
return on all capital employed

Return on Total Equity $\frac{\text{Net Income}}{\text{@ Total Equity}}$ ROE

Return on Owners Equity $\frac{\text{Net Income – Preferred Dividend}}{\text{@ Common Equity}}$

Return on Equity (ROE): DuPont System duPont formulation
ROE = NI / Equity or EAT/Equity

3 Step ROE = $\frac{NI}{Equity}$ = Net Profit Margin * Asset Turnover * Financial Leverage   a.k.a.Equity Multiplier

$$\frac{NI}{Sls} * \frac{Sls}{Assets} * \frac{Assets}{Equity}$$

Note: $\frac{(Sls)(Assets)}{(Sls)(Assets)}$

4 Step ROE = $\frac{NI}{Equity}$ = Tax Reten * Interest Burden * Oper'g Profit * Asset Turnover * Financial Leverage

$$\frac{NI}{EBT} * \frac{EBT}{EBIT} * \frac{EBIT}{Sls} * \frac{Sls}{Assets} * \frac{Assets}{Equity}$$

5 Step Equation = [Oper Profit Margin * Total Asset Turnover - Interest Expense Rate] * Financial Leverage Multiplier * Tax Retention Rate

$$\left[\frac{EBIT}{Sls} * \frac{Sls}{Assets} - \frac{Int}{Assets}\right] * \frac{Assets}{Equity} * (1 - T)$$

Financial Risk: Uncertainty of returns to equity holders due to a firm's use of fixed obligation debt securities

Debt / Equity — remember firm value is Db + Eq
Db=1, Eq=2, firm value = 3, D/E = ½
(not D/E=1/3, easy mistake in a hurry)

LTD / LT Cap — LTD = Long Term Debt   LT Cap = Long Term Capital

Total Debt / Total Capital

Interest Coverage — $\frac{EBIT}{Interest\ Expense}$ $\frac{NI + Tax + Int\ Exp}{Int\ Exp}$

(Note: Look for this on the exam

Cash Flow / LTD

Cash Flow / Total Debt

Growth Analysis

Retention rate — earnings retained / total earnings
(remember: growth = retention rate * ROE)

ROE — see above, profitability

Total Asset Turnover — see above, operational performance

Total Assets / Equity — note component of ROE

Net Profit Margin — see above, profitability

Sustainable growth rate — g = retention * ROE

retention rate = 1 – (Oper Inc after taxes)

Risk Analysis: uncertainty of income flows for the total firm and for sources of capital

Business Risk: Uncertainty of income caused by a firm's industry
Variability of sales due to products, customers, production methods

Business Risk Coefficient of variation of operating income CV = σ/mean

Standard Deviation of Operating Earnings (OE) / Mean Operating Earnings — need 5<Thru> 10 yrs to compute coef of variation

Sales Volatility Coefficient of Variation of Sales CV = σ/mean

sd of sales / mean sales — prime determinant of earnings variability

Operating Leverage $\%\Delta OE / \%\Delta Sls$ or $\Sigma \mid [\%\Delta OE] / [\%\Delta Sls] \mid / N$ employment of fixed production costs direction of change not important, but relative size of the change is relevant

OL = % change in operating earnings / % change in sales , calc from #'s not %

Notes:

Book Guarantee

This guarantee applies only to books published by TotalRecall Publications, Inc.! We are so confident in our products, we are prepared to offer the following guarantee to YOU our valued customer: If you do not pass your certification exam after one attempt, you will be eligible for next years book as follows!

Registered book purchasers will receive

1. Receive a 50% cash discount on next years purchase price

OR

2. Receive a free FinancialExams electronic download product of less or equal value.

To qualify for this Guarantee you must meet these requirements and perform the following tasks:

1. Register your purchase at www.TotalRecallPress.com web site before taking the Real Exam.
2. Fail the corresponding exam once.
3. Contact FinancialExams for the RMA # and to claim this guarantee
4. Send notification email to support@financialexams.com with RMA # plus reason for return.

Ship the following to claim your refund.

1. RMA # from returned email
2. A Copy of the Document identifying the exam scores failed attempt
3. Proof of passing score on the FinancialExams Simulated Test
4. Return the Book with CD-ROM to the following address

TotalRecall Publications	
Attn: Corby Tate	
1103 Middlecreek st.	
Friendswood, TX 77546	
877-654-2265	**support@financialexams.com**
281-992-3398	**http://www.totalrecallpress.com**
281-482-5390 Fax	**http://www.financialexams.com**

Thank you for using the TotalRecallPress.com Success Program.

FinancialExams Features

Using FinancialExams Quizzer

In Brief

The FinancialExams Quizzer exam software is designed to identify your personal areas of weakness relative to passing specific exam objectives. Once this software determines just what those weaknesses are, it will force you to continually face them until you can demonstrate mastery over them. Then it will find something else to haunt you with.

To use this software successfully, follow these simple steps.

1) ***Spend some time getting familiar with the program. When you're ready to settle down to work, clear the history (the button is on the main screen). Do not clear the history again until all of the following steps have been completed.***
2) ***Take four (4) Adaptive Exams. During this process, you have no choices. The software is in control. It is using its internal logic to determine your strengths and weaknesses on a topic-by-topic basis. (Note: You don't have to take all four at one sitting.)***
3) ***After the four Adaptive Exams, look at your Historical Analysis (the button is on the main screen). This will give you a graphical presentation of how you have done cumulatively in each category. Let this be your guide as to which subcategories to begin studying. Start with your weakest and work your way up.***
4) ***Begin taking Study Sessions on selected topics. Select the Category and Subcategories that you will be focusing on. You have two primary goals in Study Session mode.***

   a) See and answer every question on that topic at least once. Keep in mind that any question answered incorrectly will be in the very next Study Session you take on that topic. Once you are able to answer it correctly, it will get shuffled to the bottom of the deck. When you have cycled through available questions, correctly answered questions will begin to reappear.

   b) Achieve a minimum score of at least 85% on each and every subcategory topic before moving on to the Simulated Exam. If you want to bounce around a little between subcategories a little, that's okay. The program will remember where you left off. However, it's important that you don't cheat yourself on this step.

5) ***Take the Simulated Exam. Don't be too disappointed if you don't pass the first time. The software has been gaining knowledge about your weaknesses and has just done everything in its power to make you fail this exam. Aren't you glad that wasn't the real thing?***
6) ***Clear your history and repeat the above steps two more times. That's right… two more times. But now, achieve a minimum of 90% and 95% respectfully on each pass through before taking the Simulated Exam. You will find that the number of Study Sessions and the amount of time necessary to achieve these scores will get smaller. The better you know the material, the quicker the whole process becomes.***

The rest of this document goes into more detail on using specific features of the FinancialExams Quizzer software. Spend some time getting to know this program. It has helped thousands of people achieve their certification goals. It can do the same for you.

Study Session

FinancialExams Quizzer tests your knowledge as you learn about new subjects through interactive quiz sessions. Study Session questions are selected from a single database for each session, dependent on the subcategory selected and the number of times each question has been previously answered correctly. In this way, questions you have answered correctly are not repeated until you have answered all the new questions. Questions that you have missed previously will reappear in later sessions and keep coming back to haunt you until you get the question correct. In addition, you can track your progress by displaying the number of questions you have answered with the Historical Analysis option. You can reset the progress tracking by clicking on the Clear History button. Each time a question is presented the answers are randomized so you will not memorize a pattern or letter that goes with the question. You will start to memorize the correct answer that goes with the question concept.

Practice Exams

FinancialExams Quizzer also provides Adaptive and Simulated certification exams. Questions are chosen at random from the database. The Simulated Exam is a timed test that presents a similar number of questions as the real exam. A break from testing occurs at the mid-point of the exam. The Adaptive Exam presents a fixed number questions with a maximum time allotment. The Adaptive Exam is most helpful in identifying areas of weakness in the candidate's knowledge of the exam objectives.

After you finish an exam, FinancialExams Quizzer displays your score and the passing score required for the FinancialExams Quizzer test. You may display the exam results of this specific exam from this menu. You may review each question, display the correct answer, identify a resource, link to an available electronic book and view an explanation for the answer.

FinancialExams Quizzer Features

1. Each database contains 200 to 1200+ questions	2. Easy to install
3. Easy to upgrade	4. Multiple choice Style questions
5. Essay style questions	6. Fill-in-the-blank Style questions
7. Performance based questions	8. Flash Card Style questions
9. Questions randomized	10. Hot Spot Style questions
11. Print a category of questions	12. Drag/Drop/Mix/Match questions
13. •Single module studies	14. Answers randomized
15. Simulation exam studies	16. Print one question
17. Instant exam feedback	18. Cheat key or Flash Card option
19. Statistical analysis	20. Instant question feedback
21. Individual exam analysis	22. Adaptive exam studies
23. Font selection	24. Skills assessment
25. Graphics	26. Historical analysis
27. User Notes creation	28. Resizable screen
29. Some Links to Electronic Book content	30. Most have Explanations
31. Free version updates via e-mail	32. References

Online Help

This manual installs on your PC along with the FinancialExams Quizzer. To access it, select Contents from the Help pull-down menu. Additional help can be obtained via:

Email:

Support@financialexams.com
AskTheExpert@financialexams.com
CustomerService@financialexams.com

Telephone:

Toll Free: ***(888) 992-3398***
International: ***(281) 992-3131***
Fax: ***(281) 482-5390***

Changing subjects

FinancialExams Quizzer provides several practice exams to test your knowledge. To change exams:

1. *Click the Change Exam button in the Main window.*
2. *Select the exam for the test you want to run from the Select Exam window.*
3. *Click OK to change to the selected exam, or the Cancel to keep the current exam.*

Changing the number of questions

You can choose the number of questions presented in each quiz session. To change the number of questions:

1. ***Click on the box to the right of the Number of Questions field in the Main window.***
2. ***Type a number of questions, between 1 and 250, in the Number of Questions field.***
3. ***If the number of questions selected exceeds the number available in the chosen subcategory, all that are available will be displayed.***

Changing the subcategories

Each FinancialExams Quizzer subject has a number of categories and subcategories. You can take a test on any one or any combination of the subcategories.

1. ***From the Subcategories frame, select the desired general category from the Categories drop down list.***
2. ***Select the desired subcategory from the list box. To select multiple subcategories, hold down the CTRL key while clicking items in the list box.***

Setting up your printer

FinancialExams Quizzer allows you to customize your print jobs.

1. ***Select Options from the View pull-down menu.***
2. ***Select the Printing Options radial button. The Printing Options window appears.***
3. ***Select the options for your printer.***
4. ***Click OK to exit and save changes.***

Printing questions

FinancialExams Quizzer allows you to print questions from your tests, with or without the correct answer(s) marked. To print the question(s), select the desired print option from the File pull-down menu in the Question window.

Using FinancialExams Quizzer options

FinancialExams Quizzer provides a number of additional options to customize your test. The following options are available:

1. ***Stop On Wrong Answers***
2. ***Enable Cheat Key***
3. ***Resizable Screen***
4. ***Font Setting***

To select an advanced option, select Options from the View pull-down menu. The Exam Preferences window appears.

Adaptive Exam

Adaptive testing is a time saving option used to identify the candidate's strengths and weaknesses. Before using Adaptive testing, clear historical Analysis. Before you learn about your subject using the Quizzer Study Sessions, you should take the Adaptive exams. This exam style does not simulate all of the exam environments that are found on certification exams. You cannot choose specific subcategories for the Adaptive exam and once a question has been answered you cannot go back to a previous question. You have a time limit in which to complete the adaptive exam. This time varies from subject to subject, although it is usually 15 to 25 questions in 30 minutes. When the time limit has been reached, your exam automatically ends.

How to take advantage of Adaptive testing:

1. ***Clear the Historical Analysis***
2. ***Take four (4) adaptive exams in a row. Study the contents after each adaptive exam.***
3. ***View the historical analysis to identify your strength and weakness at the end of the four (4) adaptive exams.***
4. ***Go back to reviewing using the Study Sessions by Sub Category***
5. ***Repeat process until you are ready to pass the real exam.***

Take the Adaptive Exam

1. ***Click the Adaptive Exam radial button from the Main window.***
2. ***Click the Start button. The Adaptive Exam window appears.***
3. ***Click the circle to the left of the correct answer. There may be more than one correct answer. Text in the bottom left corner of the window instructs you to Choose the Best Answer (if there is only one answer) or Mark All Correct Answers (if there is more than one correct answer).***
4. ***Click the Next button to continue.***

After the allotted time has elapsed, the exam exits to review mode. To quit the test at any time, click the Finish button. After you have completed the Adaptive exam, FinancialExams Quizzer displays your score and the passing score required for the test. Display your exam results by selecting Details You may review each question, display the correct answer, and view an explanation for the answer (if available).

Reviewing an Adaptive Exam

After you have taken an Adaptive exam, you can review the questions, your answers, and the correct answers. You may only review your questions immediately after completing an Adaptive exam. To review your questions:

1. ***Click the Correct Answer button.***
2. ***To see your answer, click the Your Answer button.***

Starting a Study Session

After you choose a subcategory to test yourself on, start the Study Session.

To start a study session:

1. ***Select the Study Session radial button.***
2. ***Click the Start button. The Question window appears. Optionally, you can select Study Session from the Start pull-down menu. Click the checkbox to the left of the correct answer. There may be more than one correct answer. Text in the bottom left corner of the window instructs you to Choose the Best Answer (if there is only one answer) or Mark All Correct Answers (if there is more than one correct answer).***
3. ***Click the Next button to continue. FinancialExams Quizzer provides immediate feedback on your answer at the bottom of the window.***

If you answered the question correctly, a new question appears. If you did not answer the question correctly, you may try to guess again or move to the next question. If you have selected the Prompt on Wrong Answers option, you have the following choices:

1. ***To try again, click the Try Again button.***
2. ***To move to the next question after an incorrect guess, click the Next Question button.***
3. ***View the correct answer***
4. ***View the Explanation option***

To quit the test at any time, click the Finish button.

Checking your score during a test

The X% button displays the current percentage of questions that have been answered correctly.

1. ***Click the X% button. A window appears displaying the number of questions that have been asked and the number of questions that have been answered correctly.***
2. ***Click OK to return to the test.***

Checking your performance

Click the QID button. A window appears, displaying the number of times you have been asked this question and the number of times you have answered this question correctly.

Checking your overall progress

1. ***Click the Historical Analysis button from the Main window. The Historical Analysis window appears.***
2. ***FinancialExams Quizzer displays your progress in each test using a graphical progress bar. Hold the cursor over the progress bar and a dialog box will open. The number of times you have answered questions in that category correctly as a percentage of the total number of questions is displayed.***
3. ***To get detailed information on your performance on any subject, click and hold the progress bar for that subject. FinancialExams Quizzer displays the performance details in the bottom left hand corner of the screen.***

Simulated Exam

After you have learned about your subject using the Study Sessions, you can take a simulated exam. This exam simulates the exam environment that might be found on a certification exam. You cannot choose subcategories for a Simulated Exam. You have a fixed limit equal to that of the real exam to complete the Simulated Exam. When this time limit has been reached, your exam automatically ends.

Take the Simulated Exam

1. ***Click the Simulated Exam radial button from the Main window.***
2. ***Click the Start button. The Simulated Exam window appears.***
3. ***Click the circle to the left of the correct answer.***

There may be more than one correct answer. Text in the bottom left corner of the window instructs you to Choose the Best Answer (if there is only one answer) or Mark All Correct Answers (if there is more than one correct answer).

4. ***If you are unsure of the answer and wish to mark the question so you can return to it later, check the Mark box in the upper left hand corner. To review which questions you have marked, which you have answered, and which you have not answered, click the Review button.***
5. ***Click the Next button to continue.***

After the allotted time for testing, the exam exits to review mode. To quit the test at any time, click the Finish button. After you have completed the Simulated Exam, FinancialExams Quizzer displays your score and the passing score required for the test. Display your exam results by selecting Details. You may review each question, display the correct answer, and view an explanation for the answer (if available).

Reviewing a Simulated Exam

After you have taken a simulated exam, you can review the questions, your answers, and the correct answers. You may only review your questions immediately after a Simulated Exam.

To review your questions:

1. ***Click the Correct Answer button.***
2. ***To see your answer, click the Your Answer button.***

FlashCard Option

After you have learned about your subject using the Study Sessions, Adaptive, and Simulated exam go to the Thinking Option. The FlashCard environment is very different and will help you more that you might believe on a certification exam. **The Flash Card Option is very effect when used with Terminology or Glossary "Fill-in-the-Blank" style questions.**

Read the displayed question, Think of the answer, Hit the F4 Function key to display the correct answer, Read the Answer, Go to the next question.

1. ***You should not view the answer until you have thought about the answer.***
2. ***You have an unlimited time limit to think about each question.***
3. ***Use this option a few days before the real exam to go through a lot of questions in a short period of time.***
4. ***The FlashCard option can be used as a review of all questions in the database.***
5. ***Use the FlashCard option to provide Positive Feed Back with Correct Answers.***

Starting a FlashCard Session

After you choose a subcategory to test yourself on, start FlashCards.

1. ***Select the FlashCards Session radial button.***
2. ***Click the Start button. The Question window appears. Optionally, you can select FlashCards Session from the Start pull-down menu. You will find no answers to check or any visible area to type your answer into.***
3. ***This is the time to THINK of the answer. Pause a moment than hit the F4 function on your keyboard. (CheatKey)***
4. ***Review the displayed answer. Did you get it correct?***
5. ***When you are ready to proceed Click the Next button to continue.***

How to use a FlashCards

1. ***Read the displayed question***
2. ***Think of the answer***
3. ***Hit the F4 Function key to display the correct answer***
4. ***Read the Answer***
5. ***Go to the next question.***

To quit the test at any time, click the Finish button.

Note: Some questions may ask for more than one answer: Bypass questions that state "Which of the Following" and "Select all that apply" etc.

Taking Notes

While you are taking your exam, you may wish to write down notes about a particular question that you can use in later Study Sessions. FinancialExams Quizzer allows you to enter notes about each question. The notes will be permanently stored in the database for the subject you are studying. You can also use this feature to record any comments you have about a particular question and send it in for review. If you would like to print or view your notes, you can export your notes to a standard text editor.

Take notes from a study session

Create your own information or reference.

1. ***Click the Notes button from the Question window.***
2. ***Type your note.***
3. ***Click OK to keep the note, or Cancel to delete the note.***

Note: You cannot take notes during a Simulated or Adaptive session until you have finished the exam and have entered the Review mode.

Export your notes

Click the Notes button from the Main window and export to Note Pad or any text editor you wish to use.

CD-ROM Instructions

The Financial Certification Center (TFCC) version 4.0
Chartered Financial Analyst (CFA) Level 1 Exam

System Requirements: Windows 95 & 98, Windows NT, Windows 2000/XP, and Windows Server 2003 with a minimum of 40 MB hard disk space and 64 MB RAM

Installation: The FE practice exam will auto install. Simply place the CD-ROM in your CD-ROM drive and follow the instructions that appear on your screen, selecting the TFCC Practice Exam.

License Key

FE-JV 2005 CFA Level-I Session Style-A	= 294227865738
FE-DS 2005 CFA Level-I Session Style-B	= 293528865738
Financial Terminology Evaluation:	= 322478807587

If you have problems with the automatic installation, use the following procedure:

1) To install the program Run: \Instexe\FEQuiz32.exe
2) To install Adobe Acrobat Reader Run:
3) Software\Acrobat\AdbeRdr60enu.exe

Starting FinancialExams To start the program the next time (if it doesn't start automatically), select FinancialExams from the Program's menu. Assistance with running and using FE is available under the Help menu.

View and Download Supplemental Information:

To obtain additional printable content visit these download links.

http://snipurl.com/Workbook Preliminary Reading Assignments and Concept Question Workbook
http://snipurl.com/EI-CFA2005 ExamInsight 2005 CFA Level I eBook with two practice exams.

Good Luck with your certification!

Your Book Registration Number is IS-91501-6000

Made in the USA
Monee, IL
08 November 2026

68136728R20376

A DAY IN THE LIFE OF A TEACHER

KIDS
an imprint of mehta publishers

MEHTA
publishers

A Day in the Life of a Teacher

ISBN: 978-93-84841-21-8

Published by: Mehta Publishers
The story typeface is KB Drunk Tank

Mehta House, A-16, Naraina Phase II,
New Delhi-110028 (India)
E-mail: info@mehtapublishers.com

Printed in India by Mehta Offset Pvt. Ltd.

First Edition